C++ Programmer's Guide to the Standard Template Library

Mark Nelson

A Division of IDG Books Worldwide, Inc.

Foster City, CA • Chicago, IL • Indianapolis, IN • Braintree, MA • Dallas, TX

C++ Programmer's Guide to the Standard Template Library

Published by
IDG Books Worldwide, Inc.
An International Data Group Company
919 East Hillsdale Boulevard, Suite 400
Foster City, CA 94404

Library of Congress Catalog Card No.: 95-79565

ISBN: 1-56884-314-3

Printed in the United States of America

First Printing, September, 1995

10 9 8 7 6 5 4 3 2 1

Distributed in the United States by IDG Books Worldwide, Inc.

Distributed by Macmillan Canada for Canada; by Computer and Technical Books for the Caribbean Basin; by Contemporanea de Ediciones for Venezuela; by Distribuidora Cuspide for Argentina; by CITEC for Brazil; by Ediciones ZETA S.C.R. Ltda. for Peru; by Editorial Limusa SA for Mexico; by Transworld Publishers Limited in the United Kingdom and Europe; by Al-Maiman Publishers & Distributors for Saudi Arabia; by Simron Pty. Ltd. for South Africa; by IDG Communications (HK) Ltd. for Hong Kong; by Toppan Company Ltd. for Japan; by Addison Wesley Publishing Company for Korea; by Longman Singapore Publishers Ltd. for Singapore, Malaysia, Thailand, and Indonesia; by Unalis Corporation for Taiwan; by WS Computer Publishing Company, Inc. for the Philippines; by WoodsLane Pty. Ltd. for Australia; by WoodsLane Enterprises Ltd. for New Zealand.

For general information on IDG Books Worldwide's books in the U.S., please call our Consumer Customer Service department at 800-762-2974. For reseller information, including discounts and premium sales, please call our Reseller Customer Service department at 800-434-3422.

For information on where to purchase IDG Books Worldwide's books outside the U.S., contact IDG Books Worldwide at 415-655-3021 or fax 415-655-3295.

For information on translations, contact Marc Jeffrey Mikulich, Director, Foreign & Subsidiary Rights, at IDG Books Worldwide, 415-655-3018 or fax 415-655-3295.

For sales inquiries and special prices for bulk quantities, write to the address above or call IDG Books Worldwide at 415-655-3200.

For information on using IDG Books Worldwide's books in the classroom, or ordering examination copies, contact Jim Kelly at 800-434-2086.

For authorization to photocopy items for corporate, personal, or educational use, please contact Copyright Clearance Center, 222 Rosewood Drive, Danvers, MA 01923, or fax 508-750-4470.

is a registered trademark under exclusive license to
IDG Books Worldwide, Inc., from International Data Group, Inc.

CREDITS

Group Publisher and Vice President
Christopher J. Williams

Publishing Director
John Osborn

Senior Acquisitions Manager
Amorette Pedersen

Editorial Director
Anne Marie Walker

Production Director
Beth A. Roberts

Project/Manuscript Editor
Denise Caignon

Assistant Manuscript Editor
Tim Lewis

Technical Editor
Kaare Christian

Composition and Layout
Ronnie K. Bucci

Proofreader
Susanne Unger

Indexer
Mark Nelson

Cover Design
Kavish + Kavish

DEDICATION

To Denise

ACKNOWLEDGMENTS

I have a long list of people to thank for making this book possible. The most important contributions were those of Alexander Stepanov, Meng Lee, David Musser and the countless others who created the STL and saw it incorporated into the draft C++ standard. Kaare Christian and Denise Caignon spent way too many hours editing a manuscript that at times was more than a little rough. Chris Williams, Amy Pedersen, and the rest of the folks at IDG Books provided an author-friendly environment, proving there's more to IDG than Dummies! Many thanks to Andrew Schulman for pointing me in their direction. Most of all, I have to thank my wife Denise. She's the one who makes this all possible.

The publisher would like to give special thanks to Patrick McGovern, without whom this book would not have been possible.

About the Author

Mark Nelson has been programming since 1976. He is currently Director of Software Development at Greenleaf Software in Dallas, Texas. Greenleaf is a leading supplier of C and C++ libraries for programmers working in various desktop environments. Mark has contributed to *Dr. Dobbs Journal*, *C/C++ Users Journal*, *Computer Language*, *Windows Tech Journal*, and is a contributing editor to *Windows/DOS Developers Journal*. Mark is also the author of *The Data Compression Book* and *Serial Communications: A C++ Developer's Guide*.

TABLE OF CONTENTS

CHAPTER 15: SORTING AND SEARCHING 521

INTRODUCTION

Dear Reader:

Traditionally, the introduction to a programming book is
something of a sales pitch. Publishers like to think this prelimi-
nary stuff is going to be read in the bookstore, and therefore
they feel compelled to weave some hooks into the first few
pages. You'll find that the next few paragraphs do indeed slant
in the marketing direction, but I encourage you to read on in
spite of it! In the case of the STL, there really is substance
behind the hype. Trust me.

The Standard Template Library, or STL, is more than just a
minor addition to the world's most popular programming language; it represents a revolutionary new capability. The STL
brings a surprisingly mature set of generic containers and algorithms to the C++ programming language, adding a dimension
to the language that simply didn't exist before.

Generic programming is going to provide you with the
power and expressiveness of languages like SmallTalk while
retaining the efficiency and compatibility of C++. And I guarantee you that the STL will increase the productivity of any
programmer who uses it. The time you spend reading this
book will be returned to you the very first time you put the
STL to work.

THE RISE (AND FALL?) OF C

By many measures, C is the most popular programming language in the world today. In fact, in some circles, fluency in C is looked on as a prerequisite to being considered a "serious" programmer. How many times have you heard put-downs of programmers who work with Visual Basic, or dBASE, or COBOL? Popular opinion says if you want to be a *real* programmer, you'd better be a C programmer!

So how did C manage to get that "Most Popular" moniker in its high-school yearbook? Well, in a way, the rise of C parallels the success of *Homo Sapiens* here on Earth. Like the human race, C has become ubiquitous by being a jack-of-all-trades. (And probably master of none.) C might not be the best language for any particular type of programming, but it is usually good enough, and it is also usually available. And just as our species has done on planet Earth, C has managed to insinuate its way into nearly every programming environment in existence.

Evolution

Biologists use the theory of evolution to explain why the dominance of any species is only a temporary thing. Through mechanisms that aren't completely understood, new species rise up to compete for a position in the status quo. Likewise, species that successfully hold down a place in the environment will at times unaccountably vanish from the face of the earth. Mutations and natural selection combine to ensure that a steady stream of newcomers fight their way to the top.

A similar evolutionary process took place with the appearance of C++, just when C seemed destined to rule the earth. But the process that created C++ isn't nearly as mysterious as its biological counterpart. The process that extended standard C and created C++ has taken place in public view over the course of just a few years. And there seems to be a limitless supply of authors eager to chronicle that process in books and trade magazines. (Witness this book!)

So, at this point, it seems very likely that C++ is on the road to supplanting C as the top dog in the programming world. The fact that you are reading this book means you are part of the shift.

C++ == C with classes

When C++ took its first baby steps out of Bell Labs and into the mainstream, programmers first focused on the use of *classes*. C++ classes provide a way to encapsulate the behavior of what used to be simple structures. This ability tied in nicely with another new-fangled thing known as object-oriented programming (OOP). The fact that OOP took center stage in the late 80s and early 90s helped boost C++ tremendously. While the hard-core OOP devotees didn't buy into C++, they didn't slow down its momentum, either.

A great deal of time and money were expended on classes in C++. Programmers eagerly began writing programs that were laced with classes, programs that took advantage of C++ inheritance mechanisms. Books with the word "Object" in their title began filling the shelves of bookstores worldwide. And all was well in the world.

A joker in the deck: templates

The class-centric view of the C++ world has proven to be effective at solving a wide variety of problems. However, you will see in Chapter 1 that classes weren't able to provide optimal solutions in a couple of areas, namely, generic algorithms and containers. Existing practice in languages such as ADA pointed towards the development of a new feature in C++: *templates*.

Before the ANSI/ISO standardization process began, the *de facto* standard for C++ was defined as the AT&T cfront compiler, along with Bjarne Stroustrup's *The Annotated C++ Reference Manual*, or ARM. Chapter 14 of the ARM described a potential implementation of templates in C++. This section of the book was labeled "experimental." Since templates were not built into the cfront compiler (or any other C++ compiler, for that matter), and they were still subject to this "experimental" designation, they didn't attract much mainstream attention.

But while the bulk of C++ application programmers may have been oblivious to the significance of templates, they were attracting serious attention in some quarters. Of most interest to us is the work done by Alexander Stepanov at Hewlett Packard. Stepanov, along with Meng Lee, David Musser, and others, was developing a library of generic algorithms and containers using templates.

Generic algorithms and containers work with any data types. For example, you should be able to use a generic linked list to hold a list of integers, strings, or more complex data types. Likewise, a generic sorting algorithm should be able to sort collections of any type, from integers to complex database elements. Generic libraries could be (and were, in some cases) built with classes instead of templates, but templates provided a far superior implementation.

The C++ Standard

Stepanov's generic library came to be known as the Standard Template Library, or STL. This template-based library was offered to the ANSI/ISO committee in 1994 as a potential addition to the C++ standard library. The committee agreed to accept it, meaning that the STL will soon be part of every vendor's C++ compiler offering. This means templates are suddenly a very important thing indeed!

Despite the rigors of the standardization process, the STL hasn't yet received extensive public review as of this writing. Early indicators have been very positive, however. The STL is an elegant and efficient collection of algorithms and containers. Programs are making effective use of it right now, even before the standardization process is complete.

WHAT THE STL MEANS TO YOU

I'd wager that the STL will turn out to be very important to you as a handy C++ toolkit. Since it is defined as part of the ANSI/ISO C++ standard, it should be available whenever you are writing C++ programs. The flexibility and the power of the STL allow you to replace a great deal of custom code on any given project.

Template-based programming was introduced to allow programmers to create libraries similar to the STL. While you might never try to write such a library, you *will* be using them. This means you'll need to understand how templates work, and how they are applied to today's programming problems. Studying the STL is an excellent way to learn not just how templates work, but also how they can be applied to generic programming problems.

An Open Book

Template-based libraries are much more open than conventional C libraries. The way templates are implemented in C++ means that a great deal of code has to be exposed in header files, instead of tucked away in object libraries. The STL carries this to an extreme, as almost all of its source is found in header files; the STL is essentially an open book.

So if the STL is an open book, why do you need *this* book? Well, just because you have the source code doesn't make the STL transparent! Alexander Stepanov developed a fairly complex framework of concepts to implement this generic library, and these concepts are not immediately obvious. After reading this book, you will not only understand the individual components of the STL, but also the philosophy that led to its current implementation.

A ROAD MAP

This book is broken down into four major sections:

- An Introduction to the STL
- The Essentials: Containers, Iterators, Algorithms, Function Objects
- The Public Interface: Reference Information
- STL Specification and Source Code

The first section provides some background material that should familiarize you with the basic concepts that led to the creation of the STL. In particular, it discusses how the use of templates leads to efficient, generic containers and algorithms.

In the second part of the book, you'll find detailed discussions about the use and operation of all the important STL components. If you want to know exactly how a deque works, or how to create a compound function object, this is the place to look. For the real nitty-gritty, turn to the reference section for details about the public interface to the STL components.

Finally, the book ends with a complete copy of the STL specification, as incorporated into the ANSI/ISO C++ specification (in the draft stage at the time this book is being published). It also contains a listing of the public distribution of the STL source released by Hewlett-Packard. This release of the STL will undoubtedly be the basis of most future commercial implementations of the STL.

TRY IT, YOU'LL LIKE IT!

C++ represents a huge body of collective effort, and the STL is certainly just a small part of it. But while the STL may not get star billing when the C++ standard finally rolls out, I predict it *will* create a small revolution in the way C++ programmers get their jobs done. Try it, and see if you don't agree.

INTRODUCING THE STL

THE STL:
A HISTORICAL
PERSPECTIVE

History: An account, mostly false, of events, mostly unimportant, which are brought about by rulers, mostly knaves, and soldiers, mostly fools.

— Ambrose Bierce, *The Devil's Dictionary*

In 1982, I received my introduction to big-time team programming: I was hired by a start-up company that was designing a new digital PBX. After extensive recruiting, a highly skilled programming team was assembled, and we began work on the system architecture.

Our team of well-paid programmers got busy creating a complex software system from the ground up. We designed every single data structure, literally bit by bit. No detail was too small to escape our attention; we were determined that our software would be a showpiece of efficiency. Access routines were coded in assembly language to provide the maximum throughput with a minimum cost in system resources.

It took months to complete the design, but I believe we were successful in meeting all of our goals. We *must* have been successful, because it was almost two years before the first major layoffs took place.

I survived the experience, and learned an important lesson: an efficient, economical design doesn't mean your product is going to be a winner. Our hand-crafted product carefully conserved every last bit of memory, but it was idiosyncratic and difficult to maintain. It was also expensive; that highly paid team of programmers burned through a great deal of venture capital to produce the initial release.

Had generic data structures and algorithms such as those found in the C++ Standard Template Library been available in 1982, I might still be working at that company. When used properly, the STL can give you the efficiency and economy you expect from hand-crafted routines—and at the price of an off-the-shelf component! For C++ programmers, this is a revolutionary promise.

WHAT IS THE STANDARD TEMPLATE LIBRARY?

The STL represents a significant step forward in the development of C++. Unlike many object-oriented programming languages, such as SmallTalk, C++ did not have a standard set of classes to represent traditional data structures. A SmallTalk programmer, for example, takes for granted the ability to create linked lists, heaps, and trees without having to reinvent the wheel. Likewise, programmers in other languages have had libraries of standard algorithms that greatly facilitate many common programming operations. Until now, C++ programmers have had no choice but to start from scratch when it comes to traversing trees, generating permutations, merging lists, and so on.

The STL puts those days behind us. It gives C++ programmers a framework of carefully designed generic data structures and algorithms that finally bring to C++ the long-promised dream of reusable software components.

The Standard Template Library, or STL, is a template-based library of generic C++ data structures and algorithms that work together in an efficient and flexible fashion. The STL contains template-based container classes and algorithms. Container classes include:

- vectors
- lists
- queues
- priority queues
- stacks
- sets and maps (associative containers)

A wide variety of low-level algorithmic operations are included, as well as more complex algorithms such as:

- sorting
- merging
- permutations
- inner product
- binary search

STL templates are designed to short-circuit that average C++ programmer's urge to custom code—in the name of efficiency—any and all data structures and algorithms. As the authors state in the STL specification:

> *"Much effort has been spent to verify that every template component in the library has a generic implementation that performs within a few percentage points of the efficiency of the corresponding hand-coded routine."*

Quick understanding and early adoption of the STL by C++ programmers promises big productivity gains, without the code bloat and loss of speed we have come to expect from most productivity tools. Serious programmers should waste no time idly wondering whether the STL is a significant new tool they ought to study. Without a doubt, it is. But as you'll see in this chapter, the STL was a very late addition to the C++ standard.

STL Joins the Team

As programming languages mature, they frequently go through a standardization process. A language becomes a standard when a group of people sit down and hammer out a detailed document specifying exactly what the language does, and how it does it.

If you're like most programmers, you consider standardization to be a really good thing. You want to know you can expect certain behavior from a compiler, regardless of who's selling it. And for the companies that develop compilers, standardization provides a clear-cut, well-defined foundation their product needs to adhere to. (It also looks very impressive to be able to brag about standards conformance in advertisements!)

We have all been here before: ANSI C

The C programming language went through a fairly long childhood and adolescence before it embarked on the standardization process. When AT&T researchers first created C in the 1970s, it was used primarily as an in-house development tool. Its scope later expanded to include a significant body of users in the academic world.

At this point in the life of C, there wasn't a strong incentive to standardize. AT&T not only owned the language, it was the primary user of C as well. If people at the company felt a need to change language features, they were free to do so whenever they wished.

But eventually, C began moving out of this cloistered environment and into the mainstream of industry. Pioneering companies began developing C compilers to run on embedded systems, PCs, and even UNIX systems. As C's user base expanded, the need for standardization increased.

The standardization of C was undertaken by the American National Standards Institute, or ANSI. Here's how ANSI defines itself:

> Founded in 1918, the American National Standards Institute (ANSI), is a private, not-for-profit membership organization that coordinates the U.S. voluntary consensus standards system and approves American National Standards.
>
> ANSI consists of approximately 1,300 national and international companies, 30 government agencies, 20 institutional members, and 250 professional, technical, trade, labor and consumer organizations.

In the mid-80s, ANSI created a committee to develop a C Programming Language standard. The committee was composed of various ANSI members who had an interest in the standardization process. This committee, designated X3J11 by ANSI, met on a regular basis for several years to produce the standard. After an immense amount of discussion, argument, and compromise, the end result was ANSI X.3159-1989, the ANSI C programming standard.

The final step in the standardization of C took place when the ANSI standard was unified with the C Programming Language standard for the International Organization for Standardization, or ISO. Finally, programmers the world over could agree on exactly what a C compiler was supposed to do.

Same song, different verse

The commercialization of C++ proceeded much more rapidly than that of C. The pressure to create a standard quickly resulted in the creation of a joint ANSI/ISO committee, designated ANSI X3J16/ISO WG21. In 1994, the committee issued a Draft Report, which amounts to a dress rehearsal for the specification.

Standards bodies move in a slow, deliberate manner, and surprises are frowned upon. So in July 1994, when the ANSI/ISO C++ Standards Committee suddenly accepted the STL as part of the C++ Standard Library, the committee was acting very much out of character. The STL was a last-minute addition that greatly expanded the scope of the C++ library.

The STL, as accepted by X3J16, is the result of years of evolution and much collaborative effort, going back to early C++ libraries, as well as generic libraries for ADA and other languages. The version of the STL now incorporated into the C++ standard was developed at Hewlett Packard, and proposed to the committee by Alexander Stepanov and Meng Lee in November 1993.

WHY DID IT TAKE SO LONG?

Why is it that C and C++ don't have built-in support for generic data structures and algorithms? The answer lies in the very reasons for the success of C++: Until template-based programming was incorporated into C++, programmers could always hand-code customized versions of data structures and algorithms that were more efficient than those any library could provide.

This part of the chapter will show you how C libraries using void pointers and C++ libraries using derivation will always be slower than hand-coded routines. It's only through the use of templates that library writers can achieve parity with industrious programmers.

C, followed by C++, is one of the most widely used programming languages in the world. C and C++ have proved themselves to be remarkably versatile, fitting into a variety of niches and specialties. They are used to develop operating systems, end-user applications with millions of lines of code, and conversely, utility programs of a few lines that take as little as 15 minutes to write. C is used in projects with 100 programmers working in parallel and by one-person garage-shop operations. In many ways, C and C++ have become the *lingua franca* of programmers worldwide.

Yet in spite of their popularity, C and C++ are not particularly elegant or easy to work with. C has always been notorious for giving programmers twice as much rope as they need to hang themselves with. C syntax can be charitably described as difficult, and can be particularly troublesome for beginning programmers. C++ compounds many of C's problems by adding a seemingly endless laundry list of new features, operators, and keywords.

The code samples shown in Figure 1-1 illustrate the "progress" programming languages have made over the last 20 years. It should be evident why some people consider the progression to C and C++ to be a step backwards into obscurity and complexity!

1974 BASIC Program:

```
10 PRINT "HELLO, WORLD"
20 END
```

1984 C Program:

```
#include <stdio.h>
main()
{
   printf( "Hello, world!\n" );
}
```

1994 C++ Program:

```
#include <iostream.h>
int main( int, char *[] )
{
   cout << "Hello, world!\n";
   return 0;
}
```

Figure 1-1
This is progress?

Yet despite the complaints, C++ (along with C) is the language of choice for a huge number of professional programmers. High up on the list of reasons why are two attributes deliberately built into the original design of C: efficiency and flexibility. C was designed to compete with what is arguably the apex of efficiency: assembly language. In *The C Programming Language*, Kernighan and Ritchie have this to say:

> *"C programs tend to be efficient enough that there is no compulsion to write assembly language instead."*

Likewise, C was designed to be flexible in at least two respects. First, it was built to be easily portable to many different computer architectures, ranging from eight-bit stand-alone microcontrollers up to high-powered supercomputers. Second, it was designed to support the entire range of programming tasks. Kernighan and Ritchie staked their claim for C's flexibility:

> *"...although it has been called a 'system programming language' because it is useful for writing operating systems, it has been used equally well to write major numerical, text processing, and data-base programs."*

Today, becoming a C++ programmer still means buying into the C/C++ dogma of efficiency and flexibility *uber alles*. C++ programmers are frequently chided by adherents of other languages for their devotion to efficiency over other attributes such as readability, modularity, and maintainability. And it is this very mindset that prevented the adoption of anything like the Standard Template Library until late 1994. Until templates were introduced to C++, generic data structures and algorithms couldn't pass either of the twin tests of efficiency and flexibility. Failing these tests guaranteed not just failure to be incorporated into the C or C++ standards, but also ensured failure in the commercial marketplace.

My Wheel Is Better!

In the world of C++, reusable software is a lot like the weather: everyone is talking about it, but nobody is doing anything about it. People pay a lot of lip service to the idea of using standardized libraries, but for the most part, C++ programmers are inclined to write each and every application from scratch. The only real exception to the rule is the standard C and C++ runtime libraries, which are typically used to encapsulate I/O, freeing the programmer from having to learn the details of system-specific I/O calls.

The remainder of this chapter will first demonstrate why hand-coded algorithms out-perform their generic equivalents written using the following strategies:

- C implementations that use void pointers to define implementation-specific data

- C++ implementations that use inheritance to add implementation-specific data

After that, you'll see why template-based generic algorithms can meet expectations where the previous two strategies failed.

GENERIC ALGORITHMS IN STANDARD C

While C programmers have been reluctantly willing to turn their I/O tasks over to standard libraries, data structures have always been a do-it-yourself project. The reason for this becomes evident when you attempt to make a generic container in C.

Listing 1-1, TREE1.H, defines the public interface for a generic C implementation of a binary tree. A *binary tree* is a collection of data items that are stored as nodes in a tree. Each node can have two child nodes, one on the left and one on the right. The tree has a special node known as the *root* node. The root node doesn't have a parent node, and all the other nodes in the tree can be found by following its child pointers.

C programmers made some of their first attempts at generic data-structure implementation using the techniques shown here. A simple C data structure is defined that can be used for each node in the binary tree. Each node contains a pointer to a left node, a right node, and a data object.

Listing 1-1
TREE1.H

```
/*
 * TREE1.H
 *
 * This file defines the public interface for a generic
 * binary tree data structure. This is a relatively simple
 * interface, with just three functions.
 *
 */
typedef struct _tag_tree {
  void *data;
  struct _tag_tree *left_node;
  struct _tag_tree *right_node;
} BINARY_TREE;
/*
 * This typedef defines the comparison function. It
 * should return a negative number if the first arg
 * is less than the second arg. The add_node() routine
 * uses this function to add data to the tree.
 */
typedef int (COMPARE_FN)( void *, void * );
typedef void (ITERATE_FN)( void * );
BINARY_TREE *create_new_node( void *p );
void add_node( BINARY_TREE *root, void *p, COMPARE_FN *cmp );
void traverse( BINARY_TREE *root, ITERATE_FN *iter_fn );
```

Note that the implementation is dependent on pointers to access key user-defined functions. The add_node() function must be passed the address of a user-defined function that is used to make comparisons between the object being inserted and the current node being tested. Likewise, the traverse() function gets a pointer to a user-defined function. A programmer calls traverse() to iterate through the entire tree, calling a function at every node.

Listing 1-2, TREE1.C, contains the implementation of this class. The add_node() and traverse() functions make use of user-defined function pointers to perform object-specific operations. This means the user isn't confined to comparisons on standard C objects, such as ints or floats. This is one of the requirements for truly generic libraries: they should work equally well on built-in and user-defined objects.

Listing 1-2
TREE1.C

```
/*
 * TREE1.C
 *
 * This file contains the code that implements the binary
 * tree generic data structure package defined in TREE1.H.
 *
 */

#include <stdlib.h>
#include "tree1.h"

/*
 * Initialize the root node. After allocating the memory,
 * the left and right pointers are set to null, and the
 * data pointer is initialized to the value passed in.
 */

BINARY_TREE *create_new_node( void * p )
{
    BINARY_TREE *node = malloc( sizeof( BINARY_TREE ) );
    node->data = p;
    node->left_node = 0;
    node->right_node = 0;
    return node;
}
```

```
/*
 * The routine to add a node just walks down the tree until we
 * find an empty node that the new data can fit into. Comparisons
 * are done using the pointer to a function passed in.
 */

void add_node( BINARY_TREE *root, void *p, COMPARE_FN *cmp )
{
  BINARY_TREE *node = root;
  BINARY_TREE *new_node = create_new_node( p );
  for ( ; ; ) {
    BINARY_TREE **next_node_ptr;
    if ( cmp( p, node->data ) < 0 )
      next_node_ptr = &node->left_node;
    else
      next_node_ptr = &node->right_node;
    if ( *next_node_ptr == 0 ) {
      *next_node_ptr = new_node;
      return;
    } else
      node = *next_node_ptr;
  }
}


/*
 * The traversal function calls the user-supplied
 * function via a pointer.
 */
void traverse( BINARY_TREE *root, ITERATE_FN *iter_fn )
{
  if ( root == 0 )
    return;
  traverse( root->left_node, iter_fn );
  iter_fn( root->data );
  traverse( root->right_node, iter_fn );
}
```

Listing 1-3, TREETST1.C, shows a sample program that exercises the generic binary-tree package. In this case, standard null-terminated character strings are the objects being added to the tree. The C runtime library function strcmp() performs the comparisons when strings are being added to the tree.

Note: The tree contains character pointers, not the strings themselves. It is the responsibility of the programmer using the package to allocate storage space for the strings. This isn't a problem in TREETST1.C, because its strings are stored in a static data area that is defined at compile time.

Listing 1-3

TREETST1.C

```
/*
 * TREETST1.C
 *
 * This program tests the binary tree interface package. It
 * does so by adding a list of strings to the tree, then
 * printing out the tree contents in order. Compile this
 * program using a command line similar to one of these:
 *
 * bcc -w TREETST1.C TREE1.C
 *
 * cl /W4 TREETST1.C TREE1.C
 *
 */

#include <stdio.h>
#include <string.h>
#include "tree1.h"

/*
 * The strings to be added to the tree.
 */

char *strings[] = {
  "Arvid",
  "Thirl",
  "Loki",
  "Athena",
  "Nimrod",
  "Zima",
  "Kirin",
  0
};

/*
 * This is the function called by the tree iteration routine.
 * It simply prints the string value stored in the node.
 */

void strprn( const char *s )
{
  printf( "%s ", s );
}
```

```
/*
 * This short program adds a set of strings to a generic binary
 * tree. Note that we don't have to define a comparison function
 * for the call to add_node(), because the RTL function strcmp()
 * does the job without modifications. After the strings have
 * been added, we print the contents of the tree out in order.
 */

main()
{
  BINARY_TREE *root;
  char **p;

  root = create_new_node( strings[ 0 ] );
  for ( p = strings + 1; *p != 0 ; p++ )
    add_node( root, *p, (COMPARE_FN *) strcmp );
  traverse( root, (ITERATE_FN *) strprn );
  return 0;
}
```

The output of TREETST1.EXE shows that the objects were added in the proper order. It also gives us some assurance that the algorithm is working properly:

```
Arvid Athena Kirin Loki Nimrod Thirl Zima
```

To demonstrate the true generic nature of this library function, Listing 1-4, TREETST2.C, shows how the same library functions can be used to create a binary tree of integers, instead of strings. From the point of view of the application programmer, the main adjustment needed is the creation of two new support routines: intcmp(), used by add_node() to compare two integers, and intprn(), used to print out integers during iteration of the tree.

Listing 1-4
TREETST2.C

```
/*
 * TREETST2.C
 *
 * This program tests the binary tree interface package. It
 * does so by adding a list of integers to the tree, then
 * printing out the tree contents in order. Compile this
 * program using a command line similar to one of these:
 *
 * bcc -w TREETST2.C TREE1.C
 *
 * cl /W4 TREETST2.C TREE1.C
```

```
 *
 */

#include <stdio.h>
#include "tree1.h"

/*
 * The numbers to be added to the tree.
 */

int numbers[] = { 5, 83, -40, -100, 88, 3, 3, -1 };

/*
 * The comparison function used by the routine that adds nodes
 * to the tree.
 */

int intcmp( int *a, int *b )
{
  return *a - *b;
}

/*
 * This is the function called by the tree iteration routine.
 * It simply prints the contents of each node.
 */

void intprn( const int *p )
{
  printf( "%d ", *p );
}

/*
 * This short program adds a set of integers to a generic binary
 * tree. Note that we have to define both a comparison function
 * for the call to add_node(), and an output function for the call
 * to traverse().
 */

main()
{
  BINARY_TREE *root;
  int i;

  root = create_new_node( numbers );
  for ( i = 1; i < sizeof( numbers ) / sizeof( int ) ; i++ )
    add_node( root, numbers + i, (COMPARE_FN *) intcmp );
  traverse( root, (ITERATE_FN*) intprn );
  return 0;
}
```

As you would expect, the output of TREETST2.EXE gives the list of numbers in sorted order:

```
-100 -40 -1 3 3 5 83 88
```

WHY C FALLS SHORT

The generic library code in TREE1.C seems like a very straightforward implementation of a binary tree. Also, there aren't many obvious improvements that can be made in the interface to the calling program. So then, why isn't there a function like this in the C standard runtime library?

For part of the answer, we can look at the data structure created by the library routines. Figure 1-2 shows an internal representation of the data structure created when running TREETST1.EXE.

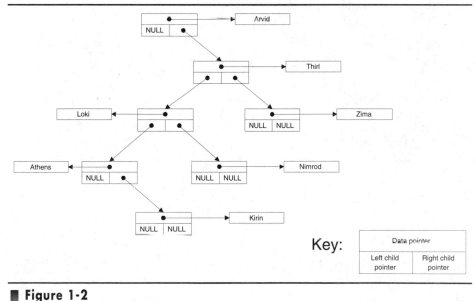

Figure 1-2
A binary tree

The data structure shown in Figure 1-2 is obviously a simple binary tree. The tree would look like this regardless of whether it contained null-terminated strings, integers, doubles, or user-defined data structures.

The important thing to note is that the data items we are storing in the tree are *not* stored in the nodes themselves. Instead, the node contains a pointer to the data item, which will have to be in storage allocated by the programmer.

The fact that data items don't reside in the nodes themselves leads to a certain amount of inefficiency. Every time the tree is being updated, the comparison routines have to dereference a pointer to get at the actual value of the data item, as opposed to looking directly in the structure under test. In our second test program, TREE2.C, we were storing integers in the tree. If those integers were being read in from a file, we would have to allocate storage for each integer, then add it to the tree, leading to unattractive code that looks something like this:

```
void store_new_element( int data )
{
  int *data_store;
  data_store = malloc( sizeof( int ) );
  *data_store = data;
  add_node( root, data_store, (COMPARE_FN *) intcmp );
}
```

This arrangement not only wastes storage space by requiring a pointer to every integer stored in the tree, it also leads to a fragmented heap as a result of numerous small allocations.

The second problem with this implementation is the inelegant practice of requiring the library user to pass a pointer to a comparison function any time a node must be added. In TREETST2.C, this meant having to write the function intcmp() which, while admittedly easy, is still an annoyance. The use of a function pointer also means we have to undergo yet another dereference every time we want to compare two data items. That is in addition to the two dereferences we need to get at the items themselves!

Hand-coded tree wins

The net result of all these difficulties is that few C programmers would ever use a routine like the one in TREE1.H. More often than not, the C programmer tasked with writing TREETST2.C would code up a few binary tree routines from scratch, resulting in code looking something like Listing 1-5:

Listing 1-5
TREETST3.C

```
/*
 * TREETST3.C
 *
 * This program replaces the binary tree interface package with
 * a hand-coded alternative. In this program, the integers
 * are stored in the tree nodes, comparisons are done inline,
 * and the printout is done inside the traversal routine.
 * Compile this program using a command line similar to one
 * of these:
 *
 * bcc -w TREETST3.C
 *
 * cl /W4 TREETST3.C
 *
 */

#include <stdio.h>
#include <stdlib.h>

/*
 * This node data structure holds the integer directly,
 * instead of using a void *.
 */

typedef struct _tag_tree {
  int data;
  struct _tag_tree *left_node;
  struct _tag_tree *right_node;
} BINARY_TREE;

/*
 * Initialize a node, and store the data simultaneously.
 */

BINARY_TREE *create_new_node( int i )
{
  BINARY_TREE *node = malloc( sizeof( BINARY_TREE ) );
  node->left_node = 0;
  node->right_node = 0;
  node->data = i;
  return node;
}

/*
 * The routine to add a node just walks down the tree until
 * there is an empty node that the new integer can fit into.
 */

void add_node( BINARY TREE *root, int data )
{
```

```c
  BINARY_TREE *node = root;
  BINARY_TREE *new_node = create_new_node( data );
  for ( ; ; ) {
    BINARY_TREE **next_node_ptr;
    if ( data < node->data )
      next_node_ptr = &node->left_node;
    else
      next_node_ptr = &node->right_node;
    if ( *next_node_ptr == 0 ) {
      *next_node_ptr = new_node;
      return;
    } else
      node = *next_node_ptr;
  }
}

/*
 * The traversal routine is just used to print out the
 * data in the tree.
 */

void traverse( BINARY_TREE *root )
{
  if ( root == 0 )
    return;
  traverse( root->left_node );
  printf( "%d ", root->data );
  traverse( root->right_node );
}

/*
 * The numbers to be added to the tree.
 */

int numbers[] = { 5, 83, -40, -100, 88, 3, 3, -1 };

/*
 * This short program adds a set of integers to a customized
 * tree. It should be much more efficient than the generic
 * equivalent.
 */

main()
{
  BINARY_TREE *root;
  int i;

  root = create_new_node( numbers[ 0 ] );
  for ( i = 1; i < sizeof( numbers ) / sizeof( int ) ; i++ )
    add_node( root, numbers[ i ] );
  traverse( root );
  return 0;
}
```

TREETST3.C requires the C programmer to define a brand-new data structure, as well as three library routines that act on that data structure. The reward for that effort is a much more efficient program that uses less data space and runs faster as well.

Truth in advertising

The additional time and space required to access data items is significant for objects like integers or single characters. But this isn't always the case. If your program is manipulating 1000-byte data records, one additional pointer dereference won't have a noticeable impact on your program. However, just looking at efficiency doesn't give you the entire picture.

One important additional benefit to hand-coding the binary tree routine is that you now have a type-safe program. TREETST3.C doesn't have the casts that were required to make TREETST1.C and TREETST2.C compile without warnings. Since the library routines in TREE1.C can't know in advance what type of data they will be manipulating, they have to use void pointers to access all data items. The library user will later be responsible for casting in the appropriate places to get around this problem.

Given that hand-coding is not only faster and more efficient but also safer, is it any surprise C programmers have done things this way for the past twenty years? While they are certainly guilty of reinventing the wheel on a regular basis, they have to be excused on the grounds that the generic wheel usually gave a pretty bumpy ride.

INHERITANCE AND C++ TO THE RESCUE

In the days before C++ even existed, Bjarne Stroustrup and his coworkers at AT&T were experimenting with an extension of C called *C with classes*. Before it evolved into C++, C with classes first introduced the class concept, then added the concept of inheritance. In the first release of C++, virtual functions were added to the mix. We finally had all the tools we needed to implement abstract classes.

The use of virtual functions to define abstract classes would seem to be a solution tailor-made for creating generic container classes. Bjarne Stroustrup pointed out one of the advantages of abstract classes:

"The importance of the abstract class concept is that it allows a cleaner separation between a user and an implementer than is possible without it."

A separation between the interface and the implementation is exactly what we want from a container class. C++ allows us to do this using derivation. A *base class* defines an abstract data type. For example, the binary tree implemented in C earlier in this chapter can be defined as a base class called BinaryTree. The header file shown in Listing 1-6 defines the complete interface this class provides.

Note that TREE2.H defines the interface to the abstract base class without any details regarding implementation.

Listing 1-6
TREE2.H

```
/*
 * TREE2.H
 *
 * This file defines the base class used to develop binary
 * trees. To make effective use of the trees, you must
 * derive a new class from this type. The derived class
 * should define the data members to be stored in the tree,
 * as well as the two pure virtual functions from this class.
 *
 */

class BinaryTree {
  protected :
    BinaryTree *left;
    BinaryTree *right;
  public :
    BinaryTree(){ left = 0; right = 0; }
    void AddNode( BinaryTree *new_node );
    void Traverse();
    virtual int Compare( BinaryTree * ) = 0;
    virtual void Display() = 0;
};
```

The base class shown in Listing 1-6 doesn't implement a useful binary tree yet. Why? First of all, it's missing a key member or members: the data that is actually being stored in the tree. Second, it is missing a couple of functions that are defined as *pure virtual* in the base class: Compare() and Display().

The missing data members and virtual functions don't show up in the base class for reasons of flexibility. A programmer uses a base class by deriving a new class from it. The derived class will contain the data members to be stored in the tree, as well as the definitions of the virtual functions used when building or traversing the tree.

The beauty of using virtual functions to define the comparison and display features used in class BinaryTree is that we can implement all the functions needed in the base class without any *a priori* knowledge about derived classes. This is because we have already defined a complete interface between the base and derived classes. It will be the responsibility of the programmer *using* the base class to define these virtual functions.

The implementation details of the base class are defined in the two functions in TREE2.CPP, shown in Listing 1-7. An examination of the BinaryTree::AddNode() function shows how the base class uses a virtual function as a key part of the algorithm. In this case, BinaryTree::Compare() tests nodes while descending the tree. The actual definition of Compare() is done by the user of a derived class. This means the developer of the base class can work with any data types that can supply a usable comparison function.

Listing 1-7
TREE2.CPP

```
/*
 * TREE2.CPP
 *
 * This file contains the code that implements the binary
 * tree generic base class defined in TREE2.H.
 *
 */

#include "tree2.h"

/*
 * The routine to add a node to the tree simply works its way
 * down the branches of the tree until it finds an open leaf
 * position where it can add the new node. To determine which
 * path to take down the tree, we need the Compare()
 * virtual function, which is defined in the derived class.
 */

void BinaryTree::AddNode( BinaryTree *new_node )
{
  BinaryTree *node = this;
  for ( ; ; ) {
    BinaryTree **next_node_ptr;
    if ( node->Compare( new_node ) < 0 )
      next_node_ptr = &node->left;
    else
      next_node_ptr = &node->right;
```

```
      if ( *next_node_ptr == 0 ) {
        *next_node_ptr = new_node;
        return;
      } else
        node = *next_node_ptr;
  }
}


/*
 * When traversing the tree we call the virtual function
 * Display(). This function is defined in the base class.
 */

void BinaryTree::Traverse()
{
  if ( left )
    left->Traverse();
  Display();
  if ( right )
    right->Traverse();
}
```

The use of a virtual function in a derived class to do comparisons has a significant advantage over the function-pointer approach in TREE1.CPP. Remember that in the C version of our BinaryTree class, comparisons were done via a function pointer cast to match the function prototype of the C add_node() function. This meant we gave up type safety when defining the function. A programmer could develop a completely inappropriate comparison function, but receive no error message when it was cast to type COMPARE_FN. For example, imagine that a C programmer was inserting integers into a binary tree. It would be relatively easy to write an incorrect comparison function, as shown in the following code. Here, the comparison function expects the integers to be passed by value, instead of via pointers:

```
int compare( int a, int b )
{
  return a - b;
}

void update_tree( int *new_data )
{
  add_node( tree, new_data, (COMPARE_FN) compare );
```

It would be nice if C compilers were able to detect this sort of bad cast, but it is simply not possible. When deriving a new class, it's impossible for the C++ programmer to cast the virtual function, thereby reducing the chances of error.

Thus, the C++ implementation of the binary tree is somewhat improved, owing to better type safety. However, the fact that it must use a virtual function means it will still lose out to the hand-coded routine when it comes to efficiency. Is this a problem? It's going to depend on the relative cost of a virtual function call when compared to the comparison function. The compare() function in this example is so short and simple that a virtual function call will look fairly costly. A complex comparison involving multiple floating-point calculations might not be so bad.

The C++ Program

Listing 1-8, TREETST4.CPP, shows what a program using class BinaryTree looks like. The program is divided into two conceptually different parts. The first part defines a derived class, in this case the class IntTree. IntTree is a very simple class, since it just has to add a data member to the base, then define four functions. Two simple virtual functions, AddNode() and Display() are used in the base class for navigating the tree and displaying data during traversal.

In addition to the two virtual functions, class IntTree defines a constructor, used to copy a data item into a new node, and an access operator, used to get the int value out of a node. Once again, these are both very simple functions.

Listing 1-8
TREETST4.CPP

```
//
// TREETST4.CPP
//
// This program tests class BinaryTree. It does so by deriving
// class IntTree, which should represent a binary tree holding
// integers as its data types. It then adds a list of integers
// to the tree, and finally prints out the integers in order.
// The derived class has just four functions defined. The
// constructor creates a new node and stores data in it, and
// a casting operator gets the data out of a node.
// The virtual functions Compare() and Display() are used by
// the base class to manipulate the tree.
```

```
//
// bcc -w TREETST4.CPP TREE2.CPP
//
// cl /W4 TREETST4.CPP TREE2.CPP
//
//

#include <iostream.h>
#include <string.h>

#include <iostream.h>
#include "tree2.h"

//
// This is the definition of the derived class. It
// is used to store integers in a binary tree. The
// base class knows how to insert items into the tree,
// and the derive class knows how to compare and display
// nodes. It takes both of them together to produce
// useful code.
//
class IntTree : public BinaryTree {
  protected :
    int data;
  public :
    IntTree( int i ){ data = i; }
    operator int(){ return data; }
    virtual int Compare( BinaryTree * );
    virtual void Display(){ cout << data << ' '; }
};

//
// During the insertion process, the base class
// has to compare nodes to determine whether to
// turn right or left from a node under test.
// This function takes care of the comparison.
//
int IntTree::Compare( BinaryTree *other_node )
{
  return data - ( int ) other_node ;
}

//
// The ints to be added to the tree.
//

int numbers[] = { 10, 15, -5, 2, 1, 100 };
```

```
//
// This short program adds a set of integers to a generic binary
// tree. After the integers have been added, the
// contents of the tree are printed out in order.
//

main()
{
  IntTree *root = new IntTree( numbers[ 0 ] );
  for ( int i = 1; i < sizeof( numbers ) / sizeof( int ) ; i++ )
    root->AddNode( new IntTree( numbers[ i ] ) );
  root->Traverse();
  return 0;
}
```

Figure 1-3 shows the tree that results from inserting the integer data in TREETST4.CPP into the tree. The tree structure still looks much like that of TREE1.CPP, but there is one crucial difference: instead of having to store data in memory allocated from the heap, TREETST4.CPP stores its data directly in the node. This means we have to perform fewer pointer dereferences when adding nodes to the tree, or when traversing the tree. So the C++ implementation shows some improvement over the C version.

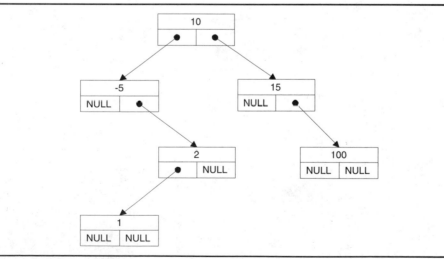

Figure 1-3
The C++ generic binary tree from TREETST4.CPP

HAND-CODING 2, LIBRARIES 0

Although the C++ implementation is somewhat safer and somewhat more efficient, it still can't compare to the hand-coded version in Listing 1-5, TREETST3. There are a couple of very important reasons why.

First, class BinaryTree is still tied to virtual functions in order to navigate the tree and display items in the tree. In terms of cost, a virtual function is somewhat less efficient than a function called via function pointer, and still worse than the inline operations that are selected when hand-coding. Figure 1-4 shows that calling a virtual function requires two pointer dereference operations, as opposed to one for calling a function via a pointer.

The customized version of the binary tree in TREETST3.C (See Listing 1-5) simply performs a direct comparison of an integer to an integer in another node while traversing the tree. Both the C and C++ generic classes have to suffer a performance penalty, since they have to first call a comparison function via pointer, then access both data items using pointers in the comparison function.

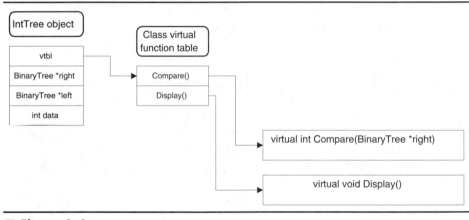

Figure 1-4
Accessing virtual functions

Another potential problem with the generic BinaryTree class used here is our old friend type safety. While it is true that we have more safety in the C++ class than we did with the C library routines, we are still vulnerable to errors when mixing types. Since anyone can derive a new class from class BinaryTree, it would be reasonable to have several types of binary trees in a single program. Without violating any type-safety rules, the programmer could inadvertently mix string nodes and integer nodes in a single tree.

When it came time to traverse the tree, or to perform comparisons while updating the tree, we would be trying to compare apples and oranges.

For example, I could add a block of integer nodes to a tree using the code from TREETST4.CPP:

```
root->AddNode( new IntTree( numbers[ i ] ) );
```

Subsequently, I might mistakenly add a string node to the same tree:

```
root->AddNode( new StringTree( "Testing" ));
```

When it came time to traverse the tree using the IntTree root node and display each node, this line of code would be called to display the contents of the node:

```
virtual void Display(){ cout << data << ' '; }
```

But in at least one case, the data member of IntTree wouldn't exist, since the node is actually an IntString node. At best, this would result in bad data being displayed. At worst, the program would crash.

RTTI to the rescue — sort of

C++ has a new feature called Run Time Type Identification, or RTTI, that can help detect these sorts of errors. You can obtain information about the type of an object using the C++ typeid() operator. With the addition of the typeid() function, we could catch errors using code like this:

```
void IntTree::Display()
{
  assert( typeinfo( *this ) == typeid( IntTree ) );
  cout << data << ' ';
}
```

While this explicit testing works, it suffers from two major problems. First, it has to be explicitly added to a program, which means it's less likely to be used. Second, the test is done at runtime instead of compile time. Static typed languages such as C++ normally do type checking at compile time, to avoid the inefficiency of doing the job at runtime.

So, although RTTI can help, it isn't really the best solution to the problem.

Inheritance won't do

With these two, and a few other, strikes against it, perhaps inheritance isn't the ideal way to implement generic container classes. Besides falling behind in the cardinal virtue of efficiency, the programmer has to define a new class, and define the virtual functions it needs.

Fortunately, there is a better way to create generic container classes, a method that solves all these problems: templates.

TEMPLATES: THE RIGHT WAY

Templates were one of the last features added to C++ before the standardization process began. As Bjarne Stroustrup says in *The Design and Evolution of C++*:

> *"Templates were considered essential for the design of proper container classes... For many people, the largest single problem with C++ is the lack of an extensive standard library. A major problem in producing such a library is that C++ does not provide a sufficiently general facility for defining 'container classes' such as lists, vectors, and associative arrays."*

Although Stroustrup was aware of the need for templates at an early stage of C++ development, templates were deliberately left out of release 2.0 of the AT&T cfront compiler in favor of multiple inheritance. Stroustrup writes that this was probably a case of mistaken priorities, but it seemed the right thing to do at the time.

The definition of templates was included in *The Annotated C++ Reference Manual*, although they weren't yet officially part of the language. Along with exceptions, templates were presented as an experimental design feature. An early attempt to investigate parameterized types (template classes) was done using the C preprocessor, along with a header file called generic.hpp. While not an actual substitute for templates, generic.hpp did provide a useful tool for experimentation.

The utility of templates was obvious and they were eventually incorporated, first into cfront, then into the draft ANSI language standard, and finally into most commercial compilers. Support for templates led directly to the development of the STL, a standardized library of container classes and algorithms using template classes and functions.

Chapter 2 takes a more detailed look at templates. For right now, if you aren't familiar with templates, you can think of them as an automated way to generate customized classes and functions. The STL uses templates to create customized containers that are built from the ground up, using your types. In both C and early versions of C++, you might have done this sort of thing using the preprocessor. Now, it's a built-in feature of the language.

Template classes: an example

Let's take another look at our BinaryTree container class design. This time we'll be using templates. The design of the BinaryTree class suffered from some obvious deficiencies in both standard C and C++ multiple inheritance. We need to see if we can correct these problems with templates.

The definition for class BinaryTree<T> is shown in Listing 1-9, TREE3.H. A striking feature of template classes is that the implementation and interface to the class are often found in the same include file. While this may be inelegant, it is a necessary by-product of C and C++'s freewheeling approach to modular programming using multiple source files.

In class BinaryTree<T>, T is the type parameter used to build the new class. You can see that T appears throughout the class definition. This parameterization is, of course, what lets us define a container class without knowing in advance what type of objects it will contain.

Listing 1-9
TREE3.H

```
/*
 ^ TREE3.H
 *
 * This header file contains the template class definition
 * for class BinaryTree<T>. Class T is the single parameter
 * used in the class definition. Note that this declaration
 * looks quite a bit like that in TREE2.H. One major difference
 * is that the header file contains all of the code defined for
 * the member functions in addition to the declaration.
 *
 */

#include <iostream.h>
#include <string.h>
```

```cpp
template <class T> class BinaryTree
{
  public :
    BinaryTree<T>( const T &t );
    void AddNode( const T & );
    void Traverse();
  protected :
    T data;
    BinaryTree<T> *left_node;
    BinaryTree<T> *right_node;
    int LessThan( const T &t );
};

//
// The LessThan function is used when inserting new
// data into the tree. Normally, this will expand
// into a simple inline comparison,
// very efficient for built-in types. This class defines
// a slightly different version for string comparisons,
// as we normally don't want to compare them just by
// pointer values.
//
template <class T>
inline int BinaryTree<T>::LessThan( const T &t )
{
  return data < t;
}

typedef char *X;

inline int BinaryTree<char *>::LessThan( const X &t )
{
  return strcmp( data, t ) < 0;
}

template <class T>
inline BinaryTree<T>::BinaryTree( const T &t )
{
  data = t;
  left_node = 0;
  right_node = 0;
}

//
// Unlike the traversal function in TREE2.CPP, this function
// doesn't have to call a virtual function to display the
```

```
// data.
//

template <class T> void BinaryTree<T>::Traverse()
{
  if ( left_node )
    left_node->Traverse();
  cout << data << " ";
  if ( right_node )
    right_node->Traverse();
}


//
// The AddNode() member function is nearly identical to that
// in TREE2.CPP. In this case, however, the comparison between
// the two data items is called using the LessThan() member
// function. LessThan() should normally expand to an inline
// function performing a direct comparison. For built-in
// data types this should be very efficient.
//
template <class T> void BinaryTree<T>::AddNode( const T &data )
{
  BinaryTree<T> *node = this;
  BinaryTree<T> *new_node = new BinaryTree<T>( data );
  for ( ; ; ) {
    BinaryTree<T> **next_node_ptr;
    if ( node->LessThan( data ) )
      next_node_ptr = &node->right_node;
    else
      next_node_ptr = &node->left_node;
    if ( *next_node_ptr == 0 ) {
      *next_node_ptr = new_node;
      return;
    } else
      node = *next_node_ptr;
  }
}
```

The first good thing we achieve by using templates is that the data member can be incorporated directly into the BinaryTree<T> class. These lines in the class declaration make that possible:

```
protected :
  T data;
```

Any time the member functions of the class want to access the data item, they can do so by looking directly at the data member. Recall that with C implementations of the binary tree, the data members had to be accessed via a void pointer. Not only was this more inefficient, due to the necessary pointer dereference, but caused us to lose type safety as well.

Note also that a template-based class can just as easily store pointers to data if necessary. For example, if my data objects were difficult to copy or manipulate, template-based containers allow me to define type T as either Myclass or Myclass *.

The C++ derived class implementation of the BinaryTree class had the advantage of storing the data as a member of the derived class, but the base class still didn't know anything about the type of the data member. So any functions that accessed the data had to be virtual functions.

In contrast, when we instantiate an instance of BinaryTree<T>, the created class knows everything about the type of the data member. The benefits of this show up in several places. First, in function BinaryTree<T>::AddNode(), we can make an immediate comparison of two data items to determine which branch of the tree to take:

```
if ( node->LessThan( data ) )
   next_node_ptr = &node->right_node;
else next_node_ptr = &node->left_node;
```

For every built-in data type (with the exception of character strings), LessThan() is a template function that expands inline to a simple comparison. Thus, for a tree class such as BinaryTree<int>, this section of code becomes:

```
if ( node->data < data )
   next_node_ptr = &node->right_node;
else
   next_node_ptr = &node->left_node;
```

Compare this to our earlier attempts at defining a container class. First, we have direct access to the data member when we're making comparisons. Second, not only do we avoid calling a virtual function to compare the two data elements, in many cases we can avoid calling a function at all! Built-in data types such as int or double will frequently be compared using inline code. Even user-defined classes or types can potentially have inline LessThan functions.

Another piece of code that benefits from the built-in knowledge of the container data type is the Traverse() function. In the template version of the Binary Tree class, the Traverse() function doesn't have to call any virtual functions; it simply uses the stream insertion operator to display the character. All built-in types have library support predefined for the insertion operator, so no new coding is necessary. Once again, this means that the code gains both efficiency and type safety.

SEE IT AND BELIEVE

Listing 1-10, TREETST5.CPP, tests the BinaryTree<T> class. It is essentially a combination of two programs, one to test BinaryTree<int>, and another to test BinaryTree<char *>.

Listing 1-10
TREETST5.CPP

```
//
// TREETST5.CPP
//
// This program tests class BinaryTree<T>. It does so by
// instantiating a BinaryTree<int>, and another BinaryTree<char *>.
// It then performs the same operations done by the other
// test programs in this chapter, namely adding a list of data,
// then displaying it using the Traverse() function.
//
// Build this program using command lines similar to this:
//
// bcc -w TREETST5.CPP
//
// cl /W4 TREETST5.CPP
//
//

#include "tree3.h"

int numbers[] = { 5, 12, 4, 4, -1, 10 };
char *strings[] = { "Burma", "Thailand", "Laos",
                    "Viet Nam", "Cambodia" };
```

```
main()
{
  BinaryTree<int> tree1( numbers[ 0 ] );
  for ( int i = 1 ; i < sizeof( numbers ) / sizeof( int ) ; i++ )
    tree1.AddNode( numbers[ i ] );
  tree1.Traverse();
  BinaryTree<char *> tree2( strings[ 0 ] );
  for ( i = 1 ; i < sizeof( strings ) / sizeof( char * ) ; i++ )
    tree2.AddNode( strings[ i ] );
  tree2.Traverse();
  return 0;
}
```

This program illustrates the advantages of templates over the previous methods we experimented with:

- You have complete type safety, both in the interface and implementation of the library. No casting or void pointers are used anywhere. This prevents many common mistakes caused by improper type conversions.

- Unlike in the ANSI C implementations, you don't have to write comparison functions or display functions. Since the container is holding built-in types, you can take advantage of the built-in comparison operators. Likewise, the iostreams library has display support for built-in types.

- You don't have to define a new class that is derived from a library base class. While this is a relatively low-cost operation, it is still an inconvenience better avoided.

- The template version of the Binary Tree class works just as well as the hand-coded version, since you don't have to make any calls via virtual functions, and no extraneous pointers are created.

- Finally, the language definition has expanded to the point where you can automatically generate code that is just as efficient and easy to use as the hand-coded equivalent. Easy, that is, once you master the slightly awkward syntax required to use templates.

Once templates were in place as part of the language, a standard library of template classes was inevitable. While there are others on the market, the STL is the library that has been accepted as part of the C++ standard. In Chapter 2, "An Overview of the Standard Template Library," we'll take a look at exactly what the STL is and what it has to offer.

AN OVERVIEW OF TEMPLATES

Nam et ipsa scientia potestas est. (Knowledge is power.)
— Francis Bacon, *Meditationes Sacrae [1597] De Haeresibus*

As we saw in Chapter 1, "The STL, A Historical Perspective," the STL accomplishes its mission through the use of templates. Looking at the STL specification, you can see that templates are the very *raison d'etre* of the Standard Template Library:

> "The Standard Template Library provides a set of well-structured, generic C++ components that work together in a seamless way. Special care has been taken to ensure that all the template algorithms work not only on the data structures in the library, but also on built-in C++ data structures."

Without templates, it is much more difficult to implement and use a library containing standard containers and algorithms that work in an efficient and seamless fashion—efficient enough to be attractive to C++ programmers.

In simplest terms, a *template* is a definition of either a class or a function that has one or more C++ types (a class or built-in type) as parameters. To use templates, we need some new syntax and terminology in the C++ language definition, as you'll soon see.

This chapter will give you an overview of what templates are, how they are used, and why they are important to the STL.

BJARNE'S CLAIRVOYANCE

In the introduction to Chapter 8 of *The C++ Programming Language, Second Edition*, Bjarne Stroustrup says:

> *"The template concept allows container classes, such as lists and associative arrays, to be simply defined and implemented without loss of static type checking or run-time efficiency. Similarly, templates allow generic functions, such as sort(), to be defined once for a family of types."*

It sounds as though Stroustrup is referring to the STL, and in a way, he is. The introduction of templates made the STL possible and virtually assured its creation and adoption. Given this tight linkage, you can be sure that if you don't understand templates, you won't understand the STL. Without having a good comfort level with templates, library declarations and source code will, at best, be confusing. Once you achieve that comfort level, the STL will show itself to be a simple, well-designed library.

As you saw in Chapter 1, templates, along with exceptions, were one of the last features to be added to the C++ language. Templates were discussed as a proposed language extension in Stroustrup's *The Annotated C++ Reference Manual*, (commonly known as the ARM), and first appeared in the 3.0 release of cfront (AT&T's UNIX-based C++ preprocessor/compiler). At the time of this writing, templates are still not supported in the most popular MS-DOS/Windows C++ compiler (Microsoft Visual C++ 1.5). Also, the ANSI/ISO C++ committee has just added the finishing touches to the draft C++ standard, which added a few new features to templates. This means compiler vendors will have to update their implementations in upcoming releases to be fully compliant.

In the face of all this activity in the area of templates, it seems appropriate to briefly discuss their essential points. To supplement this chapter with a more detailed reference, you can refer to Chapter 8 of *The C++ Programming Language, Second Edition*. If you are comfortable with templates, feel free to skip this brief review.

Exactly What *Is* a Template?

One of the early advances in symbolic programming languages was the ability to write functions and procedures that took arguments. This meant that a programmer working with FORTRAN in the 1960s could write one routine to multiply matrices, then call it repeatedly with different arguments. A matrix multiplication routine might expect to have six arguments:

- An input array of dimensions R_1 by C
- A second input array of dimensions C by R_2
- An output array of dimensions R_1 by R_2
- The value of R_1
- The value of C
- The value of R_2

Typical calls to this function could look like this:

```
CALL MATMUL( A, B, C, 3, 4, 5 )
CALL MATMUL( D, E, F, 8, 1, 9 )
CALL MATMUL( NODES, WEIGHTS, OUTPUT, 100, 100, 100 )
```

Without the ability to pass arguments to subroutines, the matrix multiplication code would have to be repeatedly written in-line, resulting in an enormous duplication of effort.

Passing parameters to subroutines not only makes life easier when writing programs, it also helps make programs more reliable and easier to maintain. A programmer can write a highly optimized matrix multiplication routine, test it thoroughly, then supply it as a library function. As long as programmers pass it the appropriate arguments, the chances of it working properly are excellent.

Procedural abstraction with parameter passing is such a useful programming concept that today it is nearly universal. Modern programming languages (even assembly languages) nearly always support this idea in one form or another.

C++ templates use parameters in an entirely new way: to create new functions and classes. And, unlike parameter passing to procedures, templates create these new functions and classes at compile time, rather than runtime.

Creation, not evolution

The idea of creating new classes and functions using types as parameters isn't entirely new. For example, you could have used the C preprocessor to define new types based on the BinaryTree class you saw in Chapter 1:

```
#define BinaryTree( t )          \
typedef struct _tree_##t {       \
  t data;                        \
  struct _tree_##t *left;        \
  struct _tree_##t *right;       \
} BinaryTree_##t;

BinaryTree( int );
BinaryTree_int a;
BinaryTree_int b;
```

Templates accomplish the same thing without the use of the preprocessor. But, you may ask, since both templates and the preprocessor can be used to generate new functions and types, why are templates so much better?

- **Templates generate new classes and functions automatically.** My example that used the preprocessor to generate BinaryTree classes required the programmer to explicitly call a macro to create a new type.

- **The syntax used to create new types is built into the language.** The preprocessor example created new type names using an arbitrary syntax, giving names like BinaryTree_int to the resulting classes. If you used the preprocessor, you'd have to develop or learn a new idiosyncratic naming methodology every time you wrote or used a new class/function-generation macro!

- **Template functions deduce the types of their arguments automatically.** You'll see later in this chapter that calling template functions is exceptionally easy. You don't even have to be aware of the fact that a function *is* a template function.

- **Template functions are generated automatically by the compiler, with no effort on your part.** For example, a template function used to raise a number to a given power might have a prototype that looks like this:

```
template<class T>
T pow( T x, int n );
```

If you write a program that calls this function three times, using different argument types, the compiler actually generates three specific versions of the function for you. Figure 2-1 shows the functions that are generated for various invocations of pow(). Remember, this is all done automatically by the compiler!

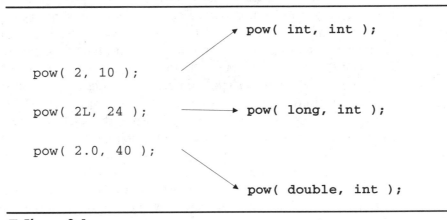

```
                                        pow( int, int );

pow( 2, 10 );

pow( 2L, 24 );          ────────►    pow( long, int );

pow( 2.0, 40 );

                                        pow( double, int );
```

Figure 2-1
Template function generation by the compiler

TEMPLATE SYNTAX

Like procedures, templates take parameters. However, the syntax for both the definition and use of templates is different from that of a C++ function. A template definition looks like this:

```
template <argument-list> declaration
```

The new keyword, *template*, clearly marks the location of a template definition. In fact, as Stroustrup says, it's easy to find places where you are using templates with automated tools like *grep*.

The argument list for a template is similar to the argument list for a function, with one important exception. An argument list for a template can have not only "normal" function arguments, but type arguments as well. You create a type argument in the list by specifying the keyword *class* followed by an identifier:

```
template <class T, int size> ...
```

In this template declaration there are two arguments; they construct a new class or function based on the values passed when the template was invoked. There are a couple of very important things to note about this. One is that the first argument in the template is actually a *type*, not a value. Wherever the template declaration has identifier *T*, the compiler will substitute the type or class name passed as an argument. The other important thing is that the substitution takes place at compile time, not runtime.

Despite the fact that template declarations use the word *class*, the type argument you provide can be any valid C++ type, including built-in types such as int or double. (This is yet another example where a C++ keyword is pressed into service with a slightly different meaning.)

This substitution of type arguments in the declaration is the reason for the power of templates. Until templates existed, the safest way to write C++ code that supported multiple types was through virtual functions. With templates, the compiler lets you specify types the same way you pass arguments to functions and procedures.

Note that the creation of new classes and functions takes place at compile time, not runtime. This makes it convenient to think of the template facility as a sort of macro preprocessor with superpowers. In fact, earlier experimental versions of templates were implemented using the C preprocessor, cpp. Stroustrup says it is reasonable to think of a template as *"a clever kind of macro that obeys the scope, naming, and type rules of C++."*

It's also important to note the distinction between macros and templates. It is difficult to write macros that work properly under all circumstances. Macros don't check argument types, generate unpleasant side effects, and can be just plain dangerous to use. For example, consider a macro that implements a max() function:

```
#define max( a, b ) a > b ? a : b
```

Even a simple macro like this can cause all sorts of problems. For example:

```
*p++ = max( *r++, *s++ )
```

An innocent little code fragment such as that shown above will wreak havoc on your program, since it will cause one of its two arguments to be incremented twice! Each time argument macro argument *a* is evaluated, it will cause pointer *r* to be incremented.

Experienced C programmers learn to recognize these situations and work around them, but templates provide an even safer approach.

The template declaration

After the template keyword and the argument list, you supply the template declaration, where you define the parameterized version of a class or function. It's up to the C++ compiler to generate different versions of the class or function based on the arguments passed to the template when it is used.

Here is an example of a simple class template:

```
template <class T, int size>
class Array {
    protected :
        T *data;
    public :
        Array(){ data = new T[ size ]; }
        ~Array(){ delete[] data; }
        T &operator[]( int index ) {
            if ( index < 0 || index >= size )
                throw( "Bad index" ); //Generate a runtime error
            else
                return data[ index ];}
    };
```

This template definition creates array classes of a given type. The two arguments passed to the array are T, which is the type of object the array is made of, and size, which defines the number of elements in the array. T appears in three different places in the definition and size is found in two more places.

The compiler generates a new version of this class for every different combination of types passed to it. It does this at compile time by performing a substitution of the arguments wherever they appear in the declaration. If somewhere in the program an array of doubles is generated containing 25 entries, the compiler will create an instance of this class equivalent to this:

```
class Array__double__25 {
    protected :
        double *data;
    public :
        Array(){ data = new double[ 25 ]; }
        ~Array(){ delete[] data; }
        double &operator[]( int index ) {
            if ( index < 0 || index >= 25 )
                throw( "Bad index" );
            else
                return data[ index ];}
    };
```

The analogy of a macro preprocessor shows how a simple template such as this is created. Of course, the internal details differ from compiler to compiler. The important point is that the compiler will generate a completely new class every time it needs to. Multiple uses of the template with the same arguments shouldn't generate new classes, since one is sufficient.

This simple class template can create arrays that will generate exceptions if an illegal index is used. A sample program using this class might look like this:

```
main()
{
    Array< int, 25 > a;

    a[ 0 ] = 0;
    a[ 1 ] = 1;
    a[ 100 ] = 100; //Should generate an exception
    return 1;
}
```

In this example, the strength of the template concept is shown in a class like Array. With a single header file and one class definition, we can create a range-checked array that can be used with any type of data. The extra work needed to handle creation of the array classes is done at compile time, with no penalty placed on our program at runtime.

THE TWO TYPES OF TEMPLATES

To understand how templates function in the STL, you need to understand the two major types of templates: *class templates* and *function templates*. Both act as factories for their particular type of objects. That is, class templates generate classes and function templates generate functions.

You use the two types of templates in different ways. Since function templates automatically determine their type parameters, you might not even know a given function is a template function. For example, older C compilers usually had a max() macro defined in stdlib.h. When Borland introduced template support to their C++ compiler, they redefined max() to be a template function. Consider a line like this in your program:

```
int a = max( b, c );
```

You don't have any easy way to know whether this is a macro call or an invocation of a template function.

On the other hand, class template users should always be aware that that they are constructing classes using a template. This is because the syntax of a template class declaration requires you to specify any type parameters:

```
vector<double> a;
```

It's hard to miss the obvious use of a template parameter in an example like this!

Class templates

The class template for class BinaryTree from Chapter 1 is shown in the following code example. BinaryTree is similar to the container classes defined in the STL. In fact, it is a container class that holds objects of the type defined by the single parameter. The public interface to the class includes a function to add nodes to the tree and to traverse the tree.

```
template <class T>
class BinaryTree
{
    public :
        BinaryTree<T>( const T &t );
        void AddNode( const T & );
        void Traverse();
    protected :
        T data;
        BinaryTree<T> *left_node;
        BinaryTree<T> *right_node;
        int LessThan( T t );
};

template <class T>
inline int BinaryTree<T>::LessThan( T t )
{
    return data < t;
}

inline int BinaryTree<char *>::LessThan( char *t )
{
    return strcmp( data, t ) < 0;
}
```

The first thing to notice about this class template is the pair of function definitions immediately following it. Often, these inline functions are embedded within the class declaration, but the template syntax allows us to declare them outside the declaration as well.

For the sake of efficiency, many member functions of the class are declared as inline. If the compiler is able to generate the code for these functions inline, it can lead to implementations of algorithms every bit as efficient as hand-coded versions.

In addition, these class templates can define customized versions of member functions for specific data types. Class BinaryTree normally sorts its entries based on comparisons with the LessThan() function, which performs a simple arithmetic comparison. For character pointers, it is preferable to compare strings via the standard library function strcmp(). You do this by writing a specialized function to be used when instantiating class BinaryTree<char *>.

Built-in types welcome

The single template argument for class template BinaryTree is referred to in the argument list as class T. This argument could be any class defined by the user or in the standard libraries. However, the type argument for BinaryTree could as easily be a built-in type such as int or double. It is clear from the declaration that everywhere you insert a T, you could use a defined class or a built-in type.

Since all container classes for the STL are built using templates, they have a real advantage over container classes that use inheritance. If you want to use the STL to create an array of a built-in type such as float, you simply declare the class using the built-in type.

```
Vector<float> iv;
```

If you use inheritance to create a container, you have to go to the trouble of defining a new class that inherits the tree behavior. The new class would contain the integer data as a data member. This amounts to extra work you would rather not have to do. It also opens the door for mistakes in the class definition, regardless of how simple it is.

Putting class templates to work

Whenever you want to use a class template in your program, simply use the class template name with the type arguments enclosed in angle brackets. For example, a BinaryTree template that holds C++ string objects would be declared like this:

```
BinaryTree<string> names;
```

Anywhere you want to refer to this type, use the compound identifier BinaryTree<string>. You can specify it as a type being passed to functions, or even as a type being passed to a template definition. For example, under the STL you might declare a two-dimensional array as:

```
vector< vector<int> > array2d;
```

This might look forbidding if you aren't accustomed to template syntax. The declaration vector<T> declares a vector (an STL array) of type T. So vector<int> is a vector of integers. This means that vector< vector<int> > is a vector of integer vectors. The resulting object is very similar to the C++ two-dimensional array of integers:

```
int *array2d[n];
```

Template definitions are frequently employed to create shorter names using typedef statements. The STL makes heavy use of nested typedefs inside class template declarations. This cuts down on the amount of heavily "templated" text and, if done well, contributes to the overall readability of the code. A typical typedef might look like this:

```
typedef vector< char > stl_string;
```

This type definition instructs the compiler to use the template class vector<char> anywhere it sees the type stl_string used. You can then use stl_string *as if* it were a new type:

```
main()
{
    stl_string first_name;
    stl_string last_name;
```

When the compiler encounters a definition using stl_string, it will automatically use vector<char> as the type. vector<char> is an STL array-like container filled with C++ characters, so the sample code represents a typical use.

A typedef as simple as this probably isn't very useful, since vector<char> is nice and easy to read. But complex definitions can be long and intimidating, so a simpler name created via type definition is a big improvement.

Function templates

A function template takes the same general format as a class template: the template keyword, followed by an argument list, followed by the declaration:

```
template <class T>
T square( T x ){ return x * x; }
```

A template like this defines a group of functions. The particular function created and called is determined by the type of the arguments passed to the function. For example, the function could be called using the following invocations:

```
cout << square( 1 ) << "\n";
cout << square( 200U ) << "\n";
cout << square( 1000.0 ) << "\n";
cout << square( 20000L ) << "\n";
```

These calls will invoke, in respective order:

```
int square( int x );
unsigned int square( unsigned int x);
double square( double x );
long square( long x );
```

It's up to the compiler to create these functions, based on their use in the source code. The compiler has to determine which function to instantiate, based on the type of the arguments passed in the call. In the example just shown, the compiler has a very easy time selecting and instantiating the appropriate function, since there is only a single argument. More complex function templates can be more difficult to resolve.

Who you going to call?

With the addition of templates, C++ compilers now have to deal with a lot of choices when it comes time to decide which version of a function to call. In the case of the square() function shown above, you could assume that the compiler only had one choice: a single template function called square(). But what if there are non-template versions of square(), or perhaps multiple template versions of square()?

No problem. The compiler follows three simple rules when selecting a function:

1. The compiler first attempts to find an exact match for the function, given the arguments that are being used. In the above case, if you attempted to call square(1), it would look for a function named square() with a single integer or integer reference argument.

2. If no exact match can be made, the compiler will then try to create a template function with the appropriate argument types. The compiler uses the exact argument types being passed by the caller. This is why a call to square(2L) would cause the compiler to create the following expansion of the template function:

```
long square( long x ) {
return x * x;
}
```

3. Finally, the compiler tries to make the function call fit into existing functions through the various type conversions it has available. If no match can be found this way, an error occurs.

FUNCTION TEMPLATES VS CLASS TEMPLATES

While class templates and function templates are logically grouped together, they are invoked quite differently in a program. A class template is instantiated using an invocation that specifies all the type and symbolic parameters:

```
BinaryTree<string> names;
```

In contrast, function templates can be called without any mention of types (just as if they were normal functions):

```
complex t = square( x );
```

This means the user can be calling a parameterized function without even knowing it. For example, Borland replaced the ANSI C min() and max() macros with template functions that look something like this:

```
template <class T>
```

```
T &max( const T &a, const T &b )
{
    if ( a > b )
        return a;
    else
        return b;
}
```

Users of Borland's runtime library may not be aware of this change, since their use of min() or max() doesn't give any clue. The first indication that templates are in use may occur when stepping into min() or max() while using the debugger.

Do-nothing arguments

When creating class template objects, you normally pass parameters to the template that simply have type information, with no reference to data whatsoever. However, creating a variable of type BinaryTree<int> causes the type int to be passed to the class template, enabling class BinaryTree to embed an int in the resulting class.

Function templates don't have the luxury of doing this. Their syntax doesn't support a function call like this:

```
x = square( 100, long );
```

Despite this restriction, there are times when you need to pass type information to a function template. For example, imagine a slightly modified version of the square() function that displays the results of the arithmetic operation. You might start with a function template like this:

```
template <class T>
void display_square( ostream &s, T t )
{
    s << (t * t) << "\n";
}
```

This would work well for many function calls, but imagine what would happen if you called it like this:

```
display_square( cout, 256 );
```

This function call *should* display a value of 65536, but unfortunately it prints 0, because squaring 256 gives a value that doesn't fit into a 16-bit int. The solution is to add an additional piece of type information to the function template that tells us what internal data type to use when calculating the square:

```
template < class T, class R>
void display_square( ostream &s, T x, R )
{
    R temp = x;
    temp *= x;
    s << temp << '\n';
}
```

The *value* of the third argument to display_square() is never employed, but the *type* of the argument is used to determine the type of the internal variable. The correct way to call this function is:

```
display_square( cout, 256, (long) 0 );
```

Now, the correct result of 65536 is displayed.

The STL frequently uses this technique in internal library routines. If you look at the declarations for iterators, you will see functions with names like value_type() that just return a 0 cast to a certain type. Functions such as value_type() are often used to pass types to function templates.

COMPILER HOUSEKEEPING

Template declarations are contained in header files, so the compiler can be aware of the entire definition of a template at compile time. Libraries such as the STL frequently contain nothing but header files, leading more than one library user to comment, "I received the STL header files, but I can't seem to find the source code!"

Keeping all the works in a header file makes life more difficult for the compiler writer for several reasons. First of all, the C++ compiler has to process a huge amount of code every time the appropriate header files are included. But even worse, there is an instantiation proliferation problem.

Imagine you have a class template for class BinaryTree that has a fairly long routine used to balance the tree. Then imagine you call BinaryTree<string>::balance() in 20 different source modules of your project. The compiler would create 20 different copies of this function, one per source file. If standard C linkers are used with a project like this, you would probably get an executable that was much larger than necessary.

Different compiler vendors handle this problem in different ways. Probably the most common is to modify the linker to be aware of templates. If more than one occurrence of a member function or template function appears, the linker can be written to disregard multiple copies. Other solutions to this problem require the user to hand-instantiate occurrences of functions.

Just as the ads say, your mileage may vary! If you are using a compiler that hasn't got the hang of templates yet, you may suffer code bloat in those projects that use the library. As compilers mature, however, this problem ought to evaporate, particularly if you keep up with new releases from your vendor.

STAYING ALIVE

If you are a new C++ programmer, you probably have already been bombarded with information about classes, virtual functions, multiple inheritance, and so on *ad nauseum*. Since the human brain can only absorb new information so fast, this chapter may leave you vulnerable to the YEGO effect: you read it and Your Eyes Glaze Over.

Don't despair if this happens. I believe that templates are easier to digest than a lot of other C++ concepts. Just remember the basic idea: templates turn your compiler into a factory that builds new classes and functions as needed. Refer back to this chapter and the ARM as you read through the rest of the book, and templates should begin to lose their aura of mystery (aggravation?) by the time you finish the book.

AN OVERVIEW OF THE STANDARD TEMPLATE LIBRARY

li·brar·y (lì´brèr´ê) noun
5. Computer Science. A collection of standard programs, routines, or
subroutines, often related to a specific application, that are available for
general use.
— The American Heritage Dictionary of the English Language, Third Edition

FIVE EASY PIECES

Niklaus Wirth wrote a book that is well known, if for no other reason than its compelling title, *Algorithms + Data Structures = Programs*. The title is more than just a clever bit of wordplay. It also concisely communicates much of the essence of writing computer programs. Programming requires the effective development of data structures, which are then used by algorithms to achieve some desired result. Modern programming methodologies are concerned with developing paths that lead us to well-designed data structures and algorithms.

The STL puts this into practice with its two core components:

- container classes
- algorithms

These two pieces of the STL are connected via a third piece of the puzzle:

- iterators

To round out the list of components, there are two additional pieces:

- function objects
- adaptors

The interaction between these five components defines the STL. In this chapter, you'll get a high-level look at these core components.

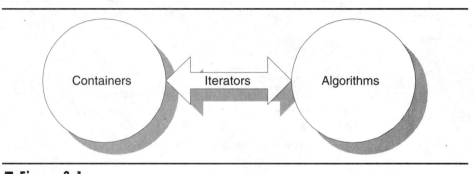

Figure 3-1
The three core components of the STL

STL CONTAINERS

The first of the five STL core components is a family of container classes. *Containers* are what they sound like: generic objects used to store other objects. The STL specification puts it simply:

> *"Containers are objects that store other objects. They control allocation and de-allocation of these objects through constructors, destructors, insert and erase operations."*

Most programmers have studied, or are familiar with, classic data structures such as arrays, linked lists, and trees. The STL has taken some of the most useful data structures and created efficient and easy-to-use implementations of them.

The declaration of a container in a program defines the type of object it will hold. For example, to create a vector of integers, an STL vector might be declared like this:

```
int main()
{
    vector<int> vec;
    ...
```

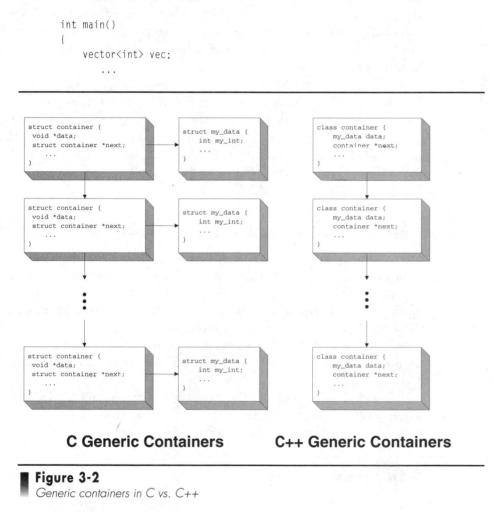

C Generic Containers   **C++ Generic Containers**

Figure 3-2
Generic containers in C vs. C++

To have and to hold

As discussed in Chapter 1, STL containers don't hold objects via pointers. Rather, objects are stored in containers as data members, which gives both efficiency and type safety. Data members held in the container are defined at compile type via template use. Because of this strategy, STL containers can store both user-defined classes and built-in objects such as ints or void * objects.

Because the STL is designed to contain whole objects, it's easy to overlook the fact that it can also be used to store *pointers* to objects as well. Container classes that hold references or pointers to objects instead of complete objects are sometimes referred to as *collection classes*. The STL is perfectly capable of operating in this mode.

If you store complete objects in STL containers, the STL takes care of creating, copying, and destroying the objects, which means you don't have to worry about it. If you store pointers to objects in your STL container, you will probably have to create and destroy the objects yourself, which gives you more chances for mistakes. But this may actually be an advantage, if the cost of creating and destroying the object is high.

Separate but equal: the two container families

STL containers come in two flavors: *sequence containers* and *associative containers*. These container families have distinct properties and are designed for different kinds of work. Sequence containers store objects in sequential order, while associative containers store objects based on an ordering function.

Sequence families contain data organized as an array or linked list. It's easy to traverse the list and access data members sequentially. If you access an object at a given point in a sequence container, it's simple to move to the next, or previous, item in the list.

Associative containers make it easy to look up a data object based on a given key. Objects in an associative container are stored using a tree organization, making searches for a given item very efficient.

Sequence containers

The STL defines three different sequence containers:

- vector<T>
- deque<T>
- list<T>

Note: Standard C array types are like sequence containers. They obey the characteristics of STL containers and can be used with algorithms that expect STL containers as arguments.

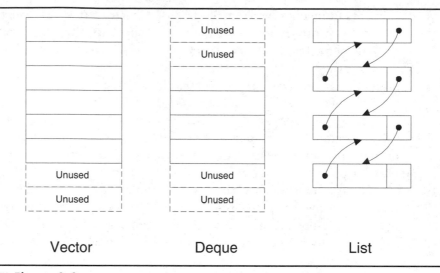

Vector   Deque   List

Figure 3-3
STL sequence containers

These three containers represent data structures that you are probably already comfortable with.

- vector<T> is a standard array that can change size transparently as needed.
- deque<T> is a queue data structure that efficiently inserts and removes objects from either end.
- list<T> is a doubly linked list.

The fundamental operations performed with sequence containers are the insertion and removal of objects. You do this with the insert() and erase() member functions. insert() takes an argument indicating the object in the container that the *new* object will be inserted in front of. The important differences between these containers relate to the cost of accessing objects, and the insertion and erasure of objects.

vector<T> objects look like normal C arrays; to access elements within the array, what's needed is a simple offset of a pointer plus an offset. Inserting or erasing elements at the end of the array is also easy since, most of the time, it can be accomplished by simply adding or removing an element from the unused space at the end of the vector.

However, inserting or erasing a new element at a position inside the vector is more difficult. This operation requires a block move of the array elements immediately following the insertion/erasure point. Thus, the time expense is proportional to the number of elements after the insertion point.

The performance characteristics of vector<T> make it useful, not only as a smart array that manages its own storage, but also as a stack. The template implementation gives it speed comparable to an array, with the bonus that a programmer doesn't have to hand-code the allocation and reallocation code.

deque<T> has most of the characteristics of the vector<T> container, and it features quick access to individual elements and quick insertion/erasure at the start *or* end of the list. This makes deque<T> a useful data structure for implementations of FIFOs.

The list<T> container features forward and reverse links between elements. This means access of individual elements in the list will not be done in fast constant time, as with vector<T> and deque<T>. list<T> has one important advantage over its two siblings: it can insert or erase elements quickly from the *middle* of the container.

A summary of the speed characteristics of the three sequence containers (in comparison to a C array) is shown in Table 3-1. Note that the operations take place in either *linear* or *constant* time. When an operation is constant, it consumes a specific amount of time that is independent of the number of elements in the container (the cost is $O(k)$). When an operation is described as linear, it takes an amount of time that is directly proportional to the number of elements in the container (the cost is $O(N)$).

Table 3-1

Cost of container operations

	array	vector<T>	deque<T>	list<T>
Insert/erase at start	n/a	linear	constant	constant
Insert/erase at end	n/a	constant	constant	constant
Insert/erase in middle	n/a	linear	linear	constant
Access first element	constant	constant	constant	constant
Access last element	constant	constant	constant	constant
Access middle element	constant	constant	constant	linear

Note: With vector<T> or deque<T> containers, you can use operator[] to access elements, just as if the container were an array. To access an element in list<T>, you must traverse the list one link at time until you reach the desired position.

An example of a short program written with a sequence container follows. Don't worry if the code seems somewhat cryptic. The next few chapters in the book will cover sequence containers in depth.

```
#include <iostream.h>
#include <list.h>
main()
{
    vector <char *> v;

    v.insert( v.end(), "Washington" );
    v.insert( v.end(), "Dallas" );
    v.insert( v.end(), "New York" );
    v.insert( v.end(), "Philadelphia" );
    for ( int i = 0 ; i < 4 ; i++ )
        cout << v[ i ] << " ";
    return 1;
}
```

Associative containers

Associative containers store objects based on a key value; the objects can be quickly retrieved via the same key value.

The STL defines four different types of containers to implement associative containers:

- set<Key>
- multiset<Key>
- map<Key,T>
- multimap<Key,T>

These four container types are implemented as balanced, sorted trees, featuring access of a given element in $\log(N)$ time—a fast and efficient way to look up data based on a key.

The four different containers are created by varying two characteristics. The distinction between sets and maps is that a map consists of a collection of data objects that can be referenced by a key, while a set is simply an ordered collection of keys. The distinction between singular and multi-implementations of sets and maps is that singular versions (set<Key> and map<Key,T>) only contain a single copy of a given key. multiset<Key> and multimap<Key,T> allow multiple copies of a single key. A summary of these characteristics is shown in Table 3-2.

Table 3-2

Associative container characteristics

	Duplicate Keys	Data w/Key
set<Key>	No	No
multiset<Key>	Yes	No
map<Key,T>	No	Yes
multimap<Key,T>	Yes	Yes

My four containers

Looking at Table 3-2, you can see that set<Key> doesn't store additional data with its key, and it doesn't allow duplicate keys. This means set<Key> might be your container of choice when you want to keep a group of unique records in sorted order. This could range from something as simple as a list of students enrolled in a class, or more complex records, such as a purchase order for several multimedia computers.

Like all the associative containers, multiset<Key> keeps objects in sorted order. The underlying tree structure used in the container maintains this ordering while keeping the cost of inserting and removing objects relatively low. multiset<Key> differs from its sibling set<Key> in that it allows multiple copies of the key value to appear in the set. The two map classes, map<Key,T> and multimap<Key,T> both store a data record based on a key. multimap<Key,T> is used in cases where you want to allow multiple copies of a given key value, just as was the case with the set containers.

One of the best ways to use map<Key,T> classes is as associative arrays, so a programmer can look up non-sequential elements. Associative arrays look a lot like conventional arrays, with one important difference: the index of an associative array doesn't have to be an integer or other scalar type. It can be any type, ranging from a string. And even if you *do* use an integer or other scalar as an index, you don't have to use a contiguous range as you do for built-in arrays.

The secret? It's simply that map<Key,T> defines operator[]() to perform a lookup function that finds the given data element for a specific key. Thus, it appears as if the map container is an array with a non-standard indexing mechanism!

Following is an example of how associative arrays can be used in a program.

```
#include <iostream.h>
#include <cstring.h>
#include <map.h>


main()
{
    map< string, int, less<string> > m;

    m[ "Jay" ] = 1;
    m[ "Dave" ] = 3;
    m[ "Johnny" ] = 5;
    m[ "Jack" ] = 7;
    cout << "Value of Jack = " << m[ "Jack" ] << "\n";
    return 1;
}
```

Associative containers should prove useful whenever you need to maintain a data structure with sorted objects. It's easy to keep lists of employee data, phone numbers, symbol tables, and so on using associative containers.

You now have a variety of associative containers you can use, depending on the specific needs in your application. Later in the book you'll get a detailed look at how these containers work.

PREST-O, CHANGE-O: CONTAINER ADAPTORS

The STL introduces a new type of component known as an *adaptor*. Adaptors are defined in the STL specification as "template classes that provide interface mappings." Adaptors might seem a little mysterious at first, if only because they have an unfamiliar name. However, they aren't much of an enigma once you realize they're nothing more than a new type of widget that can be used to modify existing STL containers, iterators, or functions.

The STL has three container adaptors:

- stack< Container >
- queue< Container >
- priority_queue< Container >

The stack<Container> adaptor implements a simple LIFO stack, with push and pop operations. The queue<Container> adaptor implements the logical sibling of the stack, a FIFO queue. Finally, priority_queue<Container> implements a queue whose elements are removed in priority order.

These adaptors create new containers from existing container types. This means you can create a stack<Container> from a vector<T>, deque<T>, or list<T> type. Likewise, queues and priority queues can be created from other sequence containers.

The nice thing about adaptors is that a simplified interface can make new container types with just a few new member functions. The bulk of the work in the new class created by the adaptor will be done using the existing class. So you get new containers without too much extra work.

The use of a container adaptor is shown in the following example. The stack<Container> adaptor only defines a few functions (as you would expect, given the narrow scope of a stack). This program uses the push(), pop(), and top() members to implement a short test program.

```
#include <iostream.h>
#include <vector.h>
#include <stack.h>
main()
{
    stack< vector< char * > > s;

    s.push( "Dallas" );
    s.push( "New York" );
    s.push( "Philadelphia" );
    s.push( "Washington" );
    while ( !s.empty() ) {
        cout << s.top() << " ";
        s.pop();
    }
    return 1;
}
```

Making Room: Memory Allocators

One very important aspect of STL design is the use of memory allocators. Each container is given a memory allocator when constructed and uses that allocator whenever it needs to allocate storage for new objects.

Allocators are so important because programmers working with unusual memory models under MS-DOS or Windows can easily mix and match objects using different memory types. For example, a single program could have one vector containing near objects and other vectors containing far objects. This is easily accomplished with allocators.

The allocator class encapsulates the size of pointers, the maximum size of a memory object, the method used to allocate and free raw memory, and so on. As a result, the container doesn't have to know anything about memory models, regardless of which was used.

Many programmers won't have to use anything except the default allocator supplied with the library. All you'll need to know about the allocator template class is what the various functions do, so you won't be mystified when you encounter them in the debugger.

THE STAR OF THE STL: ITERATORS

The Standard Template Library would have been reduced to a pale shadow of its present self if not for the inclusion of *iterators*. Iterators provide a measure of flexibility and power that would be difficult to express if we had to use member functions to navigate through containers.

What is an iterator? For all practical purposes, it is a smart pointer; it points to objects in a container. An algorithm or user of a container can access objects in the container by using the dereference operator*(). The increment and decrement operators can be used to move forward or backward through the container.

The design of iterators is so pointer-like, in fact, that actual pointers can be used as iterators by STL algorithms. This is one more factor that gives the STL complete functionality with built-in C data types. Therefore, you can call STL algorithms such as sort() or copy() with pointers into an array, just as you would with iterators that point into a container.

Figure 3-4 shows an example of the use of iterators. The deque<T> container (like all other STL containers) has a begin() and end() member function. Each of these functions returns an iterator that points into the deque object. The begin() and end() member functions are used frequently in the STL, since many algorithms need pointers to the beginning and end of an object.

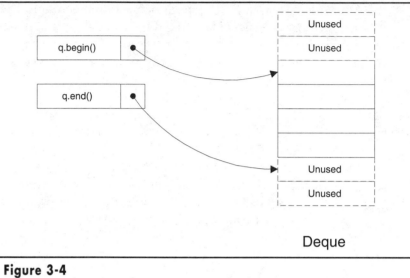

Deque

Figure 3-4
Iterators into a deque

All iterators are not created equal

It would be nice if all iterators had the same properties and capabilities, but this isn't the case. An obvious example is to compare iterators used to point into list<T> with those that point into vector<T>. With vector<T> iterators, it's easy to use an iterator as a random access pointer into the vector. An expression such as iterator[n] can easily be evaluated by adding n*sizeof(T) to the base address of the vector. Calculating iterator[n] for a list<T> object is much more difficult, since you have to scan through the list one element at a time until the nth element is located.

As a result of this type of problem, iterators are divided into a simple hierarchy. Figure 3-5 shows this structure. The most powerful iterator type is at the top and the simplest at the bottom.

As you can see, random access iterators are the most powerful. They support dereferencing operations, operator[], increment, and decrement operations. Native C pointers are random access pointers, which means that any algorithm requiring random access iterators can also work with pointers. The sequential containers vector<T> and deque<T> support random access iterators.

Bidirectional iterators lack one capability that random access iterators enjoy: it isn't possible to use operator[] on a bidirectional iterator. The sequential container list<T> supports bidirectional iterators. The structure of list<T> makes it easy to increment or decrement an iterator if you want to point to the previous or next object in a list<T>, but not so easy to evaluate iterator[n].

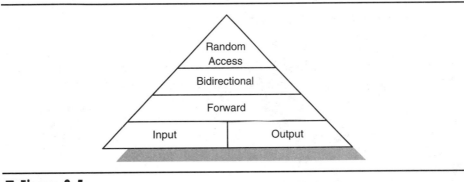

Figure 3-5
The hierarchy of iterators

Forward iterators lose one additional capability, namely the ability to handle operator--(). Forward iterators are more restricted, but can still be used in many STL algorithms. Care was taken by the STL designers to ensure most STL algorithms could perform their work in a single pass, so forward iterators are more useful than they first appear.

Input and output iterators are highly restricted versions of pointers. Not only do they have the restrictions of forward iterators, but there are additional restrictions on when and how they can be dereferenced. In addition, I/O iterators don't follow many of our customary pointer semantics. For example, you can't expect input iterators to work properly if two iterators are reading from the same source. Similarly, you can and must write once, and only once, to an output iterator before incrementing.

Although input and output iterators are greatly restricted in many respects, they bring a high level of extra capability to the STL. By connecting output iterators to a stream, you can invoke STL algorithms and have them write their output to a file, instead of to another object. Likewise, some STL algorithms can read their input directly from a file.

Furthermore, if you write an algorithm that only operates with input and output iterators, you guarantee it will work with all STL containers, including containers that haven't been designed yet.

Of course, any iterator in the hierarchy can be downgraded in type. For example, if there is an algorithm that requires a forward iterator, you can pass a random access iterator with every expectation that things will work properly. This means that normal C pointers will work properly with all STL algorithms.

Iterator adaptors

Iterator adaptors are based on the same philosophy as container adaptors: they are classes based on existing iterator classes. The adaptor classes provide new functionality with few modifications. Iterator adaptors defined in the STL are:

- reverse_iterator
- back_inserter
- front_inserter
- inserter
- raw_storage_iterator

The reverse_iterator is based on a bidirectional iterator; it reverses the normal direction of the increment operator. This gives the programmer a way to reverse the normal direction of STL algorithms by passing a reverse_iterator where a forward iterator is expected.

The three insertion iterators convert a normal iterator into one that inserts new objects into a container. They insert new objects at the front, rear, or at a given point in the container.

The raw_storage_iterator adaptor allows algorithms to insert objects into uninitialized memory.

Putting iterators to work

As you might expect, iterators end up looking a lot like pointers when used in a program, as shown in the following code example.

Note: The type of the iterator is defined in class deque<char*>. The reason for this somewhat awkward definition is that *iterator* is a type defined in the class declaration for deque<T>. Since this is a nested type definition, it must be declared with the slightly more complicated syntax.

```
#include <iostream.h>
#include <list.h>
#include <deque.h>

main()
{
    deque<char *> q;

    q.push_front( "Dallas" );
    q.push_front( "New York" );
    q.push_front( "Philadelphia" );
    q.push_front( "Washington" );
    q.push_front( "Arizona" );
    for ( deque<char*>::iterator i = q.begin() ;
          i != q.end() ; i++ )
        cout << *i << " ";
    return 1;
}
```

A Familiar Beat: STL Algorithms

STL containers and iterators introduce certain new concepts, particularly for programmers new to the turbulent waters of C++. However, the algorithms included in the STL should be more familiar. If you understand the basic idea behind containers and iterators, STL algorithms won't present any difficulties.

STL algorithms generally don't know anything about containers—and they don't *need* to know anything. These are stand-alone template functions that perform their container access via iterators. The prototype for a typical STL algorithm looks something like this:

```
template <class BidirectionalIterator>
void reverse( BidirectionalIterator first,
              BidirectionalIterator last );
```

When this function is invoked, the compiler instantiates it using the class definition of the iterator as the type parameter. A function like reverse doesn't need to know it is reversing the elements in a deque<T>or a vector<T>; it just needs to know it can access all the elements sequentially, using the ++ and – – operators on the two iterators.

If you try to pass a forward iterator to the reverse() function, you'll get a compile-time error. The instantiated function will try (and fail) to apply operator––() to the iterator.

All in the algorithm family

STL algorithms are loosely gathered into seven families. This section briefly discusses each family. You'll find more detail about what each function accomplishes in the appropriate chapter in the remainder of the book. There is a chapter for each of the categories listed here, so you should be able to locate specific algorithms easily.

Non-mutating sequence algorithms

These algorithms apply to sequence containers, and the "non-mutating" designation lets you know that they don't modify the containers as they operate. They either don't work properly with the associative containers, or aren't particularly useful in that context.

Many of these algorithms (and the ones in the next section, mutating sequence algorithms) come in two versions. Which one is generated depends on the set of arguments passed to the function.

- a standard version that uses the comparison operators == and < to make comparison tests. This version of the algorithm is used when the caller supplies an object of type T as the last argument to the function.

- a second version that takes a user-supplied function object to make comparisons. This version of the algorithm is used when the caller supplies a comparison function as the last argument to the function.

Here is the list of non-mutating sequence algorithms:

- for_each()
- find()
- find_if()
- find_end()
- find_first_of()

- adjacent_find()
- count()
- count_if()
- mismatch()
- equal()
- search()

Mutating sequence algorithms

These algorithms also apply to sequences, but in this case they *do* modify the contents of the container. Many of these functions have an if variation or a copy variation. The if variations (for example, copy_if()) only perform their function if the data member in the container evaluates as true when passed to a predicate function. The copy versions of the functions (such as replace_copy()) copy their output to a new container instead of modifying the existing container.

Here is the list of mutating sequence algorithms:

- copy()
- copy_backward()
- swap()
- iter_swap()
- swap_ranges()
- transform()
- replace()
- fill()
- generate()
- remove()
- unique()
- reverse()
- rotate()
- random_shuffle()
- partition()
- stable_partition()

Sorting and searching algorithms

These algorithms are used either to search or sort the contents of containers. As is the case with non-mutating sequence algorithms, most come in two versions:

- The first version uses the standard operator < for comparisons.
- The second uses a user-supplied comparison function object.

Which function is chosen is determined by the arguments passed when the function is invoked. Here are the sorting and searching algorithms:

- sort()
- stable_sort()
- partial_sort()
- partial_sort_copy()
- binary_search()
- merge()
- inplace_merge()
- nth_element()
- lower_bound()
- upper_bound()
- equal_range()

Set operations

The following functions work on all sorted STL containers:

- includes()
- set_union()
- set_intersection()
- set_difference()
- set_symmetric_difference()

Heap operations

Heap operations work much like a container adaptor. They allow you to treat a range in a sequence adaptor as a heap, and provide the basic functions to insert and remove elements:

- push_heap()
- pop_heap()
- make_heap()
- sort_heap()

Numeric algorithms

These algorithms consists of a few general-purpose numeric functions:

- accumulate()
- inner_product()
- partial_sum()
- adjacent_difference()

Miscellaneous/other functions

These are functions that don't fit well into any other group. Apart from that, they have nothing in common:

- min()
- max()
- min_element()
- max_element()
- lexicographical_compare()
- next_permutation()
- prev_permutation()

HARD WORKERS: STL FUNCTION OBJECTS

Function objects are the worker bees of the STL; they are low-level objects that aren't very visible and don't get much credit or glory. But despite their lowly status, they *should* get credit for doing much of the work in the STL, as you'll soon see.

When writing library routines in C, we frequently resort to function pointers to pass needed functionality into a library routine. This works fairly well, but library functions like qsort() that rely on this technique have two serious problems.

The first problem is efficiency. Having to call a function indirectly via a pointer is slower than invoking it directly by name. The comparison becomes worse if we could have called the function inline, which is often the case in C++.

The second problem is loss of type safety. The library routine has a prototype for function pointers and since this is usually fixed before compile time, it employs void pointers to refer to any data objects. You not only lose type safety because of this, but might lose efficiency by passing smaller (that is, built-in types such as int or char) data objects via pointers.

Function objects solve this problem. They are defined by creating classes that have no purpose other than to carry around the definition of a function. The function is defined using operator()(), and invoked as such. A class that defines a function object usually has no data members, no constructor or destructor, and doesn't exhibit much class-like behavior at all.

These characteristics mean function objects are an ungainly addition to the STL syntax, but they do their job well. They allow a much higher degree of efficiency than function pointers, in large part because their definitions can usually be expanded inline. A typical STL function object looks something like this:

```
template <class T>
struct less : binary_function<T, T, bool> {
    bool operator()(const T& x, const T& y) const { return x < y; }
};
```

When working with the STL, you will frequently have to write your own function objects. This isn't difficult; you just have to properly wrap your function definition up in a class declaration. However, the STL provides many useful pre-built functions, including function objects that encapsulate most of the arithmetic and logical operators. See Table 3-3.

Table 3-3

STL built-in function objects

Arithmetic Operators	Logical Operators	Comparisons
plus<T>	logical_and<T>	equal_to<T>
minus<T>	logical_or<T>	not_equal_to<T>
times<T>	logical_not<T>	greater<T>
divides<T>		less<T>
modulus<T>		greater_equal<T>
negate<T>		less_equal<T>

How might you use a function object? Here's a typical example. To negate every element of a vector<double>, you could make a single function call like this:

```
transform( a.begin(), a.end(), a.begin(), negate<double>() );
```

Note: The fourth parameter to this function call invokes the constructor for the negate<T> function object, which has no members. Presumably, this makes it a very low-overhead constructor. In fact, with luck, it will generate no code at all!

Function adaptors

Similar to other adaptors, function adaptors create new function objects from existing functions. The three supplied adaptors are:

- negators
- adaptors for function pointers
- binders

Negators create a new function object class that inverts the result of a function. If you have already defined a logical function, you can use a negator to invert the sense, giving you a second function without too much work.

Adaptors for function pointers are useful if you already have a function defined (as opposed to a function object), and want to create a function object out of it. This allows you to create the new class without having to perform any work.

Finally, binders convert function objects that take two arguments into function objects that take one. They permanently bind any object the user supplies to either the first or second argument of a function. So, if you wanted to add 10 to every member of an integer array, you could do so in a program like this:

```
#include <iostream.h>
#include <algo.h>

main()
{
    int a[] = { 1, 2, 3, 4, 5 };

//
// Print the array to cout using an output stream iterator
//
    copy( a, a + 5, ostream_iterator<int>(cout," " ) );
    cout << "\n";
//
// Now add 10 to each item in the array using a function object
//
    transform( a, a + 5, a, bind1st( plus<int>(), 10 ) );
//
// Print out the resulting array using another stream iterator
//
    copy( a, a + 5, ostream_iterator<int>(cout," " ) );
    cout << "\n";
    return 1;
}
```

The output from this program looks like this:

```
1 2 3 4 5
11 12 13 14 15
```

How's It Going?

If you are still new to C++, and particularly to templates, this chapter may have raised just as many questions as it answered. The remainder of the book will go over all this material in significantly greater detail, so don't worry if it seems a bit fuzzy right now. With patience (and many sample programs to work with), the STL will become clear before the book is over.

THE ESSENTIALS: CONTAINERS, ITERATORS, ALGORITHMS, FUNCTIONS

The Vector Container

> Yet what are all such gaieties to me
> Whose thoughts are full of indices and surds?
> — Lewis Carroll, Four Riddles, no. 1

This chapter looks at the first of the three STL sequence containers: vector<T>. We'll start by examining what vector<T> is, then look at some of the things it has to offer. We'll then go over some of its internal workings, using sample code for illustrative purposes.

The last part of the chapter discusses in detail the public member functions of vector<T>, along with sample code showing ways to use the functions.

For a straight-ahead reference to the members of vector<T>, see Chapter 20.

What Is Vector<T>?

vector<T> is an STL container that, internally, is a contiguous array of elements. You can perform all the operations on vector<T> that you would normally perform on a C array, but vector<T> has the advantage that it can grow transparently.

As discussed in Chapter 3, the STL defines three container classes for data accessed in a sequential manner: vector<T>, list<T>, and deque<T>. STL algorithms also work with conventional arrays such as T[], so arrays can be thought of as a fourth type of sequence container.

These objects present various strengths and weaknesses to programmers, and they have one thing in common: the objects in the container are stored in a linear fashion, so it will always be easy to walk forward or backward through all the elements of a sequence container.

Vive la différence!

There wouldn't be much point in having four different containers if they were all exactly the same. In case you breezed past the overview in Chapter 3, Table 4-1 gives a quick recap (with vector<T> highlighted) of the costs of various operations on STL containers. Be sure to note that standard C/C++ arrays are considered to be STL containers as well!

Table 4-1

The cost of various container operations

	C array, T[]	vector<T>	deque<T>	list<T>
Insert/erase at start	n/a	**linear**	constant	constant
Insert/erase at end	n/a	**constant**	constant	constant
Insert/erase in middle	n/a	**linear**	linear	constant
Access first element	constant	**constant**	constant	constant
Access last element	constant	**constant**	constant	constant
Access middle element	constant	**constant**	constant	linear
Overhead	none	**low**	medium	high

There are a couple of important things to note about vector<T> when looking at this table. First, vector<T> has constant access time for any element in the container, including elements at any location in the vector (referred to as *random access*). This means you can use operator[] to retrieve any element in the container with a fixed cost, regardless of the container size.

```
char letters[ 128 ];

    fill( letters );
    char c = letters[ 20 ];
    char d = *(letters + 10 );
```

We take this operation for granted when using simple C/C++ arrays, but can also use random access freely on objects of class vector<T> or deque<T>. By comparison, list<T> is implemented as a linked list, which means random access has to be implemented using an inefficient list traversal.

Table 4-1 also shows what vector<T> *isn't* particularly good at: inserting elements anywhere other than the end of the container. Just as with a standard C container, inserting objects in the middle of a vector means you have to shuffle every element after the insertion point to make room.

Accessing elements of vector<T>

vector<T> has a simple internal data structure. Figure 4-1 shows the important public data members that define a vector<T> object. These three members, start, finish, and end_of_storage, are all *iterators*. Iterators share the syntax and semantics of standard C pointers, and in some cases actually *are* pointers. An example is when vector<T> is created using an allocator built around standard memory models. In Chapters 9 and 10, you'll see some of the more exotic programs that can be created using different allocator/iterator schemes.

The three iterators found in a vector<T> object are pointers into a contiguous block of memory:

- *start* points to the start of the block of memory
- *finish* points to the first unused location in the reserved memory, or to one past the last allocated object
- *end_of_storage* points just past the end of reserved memory

All objects being stored in the block of memory are in a contiguous sequence of storage locations that begin at start and end at finish.

The fact that both the finish and end_of_storage iterators point *past* the last elements, instead of pointing *to* the last element, may not seem like the conventional way to implement these members. However, this is the convention in the STL; iterators that denote the end of a sequence always point one past the last object. Because of this, the conventional way to test for the end of an iterator walking through a sequence is to see if the iterator is not equal to the end value, instead of using the less–than operator.

By using the one-past-the-end strategy to mark the end of containers, STL implementors and users don't ever have to use operator<() when testing iterators. This is a good thing, because some iterators may not have a defined operator<(). For example, consider the iterator pointing into a linked list. Since list members are allocated independently, and can occur anywhere in memory, implementing operator<() could be quite a problem!

```
while ( i != my_list.end() ) {
cout << *i;
  i++;
  }
```

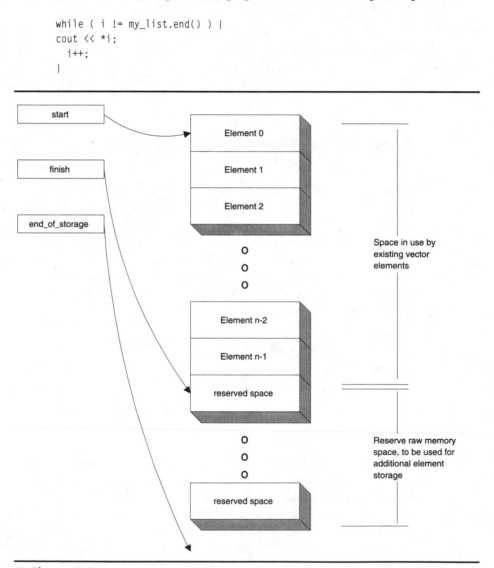

Figure 4-1

Internal structure of vector<T>. Start, finish, and end_of_storage are the three iterators that define the current storage state of the vector.

Two of the iterators can be accessed with standard member functions of vector<T>:

```
iterator begin();    //returns start
iterator end();      //returns finish
```

Note: begin() and end() are defined for *all* containers, not just the sequence containers. The code used to iterate through a vector will also work with a list, a map, a multiset, or any other container.

The end_of_storage iterator is not directly accessible with a member function. However, the capacity() member function returns the difference between end_of_storage and start, given a count of the number of objects the block of memory can hold.

What's So Great About Vector<T>?

Considering that the start member of vector<T> will ordinarily be a pointer, vector<T> looks a lot like an array implemented using a pointer into the heap. In fact, you can write code that treats vector<T> as equivalent to an array of type T:

```
vector<char> s;
  .
  .
  .
char *p = s.begin();
int count = s.end() - s.begin();
for ( int i = 0 ; i < count ; i++ )
cout << p[ i ];
```

So why use a vector instead of a simple array? Well, the list of advantages is fairly impressive:

- vector<T> can be dynamically resized; when you run out of space, vector<T> automatically grows.
- Elements of vector<T> can be added or removed from the interior of a vector without the need to write new code.

- You not only have easy access to the start of the vector, but you can get to the end of it quickly using end() or rend(). You can only do this with an array if you have prior knowledge of its size. A subroutine that expects a pointer to an array won't know its length implicitly.

- You can iterate through the vector in forward or reverse.

- It is a simple matter to add bounds checking to both operator[] and pointer dereferencing.

- vector<T> objects can reside in any type of memory, as well as types not directly supported by your compiler. For example, a custom allocator class might know how to locate STL objects in EMS memory.

- Unlike arrays, vector<T> has a usable assignment operator, as well as comparison operators.

The price for this list of advantages is relatively small. A standard C array allocated from the heap has to keep one pointer to the start of the array. An object of type vector<T> has to maintain two additional pointers. For most objects, this extra cost is insignificant.

All other access operations—including dereferencing, incrementing pointers, and so forth—take place via inline functions, and should be just as efficient as accessing a standard array.

A ROAD TEST

vect0401.cpp, shown in Listing 4-1, illustrates some of the most important properties of vector<T>.

Listing 4-1
VECT0401.CPP

```
// VECT0401.CPP
//
// This example program is used in Chapter 4 to test some
// of the features of vector<T>. It creates a
// vector<T> object, then performs some insertions
// and erasures, dumping the contents of the vector
// after each step.
//
```

```
//
// Borland 4.x workarounds
//
#define __MINMAX_DEFINED
#pragma option -vi-

#include <vector.h>
#include <iostream.h>
#include <iomanip.h>

template<class T>
void dump_array( char *title, vector<T> &data );

//
// This test program creates a vector of doubles. It
// inserts three doubles using the conventional
// vector<T>::push_back() function. It then modifies one
// of the saved doubles using operator[], erases the
// same object, then inserts a new object at the start
// of the vector.
//
main()
{
    vector<double> a;

    dump_array( "At creation", a );
    a.push_back( 1.0 );
    dump_array( "Added 1 object", a );
    a.push_back( 2.0 );
    a.push_back( 3.0 );
    dump_array( "Added 2 more objects", a );
    a[ 1 ] = 2.5;
    dump_array( "Modified a[1]", a );
    a.erase( &a[ 1 ] );
    dump_array( "Erased a[1]", a );
    a.insert( a.begin(), 0.5 );
    dump_array( "Inserted at a[0]", a );
    a.insert( a.begin() + 2, 2.6 );
    dump_array( "Inserted at a[2]", a );
    while ( a.size() > 0 ) {
        a.pop_back();
        dump_array( "After pop_back()", a );
    }
    cout << "\n";
    return 1;
}
```

```
//
// This routine is called to print out the contents of
// a vector. It was created as a template function so
// that it would be easy to test different types of
// vectors without a rewrite.
//

template<class T>
void dump_array( char *title, vector<T> &data )
{
    static int first_time = 1;
    if ( first_time ) {
      first_time = 0;
      cout << "          Event           Begin    End      "
           << "Size  Capacity          Data\n"
           << "--------------------  -------- ------- "
           << "----- --------  --------------------\n";
    };
    cout << setw(21) << title
         << "  " << (void *) data.begin()
         << "  " << (void *) data.end()
         << "  " << setw( 6 ) << data.size()
         << "  " << setw( 6 ) << data.capacity()
         << "  ";
    for ( vector<T>::iterator i = data.begin();
          i != data.end();
          i++ )
       cout << setw( 4 ) << *i;
    cout << endl;
}
```

vect0401.cpp has a simple dump routine that displays several of the most important properties of a vector<T> object. Calls to the dump routine were inserted after most of the operations performed on the vector. The output from vect0401.cpp is shown in Figure 4-2.

vect0401.cpp produces six columns of output. The first column is a simple character string that indicates what was happening in the program when dump_array() was called. The next two columns give the values returned from the begin() and end() member functions. These correspond to the start and finish protected data members.

The next two items listed in the output are the returns from the size() and capacity member functions of vector<T>. Size tells us how many objects are actually present in the container, and capacity tells us the total number of objects the vector can contain at its present size. The last column lists all the data stored in the vector.

Event	Begin	End	Size	Capacity	Data			
At creation	0x0000	0x0000	0	0				
Added 1 object	0x1ad4	0x1adc	1	512	1			
Added 2 more objects	0x1ad4	0x1aec	3	512	1	2	3	
Modified a[1]	0x1ad4	0x1aec	3	512	1	2.5	3	
Erased a[1]	0x1ad4	0x1ae4	2	512	1	3		
Inserted at a[0]	0x1ad4	0x1aec	3	512	0.5	1	3	
Inserted at a[2]	0x1ad4	0x1af0	4	512	0.5	1	2.6	3
After pop_back()	0x1ad4	0x1aec	3	512	0.5	1	2.6	
After pop_back()	0x1ad4	0x1ae4	2	512	0.5	1		
After pop_back()	0x1ad4	0x1adc	1	512	0.5			
After pop_back()	0x1ad4	0x1ad4	0	512				

Figure 4-2
vect0401.cpp output

SMART POINTERS: VECTOR<T> ITERATORS

vect0401.cpp shows how containers and iterators interact in a couple of different ways. Since iterators have both the syntax and semantics of pointers, they can be thought of as *smart pointers*. Smart pointers are C++ objects that can be used just like regular pointers, but conceal some additional intelligence inside their member functions. For example, a smart pointer into a linked list would implement operator++() as a short piece of link traversal code.

In the case of vect0401.cpp, iterators are in fact just pointers to objects of type double. The internal structure of vector<T> means that standard memory pointers have all the intelligence needed to navigate through the container.

This might lead you to wonder why you should care about iterators, if you can simply use pointers to work your way through a vector. The important thing to remember about iterators is that they can conceal additional complexity used to structure a container. When you increment an iterator, you may be taking advantage of a substantial amount of code that implements a new storage type. Perhaps someone will design an allocation class that allows you to store a vector<T> in an object-oriented database. In that case, your code that increments the iterator will be taking advantage of a great deal of power, without having to modify the code that works with standard memory vectors.

The actual type of an iterator in a container class is composed of a couple of definitions found in two different places. For example, in the header file vector.h, the class declaration for vector<T> contains a long sequence of type-defs. The two lines that provide the definition for an iterator in vector<T> are:

```
typedef Allocator<T> vector_allocator;
typedef vector_allocator::pointer iterator;
```

This means a line of code that declares a vector<T> iterator (using a declaration such as this: vector<int>::iterator i) is using a pointer type, as defined by the class's allocator object.

Chapter 3 explains that container classes have *allocator* classes which are in charge of managing raw memory for containers. Container classes can be constructed using different memory allocation classes but, in this chapter, we will only use the default allocator object, defined in defalloc.h. In that header file, the class declaration contains another series of typedefs. They look something like this:

```
template <class T>
class allocator {
public:
    typedef T value_type;
    typedef T* pointer;
...
```

In vect0401.cpp, we have constructed a vector<double> object using the default memory allocator. As a result, iterators in vector<double> will, in fact, be pointers to doubles. But don't forget, you can construct a vector using a more complex allocator, in which case vector<T>::iterator could have a completely different definition.

begin() and end()

One of the most common operations we do as programmers is to iterate through a data structure (or container, using STL terminology). Iterating through a vector in the STL usually means writing a loop that uses the member functions begin() and end() to mark the starting and ending points. begin() returns an iterator that points to the first defined object in the vector, and end() returns an iterator that points one past the last allocated object.

In Figure 4-2 you can see the various values that begin() and end() return during the lifetime of a vector object. Before anything is inserted into the vector, both begin() and end() are set to 0. This special case indicates that, not only have no objects been stored, but no memory has been allocated yet.

When the program inserts the first double into the vector, vector<T> has to allocate some actual storage space. The first double is stored at the start of the raw memory block. start is set to point to that location, and finish is set to point to start + n, where *n* is sizeof(T). In the case of vector<double>, after inserting the first object, end() returns a value eight bytes past begin(). Eight bytes is the same as sizeof(double), so things all add up.

Throughout the program, end() is always equal to begin() + n * sizeof(T), where *n* is the number of objects currently being stored in the vector. This holds true before any storage space has been allocated for the vector, and also after all objects have been removed from the vector.

Regardless of the state of a vector<T> object, you can be assured that a loop of this type will iterate through all positions of the vector:

```
for ( vector<T>::iterator i = object.begin();
      i != object.end();
      i++ )
   ...
```

The only time this sort of loop could run into trouble is when objects are inserted or removed from the vector while inside the loop. These operations can dynamically change the values returned by begin() and end().

size() and capacity()

The fourth and fifth columns in Figure 4-2 show the return values for the size() and capacity() member functions. size() is used to indicate how many objects are presently stored in the vector. capacity() returns a number indicating how many objects *could* be stored in the vector without any further memory allocations. Both functions have short definitions as inline functions:

```
size_type size() const {
      return size_type(end() - begin());
}
size_type capacity() const {
      return size_type(end_of_storage - begin());
}
```

Like begin() and end(), these two functions are partially defined by the allocator being used for vector<T>. The definition of size_type is a typedef in the allocator class. In the case of the default allocator, size_type is defined as size_t. This is the size type for standard memory objects.

The definitions for these functions are shown above. They both perform simple pointer math using member iterators. Since the iterators are random access, the difference between pointers can be calculated, to get a count of objects.

The data elements

The data elements in vect0401.cpp are printed using the standard iteration loop:

```
for ( vector<T>::iterator i = data.begin();
      i != data.end();
      i++ )
    cout << sctw( 6 ) << *i;
```

This loop starts at the iterator value returned by vector<double>::begin(), and ends at the iterator value returned by vector<double>::end(). The value of the object stored in the vector is retrieved by a pointer dereference on iterator *i*. This highlights the fact that iterators must *act* like pointers, even if they aren't really pointers.

Note: You could just as easily access the data objects in this loop using a[*i*], (operator[]) while looping from *i* = 0 while *i* < a.size().

DEEP DOWN: INTERNALS

In the dark past of C++ (before templates), vendors of C++ libraries were able to supply end users with implementations of their libraries in object form only. Programmers using vendor-supplied libraries could link the libraries to their applications, despite having no access to the library's source code.

Template-based libraries can't be supplied in object form, since the compiler must be able to access the source code at compile time, in order to generate code for user-defined types. While library vendors can still conceal non-parameterized code in object libraries, this in some ways defeats the advantages of templates.

Fortunately, the STL exposes *all* its source code to its users. Nearly all the code in the STL is found in either template functions or as member functions of template classes. So the code is found in header files, not in C++ source files. This is different enough to prompt occasional messages in comp.lang.c++ that look like this:

> *"I downloaded the STL header files from the distribution site, but I didn't get any of the source code. Does anyone know where it is?"*

Of course, the slightly confused user got the *entire* STL, not just the header files. And therein lies much of the charm of the STL. It keeps no secrets from its users; you won't see any books titled *Undocumented STL* or *Secrets of the STL*. It's all there for anyone to look at, analyze, criticize, and improve on. vector.h takes up only 300 lines or less, so we should be able to make sense of most of what we see there.

Memory management

C++ programmers are in a rut when it comes to object creation. Virtually every C++ book or tutorial describes the standard three ways to create an object: static objects use a fixed memory, allocated when a program starts; automatic objects are created on the stack; and dynamic objects are created using memory from the heap. These three methods of memory allocation all assume that the memory is allocated and the constructor is called to initialize the object at approximately the same time.

```
int static_array[ 25 ];

main()
{
    int auto_array[ 24 ];

    char *dynamic_array = new int[ 23 ]
```

Figure 4-3
The three traditional object-creation methods

All three of these object creation methods perform memory allocation and object initialization at the same time. vector<T> (and other STL containers) does things a little differently. While memory is still allocated using the C++ *new* operator, the allocation step is separated completely from the initialization (constructor) process.

How does vector<T> (and the rest of the STL) accomplish this? By using a couple of different techniques. First, raw memory allocation for use by STL containers is delegated to an allocator class. Each instantiation of an STL container employs a specific allocator class to create usable memory blocks. The allocator class is a template class that defines pointer-like objects that can be used to access an object of type T. The allocator class also has member functions that can be called to allocate and destroy raw memory.

If the allocator class simply allocates blocks of raw memory, how does the STL turn that memory into useful objects? By utilizing *placement syntax* to coerce operator new into using the memory locations you chose, instead of random locations off the heap.

Your place or mine: placement syntax

If you haven't heard of placement syntax before, don't worry. Placement syntax has been part of C++ for some time now, but it hasn't seen wide use. Libraries like the STL represent one place where placement syntax has been found to be quite useful.

Dynamic creation of C++ objects is usually done with the *new* operator. new does two things: first, it allocates enough memory to contain the object, then it calls the constructor for that specific object. The use of the placement syntax lets you tell the new operator that you don't want to use the default heap routines to allocate the object's memory. Instead, the placement syntax invokes a custom version of new that does whatever you desire. A new object using the placement syntax might look something like this:

```
void* operator new(size_t, void* p) { return p; }

void *p = malloc( sizeof( foo ) );
foo *fp = new( p ) foo;
```

The example above creates a new object in the block of memory allocated with malloc. Note that the placement syntax doesn't really do anything on its own. Instead, it calls a customized version of ::new() to return the memory. The two parameters passed to this customized version of ::new() are the size of the desired memory object, and a second argument that corresponds to the type of argument passed as part of the placement syntax. Your program can implement this version of ::new() however it likes. In the code fragment shown above, my version of new assumes that the void pointer being passed as an argument points to a valid block of memory, and just returns its value to the calling program.

Placement syntax also uses another C++ obscurity: the explicit destructor call. Normally, dynamically created objects are destroyed with the delete operator. delete first calls the destructor for the object, then frees the memory used by the object. But an object created using placement syntax might not reside in a block of memory that can be returned to the heap. So instead, you must call the explicit destructor, using the following syntax:

```
fp->foo::~foo();
```

An example of how placement syntax is used is shown in Listing 4-2. This short program creates an object of class foo. Instead of calling the default new operator to allocate memory from the heap, this program uses an integer array allocated on the stack to hold the newly created objects. Likewise, when it's time to delete the object, an explicit call is made to the destructor, instead of either calling the delete operator, or letting the object pass out of scope.

There are a few oddities in this program that are used to illustrate the way the program works. First, the constructor fills the object with a set of predefined values, and the destructor changes those values. This is done for just one reason: when the program prints out the data in the x array, you will be able to tell whether or not an object has been created or destroyed in the given memory.

The fact that this program constructs the objects in the x array also highlights the need for the explicit destructor call. If you were to try to delete the foo *p using a normal call to delete, the delete operator would presumably attempt to free the memory location pointed to by p, which is the x array on the stack. Since x wasn't allocated from the heap, this would be a bad thing!

Listing 4-2

plac0402.cpp: A demonstration of object creation using placement syntax

```
//
// PLAC0402.CPP
//
// This short program shows how placement syntax
// can be used with the new operator to create objects
// anywhere in memory. This allows the programmer
```

```
// to control precisely where and how objects are
// created, instead of leaving things up to the
// heap manager. This program creates an object of type
// foo in an integer array on the stack. It then
// deletes the same object using an explicit call to
// the destructor. The program prints out the contents
// of the integer array to verify that the ctor and
// dtor have been invoked.
//
#include <iostream.h>

class foo {
        int a, b, c;
    public :
        foo() : a(101), b(202), c(303) {}
        ~foo(){ a = 404; b = 505; c = 606; }
};


//
// This version of new will be called when I create
// an object of type foo using the placement syntax.
//
inline void* operator new(size_t, void* p) { return p; }

main()
{
    int x[ 10 ];
//
// Create an object using the memory in x
//
    foo *p = new( x ) foo; //new using placement syntax
    for ( int i = 0 ; i < 10 ; i++ )
        cout << x[ i ] << ' ';
    cout << endl;
//
// Now destroy the same object
//
    p->foo::~foo();  //explicit destructor call
    for ( i = 0 ; i < 10 ; i++ )
        cout << x[ i ] << ' ';
    cout << endl;
    return 1;
}
```

The output from this program confirms the object was created and then destroyed using the memory allocated for integer array *x*:

```
101 202 303 15 0 -8 14847 -10 -32370 -8
404 505 606 15 0 -8 14847 -10 -32370 -8
```

Note: Only the first three integers are relevant. In this particular case, objects of class foo() only occupy the first three locations in the array. The remaining bytes displayed here are uninitialized memory. Most importantly, you can create and destroy an object dynamically without using heap storage.

So what does this placement syntax have to do with vector<T>? Simply this: vector<T> relies on an allocator class to allocate a block of raw storage. Objects of type T are then created, using the storage locations in this raw memory, by way of the new operator with the placement syntax. When it comes time to delete an object, it is destroyed with an explicit call to the destructor that leaves the raw storage intact.

Inserting objects: A walkthrough

A good way to understand how these components work together is to walk through the process of inserting new objects into the container. The test program shown earlier in this chapter, vect0401.cpp, can shed light on this topic.

One of the common ways to add a new object to the vector is with the push_back() routine. vec0401.cpp adds the first three objects to the vector<double> container. After the first call to push_back() with a parameter of 1.0, the internal state of the vector should look like Figure 4-4.

The first call to push_back() resulted in the allocation of a block of memory (in this case, enough to hold 512 doubles). The first object was constructed at the start of the vector, but the rest of the space in the vector has not been used. You can determine that the vector has only one element because data member finish—which we can see via member function end()—points to position 1 in the array.

The second call to push_back() passes an argument of 2.0. In vector.h, the code to implement push_back looks like this:

```
void push_back(const T& x) {
    if (finish != end_of_storage)
        construct(finish++, x);
    else
        insert_aux(end(), x);
}
```

By looking at the data in Figure 4-2 and the diagram in Figure 4-4, you can see that finish is not equal to end_of_storage, so there is room for the new object in the vector. The STL code will call construct(finish++, 2.0) to add the new object to the vector.

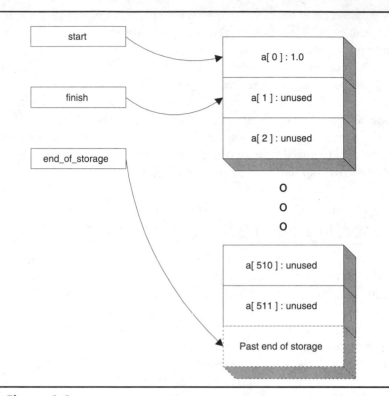

Figure 4-4

vector<double> a after the first call to push_back()

Remember, finish is an iterator that points to objects of type double, and 2.0 is a double.

It is logical to expect construct() to be a member function of vector<T>, since it will create new objects of class T. In fact, construct() is a template function customized to work with a specific allocator. The first argument passed to construct() is a pointer to the type of object being constructed. You can see in the following default memory model construct() code that the argument is just a standard pointer. Allocators that use a different memory model (for example, huge model) might use something like T1 _huge *p as the first argument of the construct template function.

```
template <class T1, class T2>
inline void construct(T1* p, const T2& value) {
    new (p) T1(value);
}
```

The second argument to construct is simply a reference to an object of type T2. For the vector<double> object we are working on, the second parameter is a reference to the double value 2.0.

The internals of construct() are deceptively simple. A new object is created using the copy constructor of object value, the second parameter to construct. The placement syntax is used to place the new object in the memory location we have chosen, instead of a location allocated from the heap. When we call push_back(2.0) in vect0401.cpp, the call to construct() will end up working more or less like this:

```
new (&a[1]) double(2.0);
```

This has the effect of copying 2.0 to the memory location at a[i].

Remember, after push_back() calls construct() it increments finish. After the new object is inserted, the vector<double> a object looks like Figure 4-5:

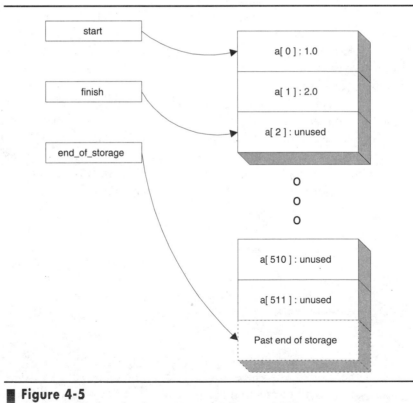

Figure 4-5

vector<double> a after the insertion of 2.0 in vect0401.cpp

The going gets tough: vector<T>::insert()

Adding an object to the end of vector<T> object is easy, as long as there is spare room at the end. By walking through the code, you can see this is a fairly low-cost operation. The code in vector.h had to call the copy constructor for the object, increment the finish pointer, and not do much else. Since these are both inline functions, it is correct to assume vector<T>::push_back() is an efficient operation.

The natural question to ask next is: how does vector<T> handle insertions in the middle of the vector? In Table 4-1 (which lists relative expense of operations), vector<T> was only optimized for insertion at the end of a vector.

Let's look at the following line of code in vect0401.cpp:

```
a.insert( a.begin() + 2, 2.6 );
```

Before we call this insert function, vector<double> a contains three doubles, and looks like the diagram in Figure 4-6.

vector<T>::insert() is shown in the following code excerpt. The function takes two arguments. The first is the position where the object will be inserted. The second is a reference to the object to be inserted into the vector.

If insert() is called to insert an object at the end of the vector, it is functionally equivalent to push_back(). The code at the start of the function tests to see if there is a request for an insertion at the end of the vector. If there is, and if there is more space available, the call to construct is executed. As with the previous example, construct() is a very efficient invocation of the copy constructor for type T, using the placement syntax.

```
iterator insert(iterator position, const T& x) {
    size_type n = position - begin();
    if (finish != end_of_storage && position == end())
        construct(finish++, x);
    else
        insert_aux(position, x);
    return begin() + n;
}
```

Unfortunately, the insertion in question from vect0401.cpp isn't at the end of the vector. Therefore, the call has to be made to insert_aux(). insert_aux() is a private member function that does all the difficult work of an insertion into the middle of a vector. It also handles insertion at the end of a vector when no free space is available.

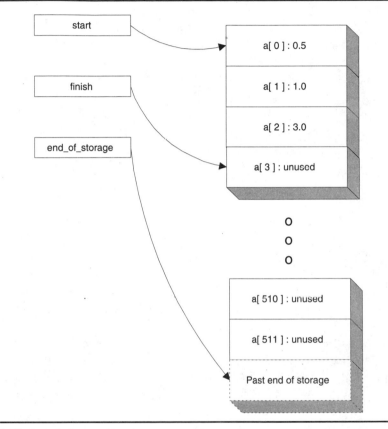

Figure 4-6
vector<double> a just before inserting 2.6

In this case, the first test in insert_aux() is to see if finish and end_of_storage are equal. If they are, there is no free storage left in the vector, so more memory will need to be allocated. In this instance, they are not equal, since we still have 509 free slots in our raw storage waiting for new doubles.

```
template <class T>
void vector<T>::insert_aux(iterator position, const T& x) {
  if (finish != end_of_storage) {
      construct(finish, *(finish - 1));
```

```
        copy_backward(position, finish - 1, finish);
        *position = x;
        ++finish;
    } else {
        size_type len = size() ? 2 * size()
            : static_allocator.init_page_size();
        iterator tmp = static_allocator.allocate(len);
        uninitialized_copy(begin(), position, tmp);
        construct(tmp + (position - begin()), x);
        uninitialized_copy(position,
                           end(),
                           tmp + (position - begin()) + 1);
        destroy(begin(), end());
        static_allocator.deallocate(begin());
        end_of_storage = tmp + len;
        finish = tmp + size() + 1;
        start = tmp;
    }
}
```

Since the first comparison is passed, only four lines of code in insert_aux have to be executed. The first line is construct(finish, *(finish - 1)). Because finish - 1 is a pointer to the last element of the array, the call to construct() will use the copy constructor to move the last element of the vector into the first free block of raw storage.

The resulting vector is shown in Figure 4-7. It still needs some work before it's a usable object, and the next operation will take care of some of this problem. insert_aux() needs to open some space for the new object at position. It does this through the call to copy_backward(position, finish-1, finish).

copy_backward() is shown in the following code excerpt. It is a simple template function found in algobase.h which copies one sequence to another, while moving in the reverse direction. To make space for a new object in a vector when doing a copy_ backward(), the program sits in a loop and copies all the objects from position to finish-2, up one slot in the raw memory block.

```
template <class BidirectionalIterator1, class BidirectionalIterator2>
BidirectionalIterator2 copy_backward(BidirectionalIterator1 first,
                                     BidirectionalIterator1 last,
                                     BidirectionalIterator2 result) {
    while (first != last) *--result = *--last;
    return result;
}
```

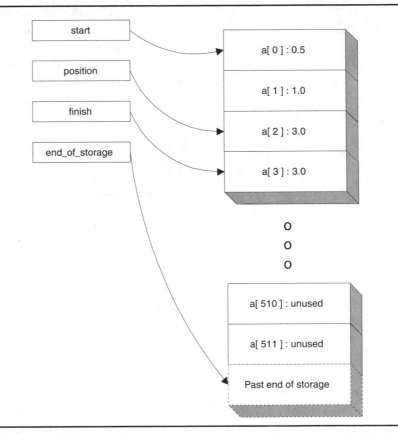

Figure 4-7

*vector<double> a after the call to construct(finish, *(finish - 1)*

In this algorithm, there's no need to worry about calling operator new with the placement syntax, because new values are being assigned to objects that already exist. We did have to call operator new for the very first move, when the object at finish - 1 was moved to finish. The call to construct() had to take care of this, since there was no object already created at position finish.

The last two lines the insert() call passes through in insert_aux() are:

```
*position = x;
++finish;
```

The first is the assignment that (finally!) stores the new value in the vector. finish is incremented so the vector<double> object will accurately indicate that it has a new object. The only remaining step is to return begin() + n to the calling program. The reason to do this, is that the iterator position may no longer be valid. In the event that vector<T>::insert_aux() had to allocate more memory, all old iterators pointing into the vector are now dangling pointers and should be discarded. begin() + n will accurately reflect the new location of start in the event of a move.

Figure 4-8 shows the final vector. The value 3.0 has moved up from a[2] to a[3] and the new value of 2.6 has been stored in a[2].

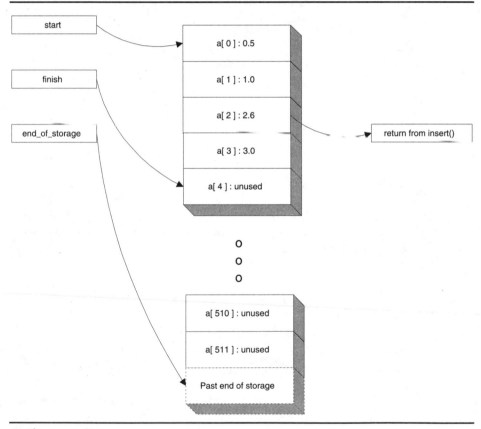

Figure 4-8
The vector after the insert() operation is complete

insert() efficiency

If you look at the code used to accomplish this operation, you'll see that insert() may require a fair amount of processing time. If the insertion requires memory to be shuffled using the copy_backward() algorithm, the algorithm will have to execute T::operator=() once for each object needing to be shuffled. Accordingly, this algorithm should run in time linearly proportional to the number of elements to be shuffled.

The fact that we sit in a loop copying elements sheds light on the objects to be inserted into a vector. If many insertions need to be performed, operator=() is going to be executed quite a bit, making it important to have an efficient implementation.

For example, imagine a String class written without much thought given to efficiency. I've written utility code very similar to this when I need a quick implementation of strings:

```
String::operator=(const String &rhs )
{
  if ( *this != rhs ) {
    free( p );
    p = malloc( strlen( rhs.p ) );
    if ( p )
        strcpy( p, rhs.p );
  }
}
```

This version of string makes an individual copy of each string. It has to perform a heap operation and a string copy every time the assignment operator is called. If an insert() operation is performed on a vector<String> object, as designed here, the heap is going to be beaten to death!

Compare the overhead caused by that assignment operator with that of a String class using reference counting:

```
String::operator=(const String &rhs )
{
  if ( *this != rhs ) {
    if ( --p->ref_count == 0 )
      delete p;
    p = rhs.p;
    p->ref_count++;
  }
}
```

While this kind of code is much more difficult to write, it usually makes better library code. Most good string classes use reference counting along with a *copy on write* strategy. This more complex version of a String class has considerably less overhead, resulting in much faster insertions. The lesson is this: in many C++ programs, the assignment operator is not a potential bottleneck. However, a study of STL internals reveals that the operator is used heavily during certain operations.

Allocating new memory

Fortunately, the previous examples of vector<T>::push_back() and vector<T>::insert() were called when there was already plenty of room available for new elements. insert_aux() has to do a little shuffling of existing elements, but we could ignore memory allocation.

As you've seen, memory allocation for STL container classes is done via the allocator class associated with each container. The allocator is responsible for allocating the blocks of raw memory to be filled with objects. In the case of vector<T>, the objects are stored in the memory by the construct() template function.

Another short test program, vect0403.cpp (shown in Listing 4-3) illustrates some of the steps vector<T> goes through when it's time to reallocate memory. vect0401.cpp created an empty vector<double>, then added new objects by using push_back() and insert(). Instead, vect0403.cpp creates a vector<char> object and uses a different constructor, in order to create the new vector with some preinitialized storage.

Listing 4-3

vect0403.cpp: Demonstrating an insert() call that requires memory allocation

```
//
// VECT0403.CPP
//
// This example program is used in Chapter 4 to test
// some of the features of vector<T>. It creates
// a vector<T> object with some predefined objects,
// then performs a single insertion, which will force
// a reallocation of memory.

//
// Borland 4.x workarounds.
//
```

```
#define __MINMAX_DEFINED
#pragma option -vi-

#include <vector.h>
#include <iostream.h>
#include <iomanip.h>

template<class T>
void dump_array( char *title, vector<T> &data );

main()
{
    char init[] = "ABDE";
    vector<char> a( init, init + 4 );

    dump_array( "At creation", a );
    a.insert( a.begin() + 2, 'c' );
    dump_array( "After insertion", a );
    a.pop_back();
    dump_array( "After pop_back", a );
    a.erase( a.begin() + 1, a.end() - 1 );
    dump_array( "After erase", a );
    return 1;
}

// The routine dump_array() in this program is identical
// to the same routine in VECT0401.CPP.  It isn't shown
// here, to save space.
```

As the output of vect0403.cpp in Figure 4-9 demonstrates, the constructor used for vector<char> allocates exactly the amount of memory needed to hold the initializer. In this case, it is the four character string "ABCD" (the terminating '\0' normally found in C strings wasn't copied). After the object has been constructed, it has a size of 4 and a capacity of 4, meaning that internally, finish == end_of_storage.

Event	Begin	End	Size	Capacity	Data			
At creation	0x164a	0x164e	4	4	A	B	D	E
After insertion	0x1652	0x1657	5	8	A	B	c	D	E
After pop_back	0x1652	0x1656	4	8	A	B	c	D
After erase	0x1652	0x1654	2	8	A	D		

Figure 4-9
The output from vect0403.cpp, demonstrating an insertion into a full object

In the source code for vector<T>::insert() (see vector.h in the STL distribution), the first thing insert() checks is whether finish is equal to end_of_storage. If this is the case, there is no room for a new object, and insert() has to delegate the hard work to insert_aux().

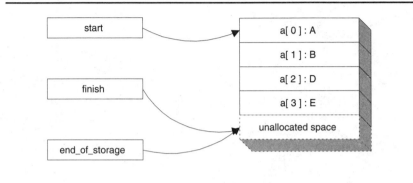

Figure 4-10

vector<char> A immediately after its croation

Once insert() calls insert_aux(), we immediately move to the code shown below. This code allocates more space for an existing vector (although it also works if no vector has been allocated yet), and moves all the old and new elements into the new storage space.

```
size_type len = size() ? 2 * size()
          : static_allocator.init_page_size();
iterator tmp = static_allocator.allocate(len);
uninitialized_copy(begin(), position, tmp);
construct(tmp + (position - begin()), x);
uninitialized_copy(position,
                   end(),
                   tmp + (position - begin()) + 1);
destroy(begin(), end());
static_allocator.deallocate(begin());
end_of_storage = tmp + len;
finish = tmp + size() + 1;
start = tmp;
```

This code has to perform six distinct tasks:

- allocate a new block of storage
- copy all existing vector elements to the new storage space

- store the new object [passed as a parameter to insert_aux()] in the storage space
- destroy all objects in the old vector
- free the memory used to hold the vector
- update the three member iterators to point to the new block of memory

This is much more complicated than the code segments of push_back() and insert_aux(). They were able to execute without allocating more memory. Let's take a look at these sections of code, one at a time.

Task #1: Allocate a new block of storage

```
size_type len = size() ? 2 * size()
            : static_allocator.init_page_size();
iterator tmp = static_allocator.allocate(len);
```

These two lines of code allocate a new block of memory by using the allocator object associated with this instance of vector<T>. (As you will see more of in Chapter 8, every container object in the STL is assigned an allocator upon creation.) The big decision to make is: how much new memory should be allocated? The simplest and most space-efficient strategy is to allocate enough memory for the new objects to be inserted into the vector. This would mean, in insert_aux(), always asking for size()+1 elements of raw memory.

However, using the size()+1 strategy could be a serious mistake. The entire vector has to be copied from one array to another every time memory is reallocated. This is an expensive operation that should be avoided. So, when the STL needs more memory for a vector, it always requests more than it has an immediate need for.

The amount insert_aux() requests is determined in the first line of code shown above. If there is already memory allocated for the vector, a new amount should be requested, double that size. If no space has been allocated before, we instead ask for an initial allocation of init_page_size() elements. init_page_size() is a member function of the allocator that returns an arbitrary amount. It returns an *element* count, not a *byte* count. The default allocator in the STL will *always* return a count of 512 for the initial page size. (Note that requesting twice as much storage when performing allocation might not be an optimal strategy on machines with real memory limitations.)

Finally, memory is allocated using the allocator member function allocate(). The version of allocate shown here is from defalloc.h in the STL distribution, which contains the code for the default allocator. allocate simply calls global operator new and allocates the correct number of bytes. The raw memory is then passed back to the calling routine which, in this case, is insert_aux().

```
template <class T>
inline T* allocate(ptrdiff_t size, T*) {
  set_new_handler(0);
  T* tmp=(T*)::operator new((size_t)(size * sizeof(T)));
  if (tmp == 0) {
    cout << "out of memory" << endl;
    exit(1);
  }
  return tmp;
}
```

In vect0403.cpp, the initial vector had room for four characters. Now, we have to request a new vector with room for eight characters. This will accommodate our current request, as well as up to three more. After the memory has been allocated, the internal structure of vector<char> a appears as in Figure 4-11.

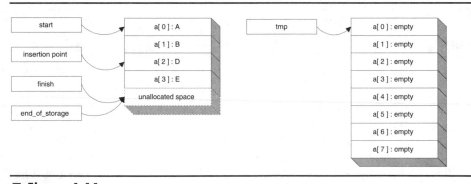

Figure 4-11
vector<char> a after new memory has been allocated in insert_aux()

Task #2: Copy existing elements to new storage

After insert_aux() has created the new storage array for the vector, the iterator tmp simply points to a block of its raw memory. The next step is to copy the existing elements from the old vector to the new memory, using two calls to the general-purpose template function uninitialized_copy(). The function has to copy two ranges to the new vector. First, it copies all the elements up to, but not including, the insertion point. Then it copies all the elements from the insertion point to the end of the vector to the new vector. The second copy is skewed by one element, so there is room for the new object to be inserted.

```
uninitialized_copy(begin(), position, tmp);
uninitialized_copy(position,
                   end(),
                   tmp + (position - begin()) + 1);
```

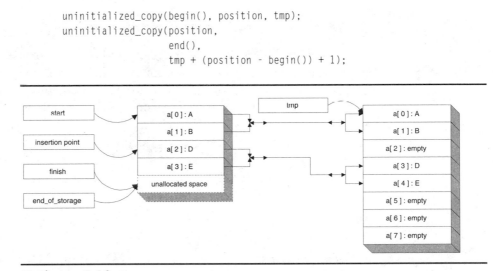

Figure 4-12
The effect on vector<char> of the two calls to uninitialized_copy()

Task #3: Copy the new object into the correct location

This step is accomplished by a function call to the construct() template function. construct() needs only two things to accomplish its task: an iterator to point it to the correct location in the new block of memory, and a reference to the object it will copy.

The location in the new vector memory is presently pointed to by the iterator tmp. Since tmp acts like a pointer, we can locate the correct offset into it by doing pointer math and calculating the difference between position and start. This gives the offset in elements (not bytes) to the desired insertion point. Adding this offset to tmp gives the desired insertion point in the new array.

```
construct(tmp + (position - begin()), x);
```

Given the correct offset into the temporary array, construct() does exactly what it did when it added a new element to the end of the vector in push_back(). It creates a new object by calling operator new, and uses the placement syntax to store the newly created object in the new memory array. Operator new will call the copy constructor for the object, since we are copying an existing object of the same type. Once this copy constructor returns, the new vector is complete.

Task #4: Destroy the old vector's contents

At this point, we have a brand-new vector ready and waiting for use, pointed to by iterator tmp. But before we can exit the insert_aux() routine, we have to destroy the contents of the old vector. It isn't enough to delete the memory used by the old vector. It's necessary to go through and call the destructor for each of the objects in the vector.

This is accomplished when insert_aux() calls the template function destroy() with a pair of iterators. As always in the STL, the first iterator points to the first object to be destroyed, and the second iterator points one past the end of the list of objects.

```
destroy(begin(), end());
```

Again, it's important to note here that objects stored in STL containers run the risk of being copied, created, and destroyed as containers are resized. It's crucial that these operations be fairly efficient. Your classes should also be set up to efficiently work with this type of storage management, as mentioned earlier in this chapter.

The following code excerpt shows the template function that accomplishes this. It sits in a loop and calls the destroy(T *pointer) template function for each iterator between the two values. This calls the destructor for each old object in the list.

```
template <class ForwardIterator>
void destroy(ForwardIterator first, ForwardIterator last) {
    while (first != last) destroy(first++);
}
```

The destroy(T *pointer) template function has to make an explicit call to the destructor, if it is to destroy the object without attempting to delete memory from the heap.

Note: When the vector<T> functions create STL objects, they use the placement syntax in conjunction with the new operator.

The destroy() function uses an equally unfamiliar syntax to make the explicit destructor call:

```
template <class T>
inline void destroy(T* pointer) {
    pointer->~T();
}
```

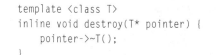
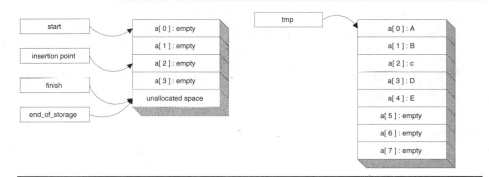

Figure 4-13
vector<char> a after all objects in the original vector have been destroyed

Task #5: Delete the old vector

Now that all objects in the old vector have been destroyed, the memory for that vector is no longer needed. The task of deleting memory is delegated to the allocator object associated with this vector<T> object:

```
allocator.deallocate(begin());
```

defalloc.h contains the deallocate() function that will be used by default. It calls the global delete operator to return the vector to the heap manager.

```
template <class T>
inline void deallocate(T* buffer) {
    ::operator delete(buffer);
}
```

Task #6: Update the member iterators

The final step in this long process is to update the three data members that define vector<T>. Once this is complete, insert_aux() can return and the new vector will be ready for use. The new iterators will point into the new vector storage pointed to by tmp:

```
end_of_storage = tmp + len;
finish = tmp + size() + 1;
start = tmp;
```

Figure 4-14 shows how the vector finally appears after the insert() operation is complete. The capacity() of the vector has doubled from four elements to eight; the previous four elements have been copied and the new element has been inserted.

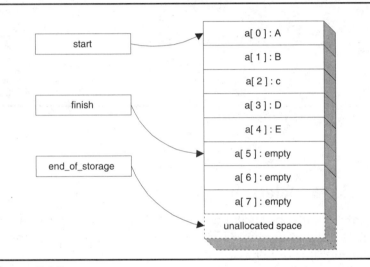

Figure 4-14
The final view of vector<char> a from vect0403.cpp after the new object has been inserted

Getting rid of objects

Objects are normally deleted from a vector<T> container by one of two methods:

- member function pop_back deletes from the end
- member function erase() deletes from the middle

Deleting is somewhat simpler than inserting because we don't have to deal with some of the memory management issues. The STL does not free up memory when objects are destroyed.

The test program vect0403.cpp demonstrates both types of deletions. A simple walk through the code in vector<T> shows how objects are deleted from the vector. As with memory allocation, the STL has divorced the tasks of object deletion and memory management. So object deletion is always done with an explicit call to the destructor. This leaves the memory intact.

vector<T>::pop_back()

Since the container class vector<T> is optimized for insertion and removal from the end of the vector, it should be no surprise that pop_back() is a very simple function. pop_back() is called to delete the last object from the vector, which it does quickly and easily. The function is implemented with just one line of code in vector.h:

```
void pop_back() { destroy(--finish); }
```

Since this destroys the last object in the vector, no copying or shuffling of objects is required. It is only necessary to decrement the finish iterator, moving the pointer to the next free element back by one. destroy()calls the explicit destructor for the object in question, deleting the object but leaving its memory intact:

```
template <class T>

inline void destroy(T* pointer) {
    pointer->~T();
}
```

Note: The template function destroy() is customized to work with the allocator. The version shown here is the one found in defalloc.h. In contrast, the destroy() function designed to work with the huge memory allocator, for example has to declare the pointer to T as huge.

The erase() functions

The erase functions have a more complicated job than pop_back(). When deleting objects from anywhere but the end of the array, erase() will shuffle the rest of the objects in the vector to fill the gap caused by the erasure. It then destroys objects left at the end of the vector. This procedure is efficient but may not be entirely intuitive, so here is a representative example.

The last vector<char> member function called in vect0403.cpp is:

```
a.erase( a.begin() + 1, a.end() - 1 );
```

As with all STL functions that accept a range defined by two iterators, erase() expects the first iterator to point to the first item to be deleted, and the second iterator to point one past the last item to be deleted.

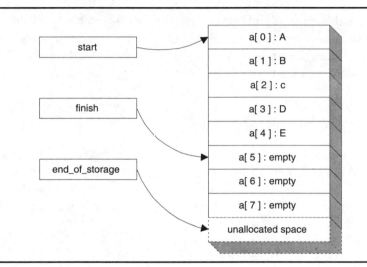

Figure 4-15
vector<char> a from vect0403.cpp just before the call to a.erase()

Given this convention, a call to vector<T>::erase(), with the first iterator set to begin()+1, and the second iterator set to end()-1, will be attempting to delete all but the first and last elements of an array. Figure 4-16 shows where the iterators point just before execution of the erase command.

```
void erase(iterator first, iterator last) {
    vector<T>::iterator i = copy(last, end(), first);
    destroy(i, finish);
    finish = finish - (last - first);
}
```

The erase() member function of vector<T> accomplishes its work with two function calls and an assignment statement. The first call is to the template function copy(), which uses the assignment operator to copy a block of elements in a container to a different position in the container.

Note: We must be copying to and from objects that have already been created if this function is to work properly. (uninitialized_copy() copies objects to raw memory.)

```
template <class InputIterator, class OutputIterator>
OutputIterator copy(InputIterator first,
                    InputIterator last,
                    OutputIterator result) {
  while (first != last)
    *result++ = *first++;
  return result;
```

After the call to copy() is complete, half the work is done. The elements of the vector that came after the range to be erased have been moved down in the vector. They are now in the positions starting at the erasure range. This obliterates some or all of the range to be erased by assigning new values to those elements.

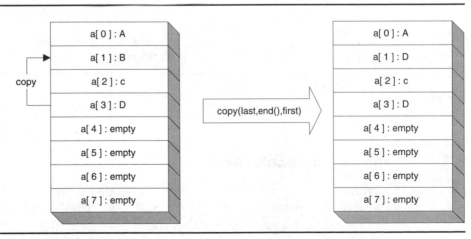

Figure 4-16
The vector after the copy() function is called

After copying the tail-end of the vector down to its new position, we have to perform the second part of the operation: destroying the old tail-end of the vector. A single call is made to the template function destroy(). erase() has to pass destroy() two iterators to define the range of elements to be destroyed. The first iterator is *i*, returned from the copy() function. copy() returns an iterator that points to the next element to be accessed immediately after the copy range. The second iterator is finish, the last constructed element in the array.

After destroy() completes its work, all that remains to be done is an adjustment of the finish iterator so it points to the new end of the array. The final vector for the example in vect0403.cpp is shown in Figure 4-17.

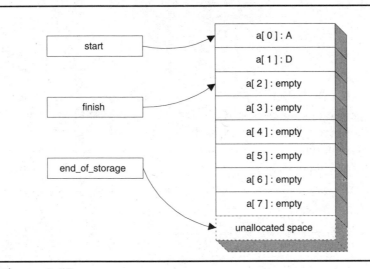

Figure 4-17
The final vector after erase() is complete.

Type requirements for T

When you create a container, the object capabilities it requires may not be immediately obvious. To learn a little about those requirements, let's look at a test program that has a class with a very limited user interface.

In this example, I am trying to develop a class foo that prevents users from utilizing the copy constructor and assignment operator. In addition, I avoided creating a default constructor, foo(), by specifying a constructor that requires a single character pointer as an argument.

Note: If you don't define the copy constructor and assignment operator, the compiler will generate default versions for you.

Listing 4-4

vect0404.cpp: A test of the features a class requires to be inserted in a container

```
//
// VECT0404.CPP
//
// This example program is used in Chapter 4 to demonstrate
// some of the requirements that an object must fulfill
// to be inserted in a container class.

//
// Borland 4.x workarounds
//
#define __MINMAX_DEFINED
#pragma option -vi-

#include <iostream.h>
#include <iomanip.h>
#include <vector.h>

class foo {
    private :
        char *operator=(const foo& rhs){ return p = rhs.p; }
        foo( const foo& rhs );
        char *p;
    public :
        foo( char *name ){ p = name; }
        ~foo(){;}
};

main()
{
    vector<foo> foovec;

    foovec.push_back( foo( "a" ) );
    foovec.push_back( foo( "b" ) );
    foovec.push_back( foo( "c" ) );
    foovec.insert( foovec.begin(), foo( "d" ) );
    foovec.erase( foovec.end() - 2 );
    foovec.pop_back();
    return 1;
}
```

vect0404.cpp doesn't attempt to use the default constructor, assignment operator, or copy constructor anywhere in its code. However, if you try to compile vect0404.cpp, the compiler will give the following response:

```
Borland C++ 4.5 Copyright (c) 1987, 1994 Borland International
vect0404.cpp:
Error ..\source\vector.h 75:
Could not find a match for 'foo::foo()' in function main()
*** 1 errors in Compile ***
```

Apparently something in vector.h uses the default constructor. The
offending code is in the argument list for a vector<T> constructor:

```
vector(size_type n, const T& value = T()) {
    start = static_allocator.allocate(n);
    uninitialized_fill_n(start, n, value);
    finish = start + n;
    end_of_storage = finish;
}
```

This version of the vector<T> constructor fills the vector with an
array of *n* initialized objects. Even though this constructor isn't used in
vect0404.cpp, the compiler still knows it might need it, so it refuses to
compile the program.

vect0405.cpp remedies this shortcoming by modifying the constructor
so that the argument has a default value. The only line that changes
between these two programs is the definition of the constructor:

```
foo( char *name = "" ){ p = name; }
```

Now the code at line 75 in vector.h should compile without a problem.
However, getting past this code only opens the door for a host of new error
messages:

```
Borland C++ 4.5 Copyright (c) 1987, 1994 Borland International
vect0405.cpp:
Error ..\source\vector.h 189: 'foo::operator =(const foo &)' is not acces-
sible in function vector<foo>::insert_aux(foo *,const foo &)
Error ..\source\defalloc.h 121: 'foo::foo(const foo &)' is not accessible
in function construct(foo *,const foo &)
Error ..\source\algobase.h 146: 'foo::operator =(const foo &)' is not
accessible in function copy(foo *,foo *,foo *)
Error ..\source\algobase.h 154: 'foo::operator =(const foo &)' is not
accessible in function copy_backward(foo *,foo *,foo *)
Error ..\source\algobase.h 146: 'foo::operator =(const foo &)' is not
accessible in function copy(const foo *,const foo *,foo *)
Error ..\source\algobase.h 160: 'foo::operator =(const foo &)' is not
accessible in function fill(foo *,foo *,const foo &)
*** 6 errors in Compile ***
```

There are several places in the STL where vector<T> objects need both a copy constructor and an assignment operator, such as in the construct() and copy() functions. (See the code walkthroughs described earlier in this chapter.) The need for a destructor in the walkthroughs was also described, but that isn't a problem for vect0405.cpp.

Making these two functions publicly accessible results in vect0406.cpp, shown in Listing 4-5. This program meets the requirements for vector<T>:

- a public copy constructor
- a public default constructor
- a public destructor
- a public assignment operator

There is some latitude in the construction of an assignment operator. As you can see in vect0406.cpp, the assignment operator for class foo is unorthodox. It returns an int instead of a reference to a foo object.

Listing 4-5

vect0406.cpp: Class foo now has all the required public member functions

```
//
// VECT0406.CPP
//
// This example program is used in Chapter 4 to demonstrate
// some of the requirements that an object must fulfill in
// order to be inserted in a container class.

//
// Borland 4.x workarounds
//
#define __MINMAX_DEFINED
#pragma option -vi-

#include <iostream.h>
#include <iomanip.h>
#include <vector.h>

class foo {
        char *p;
    public :
        int operator=(const foo& rhs){ p = rhs.p; return 1; }
        foo( const foo& rhs ){ p = rhs.p; }
```

```
            foo( char *name = "a" ){ p = name; }
            ~foo(){;}
    };

    main()
    {
        vector<foo> foovec;

        foovec.push_back( foo( "a" ) );
        foovec.push_back( foo( "b" ) );
        foovec.push_back( foo( "c" ) );
        foovec.insert( foovec.begin(), foo( "d" ) );
        foovec.erase( foovec.end() - 2 );
        foovec.pop_back();
        return 1;
    }
```

BUILT-IN TYPES

Note: This whole section only exists because of a compiler bug that causes problems for the STL. Once all C++ compilers properly support the STL, this information won't be needed.

In general, built-in types such as double, unsigned char, and int *, work properly with the STL. However, there is a small problem with explicit destructors in the template function destroy(): destroy() attempts to call the explicit destructor for vector<T> objects with code that looks like this:

```
    pointer->~T();
```

This code works fine for user-defined types that have a destructor, but it doesn't work for built-in types. Because of this, defalloc.h defines specialized versions of destroy() for most built-in types, contained in a sequence like this:

```
        inline void destroy(char*) {}
        inline void destroy(unsigned char*) {}
        inline void destroy(short*) {}
        inline void destroy(unsigned short*) {}
        inline void destroy(int*) {}
```

As you would expect, destroy() turns into a do-nothing function when asked to destroy a built-in type.

This snag in the implementation of the STL can lead to another problem. While defalloc.h does try to develop special versions of destroy() for built-in types, it can't possibly cover *every* kind of built-in type. After all, a pointer to a user-defined class is a built-in type, but there is no way the STL can know about it in advance.

So a program that attempts to create a vector<foo *> will see some peculiar error messages:

```
    Error ..\source\defalloc.h 74: Pointer to structure required on left side
of -> or ->* in function destroy(foo * *)
    Error ..\source\defalloc.h 74: Statement missing ; in function destroy(foo * *)
    Warning ..\source\defalloc.h 75: Parameter 'pointer' is never used in function
destroy(foo * *)
    *** 2 errors in Compile ***
```

These messages are displayed because the destroy() function is trying to invoke the destructor for the built-in type foo *. This should be legal C++, but in Borland's case it doesn't compile. So you have to implement a special version of destroy() just to accommodate foo*. The code is as simple as all the other specializations found in vector.h:

```
    inline void destroy(foo **){}
```

The resulting program is in vect0407.cpp.

Note: This problem is an annoyance that should disappear in the future when the STL, compilers, and the ANSI specification begin to work better together.

Listing 4-6

vect0407.cpp: Destroy(foo**) must be defined for vector<foo*> to work

```
//
// VECT0407.CPP
//
// This example program is used in Chapter 4 to demonstrate
// some of the requirements an object must fulfill in
// order to be inserted in a container class.

//
// Borland 4.x workarounds
//
#define __MINMAX_DEFINED
#pragma option -vi-
```

```
#include <iostream.h>
#include <iomanip.h>
#include <vector.h>

class foo {
    private :
        char *p;
    public :
        int operator=(const foo& rhs){ p = rhs.p; return 1; }
        foo( const foo& rhs ){ p = rhs.p; }
        foo( char *name = "a" ){ p = name; }
        ~foo(){;}
};

inline void destroy( foo ** ){}

main()
{
    vector<foo> foovec;
    vector<foo*> foopvec;

    foovec.push_back( foo( "a" ) );
    foovec.push_back( foo( "b" ) );
    foovec.push_back( foo( "c" ) );
    foovec.insert( foovec.begin(), foo( "d" ) );
    foovec.erase( foovec.end() - 2 );
    foovec.pop_back();
    return 1;
}
```

Vector<T> Potpourri

Before concluding this chapter, there are a few miscellaneous topics regarding vector<T> that need to be addressed. They include the specialization for vector<bool>, bounds checking, and deviations from the standard.

vector<bool>

The ANSI committee for the standardization of C++ added a new built-in type to C++: bool. The creation of a new type with a simple true or false value is probably a good thing, but at the moment, most compiler makers haven't had a chance to implement type bool. This makes the implementation of vector<bool> a problem. Admittedly, you could use a type definition that implements bool as a simple integer or char. The problem is, this makes vector<bool> grossly inefficient, using as many as 32 bits to implement a value that could be stored in 1. If you are creating a small vector of bools on a Pentium-class server with 32M bytes of memory, this isn't a problem. But what if you are an embedded systems programmer targeting an 8051 with 32K of RAM? The wasted space could very well prevent you from using vector<bool>. Remember that C++ is meant to support a wide range of different environments.

The recommended solution to this problem is to implement a specialized version of vector<bool>. C++ allows you to instantiate specific versions of a template class or function, which allows you to optimize things that might not be inherently obvious to the compiler. For example, you can pack multiple bool values into a single int, saving space.

The STL distribution from HP has a version of vector<bool> that takes advantage of this fact. It required the creation of a respectable amount of customized code, but will definitely do a better job of storage management.

Bounds checking for dereferencing operations

The STL acts like standard C++ when it comes to array bounds checking: any time you attempt to access an element in a vector, the STL trusts that you are making a legal reference. If the access is before the start or after the end of a vector, the STL won't do anything to stop you. This applies to references using an iterator or operator[]. While the result of an illegal access will vary depending on your environment, you can be sure nothing good will come of it.

All is not lost, however. The STL is implemented using templates, so you have complete control over the source code. User or vendor modifications to the STL files to implement bounds checking seems like a good idea. For example, you could use the assert facilities included as part of the C++ compiler to add bounds checking directly to your STL source files.

As an example, consider this modified version of vector<T>::operator[]:

```
reference operator[](size_type n) {
    assert( n < size() );
    return *(begin() + n);
}
```

This version of the array reference operation will check if the index is valid before attempting to perform the dereference operation. An illegal attempt will issue the standard message seen when an assertion fails:

```
Assertion failed: n < size(), file myvect.h, line 74
Abnormal program termination
```

This error message is not particularly enlightening, but it *does* catch the error when it happens. Now, it's just a matter of tracking down where it occurred in the program.

If you don't like the idea of hacking away at your copy of the STL, you can always use a commercial implementation. Modena Software sells a version of the STL that has added features, such as bounds checking, embedded in the library. Modena's error messages are also more informative:

```
STL++: Container Bounds Violation at line 83 in file vector.h
:::::: cannot access container before begin() :: ABORTING
```

ObjectSpace's version of the STL, STL<ToolKit>, can be configured to throw exceptions when an out-of-bounds access occurs. This allows you to recover from errors in a structured fashion.

On the Bandwagon Yet?

The vector container is the STL replacement for built-in arrays in C and C++. Once you are confident that your compiler properly supports the STL, you should start trying to use vectors everywhere you would normally use arrays. You should immediately start reaping the benefits, including efficient use of memory, bounds checking (if your version of the STL supports it), and easy expansion of vectors. The vector container by itself would be more than enough reason to start using the STL. The next few chapters discuss some other containers that make adoption even more worthwhile.

THE DEQUE CONTAINER

queue (kyo̅o̅) noun
1. *A line of waiting people or vehicles.*
2. *A long braid of hair worn hanging down the back of the neck; a pigtail.*
3. *Computer Science. A sequence of stored data or programs awaiting processing.*

— The American Heritage Dictionary of the English Language, Third Edition

deque<T> is the second of four container types defined by the STL. Like vector<T>, this container is designed for sequential storage of C++ objects, including built-in types. However, it has a unique set of characteristics that make it the appropriate container for certain jobs, and a completely inappropriate container for others.

The name *deque* is shorthand for "double-ended queue." A queue is a common data structure used in programming, designed to hold a list of objects that are waiting for some type of servicing. Usually objects are inserted one at a time at one end, and removed one at a time from the other end. This type of data structure is ideal for a consumer/producer situation. For example, print jobs are often kept in a queue by an operating system. Various programs *produce* print jobs, and one or more printers *consume* the same print jobs.

The STL's deque container is a slightly more versatile version of the traditional queue known to computer programmers. The deque is set up to efficiently handle insertions and removals at either end of the container. Although you might only use deque<T> as a normal queue, it retains this bidirectional capability, at a very minor cost.

In the first part of this chapter, we'll look at the structure and function of deque<T>. This will give you the information you need to use the next section—a discussion of the advantages and disadvantages of deque<T>.

Following that, some sample code will be presented that uses deque objects as containers. We'll investigate the performance of the resulting program. After that, we'll examine the internals of deque<T> in detail, with particular attention to the iterators.

For a straight-ahead reference to the elements of deque<T>, see Chapter 20.

WHAT IS DEQUE<T>?

Table 5-1 highlights the cost of operations performed on deque<T>. You can see that deque<T> has its own unique set of characteristics. You can perform constant time insertions and removals at both ends, whereas vector<T> only has constant time insertions and removals at one end. And unlike list<T>, deque<T> features constant time for random access, which means operator[]() is defined for this container.

Table 5-1
The cost of various container operations

	C array, T[]	vector<T>	**deque<T>**	list<T>
Insert/erase at start	n/a	linear	**constant**	constant
Insert/erase at end	n/a	constant	**constant**	constant
Insert/erase in middle	n/a	linear	**linear**	constant
Access first element	constant	constant	**constant**	constant
Access last element	constant	constant	**constant**	constant
Access middle element	constant	constant	**constant**	linear
Overhead	none	low	**medium**	high

A peek at the structure of deque<T>

The basic structure of deque<T> is shown in Figure 5-1. Unlike vector<T>, data in a deque is not stored in a single variable-length block of memory.

Instead, deque<T> allocates sets of fixed-size blocks that hold collections of objects. A member of deque<T>, map, points to a block of pointers, which in turn point to each of the data blocks presently in use. The pointers stored in the map are arranged sequentially, so that moving from the block pointed to in map[m] to the block pointed to in map[$m+1$] will let you traverse from data item n to $n + 1$.

Just like vector<T>, deque<T> has two important data members that keep track of where stored data begins and ends: start and finish. These two members are of type deque<T>::iterator.

vector<T> also has an end_of_storage member to indicate where the end of the raw allocated memory is. deque objects can make do without this, since they inherently know the size of each block being used to hold objects of type T.

As with a vector, the data stored in deque<T> goes sequentially from start to finish without any gaps. However, in deque<T>, the data may span several data blocks, so it can't be truly described as contiguous.

vector<T> can expand the number of objects it contains by moving the finish iterator into raw memory not yet initialized. deque<T> has this capability as well, but it can also store additional data before the start iterator. This means deque<T> can grow in either direction, not just from the back.

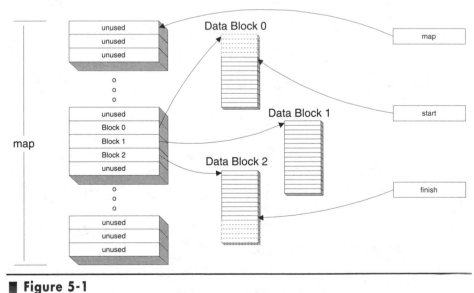

Figure 5-1
A view of deque<T>

Read the fine print before signing

Of course, there is a price to be paid for the additional capabilities just described: the cost of iterator operations.

In the previous chapter we saw that, when using the default allocator, iterators in vector<T> are standard pointer types. So normal pointer operations such as dereferencing, incrementing, and decrementing are very efficient. The efficient use of standard pointers (like those used for vector iterators) is the reason C is often called a high-level assembly language.

But iterators in deque<T> aren't nearly as efficient, and it's easy to see why. It isn't a good idea to try to use a standard built-in pointer to reference an object inside a deque container. For example, in Figure 5-1, you could try using a pointer for the start iterator. You could dereference the pointer and get the value you wanted. However, after incrementing the pointer a few times, you would point past the end for data block 0, leaving you with an invalid pointer. So while it is certainly possible to use a pointer (as defined by the container's allocator) to point to an item in a deque<T>, you can't expect normal pointer operations to navigate through the container in a reliable manner.

A slightly smarter pointer is really needed as an iterator in deque<T>. Iterators in this class have to detect when they have reached the end of a block, and then move on seamlessly to point into the next data block. While this isn't a difficult job, it will certainly have considerably more overhead than a built-in pointer.

ADVANTAGES OF DEQUE<T>

Chapter 3, "An Overview of the Standard Template Library," has a discussion comparing the STL to other C and C++ container and collection classes. The advantages of vector<T> described there (and in Chapter 4) apply to deque<T> as well. This section looks at some of the unique things deque<T> can bring to the party.

Efficient operator[]

One of the really nice things about C/C++ arrays is our old friend, the subscripting operator. We take it for granted that the compiler can generate efficient code to reach any element in an array, given its base address:

```
extern char *first_name[];
extern char *last_name[];

string get_user( int record_num )
{
    string name = first_name[ record_num ];
    name += " " + last_name[ record_num ];
    return name;
}
```

As expected, this turns out to be an efficient operation. At the assembly code level, accessing first_name[record_num] means adding record_number*sizeof(char *) to the base of the array first_name, then doing a lookup on the resulting address. This is a very low-cost operation when considered in the grand scheme of things.

Both vector<T> and deque<T> implement operator[] as well. So either of these two containers can be treated like an array.

The previous chapter pointed out that vector<T> can perform data access using operator[] as efficiently as an array. It would be nice if deque<T> could perform the same simple pointer math as in vector<T>, but this isn't the case. It takes quite a bit more work. However, it is still efficient enough to include operator[] as a member of the class.

The man behind the curtain

The mechanics of operator[] for deque<T> are more complicated than those for normal pointer arithmetic, but that doesn't mean they have to be forbidding. In fact, they are still relatively easy to understand.

Figure 5-2 shows the layout in memory of a typical deque<T> object. The components of the relevant object are:

- An iterator, start, that points to the first valid object in the container.

- The blocks of data used to contain the objects currently in the container. Each data block has room for exactly five objects (in this example). There may be empty space at the beginning of the first block, as well as at the end of the last block. The mechanism that decides the block size is discussed later in this chapter.

- An array of pointers known as the map. There is a range of active pointers in the middle of the map, with unused pointer space at the beginning and end. Each allocated data block is pointed to by the map.

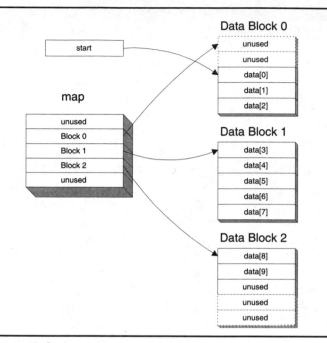

Figure 5-2
Performing calculations for operator[]

Given this memory layout, we need to determine what has to occur for the program to perform a dereference such as:

```
main()
{
    deque<foo> a;
    ....
    b = a[ 9 ];
```

The internal structure of deque iterators hasn't been discussed yet, but it's clear that each iterator needs to know which data block to point to, as well as the offset within that block. So, when applying operator[], you are calculating a block number, as well as an offset within that block. The algorithm the STL uses to calculate this new address is:

```
operator[ n ] :
    total_offset = n + ( index of data[0] in Data Block 0 )
    block_size = number of elements in each Data Block
    data_block_number = total_offset / block_size
    offset_in_block = total_offset-(data_block_number*block_size)
    return iterator( data_block_number, offset_in_block )
```

This code example tries to dereference $a[9]$, which is the same as (start + 9). The first step in the pseudocode is to calculate the offset from the start of Data Block 0—the first line in the algorithm. In this case, the result is 9 + 2, i.e., 11.

The next step is to calculate the block number that the element 9 will reside in. This is done in the third line of pseudocode, which simply divides the offset by the number of elements in each Data Block. In this case, that is 11/5, or 2. This yields a data_block_number of 2, and an offset_in_block value of 1. The resulting iterator points to $a[9]$, which is what we wanted.

This calculation is clearly not as easy as the pointer math used for vectors and arrays, but it *does* limit itself to a few integer math operations. Most importantly, the calculation time is constant, so you don't have to worry about an increasingly balky response as the container grows large.

Growth in either direction

When using vector<T>, inserting new objects into a container is an expensive operation. The only place new objects can be added without paying a higher price is at the end of the vector. This isn't necessarily a bad thing. Some data structures, such as a stack, *need* to grow in only one direction.

However, other data structures aren't happy when restricted to growth in a single direction. Some, such as a FIFO queue, want to add elements at one end and remove from the other. This can be done with a vector using insert() and erase(), but you will pay the price! Insertions and erasures from anywhere but the end have linear, or O(N) complexity. (The O(N) designation is a standard way of referring to the complexity of an algorithm. It is usually referred to as the *Order* of the algorithm, using *big-O* notation.)

Clearly, in Figure 5-2, you can see that adding new objects to either end of the data structure is a low-cost operation. Since there is unused space in the data blocks at both ends of the vector, you can insert data there by first calling the constructor, then either incrementing the finish iterator, or decrementing the start iterator. In deque<T>, these operations are performed with the push_back() and push_front() operations. The corresponding member functions to remove data are pop_back() and pop_front().

But what happens when you completely fill a data block at the start or end of the container? The next time you want to add a new object, you will first need to allocate a new block of memory, add it to the map, and update the member iterators. Then the normal insertion can take place.

As an example, consider the data structure from Figure 5-2. If two consecutive push_front() function calls are performed, the original Data Block 0 is not completely filled. When the next push_front() is called, the following sequence of events takes place:

1. A new data block is allocated. It is now the first data block in the structure, so it gets labeled Data Block 0.

2. The map gets a pointer to the new data block 0 in the first open position up from the existing block of pointers.

3. The deque start iterator is set to point to the last element in Data Block 0.

4. The object to be added to the container is constructed in the location pointed to by start.

A similar operation takes place when data has to be added to the end of the container with push_back().

Figure 5-3 shows what the deque object from Figure 5-2 might look like after three calls to push_front(), and five calls to push_back().

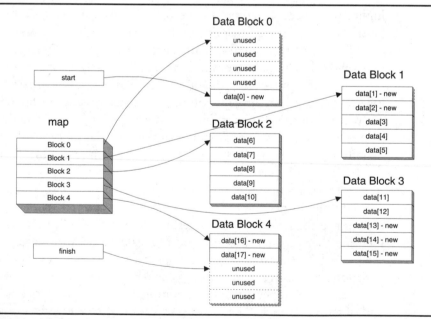

Figure 5-3

The structure from Figure 5-2 after several new objects have been added

One last detail...

The one detail left uncovered in this explanation concerns what happens when the map gets full. The map can only hold a finite number of pointers to data blocks. In Figure 5-3, the fourth call to push_back() will provoke a crisis in the container management. Fortunately, the STL handles this with grace.

When a new allocation takes place, but the map is full at the end in question, a new map is allocated. The existing map is copied into the center of the new map. This leaves plenty of room for expansion in both directions. Figure 5-4 shows what the map looks like after the addition of a new block at the end of the deque.

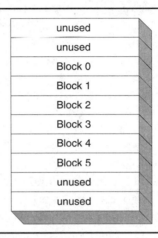

Figure 5-4
The new map after it has been allocated and initialized

No shuffling!

vector<T> is a very nice container, but it does have a bad habit: Whenever it outgrows its current storage space, it has to allocate a new block of raw memory, then copy all the objects from the old vector to the new vector. After this, it has to call the destructor for each object in the old vector. This adds up to a lot of work!

With deque<T>, this shuffling, copying, creating, and destroying doesn't have to take place. Once an object is constructed, it can stay in the same memory location as long as it exists. As new objects are added or removed from either end, there will be many new allocations of data blocks, but existing data blocks won't be tampered with. This will always be true as long as you use deque<T> for its most efficient operations, which are insertions and removals from either end. But insert or remove an element from the middle of the container—and all bets are off!

So what's the catch? Doesn't some shuffling have to occur? In a way, it does. In the deque container, it is the *map* that gets shuffled. When the existing block of pointers in the map becomes too large, a new map is allocated and the pointers have to be copied into it. The old map is then deallocated.

If you have to shuffle something, shuffling the map is a lot better than shuffling container contents. The map holds only pointers. Since the pointers in the map are of a built-in data type, there aren't any constructors or destructors to call, and assignments are done using efficient machine code.

Demo program dequ0501.cpp shown in Listing 5-1 compares benchmarks of deque containers with vector containers. The program highlights the cost that vector<T> has to pay in extra copying operations as the container grows. For example, when inserting 511 objects into a deque container, 511 calls are made to the copy constructor.

Inserting the same 511 objects into a vector requires 991 calls to the copy constructor, an increase of 480 calls—almost 100% additional overhead! Naturally, this also requires an extra 480 calls to the destructor. The additional copies are a result of multiple resizing operations on the vector.

This additional overhead can become very painful if your constructors and destructors are costly. The net effect can more than erase any gains vector<T> achieves by virtue of using pointers for iterators.

Listing 5-1

dequ0501.cpp: Comparing benchmarks

```
//
//  DEQU0501.CPP
//
//  This demo program is used in Chapter 5 to compare the
//  number of constructor calls that are made when
//  filling a deque vs. the number when filling a vector.
//

//
// Borland 4.5 workarounds
//
#define __MINMAX_DEFINED
#pragma option -vi-
```

```
#include <vector.h>
#include <deque.h>
#include <iostream.h>
#include <iomanip.h>
#include <strstrea.h>
#include <string.h>

class foo {
    public :
        int a[ 64 ];
        foo( int i = -1 ){ ctor_count++; }
        foo( const foo &rhs ){ copy_count++; }
        void operator=( const foo & ){ assign_count++; }
        ~foo(){ dtor_count++; }
        static long ctor_count;
        static long copy_count;
        static long dtor_count;
        static long assign_count;
};

long foo::ctor_count = 0;
long foo::copy_count = 0;
long foo::dtor_count = 0;
long foo::assign_count = 0;

template<class T1, class T2>
void exercise( T1 &container, T2 * )
{
    for ( int j = 0 ; j < 511; j++ )
        container.push_back( T2( j ) );
    container.erase( container.begin(), container.end() );
}

main()
{
    cout << "Testing vector<foo>\n";
    vector<foo> a;
    exercise( a, (foo *) 0 );
    cout << "Ctor count:   " << foo::ctor_count   << "\n";
    cout << "Copy count:   " << foo::copy_count   << "\n";
    cout << "Assign count: " << foo::assign_count << "\n";
    cout << "Dtor count:   " << foo::dtor_count   << "\n";

    foo::ctor_count = 0;
    foo::copy_count = 0;
    foo::assign_count = 0;
    foo::dtor_count = 0;
```

```
    cout << "\nTesting deque<foo>\n";
    deque<foo> b;
    exercise( b, (foo *) 0 );
    cout << "Ctor count:   " << foo::ctor_count   << "\n";
    cout << "Copy count:   " << foo::copy_count   << "\n";
    cout << "Assign count: " << foo::assign_count << "\n";
    cout << "Dtor count:   " << foo::dtor_count   << "\n";
    return 1;
}
```

dequ0501.cpp produces the following output:

```
Testing vector<foo>
Ctor count:   511
Copy count:   991
Assign count: 0
Dtor count:   1502

Testing deque<foo>
Ctor count:   511
Copy count:   511
Assign count: 0
Dtor count:   1022
```

MS-DOS-friendly

deque<T> has a few additional advantages when it comes to memory allocation. Once again, these concerns may not rate as terribly important to programmers with acres and acres of available RAM. But people programming for old MS-DOS systems, or working with price-constrained embedded systems, will appreciate these aspects of deque<T>:

- deque<T> frees data blocks when they are emptied. Its sibling, vector<T>, only grows; it never shrinks. So deque containers will always have less than two blocks of unused memory in use.

- deque<T> works well with fixed-length memory allocations. Many real-time operating systems parcel out memory from pools of fixed-size blocks, due to their reliable performance characteristics. Even when using standard C heaps (because the memory allocator is parameterized by type T) wasted space is minimized.

- When a vector container of size n has used all of its free storage, it will resize to size $2n$. Until it has finished copying the elements to the new storage area, the vector will temporarily be using space for $3n$ elements to hold $n+1$!

- The total overhead for an object of deque<T> is small. A typical implementation needs two iterators, two integers, a pointer, and a block of pointers.

While vector and deque containers won't solve every problem associated with array-like data structures, they do take care of the biggest ones.

A ROAD TEST

The public interface to deque<T> is relatively simple, and nearly identical to the interface you've already seen for vector<T>. It includes the standard push_back() and pop_back() functions, the same set of constructors, and the insert() and erase() functions. In addition, deque<T> adds the push_front() and pop_front() functions for adding and removing elements from the front of the list. These two functions reflect the additional capabilities found in this new container.

The test program presented in Listing 5-2, dequ0502.cpp, serves two purposes. First, it illustrates some of the basics of creating and using deque<T>. Second, this program shows how to peek inside the protected data members in the deque container itself.

dequ0502.cpp looks at some of the deque data members, including the map data structure. This program doesn't look at the internals of iterators. They'll be taken up in the next section.

The long code example in Listing 5-2 goes through several different stages. First, it creates an empty deque<foo> container. Then it adds 32 foo objects to the container, taking up about 64K of space (the maximum allowed under 16-bit MS-DOS). Finally, the program sits in a loop, adding objects to the end of the container while removing them from the beginning. At the end of the program, all the objects are erased from the container and some final statistics are printed out.

Note that most information this program prints out is normally inaccessible to users of this STL class. If objects truly of class deque<T> were created, it wouldn't be possible to look at the map pointer, the buffer_size, or any other protected members.

Listing 5-2

dequ0502.cpp

```
//
// DEQU0502.CPP
//
// This example program is used in Chapter 5 to demonstrate
// some features of deque<T>. It looks at the internals of
// deque<T> by creating a derived class called public_deque<T>.
// This public function has access to all of the deque<T>
// member data, and provides member functions to copy their
// values.
//

//
// Borland 4.x workarounds
//
#define __MINMAX_DEFINED
#pragma option -vi-

#include <deque.h>
#include <iostream.h>
#include <iomanip.h>
#include <strstrea.h>
#include <string.h>

//
// class public_deque<T> does nothing useful on its own.
// It exists solely to allow us to look at the protected
// members of deque<T>. The various access functions
// defined below provide read-only access.  Note that
// the other constructors supported by deque<T> can all
// be added to this class fairly easily. At this time,
// only the default ctor is defined.
//

template<class T>
class public_deque : public deque<T> {
  public :
    public_deque() : deque<T>() {}
    deque<T>::map_pointer get_map(){ return map; }
    deque<T>::size_type get_map_size(){ return map_size; }
    deque<T>::size_type get_length(){ return length; }
    deque<T>::size_type get_buffer_size() {
        return buffer_size;
    }
};
```

```
//
// This class keeps track of how often its member functions
// are called.  This helps provide an indication of how
// efficiently the class is being used.
//

class foo {
    public :
        static int ctor_count;
        static int copy_count;
        static int assign_count;
        static int dtor_count;
        char a[ 2000 ];
        foo(){ ctor_count++; }
        foo( const foo& ){ copy_count++; }
        void operator=(const foo&){ assign_count++; }
        ~foo(){ dtor_count++; }
};

int foo::ctor_count = 0;
int foo::copy_count = 0;
int foo::assign_count = 0;
int foo::dtor_count = 0;


foo static_foo;

//
// This routine displays some of the member functions
// of the deque<T> object.
//
template<class T>
void dump_public_deque( public_deque<T> & a, char *note )
{
    cout << "\nDump of deque<T> " << note << ":" << endl;
    cout << "map = "          << a.get_map() << "   "
        << "map_size = "      << a.get_map_size() << "   "
        << "deque_length = " << a.get_length() << endl;
}


//
// The body of the test program.
//
main()
{
    public_deque<foo> a;

    cout << "deque<foo>::buffer_size  = "
        << a.get_buffer_size()
```

```
              << endl;
        cout << "deque<foo>::max = "
              << a.max_size()
              << endl;
        dump_public_deque( a, "just after creation" );
//
// First I add 32 elements to the deque.
//
        for ( int i = 0 ; i < 32 ; i++ ) {
            cout << i;
            a.push_back( static_foo );
            cout << '\r';
        }
        dump_public_deque( a, "after adding 32 blocks" );
//
// Now we can add to the end and take away from the
// beginning.  We do this more than 1K times so that
// we are sure to reach the end of the 1K map.
//
        for ( i = 0 ; i < 1024 ; i++ ) {
            cout << i;
            a.pop_front();
            a.push_back( static_foo );
            cout << '\r';
        }
        dump_public_deque( a, "after 1024 add/delete cycles" );
//
// Now erase all of the elements in the deque, and see
// what it looks like afterwards.
//
        a.erase( a.begin(), a.end() );
        dump_public_deque( a, "after erasing all elements" );
//
// Finally, dump the class statistics.
//
        cout << endl;
        cout << "ctor count = " << foo::ctor_count << endl;
        cout << "copy count = " << foo::copy_count << endl;
        cout << "assign count = " << foo::assign_count << endl;
        cout << "dtor count = " << foo::dtor_count << endl;
        return 1;
}
```

Normally, this restricted access isn't a problem. After all, one of the nice things about using a container class is that we can remain blissfully ignorant of the internal workings of the class. However, in this case, we *want* to snoop, so it's necessary to take extreme measures.

The data members of interest in deque<T> are protected members, so classes derived from deque<T> can access these members. All that was done in dequ0502.cpp is to create a new class derived from deque<T>. Class public_deque<T> inherits the functionality of deque<T>. So, all that has to be added are constructors, plus access routines for the required protected members. The code to do this is shown near the top of the listing for dequ0502.cpp.

Initialization

The first line of functional code in main() creates a container of type public_deque<foo>. class foo is a dummy class created solely for the purpose of exercising this container. Since the default allocator has a preferred page size of 4096 bytes, the container should be able to hold two objects per buffer.

The first diagnostic line output from the program confirms that calculation:

```
deque<foo>::buffer_size  = 2
```

Note: A buffer_size member of 2 doesn't mean each block will be 4096 bytes long, with only 4000 in use. The default allocator will be parameterized by class foo, so it will allocate blocks large enough to hold 2 foo objects, but no more.

The next line in main() calls the dump routine to show the current state of the map, as well as the number of objects contained by the public_deque<foo>. As you would expect, the map has not been allocated yet, and the length of the container is 0:

```
Dump of deque<T> just after creation:
map = 0000:0000  map_size = 0  deque_length = 0
```

Fill 'er up!

dequ0502.cpp then sits in a loop adding objects to the container. The total amount of storage added to the container is roughly 32 * 2000 bytes, or just under the 65535 byte limit.

The dump output after completing this operation confirms that the map has been allocated, and that we have successfully added 32 objects to the container:

```
Dump of deque<T> after adding 32 blocks:
map = 0x17df0004  map_size = 1024  deque_length = 32
```

This information indicates that the initial allocation for the map created room for 1K worth of pointers to data blocks. Since only 32 are being employed at this point (since each foo object takes up an entire data block), only a small subset of the available pointer space in the map should be used.

map

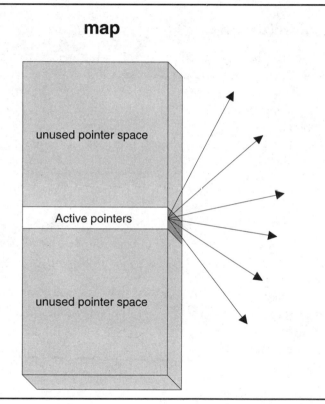

Figure 5-5
The map after 32 objects have been added

Exercising the container

The next loop in the test program repeatedly adds objects to the end of the container, while removing them from the beginning. The reason is to force a map reallocation.

Adding each object to the end of the container takes up one more pointer in the map, until we arrive at the end of the map. At that point, a new map has to be allocated, and the pointers will all be copied to it.

The output of the dump routine after the exercise loop confirms that a reallocation has taken place:

```
Dump of deque<T> after 1024 add/delete cycles:
map = 0x1bbf0004  map_size = 32  deque_length = 32
```

In this case, not only does the map have a new address, but it also has a new size! Whenever the map is reallocated, the container allocates enough space to hold twice as many pointers as it needs. In this example, there were 16 blocks in the container when the reallocation took place, so the new map had space for 32 pointers. (Remember that each block holds two objects, and there are 32 objects in the queue.)

Figure 5-6 is a graphical view of the map reallocation process. When the last pointer in the map was at the very end of the map, deque<T> asked for a new map with a new smaller size. It then copied the current set of block pointers into the new map, and deleted the old memory.

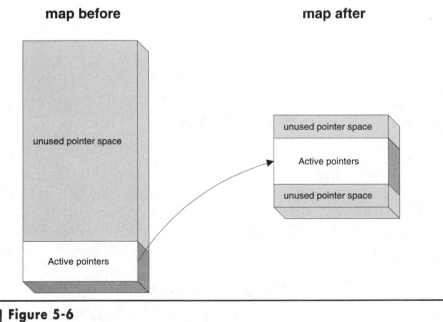

map before   **map after**

unused pointer space

Active pointers

unused pointer space

Active pointers

unused pointer space

Figure 5-6
The map after reallocation

Clean-up

The final clean-up code in main() erases all existing objects from the container. Once this is done, the length of the deque<foo> container is 0, which means it has no active block pointers in the map. The map still exists, and still has room for 32 new entries. The only way to delete the map is to delete the container.

```
Dump of deque<T> after erasing all elements:
map = 0x1bbf0004  map_size = 32  deque_length = 0
```

At the end of the program, the member function counters for class foo are printed out. The two loops in the main program allocated a total of 1024 + 32 (1056) new objects. The copy constructor is called exactly 1056 times, in order to copy the object into the container.

After erasure, the destructor is called exactly 1056 times as well. No extra function calls were generated to move objects around inside the container, despite the need to relocate the map. (The single default constructor call was to allocate static_foo, the object that was repeatedly copied.)

```
ctor count = 1
copy count = 1056
assign count = 0
dtor count = 1056
```

THE MYSTERY GUEST: DEQUE<T> ITERATORS

As mentioned earlier in the chapter, deque<T> can't use standard pointer types as iterators. In the process of iterating from the start to the end of a deque object, the iterator may have to jump from block to block. Normal pointer increment operations won't work properly under these conditions.

So it's now time to take a look at the mysterious type deque<T>::iterator.

Not your father's iterator

If you look at the header file deque.h, you'll notice right away that the definition of an iterator isn't going to follow the form we saw in vector.h. deque.h starts off with a list of type definitions, as in the definition of vector<T>:

```
typedef T value_type;
typedef Allocator<T> data_allocator_type;
typedef Allocator<T>::pointer pointer;
typedef Allocator<T>::reference reference;
typedef Allocator<T>::const_reference const_reference;
typedef Allocator<T>::size_type size_type;
typedef Allocator<T>::difference_type difference_type;
typedef Allocator<pointer> map_allocator_type;
```

There is something missing from this list. Where is the definition of type iterator?

The STL specification says that a container class is required to have a type definition for iterator. If this type was left out of deque<T>, standard algorithms couldn't be used on this container.

Fortunately, deque<T> *does* define an iterator type. But instead of defining its iterator as a built-in type, deque containers have a nested class definition. Nested classes are a feature recently added to C++. It simply means that the scope of the iterator class is confined to the container class that defined it. Here's the definition from deque.h:

```
template<class T>
class deque {
    ...
class iterator
    : public random_access_iterator<T, difference_type> {
friend class deque<T>;
friend class const_iterator;
protected:
    pointer current;
    pointer first;
    pointer last;
    map_pointer node;
    iterator(pointer x, map_pointer y)
        : current(x), first(*y), last(*y + buffer_size), node(y) {}
public:
    iterator() : current(0), first(0), last(0), node(0) {}
    reference operator*() { return *current; }
    ...
```

The class definition goes on for quite a while. To function effectively as an iterator, this new class has to implement the following list of operators:

```
reference operator*();
difference_type operator-(const iterator &);
iterator& operator++();
iterator& operator++(int);
```

```
iterator& operator--();
iterator& operator--(int);
iterator& operator+=(difference_type);
iterator& operator-=(difference_type);
iterator& operator+(difference_type) const;
iterator& operator-(difference_type) const;
reference operator[](difference_type);
bool operator==(const iterator&) const;
bool operator<(const iterator&) const;
```

Note: In addition to this lengthy definition, deque<T> has to create a nearly identical class definition for deque<T>::const_iterator(). It has the same member functions, with only a few very small differences. (The extra work required to support this *const*-ness is a necessary chore that isn't limited to just the STL!)

A look under the hood

An iterator is used as a pointer to an object of type T. In the case of deque containers, objects of type T are stored in fixed-size blocks. Each block is, in turn, pointed to by a pointer in the map object. An iterator has to contain enough information to tie all this together in a usable manner.

The deque<T>::iterator accomplishes this by manipulating its four protected data members. They are:

current: This is a pointer to the object of type T. When it's time to dereference an iterator, in order to access the object, this is the pointer used. current points to a location inside one of the allocated data blocks.

first: This is a pointer to the first location of storage in the data block pointed to by current. The iterator needs to keep this information on hand so that, when it is performing a decrement operation, it can detect when it needs to move to the previous block.

last: This is a pointer one past the last storage location in the data block pointed to by current. Like *first*, the iterator needs to keep a copy of *last* so that increment operations can detect when they have moved past the end of a block.

node: The node pointer differs from the other three: it is not a pointer to type T. Instead, it points into the map. The map structure is simply an array of pointers to the data blocks that collectively constitute the container. That makes node a pointer-to-a-pointer to T. When an increment or decrement operation on the iterator passes outside the current data block boundaries (as defined by first and last), the next data block can be reached by either incrementing or decrementing node.

Even though these members are referred to as pointers, they are, in fact, of a type defined by the currently used allocator. For normal memory models they will usually be standard pointer types, but more exotic allocators are free to use other objects, as long as they obey the syntax and semantics of pointers.

Figure 5-7 shows how the components of a deque<T>::iterator might look in action:

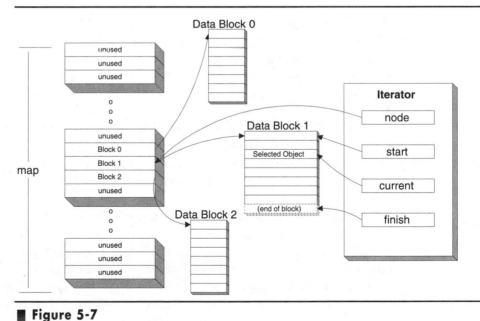

Figure 5-7
An iterator in action

- the current member points to the selected object—the third object in a selected data block.

- first and last point to the start and finish of the selected block (not the start and finish of the entire deque container).

- node points into the map, to the pointer to the current block.

All four pointers work in harmony to provide the semantics of a normal pointer. A simple illustration is the increment operator for an iterator in this container class. Here is the code from deque.h:

```
iterator& operator++() {
    if (++current == last) {
        first = *(++node);
        current = first;
        last = first + buffer_size;
    }
    return *this;
}
```

The whole purpose of the increment operator is to move the pointer to the next object in the container. Since current points to the selected object, the first thing the operator code does is increment that pointer. It then tests to see if current now points to the same position pointed to by last. If not, we are presumably pointing to a valid object in the current data block, and the function is finished.

However, if current was *already* pointing to the last object in the data block, this increment operation needs to move us to the next data block. Since node points to the pointer to the current data block, we know that we can increment it, at which point node will point to a pointer to the next data block.

Since node now points to the next data block, dereferencing it gives us the next value of first, which is the first position in the next block. current should also point to the first position. Finally, last is updated using simple pointer math until it points to the end of the new data block.

This is a very simple operation, but it will always be slower than the increment operation on a vector<T> iterator. Having to perform a comparison after every increment operation will, by itself, slow things down. The code executed when the end of a block is reached slows things down even more. However, these are unlikely to prove to be major bottlenecks.

The decrement operation looks very similar to this, and is of equal complexity.

A sneaky peak inside the iterator

As was the case with deque<T>, the interesting members of this iterator are protected. They are not accessible when writing programs that use this container.

A program called dequ0503.cpp has been created to get around this problem by using derivation. The template class public_iterator has special member functions and friends that allow it to look at protected data members. You just copy the deque iterator into a public_iterator<T> object and print out the members in the copy.

dequ0503.cpp is very similar in content to dequ0502.cpp. However, instead of printing out information regarding the map, it prints out the contents of the start and finish iterators. It also looks at the node pointers of the two iterators to determine how many blocks of memory are in use. The listing for dequ0503.cpp follows.

Listing 5-3

dequ0503.cpp: A program to print iterator contents

```
//
// DEQU0503.CPP
//
// This example program is used in Chapter 5 to demonstrate
// some features of the deque<T>::iterator. It looks at the
// internals of these iterators by creating a derived class
// call public_iterator<T>. This public function has access
// to all of the deque<T>::iterator member data, and provides
// member functions to copy their values.
//

//
// Borland 4.x workarounds
//
#define __MINMAX_DEFINED
#pragma option -vi-

#include <deque.h>
#include <iostream.h>
#include <iomanip.h>
#include <strstrea.h>
#include <string.h>
```

```
//
// Class public_iterator is used to let us look at
// the contents of a deque<T> iterator.  The iterator
// members are protected, so we derive this new
// class that gives us access to all of the protected
// members of the iterator. To look at the members,
// just copy the iterator into one of these, using
// either the copy constructor or the assignment operator.
//

template<class T>
class public_iterator : public deque<T>::iterator {
  public :
    public_iterator( const deque<T>::iterator &a )
        : deque<T>::iterator( a ) {}
    friend ostream& operator<<( ostream&,
                                public_iterator<T>&);
    deque<T>::pointer *get_node(){ return node; }
};

//
// Once we create a public_iterator object, this routine
// is called to print its members.  There are four components
// to any given iterator.
//

template<class T>
ostream& operator<<(ostream& s, public_iterator<T>& i )
{
    s << "Curr: " << i.current << "  "
      << "1st: "  << i.first << "  "
      << "Last: " << i.last << "  "
      << "Node: " << i.node;
    return s;
}

//
// This template function does a dump of some of the iterator
// data for a container.  It accomplishes this by assigning the
// begin() and end() iterators from the container to iterators
// in my derived class.  I have access to the information from
// the derived class, so it gets printed out.
//
template<class T>
void dump_iterators( deque<T>& a, char *label )
{
    cout << "\nIterator dump: "
```

```
                    << label
                    << endl;
        public_iterator<T> start = a.begin();
        public_iterator<T> finish = a.end();
        cout << "Start:   " << start << endl;
        cout << "Finish: " << finish << endl;
        cout << "Number of allocated_blocks : ";
        if ( finish.get_node() == 0 )
            cout << "0";
        else
            cout << (finish.get_node() - start.get_node() + 1);
        cout << endl;
}


//
// This program creates a deque<double> container.
//
main()
{
    deque<double> a;

    dump_iterators( a, "Immediately after ctor" );
    a.push_front( -1 );
    dump_iterators( a, "After one push_back()" );
    for ( int i = 0 ; i < 8000 ; i++ ) {
        if ( ( i % 1024 ) == 0 )
            cout << i;
        a.push_front( i );
        if ( ( i % 1024 ) == 0 )
            cout << '\r';
    }
    dump_iterators( a, "After filling container" );
    a.erase( a.begin(), a.end() );
    dump_iterators( a, "After erasure" );
    return 1;
}
```

dequ0503.cpp creates a deque container that holds doubles. It dumps the contents of the container's iterators when it is first created, after a single insertion. And it dumps them again after 8000 doubles are inserted.

Finally, the program erases all members of the deque<double> container and prints the contents again. The results are shown in Figure 5-8.

The dump output gives visible confirmation of the iterator operations. When the container is first created, the pointers inside the iterator are set to 0, the NULL pointer value. As soon as the first object is added to the container, a data block is allocated, and the pointers are initialized.

```
Iterator dump: Immediately after ctor
Start:  Curr: 0x00000000  1st: 0x00000000  Last: 0x00000000  Node: 0x00000000
Finish: Curr: 0x00000000  1st: 0x00000000  Last: 0x00000000  Node: 0x00000000
Number of allocated_blocks : 0

Iterator dump: After one push_back()
Start:  Curr: 0x1a690804  1st: 0x1a690004  Last: 0x1a691004  Node: 0x1b6a0804
Finish: Curr: 0x1a69080c  1st: 0x1a690004  Last: 0x1a691004  Node: 0x1b6a0804
Number of allocated_blocks : 1

Iterator dump: After filling container
Start:  Curr: 0x2b7a0e04  1st: 0x2b7a0004  Last: 0x2b7a1004  Node: 0x1b6a07c4
Finish: Curr: 0x1a69080c  1st: 0x1a690004  Last: 0x1a691004  Node: 0x1b6a0804
Number of allocated_blocks : 17

Iterator dump: After erasure
Start:  Curr: 0x00000000  1st: 0x00000000  Last: 0x00000000  Node: 0x00000000
Finish: Curr: 0x00000000  1st: 0x00000000  Last: 0x00000000  Node: 0x00000000
Number of allocated_blocks : 0
```

▎ Figure 5-8
The output from dequ0503.cpp

After that first block is inserted, both the start and finish iterators have the same node pointer, since start and finish are in the same block. The difference between the start and finish of the data block is 0x1000, or 4096 bytes. 4096 is the preferred page size of the default allocator.

One final thing to note about the first insertion is that current is set to 1a69:0804. This is exactly in the middle of the data block. The first object is inserted in the middle of the data block and the pointer to the data block is stored in the middle of the map. This ensures that the deque<T> object will not be biased towards insertions from the front or back of the queue.

After 8000 more insertions, the start and finish iterators point to two blocks that are nowhere near one another. It is clear from their node pointers that there are 17 data blocks allocated. Under the large 16-bit memory model of MS-DOS, each pointer in the map takes up 4 bytes, and there are 68 bytes occupied in the map.

When all objects have been deleted, start and finish are once again set to 0, indicating that no data blocks have been allocated. The map will have been freed, so the container will drop its memory use down to nearly 0.

CLEVER WAYS: MEMORY ALLOCATION

Memory allocation represents the core of the sequential container classes. If all they had to do was store and retrieve objects, these classes wouldn't be very exciting. What makes them useful are the clever ways they manipulate memory, in order to handle the demands placed on them.

Of course, you don't need in-depth understanding of the memory allocation issues in deque<T> to use the class. However, like all containers in the STL, the more you understand the underpinnings of the library, the more effectively you can use it. When it comes to the STL, ignorance is not bliss!

Creating and destroying

Chapter 4 explained how vector<T> has separated the two tasks of memory allocation and object creation. Normally, C++ programmers consider the two jobs to be the same, but with the help of the placement syntax for operator new, and explicit destructor calls, vector<T> manages to subdivide the effort.

deque<T>, like all STL containers, takes exactly the same approach to memory management. Whenever memory is allocated for either a deque data block or a new map, it's done by a call to a raw memory allocator. The memory is allocated in the default allocator using the global new operator. This returns a block of untyped raw memory. For example, when a new data block is allocated, it may have room for hundreds of objects, but it won't immediately have any objects in the storage area.

After deque<T> has allocated a data block consisting of raw memory, it can create objects by calling the construct() template function. This function is defined as part of the memory allocator, which is passed to the constructor of the deque container. The construct() function, as defined in the default allocator class (in defalloc.h), looks like this:

```
template <class T1, class T2>
inline void construct(T1* p, const T2& value) {
    new (p) T1(value);
}
```

This function is called whenever a new object has to be inserted into the data block. Argument T1* p is a pointer to the raw memory area that will get the new object, and T2& value is the object that will be copied into the memory. The placement syntax used with operator new allows it to create a new object in a section of preexisting memory.

An example of how the construct() template function is called is shown in the following section of code, for deque<T>::push_front().

First, this function checks if the container is currently empty, or if the start member of the container, as accessed by begin(), is pointing to the first location in a block. Since this function wants to add a byte to the front of the container, either one of these conditions will require more memory to be allocated. The function does so at this point.

```
void push_front(const T& x) {
    if (empty() || begin().current == begin().first)
        allocate_at_begin();
    --start.current;
    construct(start.current, x);
    ++length;
}
```

Once the function gets past the memory allocation, it decrements the current member of the start iterator, to point to the next available storage item in the front section of the data block. The construct() function is then called to initialize the new location with a copy of the object that was passed as a reference parameter. construct() is called by both push functions. It is also called indirectly when one of the insert() functions is called.

Destruction of objects is done using the destroy() member function, which is also defined in the allocator. The explicit call to the destructor is used to destroy the object without freeing any memory associated with the object:

```
template <class T>
inline void destroy(T* pointer) {
    pointer->~T();
}
```

The destroy() function is called when either of the pop functions is called, or indirectly when one of the erase() functions is invoked. The code in the following excerpt shows the pop_back() function, which destroys the last object in the container.

```
void pop_back() {
    --finish.current;
    destroy(finish.current);
    --length;
    if (empty() || end().current == end().first)
        deallocate_at_end();
}
```

The pop_back() function is similar to vector<T>::pop_back(), except that it has a little more bookkeeping to do when it destroys an object. First, it has to decrement the finish pointer. Since finish points one past the last object—the convention in the STL—we need to decrement it first, then call destroy for the resulting location. Next, the routine needs to decrement the length member that keeps track of how many elements are presently stored in the container.

The storage in use by the current block can be freed if there are no more elements in the container, or if the finish pointer, as referenced by end(), is pointing to the start of the block. This is done by calling deallocate_at_end().

In a class of its own: Adding data blocks

The push and pop functions in deque<T> are similar to those in the vector container class. The code in the deque container really deviates from that in the vector class in the memory allocation routines. There are four routines defined for use by this class:

```
allocate_at_begin()
allocate_at_end()
deallocate_at_begin()
deallocate_at_end()
```

These routines differ from those that grow and shrink a vector in the way the two containers handle their memory. When a vector object needs to allocate more memory, it has to allocate an entire new vector, and copy all the old data into the new vector.

A deque container gets out of doing any of this work. It simply has to allocate the new storage area and update the start and/or finish iterators to properly point to the new block. This represents a big difference in the way the two containers work. You saw a lot of similarity between vector<T> and deque<T> when comparing member functions like push_back(). But these new memory management routines have to operate in an entirely different manner than memory management routines in vector<T>.

So let's check now to see how allocate_at_begin() works. This function is only called from push_front(), under one of two different circumstances:

■ when the container is completely empty, meaning no data blocks have been allocated

■ when the start iterator points to an object that is the first object in a data block

Either situation means a new data block has to be created and added to the map. The start iterator then needs to be pointed into the map. Figure 5-9 shows what a deque container might look like immediately before the allocation takes place.

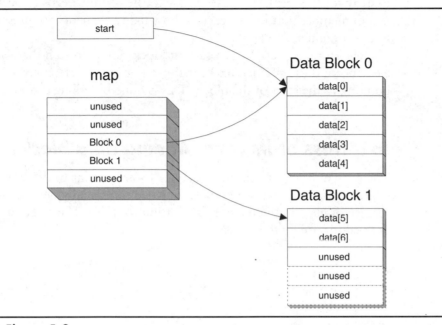

Figure 5-9
A deque<T> container that will need more memory to perform a push_front()

It's clear from Figure 5-9 why you need to allocate a new block before performing a push_front(). The first thing necessary when performing a push_front() is to decrement the start iterator. But in its present position, decrementing start will leave an invalid iterator, since there isn't another block ahead of the current block.

To see how this is handled, look at the source code for allocate_begin(), which is found in deque.h. It may look a bit long to digest in one gulp, but it is composed of three distinct, mutually exclusive parts. You can gain a good understanding of the function by looking at the three parts separately.

```
template <class T>
void deque<T>::allocate_at_begin() {
  pointer p = data_allocator.allocate(buffer_size);
  if (!empty()) {
    if (start.node == map) {
```

```
        difference_type i = finish.node - start.node;
        map_size = (i + 1) * 2;
        map_pointer tmp = map_allocator.allocate(map_size);
        copy(start.node, finish.node + 1, tmp + map_size / 4 + 1);
        map_allocator.deallocate(map);
        map = tmp;
        map[map_size / 4] = p;
        start = iterator(p + buffer_size, map + map_size / 4);
        finish = iterator(finish.current, map + map_size / 4 + i + 1);
      } else {
        *--start.node = p;
        start = iterator(p + buffer_size, start.node);
      }
    } else {
      map_size = map_allocator.init_page_size();
      map = map_allocator.allocate(map_size);
      map[map_size / 2] = p;
      start = iterator(p + buffer_size / 2 + 1, map + map_size / 2);
      finish = start;
    }
  }
}
```

The one thing all three parts of allocate_at_begin() share is a need to allocate a new block of raw memory. This is done at the top of the function, with a call to the allocate() function of the data allocator. (Unlike vector<T>, this function has two allocators: one for data blocks, and one for the map.)

The function then breaks down into one of three different sections, depending on the results of a pair of tests:

- If the container isn't empty, but there is no more room at the front of the map, you have to perform a map reallocation, followed by insertion of the new block.

- If the container isn't empty and there is room in the map, you have to perform a simple insertion of the new block.

- Finally, if the container *is* empty, you have to allocate a new map and insert the new block.

Map reallocation

This is the most difficult of the three possibilities. Figure 5-10 shows a container that will need to reallocate its map before it can add a new block to the front. While there's no problem with allocating the new block, there's no room at the front of the map to add a new pointer.

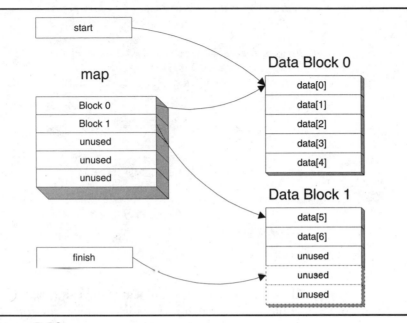

Figure 5-10
A container that will need map reallocation

The code that allocates the new map is shown in the next excerpt. The first line calculates the number of elements currently in use in the map.

Each iterator, including start and finish, has a pointer (the node member) back to the location in the map that points to its block. By finding the difference between the node members of start and finish, you get a count of how many pointers are in use in the block.

The next two lines manage to allocate a new map with twice as many blocks as are presently in use:

```
difference_type i = finish.node - start.node;
map_size = (i + 1) * 2;
map_pointer tmp = map_allocator.allocate(map_size);
copy(start.node, finish.node + 1, tmp + map_size / 4 + 1);
map_allocator.deallocate(map);
map = tmp;
map[map_size / 4] = p;
start = iterator(p + buffer_size, map + map_size / 4);
finish = iterator(finish.current, map + map_size / 4 + i + 1);
```

Once the new map has been allocated, the rest of the work is simple. All the pointers in use in the old map are copied to the middle of the new map, and the new map is freed up. The pointer to the new map is installed in the map, and start and finish are adjusted to reflect the new reality.

It's important to note that this operation has invalidated any iterators pointing into this container. Any operation with the potential to reallocate the map can have this effect, so it's important to recognize if, and when, it can happen. In general, when you're using an iterator to work through any STL container, you can't expect your iterator to remain valid after inserting or removing data.

Figure 5-11 shows the same container after the map has been updated. It is now ready to receive a new object at the location pointed to by start.

Note: Immediately after the reallocation, the container is in an invalid state. The object pointed to by start has not been constructed yet; it is just an empty raw memory location. However, this can only occur while we are inside push_front(), and it will immediately call construct().

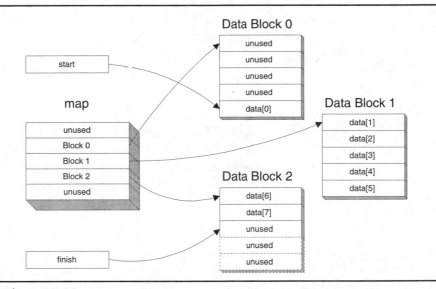

Figure 5-11
After map reallocation

Simple insertion

If the map has space for the new data block, a simple insertion takes place, an operation that only takes two lines of code.

First we put the pointer to the data block into the map by dereferencing the node member of the start iterator, after a predecrement. Then, the start iterator is updated to point to the new data block, using the iterator constructor that assigns new values to the first and last iterator members. first and last must point to the start and end of the new data block.

```
*--start.node = p;
start = iterator(p + buffer_size, start.node);
```

Map creation

If the container was completely empty when push_front() was called, a new map must be allocated to hold the new pointer. The initial size of the map is determined by the allocator used by this container.

The following piece of code allocates a map block, then puts the pointer to the new block, right in the middle of the map.

```
map_size = map_allocator.init_page_size();
map = map_allocator.allocate(map_size);
map[map_size / 2] = p;
start = iterator(p + buffer_size / 2 + 1, map + map_size / 2);
finish = start;
```

The only remaining work to do after the map is allocated is to initialize the start and finish iterators. You can see from the last code excerpt that, not only was the pointer to the new block put in the very center of the map, but the iterator pointing to the first element was put right in the middle of the new block. This illustrates the point that deque<T> tries when possible to avoid favoring push_front() or push_back().

Removing data blocks

Just as allocate_at_begin()/allocate_at_end() was called from push_front()/push_back(), there are a pair of routines that remove an object from the begin and end of the container. These two routines are called deallocate_at_begin() and deallocate_at_end().

The two deallocation routines are completely symmetrical, so it's only necessary to look in depth at one of them; the other is its twin (with references to the start and end of the container reversed).

```
void deque<T>::deallocate_at_end() {
    data_allocator.deallocate(*finish.node--);
    if (empty()) {
        start = iterator();
        finish = start;
        map_allocator.deallocate(map);
    } else
        finish = iterator(*finish.node + buffer_size, finish.node);
}
```

This routine is simpler than allocation routines; the deallocator doesn't include any code for resizing the map. Thus, a map will never change size until a reallocation is forced by a push_back() or push_front() that pushes it past its present boundaries.

The deallocation routine handles two possibilities. First, it always deallocates the data block in question (the first or last block, depending on which deallocation routine is being called). Then it has to determine whether removing the last data block left an empty container. If the container is empty, the map is deleted, and both iterators are set to 0. If the container isn't empty, either the start or finish iterator is updated, depending on which of the two deallocation routines is being called.

insert() and erase()

The only other routines that cause memory to be allocated or freed are the various versions of the insert() and erase() member functions.

While there is a sizable portion of the deque.h header file dedicated to supporting these routines, they don't do anything difficult on their own. Instead, they do all their insertions and erasures through repeated calls to one of the four push or pop routines. These are followed by copies to move data up or down in the container.

The only reason routines such as these occupy as much space as they do is because they have to make a large number of choices regarding where to push, where to pop, where to copy from, and where to copy to. These choices are fundamentally easy to understand; they are simply bookkeeping.

This is the source code for one of the standard erase() routines:

```
template <class T>
void deque<T>::erase(iterator first, iterator last) {
    difference_type n = last - first;
    if (end() - last > first - begin()) {
        copy_backward(begin(), first, last);
```

```
            while(n-- > 0) pop_front();
        } else   {
            copy(last, end(), first);
            while(n-- > 0) pop_back();
        }
    }
```

This version of erase() is called to erase a range of elements from the container, starting at the first parameter and ending just before the last parameter.

The only decision this routine has to make is whether it is more efficient to move the top of the range down, or the bottom of the range up. Figure 5-12 shows two different potential ranges to be erased. Clearly, in Range A, the best choice would be to copy the bottom of the range so it overlaps the erase range, then delete the end of the range using pop_back(). Range B would require the reverse operation.

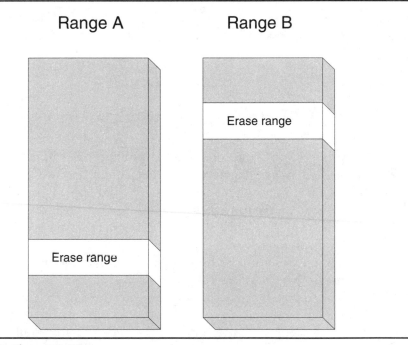

Figure 5-12
Two possibilities for an erasure

The insertion routines have to make similar decisions about where and how to copy. But this, too, is nothing but bookkeeping.

BENCHMARKS: VECTOR VS. DEQUE

A lot of comparisons are made in this chapter between vector<T> and
deque<T>. If you've read it through, you should now have a good understanding of the relative strengths and weaknesses of the two classes.
Knowing the merits of each class will help ensure you use STL containers
when they work well and bypass them when they do not.

But all this talk about the performance of vector and deque is just talk
so far. Let's back it up with some benchmark testing, shown in Listing 5-4.

Listing 5-4

dequ0504.cpp: A benchmark to test container access speed

```
//
// DEQU0504.CPP
//
// This example program is used in Chapter 5 to
// perform some *extremely* crude benchmarks on classes
// vector<T> and deque<T>.  I throw in testing of T[]
// to use as a baseline.  This routine just puts
// a bunch of ints into an array, then adds them
// up.  The goal is to see how fast we are able to
// iterate through the array.
//

//
// Borland 4.x workarounds
//
#define __MINMAX_DEFINED

#include <deque.h>
#include <vector.h>
#include <iostream.h>
#include <iomanip.h>
#include <stdlib.h>
#include <time.h>

const int runs = 25;
long results[ runs ] = { 0 };

//
// This template function performs the actual test.
// To get reasonable run times, you may have to
// tinker with "runs" to get decent multiples of
// a second for each of the three types tested here.
//
```

```
template<class T>
void test( T begin, T end )
{
    srand( 1 );
    time_t t1 = time( 0 );
    int i = rand();
    for ( int j = 0 ; j < runs ; j++ ) {
        for ( T p = begin; p != end; p++ )
            *p = i++;
        long total = 0;
        for ( p = begin; p != end; p++ )
            total += *p;
        cout << '.';
        if ( results [ j ] == 0 )
            results[ j ] = total;
        else if ( results[ j ] != total )
            cout << "Error!\n";
    }
    long delta = time( 0 ) - t1;
    cout << " elapsed time: "
        << delta
        << " seconds"
        << endl;
}
//
// Main just sets up the containers, then calls
// the template function to test them out.
// Note that the allocation of *all* the space
// for the container is done here, so it doesn't
// come into play in the benchmarks.
//
main()
{
    short int *a = new short int[ 32000 ];
    cout << "Testing T[]        ";
    test( a, a + 32000 );

    cout << "Testing vector<T> ";
    vector<short int> b( 32000 );
    test( b.begin(), b.end() );

    cout << "Testing deque<T>   ";
    deque<short int> c( 32000 );
    test( c.begin(), c.end() );

    return 1;
}
```

dequ0504.cpp has a single template function, test(), that iterates through a container multiple times. It inserts a series of integers into the container, then adds them up. A quick sanity check is performed to be sure that all the different containers come up with the same totals on each pass through the test.

Template function test() isn't very complex, but it provides a good example of the flexible functions you can write with the STL. It is parameterized on the type of the container iterator, so it can accept any pair of objects that obey pointer semantics. test() isn't as general-purpose as it could be, since it assumes the iterators will dereference to numbers that can be added to a long. The important thing to note is that a single function will work properly with standard C arrays, STL vectors, and STL deques.

After compiling dequ0504.cpp in a standard MS-DOS 16-bit memory model, the program produces this output:

```
Testing T[]         ....................... elapsed time: 2 seconds
Testing vector<T>  ....................... elapsed time: 2 seconds
Testing deque<T>   ....................... elapsed time: 13 seconds
```

The first two classes of objects, T[] and vector<T> have nearly identical performance. This isn't surprising; a vector is almost identical to a standard C array. Any differences come into play only when it's time to resize the vector, and that doesn't happen in this test.

But when it comes to class deque<T>, there is a big difference in performance. Once again, this isn't surprising, since iterators for deque<T> have to do much more work when being incremented or decremented, compared to those for T[] or vector<T>.

Remember, this particular example is doing nothing but iterator operations. When you use deque<T> in a program, the performance hit is likely to be diluted considerably by other processing. For example, if you are using deque<T> as a message queue in your operating system design, you may spend far more time processing each message in the queue than you spend incrementing the iterator to get to it.

The important thing to remember is that deque<T> might be a more efficient consumer of memory in your environment. It uses small pieces, gives memory back when it is done, and won't have to shuffle data elements if you confine your insertions and removals to the front and back of the queue. If those criteria are important to your design, deque<T> may be precisely what you need. On the other hand, if you need speedy access to your array, and you don't have to worry about its size, vector<T> may be the better alternative.

Type Requirements for T

Chapter 4 goes into considerable detail about the requirements vector<T> has for type T. The member functions and operators of the vector class expect to do certain things with objects of type T. If you attempt to create a class parameterized by a type T that doesn't meet these requirements, you will get hard-to-interpret errors in the STL header files. Depending on your compiler, the message you get may leave you scratching your head in bewilderment.

The requirements for deque<T> are identical to those for the vector class. Refer to Chapter 4 for the full explanations behind them. In a nutshell, any type T that is used to construct a deque container must have:

- a public copy constructor
- a public default constructor
- a public destructor
- a public assignment operator

In addition, built-in types may require a destroy() function defined, for the reasons described in Chapter 4. Borland 4.x users should refer to the earlier discussion for details.

Deque<T> Miscellany

Please refer to Chapter 4 and Appendix A for more detailed information about these topics:

- **Bounds checking for iterator operations.** This is not offered as part of the standard STL, but may be present in third-party and compiler vendor packages.
- **Selection of an allocator class.** This is currently done using the preprocessor, although the STL specification says it should be done with a template parameter. This will be changed when compiler vendors can conform to the C++ template standard.
- **Using a user-defined allocator in the constructor.** Allowing the user to instantiate an allocator for a specific container was a last-minute change made by the ANSI/ISO standardization committee. At press time, this feature was not supported in the public HP release of the STL.

THE LIST CONTAINER

Early to bed, early to rise, work like hell and organize
— Albert Gore. Jr.

The list<T> sequence container uses a linked list structure to store elements in a container, which makes it very efficient at inserting elements anywhere in the container. You might use this container to keep track of processes running under an operating system, or windows on a screen. Because of the low overhead incurred when deleting an item in the middle of the list, list<T> is better than either vector or deque for applications of this type.

This chapter starts with a look at the internal structure of list<T> and its advantages and disadvantages. There's also some sample code that will help you examine the internals of list<T>. The chapter also presents some benchmarks to compare the performance of list<T> to the other sequence containers.

For more information on the public interface to list<T>, see Chapter 20.

WHAT IS LIST<T>?

list<T> implements a doubly linked list container. Its internal structure is significantly different from vector<T> and deque<T>.

Since these other two containers are variations on an array, their data is stored in sequential blocks.

With a linked list, data is stored in random locations in memory, and no two blocks need be contiguous. To navigate either forward or backwards through the list, you must follow links between individual elements in the container.

Figure 6-1 shows the basic structure of a doubly linked list, such as the one used in list<T>. Each of the list nodes contains a data object and two pointers. The pointers point to the previous and next elements in the linked list.

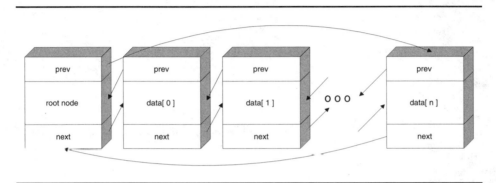

Figure 6-1
The essentials of a linked list

If you create a linked list using standard C, and perhaps C++, the prev and next pointers are exposed as part of the node structure. When you want to move from one node to the next, you usually dereference the next member of the structure. If you're using C++, you can call a next() function to get the pointer.

In the STL, the prev and next pointers aren't just *partially* hidden from the user. To use list<T>, you don't need to be aware of the link pointers at all. Instead, the list is navigated with the same iterator syntax used for the other sequence containers.

A peek at the list<T> structure

In Figure 6-1, the linked list is composed of a bunch of little boxes, each of which holds a data item and two pointers. In list.h, the same structure is defined as struct list_node:

```
struct list_node {
    void_pointer next;
    void_pointer prev;
    T data;
};
```

struct list_node contains the two link pointers (defined as a typedef from the allocator definition), and a data element. Given this structure, all that is needed to define a complete list is a head and tail pointer, to point to the first and last elements in the list. list.h defines this, along with a length counter, as protected data members in class list:

```
protected:
    link_type node;
    size_type length;
```

node defines the root node of the linked list. It doesn't contain a valid object of type T, but instead provides root pointers to the first and last nodes.

A frequent technique used in linked lists is to terminate the list with a node that has a null value in its next pointer. In that case, the prev pointer of the first node also points to 0.

This isn't the method used in list<T>. Instead, it implements a list as completely circular. If you look at Figure 6-1, the last node in the list points back to the root. Likewise, the prev pointer in the root node points to the last node.

Figure 6-2 shows how the list looks immediately after it is created. It simply has prev and next pointers that point back to itself.

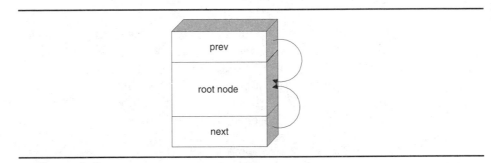

Figure 6-2
A list<T> immediately after construction

Given this, how do you know when you're at the end of the list? Using old-fashioned C linked lists, you can iterate through a list, using code that checks for a NULL pointer in a link:

```
NODE *node;

for ( node = root->next ; node != NULL ; node = node->next )
    printf( "%s\n", node->data );
```

But this code doesn't work with list<T>, since you can't look at next, the protected member. How do traditional C++ classes handle this? First, by hiding the next pointer as a protected class member. Second, by allowing navigation using a get_next() member function. The class definition, and some code that used it, might look like this:

```
class node {
    protected :
        node *next;
        node *prev;
    public :
        node *get_next(){ return next; }
        T data;
    .
    .
    .

void dump_list( node *list )
{
    while ( list ) {
        cout << list->data << endl;
        list = list.get_next();
    }
}
```

This code is fairly straightforward, but it doesn't meet the design goals for the STL. It's incompatible with the code needed to iterate through a vector<T> or deque<T> container.

To make the linked list containers compatible with other sequence containers, the STL requires that navigation through the container be done with iterators. The C++ code we just saw would look like this for the STL:

```
void dump_list( list<string>& a )
{
    list<string>::iterator i;

    for ( i = a.begin(); i != a.end() ; i++ )
        cout << *i;
}
```

If you wrote a dump_vector() routine, it would look nearly identical to the code shown above. In fact, templates can be used to write a generic version that will work with linked lists, deque containers, and vectors:

```
template<class T>
void dump_list< T& a )
{
    T::iterator i;

    for ( i = a.begin; i != a.end() ; i++ )
        cout << *i;
}
```

This generic ability to navigate data structures is one of the hallmarks of the Standard Template Library, and is one of its most important features.

list<T>::begin(), list<T>::end()

So what are the values of begin() and end() used in list<T>? begin() looks for a reference to the first node in the list. Since the root node (member node) *points* to the first node, list<T>::begin() simply has to follow that pointer and return the node it is pointing to:

```
iterator begin() {
    return (link_type)((*node).next);
}
```

Once you get a node iterator back from begin(), you need to test whether the iterator points to the end of the list. The value for end() is an iterator pointing to the root node:

```
iterator end() { return node; }
```

Remember that the root node (member node) doesn't contain an initialized data object. This means end() returns an iterator that shouldn't be dereferenced—as applies to all other STL container classes.

ADVANTAGES OF LIST<T>

Table 5-1 is another appearance of our old friend, the STL sequence container benefit chart. This is where you finally get to see what a list<T> container can do.

Since list<T> uses an internal structure that has little in common with the other two container classes, there should be some important differences. And in fact, this is the case. I'll cover several of these differences in this section.

Table 5-1

Container characteristics

	T[]	*vector<T>*	*deque<T>*	**list<T>**
Random access, operator[]	√	√	√	
Sequential access	√	√	√	√
Insert/delete at front			√	√
Insert/delete in middle				√
Insert/delete at end		√	√	√
Overhead	lowest	low	low	**High**

No random access

In some ways, the table is better at showing what list<T> *doesn't* do. One shortcoming appears in the first row of the table. The three other types of containers—standard arrays, vector<T>, and deque<T>—have random access capabilities, so they can use operator[].

vector<T> and deque<T>, along with standard C arrays, can perform random access lookups based on the value of an iterator. To look up a random element in a vector requires a simple bit of pointer addition. Looking up a random element in a deque<T> is more complicated, but still only requires a constant amount of time.

list<T> iterators aren't so lucky. Because of the way list elements are organized, finding the *n*th element of a list requires *n* sequential pointer dereferences. There simply isn't any shortcut.

Since the STL actively discourages the use of $O(N)$ operations, you won't find operator[] in list.h, and you won't find operator+() defined for list<T>::iterator.

Mean...but not lean: Higher overhead

Since we're discussing the negatives affecting list<T>, you also need to be aware of overhead. vector<T> can proudly boast of virtually no overhead. Other than a few pointers that keep track of storage allocation, it runs lean and mean.

deque<T> is not quite as lean. It has a map structure, which takes up a page of memory (as defined by the allocator). Also, it has more overhead in its iterators, which have to carry around pointers to the map, as well as pointers to the start and finish locations for the current block.

When it comes to overhead, list<T> really eats up the extra bytes. Its data elements are stored in objects of type link_node. Every link_node object is burdened with two pointers, one to the previous node in the list, and one pointing to the next node.

This is a particularly large burden when the objects contained in list<T> aren't very big. For example, when storing char objects in a linked list with 32-bit pointers, each node has eight bytes of overhead for a single byte of storage. Obviously, the burden becomes lighter as the size of the object increases, but it remains a significant factor—unless the objects of type T get *really* big.

Node allocation

Memory allocation is discussed in detail later in this chapter, but there are two important things to be aware of concerning node allocation:

- list<T> allocates its own private memory blocks for allocation of new nodes

- list<T> doesn't return nodes to the program's heap when they are freed. Instead, it keeps a private list of freed nodes that are recycled by future allocations

Private memory allocation schemes can often be managed more efficiently than the C runtime library heap. This is particularly true when objects to be allocated are of a fixed size, known in advance. list<T> takes advantage of this when allocating nodes.

Instead of allocating one node at a time from the heap, list<T> allocates a page at a time. The size of the page is determined by the allocator. Individual nodes are taken from the page one at a time, as they are needed. When nodes are freed, they're added to a list of free nodes; any free elements on the list are used first, before another page is taken from the heap.

This memory management scheme is much more efficient than the runtime heap, for several reasons. First, when a new block is needed, the first free block is guaranteed to be a fit. You don't have to search through the heap for a block of the right size, because *every* block is the right size. Second, when freeing blocks, there's no need to coalesce adjacent blocks. Both of these features contribute to the overall speed and efficiency of the class.

These are useful features for list<T>, but they point to additional overhead and complexity. The memory blocks that list<T> allocates require pointers and lists of their own, so they can be managed properly. The freed nodes require another list of their own.

Of course, normal heap storage comes at a cost as well, but the cost is usually hidden from C++ programmers. If you plan to maintain a list with a large number of nodes, list<T> may well do a better job of managing its storage than ordinary heap storage would.

Growth in either direction, and the middle

Rising through the hierarchy of sequential containers, you find more and more flexibility when adding new elements to a container. Standard C arrays can't grow at all. With vector<T>, you gain a push_back() function, which allows you to add elements to the end of the vector. deque<T> has an additional function, push_front(), which enables easy addition to the start of the container as well.

list<T> has an additional group of constant time functions, the insert() family. insert() adds a new node or nodes to any point in the list without any O(N) shuffling of existing elements.

The reason inserting new nodes into a list takes constant time is precisely because there is no shuffling. Figure 6-3 shows some elements in the middle of an existing list. A new node is added to the list just before element *m*. This is done with a function call like this:

```
a.insert( node_m, new_element );
```

When calling insert() for either a vector or a deque, you go into a function that moves all the elements before or after the insertion point up or down. As a result, a new element of free space is opened.

But with a list, it's only necessary to break the two links between data[*m*-1] and data[*m*]. The links are moved to point to the new node. Then, the new node adds a prev and next link that point to data[*m*-1] and data[*m*]. This means the new node is inserted with just a small amount of effort. Figure 6-4 shows the state of the list<T> container immediately after a new node has been inserted.

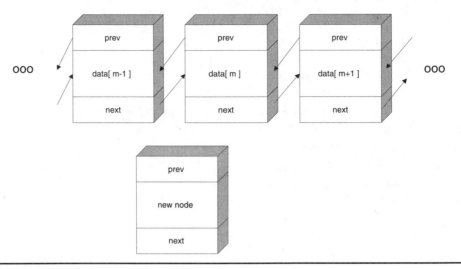

Figure 6-3
Just before adding a new node to a list<T>

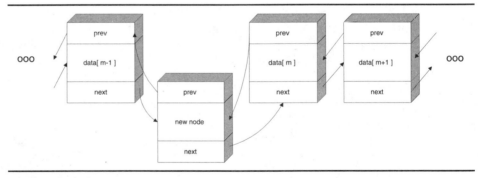

Figure 6-4
After the node has been added

This ease of insertion has a corresponding function for the removal of elements from a list<T> container. With vector<T>, it's easy to remove elements from the end of a container. deque<T> adds the capability to remove elements from the front of the container. And list<T> can call the erase() family of functions to remove an element or multiple elements from the inside of a container. No shuffling necessary. It's simply a matter of redirecting a pair of pointers to break the target elements out of the chain.

Windows-friendly

list<T> offers some advantages to PC programmers in Windows memory management. Under MS-Windows, there are a finite number of selectors available in the system memory pool. For this reason, applications that use the Windows API function GlobalAlloc() can run out of selectors long before available memory is exhausted.

The normal solution is to provide a subsegment allocator in the heap manager. This allocates big blocks of memory and then parcels them out to your application in smaller chunks.

list<T> has its own version of a subsegment allocator. Instead of going to the operating system every time a new node needs to be allocated, list<T> asks for larger blocks of memory and parcels them out to nodes when necessary. This can be helpful under MS-Windows, as well as in embedded systems that lack sophisticated O/S memory allocation algorithms.

A ROAD TEST

list0601.cpp is a sample application that makes use of list<T>. One of the big advantages of list<T> is that you can insert and remove elements from the interior of the container in constant, or O(*k*), time. This program provides a shell for a possible text processing program.

Listing 6-1

list0601.cpp: A Road test

```
//
// LIST0601.CPP
//
// This example program is used in Chapter 6 to demonstrate
// some features of list<T>. The program reads in a text file,
// strips out all lines that start with a comment, then
// prints the resulting file back out to cout. Borland defines
// their string class in cstring.h, other compilers may use a
// different file.
//

//
// Borland 4.x workarounds. Note that when using STL with
// Borland 4.x, you must include the RTL headers
// (fstream and cstring) before list.h.
//
#define __MINMAX_DEFINED
#pragma option -vi-
```

```
#include <fstream.h>
#include <cstring.h>
#include <list.h>

//
// These comment lines should be stripped from the
// output file.
//

main()
{
    ifstream input( "list0601.cpp" );
    if ( !input ) {
        cerr << "Open file error, list0601.cpp not found!\n";
        return 1;
    }
    list<string> text;

    while ( input ) {
        char buf[ 133 ];
        input.getline( buf, 132, '\n' );
        text.push_back( buf );
    }
    input.close();
    list<string>::iterator i = text.begin();
    while ( i != text.end() ) {
        if ( (*i).substr( 0, 2 ) == "//"  )
            text.erase( i++ );
        else
            i++;
    }
    for ( i = text.begin() ; i != text.end() ; i++ )
        cout << *i << endl;
    return 0;
}
```

list0601.cpp reads in all the lines of text from a file, in this case
list0601.cpp. The lines are stored in a container of type list<string>. Once the
whole file is read into the container, list01.cpp steps through the entire list,
and deletes any line that starts with the "//" single line comment delimiters.

There are a couple of things to note here. First, even though this same
program could be written with vector<string> or deque<string> containers,
list<string> is much more efficient. The above example might not show it
effectively, but reading in a source file with thousands of lines would
undoubtedly point out the difference. Calling the erase() function in the

middle of a vector<T> will always cause a massive memory shuffle, resulting in a delay of O(*N*), where *N* is the size of the container.

Second, while list0601.cpp could call the erase() function, it continues to use an existing iterator. Once you perform an erase() or insert() operation on a deque<T> or vector<T>, your shuffle operation renders any existing iterators invalid. This isn't the case with list<T>. The only iterator made invalid by the erase() operation is an iterator pointing to the node being erased. In list0601.cpp, iterator *i* is incremented just before the node it points to is erased. Since the iterator now points to the next node, you can continue using it.

Listing 6-2 shows the output from list0601.cpp. As promised, it has printed out the contents of the source file with all single line comments stripped out.

Listing 6-2

The output from list0601.cpp: A copy of its own source with single line comments stripped

```
#define __MINMAX_DEFINED
#pragma option -vi-

#include <fstream.h>
#include <cstring.h>
#include <list.h>


main()
{
    ifstream input( "list0601.cpp" );
    if ( !input ) {
        cerr << "Open file error, list0601.cpp not found!\n";
        return 1;
    }
    list<string> text;

    while ( input ) {
        char buf[ 133 ];
        input.getline( buf, 132, '\n' );
        text.push_back( buf );
    }
    input.close();
    list<string>::iterator i = text.begin();
    while ( i != text.end() ) {
        if ( (*i).substr( 0, 2 ) == "//" )
            text.erase( i++ );
```

```
        else
            i++;
    }
    for ( i = text.begin() ; i != text.end() ; i++ )
        cout << *i << endl;
    return 0;
}
```

LOVE ME, LOVE MY ITERATOR

Understanding an STL container is easy if you understand its iterator. Since an iterator has to navigate through the container, its code, in some sense, provides an encapsulation of the container structure.

For example, in Chapter 5, "The Deque Container," the code for the operators of deque<T>::iterator is much more complicated than for a simple pointer. When the iterator is incremented from one location to the next, the code considers whether it has reached the end of a block. If it has, the address of the next block must be loaded from the map block of pointers.

Listing 6-3 is a complete listing of the list<T>::iterator class. It isn't as long or complex as deque<T>::iterator, nor is it as simple as the pointer type used as a vector<T>::iterator. The simplicity in this class is a reflection of the simplicity inherent in a doubly linked list.

Listing 6-3

The list<T>::iterator class definition

```
class iterator : public bidirectional_iterator<T, difference_type> {
  friend class list<T>;
  friend class const_iterator;
protected:
  link_type node;
  iterator(link_type x) : node(x) {}
public:
  iterator() {}
  bool operator==(const iterator& x) const;
  reference operator*() const { return (*node).data; }
  iterator& operator++() {
    node = (link_type)((*node).next);
    return *this;
  }
```

```
iterator operator++(int) {
  iterator tmp = *this;
  ++*this;
  return tmp;
}
iterator& operator--() {
  node = (link_type)((*node).prev);
  return *this;
}
iterator operator--(int) {
  iterator tmp = *this;
  --*this;
  return tmp;
}
};
```

Middleweight power

The most powerful iterator of all is a random access iterator. A standard pointer is an example of a random access iterator. As discussed briefly in Chapter 3, "An Overview of the Standard Template Library" (and in depth in Chapter 9, "Allocators"), random access iterators implement all conventional pointer operations.

In a nutshell, a random access pointer can be incremented, decremented, and have an offset added to or subtracted from it. This implies the ability to support operator[].

Listing 6-3 shows that list<T>::iterator is a little deficient in this list of operators. It doesn't support any operation that allows you to add or subtract a random offset from an iterator. It does still have the increment and decrement operations defined, so you can move forward or backwards through the container. You just can't take big jumps.

By definition, this makes list<T>::iterator a *bidirectional iterator*. In the first line of the class definition, the iterator is derived from the template class bidirectional_iterator<T,difference_type>.

Bidirectional iterators are useful, but their lack of power restricts the use of list<T> objects to algorithms that don't depend on random access. For example, the STL sort() requires its input iterators to be random access iterators. If you try to pass list<T> iterators to sort(), you'll generate compiler errors caused by an attempt to use underpowered iterators.

```
void foo( list<string> &a )
{
    sort( a.begin(), a.end() );
```

A piece of code such as this would compile and run without question if the container were a vector<string> or a deque<string> type. Since list<string> doesn't have random access operators, it generates a compile-time error instead. In the case of Borland C++, this causes a tangled web of sometimes confusing messages:

```
    Error ..\source\algo.h 744: Illegal structure operation in function
__final_insertion_sort(list<string>::iterator,list<string>::iterator)
    Error ..\source\algo.h 745: Illegal structure operation in function
__final_insertion_sort(list<string>::iterator,list<string>::iterator)
    Error ..\source\algo.h 745: Could not find a match for '
__insertion_sort(list<string>::iterator,undefined)' in function
__final_insertion_sort(list<string>::iterator,list<string>::iterator)
    ...
    ... etc.
    ...
    *** 14 errors in Compile ***
```

Does this mean that list<T> is somehow inferior to other containers? No, it simply means that it is specialized for certain types of activity. Random access of elements in the container isn't one of them.

Behind the curtain

An iterator in class list<T> has a single member, *link_type node*. link_type is a type definition for a pointer to a linked list node. Accordingly, list<T>::iterator::node is essentially a pointer to one of the nodes in the linked list.

One of the most important things an iterator in a container class does is provide a pointer to the data object contained in the container. Since node doesn't point to a data object, the dereferencing operator for list<T>::iterator has to work to get at the data stored in the list_node:

```
    reference operator*() const { return (*node).data; }
```

Since node points directly to a list_node object, navigating forward and backwards through the list is an easy operation. The increment and decrement code is simple. The only complication in the HP implementation is that a cast is required for type safety:

```
iterator& operator++() {
  node = (link_type)((*node).next);
  return *this;
}
iterator& operator--() {
  node = (link_type)((*node).prev);
  return *this;
}
```

Based on these definitions, it isn't hard to implement operator[] for list<T>. A simple loop that walked up the pointer chain would do the job. But such an operator would be inefficient, requiring $O(N)$ time to look up a single data element. For this reason, it isn't defined, and should not be defined. If you find that you need random access into your data, you need to think about using deque<T> or vector<T> instead.

More Than Meets the Eye: Memory Allocation

While list<T> seems a simple class on the surface, it hides a complex memory allocation system. In an attempt to eliminate the inefficiency of using the standard library heap manager for large numbers of allocations, list<T> takes over memory management at the list_node level. There are two major components to the list<T> allocation scheme:

- allocation of new blocks (buffer pool)
- recycling the storage space of deleted nodes (free_list)

The list<T> manager function creates memory from buffers. When the list is created, this memory is used to allocate new nodes. add_new_buffer() brings in the data blocks, which provide raw storage for initial calls that add new nodes to the list.

When nodes are freed from a list by calls to erase(), pop_front(), or pop_back(), their storage is not returned to the 'heap. Instead, the node is added to the list of free nodes. It can be used the next time a new node is added to the container. The free space won't be returned to the heap until the list container itself is destroyed.

Storage management is static

When you create a list of a given type, such as list<foo>, the STL has to put in place the memory management for the list elements that will be used to store objects of type foo in the list. Now, when you create a second list of type foo, does it make sense to create a new pool of nodes and blocks in order to store the second list?

Since the two lists need identical size storage elements, the answer is no. Instead, all of the buffers allocated for a given type of list, such as list<foo>, will be shared among all containers of type list<foo>. And when discarded storage used by freed nodes is added to the free list, the buffers become available to all lists of a certain type.

list<T> accomplishes this by using *static* members to create the storage pool. Remember that static members in C++ are shared by every object in that class. This provides a great way for the STL to manage storage for an entire class of lists, instead of duplicating the effort each time a new list is created.

Figure 6-5 clarifies this. In a program with eight different objects in the list<T> family, there are only two copies of storage management members. One set of storage is shared amongst all members of list<foo>, the other amongst list<bar>.

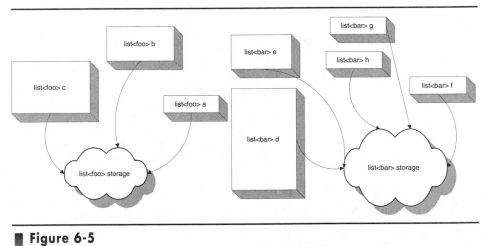

Figure 6-5
Storage management is shared among all members of a class

It is important to consider this when evaluating the overhead for storage management of list<T>. If many objects of a specific type are created, the cost of storage management is spread over all the objects, making the burden less onerous.

Allocation of new nodes

When an object of list<T> is instantiated, both the buffer pool and free list are empty. The first time a new object is stored in the container, you must load the buffer pool with some memory returned by the allocator object.

This is triggered by the function list<T>::get_node(). get_node() is called whenever a member function of list<T> adds a new node to the container. For example, the function used to insert a single object of type T in the container starts like this:

```
iterator insert(iterator position, const T& x) {
    link_type tmp = get_node();
    construct(value_allocator.address((*tmp).data), x);
```

To insert the new object, you need an object of type list_node to hold the data and the pointers. get_node() is responsible for providing this.

How does get_node() interact with these two entities? The following code excerpt gives an interpretation of list<T>::get_node().

```
link_type get_node() {
    if ( free_list ) {
        link_type tmp = free_list;
        free_list = (link_type)( free_list->next );
        return tmp;
    } else {
        if ( next_avail == last )
            add_new_buffer();
        return next_avail++;
    }
}
```

The first thing this code does is check the free_list pointer to see if any nodes are ready to be recycled. At the time the list container is created, this pointer will be set to 0. So, you will fall through to the second half of the function. Since there aren't any list_node size objects in the free list, the new piece of memory must come from the buffer pool.

The buffer pool always has a pointer called next_avail. It points to the next free node in the pool and, in addition, has a standard pointer called last that points one past the last available node in the pool.

When next_avail is equal to last, there are no nodes left in the buffer pool, so the add_new_buffer() function is called. This adds a new buffer to the list, updates next_avail and last, and returns with a newly replenished pool.

Once add_new_buffer() puts the buffer pool in order, get_node() returns the next_avail pointer, and increments it to point to the next free node. The next time get_node() is called, next_avail will point to a memory block ready to be used.

Note: The number of nodes stored in a single buffer is determined by the page size of the allocator. The default allocator has a page size of 4096 bytes.

One additional detail

As long as at least one container has the correct type instantiated, all buffers allocated for that type will be left in memory. Memory buffers are never returned to the standard library heap until the last object is destroyed.

This may seem like a bad strategy to you. Whether it is or not depends a lot on both your environment and your use of lists. The worst case will be if you build a huge list, then remove *almost* all the nodes. Your list buffer pool will still be using the same amount of space as when the list was at its largest, despite having no current need for it. The only way to be sure the space is restored to the standard library's heap is to delete every list of that type.

The job isn't over...

When the last list<T> object is destroyed, the list<T> buffer pool manager needs to delete all the buffers. But how does it know which buffers have been allocated? Fortunately, the buffer pool management code keeps each buffer that it allocates in a simple list.

list.h defines a structure type list_node_buffer that defines the data structure used to hold the buffer list. It creates a typedef for this structure called buffer_pointer. It also defines the root node of the list, buffer_list. Figure 6-6 shows the relevant declarations from list.h.

Note: buffer_list is static. The buffer pool is shared among all instances of a given list type, so the buffer pool must be static.

This section of code shows how the buffer list might look when used in a program:

```
struct list_node_buffer {
        void_pointer next_buffer;
        link_type buffer;
    };
typedef Allocator<list_node_buffer>::pointer buffer_pointer;
static buffer_pointer buffer_list;
```

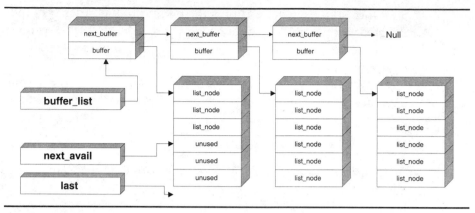

Figure 6-6
The buffer pool in action

The linked list of buffer pointers is rooted in buffer_list. buffer_list points to a list of list_node_buffer objects, each of which points to a buffer allocated for the pool.

Since list<T> needn't do any sophisticated traversals of this list, it is a simple, singly linked list. The code for add_new_buffer() shows what happens when a new list is added:

```
void add_new_buffer() {
    buffer_pointer tmp = buffer_allocator.allocate((size_type)1);
    tmp->buffer = list_node_allocator.allocate(buffer_size());
    tmp->next_buffer = buffer_list;
    buffer_list = tmp;
    next_avail = buffer_list->buffer;
    last = next_avail + buffer_size();
}
```

add_new_buffer() takes care of two different data structures at the same time. First, it allocates a new list_node_buffer structure, done via the allocate() call performed on the buffer_allocator. After that, the new buffer is allocated by the call to list_node_allocator::allocate(). This call returns a page of list_node objects that will be used every time get_node() is called.

Once the two buffers are allocated, the newly allocated list_node_buffer object is inserted to the front of the buffer list. The next_avail and last pointers are initialized to point to the first and last elements in the newly allocated buffer. When add_new_buffer() returns to get_node(), get_node() uses the node pointed to by next_avail, and decrements next_avail.

Freeing the buffer pool

When does the buffer pool get deleted? Not until the last object of the specific type of list<T> is deleted. How this happens can be seen in the destructor for list<T>:

```
~list() {
    erase(begin(), end());
    put_node(node);
    if (--number_of_lists == 0) deallocate_buffers();
}
```

list<T> has a static data member called number_of_lists, which keeps track of how many lists have been instantiated. When that number drops to 0, it's time to delete all the buffer space. Until then, nodes in the buffers might be in use by other lists, so you can't afford to free them.

The deallocation code removes all the buffers by iterating through the list of buffers, starting at buffer_list. At each list_node_buffer in the list, deallocate_buffers() frees the buffer that the node points to, and then frees the list_node_buffer itself.

```
template <class T>
void list<T>::deallocate_buffers() {
    while (buffer_list) {
        buffer_pointer tmp = buffer_list;
        buffer_list = (buffer_pointer)(buffer_list->next_buffer);
        list_node_allocator.deallocate(tmp->buffer);
        buffer_allocator.deallocate(tmp);
    }
    free_list = 0;
    next_avail = 0;
    last = 0;
}
```

The free list

The second component of memory management in list<T> is the free pool. Objects can be freed from a list<T> object by calling pop_back(), pop_front(), or erase(). After these functions destroy the object and remove it from the list, they return the memory occupied by the object to the free pool, by calling put_node().

The entire contents of put_node() are shown below. Since the free list is a singly linked list, and new nodes are always added to the front of the list, the code is very simple:

```
void put_node(link_type p) {
    p->next = free_list;
    free_list = p;
}
```

The free list is navigated starting with the static member list<T>::free_list. Each node in the list uses its next pointer to point to the next node in the free list. These free nodes are all found in the middle of existing buffers. Figure 6-7 shows how the free list winds its way through the existing set of buffers.

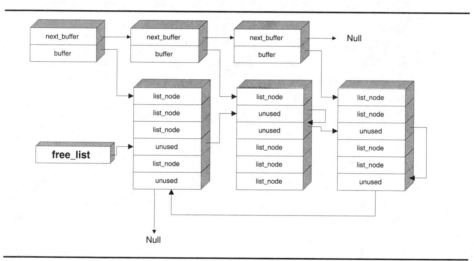

Figure 6-7
The free list

When get_node() is called to return a memory block for a new list node, the free list is always the first choice for the node. Before get_node() even worries about the buffer pool, it checks if free_list contains a valid pointer. If it does, that node is removed from the list and returned to the caller:

```
link_type get_node() {
    if ( free_list ) {
        link_type tmp = free_list;
        free_list = (link_type)( free_list->next );
        return tmp;
```

This looks the same as the operation performed by the C runtime library, when either malloc() or ::operator new are called. However, get_node() is considerably more efficient.

get_node() doesn't have to check whether nodes in the free list are large enough to hold a node; the entire free list consists of blocks just the right size! Nor does it worry about coalescing adjacent blocks to create larger blocks, because it never needs larger blocks.

Note: There is no cleanup code for the free list. When the last list<T> destructor is called, it isn't necessary to go through and return free nodes to the heap. That work is taken care of by the buffer manager. At the point where all the buffers are being returned, the free list should contain every node in the buffer pool.

Creating and destroying

As with all STL containers, list<T> completely separates memory allocation and object creation. Memory, for all objects, is created and destroyed by using the memory allocator object defined as part of the class. Memory is returned to the buffer pool management code in a raw state. It doesn't contain constructed objects. Likewise, when memory is returned to the allocator, the allocator can safely assume all objects have been destroyed—the memory is nothing more than empty memory.

So how and when do objects get created and destroyed? Let's look at the process of creation first. When a single object is being inserted into the linked list, even if the actual function call is to push_front() or push_back(), the work is done via the insert() call. insert() for a single object starts out like this:

```
iterator insert(iterator position, const T& x) {
    link_type tmp = get_node();
    construct(value_allocator.address((*tmp).data), x);
```

The first line of insert() should be familiar. get_node() is called so a new block of memory can hold a list_node. This memory comes directly from the free list or the buffer pool, and is a big batch of uninitialized bytes. These bytes get turned into an object with a call to construct(). construct() is a template function defined by the allocator. The version of construct() defined in the default allocator is shown below:

```
template <class T1, class T2>
inline void construct(T1* p, const T2& value) {
    new (p) T1(value);
}
```

construct() calls the new operator using the placement syntax. The placement syntax allows new to call the constructor for an object and, at the same time, specifies a location where the new object will be created.

More details on how the placement syntax works can be found in Chapter 4.

One confusing aspect of the call to construct() in the insert() function is the first argument. Usually, you would expect it to be a simple pointer, but here you need this frightening creation:

```
value_allocator.address((*tmp).data)
```

While this may look formidable, the work being done here is simply a type-safe way to take the address of the data member of the link_node returned by the call to get_node(). address() is a function in that returns the address of an object, using the pointer type defined by the allocator.

Destructors

When destroying an object in the list, you will work your way down to one of the erase() functions, regardless of whether you called pop_front(), pop_back(), or erase(). An example of the final few lines of one version of erase() that destroys a single item in the list is shown here:

```
destroy(value_allocator.address((*position.node).data));
put_node(position.node);
--length;
}
```

The process of destroying an object is similar to constructing one. Normally, objects are destroyed by a call to the delete operator, but operator delete wants to free memory as soon as the object is deleted. This, of course, isn't how STL container classes work; it's necessary to retain the memory used by the object and add it to the free list. The STL manages this by calling the destroy() template function found in the allocator for the class. The template function destroy() makes an explicit call to the destructor for type T, leaving the memory intact:

```
template <class T>
inline void destroy(T* pointer) {
    pointer->~T();
}
```

Once the object is destroyed, the data in the list_node object is simply a collection of uninitialized bytes, and is ready to be added to the free list.

A look at the buffer pool and free list

Here is a simple test program that looks at the inside of the list<T> memory management data structures.

list0602.cpp derives a new class from list<T> called public_list. The public list class has member functions that examine the buffer pool and the free list. Information can be printed out about them at various points during the lifetime of an object of that class.

Listing 6-4

list0602.cpp: A program that examines the memory allocation members of list<T>

```
//
// LIST0602.CPP
//
// This example program is used in Chapter 6 to demonstrate
// the internals of the memory allocation system used in
// list<T>. It creates a couple of list<double> containers,
// and dumps their memory statistics after various operations.
//

//
// Borland 4.x workarounds.
//
#define __MINMAX_DEFINED

#include <list.h>

//
// Note that list<T> doesn't allow access to the
// data members that control memory allocation.
// So that we can get at them, I derive a new class
// here that has some public functions that let
// us look at buffer pools and the free list.
//
```

```
template<class T>
class public_list : public list<T> {
    public :
        public_list() : list<T>() {}
        size_t buffer_pool_free();
        size_t buffer_pool_total();
        size_t buffer_size(){ return list<T>::buffer_size(); }
        long free_count();
        list<T>::link_type get_free_list(){ return free_list; }
};


//
// This function is used to calculate the total number
// of nodes in the buffer pool. It simply iterates
// through the list of buffers, adding to the total
// count of nodes along the way. Note that these
// nodes may be in use or may be in the free list, we
// don't know at this point.
//
template<class T>
size_t public_list<T>::buffer pool_total()
{
    size_t total = 0;
    buffer_pointer list = buffer_list;
    while ( list ) {
        total += buffer_size();
        list = (buffer_pointer)( list->next_buffer );
    }
    return total;
}


//
// This function returns the total number of nodes
// available for immediate allocation from the buffer
// pool.
//
template<class T>
size_t public_list<T>::buffer_pool_free()
{
    if ( next_avail == 0 || next_avail == last )
        return 0;
    else
        return last - next_avail;
}
```

```
//
// This function returns the total number of nodes
// in the free list. We do it the hard way, by
// counting every single one.
//
template<class T>
long public_list<T>::free_count()
{
    long count = 0;
    link_type free_guy = free_list;
    while ( free_guy ) {
        count++;
        free_guy = (link_type) free_guy->next;
    }
    return count;
}


//
// This function dumps out the memory stats for
// a given list<T> object. The caller gets to
// add a short message to the start of the printout.
//
template<class T>
void dump_memory( char *message, public_list<T> &a )
{
    cout << message << " ";
    cout << "size= " << a.size() << " ";
    cout << "buffer pool (total/free)= "
        << a.buffer_pool_total()
        << "/"
        << a.buffer_pool_free()
        << "  free_count= "
        << a.free_count()
        << endl;
}


//
// This program prints out the memory stats for
// the list<double> class at several points during
// the lifetime of the objects.
//
main()
{
    public_list<double> a;
    public_list<double> b;
    public_list<char> c;
```

```
dump_memory( "a, constructed  ", a );
a.push_front( -2 );
dump_memory( "a.push_front()  ", a );
a.push_back( -3 );
dump_memory( "a.push_back()   ", a );
a.pop_back();
dump_memory( "a.pop_back()    ", a );
a.push_front( -4 );
dump_memory( "a.push_front()  ", a );
for ( long i = 0 ; i < 5000 ; i++ ) {
    if ( !( i % 1024 ) )
        cout << '\r' << i;
    a.insert( a.begin(), i );
}
cout << '\r';
dump_memory( "a.insert()*5000 ", a );
a.erase( a.begin(), a.end() );
dump_memory( "a.erase()       ", a );
dump_memory( "b, constructed  ", b );
dump_memory( "c, constructed  ", c );
return 1;
}
```

list0602.cpp prints out several pieces of information about the list<double> objects it uses. Each time dump_memory() is called, it prints out the size of a given object, i.e. the number of nodes it contains. It also prints out the number of nodes presently in the buffer pool for list<double>, and the number of unused nodes remaining in the buffer pool. As well, it counts up the total number of free nodes in the free list for list<T>. The output from a run of list0602.cpp is shown in Figure 6-8.

```
a, constructed   size= 0 buffer pool (total/free)= 256/254  free_count= 0
a.push_front()   size= 1 buffer pool (total/free)= 256/253  free_count= 0
a.push back()    size= 2 buffer pool (total/free)= 256/252  free_count= 0
a.pop_back()     size= 1 buffer pool (total/free)= 256/252  free_count= 1
a.push_front()   size= 2 buffer pool (total/free)= 256/252  free_count= 0

a.insert()*5000  size= 5002 buffer pool (total/free)= 5120/116  free_count= 0
a.erase()        size= 0 buffer pool (total/free)= 5120/116  free_count= 5002
b, constructed   size= 0 buffer pool (total/free)= 5120/116  free_count= 5002
c, constructed   size= 0 buffer pool (total/free)= 455/454  free_count= 0
```

■ Figure 6-8
The output from list0602.cpp

The first line of output from list0602.cpp shows that, even though no data has been put into either of the lists, there are still two nodes used from the list<double> buffer pool. This is because each list has to allocate a root node that anchors the linked list, even before any data has been added to the list.

The next two lines of output show that, as new nodes are allocated, they are removed from the store of available nodes in the buffer pool. Each time a node is added, the number free in the pool is decremented.

Finally, after several insertions, a node is deleted from the list. As expected, the free node doesn't get pushed back into the buffer pool; instead it goes to the free list. And when the next node is added to the list, the node is taken from the free list, not from the available nodes in the buffer pool.

The next few lines of output from list0602.cpp serve to amplify the points made about memory allocation. After adding 5,000 nodes to one of the containers, then erasing them, we have all 5,000 nodes in the free list. They show up as having been allocated from the buffer pool.

A peek at the memory structures for container *b*, which has done nothing during this time, shows that the memory structures are static. They are shared among all members of the class. This can be verified because the memory pool for list<char> has completely different statistics.

BENCHMARKS

Since list<T> uses a radically different internal structure from vector<T> or deque<T>, you might find it useful to see how list<T> compares to the other containers.

The first test program, list0603.cpp, creates containers, then iterates through them. This gives some idea of how fast the increment and decrement operators are for the given type of container. list0603.cpp uses exactly the same test routines and timing code as dequ0504.cpp, so the listings for the bulk of the program have been omitted here, although the entire code is on the disk. The only part of the program different from that used in the last chapter is the main() routine, which has added list<short int> to the containers it tests.

Listing 6-5
The relevant part of list0603.cpp (the remainder is identical to dequ0504.cpp)

```
//
// Main sets up the containers, then calls
// the template function to test them.
// Note that the allocation of *all* the space
// for the container is done here, so it doesn't
// come into play in the benchmarks.
//
```

```
main()
{
    short int *a = new short int[ 32000 ];
    cout << "Testing T[]        ";
    test( a, a + 32000 );
    delete a;

    cout << "Testing vector<T> ";
    vector<short int> *b = new vector<short int>( 32000 );
    test( b->begin(), b->end() );
    delete b;

    cout << "Testing deque<T>   ";
    deque<short int> *c = new deque<short int>( 32000 );
    test( c->begin(), c->end() );
    delete c;

    cout << "Testing list<T>   ";
    list<short int> *d = new list<short int>( 32000 );
    test( d->begin(), d->end() );
    delete d;

    return 1;
}
```

The test program repeatedly loops through the entire container, adding up the contents. A gross timing measurement gives the relative iteration times for the four different containers. The results of a typical run through the program are shown here:

```
Testing T[]        ....................... elapsed time: 3 seconds
Testing vector<T> ....................... elapsed time: 3 seconds
Testing deque<T>   ....................... elapsed time: 7 seconds
Testing list<T>    ....................... elapsed time: 4 seconds
```

As expected, the vector container and the built-in array types are faster than list<T>. But the list container does considerably better than the deque container. This makes sense, since the deque<T> iterator has to perform a comparison before it can increment, whereas the list<T> iterator just has to follow a pointer. Perhaps it's also easier for the compiler to optimize or inline the list<T> iterator code.

Insertion and removal

list<T>should really perform well in the area of insertions and removals. deque<T> and vector<T> have to move large amounts of data when they insert or erase, so their algorithms are going to have O(*N*) runtime.

list<T> only has to break the links between two nodes, then establish new links for the insertion node. This means it can run in O(*k*) time. Even if there isn't much difference in insertion speed for small containers, there ought to be a big difference as the containers fill up.

list0604.cpp is designed to test this assertion. It's similar to list0603.cpp and dequ0504.cpp. The template function test() is executed for each of three container types — list<double>, deque<double>, and vector<double>.

The test function sits in a loop, inserting doubles into the very middle of the container. This should cause a lot of stress for the vector and deque containers, but the list container ought to be able to handle it effortlessly.

Listing 6-6

list0604.cpp: A performance test of insertion speed

```
//
// LIST0604.CPP
//
// This example program is used in Chapter 6 to
// perform some *extremely* crude benchmarks on classes
// vector<T>, deque<T>, list<T>. This routine just inserts
// a load of doubles into a container, then checks to see
// how long the entire operation took.
//


//
// Borland 4.x workarounds
//
#define __MINMAX_DEFINED

#include <deque.h>
#include <vector.h>
#include <list.h>
#include <iostream.h>
#include <iomanip.h>
#include <stdlib.h>
#include <time.h>
```

```
//
// This template function performs the actual test.
// The insertion point is determined by iterator j.
// I fiddle with j to ensure that all insertions are
// done in the very middle of the container.
//

template<class T>
void test( T& a )
{
    time_t t1 = time( 0 );
    T::iterator j = a.begin();
    for ( int i = 0 ; i < 8000 ; i++ ) {
        if ( ( i % 256 ) == 0 )
            cout << '.';
        j = a.insert( j, i );
        if ( i % 2 )
            j++;
    }
    cout << "\n";
    cout << "Size = " << a.size() << endl;
    cout << "Elapsed time: "
        << time( 0 ) - t1
        << " seconds"
        << endl;
    a.erase( a.begin(), a.end() );
}


//
// Main just sets up the containers, then calls
// the template function to test them out.
//

main()
{
    cout << "Testing vector<T> ";
    vector<double> *a = new vector<double>;
    test( *a );
    delete a;

    cout << "Testing deque<T>  ";
    deque<double> *b = new deque<double>;
    test( *b );
    delete b;

    cout << "Testing list<T>   ";
    list<double > *c = new list<double>;
    test( *c );
    delete c;

    return 1;
}
```

Even knowing what we do about these containers, the results of the test are a little startling. 8000 insertions are very time-consuming for both the vector and deque containers. The same test on a list container is executed so quickly, it doesn't pass a single second of execution! Clearly, if you are going to be inserting things into the middle of a container, list<T> is a good candidate for the job. The results of list04.cpp run are shown in Figure 6-9.

```
Testing vector<T> ..............................
Size = 8000
Elapsed time: 14 seconds
Testing deque<T>  ..............................
Size = 8000
Elapsed time: 77 seconds
Testing list<T>   ..............................
Size = 8000
Elapsed time: 0 seconds
```

Figure 6-9
The results of a run of list04.cpp

TYPE REQUIREMENTS FOR T

Like the other container classes, list<T> requires access to the five basic functions that are usually defined for any class:

```
T();                        //Default constructor
T(const T&);                //Copy constructor
T& operator=(const T&);     //Assignment operator
~T();                       //Destructor
To& operator&();            //Address of operator
```

By default, the compiler creates all these functions for a given class, so they are often overlooked. However, in some cases, these functions may be protected or private. Programmers often define a class that doesn't have a constructor with no arguments. This is usually due to the definition of some other constructor that takes one or more arguments.

If you try to create a container without an accessible version of one of these functions, you may be victimized by a long series of incomprehensible error messages. However, with list<T>, there are two additional stand-alone functions you may need to have defined:

```
int operator<(const T& f1, const T& f2);
int operator==(const T& f1, const T& f2);
```

There are a few member functions of list<T>—unique(), merge(), sort(), and remove()—that use these functions. vector<T> and deque<T> don't have these requirements.

If your program doesn't use these functions, your compiler may be smart enough to realize it doesn't need the operators defined. If it does, it will make you aware of the problem in the usual fashion.

Chapter 4 goes into great detail on this topic. If you need more insight into why these type requirements exist, please refer to the appropriate section of that chapter. In addition, built-in types will have to have a destroy() function defined, for the reasons described in Chapter 3.

LIST<T> MISCELLANY

Please refer to Chapter 4 and Chapter 20 for more information on these topics:

- **Bounds checking for iterator operations.** This is not offered as part of the standard STL, but may be present in third-party and compiler vendor packages.

- **Selection of an allocator class.** This is currently done using the preprocessor, although the STL specification says it should be done using a template parameter. This will be changed when compiler vendors can conform to the C++ template standard.

- **Using a user-defined allocator in the constructor.** Allowing the user to instantiate an allocator for a specific container was a last-minute change made by the ANSI/ISO standardization committee. At press time, this feature was not supported in the public HP release of the STL.

CONTAINER ADAPTORS

According to the STL specification:

> *"Adaptors are template classes that provide interface mappings. For example, insert_iterator provides a container with an output iterator interface."*

This definition is accurate, but vague if you don't have much STL experience. The first part of this chapter is concerned with figuring out just what a *container adaptor* is. Function and iterator adaptors get their own chapters later.

After defining a container adaptor, the remainder of the chapter looks at the three types of container adaptors supplied with the STL: stack, queue, and priority_queue. For straight-ahead reference information about the adaptors, see Chapter 21.

Whatever you do, don't skip this chapter. Once you've read and understood what's written here, you may find that adaptors will considerably simplify your life.

WHAT IS A CONTAINER ADAPTOR?

The STL definition of an adaptor says it's a template class that provides an interface mapping. In plain English, that means STL adaptor classes are simply classes that act as a wrapper around *another* class. Container adaptors are classes that encapsulate an existing container, and provide a new user interface. This makes it seem like the adaptor is a completely new and different container type. But in fact, all the underpinnings are simply mechanisms found in the class that has been wrapped.

The three container adaptors defined in the STL are stack, queue, and priority_queue. But what's new about this? These three elements sound (to the experienced programmer) like simple containers, not some new thing we don't know about. What is it that makes, say, a stack an adaptor and not just a container?

The only difference that matters to us is that stack, queue, and priority_queue don't implement containers themselves. Instead, they use the existing members of the other three sequential containers to implement what appear to be new containers. As an end user of containers, this sort of argument may seem nothing more than an exercise in splitting hairs. But it *is* important to understand the underlying concept behind container adaptors. Knowing what lurks beneath the surface of a stack will help you avoid making decisions that lead to inefficient implementations. It can also help you develop your own adaptors, a worthy goal in itself.

How to recognize an adaptor when you see one

Normal STL container classes take a type name as one of their template arguments:

```
list<int> a;      // Template arg is a built in type
vector<employee> b; // Template arg is a user-defined class
deque<record, faralloc> c; //Class type and allocator
```

Container *adaptors* have a completely different appearance. Instead of taking a single type T as a template argument, a container adaptor takes a *container type* as an argument:

```
#include <vector.h>
#include <stack.h>

int main()
{
    stack< vector<int> > a;
```

In the above example, a stack of integers is created. To do this, you can't simply declare an object of type stack<int>. A stack<> has to be defined with an existing container as a template argument.

In this particular case, a vector was chosen, but a list or deque object could just as easily be used to provide the foundation for the stack. In any case, the container you choose to provide storage for your adaptor should have attributes suitable to the capabilities needed for a given application.

Remodeling, STL style

As just mentioned, a container adaptor provides a completely new interface to an existing container type. Figure 7-1 shows how this concept works. An existing container type is encapsulated in a container adaptor. The adaptor provides an API that defines the interface to the container and, at the same time, conceals the existing interface to the container. This creates what appears to be an entirely different type of container.

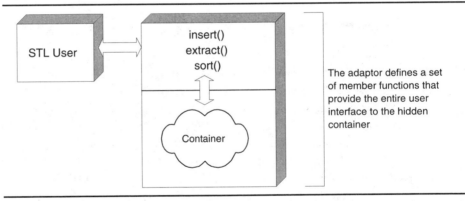

■ Figure 7-1
A hypothetical container adaptor

In Figure 7-1, the cloud-like apparition in the bottom of the container adaptor is a standard STL container. This container is of the type specified as a template argument when the adaptor object was declared. In this hypothetical case, the container adaptor's job is to present an interface to the outside world that has insert(), extract(), and sort() member functions.

It's important to note that an adaptor uses the container through *composition*, not inheritance. That means the container is a data member of the adaptor, not a base class. In C++, composition is used when an object of class *a has* a member of class *b*. In contrast, inheritance is used when an object of class *a is* an object of class *b*.

```
Composition:   class A {
                   B b;
                   ...

Inheritance:   class A : public B {
                   ...
```

STL container adaptors always use composition. This means that if you declare an object as being of type queue< list<foo> >, your queue has a list as a member. Because the container is a protected member of the adaptor, the STL user (you) can't access the member functions of the original container.

For example, you can create a stack that uses a list as its container. list<T> contains somewhere in the neighborhood of 30 publicly accessible member functions. Once you put the list<T> object inside the stack, you hide those 30 functions and replace them with public stack member functions. stack<T> has only six member functions, so it has a replacement API considerably simpler than the one its container started with.

Like a virus

Biological viruses (and to some extent their digital siblings) exist on the hazy edge of the family of living organisms. Viruses don't have the cellular machinery that plants and animals use to reproduce. Instead, a virus has to co-opt the machinery of an existing host cell to reproduce itself. So a virus by itself is not an effective organism. It only achieves the goals of living creatures when it takes over another living being's cells.

STL container adaptors are like viruses. They lack the memory management features found in container classes, and so an object like a queue knows absolutely nothing about adding or deleting objects from a container. Instead, it relies on a host class to take care of the low-level details it lacks.

An example of this is shown in the following listing of public functions from the queue container. The queue adaptor has a data member, c, that is the container holding all the queue data.

Note: *Every* public function for queue is implemented using member functions of c, the container member.

```
template<class Container>
class queue {
protected :
    Container c;
public :
```

```
bool empty() const { return c.empty(); }
size_type size() const { return c.size(); }
value_type& front() { return c.front(); }
const value_type& front() const { return c.front(); }
value_type& back() { return c.back(); }
const value_type& back() const { return c.back(); }
void push(const value_type& x) { c.push_back(x); }
void pop() { c.pop_front(); }
```

So how do you know what sort of container can be used with a given adaptor? The vocabulary of C++ doesn't give us an easy way to do this. It boils down to two steps. First, you must determine what the list of container requirements are for the adaptor. Second, you see if the container class you would like to use fills these requirements.

For example, in the partial listing of the stack class shown above, eight different member functions in the container are called by the adaptor. This means you can use any container as a basis for the adaptor, as long as it provides all eight of those member functions.

This is a straightforward system, but it does make it a little hard to match up containers with adaptors. If you want to know if container *a* will work with adaptor *b*, you have three choices:

- You can sit down and try to map out the functions required and provided.

- You can just run the combination through your compiler and see what happens.

- You can rely on your STL documentation, including this book.

What it is!

To sum up, a container adaptor is simply a template class that encapsulates an existing container class. It exposes a set of public member functions that perform a given set of operations, such as those of a stack or queue. The member functions provide the internal operations needed to perform the new set of functions defined by the container adaptor.

At the same time, the encapsulation of the container conceals its member functions from the end user. This simplifies the view the outside world has of the container adaptor and, at the same time, conceals the inner workings of the adaptor. So it isn't clear whether the container adaptor is built on a vector, a deque, or a list. The type of container is selected when the object is created, and you shouldn't have to worry about it anymore.

THE STACK ADAPTOR: STACK<T>

The first container adaptor we'll look at is stack<T>. A stack can be made from any of the three sequential containers described in Chapters 4, 5 and 6—vector<T>, deque<T> and list<T>. The external appearance of the stack container is the same, regardless of the type of container used.

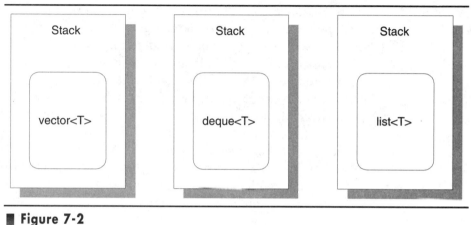

Figure 7-2
The Three Faces of Stack

stack<T> makes a great case study in container adaptors, because it's so simple. If all you need from a container is the functionality of a stack, stack<T> provides a clean interface that minimizes the number of ways things can go wrong. And aren't good interfaces the key to success for container classes?

What it does

The stack<T> container adaptor implements a stack using a container of type T. The objects actually stored in the stack will be decided by the type of object used in the template parameter of container T. Objects are inserted and removed from the stack using the two fundamental functions:

- push(), to insert objects on top of the stack
- pop(), to remove objects from the top of the stack

The pop() function isn't implemented exactly the way you might think. It would be reasonable to suppose that pop() returns the value from the top of the stack, because that is the canonical way pop functions work on stacks. However, this isn't that case in the STL! If you want to access the top element of the stack, you must use:

- top(), which returns a reference to the top item on the stack. Note that since this is a reference, you can use top() on the left side of an assignment, as in a.top() = 0.

You can check the number of elements contained in the stack with a couple of metric functions:

- empty(), which returns a bool indicating whether or not the stack is empty.
- size(), which returns a count indicating how many items are presently in the stack.

In addition, there are two friend functions that perform logical comparisons of stack<T> objects. operator==() and operator(T)<() perform the comparisons as defined by the container class providing the foundation for the stack.

Tall and elegant: Using the stack

Listing 7-1 shows the entire implementation for stack<T>. It consists of a pair of friend functions, another pair of type definitions, a data member, and six one-line member functions. The elegance of the stack class is a tribute to the design of the container classes used to build it. The strength of the underlying container design made development of adaptor classes an easy job.

Listing 7-1
The stack<T> definition

```
template <class Container>
class stack {
friend bool operator==(const stack<Container>& x,
                       const stack<Container>& y);
friend bool operator<(const stack<Container>& x,
                      const stack<Container>& y);
```

```
public:
    typedef Container::value_type value_type;
    typedef Container::size_type size_type;
protected:
    Container c;

public:
    bool empty() const { return c.empty(); }
    size_type size() const { return c.size(); }
    value_type& top() { return c.back(); }
    const value_type& top() const { return c.back(); }
    void push(const value_type& x) { c.push_back(x); }
    void pop() { c.pop_back(); }
};

template <class Container>
bool operator==(const stack<Container>& x,
                const stack<Container>& y)
{
    return x.c == y.c;
}

template <class Container>
bool operator<(const stack<Container>& x, const stack<Container>& y) {
    return x.c < y.c;
}
```

Which types of containers can be used to create stack containers? To answer this question, brute force is required: you have to look through the class definition to see what operations are performed on the container. Given that, you can come up with a list of requirements you can then apply to other STL containers.

The first few requirements of class Container can be gleaned directly from the listings. Table 7-1 lists the functions that are called by the member functions of stack<T>, and therefore must be part of the underlying container.

The three sequential containers defined by the STL (vector<T>, deque<T>, and list<T>) all meet these qualifications, although standard C/C++ arrays do not. Associative containers (covered in Chapter 8, "Associative Arrays") don't qualify, so they can't be used as the basis of a stack.

Table 7-1

stack<T> container required functions

Required function	Additional requirements
empty()	returns a boolean value
size()	return type is Container::size_type
back()	returns a reference to Container::value_type
back()	returns a const reference to Container::value_type
push_back()	takes argument of type const Container::value_type
pop_back()	takes no argument
operator<()	either a member or friend function
operator==()	either a member or friend function
Container()	a publicly accessible default constructor

Where's the constructor?

In the previous section, we saw that stack<T> doesn't have a constructor. Since the only data member in the stack container is Container *c*, there isn't a pressing need to define a constructor. However, this means you will always start out with an empty stack.

If you have a need to initialize your stack with some data, you can do so without modifying the definitions found in stack.h. You can derive a new class of Container, giving it a default constructor that performs custom initialization. Listing 7-2 shows a short program that does this with container class deque<char>.

Listing 7-2

stac0702.cpp: Demonstrating a derived class with a different constructor

```
//
// STAC0702.CPP
//
// This program is used in Chapter 7 to demonstrate
// one method of overcoming the lack of a
// constructor for the stack<Container> container
// adaptor. When creating a stack based on container
// type deque<char>, I derive a new class called
// my_deque. my_deque<> is exactly like deque<char>,
// except that its default constructor initializes
// the deque with the correct initial number of
// elements.
//
```

```
//
// Borland 4.x workarounds
//
#define __MINMAX_DEFINED
#pragma option -vi-

#include <deque.h>
#include <stack.h>
#include <iostream.h>

//
// This derived class is used to force the
// deque<char> container used to build the
// stack to start life with 15 copies of
// the letter 'a'.
//

class my_deque : public deque<char>
{
    public :
        my_deque() : deque<char>( 15, 'a' ){}
};

//
// This short program demonstrates that the
// stack does in fact start out with 15
// predefined elements.
//
main()
{
    stack<my_deque> a;

    a.push( 'X' );
    a.push( 'Y' );
    a.push( 'Z' );
    cout << "a.size() = " << a.size() << endl;
    while ( !a.empty() ) {
        cout << a.top();
        a.pop();
    }
    cout << endl;
    return 1;
}
```

In stac0702.cpp, the intention is to initialize the stack to contain a string of 15 appearances of letter 'a'. The container created would normally be of type stack<deque<char> >. But to force the preferred initialization, a new derived container class is created called my_deque, and a stack of type stack<my_deque>.

my_deque is directly derived from deque<char>, and only defines a single constructor. This constructor allows us to force a default initialization of the container.

Following is the output of stac0702.cpp. Clearly, the stack underwent the desired initialization.

```
a.size() = 18
ZYXaaaaaaaaaaaaaaa
```

Design considerations

The obvious question when constructing a stack<T> object is: which type of container should you use? Since each of the three container types has different performance characteristics under different circumstances, which container you select will be based on the sort of work you expect it to do.

As a general rule, vector<T> gives the best performance as a stack, especially for small stacks. However, it loses some of its advantages if it has to be resized frequently. If you know in advance that your stack will need a certain number of elements, you can use the derivation technique from stack0702.cpp to reserve that amount of space in your constructor.

If vector<T> can't do the job for some reason, deque<T> is the only other realistic choice. deque<T> allows you to create larger objects on a system with segmented memory. It also returns unused blocks of memory to the operating system, resulting in more efficient use of memory.

There isn't much incentive to construct a stack out of list<T>. The design list<T> gives up speed and efficiency for flexibility; it can insert objects into the middle of the list. Since this will never be done with a stack<T> object, there's no good reason to use a list.

THE QUEUE ADAPTOR: QUEUE<T>

stack<T> and queue<T> are siblings; they are both container adaptors that create very simple containers. In an introductory data structures course, you might study stack containers on the second day of class, and queues on the third—the first day is for handing out the syllabus! Neither one is challenging, either to understand or to implement. The relative simplicity of these containers makes them perfect candidates for implementation using adaptors.

queue<T> implements a traditional single-ended queue. A *queue* is a data structure that has two fundamental operations: you insert an object at one end of the queue, and remove objects at the other end. This is referred to as a First In, First Out (FIFO) processing model. A grocery store checkout line is a pretty good example of a queue.

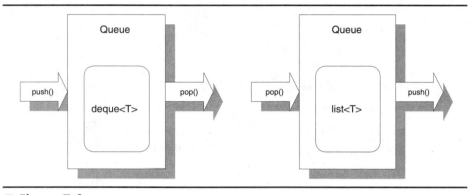

Figure 7-3
The Two Faces of Queue

queue<T> must be able to efficiently insert data at one end of the container, and remove it from the other. Only two of the four sequential containers are able to meet these requirements. (See Chapters 4, 5 and 6.) C arrays can't perform insertions or removals at either end, and vector containers can only grow or shrink from the back. This leaves deque<T> and list<T> as the two containers capable of forming the basis for a queue<T>.

The queue<T> container adaptor implements a queue that holds objects of the type defined by the container class passed as the template parameter. Objects are inserted and removed from the stack using the two fundamental queue functions. Figure 7-4 shows the general flow of objects in and out of the container.

Note: stack<T> continually recycles the same area in memory, since push() and pop() operate on the same end of the container. queue<T> keeps moving into new memory areas as new data is inserted and old data is deleted. However, both deque<T> and list<T> perform well under these circumstances.

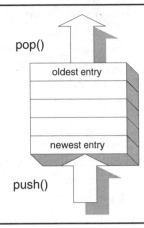

Figure 7-4
queue<T> object flow

The queue<T> container holds objects of the type defined by the type of container underlying the queue. Again, objects are inserted and removed from the FIFO using the two fundamental functions:

- push(), to insert objects at the back end of the queue
- pop(), to remove objects from the front end of the queue

stack<T> can access the top item on the stack. queue<T> improves on this, since it has defined functions to access the items at the front and the back of the container:

- front(), which returns a reference, or a const reference, to the oldest item in the FIFO. This object of type T is the one which will be removed by the next call to pop().
- back(), which returns a reference, or a const reference, to the newest item in the FIFO. This object is the one inserted by the most recent push() call.

Finally, you can check on the number of elements presently contained in the queue with a couple of capacity functions:

- empty(), which returns a bool indicating whether or not the stack is empty.
- size(), which returns a count indicating how many items are presently in the stack.

In addition, there are two template friend functions that perform logical comparisons of queue<T> objects. operator==() and operator<() perform the comparisons as defined by the container class providing the foundation for the stack. These two functions allow you to perform two different types of comparisons on queue containers.

Using the queue

Listing 7-3 shows the entire implementation for queue<T>. This container adaptor has a complement of members and definitions that are very nearly identical to those of stack<T>.

Listing 7-3

The queue<T> definition

```
template <class Container>
class queue {
friend bool operator==(const queue<Container>& x,
                       const queue<Container>& y);
friend bool operator<(const queue<Container>& x,
                      const queue<Container>& y);
public:          .
    typedef Container::value_type value_type;
    typedef Container::size_type size_type;
protected:
    Container c;
public:
    bool empty() const { return c.empty(); }
    size_type size() const { return c.size(); }
    value_type& front() { return c.front(); }
    const value_type& front() const { return c.front(); }
    value_type& back() { return c.back(); }
    const value_type& back() const { return c.back(); }
    void push(const value_type& x) { c.push_back(x); }
    void pop() { c.pop_front(); }
};

template <class Container>
bool operator==(const queue<Container>& x,
                const queue<Container>& y) {
    return x.c == y.c;
}

template <class Container>
bool operator<(const queue<Container>& x, const queue<Container>& y) {
    return x.c < y.c;
}
```

The class definition starts with a pair of friend functions, another pair of type definitions, a data member, and eight one-line member functions.

There are two places where we see a difference between stack<T> and queue<T>. First, the stack adaptor has a single type of access function to refer to the top of the stack. queue<T> has front() to access the start of the container, and back() to access the end.

The second place where we see a difference is in the pop() function. As expected, stack<T> pops data from the top (or back) of the container, but queue<T> pops from the front of the container.

Container requirements

The container requirements for queue<T> are identical to those for stack<T>, with these additions:

Table 7-2

Additional queue<T> container required functions

Required function	Additional requirements
front()	returns a reference to Container::value_type
front()	returns a const reference to Container::value_type
pop_front()	

queue<T> also drops the requirement that the container have a pop_back() function.

This new set of requirements means vector<T> must be dropped from the list of sequential containers that can support a queue<T>.

If you were to somehow attempt to implement a queue<T> with vector<T>, you would quickly run into major performance problems. A queue< vector<T> > that contained a large number of elements would spend enormous amounts of time shuffling data every time an element was popped from the front of the queue. Both list<T> and deque<T> can pop elements from the front end of themselves in linear time, since they don't perform any shuffling.

Design considerations

In the previous section, it looked like the best container for small stack containers is vector<T>. But this choice won't work for queue<T>, since vectors have been crossed off the list of eligible containers. Where does this leave us?

Both of the remaining container classes are efficient at inserting and removing items from the container. The place they differ drastically is in the area of memory management. In general, list<T> is more efficient than the standard library routines, particularly when performing large numbers of allocations and removals. But there is a price to be paid for this, in overhead for the pointers to maintain the list, and in the inability of list<T> to free up unused memory.

deque<T> doesn't have to maintain prev and next pointers for each object, which means it will use less memory. It also frees up pages of memory when they are no longer in use. The downside of deque<T> is that it will be continually exercising the heap, as old blocks are discarded and new ones are allocated.

Since the two container classes differ so drastically in the way they handle memory, you should experiment with the two types to see which suits your application. Fortunately, the design of the STL allows you to switch back and forth between the two container types simply by changing a single line of code. You should take this as the designer's implicit encouragement to tinker with types!

THE PRIORITY QUEUE ADAPTOR: PRIORITY_QUEUE<T>

This chapter started with a look at two different container adaptors, stack<T> and queue<T>. Both were characterized as being lightweight, since the data structures they create are very simple.

Well, priority_queue<T> is a much more powerful container adaptor, and isn't something you can easily whip up yourself in five or ten minutes. This section of the chapter looks at just what priority_queue<T> has to offer.

What is a priority queue?

A standard FIFO queue is simply a big buffer. The first object pushed into the queue is also the first object removed. This is the kind of data structure a simple operating system might use to handle, say, requests to access a hard drive.

The same operating system may also have a queue to decide which task gets the next slice of CPU time. A simple round-robin scheduler may be built around queue<T>. However, most operating systems want to include the concept of a *priority* attached to each task. The scheduler would then give the next slot of CPU time to the task with highest priority.

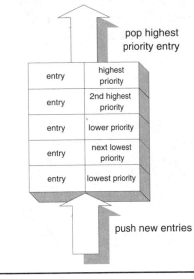

Figure 7-5
A hypothetical priority queue

How does it do that?

There are a number of ways to implement a priority queue. It's easy to imagine a trivial implementation that simply stores all the entries in a list<T>. Here, inserting entries would be done with a call to push_back(). The highest() function would iterate through the entire list, and find the entry with the highest priority:

```
template<class Container>
Container::iterator begin()
{
    Container::iterator maxi = c::begin();
    for ( Container::iterator i = c::begin();
        i != end();
        i++ )
      if ( *i > *maxi )
          maxi = i;
    return maxi;
}
```

This is a nice, simple implementation, but it has one unfortunate drawback: it's relatively inefficient. The code will run in $O(N)$ time, where N is the length of the queue. We can do much better than this.

Meet the heap

The STL implements the priority queue by storing the elements in a *heap*. Since Chapter 17, "Heap Operations," provides detailed information on this process, in this chapter you'll just get the quick tour.

Figure 7-6 gives an illustration of a heap with six elements. Although it's presented here as a tree, the heap is actually a sequential container with N elements.

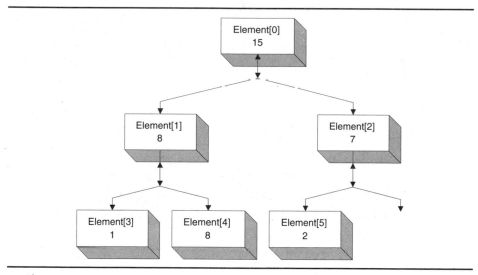

Figure 7-6
A heap

Any list containing N elements is considered a heap if each element i is greater than, or equal to, each of its two children, elements $2i+1$ and $2i+2$. These two nodes can be considered to be children in a binary tree.

The heap shown in Figure 7-6 meets this requirement. For example, Element 1 has a value of 8, which is greater than or equal to each of its two children, Elements 3 and 4. The heap structure frequently makes it appear that the heap is a sorted binary tree, but that isn't exactly true. For example, Element 4 in this figure is larger than Element 2, which would violate the rules for a sorted binary tree.

Why use a heap?

There are several good reasons to use a heap as the basis for a priority queue. The most important is that, for any given heap, element 0 *must* be the largest element in the array. As long as you ensure your data structure is a heap, you can access the highest priority element in constant time.

But there are plenty of other data structures with this characteristic. You can take your pick from dozens of different balanced tree implementations. What's so great about a heap?

- There are no additional storage requirements. The shape of the heap is a simple binary tree, with each node's children always residing in the same spot. You can always find children or parents using simple index math.
- Adding a node to the heap is an O(log$N$) operation.
- Removing a node from the tree is an O(log$N$) operation.

The reason the heap out-performs other sorted tree implementations is simple: the heap doesn't sort the whole tree. Instead, it just ensures that the element at the top of the tree is the largest in the heap. Because of this, heap operations that add or delete a leaf node don't have to shuffle the entire tree.

So using the heap gives us guaranteed insertion and removal time, without requiring any new storage in the data structure. Implementing priority_ queue<T> is simply a matter of imposing this heap discipline on an existing sequential container. And that is exactly what container adaptors are made for.

Using priority_queue<T>

Creating and using priority_queue<T> is not much different from using queue<T>:

- Instantiate the queue using the container type of your choice.
- Use push() to insert new objects into the queue.
- At any time, you can access the highest priority object using top().
- You can use pop() to remove the highest priority item.

A sample program that uses priority_queue<T> is shown in Listing 7-4. This program utilizes the priority queue to read in the contents of a file, then remove the characters from the queue. Since the characters are retrieved in priority order, the program returns a sorted list of all the letters it contains.

Listing 7-4

pque0704.cpp: A sample program using priority_queue<T>

```
//
// PQUE0704.CPP
//
// This program is used in Chapter 7 to demonstrate
// the use of a priority queue. I create a priority
// queue based on deque<char>, then place the contents
// of this file (PQUE0704.CPP) into the queue. I pull
// the characters out one at a time to demonstrate
// the fact that they will be removed in sorted order.
//
// Note that I use greater<T> instead of the conventional
// less<T>, so that the queue stores items smallest
// first instead of largest first.
//


//
// Borland 4.x workarounds.
//
#define __MINMAX_DEFINED
#pragma option -vi-

#include <deque.h>
#include <stack.h>
#include <function.h>
#include <iostream.h>
#include <fstream.h>

main()
{
    priority_queue< deque<char>, greater<char> > a;
    ifstream infile( "pque0704.cpp" );

    while ( infile ) {
        char c;
        infile >> c;
        if ( c != '\n' && infile )
            a.push( c );
    }
    while ( !a.empty() ) {
        cout << a.top();
        a.pop();
    }
    cout << endl;
    return 1;
}
```

Here's the accurate, although uninspiring, output from the program:

```
!!""#######&&''((((((((((()))))))))),,,-................./
//////////////////////////////////////000000144447777;;;;;;;;;;<<
<<<<<<<<<<<<<=>>>>>>>>>>>ABCCCDDEEEEFIIIIIMMNNNPPPPPQQTT
TUUX\____aaaaaaaaaaaaaaaaaaaaaaaaaaaaaaaaaaaaaaaaaaabbcccccc
ccccccccccccccccccddddddddddddddddddddddeeeeeeeeeeeeeeeeeee
eeeeeeeeeeeeeeeeeeeeeeeeeeeeeeeeeeeeeeeeeeeeeeeeeeeeeeeeeee
eeffffffffffffffffffggggghhhhhhhhhhhhhhhhhhhhhhhhhhhhiiiiiii
iiiiiiiiiiiiiiiiiiiiiiiiiiiiiiiiiiiiiiikkllllllllllllllllll
lllllmmmmmmmmmmmmmmnnnnnnnnnnnnnnnnnnnnnnnnnnnnnnnoooooooo
ooooooooooooooooooooooooooooppppppppppppppppppqqqqqqqqqrrrr
rrrrrrrrrrrrrrrrrrrrrrrrrrrrrrrrrrsssssssssssssssssssssssss
sssssssttttttttttttttttttttttttttttttttttttttttttttttttttt
tttttttuuuuuuuuuuuuuuuuuuuuuuuuuuuuuuuuvvvwwwwxyyyyy{{{}}}
```

What is this function object thing?

If you have been exploring the container classes discussed in previous chapters, you should feel very comfortable with the code shown in Listing 7-4. It uses standard access routines to add and remove objects from the container. However, the constructor for the container is different from anything we've seen before:

```
priority_queue< deque<char>, greater<char> > a;
```

All other container adaptors seen so far take a single type argument in the template name. This argument has always been a standard container, and you can see that priority_queue is no exception. But the second type argument is something called greater<char>. What exactly is that?

The template definition for class priority_queue gives a hint:

```
template <class Container, class Compare>
class  priority_queue {
public:
```

We see here that the name of the first class type is a container, and the second is a comparison class. Later on in the class definition, these two class parameters are used to instantiate members of the class:

```
protected:
  Container c;
  Compare comp;
```

It's no surprise to see that the class contains a data member of the container type. But what exactly is the data member called *comp*?

Compare comp is a data member referred to as a *function object*. In this case, the greater<char> function object is a member of a class that knows how to compare two integers, and return a true value if the first is greater than the second. The entire class definition for greater<T> is shown in this piece of code:

```
template <class T>
struct greater : binary_function<T, T, bool> {
    bool operator()(const T& x, const T& y) const { return x > y; }
};
```

It is clear from the class definition that greater<T> isn't the everyday type of class we are accustomed to. It doesn't have data members, constructors, or anything else. All it *does* have is a single member function: operator()(). (You might be tempted to think this odd looking thing is a misprint, but it isn't! operator()() is the name of the function that is called when the () operator is applied to an object.)

This is what function objects always look like: a nearly empty class definition, with a single operator()() function. The place we always see function objects is as class parameters passed to template functions or template classes. Function objects take the place of what would normally be function pointers in C, or even early C++.

What the function object does

One of the things needed to create a heap, as in priority_queue<T>, is a way to compare two elements of the container. You can do this with the normal operator<() provided for built-in data types. You simply have to define operator<() for any user-defined types you intend to use in a queue.

Being limited to operator<() seems kind of restrictive, however. In a world without function objects, the user of a priority_queue<T> would probably be allowed to pass a pointer to a comparison function to the constructor. You might end up with source code something like this:

```
bool compare_guy( const int &i, const int &j )
{
    return i > j;
}
```

```
main()
{
    priority_queue< vector<int> > a( compare_guy );
    .
    .
    .
```

In this sort of system, you would keep track of the function pointer, calling compare_guy() with the pointer whenever you wanted to see which of two values was smaller. This is the system that has been in use by C programmers for years. For example, qsort() is a sorting routine that takes a function pointer as one of its arguments.

There are several negative factors regarding the use of function pointers. Perhaps the two most important are inefficiency and inconvenience. Efficiency is lost because every comparison requires an indirect function call. Convenience is lost because you have to manually create a function for what is essentially a built-in operation. Type safety can be an issue as well, as function pointers used by qsort() and the like typically pass pointers to objects using void (typeless) pointers.

Function objects get around all of these problems easily. Instead of passing a function pointer to the constructor for a priority_queue<T> object, a class name is passed as a template argument. In the case we are studying, the class name is greater<int>. The constructor for the queue then creates a member of that class called *comp*. This can be used any time you want to compare two objects in the container, and is done with a call such as this:

```
if ( comp( *i, *j ) ) {
    .
    .
    .
```

This method overcomes three problems. First, it should generate inline code instead of an indirect function call. Second, you don't have to write the comparison function, since the STL has already provided template functions for all common operations. And finally, the function is fully prototyped for complete type safety.

Where can I get a function object?

Function objects are discussed in detail in later chapters, starting with Chapter 12, "Function Objects and Function Adaptors." The STL has dozens of predefined function objects, making it easy to create priority queues, heaps, trees, and other data structures. Comparison objects are used extensively in the next chapter, when we'll be looking at associative containers.

Most of the function objects can be found in functions.h. The predefined template function class definitions used in creating functions include:

- equal_to<T>
- not_equal_to<T>
- greater<T>
- less<T>
- greater_equal<T>
- less_equal<T>

Do it yourself!

If you're creating a priority queue to hold objects of your own definition, you will probably need to create a function object class. This is a pretty easy job; you just need to define a class with a single operator() member function. This isn't much different from writing a function and passing a pointer to it, but the implementation is a little more efficient.

Listing 7-5 shows pque0705.cpp. This program creates a priority queue that contains objects from a user-defined type, called foo. You can't use a built-in function object on class foo, so creating the priority queue with an argument such as less<foo> is not an option. Instead, you have to create a comparison class of your own.

Listing 7-5

pque0705.cpp: Using function objects with a priority queue.

```
//
// PQUE0705.CPP
//
// This program is used in Chapter 7 to demonstrate
// the use of function objects with a priority queue.
// Since the queue is built to contain objects of a user-
// defined type, we can't use a built-in function
// such as less<T>. Instead, I have to define a class
// dedicated to performing the comparison between
// two objects of type foo.
//
```

```
//
// Borland 4.x workarounds.
//

#define __MINMAX_DEFINED
#pragma option -vi-

#include <vector.h>
#include <stack.h>
#include <function.h>
#include <iostream.h>

struct foo {
    char *name;
    int age;
    foo( char *n = "", int a = 0 ){ name = n; age = a; }
};

//
// The function object used to compare two objects
// of type foo will be created from this class.
// class test_foo doesn't do anything useful except
// compare objects of type foo.
//
class younger_foo {
  public :
    int operator()( const foo &a, const foo &b )
    {
        return a.age > b.age;
    }
};

main()
{
    priority_queue< vector<foo>, younger_foo > a;

    a.push( foo( "Mark", 38 ) );
    a.push( foo( "Marc", 25 ) );
    a.push( foo( "Bill", 47 ) );
    a.push( foo( "Andy", 13 ) );
    a.push( foo( "Newt", 44 ) );
    while ( !a.empty() ) {
        cout << a.top().name << endl;
        a.pop();
    }
    cout << endl;
    return 1;
}
```

In pque0705.cpp, the comparison class is called younger_foo. This class doesn't have a defined constructor or destructor, nor any data members. It only has a single member function, operator()(), which is used by functions that manipulate the heap to compare two objects of type foo.

In the particular example being studied, the comparison object compares the age members of two foo objects. It returns a logical true if the first is less than the second. When the program runs with this comparison object installed, the output looks like this:

```
Andy
Marc
Mark
Newt
Bill
```

Inside priority_queue<T>

Although this is a much more powerful adaptor than the other two in this chapter, its definition is still very simple. The difficult work in class priority_queue is done by the heap functions, which are defined in heap.h, and discussed in detail in Chapter 17. The code defining the priority queue is found in stack.h, and is shown here:

Listing 7-6

The implementation of priority_queue<T>

```
template <class Container, class Compare>
class  priority_queue {
public:
  typedef Container::value_type value_type;
  typedef Container::size_type size_type;
protected:
  Container c;
  Compare comp;
public:
  priority_queue(const Compare& x = Compare()) :  c(), comp(x) {}
  priority_queue(const value_type* first,
                 const value_type* last,
                 const Compare& x = Compare()) : c(first, last),
                                                 comp(x) {
    make_heap(c.begin(), c.end(), comp);
  }
```

```
      bool empty() const { return c.empty(); }
      size_type size() const { return c.size(); }
      value_type& top() { return c.front(); }
      const value_type& top() const { return c.front(); }
      void push(const value_type& x) {
        c.push_back(x);
        push_heap(c.begin(), c.end(), comp);
      }
      void pop() {
        pop_heap(c.begin(), c.end(), comp);
        c.pop_back();
      }
  };
```

For the most part, the source code in the definition of priority_queue<T> looks very similar to stack<T> and queue<T>. The only places there are differences are in functions used either to add or remove data from the container:

```
    priority_queue(const value_type* first,
                   const value_type* last,
                   const Compare& x );
    void push(const value_type& x);
    void pop();
```

Each of these three functions either adds or removes data from the container.

Note: The container in priority_queue<T> needs to be a heap at all times. Thus, any time you add or remove data, you should perform the adjustments needed to ensure the data is still a heap.

For the constructor shown in Listing 7-6, we copy all the initialization data into the container, then call the make_heap() template function. make_heap() takes an ordinary container with a random access iterator and rearranges the elements, so as to create a valid heap.

The push() function uses the container's push_back() function to add an object to the end of the heap. The heap function push_heap() is then called. It incorporates the new element into the heap by working its way up the tree, switching nodes as necessary.

The pop() function works in reverse order. First, it has to call pop_heap(). This removes the first element from the heap and puts it in the end of the container. The last element can then be safely removed.

Note also that you can pop the first element from the heap without having to call pop_front(). This is the reason you can use objects of class vector<T> as priority queues, even though vector<T> can't be used as the basis for a queue<T>.

Container requirements

priority_queue<T> has the same set of requirements for its container as stack<T>. The container has to support the push_back() and pop_back() operations, as well as functions such as front(), begin() and end().

Due to the use of the heap functions, priority_queue<T> has some additional requirements that place more restrictions on the type of container it can use as a foundation.

Heap functions do their work using indices into the container, so the container must support random access iterators. This means deque<T> and vector<T> will work properly, but not list<T>. Thus, you have only two choices for the foundation of a priority_queue<T>.

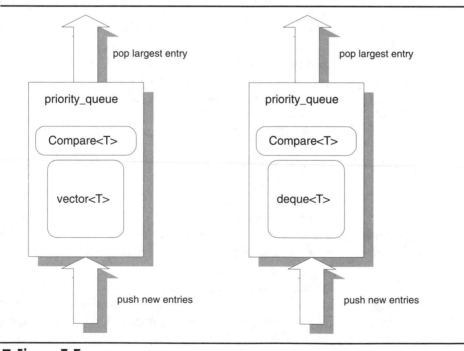

Figure 7-7
The two versions of priority_queue<T>

Design considerations

You can use either a vector<T> or a deque<T> as the container to provide storage for a priority_queue<T>. If it's feasible, the vector<T> object usually makes a better container.

The heap operations performed every time the container is modified make heavy use of random access iterators. A number of the test programs in this book have shown that random access iterators are considerably slower for objects of type deque<T> than for vector<T>, so if access time is your primary consideration, vector<T> makes an excellent host class for priority_queue<T>.

The one place where deque<T> might be the class of choice is when you expect the size of the queue to vary greatly. deque<T> deals efficiently with this situation, and most importantly, returns unused memory to the system when it is done with it.

HOOKED ON ADAPTORS

One of the things I hope you've picked up in this chapter is that container adaptors are a little less forbidding than the STL container classes. They all feature simple interfaces that make them a real breeze to plug into your programs. When you find yourself looking through the STL specification to find just the right container for your program, be sure not to overlook the gems found in this chapter!

ASSOCIATIVE CONTAINERS

Thus is his cheek the map of days outworn.
— William Shakespeare (1564–1616), Sonnet 68.

The sequential containers we looked at in Chapters 4 through 7 provide incremental improvements in the lives of everyday C++ programmers. Once you become familiar with them, you'll probably see new uses for vector<T>, list<T>, and deque<T> every time you sit down to write some code.

But while these containers are useful, they aren't revolutionary. They're well designed, and the occasions you'll feel compelled to write your own version of a sequential container class are going to be few and far between. However, you know you *could* write your own version of vector<T> if you had to. It might not be as versatile as vector<T>, and it probably wouldn't integrate as well with the rest of the STL, but at least it would work. After all, many programmers were writing their own versions of these containers—although probably not generic versions—long before the STL came along.

With the associative containers, set<Key, Compare> and map<Key, T, Compare>, the STL takes the process one step further. These containers provide functionality that isn't so easy to duplicate with a few hours of coding.

WHAT IS AN ASSOCIATIVE CONTAINER?

An *associative container* stores objects based on *keys*. This is a very convenient way of organizing data, but isn't built into C or C++. Large databases that contain megabytes of data on disk almost always have the ability to look up records based on keys. And languages like PERL have built-in support for associative arrays. But until now, C++ programmers who want to use associative data structures in their programs have had to use third-party libraries or write the code themselves. In the STL, associative data structures are available as a template class, so it's easier than ever to use.

To C programmers, a natural paradigm for this type of container is the *associative array*. Associative arrays store data based on a key value, not an index into a sequence of memory objects. For example, if you are writing a C compiler, you may wish to add values to your symbol table using syntax such as this:

```
table[ "main" ] = 0x00000322;
table[ "_foo" ] = 0x000009a2;
table[ "_exit" ] = 0x00000e31;
```

Then, when it's time to access a value in the symbol table, you can write code like so:

```
long jump_address = table[ "_foo" ];
```

This is a very intuitive way to code, but it isn't supported in standard C++. But given the flexibility of C++, and the ability to overload operators, you can implement associative arrays that use this syntax.

The example shown above uses strings as an index into the associative array, but with the STL, you can create associative arrays that use *anything* as an index: built-in types, user-defined structures, classes, and so on.

Program map0801.cpp uses the map<Key,T,Compare> associative container to show how the associative arrays defined in the STL can be used in a C++ program. This particular implementation is of a map, which is a container that has a key value and a data object for each entry in the array. So, for example, the key value of "Bill Gates" is used to access the entry "Microsoft".

Listing 8-1

map0801.cpp: Some example code that shows an associative array in action

```cpp
//
// MAP0801.CPP
//
// This program is used in Chapter 8 to demonstrate
// the use of associative containers. In this case,
// the container is a map which holds two strings.
// The first string contains a person's name, and the
// second holds a company name.
//
// The program shows how an associative array
// can be initialized using conventional syntax.
// The contents of the array can then be accessed
// using several different techniques.
//
// Note that this program uses Borland's string class,
// which may differ slightly from the standard.
//


//
// Borland 4.x workarounds
//
#define _ MINMAX_DEFINED
#pragma option -vi-

#include <cstring.h>
#include <iostream.h>

#include "map.h"

main()
{
    typedef map< string, string, less<string> > my_map;
    my_map a;

    a[ "Bill Gates" ] = "Microsoft";
    a[ "Steve Jobs" ] = "Next";
    a[ "Bob Frankenberg" ] = "Novell";
    a[ "Charles Wang" ] = "Computer Associates";
    for ( my_map::iterator i = a.begin() ;
          i != a.end() ;
          i++ )
        cout << (*i).first
            << " is CEO of "
            << (*i).second
```

```
                    << endl;
        cout << "John Sculley is the CEO of ";
        my_map::iterator j = a.find( "John Sculley" );
        if ( j == a.end() )
            cout << "nobody";
        else
            cout << (*j).second;
        cout << endl;
        cout << "Bill Gates is CEO of "
            << a[ "Bill Gates" ]
            << endl;
        return 1;
    }
```

There are several ways to insert and extract data from an associative container. One of the simplest is with the overloaded operator[]() function. The associative class map<Key,T,Compare> lets you use operator[]() to insert objects into the array, as well as obtain a reference to an object already in the container.

The first four lines of code after the variable declarations in main() use operator[]() to insert company names in the array, employing CEO names as keys:

```
        a[ "Bill Gates" ] = "Microsoft";
        a[ "Steve Jobs" ] = "Next";
        a[ "Bob Frankenberg" ] = "Novell";
        a[ "Charles Wang" ] = "Computer Associates";
```

Once the data has been inserted in the array, you can iterate through the items using the standard iterator loop that you have seen in many of the example programs in this book. Note, however, that dereferencing the iterator for a map<Key,T,Compare> object yields a pair<> object. The pair object has two data members called first and second, which are used to access the key and data, respectively. This is the somewhat awkward syntax used consistently throughout the STL when two objects are returned in a single function call.

The remainder of map0801.cpp shows two other ways data can be found in an associative array:

- the find() function looks up a key value using a syntax oriented to a more conventional C function

- operator[]() looks up a value that has previously been stored in the array

Here's the output from map0801.cpp:

```
Bill Gates is CEO of Microsoft
Bob Frankenberg is CEO of Novell
Charles Wang is CEO of Computer Associates
Steve Jobs is CEO of Next
John Sculley is the CEO of nobody
Bill Gates is CEO of Microsoft
```

Looking through map0801.cpp should quickly convince you that associative containers are a powerful new addition to C++. The rest of this chapter will explain the different uses of the four different types of associative containers found in the STL.

A DYNAMIC FOURSOME

There are four associative containers defined in the STL. They represent all the permutations of an associative container based on the values of two true/false parameters. The two parameters answer the following questions:

- Are multiple appearances of the same key allowed?
- Does the container hold just the key, or the key and associated data?

Table 8-1 shows the names of containers that result from the four possible states of this two-variable system. The *set* and *multiset* containers hold just a key value, whereas *map* and *multimap* hold both a key and an associated data element.

All four containers share one common purpose: storage and retrieval of data based on a key. The examples you saw in map0801.cpp did both of these things, using a CEO name as a key. Storage and retrieval can be done with member functions like insert() and find(), or for one of the two map classes, operator[]().

The two set classes store only their key, while the map classes store an additional data item based on a key. Thus, when you search for a key in a set class, you find a copy of the key value, but nothing else. When you search for a key in a map class, you are looking up an additional piece of data. This process will be explored in more detail later in this chapter.

Table 8-1

The four associative containers

	One instance of a key	Multiple instances of a key
Key only	set<Key,Compare>	multiset<Key,Compare>
Key and associated data	map<Key,T,Compare>	multimap<Key,T,Compare>

Table 8-1 also shows that all four containers have a template parameter called *Compare*. Compare is a function object that compares two key values. Ordinarily, the function object is operator<() for the Key type. For built-in types, this means you can pass a function object based on the less<> function object template:

```
set< long, less<long> > a;
```

It's very important to note here that the STL does all its comparisons using either operator<() or a user-supplied equivalent. Since the STL was designed to do its ordering comparisons with this operator, it won't apply operator==() at any time. This has one unusual side-effect: when looking up a key value in an associative container, two keys are assumed to be equal if both (Key1<Key2) and (Key2<Key1) evaluate to false!

If you compare key values that are of some user-defined type, you'll probably have to create a function object tailored to your particular classes. Some classes, such as the string class supplied with the standard library, will already have operator<() defined. Classes you create yourself won't have this operator defined until you write a function object to do the job.

ONE BIG, HAPPY FAMILY: ITERATORS

Despite the fact that these containers seem so different when placed alongside sequential containers, their inclusion in the STL leads us to expect that certain fundamental container properties will still apply to them. Most of these properties relate to the behavior of the iterators defined for the container, as well as the functions that return iterators.

Each container has an iterator type that can be used to sequentially step through the entire container, just as we have been doing with the sequential containers. The containers have begin() and end() functions that return the appropriate iterators, as well as rbegin() and rend(). Thus, many of the functions and algorithms built into the STL that work with sequential containers also work with associative containers. (The determining factor will be the type of iterator, which is covered in detail in Chapter 10.)

The associative containers are similar to list<T>, in that their iterators are not random access iterators. Thus, you can't use the iterator returned by begin() as an offset to the fifth element of the array by looking up *i*[5]. However, any algorithm that uses only the increment or decrement functions of iterators will work properly. (This means associative containers have *bidirectional iterators*, also covered in Chapter 10.)

RED-BLACK TREES

All four associative classes in the STL are variations on a common theme. Because of this, they can be implemented using the same foundation: the *red-black tree*. This is a form of balanced tree that has O(logN) time for insertion, removal, and access of keys. Accordingly, when you iterate through the tree, you see all the elements appear in sorted order.

While the red-black tree does all the hard work, the containers—map, set, multimap, and multiset—get to provide the public API and so take all the credit.

Each associative class incorporates a red-black tree as a private data member. map and multimap use the type definition and member declaration shown in the next code excerpt:

```
public:
    typedef Key key_type;
    typedef pair<const Key, T> value_type;
    typedef Compare key_compare;
private:
    typedef rb_tree<key_type,
                    value_type,
                    select1st<value_type, key_type>,
                    key_compare> rep_type;
        rep_type t;  // red-black tree representing multimap
```

For all four associative containers, a private data member is constructed using a variation of the template class rb_tree. This class is discussed in more detail later in this section. For now, if you look at the map and set declarations, you can see they are very similar. The only significant difference between them is that set and multiset trees only hold an object of type

Key. map and multimap hold a pair<>, consisting of a Key object and an object of class T.

```
public:
    typedef Key key_type;
    typedef Key value_type;
    typedef Compare key_compare;
private:
    typedef rb_tree<key_type,
                    value_type,
                    ident<value_type, key_type>,
                    key_compare> rep_type;
    rep_type t;  // red-black tree representing multiset
```

Exactly what is a red-black tree?

Before we look at the STL-specific implementation of a red-black tree, you should have a general idea of this type of data structure.

Associative containers need to store data in a structure without knowing in advance how much data the structure will be asked to hold. They also need to quickly insert, delete, or find objects, based on a given key. There are many kinds of data structures that can do this, including various balanced trees and hash tables.

The choice of red-black trees is a good compromise. While some data structures, such as those based on hash tables, can run much faster under optimal conditions, they are *much* slower in some circumstances. Red-black trees aren't the fastest or the most efficient sorted data structures on Earth. However, you don't have to worry about pathological slow performance in the worst cases, and you aren't subjected to a great deal of overhead in exchange for speed.

2-3-4 trees

The red-black tree is actually just a clever representation of a *2-3-4 tree*. In a 2-3-4 tree, each node contains one, two or three data objects, and two, three or four descendants. The nodes are labeled according to the number of descendants, with each node having one less data object than descendant nodes. Thus, a 2-node contains one data object and two descendants. The nodes and descendants obey the following rules:

- A 2-node has two descendants. The left-hand descendant has a key less than, or equal to, its 2-node's key. The right-hand descendant has a key greater than the 2-node's key.

- A 3-node has three descendants. The left-hand descendant has a key value less than, or equal to, the *smaller* of the two data members in the 3-node. The right-hand descendant has a key value greater than the *larger* of the two data members. The center descendant has a key value between or equal to the two values in the 3-node.

- The rules for a 4-node are a logical extension of the previous two rules. The 4-node descendants span the ranges defined by the three data objects contained in the node.

A 2-3-4 tree with just a few elements is shown in Figure 8-1. Note that this tree is presently *balanced*; that is, all terminating nodes are at the same depth in the tree. When adding nodes to the tree, we need to continually adjust the tree so that the 2-3-4 characteristics are still present, while also keeping the tree balanced.

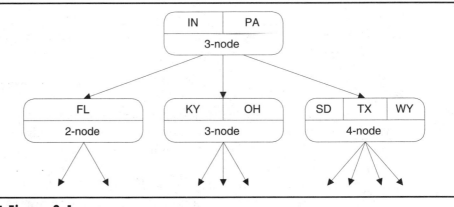

Figure 8-1
A 2-3-4 tree containing postal abbreviations for states in the USA

Adding nodes means starting at the root of the tree and continuing down, until we reach a terminating node. The insertion of a new object into an existing node follows these rules:

- If the target node is a 2-node, you add the new data object to the node, making it a 3-node.

- If the target node is a 3-node, you add the new data object to the node, making it a 4-node.

(If you're wondering about the 4-node, hang on a bit longer!)

Figure 8-2 shows how the first two rules affect the tree from Figure 8-1 when two new nodes, "CA" and "NY", are added. "CA" is added to the 2-node on the far left, making it a 3-node. "NY" is added to the 3-node in the center, making it a 4-node.

In both cases, the balance of the tree hasn't been affected, because we haven't created any new nodes. This means the existing nodes remain at the same depth, so balancing isn't a problem.

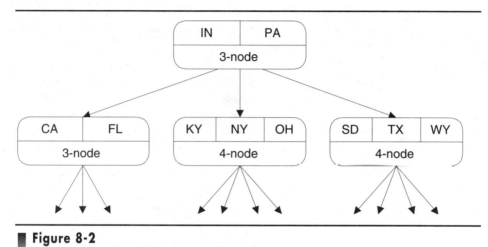

Figure 8-2
The same tree after adding "CA" and "NY" to the 2-node and 3-node

This is nice and simple, but a big problem has clearly been overlooked. What happens when it's time to add a new node to a 4-node? Does it suddenly become a 2-3-4-5 tree? For example, how would you add "WA" to the tree in Figure 8-2?

The solution is a two-step process. First, the 4-node that will accept the new data object is split into two 2-nodes. The smallest and largest keys become 2-nodes at the same level, and the center object is moved up to the parent node. In this case, that means "TX" is moved up, leaving "SD" and "WY" as new 2-nodes. Figure 8-3 shows the tree in this intermediate state.

Once the tree has been adjusted, the new node can be added to one of the two resulting 2-nodes. The final result is shown in Figure 8-4.

Once again, this glosses over an additional detail. What happens if you try to pass up an object to a parent node, and the parent node is already a 4-node?

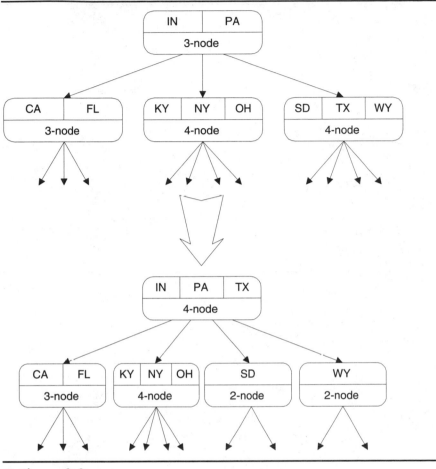

Figure 8-3
Splitting the rightmost 4-node

For example, what if you tried to add "NC" to the tree shown in Figure 8-4? "NC" would need to be stored in the 4-node containing "KY NY OH". This would mean splitting it into a 2-node containing "KY", and another 2-node containing "OH", while passing "NY" up to the parent node. But in this case, the parent node is a 4-node! So what do you do now?

You simply keep on splitting nodes and passing up until you either reach the root or run out of 4-nodes. The result of this process is shown in Figure 8-5. In this case, it was only necessary to split an additional level at the root node. This has resulted in a tree that is still balanced, but is one level deeper.

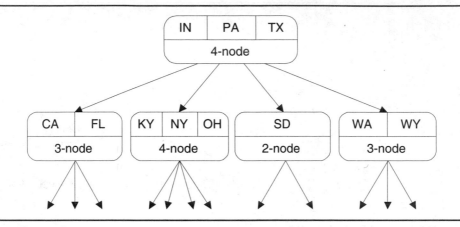

Figure 8-4
After adding the new key to the resulting 2-node

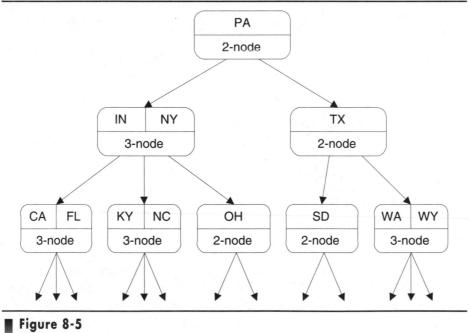

Figure 8-5
The tree after adding "NC"

The process of deleting nodes follows a similar course. Any deletion from a 2-node would result in an unbalanced tree, so an adjustment has to be made. In the case of a deletion, you must move a parent object down the tree, instead of moving a child object up the tree. If the parent is a 2-node, you need to work your way up the tree, moving nodes down. The process keeps on going until you either get to the root node, or reach a 3-node or a 4-node.

2-3-4 trees morph to red-black

2-3-4 trees are conceptually very simple and are easy to follow on paper. However, implementing a 2-3-4 tree is a sloppy process. Every node in the tree has to remember whether it is a 2-node, a 3-node, or a 4-node. Conversion between all three types of nodes must be easy, and the individual objects in each node must be kept in sorted order. It can be done, but it won't be as tidy as you might like.

Once you leave pencil and paper behind, and move to a programming language like C++, there's a considerably simpler alternative way to represent 2-3-4 trees. You create a special form of binary tree, the red-black tree.

A red-black tree appears to be a standard binary tree, but there is one important difference: every link between nodes in the tree has a color—either red or black.

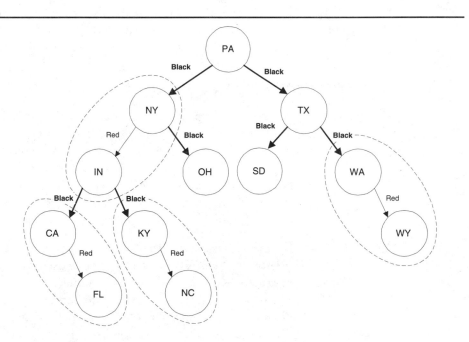

Figure 8-6
A 2-3-4 tree represented as a red-black tree

A black link in a red-black tree is a normal link connecting two levels of the tree. A red link, on the other hand, is a special link that connects the members of a 3-node or a 4-node.

Figure 8-6 shows the tree from Figure 8-5 when represented as a red-black tree. It looks much like a standard binary tree, with an important difference. The figure shows that each link has been colored to be red or black. The red links are used to connect nodes that are actually part of the same 3-node or 4-node. (The figure encloses these nodes to enhance readability.)

When searching the tree for a particular key, the color of a link is irrelevant; you simply perform a search as if it were a binary tree. However, when inserting or removing keys, red-black algorithms use the link color to properly follow the 2-3-4 tree guidelines.

The algorithms that insert or remove nodes in the red-black tree are just as complicated as those which manipulate a 2-3-4 tree. Although in principle they are doing the same thing, the red-black algorithms can be difficult to follow, owing to the non-intuitive nature of the read and black links.

The algorithms won't be discussed here; instead, you're recommended to look at one of the algorithms books listed in the bibliography. Reading those texts with the STL code close at hand should help you puzzle your way through the implementation of a red-black tree.

Implementation in rb_tree

Red-black trees are defined for the STL in the header file tree.h. The class definition includes a formidable list of classes that have to be defined for class rb_tree. Briefly, the type parameters needed to define class rb_tree are:

Key: This is the class of object used to order the nodes in the tree. Objects of class Key are compared against each other to determine which nodes are greater than others.

Value: Objects of class Value are those actually contained in each node of the tree. When class rb_tree is used to build set<> containers, Key and Value are the same, since it is the objects of class Key that are actually stored in the tree. When building containers of type map<>, Value is set to pair<Key,T>, a construct made up of the key and value collected together.

KeyOfValue: This is the type of function object that extracts the Key object from the Value object. For sets, its type is ident<>, and it returns the Value object, which is the same as the Key object. For maps, its type is select1st<>, which extracts the first object from pair<Key,T>.

Compare: This is the type of the function object used to compare two keys.

The next piece of code shows the start of the class definition:

```
template <class Key, class Value, class KeyOfValue, class Compare>
class rb_tree {
```

The nodes in class rb_tree<> are defined by the nested class rb_tree_node:

```
enum color_type {red, black};
struct rb_tree_node {
    color_type color_field;
    void_pointer parent_link;
    void_pointer left_link;
    void_pointer right_link;
    Value value_field;
};
```

The important thing to note here is that the tree defines rb_tree_node, the data structure that defines a node in a red black tree. rb_tree_node has a color, links to its parents and children, and the value of the node.

How rb_tree is used in associative containers

The foundation provided by class rb_tree includes an iterator and a set of utility member functions. So it's an easy job to build the four associative classes. Each one has a private data member that consists of a properly defined rb_tree instance.

In the two versions of the map class, the declaration of the tree type is:

```
typedef rb_tree<key_type,
                value_type,
                select1st<value_type, key_type>,
                key_compare> rep_type;
```

We haven't looked at function objects in any detail yet. However, you've probably figured out that the select1st<> function object extracts the key object from the pair<Key,T>. It is the pair<> object that is actually stored in the tree.

The set classes use this declaration:

```
typedef rb_tree<key_type,
                value_type,
                ident<value_type, key_type>,
                key_compare> rep_type;
```

Once again, you have to contend with an unfamiliar function object. In this case, ident<> extracts the key value from Key; it simply returns its only argument. ident<> is a function object that returns a reference to its input, so it's pretty simple! Since the template code will be called inline, the ident<> function will, ideally, generate no code at all.

As all four associative classes keep their tree members private, their functions are exposed to the programmer via a set of member functions. For the most part, member functions of the associative functions result in short translations to function calls to member functions to class rb_tree<>. We'll look at these function calls in more detail in the next four sections.

SET<KEY,COMPARE>

The first associative container is, in many ways, the simplest. set<Key,Compare> is a sorted container that holds unique objects of type Key. Because objects need to be unique, an insertion operation with a key already in the set will fail; the method to indicate the failure varies depending on the insertion function called. And unlike the map<> container, set<> doesn't have separate key and data objects.

When inserting objects or searching the set<> container, the performance is O(logN). And because of the characteristics of a red-black tree, you don't have to worry about a worst-case performance more severe than O(logN).

The basics

Associative containers differ in some ways from the sequential containers, list<>, deque<>, and vector<>. Yet they share the elements common to *all*

STL containers, the standard access functions and iterators described in the previous chapters. The access functions are:

- begin()
- end()
- rbegin()
- rend()
- empty()
- size()
- max_size()

Functions such as begin() and end() return iterators, just like their counterparts in the sequential containers. The iterators are used to work through every element in the set. Of course, the elements in set<> are ordered, so the iterator returns keys in sorted order. set0802.cpp, in Listing 8-2, shows how these functions are used with a set.

Note: The loop that prints out values in the container is identical to the code that prints out the contents of any other type of container. This is one of the important properties of the STL: iterators provide a form of universal access to containers.

Listing 8-2

set0802.cpp: Access functions in set<Key,Compare>

```
//
// SET0802.CPP
//
// This program is used in Chapter 8 to demonstrate the
// access functions used in set<Key,Compare>. I use a
// constructor that initializes the set, then print
// out some of its metrics, as well as all of its elements.
//

//
// Borland 4.x workarounds
//
#define __MINMAX_DEFINED
#pragma option -vi-

#include <iostream.h>
#include "set.h"
```

```
main()
{
    int init[] = { 4, 10, 1, 3, 22, 1, 100, -100 };
    set<int, less<int> > a( init, init + 8 );

    cout << "a contains "
         << a.size()
         << " elements"
         << endl;

    cout << "The maximum size is "
         << a.max_size()
         << endl;

    cout << "a is "
         << ( a.empty() ? "" : "not " )
         << "empty"
         << endl;

    cout << "a contains : ";
    for ( set<int, less<int> >::iterator i = a.begin() ;
          i != a.end() ;
          i++ )
        cout << *i << " ";
    cout << endl;

    cout << "a reversed contains: ";
    set<int, less<int> >::reverse_iterator j;
    j = a.rbegin();
    while ( j != a.rend() )
        cout << *j++ << " ";
    cout << endl;

    return 1;
}
```

The output from set0802.cpp shows that, even though associative containers behave quite differently from sequential containers, they still present an interface that is standard among all STL containers:

```
a contains 7 elements
The maximum size is 4095
a is not empty
a contains : -100 1 3 4 10 22 100
a reversed contains: 100 22 10 4 3 1 -100
```

set<>::iterator

One of the critical pieces needed to make set<> look like a standard STL container is the presence of an iterator. All four associative classes share the iterator defined by the rb_tree<> class. Traversing the nodes of a binary tree results in code slightly more complicated than for any of the sequential classes.

Most algorithms normally used to traverse trees are designed to visit every node in a tree while in a single subroutine. They tend to rely on recursion, with slightly different setups for the various methods of tree traversal. It's unusual to traverse trees by using a structure like an iterator. Here, the entire state of the iteration has to be stored in a variable, so it can be used on an asynchronous basis.

As it turns out, rb_tree::iterator manages to do this while keeping track of nothing more than the currently selected node. The next code excerpt gives an example of how this works for operator++():

```
protected:
    link_type node;
public:
iterator& operator++() {
        if (right(node) != NIL) {
            node = right(node);
            while (left(node) != NIL)
                node = left(node);
        } else {
            link_type y = parent(node);
            while (node == right(y)) {
                node = y;
                y = parent(y);
            }
            if (right(node) != y) // necessary because of rightmost
                node = y;
        }
        return *this;
}
```

rb_tree<>::iterator::operator++() needs to navigate through the binary tree from one node to the next—and it can ignore the color of the links. As you can see from the code above, there are two distinct paths through this navigation process.

When it's time to move to the next node, operator++() checks if the current node has a right-hand descendant. If it does, it moves to that node, then follows all the subsequent left-hand links, until it reaches the end of the chain. In Figure 8-7, an iterator pointing to "PA" moves to "TX", then follows the left-hand descendants until it reaches "SD". "SD" is the next node after "PA".

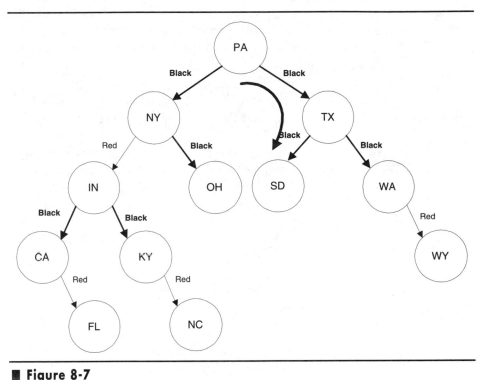

Figure 8-7
operator++() with a right-hand descendant

Look again at the last piece of code. A completely different branch is taken if there is no right-hand descendant for the given node. The section of code called is slightly more complicated; it sits in a loop, moving to consecutive parent nodes. It continues moving up the chain until it finds a parent node linked on the left-hand side, instead of the right-hand side.

Figure 8-8 shows this process. The current node is "NC", which has no right-hand or left-hand descendant. So the iterator code moves up the chain from parent to parent. Each time it arrives at a new parent, it checks to see if it arrived by a right-hand link or a left-hand link. When it finally arrives by a left-hand link, it terminates. Indeed, this happens at "NY", the next node in the chain.

When decrementing an iterator (navigating the tree in reverse), the operations you've seen here are simply translated into a mirror image of themselves: every left changes to right, and every right changes to left.

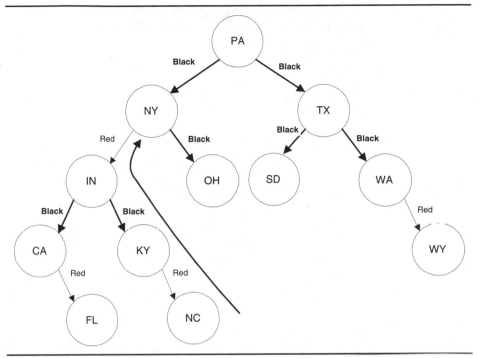

Figure 8-8
operator++() with no right-hand descendant

What's my iterator?

The rb_tree<> iterator is capable of operating in either direction, but it can't be incremented or decremented by a constant offset. This makes it look like the iterator for list<T>—a *bidirectional iterator*.

Because it can't be employed as a random access iterator, it can't use many of the algorithms supplied with the STL. However, many of the algorithms that need a random access iterator are sorting and searching algorithms. Since the associative containers are already sorted, these capabilities are already available in the class, without the need for external algorithms.

What does it point to?

In the STL, we assume that iterators are pointer-like objects. In fact, iterators for classes such as vector<T> *are* pointers.

Clearly, a red-black tree uses iterators that aren't pointers. The underpinnings needed for code as complex as the iterator's operator++() are way over the heads of built-in objects.

With a real pointer, you can be pretty sure of what happens when you perform a dereference operation. But with an iterator object, it's a good idea to take a closer look. In the case of rb_tree<>::iterator, the dereference code looks like this:

```
reference operator*() const
{
    return value(node);
}
```

The value function used in this operation is defined in tree.h:

```
static reference value(link_type x)
{
    return (*x).value_field;
}
```

Following this even further back in header file tree.h, you find that the argument, link_type, is simply a pointer to an object of type rb_tree_node. The node type holds the value contained in the node. This is the Value field in the template class rb_tree<Key,Value,KeyOfValue,Compare>.

It takes a lot of work to get there, but the upshot of all this is that dereferencing the iterator returns a const reference to the key value stored in the node. This is what we should have been expecting.

What's missing?

The first part of this section describes the facets of set<> that are similar to the sequential containers in the STL. Functions like begin() and size() are universally used among all containers, including associative containers.

Does this similarity extend throughout the class? Not quite. Associative containers part company with sequential containers in the functions they use to insert and remove objects from the container. With sequential containers, you have access to routines that manipulate specific portions of the containers:

- push_front()
- push_back()

- pop_front()
- pop_back()

Not one of these functions is available in the associative containers. push_front() and push_back() are irrelevant, because you can't arbitrarily place an object at the beginning or end of the container. It goes where it belongs according to the sorting order, which could be anywhere in the container.

Old functions, new returns

The functions set<> uses to insert and remove objects should be familiar; they are simply variations on the traditional insert() and erase() functions. Probably the most confusing thing is the new type of return value introduced by one of the insert() functions. The body of this function is shown in the next piece of code:

```
pair_iterator_bool insert(const value_type& x) {
    pair<rep_type::iterator, bool> p = t.insert(x);
    return pair<iterator, bool>(p.first, p.second);
}
```

Note the odd return type for this function. All other insert() functions for the sequential containers returned normal iterators, which makes sense. But this function returns some strange object of type pair<iterator,bool>!

This is definitely a less-than-elegant solution to an age-old problem for C programmers: What do you do when a function needs to return two or more things, instead of just one?

When it comes to inserting objects into a set<>, you are faced with a possibility that didn't exist with sequential containers. Namely, set<> doesn't allow multiple copies of the same Key value to be inserted. Thus, it's possible for a call to insert() to fail, if it's attempting to insert a key already in the container.

This leaves you with a problem. If an insertion operation succeeds, it returns an iterator pointing to the element just inserted. If the operation fails, it returns an iterator that points to the *previously inserted* identical element. In both cases, you'll get back a legitimate iterator. So, how do you know when a failure has occurred?

The answer is simple. You modify the function so it returns *two* values instead of one. Although this sounds an unlikely solution, with the help of a template class it isn't too hard.

pair<T1,T2>

The STL header file pair.h defines a new template class:

```
template <class T1, class T2>
struct pair {
    T1 first;
    T2 second;
    pair(const T1& a, const T2& b) : first(a), second(b) {}
};
```

As you can see by looking at this definition, pair<T1,T2> is the simplest of containers. It doesn't do anything other than initialize two members to two different values. Since it's defined as a struct instead of a class, both members are publicly accessible. This means a function that returns a pointer and a boolean value can use code like this:

```
return pair<iterator, bool>(i, false);
```

Likewise, a function that receives this pair can test for the two values simply by accessing the *first* and *second* members:

```
pair<iterator,bool> result = foo( a );
if ( result.second )
    cout << result.first;
else
    cerr << "Failure";
```

Ideally, the compiler will inline all this code, making it a very efficient way to return arguments. It doesn't suffer from the semantic ambiguity you run into with reference arguments. After all, C and C++ programmers are used to seeing inputs passed as arguments and outputs returned as results from functions. You *aren't* used to seeing reference arguments in functions that can change your parameters without you knowing about it.

So, even if the pair<> construct is a little untidy, and maybe not as elegant as you'd like, it *does* work. It's efficient and it *is* semantically consistent with the practice of C and C++. It's here to stay.

An example using pair<T1,T2>

Listing 8-3 shows a listing of set0803.cpp, a program that inserts a list of integers into a set<int>. Since some of the integers are duplicated, some of the insertion attempts will be failures.

Listing 8-3

set0803.cpp: An example program that demonstrates the pair<T1,T2> class

```
//
// SET0803.CPP
//
// This program is used in Chapter 8 to demonstrate the
// insertion function for containers of type set<>.
// This program introduces the oddball return type
// of pair<iterator,bool> that is used by some of
// the insertion functions in the associative classes.
//

//
// Borland 4.x workarounds
//
#define __MINMAX_DEFINED
#pragma option -vi-

#include <iostream.h>
#include "set.h"

main()
{
    typedef set<int, less<int> > my_set;
    my_set a;
    int data[] = { 1, 2, 3, 4, 3, 4, 5, 6, 0 };

    for ( int i = 0 ; data[ i ] != 0 ; i++ ) {
        pair< my_set::iterator, bool> x = a.insert( data[ i ] );
        cout << "insertion of "
             << data[ i ]
             << ( x.second ? " worked" : " failed" )
             << endl;
    }
    return 0;
}
```

The output from set0803.cpp is shown in the next code excerpt. As you can see, the insertion failures were detected and printed out properly:

```
insertion of 1 worked
insertion of 2 worked
insertion of 3 worked
insertion of 4 worked
insertion of 3 failed
insertion of 4 failed
insertion of 5 worked
insertion of 6 worked
```

Like a map, but simpler

The examples of set<> containers shown in this chapter so far have used simple, built-in data types as the objects contained by set containers. There will probably be times when you want to store ints, floats, strings, or some other simple type in a set. But it's just as likely you'll want to store more complex objects built out of classes of your own devising. set<> does this job as well, but it requires a little more effort on your part.

When creating a set<> for a user-defined type, you'll have to define a comparison object that works properly with your value. When utilizing built-in types, you've always used less<T> as a comparison class in the template definition. But less<T> only uses operator<() to compare the two objects. It will only work if you can do this:

```
less( const T& x, const T& y)
{
    return x < y;
}
```

If your object doesn't have operator<() defined, you'll have to create your own comparison class. Fortunately, this is an easy job. You'll need to create a class, but the class only requires a single member function definition.

Listing 8-4 shows set0804.cpp, a program that creates a user-defined class called *employee*. By default, there is no operator<() defined for a new type, so you can't create a set called set<employee,less<employee> >. Instead, you have to define a new comparison class.

In this program, the comparison class is called less_employee. less_employee has only a single member function, operator()(), which is used to compare two employee records. In this case, it compares the two name fields.

Listing 8-4

set0804.cpp: Using set<> with user-defined data types

```
//
// SET0804.CPP
//
// This program is used in Chapter 8 to demonstrate the
// use of set<> with user-defined data types. The program
// creates a user-defined type, class employee. Then, it
// creates a comparison class that can be used to order
// objects of this type.
//
```

```
//
// Borland 4.x workarounds
//
#define __MINMAX_DEFINED
#pragma option -vi-

#include <iostream.h>
#include <cstring.h>
#include "set.h"

class employee {
    public :
        string name;
        long id_number;
        employee( char *n, long id )
          ·  name( n ), id_number( id ){}
};

class less_employee {
    public :
    bool operator()(const employee& x, const employee& y) const
    {
        return x.name < y.name;
    }
};
main()
{
    set<employee,less_employee > a;

    a.insert( employee( "Bill Gates", 123 ) );
    a.insert( employee( "Phillipe Kahn", 456 ) );
    a.insert( employee( "Bill Clinton", 789 ) );
    set<employee, less_employee>::iterator i;
    i = a.find( employee( "Bill Gates", 0 ) );
    if ( i == a.end() )
        cout << "Bill Gates not found!" << endl;
    else
        cout << "find() returned: "
            << (*i).name
            << ", "
            << (*i).id_number
            << endl;
    return 0;
}
```

This example highlights the fact that you can use the set<> container to hold more than just simple types. In this case, the set<> holds an entire employee record. But the ordering in the set is done using just the name. This means you can use set<> by itself to perform some of the same functions performed by map<Key,T>.

set0804.cpp also uses a lookup function at the end of the program to search for a specific record. Note that when searching for the employee record for "Bill Gates", you don't have to pass valid information in any data members of the employee record, except the name. None of the other members of the class take part in the key inequality function.

The output from set0804.exe is:

```
find() returned: Bill Gates, 123
```

MULTISET<KEY,COMPARE>

The standard set<> container refuses to add objects with duplicate keys to the container. Even if the two objects differ in some other respect, if they have the same key values, they can't reside in the same set, period.

Obviously, there will be times when you want to store multiple objects with the same key. You don't want duplicate entries when you're a compiler writer generating a symbol table. On the other hand, you probably *do* want to handle duplicate keys if you're building a database that will contain your baseball card collection. After all, if you're lucky enough to have two copies of the 1978 Bill Gates rookie card, you want your database to be able to handle that.

Inside the multiset<>

The internal representation of multiset<> is the same as for set<>; both depend on class rb_tree to do the real work. So why are multiple insertions allowed in one class and not in another?

rb_tree has a single data member that is defined when a tree is constructed. This data member, called insert_always, controls whether the red-black tree code allows copies of existing keys to be inserted. It is initialized by a single argument to the constructor, and is never modified during the life of the red-black tree. The constructor for rb_tree in the next piece of code shows how this is done:

```
rb_tree(const Compare& comp = Compare(), bool always = true)
      : node_count(0), key_compare(comp), insert_always(always) {
   init();
}
```

All multiset<> and set<> need do to distinguish themselves is vary the *always* parameter they pass to the rb_tree constructor when they call it. The next code excerpt shows a pair of constructors that demonstrate this.

Note: The rb_tree member of set<> and multiset<> is named *t*.

```
set(const Compare& comp = Compare()) : t(comp, false) {}
multiset(const Compare& comp = Compare()) : t(comp, true) {}
```

Because of the possibility of error (an attempt to insert a duplicate key), set<> has to check for errors in the insert() function. It must return a pair<> value containing both the resulting iterator and the boolean result code.

multiset<> gets to skip this process, which means it can just return an iterator. Accordingly, the return type of the insert() function is different for set<> and multiset<>. The access, insertion, and deletion functions for the two classes are otherwise nearly identical.

When you're selecting the insertion routine you wish to use, be sure to keep track of what value it returns. multiset<> and set<> have slightly different return values, and the various versions of insert() within each class differ in their return values as well. The actual value returned will affect how you go about detecting errors.

A multiset example

Listing 8-5, mset0805.cpp, creates a multiset and adds a few entries to it. Once the multiset contains data, two different lookups are performed on data elements. The first is done with a call to lower_bound(). This function returns an iterator pointing to the first element that matches the single parameter to this function.

The second call gets two iterators that define the entire range between the first match of the key and the last match. In STL style, the first iterator points to the first match, while the last points *one past* the last match. If no entries in the multiset match the key, both iterators will be set to match end().

Listing 8-5
mset0805.cpp: Lookup functions used with multiset<>

```
//
// MSET0805.CPP
//
// This program is used in Chapter 8 to demonstrate two
// of the lookup functions used with multiset<>. The program
// creates a set containing many duplicate entries, next
// looks up a single entry, and then looks up a range of entries.
//

//
// Borland 4.x workarounds
//
#define __MINMAX_DEFINED
#pragma option -vi-

#include <iostream.h>
#include <cstring.h>

#include "multiset.h"

struct product {
    string Company;
    string Name;
    product(char *company, char *name )
        : Company( company ),
          Name( name ){}
    bool operator<( const product& a ) const {
        return Company < a.Company;
    }
};

typedef multiset< product, less<product> > Products;
typedef pair< Products::iterator, Products::iterator > ProductsRange;

main()
{
  Products p;

  p.insert( product( "Microsoft", "Visual C++" ) );
  p.insert( product( "Borland", "Borland C++" ) );
  p.insert( product( "Microsoft", "Word for Windows" ) );
```

```
p.insert( product( "Borland", "dBase" ) );
p.insert( product( "Symantec", "Norton Desktop" ) );
p.insert( product( "AT&T", "Plan 9" ) );
p.insert( product( "Microsoft", "Excel" ) );
p.insert( product( "Microsoft", "Access" ) );
cout << "Set size = " << p.size() << endl;
Products::iterator i;
i = p.lower_bound( product( "Microsoft", "" ) );
cout << "First entry matching 'Microsoft' = "
    << (*i).Company
    << ", "
    << (*i).Name
    << endl;
i = p.lower_bound( product( "Vaporware, Inc.", "" ) );
cout << "First entry matching 'Vaporware, Inc.' = ";
if ( i == p.end() )
    cout << "None" << endl;
else
    cout << (*i).Company
        << ", "
        << (*i).Name
        << endl;
ProductsRange result = p.equal_range(product("Microsoft",""));
for ( i = result.first ; i != result.second; i++ )
  cout << (*i).Company
        << ", "
        << (*i).Name
        << endl;
return 1;
}
```

There are a couple of interesting things to note about this program. The first is that, instead of defining a custom comparison operator, as in the last program, the standard STL function object less<T> is used. In theory, this ought to be simpler than creating a custom comparison class, but in practice it isn't too different. That's because, even though you get out of creating the comparison class, you still have to define operator<() for the class stored in the multiset. Without operator<(), template function object less<> can't compare the two objects.

The other point to be aware of is that pair<> objects don't have a default constructor. So you can't write code like this:

```
pair<Products::iterator,Products::iterator> result;
result = p.equal_range( test_case )
```

If you do try this, the compiler tells you it doesn't know how to construct this object.

So, how *can* you work with pair<> objects?

The answer is, you have to create a pair object with one of two constructors. You can either use the copy constructor, which the compiler has defined for pair<T1,T2>, or you can use the constructor defined in pair.h:

```
pair(const T1& a, const T2& b) : first(a), second(b) {}
```

In mset0805.cpp, the copy constructor is used. Although it looks as though the assignment operator is being used to initialize variable *result*, C++ interprets that syntax as a call to the copy constructor. Here's the output from mset0805.cpp:

```
Set size = 8
First entry matching 'Microsoft' = Microsoft, Visual C++
First entry matching 'Vaporware, Inc.' = None
Microsoft, Visual C++
Microsoft, Word for Windows
Microsoft, Excel
Microsoft, Access
```

MAP<KEY,T,COMPARE>

In theory, you could fulfill all your associative container needs by using set<> and multiset<>. But the designers of the STL wisely foresaw that the two set-based containers could be complemented by the parallel classes map<> and multimap<>. In particular, map<> provides C programmers with the powerful capabilities of associative arrays.

The basics

In the simplest format of a set<>, you simply have an ordered collection of objects. The STL doesn't tell you exactly how they're organized, only how difficult it is to look up an individual entry. Figure 8-9 is a conceptual representation of what a set might look like.

Note: Each entry consists of nothing more than a string, and the entries are sorted according to that string.

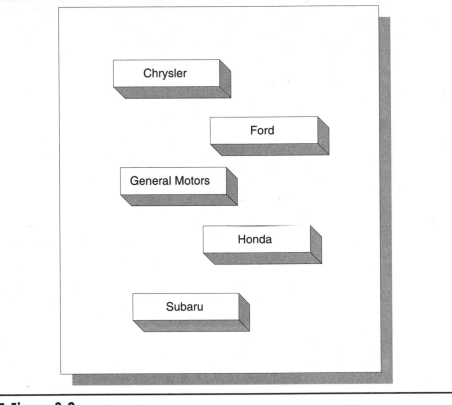

Chrysler

Ford

General Motors

Honda

Subaru

Figure 8-9
A simple set

Figure 8-10 shows the more complex method of using a set<>. In this case, the entries are larger structures, such as database entries. Only a portion of the record is being used as a key.

You can store more complex records in this manner by defining a customized comparison object that tests only the selected portion of the data structure. In the case shown in Figure 8-10, the comparison is done on a single portion of the record, or a single member of the object. The remainder of the record doesn't enter into the calculation.

Onto the map

Since you can store any sort of C++ object in a set<>, and can define your own comparison object, you are able to do anything, right? Well, that's true to some extent. Regardless of the data items you need to store, you can always come up with some way to put them into a set. You may have to define a new class to collect objects together, but even that isn't too hard.

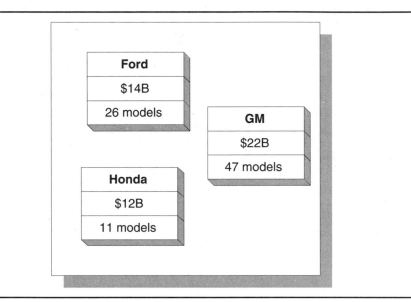

Figure 8-10
A more complex set

So why do we need map<>, a new sort of associative container? First, we'll look at what a map<> is, then we'll see the benefits you get from it.

Figure 8-11 shows the logical representation of a map<>. In the STL, a map<> container keeps its objects in order, but you don't necessarily care what sort of data structure manages that task. (One thing you *do* know is that, in the public release, it takes the form of a red-black tree.)   You can see in the structure of the map container that the key and data are handled as separate objects, with the key used as a pointer to access the data.

Map<> implementation

There are any number of ways you can represent a map data structure, and database programmers frequently develop structures like this. For instance, in dBASE, database structures hold the key values in one data structure, and pointers to the data objects in another structure. This keeps the index file much smaller than the data file, so searching and sorting is faster.

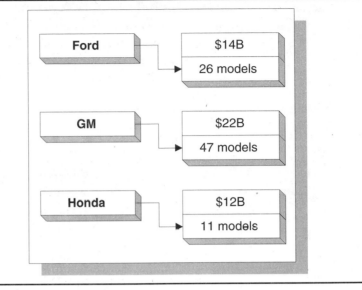

Figure 8-11
Map as stored in the red-black tree

To simplify the STL design, map<> implementation avoids this approach. Instead, it stores the data and key objects together in the red-black tree data structure used for set<> and multiset<>. It accomplishes this with the template class pair<T1,T2> introduced earlier in this chapter.

Listing 8-6 shows part of the class declaration from map.h for map<Key,T,Compare>. The definition for type rep_type is where the structure of the red-black tree is defined. The four arguments passed as type parameters to rb_tree<> are:

key_type:	The type of the key. For instance, in the example shown in Figure 8-10, the type of the key is some sort of string, since it is the name of an automobile manufacturer.
value_type:	This is the type of the values stored in the map. Note, value_type is defined to be a pair<> construct that holds a Key object and a T object together. This means a node in the tree contains both the key and the data.

select1st<value_type, key_type>:	This is the KeyOfValue comparison object type. It extracts the key value from the data stored in the red-black tree. Since the nodes in the tree defined here are a simple pair<T1,T2>, the selection function class select1st<> merely extracts the key from the pair.
key_compare:	Naturally, this is the key comparison object defined when the map<> class was instantiated.

Part of the map<> class definition is shown in Listing 8-6.

There is an important difference between this declaration and the one for set<>. The second parameter to rb_tree<> determines the type of the data object stored in the tree. In the case of set<>, the type is Key; the key itself is stored in the red-black tree. In map<>, however, value_type is defined as pair<const Key,T>. The insertion routines defined in map<> create a pair out of the key and data values and store the resulting object in the tree.

Listing 8-6
Type definitions used in map<>

```
typedef Key key_type;
typedef pair<const Key, T> value_type;
typedef Compare key_compare;

typedef rb_tree<key_type,
                value_type,
                select1st<value_type, key_type>,
                key_compare> rep_type;
rep_type t;
```

Figure 8-12 shows a conceptual view of the storage of data and key objects in map<>. Even though the two pieces of data may have no class or structural relationships, they are temporarily bound together while stored in the map<> object. The binding imposed by the pair<> template class is meaningful only in the sense that it allows you to locate a data object simply by locating the key associated with it.

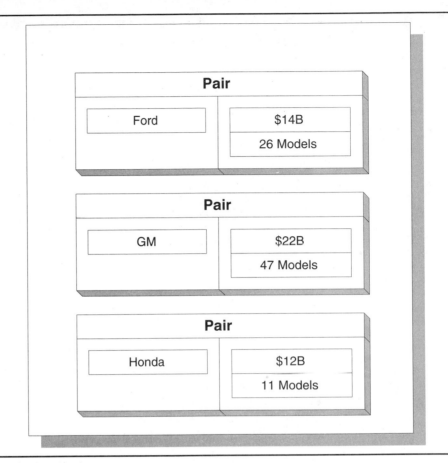

Figure 8-12
Set becomes map

Why bother?

Given that a map<> container has this neat structure, there's still the question, Why? Is this nothing more than a moderately complex set<> in sheep's clothing?

In fact, one interesting possibility is opened up by separating the key and data elements of the map<>. Because there's a one-to-one mapping between keys and data objects, it's possible to naturally define a function in this way:

```
template<class Key, class T>
T& lookup( const Key &);
```

This is nice, but not overwhelming. Things get more interesting if you rephrase the function definition to look like this:

```
T& operator[]( const Key &);
```

Now this *is* a novel idea! We can make the map<> look as if it's a big array, and use the key values as indices. This means the next piece of code is completely acceptable:

```
salary[ "Bill Clinton" ] = 2500000L;
salary[ "Al Gore" ] = 200000L;
salary[ "Newt Gingrich" ] = 130000L;
cout << "The president's salary is "
     << salary[ "Bill Clinton" ]
     << endl;
```

operator[]() considered helpful

To get an idea of the power this associative array brings to C++ programmers, look at program map0807.cpp in Listing 8-7. It reads in the entire contents of a file, word-by-word, and keeps a running count of the occurrences of each word. This is accomplished with only a dozen or so lines of code in main(). You would be hard-pressed to write the equivalent program in ANSI C in under a couple of hundred lines of code!

Listing 8-7

map0807.cpp: A program that counts words in a file

```
//
// MAP0807.CPP
//
// This program is used in Chapter 8 to demonstrate
// the use of associative containers.  In this case,
// the program scans an input file and keeps a count
// of all the strings it reads in.  Normally, you
// might want to do this with a map<string,int,...>,
// but I decided to define a special counter class.
// I get the convenience of having the counters
// initialized with a value of 0.  The first time
// I reference a string entry, it will get created
// and incremented in one operation.
//
```

```
//
// Borland 4.x workarounds
//
#define __MINMAX_DEFINED
#pragma option -vi-

#include <cstring.h>
#include <iostream.h>
#include <fstream.h>

#include "map.h"

struct counter {
    int value;
    counter() : value(0) {}
    void operator++(int){ value++; }
};

ostream& operator<<(ostream& s, counter& a )
{
    return s << a.value;
}

main()
{
    map<string,counter,less<string> > counts;
    ifstream f( "map0807.cpp" );
    string token;

    for ( ; ; ) {
        f >> token;
        if ( f )
            counts[ token ]++;
        else
            break;
    }
    map<string ,counter,less<string> >::iterator i;
    for ( i = counts.begin(); i != counts.end() ; i++ )
        cout << (*i).first
            << ", "
            << (*i).second
            << endl;
    return 1;
}
```

The line of code that takes advantage of the associative array aspect of the map<> is:

```
counts[ token ]++
```

This line looks up the counter value for a given word, then increments it. It is a deceptive piece of code that invokes a navigation of the red-black tree to find the appropriate node, selects the T portion of pair<Key,T>, then increments it.

Backstage with map<>

If you read over the previous code carefully you may see something amiss. In the input loop, I'm only too happy to increment the count for a given key, even if the key has never been seen before. But, doesn't this mean I'm starting off with a random value?

Because of the way this program has been designed, the answer is no. One characteristic of operator[]() for map<> is that it always dereferences a valid object of type T. If you invoke operator[]() for a key value that doesn't yet exist in the map<>, one is created immediately, using the default constructor. If the map in map0807.cpp had been constructed using integers as counters, I would have invoked the default constructor for an integer. Therefore, the first time I saw the word "#include" in the text, and performed this operation:

```
counts[ "#include" ]++
```

I would increment an integer constructed with the default integer constructor. This integer would have a random value. So instead, I had to go to a little trouble to use a counter that had a constructor that initialized its value to 0. This is a small price to pay for what I got in return!

The rest of map<>

Except for operator[](), map<> looks very much like set<>. The primary difference between these two containers is in the insert() functions.

Insert functions for map<> take a pair<Key,T> object as an argument. set<> and multiset<> expect a single argument of type Key. The details of these functions are discussed in Chapter 20.

MULTIMAP<KEY,T,COMPARE>

Earlier in this chapter, we made the transition from set<> to multiset<>. You may remember that the only difference between these two is that multiset<> allows duplicate copies of key entries, whereas all elements in a set<> are unique.

The distinction between map<> and multimap<> is identical. While map<> doesn't pay much attention to objects of type T inserted into the container, it *does* insist that each key value be unique; it initializes its personal red-black tree to have an insert_always member flag set to false. multimap<> constructs its red-black tree with the insert_always member set to true. Any time you insert a new value, it goes into the tree, regardless of whether or not it's a duplicate.

That sums up their differences. There are minor discrepancies in some access functions that result from this difference, but they're truly minimal. Other than that, the two classes are virtually identical.

Repercussions

Probably the biggest change in the move from map<> to multimap<> is the loss of operator[](). This function had to be thrown out due to its ambiguous position in the new multimap<> order. If operator[]() had remained defined for multimap<>, it would have been up against that ambiguity.

To see why this would be a problem, look at the multimap<> container in Figure 8-13. Clearly, if you were to use the expression cars["Checker"], you'd expect the result to be a reference to "Marathon". But what would the expression cars["Ford"] reference? It could be one of three: "Fairlane", "Pinto", or "Maverick". The syntax of the operator doesn't help us select any particular entry. For this reason, multimap does away with operator[]().

If you want to find a particular object in a multimap container, you can use the find() command. However, the ambiguity of operator[]() persists with find(), so you're better off with one of these three functions:

- iterator lower_bound(const key_type&)
- iterator upper_bound(const key_type&)
- pair<iterator,iterator> equal_range(const key_type&)

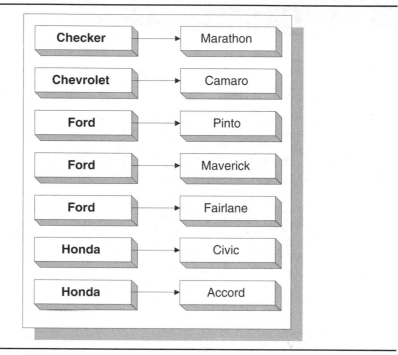

Figure 8-13

An example: multimap<string,string,less<string> >

These functions return iterators that define the range of objects that have the same key. Like all STL ranges, the upper bounds of the range are an iterator that points *one past* the last key with the specified value. For example, upper_bound("Honda") returns an iterator equal to a.end().

A multimap<> example

Listing 8-8 shows mmap0808.cpp, an example of a multimap. It's similar to map0807.cpp, which counted the frequency of each word in a text file, except this program doesn't count the occurrences of each word. Instead, it keeps track of the line number of each occurrence.

The portion of the program that records the line number of every word is straightforward. The only unusual twist is stripping all punctuation and other non-alphanumeric characters from the file. The pair<string,int> pairs are inserted into the container using the standard insert() function.

Listing 8-8

mmap0808.cpp: Another word counter

```
//
// MMAP0808.CPP
//
// This program is used in Chapter 8 to demonstrate the
// use of the multimap<> container. It does this by
// scanning this text file, and adding each appearance
// of a word to the container, along with the line
// number. After the entire contents of the file have
// been read, I go through the container and print the
// line numbers that each word appears on.
//

//
// Borland 4.x workarounds
//
#define __MINMAX_DEFINED
#pragma option -vi-

#include "multimap.h"

#include <cstring.h>
#include <iostream.h>
#include <strstream.h>
#include <fstream.h>
#include <ctype.h>
#include <cstring.h>


main()
{
    ifstream input( "mmap0808.cpp" );
    if ( !input ) {
        cerr << "Failed to open file!\n";
        return 1;
    }
    string word;
    int line;
    multimap< string, int, less<string> > words;

    for( line = 1; input ; line++ ) {
        char buf[ 129 ];
        input.getline( buf, 128 );
```

```
//
// I throw away all of the punctuation chars
// in each of the words, leaving just alphas.
//
      for ( char *p = buf ; *p != '\0'; p++ )
          if ( !isalnum( *p ) )
              *p = ' ';
      istrstream i( buf );
      while (i) {
          i >> word;
          if ( word != "" )
              words.insert( pair<const string,int>( word, line ) );
      }
  }
  input.close();
//
// This is where I print out the results. I have to
// print all the appearances of each word. The
// upper_bound() function tells me where the last
// appearance of each word will be.
//
  multimap< string, int, less<string> >::iterator j;
  multimap< string, int, less<string> >::iterator k;
  for ( j = words.begin() ; j != words.end() ; ) {
      k = words.upper_bound( (*j).first );
      cout << (*j).first << " : ";
      for ( ; j != k ; j++ )
          cout << (*j).second << " ";
      cout << endl;
  }
  return 0;
}
```

The output from this program is shown below. To format this output, a nested loop was used. The outer loop used iterator *j*, which started at lines.begin().

The test for termination of the loop is when *j* has advanced to lines.end(), past the end of the container. The inner loop advances iterator *j* from its starting position to the upper bound of the current key. The inner loop is complete at that point, and exits. The outer loop picks up again at that point, with *j* pointing to the next key in the container.

```
does : 5
each : 6 10 45 60 62
end : 66
endl : 71
```

```
entire : 8
file : 6 8 33
first : 67 68
for : 40 47 66 69
fstream : 24
function : 61
getline : 42
go : 9
h : 19 21 22 23 24 25 26
```

There isn't too much difference between multimap<> and multiset<>. Anything you can do with a multimap<> can be done with a multiset<>, without too much work. But there are times when multiset<> is more convenient. If you're lucky enough to have a key object that isn't part of your data object in class T, you'll save a few lines of code and a bit of data space by using multimap<> instead of multiset<>.

MEMORY MANAGEMENT

Memory management issues can be a little tricky for the four associative containers. If you look through the four header files, map.h, set.h, multiset.h, and multimap.h, you won't find any hints whatsoever regarding memory management. After searching for a while, you might find yourself wondering who's minding the store.

The answer is found in tree.h, the header file that defines the red-black tree structure. Not only do the four associative classes share the red-black tree container, they also use its memory allocation. Whenever a new node is inserted into the tree, it's done by red-black tree code.

The memory allocation routines that show up in tree.h are:

- add_new_buffer()
- get_node()
- put_node()

Do these names sound familiar? If not, you need to go back to Chapter 5, "The list<T> Container," and brush up on list<T>. It turns out that rb_tree has exactly the same memory management system as that defined for list<T>.

A very brief recap

Chapter 5 has an extensive discussion of the memory management system used by list<T>. Since it's identical to the system used in rb_tree<>, only its most important features are summarized here.

Associative containers must allocate space to hold objects of type value_type. For the two set containers, value_type is defined to be the same as key. For the map containers, value_type is defined as pair<Key,T>.

The memory allocation system to hold objects of value_type has the following characteristics:

- rb_tree<> doesn't allocate space for value_type objects one at a time. Instead, pages that are usually large enough to hold many objects are allocated. As necessary, individual value_type size chunks are removed from the page until it has been consumed.

- When value_type objects are destroyed, the resulting chunk of memory doesn't get returned to the block it came from. Nor is it returned to the heap, or to whatever memory management system is in use by the allocator. Instead, it gets added to a list of free blocks.

- When allocating blocks, the free list is the first choice of rb_tree<>. Chunks of memory aren't allocated from a page until the free list is empty.

- All rb_tree<> objects of the same type share a common memory pool.

- None of the memory used by a given type of rb_tree<> is returned to the heap, or to whatever memory management system the allocator is using, until every container of that type has been destroyed.

TYPE REQUIREMENTS

Both Key and T have the usual type requirements imposed by the STL. To insert and remove objects, the following functions need to be defined:

- a public copy constructor
- a public default constructor
- a public destructor
- a public assignment operator

Also, built-in types must have a destroy() function defined, for the reasons described in Chapter 4, "The vector<T> Container." If any of these functions aren't defined, you'll face the usual litany of incomprehensible compiler error messages.

Note: These functions will be generated automatically by the compiler if you fail to do so.

Generally, key objects should have operator<() defined, but this is not necessarily a requirement. Comparisons performed during insertion and search operations use the comparison object passed to the type declaration of the associative container. Naturally, the comparison object can do whatever it pleases to perform a comparison. Even so, many examples shown here use the less<> predefined comparison object, which does require operator<().

HASH TABLE CONTROVERSIES

While the STL has, in general, been well received, people have had some misgivings. The source of most confusion and irritation is the manner in which the STL was added to the ANSI C++ draft at the last minute. There are some who claim that the timing prevented adequate review of the STL, and perhaps inadequate consideration of alternatives.

Anyone who has observed the operations of standards bodies knows there is going to be a certain amount of complaining and bickering about *any* decision. The noise level surrounding the STL has, in fact, been fairly low. However, there is one complaint that seems to have struck a responsive chord among reviewers: the lack of associative containers based on hash tables.

Why hash tables?

Accessing data based on hashed keys is a mature and well-understood type of storage. In a nutshell, hashing is a way of generating an index into a storage table based on a key.

For example, if you want to store strings in a hashed table, you can create a vector<string> object with room for 256 objects. To store a given string in the table, you can XOR the first 4 bytes of the string together to create a pseudo-random address. You can then store the string at this address. The XOR function, in this case, is called the *hashing function*.

When it comes time to look up the data based on the key, you merely perform the hash function on the key, then go to the specific place in memory pointed to by the resulting index. If all is working properly, you'll immediately be able to access the data stored using the given key.

Figure 8-14 shows the result of hashing some string keys based on the 4-byte XOR algorithm. In this case, the five different strings are directed into different storage indices in a small vector. When it comes time to locate these keys in the table, it can be done easily by reapplying the hashing function.

The reason this system is so appealing is that under just the right conditions, the work needed to either store or search for a given key is constant, regardless of the size of the table.

Storing data in a red-black tree requires $O(logN)$ time, where N is the number of elements in the table. As the table grows in size, the time required to navigate the tree becomes significant. With hashing, the time required to find a key remains fixed, regardless of table size.

When it's good . . .

This system behaves really well if several things work properly. First, the hashing function has to be good at generating random addresses. In the example, this involves XORing the first four bytes of the string. In general, it means that, for a given sequence of input keys, the hashing function should generate a wide variety of keys.

Regardless of how well the hashing function works, it may generate duplicate keys from time to time. (A technique called *perfect hashing* doesn't generate any duplicates. Perfect hashing can only be used in some circumstances.) The hash container has to effectively handle these collisions. This can be done by chaining extra storage slots in a list, from the slot that was selected by the collision. It can also be handled by a secondary hashing function that attempts to generate a new address.

Even when hashing and collision management is done properly, there will still be times when the storage area fills up. When this occurs, the hashing system needs to be able to expand the storage area. And it must be able to adjust the hashing function to accommodate the new storage area.

When all these things are doing what they're supposed to be doing, you have a very fast way to access data based on keys. Just execute a simple hashing function, and you're quickly at the correct address, in constant time.

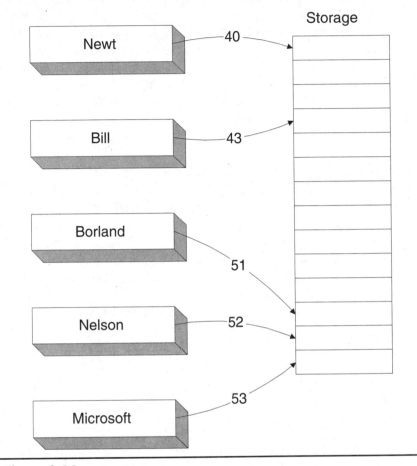

Figure 8-14
A hash table, using strings as keys

But when it's bad . . .

Most algorithms in the STL have guaranteed worst-case computation times. The overriding themes in the STL are efficiency and predictability. Hashing generally meets the criterion of efficiency, but predictability is another matter. If a stroke of bad luck occurs, and a string of keys is added which inadvertently hash to the same location, the hash table performance can lean towards O(N) instead of O(k). The only real solution to this problem is to improve the hash function. This may be difficult or impossible.

A second downside in the hash table approach is that the hashed data isn't sorted. Since hashing tends to produce pseudo-random indices, there's no effective way to iterate through the table from smallest to largest value. Even worse, there isn't any good way to iterate through the hash table at all! Since STL algorithms hinge on the ability to use an iterator to access each element in a container, this is a real problem.

A modest proposal

Despite these problems, there's some agitation in the ANSI/ISO committee to adopt hash-based containers for the STL. As this is being written, the draft standard does not include hash-based containers. Still, I think the proposal before the committee has an excellent chance of being adopted in some form. There was simply not enough time to evaluate it properly without delaying the entire standard.

The proposal would add four new associative containers to the STL:

- hash_set<>
- hash_multiset<>
- hash_map<>
- hash_multimap<>

The proposal gives some interesting solutions to a couple of the problems with hash tables. First, there needs to be a way to iterate through all members in a container, regardless of how it is stored. In the normal associative containers, this iteration is through the keys in order. However, this isn't a requirement of the containers.

As mentioned earlier, hash tables don't necessarily have a good way to perform iteration. You could conceivably modify the structure shown in Figure 8-14, so it has a usage flag of some sort. The code to increment or decrement the iterator would simply have to step over all the vacant elements in the vector until it reached one that was in use.

This approach would work, but it could be very inefficient. With a large vector that is sparsely populated, incrementing to decrementing the iterator could be a lengthy process. Instead, the current proposal stores the elements in a two-piece container. All data objects are stored in a doubly linked list.

The linked list has built-in iterators supported automatically. So that takes care of part of the problem.

The second element of the proposed hash container is a vector of pointers. This vector is the hash table you're used to seeing, with the indices into the table determined by a hashing function. But instead of an index that points directly to an object, the index yields a pointer to the object.

Figure 8-15 shows a diagram of how part of a hash_set<> might look. The container carries a little more baggage than is preferable. Even so, its proponents claim significantly faster insert, delete, and find operations over its red-black tree-based cousins.

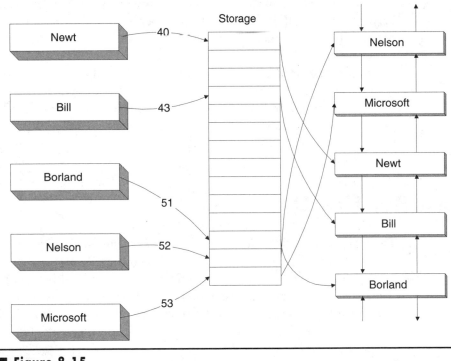

Figure 8-15
A hash_set<> example

Read the fine print

There are a couple of areas where this proposal needs to be thoroughly tested. The first concerns the built-in hashing functions that ship with the container. While the classes allow a user to supply his or her own hashing function, it's likely most people would prefer to use the default functions. These functions need analysis and testing to see how well they do under real-world conditions.

Another performance question is how well the hashed containers handle growth. Since we can't know in advance how many objects the container will need to hold, it must have the ability to grow. The simplest growth algorithm is to set a trigger point for resizing. When that trigger point is reached, a new vector is allocated with a new size. All objects are rehashed, and new pointers are created. This is a reasonable scheme, but has the disadvantage of periodically causing an insertion to be *really* slow!

Incremental growth schemes avoid this problem by spreading growth across some or all insertions, at the expense of additional complexity. As of this time, the choice of growth schemes for the STL proposal is still under debate.

If you're interested in the future of hash-based containers, you might want to check HP's distribution site for the STL (butler.hpl.hp.com, in directory /stl). Some sample code and a document have been posted. Together, they should provide you with enough information to begin experimenting with this new type of container.

Last But Not Least

The STL's associative containers provide exciting new capabilities for C++ programmers. These classes represent a considerable amount of careful work, and are well-designed and efficient. I think you'll find that associative containers do a very creditable job of simplifying many of your programming problems. But since this is a brand-new feature of C++, the hardest part might be training yourself to even recognize problems that could be solved with these containers!

ALLOCATORS

The palest ink is better than the best memory.

— Chinese proverb

The creators of the STL wanted to be sure their containers were flexible enough to support multiple memory architectures. After many design iterations, the concept of an *Allocator class* was created, and it now provides the fundamental underpinnings of memory management for the STL.

    This chapter describes exactly what a memory allocator is and how it interfaces with the various containers in the STL. It looks at several of the allocators in the current release of the STL. For detailed specifications on allocator member functions, see Chapter 21.

A BIT OF HISTORY

One of the big incentives for the creation of allocators was mixed model programming on the IBM PC; with that fact in mind, this part of the chapter will give you the background scoop on how allocators came to be.

By the way: Do you feel pretty comfortable with memory models and pointer modifiers? Feel free to skip over the next few sections; you can always come back to them later if needed. But don't think you can skip this entire chapter just because you aren't writing 16-bit programs for the IBM PC. Allocators offer a lot more than just memory-model support!

Back in the Dark Ages of C, the topic of memory models never came up. UNIX systems were the predominant platforms for program development. On these systems, a pointer was a pointer, and that was accepted as a fact of life. Usually, a pointer had a 16-, 24-, or 32-bit value that could point anywhere in main memory. You could perform ordinary math on a pointer by adding or subtracting from it. And if two pointers weren't equal, you could be confident they didn't point to the same location in memory.

This was a nice, orderly world, but it didn't last. Everything we knew about memory and pointers flew out the door when the IBM PC entered the picture.

Enter the PC

When IBM was designing the PC, they selected a microprocessor that was considered something of a dark horse: Intel's 8088. To say that some people consider this machine to have an inelegant architecture would be a drastic understatement. In particular, folks who were working on contemporary UNIX systems had nothing but scorn for the 8088 design. It seemed like a clumsy hybrid of 8-bit and 16-bit architectures that wasn't at home in either camp.

At least in the eyes of the programming public, the major problem with the 8088 was its segmented memory architecture. The 8088 could access about 1 megabyte of memory. But instead of allowing programmers to access this memory with 20-bit pointers, Intel adopted a system that used pointers made up of 16-bit segment registers combined with 16-bit offsets. A memory location was found using the following formula:

```
Physical Address = ( Segment  * 16 ) + Offset
```

Among other things, this system of calculating addresses meant it was now possible to have two different pointers referencing the same location in memory. For example, in Table 9-1, pointer 0x4000:0x0010 and pointer 0x4001:0x0000 address the same location in memory!

Table 9-1

Intel pointer math

Pointer		
Segment	Offset	Physical address
0x4000	0x0010	0x40010
0x4001	0x0000	0x40010

Early compiler writers for the IBM PC had no choice but to deal with these strange new pointers. One of the changes they made to C compiler technology was to support something called a *memory model*.

On the PC, there were four standard memory models: small, compact, medium, and large. These models are based on the concept of 16-bit (near) pointers and 32-bit, or 16:16-bit (far) pointers. Since a program using near data pointers only manipulates data addresses within a single, fixed 64K segment, the segment portion of all pointers is the same. A program using far data pointers can modify the segment portion of addresses as well as the offset portion, which is why it is referred to as a 16:16-bit pointer.

Table 9-2 shows the names of the memory models that were based on the four permutations of these pointer types.

Table 9-2

The four most commonly used memory models

	16-bit code pointers	16:16-bit code pointers
16-bit data pointers	Small model	Medium model
16:16-bit data pointers	Compact model	Large model

One additional model not shown here is the *tiny* model. The tiny model is a subset of small model in which the code, stack, and data segments are all the same. So where a small model program can access 64K each of data, code and stack, a tiny model program can only access 64K of code, data, and stack *combined*.

When using a C or C++ compiler to write 16-bit, real-mode 80x86 programs, you can ordinarily compile for one of these four memory models. If you select 16-bit pointers, all your code or data will reside in a single 64K segment. Your 16-bit pointer will simply provide an index into this segment.

16:16-bit pointers can point to any location in physical memory. However, the size of that object is still generally restricted to the same 64K size, since pointer math usually only affects the offset portion of the segment/offset pair.

The decision to support these four memory models had all sorts of ramifications for MS-DOS and Windows programmers. Among them:

- code and data pointers might not be the same size
- structures that contain pointers changed size when compiled with a new memory model
- the amount of memory or code a program could access would change radically when compiled with a different model

In the early 80s, when the first PC programs were being created, small model programs were the norm. Today, fewer and fewer small model programs are being developed. The amount of code needed to support sophisticated user interfaces has grown to the point that even simple programs are usually written in the large memory model.

MIXED MODEL PROGRAMMING

One of the nice things about the small model is that it's slightly faster and more efficient than any of the other programming models. Since pointers and function calls can all be done using 16-bit instead of 16:16-bit operations, the program runs faster and uses less memory.

The speed of the small model is a disadvantage, however. A pure small model program has to restrict its total code size to 64K, and is restricted to a total of 64K for heap, stack, and static data storage. And even small programs may need to access larger data objects, or link into large code libraries.

To get around these problems, the concept of *mixed model* programming was created. A mixed model program is a program that uses pointers of a different size than the prevailing memory model. For example, programmers using the small memory model may still need to use 16:16 pointers to access specific locations in memory, or to link to a library built using large model.

All mixed up

The way mixed model programs accomplish their work is through the use of the __near and __far keywords. For example, in a small model program, both code and data pointers are normally 16-bit values. A small model program may have a family of data structures that collectively add up to greater than 64K. The program can get around the limitations of small model programs by declaring these structures to be __far and allocating them from the far heap.

Listing 9-1 shows an example of a program that does just that. mix00901.cpp is a small model program that creates some arrays in far memory through the use of the __far keyword. The far pointers are stored in array tables, and are created using the __far keyword in conjunction with operator new.

Listing 9-1

mix0901.cpp: A mixed model program

```
//
// MIX0901.CPP
//
// This program is used in Chapter 9 to give a quick
// demonstration of mixed model programming. You can
// compile this as a small model program that still is
// able to allocate over 300K bytes of data in far
// memory.
//
// This program only works with 16-bit PC compilers!
//

#include <iostream.h>
#include <alloc.h>

int _far *tables[ 10 ];

main()
{
//
// Any allocation failures will show up
// as 0000:0000 pointers in the printout.
//
    int i;
    for ( i = 0; i < 10 ; i++ )
        tables[ i ] = new far int[ 16000 ];
    for ( i = 0 ; i < 10 ; i++ )
        cout << i
             << ": "
             << hex
             << (long) tables[ i ]
```

```
            << dec
            << endl;
  for ( i = 0; i < 10 ; i++ )
     if ( tables[ i ] )
        delete tables[ i ];
  return 1;
}
```

C++ programmers can allocate near or far pointers using model-specific modifiers to operator new. C programmers can accomplish the same through specialized calls to functions such as faralloc(). In both cases, these represent non-standard language extensions that seem to be universally supported.

In addition to near and far data pointers, programmers can declare static data, functions, member functions, and classes to be __near or __far. For example, when programming for 16-bit Microsoft Windows targets, routines in DLLs are always declared as __far functions. This means that, even when a small model program calls a DLL function, it generates a far function call. This is necessary, since the DLL will always have its own code segment.

A huge success

In addition to the __near and __far pointer types, some real-mode 80x86 compilers support __huge pointers. Various compiler vendors introduced __huge pointers as a method of allocating and accessing objects greater than 64K. Just as with __near and __far pointers, now you could declare a pointer to be a __huge pointer, using syntax like this:

```
char __huge *dictionary;
```

The most important thing about a huge pointer is that it isn't limited to accessing a single 64K block of memory, unlike a far pointer. The compiler generates code that allows this to work properly, usually by *normalizing* the pointer. A normalized pointer is a 32-bit quantity that contains the physical address of a given object.

Normalized addresses have good points and bad points. The worst problem with a normalized pointer is that dereferencing it requires the compiler to generate additional code to create a segment/offset pair. On the plus side, normalized pointers can safely be compared to one another, something that isn't possible with conventional far pointers.

Huge pointers had yet another incarnation under Microsoft Windows. The Windows memory management code can supply huge memory objects under Win16, using functions such as GlobalAlloc().

Remember that these memory models only matter to people writing 16-bit programs for Windows or DOS. Memory models under Windows 95, Windows NT, OS/2 Warp, and most UNIX platforms are a much simpler matter. These systems use linear addressing, where a single pointer type can access all memory. On the IBM PC, this type of addressing is supported in *Flat Model*, which uses simple 32-bit pointers. This is the standard model for Windows NT, Win32s, and Windows 95.

And what does it spell?

All these strange ways of managing and using memory on PCs add up to a witch's brew of esoterica, collectively referred to as memory models. The whole concept of memory models is a source of endless confusion for both novice and experienced programmers. And, in particular, standards groups such as ANSI and the ISO have left this pocket of programming alone, considering it to be an implementation issue. Unfortunately, this ignores the very real needs of millions of PC programmers.

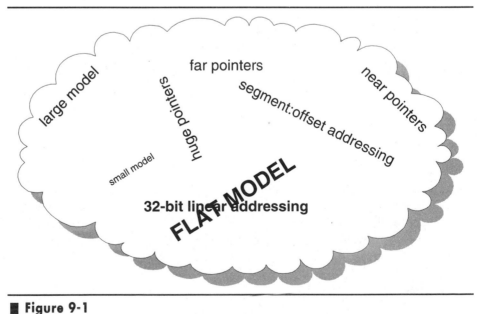

Figure 9-1
The scrambled state-of-the-art in PC memory models

THE STL UNDERSTANDS

Memory models were very much on the minds of STL designers. They knew that for a Container class to be useful, it *had* to work with this rat's nest of allocation and management systems. The question was: How to do it?

One of the first approaches to the problem was the idea that additional parameters could be added to the container template parameter lists. For example, our old friend vector<T> might end up looking like this:

```
template<class T, class Alloc, class Free, class Ptr >
vector {
```

In fact, the early designs of the STL went through several iterations experimenting with lengthy constructs like this. The rationale behind extended argument lists was that, by using default template arguments, the end user would be spared from entering these arguments in the default case. A slightly different version of the previous definition, using default template arguments, could be:

```
template<class T,
         template<class U> class Alloc = DefaultAllocator,
         template<class U> class Free = DefaultFree,
         class Ptr = T *>
class vector {
```

Admittedly, such a class definition wouldn't be too difficult for most users of vector<T>. (At least, it won't be too difficult when most C++ compilers properly support default template arguments! As this is being written, this support is promised by many, but delivered by none.) A user could create a vector<> class simply by leaving off all template arguments with defaults:

```
main()
{
    vector<foo> a;
```

This declaration indicates that you want to create a vector object that uses all default memory classes. You don't have to go to any extra work to do this. But if you want to start using __far pointers to hold all objects in the vector<>, you'll be faced with writing a horrendous declaration:

```
main()
{
    vector<foo, FarAllocator<foo>, FarFree<foo>, foo _far *> a;
```

This isn't likely to please too many users of this template class!

A better way

Nobody seemed to be satisfied with stringing together long lists of default arguments to support various memory models. The end result of much struggle was the development of the Allocator *class*. You still have to rely on default template arguments to select the appropriate memory management code, but now that involves the selection of a single class, instead of a series of functions and types:

```
template<class T, template<class U> class Alloc = allocator >
class vector {
```

In this definition, Allocator<T> encapsulates everything you need to know about the current memory model. This includes things like:

- the actual type of a pointer to class T, e.g., T __far *
- the type of a reference to an object of class T
- the function used to allocate raw memory
- the function used to free that same memory

The Allocator object is a reference data member of the Container class; a single copy of it is instantiated for each object created. That object is then called to provide various memory-related services.

The Allocator not only provides traditional C++ type functions, such as creating and destroying memory, but also parameterized type functions—for example, returning the pointer type used by objects in the vector. The actual interface the Allocator class provides is discussed in detail in the API section of this chapter, which follows shortly.

So How Do I Use It?

When writing programs that use the STL, you probably won't have any reason to use the member functions of an Allocator class. The primary place you'll be using allocators is as type arguments to container declarations. The allocators will show up in lines of code looking like this:

```
vector< foo, far_allocator > x;
list< int, near_allocator > y( 10 );
list< students > z;
```

It's also important to note that some of today's compilers won't be able to support the use of allocators in exactly this manner. Compiler vendors are working hard to bring their products into compliance with the ANSI/ISO draft, but much work remains to be done. The workarounds are discussed later in this chapter.

See right through it: Using far memory

Probably one of the most common reasons for wanting to specify an Allocator class as a template argument is to place an object in far memory. As discussed earlier in this chapter, you can combine the efficiency of a small model program while using far pointers to access objects outside the default 64K range.

The only thing you need to know to accomplish this is the name of your far memory allocator. This is a vendor-defined implementation issue, not part of the C++ specification, so you may have to consult with your vendor to find the correct class name. HP's public release of the STL uses the names *far_allocator* and *near_allocator* for the two PC-specific memory model allocators.

Given HP's naming scheme, it's simple to create a vector in far memory when building a small model program:

```
main()
{
    vector<int, far_allocator> vfi;
```

In this code fragment, vfi will now use far memory for storage, and far pointers for access of vector elements. All of this is transparent to you, and transparent to other STL components. For example, you could easily create a second vector in near memory (using the default allocator), then copy one to the other without any special treatment:

```
vector<int> vni(100);  //Using default small memory model
copy( vfi.begin(), vfi.end(), vni.begin() );
```

This sort of transparency to the memory model is one of the most powerful features of the STL. If you've ever had to grapple with the _far and _near keywords, you'll know just what an improvement this is.

Remember, in a fully compliant C++ compiler, there are no restrictions on your use of allocators. You can mix and match them at will among various containers. The compiler is able to distinguish list<int,near_allocator>

and list<int,far_allocator> because the two are completely different types, as created by the template mechanism. Not only can it distinguish them, but it can use them side-by-side in the same program.

One last wrinkle

The ANSI/ISO committee made one seemingly minor change to the STL specification before incorporating it into the draft. Under the original STL as submitted, each instantiated template class had a single static allocator that was used by all objects of that class. The committee modified the class definitions so that each *object* of a given class has its own allocator. This means all container constructors now have an additional allocator argument. The argument has a default value, which means you don't have to specify it. For example, two of the vector<T> constructors have the following prototypes:

```
vector( Allocator& = Allocator() );
vector( InputIterator first,
        InputIterator last,
        Allocator& = Allocator() );
```

You can see that you never have to specify an allocator, if you take the default value at all times. So when do you want to provide a specific allocator object for a container? The ANSI/ISO committee was persuaded that specific instances of allocators would be useful in applications such as object-oriented databases. In such cases, you would use a custom allocator provided by a third-party vendor.

ALLOCATOR API

Allocators are a helper class in the STL; they're used for all memory allocation and deallocation by the Container classes. You won't necessarily use an Allocator class yourself, but should you decide to, you'll find the class interface familiar. Although Allocator classes provide a completely different set of services than Container classes, they use canonical STL methods to provide those services.

The API of an Allocator class is provided via three different mechanisms:

- type definitions local to the Allocator class
- member functions of the Allocator class
- global template functions

Remember, the Container class has access to the *type* of the allocator by way of the template parameters passed when the Container class is defined.

In addition to the type of the allocator, all Container classes create an *instance* of the allocator. This gives them access to the member functions of the class. It usually looks like the code shown in Listing 9-2.

Listing 9-2

Typical use of the allocator by a container

```
template< class T, template<class U> class Alloc = allocator >
class container {
    public :
        typedef Alloc<T> container_allocator;
        .
        .

        .
    protected :
        Alloc<T> &allocator;

        .
        .
        .
};
```

In Listing 9-2, a Container class creates a reference to the parameterized allocator. It can be difficult to read a listing like this because of the naming conventions. The STL freely defines new types, along with functions and members, and there are no conventions for how to tell them apart. In this case, allocator is a member of the Container class, and container_allocator is a typedef.

The reference to an instance of the allocator is defined when each container is constructed. That particular allocator then provides all the memory services needed by that particular container.

Heap o' typedefs

```
typedef T value_type;
typedef T* pointer;
typedef const T* const_pointer;
typedef T& reference;
typedef const T& const_reference;
typedef size_t size_type;
typedef ptrdiff_t difference_type;
```

One requirement for an Allocator class is that it include the typedefs shown above. These samples are the definitions from the default allocator, so they're quite generic. For the most part, these type definitions are immediately recycled into a new batch of type definitions used by the container.

For example, the next piece of code is extracted from map.h. It demonstrates how allocator type definitions are used to create the definitions employed by map.h:

```
typedef Allocator<T>::pointer pointer;
typedef Allocator<T>::reference reference;
typedef Allocator<T>::const_reference const_reference;
typedef Allocator<T>::size_type size_type;
typedef Allocator<T>::difference_type difference_type;
```

It may seem that the STL has created an unnecessarily complex hierarchy of definitions, but there is a good reason for doing things this way. Imagine you want to create a vector<T> full of integers, and you want them to reside in the far heap, even though you're creating a small model program. To do this, you would ordinarily declare the vector like this:

```
vector<int,faralloc> a;
```

In the far allocator, the definition of a pointer is as follows:

```
typedef T __far * pointer;
```

This makes sense, since the allocator always works with far memory objects. In the next step, this pointer declaration gets copied down to vector<T>, using another type definition line:

```
typedef Allocator<T>::pointer iterator;
```

This line of code in vector.h says that a vector<T> iterator is going to be a pointer, using the pointer definition the allocator has decided on. When an iterator is used in a program like this:

```
vector<int,faralloc>::iterator i;
for ( i = a.begin(); i != a.end() ; i++ )
    cout << *i << endl;
```

you are actually writing the equivalent of this:

```
int __far *i;
for ( i = a.begin(); i != a.end() ; i++ )
    cout << *i << endl;
```

This means your code will dereference a far pointer instead of a near pointer, even though you're running in small model. All this, because of the type definition found in the declaration of the far allocator.

It's important to note in the code above that the iterator type definition is being done at compile time. The code created by the compiler should be just as efficient as the hand-coded version shown immediately above.

But wait — there's more!

The implications of this methodology go far beyond the ability to create mixed model programs easily. The allocator mechanism shown here allows you to use *anything* that obeys pointer semantics as a pointer in your container. So, if you think you can define a class that provides pointer-like access to a database file, extended memory, or semaphore-protected shared memory, you can use it as the basis for an STL allocator.

Member functions

```
pointer allocate( size_type n );
void deallocate( pointer p );
pointer address( reference x );
const_pointer const_address( const_reference x );
size_type init_page_size();
size_type max_size() const;
```

This list shows the required member functions for an allocator. The first two, allocate() and deallocate(), allocate and free memory that can hold objects of type T. The address() and const_address() are functions that convert a reference to an address. reference is a type defined in the typedef declarations for allocators. The remaining two functions provide information about the memory model in use. The next code excerpt gives an example of how these functions are called by the container code.

add_new_buffer() is a function from the rb_tree class. rb_tree allocates blocks of space in one fell swoop, adding them to a buffer list. It needs to allocate a big block of memory to create a buffer, and a small block of memory to contain the list item pointing to the buffer.

```
void add_new_buffer() {
    buffer_pointer tmp = buffer_allocator.allocate((size_type)1);
    tmp->buffer = rb_tree_node_allocator.allocate(buffer_size());
```

To handle these different types of allocation, rb_tree creates two different static allocator member objects. buffer_allocator is the static object used to create and destroy the buffers. rb_tree_node_allocator creates the link elements used to keep the list of buffers.

Because of the way allocators are created, classes such as rb_tree have to create a unique type of allocator for every type of object they store. This means that each Allocator class is parameterized by a type T that specifies the sort of objects it needs to work with. They aren't general-purpose objects that create random-sized blocks, as calloc() or malloc() do.

Global functions

```
template <class T1, class T2>
void construct(T1* p, const T2& value);

template <class T>
void destroy(T* pointer);
```

In addition to its member functions and typedefs, each allocator must define a pair of template functions that create and destroy objects. Both functions are parameterized according to the pointer type. construct() is also parameterized according to the type of object being constructed. (Chapter 4, "The vector<T> Container," demonstrates how construct() and destroy() are used to disconnect the two processes of memory allocation and object creation.)

Container classes use the allocate() function to allocate raw memory of a specific type (near, far, etc.), then construct new objects using construct(). The objects are destroyed with destroy(), and the memory is freed with deallocate().

Normally, construct() and destroy() simply call new with the placement syntax and the explicit destructor for their particular objects. This seems easy enough to handle with a single function template that could be used with *every* allocator. The next section shows you why this isn't possible.

Each allocator needs its own construct()

The default allocator has a nice, simple construct() function. It looks as though it ought to work properly with every memory model, not just the default:

```
template <class T1, class T2>
inline void construct(T1* p, const T2& value) {
    new (p) T1(value);
}
```

Why can't *every* allocator just use the template version of construct() when it needs to construct objects? It looks possible, but in fact, the compiler won't do it. The reason is simply a matter of type conflicts.

For example, if the construct() template function shown above were being used in a small model MS-DOS program, you could call it like this without any problem:

```
int x;
construct( &x, 15 );
```

The compiler would then create an instance of construct() using int as T1 and T2. In the same program, you could try this function call:

```
_far int y;
construct( &y, 16 );
```

In this case, the compiler would have to generate an error. This is because the first argument to construct() is "T *p", but we are trying to pass "int _far *". There is no way the compiler can safely make a near pointer out of a far pointer, so an error message results.

Listing 9-3 demonstrates this problem using a short program that compiles, links, and runs properly when compiled using the large memory model.

Listing 9-3

test0903.cpp: Demonstration of a template problem

```
//
// TEST0903.CPP
//
// This program demonstrates the problem with using
// templates to handle new pointer types, such as
// __far or __huge pointers.  The program below
// compiles properly under large model, but generates
// an error when compiled in small model.  The compiler
// won't generalize a template function for "T *" to
// include "T _far *".
//
// Note that this program is designed for 16-bit segmented
// memory models.
//

#include <iostream.h>

template<class T>
void dump( T *p )
{
    cout << "Value to dump = "
         << *p
         << endl;
}

main()
{
    char *letter = "a";
    int num = 1;
    int *number = &num;
    int __far *farnumber = &num;

    dump( letter );
    dump( number );
    dump( farnumber );
    return 1;
}
```

When you try to compile the program using the small model, the compiler generates the following error messages:

```
Borland C++ 4.5 Copyright (c) 1987, 1994 Borland International
test0903.cpp:
Error test0903.cpp 32:
Could not find a match for 'dump(int far*)' in function main()
Warning test0903.cpp 34:
'farnumber' is assigned a value that is never used in function main()
*** 1 errors in Compile ***
```

So what does all of this mean? It means that an allocator designed to use far pointers needs to define its own specialized versions of construct() and destroy(). For example, this construct() function works for a far allocator in a small model program:

```
template <class T1, class T2>
inline void construct(T1 __far * p, const T2& value) {
    new (p) T1(value);
}
```

The only difference between this version of construct() and the default version is the addition of the __far keyword in the pointer specification in the argument list. But since that's enough to convince the compiler that a new version is needed, that's what each allocator has to do.

IMPLEMENTATION KLUDGES

Current shortcomings in C++ compilers have led to a couple of not-so-pretty workarounds in today's releases of the STL. These problems should be of a temporary nature, but don't expect them to be fixed soon. Compiler vendors will have to work on bringing their C++ implementations up to the ANSI/ISO standard, which is still in a state of flux. This will involve a fair amount of work. So, in the meantime, you'll have to make do with the products that are shipping today.

No default template arguments

One feature of the Allocator classes is that they are invisible to the casual user of the STL. Say you're creating a new type of container, regardless of whether it's a vector<T>, map<T>, or something of your own devising. You should be able to define it without making any mention of the Allocator class.

The prototype defined in the specification for the list class is:

```
template< class T, template<class U> Alloc = allocator >
class list {
```

This prototype indicates a couple of things about the Allocator class list<T> is going to use. First, it says that the allocator is a template class parameterized on a single type. Second, it tells you that, if the user doesn't specify an Allocator class, the default value of allocator will be selected. This means any of these three declarations are valid:

```
list<foo> a;
list<foo, allocator> b;
list<foo, far_allocator> c;
```

The first two declarations are different, but should cause the same type of object to be generated. Since I didn't supply a second argument to the type specification, *a* (in list<foo> a;) uses the default value of allocator as its Allocator class. The second declaration shown above selects allocator explicitly, which amounts to the same thing.

The third declaration explicitly asks for the far_allocator, a class supplied with the current release of the STL. This creates a list<T> that uses far pointers, along with the far versions of new and delete, to allocate and release memory.

Trouble in paradise

This system seems easy to use, but there's a problem: the current generation of C++ compilers doesn't support default template arguments that are templates themselves. So the entire scheme defined in the specification is unworkable.

The fix in the current release is fairly easy to swallow. Instead of using the compiler to define the allocator, it uses the preprocessor. The first few lines of the class definition for vector<T> in vector.h are:

```
template <class T>
class vector {
public:
    typedef Allocator<T> vector_allocator;
    typedef T value_type;
```

Right off the bat, you can see that there isn't any allocator defined in the template parameter list. Instead, the class definition jumps right in and starts using Allocator as if it were a valid argument. And, in fact, it *is* valid, due to a definition found a few lines earlier in the header file:

```
#ifndef Allocator
#define Allocator allocator
#include <defalloc.h>
#endif
```

This piece of preprocessor magic is found at the start of each header file that defines a Container class. It substitutes the macro definition of Allocator for the template argument passed to the Container class. Since, presumably, you haven't defined the macro Allocator yourself, it will default to allocator— the name of the default allocator.

Given this system, what must you do to use a different allocator? Looking at the preprocessor code shown above, the answer is simple:

1. Define Allocator to be equal to the name of the allocator you want to use.

2. Then include the header file which defines that allocator.

3. Lastly, include the header file that defines the Container class you want to use.

That container will then use the allocator you selected with the definition of Allocator.

An example of how this works is shown in Listing 9-4. This program includes hugalloc.h, which defines the huge Allocator class. It then defines Allocator to be huge_allocator, which is the name of the class just included. Finally, it includes vector.h, which binds the allocator to the vector<T> class definition.

Listing 9-4

huge0904.cpp: Demonstration of a template problem

```
//
// HUGE0904.CPP
//
// This program is used in Chapter 9 to demonstrate
// the steps you need to take to use a non-default
// allocator class for a given container.
//
// This program defines Allocator to be huge_allocator
// *before* including vector.h.  This means that vector.h
```

```
// will use the huge allocator instead of the default
// allocator.  vector.h automatically undefines Allocator,
// which means the next include of list.h will use the
// default allocator.
//

//
// Borland 4.x workarounds
//
#define __MINMAX_DEFINED
#pragma option -vi-

#include <iostream.h>

#include <hugalloc.h>
#define Allocator huge_allocator
#include <vector.h>

#include <list.h>

main()
{
    vector<int> a;
    cout << "a.max_size() = "
         << a.max_size()
         << endl;

    list<int> b;
    cout << "b.max_size() = "
         << b.max_size()
         << endl;
    return 1;
}
```

The output from huge0904.cpp is shown below. Clearly, a.max_size()
indicates that *a* was created using a huge pointer type, since its address
space can accommodate up to 2 billion integers. *b* was created using a standard allocator, which has a limit of 64K per object. Because of this, it only
has room for about 10K list nodes.

```
a.max_size() = 2147483647
b.max_size() = 10922
```

One additional point to note is that all Container classes undefine
Allocator at the end of their header files. Any subsequent Container class
include statements will revert to the default allocator. This is shown in
huge0904.cpp, which includes list.h immediately after vector.h.

So the only way you can reliably use an allocator other than the default is to define the Allocator macro immediately before including the appropriate header file. You may end up with code that looks like this:

```
#define Allocator near_allocator
#include <vector.h>

#define Allocator far_allocator
#include <map.h>

#define Allocator huge_allocator
#include <set.h>
```

Remember, this may seem awkward, but it's only a temporary situation. As compiler vendors bring their products up to specifications, this workaround will disappear. And yes, there is a disappointing limitation inherent in this workaround. You're limited to using the same allocator for *every* container of a given type you create in a given module.

Caveat emptor

Using the preprocessor in this fashion is no more difficult than using default template arguments. You only have to type a couple of extra characters to get the same results. But there's one big problem.

The binding of the Container class to the allocator takes place when the container header file is included and the class definition is read in. When this is taking place, all lines with Allocator<T> in them are expanded to the appropriate allocator name.

But, like most header files in C++, the Container class definition files are designed to be read in only once. To accomplish this, they use wrapper code at the start of the header file, usually along these lines:

```
#ifndef VECTOR_H
#define VECTOR_H
    .
    .
    .
    body of header file
    .
    .
    .
#endif
```

Since you're effectively limited to reading in a container header file just once, you're also limited to binding just one allocator to the container. Therefore, you can't create a vector<T> that uses the default allocator, then create another that uses the far allocator.

Hopefully, this limitation won't cause too much trouble. In some situations, you can get around it by using different include/define sequences in different source modules. However, this won't help in cases where you need both types of container in a single source file. For that, you'll have to wait for the ANSI-conforming release of your favorite compiler.

Destroy problems

As you saw earlier in this chapter, each type of allocator defines a destroy() template function. destroy() destroys an object without deleting the memory in use for that object. It does this through an explicit call to the destructor. This is how the default allocator defines a version of destroy():

```
template <class T>
inline void destroy(T* pointer) {
    pointer->~T();
}
```

The call to the destructor is slightly out of the ordinary, but is perfectly legal C++. Nonetheless, some C++ compilers have a problem with a call to an explicit destructor for a built-in type. For example, if a container held integers, it would make calls to destroy() with pointers to integers. When this is the case, the explicit call to the destructor is supposed to do nothing.

To help work around this problem with non-conforming compilers, the present version of the STL defines a whole batch of specialized versions of destroy() for a host of built-in types. These specialized versions don't make the explicit call to the destructor. In fact, they don't do anything at all. Listing 9-5 shows the versions defined for the default allocator.

Listing 9-5
destroy() specializations in the default allocator

```
inline void destroy(char*) {}
inline void destroy(unsigned char*) {}
inline void destroy(short*) {}
inline void destroy(unsigned short*) {}
inline void destroy(int*) {}
```

```
inline void destroy(unsigned int*) {}
inline void destroy(long*) {}
inline void destroy(unsigned long*) {}
inline void destroy(float*) {}
inline void destroy(double*) {}
inline void destroy(char**) {}
inline void destroy(unsigned char**) {}
inline void destroy(short**) {}
inline void destroy(unsigned short**) {}
inline void destroy(int**) {}
inline void destroy(unsigned int**) {}
inline void destroy(long**) {}
inline void destroy(unsigned long**) {}
inline void destroy(float**) {}
inline void destroy(double**) {}
```

This is a pretty comprehensive list of specializations, but it isn't complete. By definition, you'll be able to create built-in types that aren't in this list, since you can always define a pointer to a user-defined type. The result is that, if you define a container that holds a pointer to a type you have defined, it may be necessary to create a destroy() function to accompany it:

```
void destroy( foo ** ){}

main()
{
    vector< foo * > a;
```

This is another problem that will go away as compilers conform more to the ANSI standard.

MORE THAN MEETS THE EYE

Allocators don't get nearly as much attention in this book as their flashy coworkers, containers and algorithms. But they *are* a vital component of the STL, and are a worthy innovation in their own right. Besides providing a workable framework for supporting today's multiple memory model environments, they hold great promise for future developments, including parallel processing and object-oriented databases. Keep on eye on allocators as C++ matures, and you can expect to see some interesting developments.

ITERATORS

vaporware: A new computer-related product that has been widely advertised but is not yet available.
> — From a list of new words in English, Merriam-Webster's
> Collegiate Dictionary, Tenth Edition

THE HEART OF THE STL

While it may not be immediately obvious, iterators are one of the most important pieces of new technology the STL has introduced to ANSI C++.

When looking at the STL, it's easy to concentrate on the different container types, so much so that it's often referred to as a Container class library. But in reality, the STL is composed of many parts, and each of them is critical to the overall success of the library. Iterators are every bit as important as containers, allocators, and algorithms. They deserve equal billing on the STL marquee.

In this chapter, you'll see what iterators are, how they're categorized, and how they work. You may have already used conventional iterators when working with the STL Container classes. In this chapter you'll work with additional types of iterators, including *stream iterators, reverse iterators, insertion iterators,* and *raw storage iterators:*

- Stream iterators let you transparently redirect STL algorithms to input or output files.

- Reverse iterators make it easy to reverse the direction an algorithm iterates through a container.

- Insertion iterators let algorithms add new elements to a container, instead of overwriting existing elements.

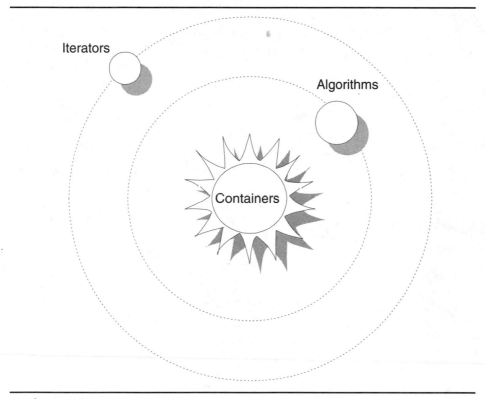

Figure 10-1
The container-centric view of the STL—popular but misleading

Once you've had a chance to see these iterators at work, you should view the STL universe as being more like Figure 10-2 than the container-biased view of Figure 10-1.

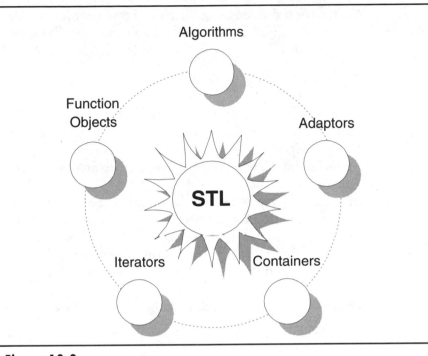

Algorithms

Function
Objects

Adaptors

STL

Iterators

Containers

■ **Figure 10-2**
A more accurate view of the STL

SEE ITERATOR, READ POINTER

The STL specification defines iterators this way:

> *"Iterators are a generalization of pointers that allow a programmer to work with different data structures (containers) in a uniform manner."*

The key point to absorb is that iterators fulfill the same role in your programs as pointers do. They have their differences, but are close enough for you to use the concept of "pointer" as a convenient mental hook to hang iterators on.

Like pointers, iterators are defined in terms of what they point to. In C and C++, a pointer p to an object of type T is defined like this:

```
T *p;
```

An iterator is defined using the type of container it's working with, so the syntax is a little different. If iterator *i* is going to point to elements in a container that holds objects of type T, the declaration will be something like this:

```
container<T,...>::iterator i;
```

For both of these declarations, dereferencing the pointer/iterator using operator*() yields a reference to an object of type T. When using traditional pointers, we expect a pointer to point to an address in memory. Dereferencing the pointer returns a reference to an object stored at that memory location.

Dereferencing an iterator is a little more opaque. We don't know exactly what sort of data structure an iterator represents, and operator*() can be anything a programmer cares to dream up. Regardless of this, we do know that operator*() returns a reference to an object of type T. In addition, for a container to be useful, it needs to return a reference in a relatively efficient manner.

The most trivial example of how this works is shown in the container definition for vector<T>:

```
template <class T>
class vector {
public:
    typedef Allocator<T> vector_allocator;
    typedef T value_type;
    typedef vector_allocator::pointer iterator;
    typedef vector_allocator::const_pointer const_iterator;
```

A class of type vector<T> depends on its Allocator class to define a pointer. When using the default allocator, vector<T>::iterator is a standard pointer to an object of type T. So for this class, there isn't any need to define operator*(); you simply use the built-in definition picked up from the allocator.

You can also see from the definition above that, for every type of iterator, there is generally a corresponding const_iterator type. A const_iterator is an iterator that returns a reference to a const object of type T instead of to a mutable object.

Not for containers only

The most obvious and visible way iterators are used in the STL is as pointers into containers. But there's nothing preventing them from being useful in other ways. For example, the STL has predefined iterators that will read and write data to and from standard streams, all the while appearing to be standard pointer-like objects. And there is no doubt that new iterator applications will appear that allow you to read and write to databases, user interfaces, on-line services, and so on. If an object can produce or consume data, it is a potential target for an iterator.

WHAT'S THE BIG DEAL?

Iterators are important because of one simple fact: *they provide a uniform way for algorithms to access the elements in a container.*

As an example of this, the following code excerpt shows the copy() algorithm found in algobase.h. This algorithm copies a range of elements to an output container.

Note: The algorithm doesn't care about the container types. For that matter, it doesn't even care what type of objects reside in the container. (Or even, what *is* type T?) Since it is a template function, it will be parameterized on the type of the iterator.

```
template <class InputIterator, class OutputIterator>
OutputIterator copy(InputIterator first, InputIterator last,
                    OutputIterator result) {
    while (first != last) *result++ = *first++;
    return result;
}
```

copy() works by using the iterator interface. It expects the input and output iterators to provide a basic set of operations, which include:

- operator*(), which should return a reference to the value_type for a container
- operator!=(); copy() needs this function to determine when it's time to exit the main loop
- operator++(), used to move to the next element in both the input and output containers.

As it happens, all the different iterator types used in the STL support these basic operations, so algorithm copy() can work on *any* container. And, just as importantly, since the iterators and algorithms are defined as template classes and functions, the algorithms should run as efficiently as hand-coded custom versions, as shown in Figure 10-3.

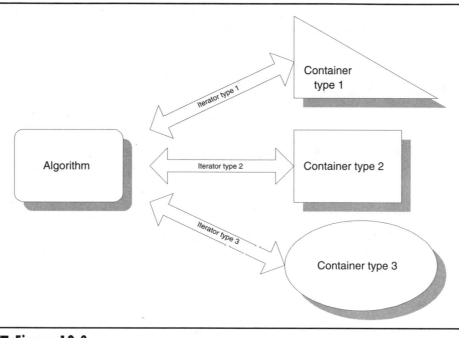

Figure 10-3
Iterators provide uniform access to containers

Since all iterators support these three operations, you now have a dramatic increase in your capabilities as a programmer. If you can write a single-pass algorithm that gets by with these operations, you'll guarantee it works with *any* container defined in the STL. So you don't have to write custom versions of your algorithm for each Container class, even for ones that haven't been invented yet.

Better yet, when you write your custom algorithms to work with the STL, you'll take advantage of a couple of key strengths of template-based functions: full type safety and efficiency that matches traditional hand-coding.

Mr. Iterator's neighborhood

Life would really be simple if all our algorithms could be written as single-pass loops that stepped through a container one element at a time. But this isn't possible to accomplish efficiently.

For instance, many of the more powerful sorting algorithms need to jump from element to element all the way through a container. Algorithms such as quicksort usually need to increment or decrement a pointer by an arbitrary amount in either direction. Of course, pointers can already perform these more sophisticated operations. So, wouldn't it be convenient if we just required iterators to support all operations defined for pointers?

This might be one approach to solving the access problem for containers, but it would eliminate some of the more creative uses of iterators in the STL. For example, the STL has a class of iterator known as a *stream iterator*. Stream iterators can be used to read objects in from a file, or write them out to a file.

For instance, you could use the copy() algorithm discussed in this chapter to easily spool a vector out to a file:

```
copy( a.begin(), a.end(), output_iterator );
```

It isn't hard to imagine implementing some pointer operations for an iterator that writes to a file. Nor to imagine how relatively simple it might be to support operator*(), and maybe even operator++() for this output stream iterator. But could you work out how to support operator-(), or operator[](? Even if you did manage to come up with definitions for these operations, you'd definitely violate the STL philosophy regarding efficiency.

The great iterator hierarchy

Iterator capabilities and algorithm requirements present us with two separate sets of operations that pull us in different directions. We have iterators that have a hard time supporting the entire set of pointer operations, and we have algorithms that have a hard time running without the entire set of pointer operations. How does the STL resolve this conflict?

The STL's solution to this problem is to create a hierarchy of iterators, with each step up the ladder adding additional capabilities. At the top of the hierarchy are *random access iterators*. These iterators support all features of pointers. Indeed, in many cases they *are* pointers. At the bottom of the hierarchy are *input* and *output iterators*. These iterators support operator*() and operator++(), but not much else.

When writing an STL algorithm, you need to know what sort of capabilities you'll require from the iterators passed as inputs and outputs. If you do, you can specify which iterators are used with a given algorithm. For instance, the copy() template function mentioned earlier in this chapter specifies that its iterator arguments are input iterators and output iterators. This means copy() can work on *any* type of iterator defined for the STL.

An example of an algorithm with more substantial requirements is sort(), and its prototype is shown in the next piece of code. Notice that it expects its input iterators to be random access iterators, meaning ones that are required to be semantically equivalent to pointers:

```
template <class RandomAccessIterator>
void sort(RandomAccessIterator first, RandomAccessIterator last);
```

Between input and output iterators at the low end, and random access iterators at the high end, there are two additional stepping stones: *forward iterators* and *bidirectional iterators*. Collectively, they form the hierarchy represented in Figure 10-4.

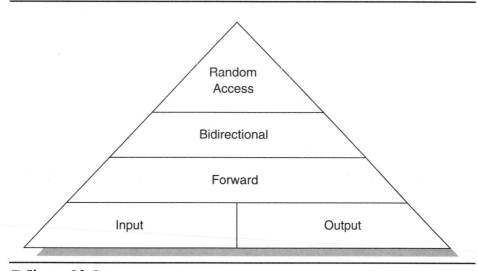

Figure 10-4
The hierarchy of iterators

The pyramid shown in Figure 10-4 does more than arrange the classes in terms of relative strength or capability. In fact, the relationships between the classes of iterators are as hierarchical as the pyramid implies. As we move up the pyramid, each new layer acquires all the capabilities of the layer below it, and adds new capabilities of its own.

The next few sections discuss in detail the features of each of the iterator types. Briefly, the four major classes have the following characteristics:

Input/Output: These iterators can only be dereferenced and incremented. Each specific location can only be dereferenced once, to load or store an object of type T.

Forward: A forward iterator returns a true reference when dereferenced, so it can be read and written to multiple times.

Bidirectional: In addition to the capabilities of the forward iterator, the bidirectional iterator can also be decremented. Any container that uses this iterator is no longer limited to single-pass algorithms.

Random: A random access iterator acts like a true pointer. It can be incremented, decremented, or have a constant value added to or subtracted from it. Because of this ability, it also supports operator[]().

Table 10-1 gives a brief description of what operations are supported by the various iterator types. These operations will be discussed in detail later in this chapter.

Table 10-1

Iterator operation requirements

Iterator Type	Supported Operations	
Input	I(i1)	i1 == i2
	I i1(i2)	i1 != i2
	I i1 = i21	++i
	*i	--i
Output	I(i1)	*i = value
	I i1(i2)	++i
	I i1 = i2	--i
Forward	I i	i1 == i2
	I()	i1 != i2
	I(i1)	i1 = i2
	I i1(i2)	++i
	I i1 = i2;	--i
	*i	
Bidirectional	All forward iterator operations	--i
	i--	
Random Access	All bidirectional iterator operations	i += scalar
	i1 - i2	i + scalar
	i1 < i2	scalar + i
	i1 > i2	i -= scalar
	i1 >= i2	i - scalar
	i1 <= i2	i[scalar]

Beyond Pointers: Using Iterators

When manipulating the contents of containers, you'll find yourself heavily dependent on iterators. This is even more true if you start using generic algorithms, or developing ones of your own.

At the beginning of this chapter, you saw that mentally equating iterators and pointers is a good tactic. And after reading the last section, you saw that random access iterators are almost indistinguishable from true pointers, but as you move down the pyramid, some weaknesses start to show up. For example, forward iterators do a lot of things that pointers do, but not *everything*.

This is an important fact to digest, because it will affect the way you write template algorithms that use iterators. When you write an algorithm, you need to be keenly aware of what operations you are asking of your iterators. To write algorithms that support all four levels of the pyramid, you have to be sure to use only the minimum set of supported functions.

The most important thing to do when you start working with iterators is to adopt the STL philosophy of an iterator's *range*. STL functions that work on containers typically do so over the range of the container, which is defined by the begin() and end() functions:

```
for ( vector<int>::iterator i = a.begin(); i != a.end() ; i++ )
```

Notice that, in a loop like this, the STL iterator is always within a valid range. It starts off pointing to a legitimate object—and always points to a well-constructed object—until it reaches the end of its range. Once at the end of its range, an iterator may point past the end of a container. This is still a valid iterator, but it cannot be dereferenced. Nonetheless, it *can* safely be compared to other iterators.

When passing a range to the STL algorithm, you pass an iterator that points to the first element to be processed, and another iterator that points one past the last element to be processed. Once again, this sentinel iterator at the end of the range may not point to a valid object, but it can safely be used to mark the end of a range.

This means most STL algorithms don't use a single iterator, they use a pair. Two iterators are used to define the range over which the algorithm operates. The prototypical STL template function has a prototype like this:

```
template<class InputIterator, class OutputIterator>
void foo( InputIterator begin;
          InputIterator end;
          OutputIterator out );
```

The programmer who implements this function continually increments the begin iterator until it reaches the end value, at which point it's no longer pointing to a valid object. This means you need to drop two common C/C++ coding habits:

- testing to see if a pointer/iterator is equal to NULL/0
- testing to see if a pointer is less than or greater than another pointer

Neither of these operations will work across the hierarchy of iterators, and in many cases they simply don't make sense.

Caveat: How will I know the requirements?

You've seen that some algorithms only support certain families of iterators. This raises the practical question: How do you know which class of iterator an algorithm requires?

This question exposes a small weakness in both the STL and C++. C++ doesn't have an elegant way to describe what sort of classes will work when trying to use a template function. For example, the sort() function described earlier in this chapter requires its arguments to be random access iterators. But there really isn't a good way to write this into the prototype of the function. Because of this, it's easy to write code that inadvertently tries to use a bidirectional iterator—one level too low in the iterator hierarchy. A typically incorrect call to sort() could be:

```
#include "set.h"
#include "algo.h"

void foo( set<int,less<int> > & a )
{
    sort( a.begin(), a.end() );
}
```

The call to the sort algorithm needs a random access iterator, which supports iterator operations such as operator[](). But a set iterator doesn't have those features, so the compiler will detect an error in this code fragment. If you were designing the perfect C++ compiler, you would like it to produce an error message like this:

```
Error in call to function sort().
Argument must be of type random_access_iterator.
```

But the compiler doesn't have any way of figuring this out. Instead, it blindly tries to generate the code for the sort() algorithm. Naturally, any code in sort() that attempts to use the iterator in random access ways will generate a compiler error. So, instead of the single tidy error message shown above, you'll get dozens of messages similar to that shown below:

```
test01.cpp:
    Error ..\source\algo.h 840: Illegal structure operation in function
__final_insertion_sort(rb_tree<int,int,ident<int,int>,less<int>>::const_itera-
tor,rb_tree<int,int,ident<int,int>,less<int>>::const_iterator)
    Error ..\source\algo.h 841: Illegal structure operation in function
__final_insertion_sort(rb_tree<int,int,ident<int,int>,less<int>>::const_itera-
tor,rb_tree<int,int,ident<int,int>,less<int>>::const_iterator)
            .
            .
            .
    Warning ..\source\algobase.h 27: 'tmp' is assigned a value that is never
used in function
__iter_swap(rb_tree<int,int,ident<int,int>,less<int>>::const_iterator,
rb_tree<int,int,ident<int,int>,less<int>>::const_iterator,int *)
    Warning ..\source\algobase.h 27: Parameter 'b' is never used in function
__iter_swap(rb_tree<int,int,ident<int,int>,less<int>>::const_iterator,
rb_tree<int,int,ident<int,int>,less<int>>::const_iterator,int *)
    *** 19 errors in Compile ***
```

In an attempt to prevent these confusing error binges, the STL has to resort to coding conventions. Since you can't tell the compiler that your function needs a certain class of iterator, you have to advise the programmer using the function. This is done by consistent naming of the class arguments used to parameterize template functions.

As an instance of this, the upper_bound() template function has the following prototype:

```
template <class ForwardIterator, class T>
inline ForwardIterator upper_bound( ForwardIterator first,
                                    ForwardIterator last,
                                    const T& value);
```

This prototype tells you that the two iterator arguments must be forward iterators, or better. If you try to call this function with input or output iterators, you'll get the massive error blitz shown earlier. Unfortunately, this is the state of the art.

BOTTOM OF THE PILE: INPUT ITERATORS

Input iterators share the bottom layer of the iterator hierarchy with output iterators. Both types of iterators are extremely limited in their capabilities and, generally, are only used to read or write objects from another form of storage. The most likely places you'll see these iterators are in the istream_iterator and ostream_iterator classes.

(Limited) capabilities

This chapter continually stresses the semantic equivalence of iterators and pointers. However, down at the bottom of the pyramid, finding this equivalence is a bit of a stretch. Input iterators miss out on most of the more interesting pointer attributes, limiting themselves to just a few operations.

The range of functionality input iterators need is fairly well summed up by the copy() function defined in algobase.h. copy() reads in a list of objects and stores them in a location specified by an output iterator:

```
template <class InputIterator, class OutputIterator>
OutputIterator copy(InputIterator first,
                    InputIterator last,
                    OutputIterator result) {
    while (first != last)
        *result++ = *first++;
    return result;
}
```

So what does copy() expect from its pair of input iterators? Not much! The following short list sums it up:

- operator != ()
- operator*()
- operator++()

copy() needs to use a comparison operator to determine when it's finished copying. It employs the dereferencing operator to read in a single value. Then, it uses the post-increment operator to advance the iterator to the next input value.

To meet the formal definition of an input iterator, a class or built-in type Iter has to perform the following operations:

Iter(Iter *y* **)** **Iter** *x*(**Iter** *y*) **Iter** *x = y*	This implies you can use the copy constructor to make a copy of a given input iterator. After being constructed, the copy should return true when the test *x*==*y* is performed.
x == y *x != y*	You must be able to test for equivalence of two input iterators. If you didn't have this test, it wouldn't be possible to define when an input iteration sequence ended, rendering functions such as copy() unable to do their jobs. **Note:** The equivalence test on two iterators is somewhat deceptive. Even though two iterators *x* and *y* may be equivalent, it doesn't mean that *x*++ and *y*++ will be equivalent. In fact, for istream_iterators this will definitely *not* be true. However, equivalence *does* imply that *x == *y.
*x	Dereferencing an input iterator returns a reference to an object of type T. It is *very important* to note that this is not necessarily an lvalue. As a result, you won't be able to put the expression *x on the left side of an assignment operation. The restriction on *x makes sense when you think of reading an input stream from a file. You don't normally expect to be able to write data back to an input stream while you are reading from it. The same holds true for input iterators. But the design of the operator*() for input iterators allows you to dereference an input iterator multiple times without altering its value. Input iterators will usually keep a copy of the current input value to ensure that this capability is met.
++*x* *x*++	This operation advances the input iterator to the next value. It may advance the iterator to the past-the-end position. Note that these two operations aren't completely equivalent. ++*x* returns a reference to itself, whereas *x*++ merely returns a copy of itself before being incremented.

It's critical that you only use input iterators for applications that can complete in a single pass. Think of an input iterator as a pointer into a set of objects that are being read in from a sequential file. That way, you'll grasp its limitations.

Also, it's generally not useful to have multiple input iterators pointing into a single object or container. Once again, it pays to think of input iterators as functions that read data from a file. If you have two iterators reading in from the same file, expect erratic results, as one iterator leap-frogs the other when each item is read in.

Do it yourself!

The odds are that, if and when you use an input iterator, it will be the istream_iterator, so that you can read data in from a file. But the simplicity of input iterators means the task of creating one of your own is quite manageable. Since input iterators only have to support a few different operations, it isn't a Herculean task.

Listing 10-1 shows iter1001.cpp, an example program that creates an input iterator for character strings. The iterator class, defined as struct input, works its way through a string of characters, returning one at a time to the caller. The old standby, copy(), tests the iterator.

Listing 10-1

iter1001.cpp: Demonstrating an input iterator

```
//
// ITER1001.CPP
//
// This program in Chapter 10 creates a simple input
// iterator class, then uses it as the input to
// the copy() function. It uses a conventional
// ostream_iterator for the output.
//

#include <iostream.h>
#include <string.h>

//
// Borland 4.x workarounds
//
```

```
#define __MINMAX_DEFINED
#pragma option -vi-


#include "algo.h"
#include "iterator.h"

//
// struct input takes a pointer to a character
// string as input to its constructor. When
// dereferenced, it returns the individual
// characters in the string. The increment
// operator advances it to the next character
// in the string. Note, this type uses the
// default copy constructor that the compiler
// generates.
//

struct input {
    char *current;
    input( char *p ){ current = p; }
    operator*(){ return *current; }
    input operator++(int) {
        input temp( *this );
        current++;
        return temp;
    }
    bool operator==(const input& y) const {
        return current == y.current;
    }
    input end() {
        char *p = current + strlen( current );
        return input( p );
    }
};

main()
{
    ostream_iterator<char> out(cout);
    input in( "This is a test" );

    copy( in, in.end(), out );
    return 1;
}
```

As you can probably divine, the output from iter1001.cpp is a copy of the string passed to the input iterator constructor:

```
This is a test
```

OUTPUT ITERATORS

The last section encouraged you to think of input iterators as iterators that could read input data from a file. Likewise, output iterators can write objects out to a file. Output iterators have more uses than this but, in general, they follow the same logic.

iter1001.cpp (shown in Listing 10-1) is meant to demonstrate an input iterator, but inadvertently shows an output iterator in use as well. The main() routine creates an ostream_iterator attached to the standard stream cout, then passes it to copy(). While it isn't particularly flashy, the ability to create an operator that allows generic algorithms to target a file for their output is a powerful addition to the library.

Capabilities

As is the case for all iterators, there isn't one particular class definition that defines an output iterator, which is defined by the list of functions it needs to support. Of course, there's no convenient way to check if you've actually met those requirements. You have to plug it into your code and take your chances with the compiler. If your creation is imperfect, you'll be greeted with the usual slew of cryptic errors.

The list of requirements for an output iterator of class Iter is short and sweet:

Iter(Iter *y*) **Iter *x*(Iter *y*)** **Iter *x* = *y***	These are the normal set of constructors.
***x* = value**	Dereferencing an output iterator is done solely for the purpose of inserting an object into whichever container is attached to the iterator. You can't dereference an iterator and return a value; the result will be undefined. Also, you must write only once to an iterator in a given state. After it has been written to, you need to increment it before writing to it again.
	Note: For ostream_iterator, the real work of inserting the value into an output stream is done by operator=(), not operator*(), as you might think. However, this is done with some sleight-of-hand using operator*(), and obeys the requirement that assignment be done with the *x* = value code. The specifics of this are discussed below.

++*x*   The increment operator is only called after a value has
x++   been written out through the iterator. It should be called
               once and only once for each element that is output. The
               increment operations return either a reference to the
               iterator or a copy of it.

An output example

A good example of an output iterator is shown below. This is the
ostream_iterator defined in iterator.h in HP's distribution of the STL. It is
usually used as a target to algorithms like copy(), allowing them to route
their output to a file or some other device.

```
template <class T>
class ostream_iterator : public output_iterator {
protected:
    ostream* stream;
    char* string;
public:
    ostream_iterator(ostream& s) : stream(&s), string(0) {}
    ostream_iterator(ostream& s, char* c)
        : stream(&s), string(c)  {}
    ostream_iterator<T>& operator=(const T& value) {
        *stream << value;
        if (string) *stream << string;
        return *this;
    }
    ostream_iterator<T>& operator*() { return *this; }
    ostream_iterator<T>& operator++() { return *this; }
    ostream_iterator<T>& operator++(int) { return *this; }
};
```

One interesting thing about this iterator is that the dereferencing opera-
tion doesn't return a reference to a value_type of type T, as you might expect.
Instead, it simply returns a reference to itself. What does this accomplish?
Two things. First, it prevents you from writing code like this:

```
T value = *iterator;
```

This will generate a compiler error—what you would like it to do, under
the circumstances. Second, it ensures that a statement like this works properly:

```
*iterator++ = value;
```

Since both the dereference and the post-increment operators simply return a reference to the iterator, the compiler does nothing with them. But it does invoke the operator=() for the output iterator type. This takes care of the actual assignment of the value.

Confused yet?

The way ostream_iterator works, in HP's implementation, isn't completely obvious, and it doesn't do things the way a normal pointer would. The important thing is that it does the right thing when it executes the key operation for output iterators:

```
*iterator = value;
```

In the section above, I mentioned that a function like the STL copy() algorithm would write to the output iterator from the inside of a loop, using a statement similar to this:

```
*iterator++ = value;
```

Using the standard C++ order of operators, the first thing that happens in the above statement is that we dereference the iterator. Looking at the class definition above, you see that operator*() for ostream_iterator does something unexpected: It simply returns a reference to itself! This means that the above line of code is equivalent to:

```
iterator++ = value;
```

Even stranger, operator++() does the same thing, which is to return a reference to itself. So ultimately, the assignment statement boils down to this:

```
iterator = value;
```

This might not seem a good thing to do, but if you look at the class definition, you'll notice that the assignment operator for this iterator generates a line of code that does this:

```
*stream << value;
```

This sends the value to the output stream, just like we wanted.

Well, this is certainly a long, strange trip, but it *does* end up in the right place. And remember, this is HP's implementation. Other vendors might implement their ostream_iterator differently. The important point is that it adheres to the output specification.

Your mileage...

There's no end to the different ways you can implement an output iterator, and the slightly eccentric implementation of ostream_iterator may not be to your taste. Even so, if you don't feel a strong urge to reinvent the wheel, this is a good model to use when developing your own output iterators. Since it's included as part of the STL release, you can expect it to be well tested and compatible with all supported algorithms.

ONWARD AND UPWARD: FORWARD ITERATORS

With a forward iterator, you are starting to see an objct that looks like a real pointer. It can do most of the things a pointer does, with just a few restrictions. The things a forward iterator can't do are often things we can live without. The two major things a forward iterator can't do (that a pointer can) are:

- no decrement or subtraction operations are supported; you can move forward through a container, but not backwards

- you can't add a scalar to a forward iterator; thus, you can't perform operator+=(int), or operator[]()

Capabilities

What *can* you do with a forward iterator? The STL specification requires the following operations for forward iterators:

Iter *x*	These operations represent the different ways a forward
Iter()	iterator can be constructed and initialized. Note that the
Iter(*x*)	two default constructors may not initialize the iterator to
Iter *x*(Iter &*y*)	a useful value. A subsequent assignment operation is
Iter *x* = *y*	required to ensure the iterator can be used.

$x == y$ $x \mathrel{!=} y$	This operation compares two forward iterators. Virtually all code in the STL relies on making comparisons to see if an iterator is at the end of a sequence, so these operations are crucial. Note that they are also supported for input iterators.
$x = y$	Forward iterators must support the assignment operator, along with the semantics of this operation. After this operation, $x == y$, and $*x == *y$. This operation enables algorithms that can perform multiple passes over a range of data (using multiple copies of an iterator), a feature missing in input and output iterators.
$*x$	As long as x is a dereferenceable value, this returns an object of value_type T. If the iterator is pointing to a const object, you can't modify the value with this operation. If it isn't, it obeys the normal semantics of a pointer when being dereferenced.
$++x$ $x++$	These operations behave with the same semantics as increment operations on a pointer. $++x$ returns a reference to x, and $x++$ returns a copy of x before the decrement. Normally, you can only perform the increment operation on a pointer that can be dereferenced.

Where are they?

If you were taking your first quick look at the STL specification, you might wonder where forward iterators are used. All containers in the STL create either bidirectional or random access iterators. And the two predefined iterators, istream_iterator and ostream_iterator, are only lowly input and output iterators. So, if nobody is creating any forward iterators, why are they defined?

The place to find these iterators is in the list of STL algorithms. Algorithms are always defined with the least powerful iterator types possible, to keep the potential domain of the algorithm as large as possible. Many of the algorithms operate with just input and output iterators, so they can work with any sort of container. However, the weakness of input and output iterators requires many algorithms to move up to forward iterators, if they are to accomplish their work.

As an example of why this is the case, look at the source code shown below for the fill() template function:

```
template <class ForwardIterator, class T>
void fill(ForwardIterator first,
          ForwardIterator last,
          const T& value) {
    while (first != last)
        *first++ = value;
}
```

This function fills a range in a container with a specific value. The range is defined in the standard STL way, using a first and last marker to delineate it. The iterator type in the type list is defined as a ForwardIterator.

Note: Remember that the type requirements for iterators are defined using a naming convention, with no compile-time support for enforcement.

If you examine the code in the function itself, you see a typical iterator loop, which runs until an iterator reaches an end point. Therein lies the reason why the iterator must be a forward iterator instead of an output iterator. Output iterators don't support the comparison operations, operator==() or operator!=(), so you can't use a loop of this type. In fact, there's a different version of fill() which accepts a numeric parameter indicating how many elements are to be filled. This version of fill uses an output iterator, since no comparisons need be performed in the inner loop.

The inability of output iterators to perform operator==() makes sense when you think about it. If you define an ostream_iterator() to connect an output stream, how can you possibly define a point in that file one past the end of the data? You have no way of knowing this information in advance, which is why this algorithm requires the more capable forward iterator.

ONE STEP FURTHER (OR BACK!): BIDIRECTIONAL ITERATORS

Bidirectional iterators take one small step closer to full pointer status. They do so by adding the ability to move backwards through a container, as well as forward. Bidirectional iterators are required to have all the functions of the forward iterator, and must support the iterator decrement operations as well:

−−*x*
x−−

These two operations should obey the same semantics as that of the decrement operations on pointers. This means the pre-decrement operation returns a reference to *x*, and the post-decrement operation returns the value of *x* before the decrement.

The decrement operation has another property: if two iterators are equal, they'll still be equal after they're both decremented. This operation assumes the operation will be performed only if there's a dereferenceable value to be pointed to after the decrement.

A big deal?

No, adding the decrement operation isn't really a big deal. It *does* make it easier to implement a few algorithms, and it means an iterator can support the reverse_iterator adaptor. But it certainly isn't a major breakthrough.

Note: For more information on this, see later in this chapter, under the section on reverse iterators.

All STL containers support either random access or bidirectional iterators. The big difference between these two pointer types is that bidirectional iterators don't support pointer math, so you can't add or subtract scalars, perform operator[](), or compare pointers.

Table 10-2 gives a quick rundown of the iterators supported for each of the container types, including standard C arrays. Remember that built-in arrays have iterators too, they are just standard pointers!

Table 10-2

Container iterator types

Container	Bidirectional iterators	Random Access iterators
standard C/C++ arrays	√	√
vector<T>	√	√
deque<T>	√	√
list<T>	√	
set<T>, multiset<T>	√	
map<T>, multimap<T>	√	

Fortunately, not too many STL algorithms require random access, so bidirectional iterators are not very restricted. But many algorithms differ in their *implementations* for random access and bidirectional iterators. If it makes a big difference, the STL algorithm library will provide specialized versions of an algorithm that take advantage of random access iterators when they are used.

Bidirectional iterators are usually considerably less efficient than random access iterators at stepping through a container. For example, compare operator++() for vector<T> and map<T>. You'll quickly see why iterating through a vector is much more efficient than iterating through a map of the same size.

KING OF THE MOUNTAIN: RANDOM ACCESS ITERATORS

Random access iterators are at the top of the heap in the STL iterator hierarchy. With virtually all the power of C pointers, they are generally efficient and easy to use. The containers that supply random access iterators are:

- built-in arrays
- vector<T>
- deque<T>

The other sequence container, list<T>, only supplies a bidirectional iterator.

Now we're talking: Capabilities

Random access iterators provide all the features defined for bidirectional iterators, plus a full complement of operations that perform various kinds of pointer arithmetic. The additional operations supported by this type of iterator are:

$x \mathrel{+}= n$	The addition or subtraction of a scalar to an iterator
$x \mathrel{-}= n$	moves the pointer by n objects. For this operation to be performed efficiently, the container needs to have storage characteristics that allow calculation of the new iterator

in constant time. Clearly, this isn't the case for the list or associative containers. These operators *could* have been implemented to run in O(N) time, but were left out in the name of efficiency.

These operations return a reference to the iterator in question.

$x + n$
$x - n$

This operation returns the value of an iterator equivalent to the existing iterator, after being moved *n* objects.

$x - y$

This operation allows you to calculate the distance between two iterators using operator-(). As with the other operations in this section, it can be performed on bidirectional iterators, but not in constant time. Thus, the associative containers and list<T> don't support this operation for their iterators.

a[*n*]

Because the random access iterators support the types of pointer math discussed here, they can be treated as if they were C arrays. This operation is equivalent to *(*a* + *n*), both in C and here. If the iterator points to mutable objects, they can be modified using this operation.

$x < y$
$x > y$
$x <= y$
$x >= y$

The pointer comparisons are used to determine which pointer appears first in a container. The sequence containers that support random access iterators can perform this operation in constant time.

Who needs 'em?

Random access iterators are powerful, but few STL algorithms require them. Four examples of algorithms that *do* insist on a random access iterator are:

- sort()
- stable_sort()
- random_shuffle()
- *n*th_element()

In addition to algorithms that require a random access iterator, there are quite a few that support specialized versions adapted to random access iterators. This is made possible by *iterator tags*.

YOU'RE IT! ITERATOR TAGS

Iterator tags are used internally by the STL to select specific algorithms based on an iterator type. If you aren't too interested in the internals of the STL, you can skip this section and jump ahead to the section on stream iterators.

Programmers who are still familiarizing themselves with templates often have a tough time following the mechanisms used to select template functions. A template function is created to match the *type* of the arguments passed to it. This makes the type of the arguments just as important as their values.

In many cases, arguments passed to a template function are never used; they are just there to parameterize some type being used in the function. A simple example is shown in Listing 10-2.

Listing 10-2

test1002.cpp: Passing a type argument to a template function

```
//
// TEST1002.CPP
//
// This program is used in Chapter 10 as an example
// of passing a type argument to a template function.
// In this case, the third argument to function sum()
// is a type argument that specifies what type the
// function will return. It isn't used anywhere in
// the function, indicated by the fact that
// the third argument to sum() has a type, but no
// parameter name.
//

#include <iostream.h>

template<class Input, class Output>
Output sum( Input a, Input b, Output )
{
    return a + b;
}
```

```
main()
{
    cout << "double average of 1, 2 is "
         << (sum( 1, 2, (double) 0 ) / 2)
         << endl;
    cout << "integer average of 1, 2 is "
         << (sum( 1, 2, (int) 0 ) / 2)
         << endl;
    return 1;
}
```

In test1002.cpp, function sum() is parameterized based on two types. The first type, class Input, is used to determine what type the first two input arguments are. The second type, class Output, determines the return type of the function.

When main() calls sum() in test1002.cpp, the third argument is a 0 cast to the return type. The actual value of the argument, 0, isn't used in the function, so it doesn't matter what is passed there. Since it has to be *something*, a value of 0 is as good as any other.

Generic, but at what price?

When writing generic functions that work with every STL container type, you're forced to code to the lowest common denominator. This may mean you have to write all your algorithms to work with those less-than-capable input and output iterators.

There are many times when this is a sub-optimal strategy. As an example, consider the STL distance() function. distance() is supposed to calculate the distance between two objects in a container. The lowest common denominator for this function might be:

```
template <class InputIterator, class Distance>
void distance( InputIterator first,
               InputIterator last,
               Distance& n )
{
    while ( first != last )
    {
        ++first;
        ++n;
    }
}
```

This version of distance() works properly with every iterator in the hierarchy except output iterators (where the concept of distance is impossible to calculate in advance). It operates by incrementing the start iterator until it reaches the end.

While this function runs properly with most iterators, it exacts a high price for working with iterators on every level of the pyramid. When trying to calculate the distance between two pointers, for instance, we would normally perform a subtraction operation. Since random access iterators can do this sort of pointer math, we would be much better off calculating their distance like this:

```
n += last - first;
```

But this code won't work with any iterators below random access iterators. So the question becomes: How do we specialize generic algorithms for different types of iterators?

Iterator tags to the rescue

The STL solves this problem with (no surprise!) templates. If you look at the definition for HP's version of the distance() function in algobase.h, you'll see this:

```
template <class InputIterator, class Distance>
inline void distance( InputIterator first,
                      InputIterator last,
                      Distance& n )
{
    __distance( first,
                last,
                n,
                iterator_category( first ) );
}
```

This version of distance doesn't do anything. Instead, it calls a helper function, __distance(), with an additional argument beyond the three that have already been defined. The extra argument, iterator_category(first), is a function that returns an iterator tag.

The purpose of the iterator tag is to select the version of __distance() that is most efficient for a given iterator type. In algobase.h, there are four different versions of __distance(). The first three are defined for input iterators, forward iterators, and bidirectional iterators. They are all virtually identical, with the input iterator version shown below as an example:

```
template <class InputIterator, class Distance>
void __distance(InputIterator first,
                InputIterator last,
                Distance& n,
                input_iterator_tag) {
    while (first != last) { ++first; ++n; }
}
```

So, how is this particular version of __distance() selected from among all the others? The last of the four arguments it uses is listed as an input_iterator_tag. Since that argument isn't used in the function (highlighted by the fact that it doesn't have an argument name), you should suspect that it's the culprit.

In fact, all four versions of the __distance() function have exactly the same argument types for the first three arguments, so the fourth argument must be the difference. If you scan through algobase.h, you'll see that these functions use the following argument types for the fourth argument:

- input_iterator_tag
- forward_iterator_tag
- bidirectional_iterator_tag
- random_access_iterator_tag

These tag types, along with one for output iterators, are defined in iterator.h:

```
struct input_iterator_tag {};
struct output_iterator_tag {};
struct forward_iterator_tag {};
struct bidirectional_iterator_tag {};
struct random_access_iterator_tag {};
```

This type definition looks a little strange, because it doesn't seem do anything useful! The types are defined as structures that contain absolutely nothing. While it may look weird, these types exist only for the purpose of selecting template functions, so they are as fleshed out as they need to be.

Evolution or creation?

When the generic function distance() calls __distance(), it selects a specific version of __distance() by calling the function iterator_category(). iterator_category() takes an iterator of any type as an argument, and returns an iterator tag that matches one of the five types shown above. The actual mechanism by which this happens is a little convoluted.

   iterator_category() is a template function with six different versions. Listing 10-3 gives you all six versions of this function, as found in iterator.h. When an algorithm calls iterator_category() with an iterator as an argument, the compiler has to select from one of these six functions. The one that gets selected determines the return type selected. The return from the function will be one of the iterator tags.

Listing 10-3

The six different versions of iterator_category()

```
template <class T, class Distance>
inline input_iterator_tag
iterator_category(const input_iterator<T, Distance>&) {
    return input_iterator_tag();
}

inline output_iterator_tag iterator_category(const output_iterator&) {
    return output_iterator_tag();
}

template <class T, class Distance>
inline forward_iterator_tag
iterator_category(const forward_iterator<T, Distance>&) {
    return forward_iterator_tag();
}

template <class T, class Distance>
inline bidirectional_iterator_tag
iterator_category(const bidirectional_iterator<T, Distance>&) {
    return bidirectional_iterator_tag();
}

template <class T, class Distance>
inline random_access_iterator_tag
iterator_category(const random_access_iterator<T, Distance>&) {
    return random_access_iterator_tag();
}

template <class T>
inline random_access_iterator_tag iterator_category(const T*) {
    return random_access_iterator_tag();
}
```

The simplest case in this process is when the iterator is just a standard C pointer. For example, the distance() function could be called like this:

```
int n = 0;
char test[] = "Random acts";

distance( test, test + strlen( test ), n );
cout << "distance = " << n << end;
```

In this case, the iterators are char pointers. This means the version of iterator_category(test) selected will be the last one from Listing 10-3. This is the one that expects an argument of type const T*.

Things are a little more complicated when we pass something like a list<T>::iterator. To see what happens first, you need to look at the definition for this iterator type in list.h. Remember that the iterator definition is a nested class of list<T>:

```
class iterator : public bidirectional_iterator<T, difference_type> {
```

This shows you that the iterator class from list<T> is derived from a class called bidirectional_iterator<>. It appears kind of odd, since derivation doesn't seem to be used in the STL. What function does this base class perform?

A quick look at the base class definition isn't too revealing:

```
template <class T, class Distance>
struct bidirectional_iterator {
};
```

From this, it would appear that the bidirectional_iterator class doesn't do a darned thing! And this isn't too far from the truth. What this class does is ensure that the compiler can figure out which version of iterator_category() to call for this iterator. Since list<T>::iterator is derived from bidirectional_iterator<>, you can assume that a call to iterator_category(list<T>::iterator) will select this version of iterator_category():

```
template <class T, class Distance>
inline bidirectional_iterator_tag
iterator_category(const bidirectional_iterator<T, Distance>&) {
    return bidirectional_iterator_tag();
}
```

This means that iterator_category() returns a bidirectional_iterator_tag which, in turn, means that a call to __distance( ) with this type of iterator will eventually go to the right function.

Between the lines

Incidentally, if you've noticed that the output_iterator_tag is a little different from all the other iterator tags, no, that isn't a typographical error. All of the other iterator tags are templates that are parameterized on the value type for the iterator (what you get when you dereference it), and optionally the difference type (the type needed to hold a distance between two iterators).

As it turns out, output iterators don't have either a value type or a difference type. You can't dereference an output iterator and get back a value, so there isn't a value type. Since you can't calculate the distance between two output iterators, there isn't a distance type either.

A price to pay

The end result of this complex web of type-based decisions can now be untangled, albeit not too easily. Going back to where this explanation started, let's look at a sample call to distance().

A call to distance() with a random access iterator—for example, deque::begin()—is made. This creates a call to template function distance(). distance() doesn't do any work itself. Instead, it calls __distance(), with a new fourth argument. The argument is iterator_category(first), where *first* is the iterator passed in. In this example, the argument passed to iterator_category() is a random access iterator.

iterator_category() is yet another template function. To determine which version of this function to call, the compiler has to decide which of the six different specializations of iterator_category() provides the best match. The choices for the argument type are:

- input_iterator<T,Distance>
- output_iterator
- forward_iterator<T,Distance>
- bidirectional_iterator<T,Distance>
- random_access_iterator<T,Distance>
- T*

In this case, the random access iterator is defined as a class derived from struct random_access_iterator. The only useful thing this derivation gives us is a way to ensure the correct version of iterator_category() is called. The version of iterator_category() that accepts an iterator of type random_access_iterator() returns a random_access_iterator_tag().

There is only one version of __distance() that expects a fourth argument of type random_access_iterator_tag. It's the version we were hoping to call:

```
template <class RandomAccessIterator, class Distance>
inline void __distance( RandomAccessIterator first,
                        RandomAccessIterator last,
                        Distance& n,
                        random_access_iterator_tag )
{
    n = last - first;
}
```

This is an awful lot of work to accomplish just one function call! In fact, this tortured path probably does more to highlight the weaknesses of C++ than its strengths. While it is certainly wonderful to be able to do what the distance() function does, there are a couple of major problems at work here:

- An enormous amount of complexity is required to solve just one problem. The fact that the STL needs classes to do nothing and (functions that return nothing useful) in order to manage all of this type information is not a good thing.

- Any time you want to specialize a function such as distance() for a particular type of iterator, you're forced to write five or six different functions: one master function for the public API, and four or five different specialized versions to handle the real work.

- This setup detracts from the generic nature of the STL. Anyone who wants to create a new category of iterator that doesn't fit into the established hierarchy has to track down all the underpinnings exposed here and add support for the new iterator type.

As an end user of the STL, you can conveniently ignore iterator tags, which is nice. The only critical point you should be aware of arises when you create a new container. Since every new container gets its own iterator, creating a container means creating an iterator. If you create a new iterator class, you must be sure to derive it from one of the five dummy classes found in iterator.h. Failure to do so would mean any existing algorithms that depend on a valid iterator tag will fail when using your new container.

Other tags

The category tag used by iterator-related functions is a little tough to handle, particularly due to the complex relationships between it and other helper classes, tags, and so on. Once you feel able to deal with category tags, the other two tags are a breeze.

value_type()

value_type() is a function that returns the type equivalent of the iterator. "Type equivalent" means that, since an iterator is analogous to a pointer to type T, value_type() returns type T*.

value_type() accomplishes this by using five template functions. As with the template function category_type(), these specializations are selected by class type. Since the standard iterator types are derived from five base classes, this selection process works. There has to be one additional specialization for objects that are standard C pointers, since they aren't generally derived from class random_access_iterator<T,Distance>.

Listing 10-4 shows the five different versions of value_type():

Listing 10-4

Five versions of value_type()

```
template <class T, class Distance>
inline T* value_type(const input_iterator<T, Distance>&) {
    return (T*)(0);
}

template <class T, class Distance>
inline T* value_type(const forward_iterator<T, Distance>&) {
    return (T*)(0);
}

template <class T, class Distance>
inline T* value_type(const bidirectional_iterator<T, Distance>&) {
    return (T*)(0);
}

template <class T, class Distance>
inline T* value_type(const random_access_iterator<T, Distance>&) {
    return (T*)(0);
}
```

```
template <class T>
inline T* value_type(const T*) {
    return (T*)(0);
}
```

Note that value_type() can't just return the type of the object the iterator is pointing to. Since this is still C++, a function has to return *some* sort of object. In this case, it's simply a 0 cast to the appropriate pointer type. Needless to say, you shouldn't use the return value from a value_type() call for anything other than as a dummy argument to a template function.

An example of how this function could be useful is found in algobase.h. This header file contains the generic function iter_swap(), which swaps the value pointed to by two pointers or iterators. The function in the next piece of code shows that this has to be accomplished in a two-step process:

```
template <class ForwardIterator1, class ForwardIterator2, class T>
inline void __iter_swap(ForwardIterator1 a, ForwardIterator2 b, T*)
{
    T tmp = *a;
    *a = *b;
    *b = tmp;
}

template <class ForwardIterator1, class ForwardIterator2>
inline void iter_swap(ForwardIterator1 a, ForwardIterator2 b) {
    __iter_swap(a, b, value_type(a));
}
```

The first part of this function accepts two iterators as arguments. It then calls a second helper function, __iter_swap(), which is parameterized on not just the iterator type, but on the type returned from value_type() as well. Since value type returns a pointer to T, the helper function can determine what type T is. This allows it to create a temporary variable of type T, which is necessary for the swap.

distance_type()

distance_type() is another function used to return a type. In this case, it returns a pointer to the type that holds the distance between two pointers. For example, with normal C pointers in a default memory model, the distance between pointers is stored in a typedef called ptrdiff_t. Thus, distance_type(char *) returns a pointer to a ptrdiff_t.

This function is very similar to value_type() and iterator_category(). It uses five template specialization functions to cover the four template categories and standard C pointers. As with value_type(), distance_type() doesn't have a specialization for output iterators, since the concept of distance hasn't been extended this far.

There's one important point to note about the distance_type() specialization for pointers. If you look at the following function, you'll notice this specialization only works properly with the default memory model. It won't work for pointer types that have been modified with qualifiers such as _far or _huge:

```
template <class T>
inline ptrdiff_t* distance_type(const T*)
{
    return (ptrdiff_t*)(0);
}
```

As a case in point, if you were using the huge pointers for a certain object in a small model program, you'd find that distance_type() wasn't working properly. Huge pointers need to use a long value to hold the distance between pointers.

The solution is to provide additional template functions for any implementation-specific pointer types. For instance, since Borland supports the huge pointer type, they would need to add the following code to their version of iterator.h:

```
template <class T>
inline long* distance_type(const T __huge*)
{
    return (long*)(0);
}
```

Incidentally, Borland doesn't have a version of iterator.h as this is being published, but the distance_type() function specialization for huge pointers is already defined in HP's public release of the STL.

PERSISTENCE PAYS OFF: STREAM ITERATORS

The STL includes a pair of iterators that support input and output to standard streams, as defined by the C++ iostreams library. While these two iterator types don't give the library full-fledged persistence, they *do* provide an easy way to read and write containers to permanent storage. (The definition of persistence is a bit slippery, but at a minimum it means objects have the ability to copy themselves in and out of files or other storage media.)

Stream iterators do their input and output to standard iostreams by using the insertion and extraction operators, << and >>. This means you must have these operators defined for any user-defined types. Built-in types come with the predefined support supplied in the C++ standard library.

istream_iterator

istream_iterator is an input iterator attached to a standard input stream, as defined in iostream.h. If you refer back to the section on input iterators earlier in this chapter, you'll find that input iterators have a very limited interface. This is an instance where having a hierarchy of iterators pays off handsomely. You can imagine how difficult it would be to write a useful iterator that could easily read and write from a stream, while at the same time supporting all the features of a pointer. In fact, the implementor of stream iterators only has to implement a few simple functions, so the istream_iterator class only takes a couple dozen or so lines in iterator.h:

```
template <class T, class Distance> // Distance == ptrdiff_t
class istream_iterator : public input_iterator<T, Distance> {
protected:
    istream* stream;
    T value;
    bool end_marker;
    void read() {
        end_marker = (*stream) ? true : false;
        if (end_marker) *stream >> value;
        end_marker = (*stream) ? true : false;
    }
public:
    istream_iterator() : stream(&cin), end_marker(false) {}
    istream_iterator(istream& s) : stream(&s) { read(); }
    const T& operator*() const { return value; }
    istream_iterator<T, Distance>& operator++() {
        read();
        return *this;
    }
    istream_iterator<T, Distance> operator++(int)  {
        istream_iterator<T, Distance> tmp = *this;
        read();
        return tmp;
    }
};
```

The operation of istream_iterator is fairly simple. When a normal istream_iterator is created, it immediately reads in an object of type T, and stores it internally in a member called value. Any time the object is dereferenced, it can return the object stored in value. When the iterator is incremented using operator++(), the current value is discarded and a new value is read in. It will be the value returned the next time the iterator is dereferenced.

In addition to reading values, istream_iterator has to handle end-of-file conditions. This is done with a two-pronged strategy:

- First, internally note when an end-of-file condition is detected, and store the value in the member named end_marker.

- When no more data can be returned, end_marker is set to false.

Note: A much better name for end_marker would be more_data_left.

But the internal end-of-file state still needs to be detected by users outside the iterator class. This is done by creating a special version of istream_iterator that can test for end-of-file conditions. Normally, an istream_iterator is constructed using code like this:

```
main()
{
    istream_iterator<string,ptrdiff_t> in( cin );
```

Note: The constructor takes an input stream as its single argument.

You can also create a special version of istream_iterator by calling the default constructor (no arguments):

```
void loop( istream_iterator<int,ptrdiff_t> &input )
{
    istream_iterator<int,ptrdiff_t> end;
```

This special iterator, *end* in this case, can't be used to read input data (it wasn't attached to a stream!). It does however, have a special quality: If you compare it to any other istream_iterator, it returns the boolean value true (if that iterator is at an end-of-file state), and false if it isn't.

As a result, you can read in a sequence of input data until an end-of-file by testing your input iterator against this special iterator:

```
void loop( istream_iterator<int,ptrdiff_t> &input )
{
    while ( input != end_of_input_istream )
        process( *input++ );
    .
    .
    .
}
```

This also makes it easy to call generic algorithms that require a starting and ending iterator:

```
copy( input_istream( cin ), eos, output );
```

istream_iterator values can be used as input for many STL algorithms. Obviously, any algorithm that needs a forward, bidirectional, or random access iterator doesn't work. However, you can use these algorithms in an appropriate manner by reading all the data into memory with the input iterator. The fact that the algorithm can't work in a single-pass fashion indicates that it's much more efficient operating out of memory anyway.

A usage note

istream_iterator has two template arguments. The first is the type of object read in on the stream, and the second is the distance type for that object. In future versions of the STL, there will be a default value for the distance type, but that isn't possible with today's compilers. (Today's compilers don't support default type arguments in template declarations.) Accordingly, you have to manually define the distance type in your istream_iterator declaration.

The samples shown in this section, plus an example program in the next section, should give you an idea of what this type declaration ought to look like.

ostream_iterator

ostream_iterators do even less work than istream_iterators. They don't even have to support the special end-of-stream values that the input streams do. So ostream_iterator only has to really work in two places: the constructor and operator=():

```
template <class T>
class ostream_iterator : public output_iterator {
protected:
    ostream* stream;
    char* string;
public:
    ostream_iterator(ostream& s) : stream(&s), string(0) {}
    ostream_iterator(ostream& s, char* c) : stream(&s), string(c){}
    ostream_iterator<T>& operator=(const T& value) {
        *stream << value;
        if (string) *stream << string;
        return *this;
    }
    ostream_iterator<T>& operator*() { return *this; }
    ostream_iterator<T>& operator++() { return *this; }
    ostream_iterator<T>& operator++(int) { return *this; }
};
```

As you saw earlier in this chapter, operator=() is where the output of objects of type T are inserted into the output stream. The operators you may have suspected of doing some serious work, such as operator*(), are nothing more than false fronts that do nothing whatsoever.

ostream_iterator() automatically inserts delimiters in the output stream it creates. The output delimiter is defined by adding a second argument to the constructor. If you don't specify a delimiter, the empty string will be used. In this case, you need to be sure your extraction function places adequate delimiter information, so the input can be properly read back at a later time.

Like its input cousin, ostream_iterator doesn't work with every algorithm. However, every algorithm that works properly with output iterators is a good match, and that includes a substantial portion of the STL library.

A case in point

Listing 10-5 is a short example that uses both the input and output stream adaptors. It creates a block of Fibonacci numbers and writes them to a file using an ostream_iterator. The file is then closed, and a copy of the vector is read back in. The two vectors are then compared for equality.

Fibonacci numbers are a favorite device used in programming classes to teach recursion (along with factorials). Remember that the sequence of Fibonacci numbers starts with F_0 and F_1, both set to a value of 1. From then on, the value of any F_n is defined as $F_{n-1} + F_{n-2}$.

Listing 10-5

iter1005.cpp: The definition of ostream_iterator

```
//
// ITER1005.CPP
//
// This program creates a vector full of Fibonacci numbers,
// then uses an ostream_iterator to write the whole vector
// to an output file.  In then uses an istream_iterator
// to read the file back in. A comparison is then done
// to ensure that the whole thing worked.
//
//
#include <fstream.h>
#include <iostream.h>
#include <string.h>

//
// Borland 4.x workarounds
//
#define __MINMAX_DEFINED
#pragma option -vi-


#include "vector.h"
#include "iterator.h"

main()
{
    ofstream outfile( "iter1005.dat" );
    ostream_iterator<long> out(outfile, " " );
    vector<long> fib( 25 );
//
// Create a vector full of fibonacci data
//
    fib[ 0 ] = 1;
    fib[ 1 ] = 1;
    for ( int i = 2 ; i < 25 ; i++ )
        fib[ i ] = fib[ i - 1 ] + fib[ i - 2 ];
//
// Write the data out
//
    copy( fib.begin(), fib.end(), out');
    outfile.close();
    ifstream infile( "iter1005.dat" );
//
// Now read it all back in.
```

```
//
    vector<long> test( 25 );
    istream_iterator<long, ptrdiff_t> in( infile );
    istream_iterator<long, ptrdiff_t> end;
    copy( in, end, test.begin() );
//
// And report on the results.
//
    if ( test == fib )
        cout << "Comparison passes!\n";
    else
        cout << "Comparison fails!\n";
    return 1;
}
```

ITERATOR ADAPTORS

Just as there is a set of adaptors for containers, there are adaptors for iterators. An adaptor is a class that can be used in conjunction with an existing object, to create some interesting behavior. In the case of iterators, there are three useful adaptors:

- reverse iterators
- insert iterators
- raw storage iterators

These adaptors provide useful extensions to the existing family of iterators, without requiring modification of the existing hierarchy.

Reverse iterators

A reverse iterator is created by applying the reverse_iterator<> adaptor to a bidirectional or random access iterator. The result is an iterator that moves through the container in the reverse direction.

Existing container families have taken advantage of this by defining types reverse_iterator and const_reverse_iterator in their class definitions. In addition, they have defined the rbegin() and rend() member functions that return reverse iterators. These are the iterators that can start and complete an exhaustive iteration loop.

Using these components, you can iterate through a container in reverse order by changing the iterator type and the start and end points of the loop:

```
container::reverse_iterator ri;
for ( ri = container.rbegin();
      ri != container.rend() ;
      ri++ )
    cout << *ri << "\n";
```

Watch me pull this rabbit

The skullduggery needed to accomplish this reverse iteration is not very sophisticated. The definition of the reverse iterator is nested inside the class definition for a container. It usually looks like this:

```
typedef reverse_iterator<iterator,
                         value_type,
                         reference,
                         difference_type> reverse_iterator;
```

This shows that a reverse iterator is created by defining a new class, based on the template reverse_iterator (or on reverse_bidirectional_iterator, for bidirectional iterator types).

The new template class redefines the operators so that operator++() and operator−−() go in the opposite direction to those you have become accustomed to. For example, the predecrement operator for a reverse_iterator is as follows:

```
self& operator++() {
    --current;
    return *this;
}
```

Thus, the reverse_iterator adaptor hijacks all the existing behavior for an iterator and turns it around. However, there is one small catch in this. Normally, an iterator starts at container.begin(), which points to the first element of the container, and continues to container.end(), which points *one past* the end. How is this implemented for reverse iterators?

The first thought that comes to mind is that rbegin() should point to the very last object in the container, and rend() should point to a position one before the first. This would be a consistent and logical way to do it, but it probably wouldn't work. The STL takes advantage of the fact that C and C++ always allow a pointer to point one element past the end of an array— even though you can't always dereference that pointer. But no such guarantee is made for the position one *before* the start of an array. A pointer decremented to a position one before the start of the array may very well generate a memory exception.

The solution to this problem is to modify the internal representation of a reverse iterator. A given reverse iterator that is supposed to point to element *n* of a container points internally to object *n* + 1. This means the internal representation of container.rbegin() is an iterator pointing one past the end of an array, and container.rend() points to the first element of the array. (See Figure 10-5.)

The reverse iterator compensates for this slightly different behavior by modifying the dereference operation for a reverse iterator:

```
Reference operator*() const
{
    return *(current - 1);
}
```

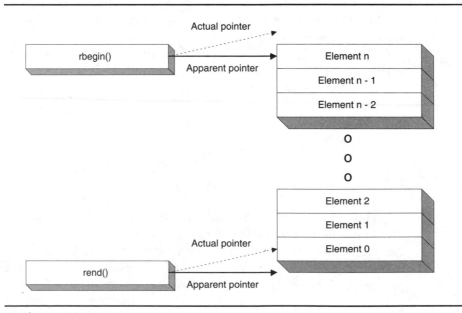

Figure 10-5

A reverse iterator for element I keeps a hidden pointer to element I - 1

This means the internal representation of a reverse iterator is subtly different from what you see as a user. However, you use reverse iterators exactly as you would forward iterators, so these implementation details are just that—details.

An example

Listing 10-6 shows ri1006.cpp. This short program not only uses a reverse iterator, but also creates the reverse iterator class for a built-in type. Normally, you won't have to do this, since all STL containers have reverse iterators already defined. But creating one from scratch helps to illustrate a couple of the key points from this section.

Listing 10-6

ri1006.cpp: Using a reverse iterator

```
//
// RI1006.CPP
//
// This test program is used in Chapter 10 to demonstrate
// how the reverse iterator adaptor can be applied to an
// existing iterator, as long as it is either a random
// access or bidirectional iterator.
//

#include <iostream.h>
#include <string.h>

//
// Borland 4.x workarounds
//
#define __MINMAX_DEFINED
#pragma option -vi-

#include "iterator.h"

char test[]= "This is a test";
typedef reverse_iterator< char *,
                          char,
                          char &,
                          ptrdiff_t > my_ri;

main()
{
```

```
    my_ri r = test + strlen( test );
    my_ri rend = test;
    while ( r != rend )
        cout << *r++;
    cout << endl;
    return 1;
}
```

The most important thing to note about ri1006.cpp is that the starting and terminating values of the loop are one off from where you expect them to be. The initial value of the iterator is *one past* the end of the array, and the terminating value is at the *start* of the array.

If a reverse iterator were identical to a standard pointer, you'd print out one null character when the loop first started, and would fail to print the first character of the array. But since the dereference operator for the iterator always selects the value one element *before* the current iterator, the loop iterates through the array the way you expect, producing the following output:

```
    tset a si sihT
```

If this seems a little confusing, you can ignore all the information about the internal structure of reverse iterators. Just remember that a reverse iterator loop looks exactly like a forward iterator loop, after you substitute rbegin() for begin() and rend() for end():

```
    container::reverse_iterator ri;
    for ( ri = container.rbegin();
          ri != container.rend() ;
          ri++ )
        cout << *ri << "\n";
```

Insert iterators

Up until this point, we've seen that iterators behave like pointers. But the three different types of insert iterators damage this concept by changing a key element of the behavior of iterators.

The three insert iterator adaptors provide special versions of standard iterators that no longer work in overwrite mode. Normally, when you assign a new value to a container by way of the assignment operator, you overwrite any value already pointed to by the iterator. However, when you're using an iterator adaptor, the new value is inserted into the iterator, and is placed into the container in previously unused space.

There are three different insert adaptors, which differ only in where they actually perform their insertion in a container. They are:

- back_insert_iterator. This iterator adaptor adds new elements to a container using the push_back() member function. This means back_insert_iterators can only be used on vector<T>, list<T>, and deque<T> containers.

- front_insert_iterator. This adaptor adds new elements to a container using the push_front() member function. Thus, front_insert_iterators can only be used on list<T> and deque<T> containers.

- insert_iterator. This adaptor adds new elements to a container using the insert() function. The location of the insertion is determined by an iterator passed to the constructor of the insert_iterator adaptor.

What they can (and can't) do

All three of these iterator adaptors create output iterators that can be used to add elements to a container. Like ostream_iterator, these iterators are extremely limited in their functionality. They are able to add new objects to the container when used with an assignment operator, but they can't do much else.

The following code excerpt contains the definition for the back_insert_iterator adaptor. There are only two things in the class that really accomplish anything. The constructor binds the iterator to a container, and the assignment operator inserts a value into the container. The rest is window dressing.

```
template <class Container>
class back_insert_iterator : public output_iterator {
protected:
    Container& container;
public:
    back_insert_iterator(Container& x) : container(x) {}
    back_insert_iterator<Container>&
    operator=(const Container::value_type& value) {
        container.push_back(value);
        return *this;
    }
    back_insert_iterator<Container>& operator*(){return *this;}
    back_insert_iterator<Container>& operator++(){return *this;}
    back_insert_iterator<Container>& operator++(int){return *this;}
};
```

You use the insertion adaptors as you would regular iterators. However, the syntax for the constructors of these iterators is slightly different, in that you must pass each a reference to a container.

The insert_adaptor requires a second argument as well—an iterator pointing into that container. Listing 10-7 is a short program that makes use of a back_insert_iterator to add elements.

Listing 10-7

ins1007.cpp: A sample program that uses an insert iterator adaptor

```
//
// INS1007.CPP
//
// This program is used in Chapter 10 to demonstrate
// the use of an insert iterator adaptor. It creates
// a back inserter and uses it to add factorial
// elements to a vector. Once the elements have been
// inserted, the vector gets dumped to cout.
//

#include <fstream.h>
#include <iostream.h>
#include <string.h>

//
// Borland 4.x workarounds
//
#define __MINMAX_DEFINED
#pragma option -vi-


#include "vector.h"
#include "iterator.h"

main()
{
    vector<long> fact;

    fact.push_back( 1 );
    back_insert_iterator<vector<long> > bi( fact );

    for ( int i = 1 ; i < 10 ; i++ )
        *bi = ( i + 1 ) * fact[ i - 1 ];
    ostream_iterator<long> out(cout, "\n" );
    copy( fact.begin(), fact.end(), out );
    return 1;
}
```

Where to use them

While ins1007.cpp does a good job of illustrating how to use an insert adaptor, it isn't much of an illustrative example. The truth is, if you were writing this program, you would just call fib.push_back() every time a new value needed to be added to the vector. There isn't any need to add a level of complexity.

The place insert iterator adaptors add something useful to the STL is when passing iterators to algorithms. This allows you to call a simple algorithm such as copy(), without worrying about having enough space to store all the elements you will receive:

```
char input[] = "Lots of input data"
vector<char> data;

back_insert_itcrator<vector<char> > bi( data );
copy( input, input + strlen( input ), bi );
```

Given that insert iterator adaptors are used most frequently as arguments to functions, the STL designers added short-cut functions that create these iterators on the fly. These are the functions you will use most frequently to create these iterators.

back_inserter(Container&)

This function creates a back inserter for the container specified as the sole argument. Since the back inserter adaptor relies on push_back() to insert elements into the container, the argument must refer to one of the three sequence containers: list<T>, deque<T>, or vector<T>.

```
copy( input.begin(), input.end(), back_inserter( output ) );
```

front_inserter(Container&)

This function returns a front inserter for the specified container. The front inserter adaptor uses push_front() to insert elements into the container. This means the container argument is limited to either a list<T> or deque<T>.

```
foo( input.rbegin(), input.rend(), front_insertor( my_list ) );
```

inserter(Container&, Iterator i);

Like its two siblings, inserter() creates an inserter adaptor suitable for passing to algorithms that accept an output iterator. But it's somewhat different, in that it requires a second argument—an iterator pointing into the container.

All elements inserted into the container that use this adaptor are inserted with the member function insert(). Insert() inserts into the middle of a container, and the iterator argument is used as the insertion point.

The only container in the STL that supports this adaptor is list<T> container. It can perform efficient insertions at the front, back, and interior of the container.

raw_storage_iterator

The final iterator adaptor in the STL is the raw_storage_iterator. Like the insertion adaptors, raw_storage_iterator creates an output adaptor and, as such, can be passed to any algorithm that can write to an output iterator.

raw_storage_iterator is used internally by several sorting and merging algorithms defined in the STL. This iterator gives the algorithms the ability to transparently use raw, uninitialized memory as the destination for an algorithm. The iterator forces a call to construct() for the correct type of object, resulting in valid memory objects.

Listing 10-8

raw1008.cpp: Using raw_storage_iterator to initialize raw memory

```
//
// RAW1008.CPP
//
// This program is used in Chapter 10 to demonstrate
// the use of the raw_storage_iterator adaptor. It creates
// five objects of type foo in raw, unallocated memory.
// Afterward, the raw contents of the memory area are
// dumped to ensure that some valid construction actually
// took place in there.
//

//
// Borland 4.x workarounds
//
#define __MINMAX_DEFINED
#pragma option -vi-

#include <iostream.h>
#include <stdlib.h>
```

```
#include <string.h>

#include "defalloc.h"
#include "iterator.h"

//
// This foo structure has a constructor that
// initializes the array.  By examining the
// array, you can tell whether it was built
// using the default constructor or using
// a single argument.
//
struct foo {
    char a[ 5 ];
    foo( char i = -1 ) { memset( a, i, 5 ); };
};

main()
{
    char *p = (char *) malloc( 5 * sizeof( foo ) );
    raw_storage_iterator<foo *, foo > rsi = (foo *) p;
    for ( int i = '1' ; i <= '5' ; i++ )
        *rsi++ = foo( i );
    for ( i = 0 ; i < ( 5 * sizeof( foo ) ) ; i++ )
        cout << *p++;
    cout << endl;
    return 1;
}
```

Listing 10-8 shows a sample program that uses a raw_storage_iterator. A block of uninitialized memory is created by malloc(), the old C-style memory allocator. New objects are then copied into it by the raw storage iterator. A final dump at the end verifies that construction did, in fact, take place:

```
11111222223333344444455555
```

POINTERS: THE NEXT GENERATION

Devoted C/C++ programmers can become quite attached to pointers. They provide a level of power that isn't found in every high-level programming language, and have helped move C/C++ to its present level of popularity.

Well, iterators could just as well be called: Pointers, the Next Generation. They attempt to retain the current power and expressiveness of pointers, while giving them a whole new level of power. The good news is that the additional power seems to be there. The bad news is that power comes at a cost, and that cost is additional overhead in both code space and time.

In this chapter, I've tried to give you an in-depth look at these souped-up pointers. Now, you can judge for yourself if you're getting your money's worth from STL iterators.

INTRODUCTION TO ALGORITHMS

"Reeling and Writhing, of course, to begin with," the Mock Turtle replied, "and the different branches of Arithmetic—Ambition, Distraction, Uglification, and Derision."

— Lewis Carroll

If you were to reduce the definition of the STL to its bare essentials, you might say it consists of three components:

- containers
- iterators
- algorithms

Until now, I've gone into a lot of detail about containers and iterators. The remainder of this part of the book will describe *algorithms* and their close relatives, *function objects*.

WHAT IS AN ALGORITHM?

In computer science, we tend to think of an algorithm as an abstract procedural concept that is realized by way of programming. This obviously leads to an immensely large and unwieldy definition of algorithms, since *any* program becomes an implementation of *some* algorithm.

In the STL, algorithms are a much more specific entity. An STL algorithm is simply a template function, parameterized by the iterator types it operates on. The STL specification spells this out plainly:

> *"...algorithms are separated from the particular implementations of data structures and are parameterized by iterator types."*

This means all algorithms in the STL are template functions. If an algorithm iterates through a container, it does so using an iterator, and the iterator will be a template parameter.

Figure 11-1 is an illustration of this view of the STL. This level of abstraction is really a wonderful thing, because it means generic algorithms will work properly with *any* container, as long as it has a properly defined iterator.

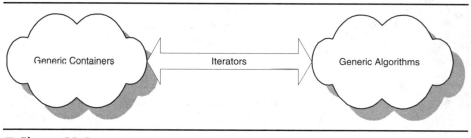

Figure 11-1
How STL algorithms work

Remember also that algorithms can specify requirements for the iterators they use without knowing anything about the containers. For example, a sort routine can specify that it needs a random access iterator, which means it will work with deque<T>, vector<T>, and built-in arrays. If you define a new container type that has a random access iterator, it will work with that as well.

Of course, one of the most important characteristics of generic algorithms is efficiency. Programmers won't use generic algorithms if they can hand-code an equivalent version that is even *slightly* faster. The STL deals with this reality in two ways. First, the template-based implementation of STL algorithms ensures efficient implementations (although code bloat is still a potential danger). Second, STL algorithms provide specializations on iterator types, meaning all algorithms don't have to work with the lowest common denominator. (Chapter 10 provides details on how this works.)

ARGUMENTS TO ALGORITHMS

A typical function prototype for an STL algorithm looks something like this:

```
template<class BidirectionalIterator>
void reverse(BidirectionalIterator first,
             BidirectionalIterator last );
```

The reverse() function reverses the order of elements in a container. There are two different specializations for this function, depending on whether the argument passed is a random access or bidirectional iterator. The implementation for the random access iterator probably looks just the way you would have written the code yourself:

```
template <class RandomAccessIterator>
void __reverse(RandomAccessIterator first,
               RandomAccessIterator last
               random_access_iterator_tag )
{
    while (first < last)
        iter_swap(first++, --last);
}
```

STL algorithms access containers via iterators, and are parameterized based on the iterator type. That is the case in reverse(). It doesn't care at all what sort of container the iterator is pointing to. In fact, all it cares about is that the iterators can be incremented, decremented, and dereferenced [in iter_swap()].

Parameterization

Algorithms such as reverse() always need to be parameterized based on the iterator type. A useful algorithm is bound to perform operations on the iterator, such as dereferencing, incrementing, decrementing, and so on. The only way for a general-purpose algorithm to make use of this functionality in the STL is through the use of template parameters.

This parameterization also gives the compiler the opportunity to generate the most efficient code possible. For instance, suppose the compiler finds this code in your program:

```
void foo( vector<int> &a )
{
    reverse( a.begin(), a.end() );
```

The compiler has read in all the template class and function definitions supplied by the STL, so it's capable of generating code that is the equivalent of this C++ code:

```
int *p1 = &a.start;
int *p2 = &a.finish;
while ( p1 < p2 ) {
    int tmp;
    tmp = *p1;
    *p1++ = *--p2;
    *p2 = tmp;
}
```

When a C++ compiler is doing its proper job, this template code should reverse the elements in a vector container every bit as efficiently as you could have done with a hand-coded routine to reverse an integer array.

Checking for legal iterators

Chapter 10, "Iterators," explains the hierarchy of iterators. This hierarchy is very important in the implementation of algorithms. In some cases, creating a generic function to work on every type of iterator isn't possible. As an example, imagine trying to implement the previously mentioned reverse() function using only a forward iterator!

In other cases, an algorithm can be implemented more efficiently using one iterator type compared to another. The reverse() algorithm provides another example of this. The implementation shown above works well for a random access iterator, but it doesn't work for bidirectional iterators. Bidirectional iterators don't have operator<(), so they can only be tested with operator==(). That restriction leads to this specialization function:

```
template <class BidirectionalIterator>
void __reverse( BidirectionalIterator first,
                BidirectionalIterator last,
                bidirectional_iterator_tag) {
    while (true)
        if (first == last || first == --last)
            return;
        else
            iter_swap(first++, last);
}
```

This algorithm is slightly inferior, because it has to make two comparisons per swap instead of one. But it does the best it can, given the limitations of the bidirectional iterator.

The main limitation of this system is the method the compiler must use to check for valid iterators. For instance, the public definition of reverse() specifies both iterators as type BidirectionalIterator. This implies to STL users that they need to call reverse() with an iterator which, at a minimum, supports the set of operations defined for bidirectional iterators.

Although the names of the arguments in the function template imply something about the argument types to us, they don't have the same significance to the compiler. If you pass a forward iterator as an argument to reverse(), the compiler won't fret. Instead, it begins trying to implement the algorithm with that iterator. If you are attempting an operation on an unsupported iterator type, you'll get the usual flood of compiler errors.

This problem is discussed in greater detail in Chapter 10. At this stage in the development of C++, it's not easy to specify the requirements of a type argument to a template class or function. This means it's incumbent upon you, the programmer, to pay attention to the argument types in the function description. The compiler isn't going to offer much help in matching up algorithms with appropriate iterators; it leaves the burden on you.

Returning data

When template functions were added to C++, one seemingly useful feature was left out: the ability to parameterize template function return types. This seems at first glance like it would be an easy enough feature to implement, but it isn't hard to think up troublesome counter-examples:

```
template<class ReturnType, class ArgType>
ReturnType foo( ArgType a )
{
    ...
```

Template function foo() looks like a reasonable function that parameterizes its return type. It's easy to see how the compiler would deduce the return type given a function call like this:

```
int test = foo( 2.0 );
```

But what is the compiler going to do when it encounters a function call like this?

```
main()
{
    foo( 0xffff );
```

In this case, the compiler has no clue what the return type ought to be. You might think this is a trivial matter, since the return from the function isn't used, but foo() may well use the return type internally when performing other calculations.

The most practical way around this problem is to use reference arguments to return values from algorithms. In the STL, this is the conventional way to return an object. The compiler has no problem deducing types when a reference is used as an argument. A case in point is shown below in the STL count() algorithm:

```
template <class InputIterator, class T, class Size>
void count(InputIterator first,
           InputIterator last,
           const T& value,
           Size& n) {
    while (first != last)
        if (*first++ == value)
            ++n;
}
```

You may feel somewhat uncomfortable returning values from functions via reference arguments, but this is simply a result of the state-of-the-art in C++.

Function objects and adaptors

The other important new argument type passed to STL algorithms is *function objects*. Function objects are a large enough topic to merit a chapter of their own (the next one, in fact). The quick explanation of function objects presented here emphasizes their role as the type-parameterized equivalent of function pointers. In fact, a function pointer works quite handily any time a function object is required.

The classic use of a function object is with the for_each() function. for_each() is categorized as an algorithm, but is really more of a helper function. It provides a convenient way to apply a function to every element in a container. This saves you the trouble of writing a few lines of code.

for_each() iterates its way through a sequence of objects defined by a pair of iterators, and applies a function object to each object in turn. If you look at the source for the for_each() algorithm, it looks as though the function argument has to be a function pointer:

```
template <class InputIterator, class Function>
Function for_each(InputIterator first,
                  InputIterator last,
                  Function f) {
    while (first != last)
        f(*first++);
    return f;
}
```

Because of the way template functions work, you aren't restricted to simply passing function pointers for this argument. It's just as valid to pass an object that has operator()() defined. Listing 11-1 shows how this works, in this case by defining a class that can be used to dump data using for_each().

Listing 11-1

for1101.cpp: A demonstration of the for_each() algorithm

```
//
// FOR1101.CPP
//
// This example is used in Chapter 11 to show how function
// objects and function pointers can be used with for_each().
// This example uses both types to do the same thing.
// The major difference between the two is that in this case
// the function pointer is limited to servicing a single
// type of object, whereas the template function object
// is able to deal with all built-in types, as well as
// any others with a defined insertion operator.
//

#include <iostream.h>
#include <string.h>

//
// Borland 4.x workarounds
//
#define __MINMAX_DEFINED
#pragma option -vi-
```

```
#include "vector.h"
#include "algo.h"

void dump( char c )
{
    cout << c;
}

template<class T>
struct dump_obj {
    void operator()(T x){ cout << x; }
};

main()
{
    char *init = "A string";
    vector<char> a( init, init + strlen( init ) );

    cout << "Using a function pointer: ";
    for_each( a.begin(), a.end(), dump );
    cout << endl;

    cout << "In reverse order, using a function object: ";
    for_each( a.rbegin(), a.rend(), dump_obj<char>() );
    cout << endl;

    return 0;
}
```

In for1101.cpp, struct dump_obj has operator()() defined, so it can be passed as a function argument as easily as a function pointer. In the STL, there are quite a few template function objects already defined that serve as building blocks that can be used as glue when calling generic algorithms. These are described in detail in the next chapter.

The output from for1101.cpp looks like this:

```
Using a function pointer: A string
In reverse order, using a function object: gnirts A
```

COPY AND PREDICATE VARIANTS

Many algorithms have one or more variant versions defined. There are two variants that can be defined for a given algorithm:

- the copy variant
- the if variant

Most STL algorithms replace the contents of a container with the result of an algorithm. However, there may be times when you want the output of an algorithm placed in a different container. Many of the standard STL algorithms have a second version that copies its results to a new container. The copy variant is always identified with the suffix "_copy" appended to the algorithm name.

An example is the rotate() algorithm. The standard rotate() function rotates the members of a container by a specified amount. rotate_copy() does the same thing, except it sends the results to a new container. In Listing 11-2, the copy02.cpp program shows how this works.

Listing 11-2

copy1102.cpp: A demonstration of a copy variant

```
//
// COPY1102.CPP
//
// This example is used in Chapter 11 to show an example
// of a copy variant of an algorithm. rotate_copy()
// rotates a container by a specified amount, and
// copies the result into a new container. This program
// also uses an inserter iterator to simplify life a bit.
//

#include <iostream.h>
#include <string.h>

//
// Borland 4.x workarounds
//
#define __MINMAX_DEFINED
#pragma option -vi-
```

```
#include "list.h"
#include "deque.h"
#include "algo.h"

void dump( char c )
{
    cout << c ;
}

main()
{
    char *init = "A new string!";
    deque<char> a( init, init + strlen( init ) );
    list<char> b;

    rotate_copy( a.begin(),
                 a.begin() + 4,
                 a.end(),
                 back_insert_iterator<list<char> >( b ) );
    for_each( b.begin(), b.end(), dump );
    return 0;
}
```

The output from copy1102.cpp shows that the rotated string has been copied correctly into the list container:

```
w string!A ne
```

The second type of variant is the "if" variant. An *if* version of an algorithm uses a function object to determine whether an operation should be applied to individual elements in a container. For instance, the replace() algorithm has a replace_if() variant. replace() simply looks through a container, and replaces any object equal to a test value. On the other hand, replace_if() uses a boolean function object to determine whether the object should be replaced.

This boolean function is referred to as the *predicate function*. A predicate function controls whether or not an algorithm applies an operation to individual objects.

rep03.cpp uses a simple function pointer as its predicate function, but you can use other kinds of function objects as well. The output from this program shows that all six-letter names were replaced:

```
Before: Bill George Gerald Jimmy Ronald
After: Bill <None> <None> Jimmy <None>
```

Listing 11-3

rep1103.cpp: A demonstration of an if variant

```cpp
//
// REP1103.CPP
//
// This example is used in Chapter 11 to demonstrate the
// replace_if() function. It goes through a set of
// names, and replaces each one that passes the test()
// function. test() just tests to see if the name has
// exactly six letters!
//
// Note that this program uses Borland's implementation
// of a string class.  You may have to make minor
// changes to adapt to your compiler.

#include <iostream.h>
//
// Borland 4.x workarounds
//
#define __MINMAX_DEFINED
#pragma option -vi-

#include <cstring.h>
#include "set.h"
#include "algo.h"

void dump( string s )
{
    cout << s << " ";
}

bool test( string s )
{
    if ( s.length() == 6 )
        return true;
    else
        return false;
}

main()
{
    set<string, less<string> > a;

    a.insert( "Bill" );
    a.insert( "George" );
    a.insert( "Ronald" );
```

```
    a.insert( "Jimmy" );
    a.insert( "Gerald" );
    cout << "Before: ";
    for_each( a.begin(), a.end(), dump );
    cout << endl
         << "After: ";
    replace_if( a.begin(), a.end(), test, "<None>" );
    for_each( a.begin(), a.end(), dump );
    cout << endl;
    return 0;
}
```

In addition, these two variants can also be combined to form a copy_if variant; both variant functions are simply performed simultaneously.

CONST? DON'T BET ON IT!

C++ supports the concept of const-ness in various ways. You can specify that pointer or reference arguments to a function are const arguments, and rest assured that the compiler will enforce the const rules. Not only will it prevent you from inadvertently modifying a variable, but it can also help the compiler generate more efficient code.

Unfortunately, STL algorithms have a tough time enforcing the rules of const-ness. There really isn't a convenient way to write template functions that mandate the use of const iterator types. Even though iterators are a lot like pointers, their similarity breaks down in this area. It's really easy to write a function declaration like this:

```
void foo( const char *arg )
{
```

But try writing a similar declaration for a template function with an iterator argument. What you really want to say is: "When I apply operator*() to arg, I promise not to modify the resulting lvalue." But there isn't a good way to say this when talking about iterator types as template arguments.

As a consequence, you'll see sentences like this in the STL from time to time:

"f() is assumed not to apply any non-constant function through the dereferenced iterator."

You can read between the lines pretty easily here. The spec is telling us that we're all on the honor system. The STL is doing the best it can, but it's very easy to subvert its prohibitions. So, when an algorithm is described as "non-mutating" (read: const), it's only a suggestion, not a law!

ALGORITHM CATEGORIES

The STL comes with a big batch of algorithms. To try to bring some order to the party, the STL specification breaks the algorithms down into four groups:

- non-mutating sequence operations
- mutating sequence operations
- sorting and related operations
- generalized numeric operations

For organizational purposes, things in this book have been subdivided a little more. A few new categories have been created:

- set operations
- heap operations
- miscellaneous

These additional categories break the list of algorithms into smaller pieces. Hopefully, these groups are not only smaller, but more coherent as well. Remember that these categories are specific to this book, and aren't part of either the ANSI/ISO or STL specifications.

Each category has its own reference chapter later on in the book. The remainder of this chapter just gives a thumbnail sketch of each category, which includes a list of algorithms. Remember that each named algorithm may have multiple manifestations. There may be overloaded versions of a function that take different types or numbers of arguments. Also, each algorithm can have if and copy variants.

Non-mutating sequence operations

These algorithms work their way through a range defined by two iterators. This range is often defined as the begin and end points of a container. The algorithms execute in O(N) time, where N is the length of the range.

These functions are termed *non-mutating* because they are not supposed to modify the objects pointed to by their iterators. (The term *mutating* seems to be derived from the new C++ keyword *mutable*.) However, they suffer from the const-ness leaks mentioned previously. Accordingly, it's possible to modify the objects with a poorly behaved predicate function.

The non-mutating sequence operations defined in the STL specification are:

- for_each()
- find()
- find_end()
- find_first_of()
- adjacent_find()
- count()
- mismatch()
- equal()
- search()

Mutating sequence operations

These algorithms are part of the same family as the previous set. They, too, work on a range defined by a pair of iterators. The critical difference is that these algorithms *do* modify the objects pointed to by the iterators.

If you read through the descriptions of these functions in later chapters of the book, you'll probably observe that there isn't much of a common thread holding them together. Collectively, they constitute a useful toolkit, but they are very different tools!

- copy()
- swap()
- transform()
- replace()

- fill()
- generate()
- remove()
- unique()
- reverse()
- rotate()
- random_shuffle()
- partition()

Sorting and searching

The sorting and searching algorithms work on built-in arrays, vectors, and deque objects. As they require a pair of random access iterators to define their ranges, lists and associative containers can't be sorted.

This isn't as much of a hardship as it might appear at first glance. list<> containers have a sort() member function tuned for linked lists, and, by design, the associative containers are always sorted.

- sort()
- stable_sort()
- partial_sort()
- nth_element()
- lower_bound()
- upper_bound()
- equal_range()
- binary_search()
- merge()

Sets

These algorithms provide basic set operations like union, intersection, and difference. As they only work on sorted structures, you need to be careful when using sequence containers with these algorithms.

In the STL specification, these functions don't merit a separate category. Instead, they are grouped with the other sorting algorithms.

- includes()
- set_union()
- set_intersection()
- set_difference()
- set_symmetric_difference()

Heaps

This set of functions is used to turn sequential containers into heaps. Heaps are a relatively efficient way to maintain a collection of data in a quasi-sorted state. These heap functions are used by the priority_queue container adaptor.

In the STL specification, these functions are grouped with the other sorting algorithms.

- push_heap()
- pop_heap()
- make_heap()
- sort_heap()

Numeric algorithms

These functions provide a varied mix of numerical functions. The four algorithms here are part of the STL as released by HP. When incorporated into the C++ draft specification, most of the STL algorithms were included in what is referred to as the Algorithms Library. These four, however, were moved to the Numerics Library, which is probably a good fit. The Numerics Library includes support for things like complex numbers and multidimensional arrays.

- accumulate()
- inner_product()
- partial_sum()
- adjacent_difference()

Miscellaneous

Finally, there are a few miscellaneous functions that don't really belong in any of the above categories. In the STL specification, they are grouped with the sorting algorithms.

- min()
- max()
- min_element()
- max_element()
- lexicographical_compare()
- next_permutation()
- prev_permutation()

WHAT'S MISSING?

The STL's algorithm library has been criticized by some, since there are dozens of fertile areas that are completely left out. These include, but aren't limited to:

- graphics
- statistics
- number crunching
- signal processing
- text processing

Even in the areas that it does cover, the STL doesn't provide extensive algorithm support. For example, sorting and searching is an area that could easily make use of dozens of functions.

While it might be nice if the STL added comprehensive support in some of these areas, it would have been extremely difficult to create and test such a library in time to be incorporated into the C++ specification. What the STL did instead is probably more important: it created a solid framework to support the *future* creation of more comprehensive standard and third-party libraries.

And when you think about it, what's lacking in the STL could be turned into an opportunity. By studying the algorithms supplied with the STL, you can begin writing generic algorithms of your own. The task has been made immensely easier for you, due to the existing STL infrastructure of iterators, containers, and allocators. Perhaps you can even take advantage of the nascent market for STL-compliant algorithm libraries!

FUNCTION OBJECTS

Nothing can have value without being an object of utility.
— Karl Marx, *Das Kapital*, Part II

The STL specification gives a short definition of *function objects*:

> *"Function objects are objects with an operator() defined...In places where one would expect to pass a pointer to a function to an algorithmic template, the interface is specified to accept an object with an operator() defined."*

This definition is accurate, but it doesn't completely capture the range of possibilities inherent in function objects. In Chapter 3, function objects are described as one of the five key components of the library. If function objects have earned such a lofty status, you probably feel this definition is a little thin, and want to flesh it out!

NOT QUITE A POINTER

It's quite true that function objects are akin to function pointers. In fact, the STL code that makes use of function objects is virtually oblivious to the existence of function objects; such code is written as if function objects were standard function pointers.

But while the STL library code doesn't care much about function objects, *you* will appreciate the difference. Using function objects instead of function pointers will allow you to avoid creating customized functions that only provide simple callback routines. Instead, you can select from the many predefined function objects included with the library.

You might ask at this point, couldn't the STL just have provided a set of callback functions, instead of these function objects? It might seem a good idea at first, but remember that the callback functions would have to be *template functions*, since they need to work with various types of objects. Since the library wouldn't know in advance which types to instantiate, you'd have to do it yourself. Instantiating function objects just happens to be an easier way of doing it, since you create the object when and where you need it.

This chapter elaborates on why function objects are useful entities, what they are, how they are used, and which predefined objects ship with the STL. In addition, you will see how function adaptors can be applied to function objects, yielding even more useful objects.

Origins

Nobody ever accused standard ANSI C of being an object-oriented programming language. But one way that standard C can make a half-hearted attempt at polymorphism is through the use of function pointers.

A good example of this is qsort(), defined as a standard library function. It can sort an array of objects in memory without knowing anything about the type of objects it's working with. A look at the prototype of qsort() gives a couple of hints as to how it works:

```
void qsort( void *base,
            size_t nelem,
            size_t width,
            int ( *cmp )( const void *, const void * )  );
```

The arguments passed to qsort() have the following definitions:

base: This is a pointer to the beginning of the array of elements to be sorted. Since this is C and not C++, qsort() has to use a void * as the argument type. C's pointer conversion rules allow you to pass any sort of pointer as a valid argument, since any type of pointer can be freely converted to a void *.

nelem: This is the number of elements in the array (the number to be sorted). Note that this is different from the way the STL provides object ranges. The STL uses a start/finish pointer pair instead of this start/count convention. qsort() could have been designed to use either approach without much difference in ease of use or efficiency.

width: This is the size of each element in the array. Since qsort() doesn't know *anything* about the array elements, you must pass it the width of each object. When qsort() exchanges elements during the sorting process, it needs the element width.

cmp: This function pointer is the key to the pseudo-polymorphism of qsort(); it's called by qsort() to compare two objects. To sort the array, qsort() has to compare elements to one another. The function must compare the two objects pointed to by the two void pointers it receives, and then return -1, 0, or 1, depending on whether the first object is less than, equal to, or greater than the second object.

    If you were to write a sorting function that took the parameters listed above, you could probably cook something up fairly easily. You'd iterate through the array, incrementing pointers *width* bytes at a time as you moved from element to element. You'd compare elements using the cmp() function passed by the caller, and shuffle objects using memcpy(), or its equivalent.

    Figure 12-1 shows how qsort() uses the comparison function it gets passed. It keeps a pair of internal pointers into the array it's sorting. Even though they are initially of type void, qsort() knows they have to be incremented *width* bytes at a time to stay properly aligned on object boundaries.

    A simple C program that uses qsort() to sort an array of integers is shown in Listing 12-1. To get qsort() to work properly with an integer array, sort1201.c has to supply a pointer to a comparison function. Although the comparison function int_cmp() is short and simple, it isn't as convenient as you'd like. For one thing, the qsort() prototype wants you to write a comparison function that takes void pointers, which means you have to cast to the type you're using. And it would really be much nicer if you didn't have to write functions like this at all!

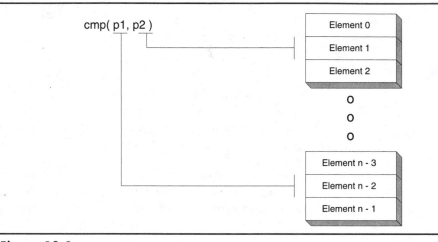

Figure 12-1

How qsort() uses the comparison function

Listing 12-1

sort1201.c: Demonstrating the use of qsort()

```
/*
 * SORT1201.C
 *
 * This program is used in Chapter 12 to demonstrate
 * how the C standard function qsort() is used.
 */

#include <stdlib.h>
#include <stdio.h>

/*
 * This is the comparison function passed to qsort().
 * qsort() expects the function to take two void
 * pointers, instead of pointers to the user-specified
 * type. This means you either have to cast the
 * function prototype in the call to qsort(), or
 * cast the arguments in the function. The
 * latter was chosen for this example.
 */
```

```
int int_cmp( const void *p1, const void *p2 )
{
    return * (const int *) p1 - * (const int *) p2;
}

int test[]={ 4, 5, 2, 4, 100, -1, 2, 8 };
#define NELEM ( sizeof( test ) / sizeof( int ) )

main()
{
    int i;

    printf( "Before sorting: " );
    for ( i = 0 ; i < NELEM ; i++ )
        printf( "%d ", test[ i ] );
    printf( "\n" );

    qsort( test, NELEM, sizeof( int ), int_cmp );

    printf( "After sorting: " );
    for ( i = 0 ; i < NELEM ; i++ )
        printf( "%d ", test[ i ] );
    printf( "\n" );

    return 1;
}
```

Wouldn't it be nice ...

qsort() manages to achieve something similar to a generic algorithm through its use of function pointers, but at a high cost. Here are some of the drawbacks to this way of doing things:

- There is a complete absence of type safety. The generic function is working with void pointers, since they're the best common denominator available to C functions.

- You have no control over the construction and destruction of objects. Instead, objects are moved around using binary copy functions.

- qsort() only sorts arrays. Container types such as those supported in the STL won't work with a function like this.

- qsort() is limited to sorting objects in memory that can be manipulated using unadorned pointers. If you store data using an unconventional memory model, qsort() can't help you.

- There is extra overhead due to the use of a function pointer to perform comparisons. For a simple comparison that just uses operator<(), a function pointer is fairly inefficient. How much of a problem this is depends on how much time is spent on comparisons, relative to the rest of the algorithm.

- You have to hand-code a comparison function every time you use qsort() with a new data type. This is true regardless of how trivial the comparison function is.

To sum up, this example of a generic function in C requires lots of trickery to outsmart the compiler. Sorting is such a common operation—there really needs to be a better way! And there are lots of other generic functions that C programmers would like to have, but these kinds of difficulties have kept them from being added to the standard library.

Not surprisingly, most of the shortcomings in qsort() go away when the sort routine is coded as a template function instead of a C-style generic algorithm. A template version acquires complete type safety, properly uses constructors and destructors, and can sort arrays regardless of what type of memory they reside in.

However, there is still one detail needed to fashion a generic sort algorithm: the *comparison function*. It might be reasonable to just hard code the use of operator<() in the sort routine, but that would cut back on the sort algorithm's flexibility. A hard-coded operator<() would make it difficult to modify the algorithm even to do something as simple as sorting in reverse order.

What would be really nice is an easy way to specify the kind of comparison operation you want to perform, without having to go to the trouble of coding a comparison operation. If C++ were just a *little* different, the STL might be able to define a template function called *less*:

```
template<class T>
bool less( T& a, T& b)
{
    return a < b;
}
```

Then, if you wanted to sort a list of employee records, you could call the sort function using a call something like this:

```
sort( start, finish, less<employee>() );
```

This same syntax might let you create more sophisticated comparisons on the fly:

```
sort( start, finish, less<employee.name>() );
```

Unfortunately, C++ doesn't work that way. You can't instantiate a template function by using it as an argument. However, C++ *does* let you instantiate a *template class object* using syntax that looks just like this. And that is what the STL refers to as a *function object*.

INTRODUCING THE FUNCTION OBJECT

In standard C, functions like qsort() have a parameter defined as a pointer to a function. Now, template functions such as sort() in the STL also take an argument that can be a function pointer, but the template function treats the comparison argument differently than C functions do. A template function in the STL is parameterized on the comparison object, which means it can be any type whatsoever.

So, does this mean the comparison object for sort() can be anything from a function pointer, to an integer, to a complex object?

Not quite. Regardless of what a function object is, the template function will use it with the syntax of a function pointer. As an example, the source for the transform() algorithm is shown in the next piece of code. transform() simply applies a function to each object in a given range, and copies the result of the function to a new range, pointed to by an output iterator.

```
template <class InputIterator,
          class OutputIterator,
          class UnaryOperation>
OutputIterator transform( InputIterator first,
                          InputIterator last,
                          OutputIterator result,
                          UnaryOperation op) {
    while ( first != last )
        *result++ = op( *first++ );
    return result;
}
```

In transform(), the type of function object op is a template parameter, so the function prototype doesn't give any hints as to the type of object it requires for that parameter. In fact, there's only one restriction on the type of object it can be: it must be possible to apply operator()() to op, with an object of type T as a parameter. (In this case, T is the type that results from dereferencing the iterator.) This implication isn't obvious from the function prototype, but it becomes clear as you study the source code.

It seems pretty obvious that op can be a function. Listing 12-2 shows sqr1202.cpp, which squares an array of numbers using the transform() algorithm. The squaring is accomplished by the square() function, which was written along with the rest of the program.

Listing 12-2

sqr1202.cpp: Demonstrating the use of a function pointer with transform()

```
//
// SQR1202.CPP
//
// This program is used in Chapter 12 to pass a simple
// function pointer to the transform() algorithm, which
// allows it to square items in the vector. The output
// from transform()is sent to cout via an ostream iterator.
//

#define __MINMAX_DEFINED
#pragma option -vi-
#include <algo.h>

int test[]={ 4, 5, 2, 4, 100, -1, 2, 8 };
const int NELEM = sizeof( test ) / sizeof( int );

int square( int a )
{
    return a * a;
}

main()
{
    ostream_iterator<int> output( cout, " " );

    cout << "Before squaring: ";
    copy( test, test + NELEM, output );
    cout << endl;

    cout << "After squaring: ";
    transform( test,
               test + NELEM,
               output,
               square );
    cout << endl;

    return 1;
}
```

The output from sqr1202.cpp confirms that it is working properly:

```
Before squaring:      4 5 2 4 100 -1 2 8
After squaring:       16 25 4 16 10000 1 4 64
```

Listing 12-3 shows sqr1203.cpp, a very similar program that uses a function object to do exactly the same work. The function object is created by defining a template class, square<T>. square<T> is extremely simple; operator()() is its only user-defined member function.

Listing 12-3

sqr1203.cpp: Demonstrating the use of a function object with transform()

```cpp
//
// SQR1203.CPP
//
// This program in Chapter 12 is nearly identical to
// sqr1202.cpp. But instead of using a function pointer to
// get transform() to square all the elements of a
// vector, it uses a function object. The function object,
// square<T>, is a local created class, not one of the
// classes provided with the library.
//

#define __MINMAX_DEFINED
#pragma option -vi-

#include <algo.h>
#include <function.h>

int test[]={ 4, 5, 2, 4, 100, -1, 2, 8 };
const int NELEM = sizeof( test ) / sizeof( int );

template<class T>
struct square {
    T operator()( T n ){ return n * n ; }
};

main()
{
    ostream_iterator<int> output( cout, " " );

    cout << "Before applying square: ";
    copy( test, test + NELEM, output );
    cout << endl;

    cout << "After squaring: ";
```

```
    transform( test,
               test + NELEM,
               output,
               square<int>() );
    cout << endl;

    return 1;
}
```

operator()() is the key ingredient in the square<T> class, since it allows an object created using this class to masquerade as a function. It means you could conceivably write code like this:

```
    square<double> f;

    cout << "value = " << f( 5.0 ) << endl;
```

Because of operator(), an object of this class looks like a function—or a function pointer.

And your point is?

Some programming language aficionados might argue that this sort of syntactic sleight-of-hand is a thing of beauty, and doesn't need to justify its existence. But if you have a more pragmatic view, you might wonder what all the fuss is about. After all, writing the function object in sqr1203.cpp looked to be just as difficult (if not more) as writing the one-line function in sqr1202.cpp. Why do we need to bother with function objects at all?

The main reason function objects are useful is, in a word, *libraries*. C++ is a language that not only allows libraries to exist, it actively supports them. The STL's collection and grouping of function objects into a library ought to make function objects near and dear to the hearts of C++ programmers. This is even more true when you consider that function pointers cannot be collected in this manner.

Why can't function pointers be collected like this? Well, to collect function pointers, you must have functions to point to. So, for the little square() function given above, you might start writing a library like this:

```
    int square_int( int a ){ return a * a; }
    long square_long( long a ){ return a * a; }
    double square_double( double a ){ return a * a; }
```

```
int (*square_int_ptr)(int) = square_int;
long (*square_long_ptr)(long) = square_long;
double (*square_double_ptr)(double) = square_double;
```

You can see where this is leading. Even for simple arithmetic functions, there is a seemingly endless collection of pointers and functions to create. And how do you handle operations on user-defined types? You can't write those functions in advance! Templates were invented to prevent exactly this sort of thing.

So can we use template functions to solve the problem? We could if this were legal:

```
template<class T>
T square( const T& a )
{
    return a * a;
}

template<class T> T (*square_ptr)(T) = square<T>;
```

The above line of code attempts to create a pointer to a template function. That way, we can let the compiler instantiate the functions as we need them, and we pick up the pointer automatically.

The trouble is, *this doesn't work!* The simple fact of the matter is that template functions and function pointers don't cooperate very well. If you want to be able to use the power of the template mechanism to create code when you need it, you are going to need to use a different mechanism. And that mechanism is the function object.

Old ways are good ways

Function objects are great when you want to create a parameterized function that can be used with lots of different types. And that's just what the STL authors did. But is there any reason to create your own function objects?

The test is simple. If your function is only going to be used with one class, just write a standard C/C++ function to do the job for you. When you call an STL algorithm, pass a pointer to the function. It should be easy to convert to a function object in the future if you need to.

On the other hand, if your function looks like it might be useful to many classes, create a template class that attaches your function to operator()(). Once you have debugged it using several different object types, you will have a component that deserves a place in your personal object library.

FUNCTION OBJECT LIBRARIES

Function objects are defined as classes. In the case of the STL, these are usually template classes. Once the class is defined, creating a function object is as simple as instantiating any other object: you simply invoke the constructor with the appropriate arguments.

So, for example, the STL has a function object defined that compares two objects using operator>(), and returns a boolean true or false. The function is called, naturally enough, greater(). When you want to use greater() to help sort a vector of integers, you can simply call the sort() algorithm like this:

```
sort( v.begin(), v.end(), greater<int>() );
```

If the designers of the STL had tried to create a library of functions that were used via function pointers, they'd have had to deal with some real difficulties. If the functions had been defined as template functions, programmers would now have to specifically instantiate a function somewhere before using it, requiring us to go through extra steps now seen as unnecessary.

Accordingly, while it might be true that creating a function object is no easier than creating a function to be used with an algorithm, the function object can easily be distributed as part of a package of pre-built objects. Standard functions lack this capability.

Later in this chapter, you'll find a description of the function objects supplied as part of the standard STL release. These functions provide the building blocks for a fairly wide variety of programming needs.

DATA ENCAPSULATION

Using function pointers as callbacks to algorithms has an additional problem: the lack of data encapsulation. For example, if you wanted to square all the elements of an array, and total them up at the same time, you could write a function like this:

```
int counter = 0;
int square_total( int i )
{
    int temp = i * i;
    counter += temp;
    return temp;
}
```

If you then passed this function to an STL algorithm such as transform(), it would total up the values in the counter variable, which is what you wanted. But it did this by using a global variable, which should have immediately raised warning flags in your mind!

The fact that the counter is a global variable spells big trouble for this function in quite a number of different circumstances. Imagine, for example, if this function were part of a shared library being accessed by several different threads or processes simultaneously. The value of the counter would be changed in an unpredictable manner.

Since function objects are created each time they're used, they can either contain unique data objects or pointers/references to unique data objects. Listing 12-4 shows the program sum1204.cpp, which totals up the sums of the squares in a vector using a unique data reference that is instantiated with each version of the object.

Listing 12-4

sum1204.cpp: Demonstrating the data encapsulation possible with function objects

```
//
// SUM1204.CPP
//
// This program is used in Chapter 12
// to demonstrate the ability of
// function objects to encapsulate data. The
// program creates a function object from the
// sum_square class, which contains a reference
// to a user-supplied counter. That counter
// will have the squared quantity added to
// it each time square() is called. After
// transform() is complete, counter will hold
// the sum of the squares of the input range.
//

//
// Borland 4.x workarounds
//
#define __MINMAX_DEFINED
#pragma option -vi-

#include <algo.h>
#include <function.h>

int test[]-{ 4, 5, 2, 4, 100, -1, 2, 8 };
const int NELEM = sizeof( test ) / sizeof( int );
```

```cpp
template<class T>
struct sum_square {
    T &counter;
    sum_square( int &c ) : counter( c ){ counter = 0; }
    T operator()( T n )
    {
        T temp = n * n;
        counter += temp;
        return temp;
    }
};

main()
{
    ostream_iterator<int> output( cout, " " );

    cout << "Before applying square: ";
    copy( test, test + NELEM, output );
    cout << endl;

    int count;
    cout << "After squaring: ";
    transform( test,
               test + NELEM,
               output,
               sum_square<int>( count ) );
    cout << endl;

    cout << "count = " << count << endl;
    return 1;
}
```

Through a glass darkly

The output from sum1204.cpp shows that it works:

```
Before applying square: 4 5 2 4 100 -1 2 8
After squaring: 16 25 4 16 10000 1 4 64
count = 10130
```

Why it works might not be so obvious. The program's goal is to square all the numbers in the test array, and sum all the squares. The summation is stored in a variable called *counter*.

The function object that does the work is an instance of the class sum_square<T>. It looks a lot like the function object found in sqr1203.cpp, with a few minor differences. First, it contains a reference to a counter variable. Second, it has a constructor that initializes that counter reference, as well as setting its initial value to 0. Finally, each time it processes a new value, it adds the squared value to counter.

An instance of sum_square<int> is created in the call to transform(). In sqr1203.cpp, you saw the constructor called with no arguments, but here it is passed a reference to the counter. The constructor will set the value of the counter to 0, which makes sense for this particular application.

From that point on, the operation of the function object is straight-forward. The transform() algorithm is going to invoke operator()() for the object once per element in the input sequence. Each time the sum_square object is called upon, it squares its input, adds it to the counter, and returns the squared value to the calling program.

Once transform() is complete, the function object will be destroyed. Since the counter is a local variable in the scope of main(), it remains in scope, and can be accessed to get the sum of the squares.

Fogged in yet?

If you've followed the explanation of how function object sum_square<T> works so far, hang on, there's just one additional detail that needs explanation. When using this function object, it might have occurred to you that it would be a good idea to make the counter a public data member of the function object. Then you could do something like this:

```
sum_square<int> f;
transform( a.begin(), a.end(), f );
cout << "total = " << f.counter << endl;
```

This would be nice, because it encapsulates the data in the object that is working with it. But this strategy would fail, for one simple reason: the function object gets passed as a value parameter to transform(), which means transform() receives a *copy* of the function object passed to it, not the object itself.

As a result, initialization and incrementing would be done on the counter in a *copy* of the function object. That same copy would be destroyed when transform() finished its work, leaving the counter in the function object curiously stuck at 0!

The net result is that any data updated or maintained by a function object needs to be accessed by a reference or a pointer, so that multiple copies of the object always access the same data element.

You can do this using a reference to data outside the function object, as you saw in sum1204.cpp. Or you can keep the data inside the function object, then create a special copy constructor that creates a reference to the data in the master object. The second solution accomplishes the encapsulation, but at the expense of more code (and tricky code, at that!).

NAMES AND PLACES

By now, you should be convinced that function objects are wonderful things, and you're probably wondering where you can start using them. The first step in this process is to see how function objects are organized in the STL. However, the STL doesn't specifically group the function objects it defines, so the organization given in this chapter should be considered *ad hoc*. The three types of function objects used with the STL are:

- predicate function objects
- comparison function objects
- numeric function objects

Each type of function object is called for in a specific place in the STL. However, they aren't rigorously defined, so using them correctly falls mostly on your shoulders as the programmer.

You need to be careful. The C++ compiler isn't able to accurately specify the types of template arguments it expects, so it's possible to use the wrong type of function object. This is an endemic problem with templates, as has been discussed in Chapter 10.

Predicate function objects

Many STL algorithms that operate over an entire range specified by two iterators only perform their operations on specific members in the range. For example, count() locates all the objects in a range that match a specific value, and find() locates the first member in the range that matches a specific value.

Algorithms that look for such a match usually take a *value* parameter of type T. Each element in the input range is compared to the value parameter so the algorithm can decide whether to perform its operation or not. For example, the remove() algorithm removes all elements from a range that match a specific value. Its function prototype is:

```
template <class ForwardIterator, class T>
ForwardIterator remove( ForwardIterator first,
                        ForwardIterator last,
                        const T& value);
```

The last argument in the function prototype is value, which tells remove() which values to remove from the sequence.

Most of the functions that perform a comparison to a value also have an *if* variant, which replaces the value argument with a predicate function object. Instead of comparing the objects in a range to the value, the if variants of STL algorithms evaluate the predicate function, using each of the elements in the range as an argument. The predicate function returns a boolean value, which tells the algorithm whether or not to perform the indicated operation.

Accordingly, the remove() function has a remove() variant, which replaces the value argument with a predicate function object argument. The prototype for remove_if() is as follows:

```
template <class ForwardIterator, class Predicate>
ForwardIterator remove_if( ForwardIterator first,
                           ForwardIterator last,
                           Predicate pred);
```

In general, you can assume that, when an algorithm has an if version, it simply replaces a value argument with a predicate function object argument. As the function iterates through the range defined by its input iterators, it applies the predicate function to each object pointed to by an iterator. Its actions are determined by whether the predicate function returns true or false.

Listing 12-5 gives a short example of the use of a predicate function object. In this case, the function object returns true if the string being tested appears anywhere in a blacklist of names. replace_copy_if() replaces any name that shows up in the blacklist with "***REPLACED***". The output from repl1205.cpp confirms that this has happened:

```
Before: FORTRAN C C++ Prolog BASIC
After: ***REPLACED*** C C++ Prolog ***REPLACED***
```

Listing 12-5

repl1205.cpp: Demonstrating the use of a predicate function object

```
/*
 * REPL1205.CPP
 *
 * This program is used in Chapter 12 to demonstrate
 * the use of a predicate function with the
 * replace_copy_if() algorithm. The function object
 * returns a value of true when the language being
 * tested is on the blacklist.
 *
 */


//
// Borland 4.x workarounds
//
#define __MINMAX_DEFINED
#pragma option -vi-

#include <iostream.h>
#include <cstring.h>
#include <algo.h>
#include <vector.h>

char *blacklist[]={ "FORTRAN", "BASIC", "JCL", 0 };

struct pred {
    bool operator()( string& s ) {
        for ( char **p = blacklist ; *p != 0 ; p++ ) {
            if ( s == *p )
                return true;
        }
        return false;
    }
};

main()
{
    vector<string> a;
    a.push_back( "FORTRAN" );
    a.push_back( "C" );
    a.push_back( "C++" );
    a.push_back( "Prolog" );
    a.push_back( "BASIC" );
```

```
cout << "Before: ";
copy( a.begin(),
      a.end(),
      ostream_iterator<string>( cout, " " ) );
cout << endl;
cout << "After: ";
replace_copy_if( a.begin(),
                 a.end(),
                 ostream_iterator<string>( cout, " " ),
                 pred(),
                 string( "***REPLACED***" ) );
cout << endl;
return 1;

}
```

Comparison function objects

Comparison function objects do just what they say: they compare two objects. They are used by algorithms that perform sorting, searching or ordering functions. In addition, comparison objects are used by container classes that store data in an ordered fashion, such as associative containers.

A comparison object is a boolean function that takes two arguments of type T. It returns true or false, based on whatever logic you decide to use to order the elements. A good example of a comparison function is supplied by the STL in functions.h. Here, less<T> simply uses operator<() to compare two objects. Since this is a template function, it adapts to any type that knows how to perform logical comparisons using operator<().

```
template <class T>
struct less : binary_function<T, T, bool> {
    bool operator()(const T& x, const T& y) const
    {
        return x < y;
    }
};
```

The STL contains a library of function objects that can really cut down on the need to write customized comparison functions. less<T> is a perfect example of this. Instead of having to write a customized version of a simple comparison function every time you create a new associative container, you can pass the name of the function object to the template definition. The class constructor either lets you pass your own function object when you create a set, or uses the default parameter mechanism to create one of its own.

In Chapter 8, where associative container classes are discussed in detail, the less<T> function object is used frequently in class declarations such as this:

```
set<int, less<int> > a( first_element, last_element );
```

Besides their use with associative containers, comparison object functions are employed in many STL algorithms in the sorting and searching categories. Many of these functions have two versions: one that uses operator<() as a default comparison function object, and another that takes a user-supplied function object to perform comparisons.

As an example of this, you can use the sort function without supplying an explicitly comparison operator:

```
sort( a.begin(), a.end() );
```

If you want to sort the objects using some criteria different from that provided by the default comparison operator, you can either pass a function object of your own creation, or one defined in the function object library.

Listing 12-6

sort1206.cpp: Demonstrating the use of a comparison function object

```
//
// SORT1206.CPP
//
// This program uses the sort() algorithm to sort an array
// of C strings (char pointers). If we use the default
// comparison operator provided by sort(), the array
// gets sorted based on the value of the pointers, which
// isn't useful! So this program provides a comparison object
// which actually compares the strings pointed to by the
// object, giving a much more useful comparison.
//

//
// Borland 4.x workarounds
//
#define __MINMAX_DEFINED
#pragma option -vi-
```

```
#include <iostream.h>
#include <string.h>

#include <algo.h>
#include <function.h>
#include <projectn.h>

char *test[]={ "Jay", "Dave", "oprah", "Ricky", "GERALDO" };
const int NELEM = sizeof( test ) / sizeof( char * );

struct cmp {
    bool operator()( char *a, char *b )
    {
        return stricmp( a, b ) < 0;
    }
};

main()
{
    sort( test, test + NELEM, cmp() );
    cout << "After sorting: ";
    copy( test,
          test + NELEM,
          ostream_iterator<char*>( cout, " " ) );
    cout << endl;

    return 1;
}
```

If you sort the array of character pointers contained in sort1206.cpp by using the standard comparison object provided by sort(), it sorts the members of the array according to the *values* of the character pointers. This isn't a useful comparison, since the values of the character pointers don't have anything to do with the contents for the strings. A sort based on this comparison produces the following "sorted" output:

```
After sorting:Jay Dave oprah Ricky GERALDO
```

Replacing it with a function object that uses stricmp() for comparisons produces a better output:

```
After sorting: Dave GERALDO Jay oprah Ricky
```

This nicely illustrates the ability of function objects to control the operation of existing STL algorithms, in a type-safe and efficient manner.

It's also worth noting in this example that you could have sorted objects from the string class without having to use a function object. The string class in the C++ draft specification supports operator<(), which is the default sorting function.

String variations

sort1206.cpp demonstrates that the default version of comparison functions supplied with this library don't work properly with character pointers. That statement really needs to be broadened, because functions such as less<T> not only have problems with character pointers, but with *any* pointer to an object.

The STL works properly with containers of pointers, but the library was created with the idea that containers are meant to hold objects, not pointers to objects. Still, all is not lost! It just means that some of the standard comparison function objects won't work properly, so you have to create versions suited to working with pointers. sort1206.cpp should give you a good idea of how to do this.

Numeric function objects

The final class of function object is used by algorithms that perform arithmetic operations over a range of objects. (To be fair, a couple of these algorithms can be used in non-numeric fashion with appropriate function objects. For example, you could use operator+() to concatenate strings, instead of adding up numbers.)

These functions take either one or two arguments of type T, perform some operation, and return a new object of type T. They are used by algorithms such as for_each(), accumulate(), and inner_product().

The STL contains predefined versions of many basic numeric function objects, such as plus<T>, minus<T>, times<T> and divides<T>. In addition, some of the function adapters discussed later in this chapter can be used to cascade existing functions to create more complex expressions.

Listing 12-7 shows a short program that uses transform() to multiply two arrays of doubles. The function object passed to transform() is an instance of the library function object times<T>, which simply multiplies two objects of type T, returning a new object of type T. times<T> multiples the two doubles and returns a new double, which then gets placed in the output vector.

Listing 12-7

tran1207.cpp: The transform() function used to multiply two vectors

```
//
// TRAN1207.CPP
//
// This program uses the transform() algorithm to multiply
// two arrays of doubles. Note that this is the binary
// version of transform(). The multiplication is done
// by the times<> function object.
//

//
// Borland 4.x workarounds
//
#define __MINMAX_DEFINED
#pragma option -vi-

#include <algo.h>
#include <function.h>

double in1[] = { 1.0, 2.0, 3.0, 4.0, 5.0, 6.0 };
double in2[] = { 1.0, 0.5, 1.0/3.0, 0.25, 0.2, 1.0/6.0 };
double out[ 6 ];

main()
{
    transform( in1, in1 + 6, in2, out, times<double>() );
    cout << "transform output: ";
    copy( out,
          out + 6,
          ostream_iterator<double>( cout, " " ) );
    cout << endl;

    return 1;
}
```

The output from tran1207.cpp correctly shows the two arrays multiplied in a piecewise fashion:

```
transform output: 1 1 1 1 1 1
```

Is the horse dead yet?

This example helps underscore the flexibility of the STL. The STL has created these new things called function objects to serve as arguments to algorithms.

But the STL is flexible with these function objects: anywhere a function object is called for, you can substitute a function pointer.

Likewise, STL algorithms that operate on STL containers will also work with standard C/C++ arrays. And any place the STL expects an iterator, you can just as easily use a pointer. This flexibility makes it easy to use the STL in your existing programs without having to redesign your entire application.

BUILD YOUR OWN

We'll now take a look at the library of built-in function objects provided with the STL. While you can save a lot of time and effort by using these canned functions, there will always be times when you need to create a call-back function tailored specifically to your own needs.

When you find that the predefined library objects don't work for you, you have two choices. Either you can build a quick and easy function that does the job for you, or you can build a general-purpose function object. In general, a template function object is the best choice. However, there will be times when you need a function to solve a problem on only one occasion. In that case, a template function object might be overkill. The real test is whether you'll have the opportunity to reuse a function in this program or elsewhere. If you do, opt for a truly reusable function object.

Function access via function pointer

Using function pointers for STL callback functions is less exciting than using a new-fangled function object. But, as a seasoned C++ programmer, you should be used to cranking out new functions at the drop of a hat, so this is an easy way to go.

The only difficulty you might face in writing callback functions for the STL is determining the appropriate argument and return types for a given function. This problem pops up repeatedly, and unfortunately there isn't a good solution. Dealing with the problem is simply a matter of knowing a few guidelines, and paying attention to compiler warnings or error messages.

Building predicate functions

Predicate functions always return a boolean value of true or false. An STL algorithm uses this to determine whether or not to perform some function, and it calls the predicate function with either one or two value arguments. The type of the argument is always the type returned by dereferencing the iterators passed to the STL algorithm.

The function prototypes for a couple of STL algorithms are shown in the following piece of code. count_if() counts the number of objects in a range that return a true value from a particular predicate function. equal() checks to see if two input ranges satisfy a predicate function for all values.

```
template < class InputIterator,
           class Predicate,
           class Size >
void count_if( InputIterator first,
               InputIterator last,
               Predicate pred,
               Size& n );


template < class InputIterator1,
           class InputIterator2,
           class BinaryPredicate >
bool equal( InputIterator1 first1,
            InputIterator1 last1,
            InputIterator2 first2,
            BinaryPredicate binary_pred );
```

You already know that any predicate function used by an algorithm has to have a boolean return type. The only two things that remain to be seen are whether it has one argument or two, and what type the argument(s) should be.

With template functions, it's often difficult for the compiler to indicate what classes or types are acceptable for a given argument. The STL works around this problem by sticking with a consistent naming convention. The compiler doesn't care much about the names, but they should be very meaningful to you, the programmer.

The predicate argument gets two names: one for the argument type or class, and another for the symbolic name of the argument. In this case, the STL uses both names to reinforce the type of argument it expects. count_if() has a predicate function argument that is described as *Predicate pred*. In contrast, equal() has a predicate function described in the prototype as *BinaryPredicate binary_pred*.

These names should be enough to indicate that count_if() has a predicate function that takes a single argument, and equal() has a predicate function that expects two arguments. Even if the names didn't tell you this, in many cases you can make an easy assumption about the function arguments by looking at the number of input iterator ranges. Functions such as count_if(), that iterate over a single range, usually pass a single value to a predicate function. Functions like equal(), that iterate over two ranges, always pass two values to their predicate function.

The only remaining question is, what should the type of the arguments to your function be? Simply put, the argument should be a value parameter of the type that is returned by dereferencing the iterator.

Note: A function that iterates over two ranges might need to take two different types of arguments.

Listing 12-8

srch1208.cpp: An example of a user-written function serving as a binary predicate

```
/*
 * SRCH1208.CPP
 *
 * This program is used in Chapter 12 to demonstrate
 * the use of a user-written function as
 * a binary STL predicate. In this case, the
 * predicate function has to use two different argument
 * types in its test for equality.
 *
 * The program uses the search() function to attempt to
 * find a match for the character array in the integer
 * array. This is a somewhat idiosyncratic function,
 * which probably doesn't belong in a library (who else
 * would ever use it?). Because of that, it is written as
 * a standard C/C++ function and passed to the search()
 * algorithms using a function pointer.
 */

//
// Borland 4.x workarounds
//

#define __MINMAX_DEFINED
#pragma option -vi-

#include <iostream.h>
#include <stdlib.h>
#include <algo.h>
#include <vector.h>

int nints[] = { 6, 7, 8, 9, 10, 1, 2, 3, 4, 5 };
char *sints[] = { "1", "2", "3" };
```

```
const int count1 = sizeof( nints ) / sizeof( int );
const int count2 = sizeof( sints ) / sizeof( char * );

bool test( int i, char *p )
{
    int j = atoi( p );
    return i == j;
}

main()
{
    int * ip = search( nints,
                       nints + count1,
                       sints,
                       sints + count2,
                       test );
    if ( ip == ( nints + count1 ) )
        cout << "Failed to find a match\n";
    else
        cout << "Found a match at position "
             << ( ip - nints )
             << endl;
    return 1;
}
```

Listing 12-8 is a program that demonstrates how to write a typical predicate function. In this case, the function has an unusual requirement, as it's comparing two different types of arrays. The search() algorithm looks through an input range to try and find the first appearance of a second range. Normally this means the function uses operator==() to test for equality between the two ranges. However, this example uses a binary predicate function, since operator==() won't work with the slightly odd combination of types passed to search().

This example program compares character pointer variables to integer variables by converting the character pointer to an integer, via the standard C function atoi(). It then performs a standard integer comparison. A quick check of the output from this program verifies that everything is working properly:

```
Found a match at position 5
```

Building comparison functions

Building comparison functions (as opposed to creating function objects) is generally not practical within the STL. The place they are primarily used is in associative containers, such as set<> and multimap<>, as these containers need comparison objects to help order their contents. The problem is, the comparison object class needs to be specified as a *class template parameter*, so that the container can instantiate a comparison object, if necessary.

This is very different from passing a function object as an algorithm argument. In that case, you are creating an object, and passing it to the algorithm in the argument list. But when you create an associative container, you have to pass the *type* of the comparison object as a template parameter. For example, a typical declaration for a set looks like this:

```
set< double, less<double> > a;
```

In this declaration, the class less<double> is the comparison class. When you pass a comparison object to an algorithm, the class name is followed by parentheses, indicating that you are constructing an object. In the template declaration, however, the absence of parentheses shows that you are just passing a type name. The red-black tree class (see Chapter 8), used to support all associative containers, creates a private data member that is an instantiation of this class. The relevant code is in the definition of template class rb_tree in tree.h:

```
Compare key_compare;
```

If you try to use a standard function instead of a comparison object, you might be tempted to write code like this:

```
bool cmp( double a, double b )
{
    return a < b;
}

set< double, bool (*)(double,double) > a;
```

Unfortunately, this code won't compile. Although you can use a function pointer specification as a type argument, you'll generate an error when the compiler attempts to instantiate it in template class rb_tree.

Because of this, if you need to create a custom comparison routine for an associative container, you'll find you have to create a *function object*, rather than a function. When you need a comparison object for an STL algorithm, you are free to choose between a function object and function pointer.

Building your own function objects

For an experienced C++ programmer, creating function objects is hardly any different than creating stand-alone functions. The main difference between a function object and a function is syntactic. The function object is actually a class definition, with the part we think of as a function defined as operator().

If you want to build a comparison function to be used with one of the associative classes, or with the priority queue container adaptor, you're more or less forced into using a function object instead of a function. If you're creating a predicate function, or a general-purpose function, you can decide between building a stand-alone function or a function object. Base your decision on the guidelines given earlier in this chapter under "Building Your Own."

There's one important point regarding the implementation of function objects that hasn't been mentioned yet. Although the stand-alone function objects you've seen so far work just fine with any algorithm supplied with the STL, they won't work properly with STL *function adaptors*.

Function adaptors are discussed in some detail in the last section of this chapter. They provide a few special classes that let you combine existing functions together into more complex functions, without writing any additional code. To work properly with function adaptors, your function objects must be derived from one of two base classes: class unary_function, or class binary_function.

These two base classes do nothing more than create a few type definitions, but these are used by all of the function adaptors. Adding this derivation to your own function objects is as simple as adding a new line of code, and makes them compatible with the rest of the library.

Since all functions used by the STL take either one or two arguments, only two base classes are needed. Your selection should depend on whether the object you're creating takes one argument or two. The definitions of these two base classes are shown in the following piece of code. Note that these classes don't contain any useful code; they are present solely to supply type definitions.

```
template <class Arg, class Result>
struct unary_function {
    typedef Arg argument_type;
    typedef Result result_type;
};
```

```
template <class Arg1, class Arg2, class Result>
struct binary_function {
    typedef Arg1 first_argument_type;
    typedef Arg2 second_argument_type;
    typedef Result result_type;
};
```

Using these function objects is simply a matter of deriving your function object class from the appropriate base class.

The header file function.h contains the definitions for all STL function objects, so that's a good place to look for usage tips. For example, the definition for function object times() is shown there. times() takes two input objects of type T, multiplies them, and returns the resulting object of type T. This would be a *really* simple function object if it weren't for two complicating factors. First, it's a template function, so it can be instantiated for any type that supports operator *(). Second, it derives itself from the binary_function base class, in order to gain the type definitions it supplies.

```
template <class T>
struct times : binary_function<T, T, T> {
    T operator()(const T& x, const T& y) const
    {
        return x * y;
    }
};
```

The binary_function base template class requires three type arguments. These create the typedefs used by function adaptors. The first two type arguments are the types of the first and second arguments to the function object. The third type argument is the return type from the function. Thus, filling in the class types for binary_function<> or unary_function<> usually boils down to cookie-cutter work.

Listing 12-9 contains a program that makes use of a function adaptor. In this program, I created a function object called add2x. It takes two arguments of type T, and returns a result of type T. The result is equal to arg1 + (2 * arg2). Since the function takes two arguments, it can be used with the version of transform() that takes two input ranges. It will apply add2x to the two input ranges, producing an output sequence.

Listing 12-9

trns1209.cpp: Used with the function adaptor bind1st()

```
//
// TRNS1209.CPP
//
// This program is used in Chapter 12 to demonstrate
// how a home-grown function object can be used with
// function adaptors. The function object add2x() is
// used to add argument 2 to argument 1 twice, and return
// the result. The first time I call transform(), add2x()
// is used in a traditional fashion. The second time,
// however, it is used with the bind2nd() function adaptor.
// This lets add2x() be used with a hard-coded value as the
// second argument. In this particular example, that
// hard-coded argument value is simply the number 2.
//

//
// Borland 4.x workarounds
//
#define __MINMAX_DEFINED
#pragma option -vi-

#include <algo.h>
#include <function.h>
#include <projectn.h>

double in1[] = { 1, 2, 3, 4, 5, 6 };
double in2[] = { 1, 3, 5, 7, 9, 11 };
const int NELEM = sizeof( in1 ) / sizeof( double );

template<class T>
struct add2x : public binary_function<T, T, T>
{
    T operator()( T a, T b ) const
    {
        a += b;
        a += b;
        return a;
    };
};

main()
{
```

```
        cout << "in1: ";
            copy( in1,
                in1 + NELEM,
                ostream_iterator<double>( cout, " " ) );
            cout << endl
                << "in2: ";
            copy( in2,
                in2 + NELEM,
                ostream_iterator<double>( cout, " " ) );
            cout << endl
                << "in1 + add2x( in2 ): ";
            transform( in1,
                    in1 + NELEM,
                    in2,
                    ostream_iterator<int>( cout, " " ),
                    add2x<int>() );
            cout << endl
                << "in1 + add2x( 2 ): ";
            transform( in1,
                    in1 + NELEM,
                    ostream_iterator<int>( cout, " " ),
                    bind2nd( add2x<int>(), 2 ) );
            cout << endl;
            return 1;
    }
```

The second call to transform() is a little more interesting. In this version of transform(), there's only one input range. So how does this work with add2x, which expects two arguments? The answer lies in the bind2nd() function adaptor. By calling bind2nd(), with add2x as the first argument, and the integer 2 as the second, you will, in effect, be calling add2x with one argument from the input range, and the integer 2 for the second argument.

This use of a function adaptor lets you modify the way the adaptor works, and is a wonderful addition to the library. The syntax isn't particularly easy to read, but it does save you from having to write lots of tiny little function objects whenever you need a slight variation on an existing object.

To use bind2nd(), the function object being called must be derived from binary_function<>. bind2nd() uses the typedefs *argument_type* and *result_type*, which are both defined in binary_function<>. If you fail to derive add2x from binary_function<>, bind2nd() will generate scads of compiler errors as it tries to use these type definitions.

The output from trns1209.cpp confirms that add2x and bind2nd() are both working properly:

```
in1: 1 2 3 4 5 6
in2: 1 3 5 7 9 11
in1 + add2x( in2 ): 3 8 13 18 23 28
in1 + add2x( 2 ): 5 6 7 8 9 10
```

Cheating const-ness

Template functions are often unable to enforce the concept of const-ness. One of the areas where this problem is particularly acute is when using function adaptors as callbacks from STL algorithms. As an example, the algorithm for_each() is defined in the STL specification as a non-mutating sequence operation, which means it's not supposed to modify any of the elements in the input range.

While this is what the specification says, there isn't a good way to enforce the rule. Whenever a template function such as for_each() is defined, there's no restriction on the classes that can be plugged into the function. This means you can't say that the iterators being passed to for_each() are const_iterators—which would prevent the callback function from modifying their value objects.

This problem is a result of the way type arguments to template functions are processed in C++. When you pass value arguments to functions, you specify a type and a name. When you specify type names to a template, you simply specify a name. What is needed is a "type of type" specification, but that simply doesn't exist.

This problem leads to loopholes in the STL. For example, one easy way to circumvent the rules is to write your callback function so it uses a reference argument instead of a value argument. This gives the callback function the ability to modify the object it's reading. Listing 12-10 shows a short example of how this can be accomplished.

Listing 12-10

bad1210.cpp: Refusing to play by the rules

```
//
// BAD1210.CPP
//
// This program is used in Chapter 12 to demonstrate
// how a non-mutating algorithm such as for_each() is
// actually at the mercy of its callback function. The
```

```
// callback can modify the objects pointed to in the input
// range, and there isn't much the compiler can do
// about it!
//

//
// Borland 4.x workarounds
//
#define __MINMAX_DEFINED
#pragma option -vi-

#include <algo.h>
#include <iostream.h>

void x2( long & l )
{
    l = l + l;
}

long a[] = { 1, 2, 3, 4, 5 };
const int nelem = sizeof( a ) / sizeof( long );

main()
{
    cout << "Before for_each: ";
    copy( a,
          a + nelem,
          ostream_iterator<long>( cout, " " ) );
    cout << endl;
    for_each( a,
              a + nelem,
              x2 );
    cout << "After for_each: ";
    copy( a,
          a + nelem,
          ostream_iterator<long>( cout, " " ) );
    cout << endl;
    return 1;
}
```

The output from bad1210.cpp shows that it is, indeed, modifying data passed to it by the for_each algorithm:

```
Before for_each:    1 2 3 4 5
After for_each:     2 4 6 8 10
```

SAVE YOUR EFFORT—USE THE BUILT-INS

One of the most important advantages enjoyed by function objects is that they can be provided as part of a library. Naturally, the STL takes advantage of this by providing a library of template function objects that can be used with existing STL algorithms. You've seen some of these functions utilized in examples in this chapter, so you should be comfortable with them by now.

The important thing to remember when using these function objects is that they are actually classes (or structures, which are nearly the same thing), not pointers to functions. To use one of them as a callback function with an STL algorithm, you must instantiate it with the default constructor. That means your code should look like this:

```
unique( a.begin(), a.end(), equal<double>() );
```

not this:

```
unique( a.begin(), a.end(), equal<double> );
```

The difference is that the invocation in the first case creates an object, whereas the second just specifies a class. That one little set of parentheses makes all the difference!

When you turn to the library for a comparison function object, things are a little different. In this case, you're actually using the class definition, not an instance of the class, as a template parameter. So, in this case, you want your code to look like this:

```
map<string,counter,less<string> > counts;
```

not like this:

```
map<string,counter,less<string>() > counts;
```

The fact that you have to pass a *type* as the template argument is the reason you can't use a function pointer in the declaration of an associative class. Once again, the only difference is in that little set of parentheses, but the compiler won't be happy if you use them.

Finally, be sure to note that these function objects will always need a type specification. In general, the type you specify between the angle brackets will be the type that is pointed to by your algorithm. When using function comparison objects, the type will be that of the key for your class.

Function Objects: A Summary

The STL specification divides function objects into three different categories:

- arithmetic operations
- comparisons
- logical operations

Logical operations and comparison objects are usually used as predicates or comparison objects. Arithmetic operations classes are used as numeric function objects. Tables 12-1 through 12-3 specify the names, types, and return values of these functions, which are all defined in functions.h. Keep in mind that the operation performed by any of these function objects is expanded by a template operation so, if a function returns 'x + y', it will use whatever overloaded operator+() is defined for the particular class.

Also, bear in mind that these simple function objects can all serve as building blocks to more complex objects, when tied together using function adaptors. The complete set of function adaptors is discussed in the next section of this chapter.

Table 12-1

Arithmetic function objects

Function object	Type	Return value
plus<T>	binary	arg1 + arg2
minus<T>	binary	arg1 - arg2
times<T>	binary	arg1 * arg2
divides<T>	binary	arg1 / arg2
modulus<T>	binary	arg1 % arg2
negate<T>	unary	- arg1
ident<T>	unary	arg1

Table 12-2

Comparison function objects

Function object	Type	Return value
equal_to<T>	binary	arg1 == arg2
not_equal_to<T>	binary	arg1 != arg2
greater<T>	binary	arg1 > arg2
less<T>	binary	arg1 < arg2
greater_equal<T>	binary	arg1 >= arg2
less_equal<T>	binary	arg1 <= arg1

Table 12-3

Logical function objects

Function object	Type	Return value
logical_and<T>	binary	arg1 && arg2
logical_or<T>	binary	arg1 || arg2
logical_not<T>	unary	!arg1

ADAPTORS—A FEW EXTRAS

Function adaptors are a little disconcerting to most C++ programmers. If you're already a little uneasy about these strange things called function objects, function adaptors aren't going to make you feel any better.

But function adaptors do serve a useful purpose. If you look at C and C++, you might see other facets of the language that are equally difficult the first time you encounter them. For example, pointers are often singled out as being tough on beginners. But once you are an experienced programmer, it's hard to imagine doing without them. You may feel the same way about function adaptors someday.

So if function adaptors really are so difficult, why do we even bother with them? Because function adaptors can perform some specific tasks that are beyond the scope of function objects alone:

- **Boolean inversion.** You can use a function object to negate the result from a function object.

- **Argument binding.** Function objects let you bind a constant value to one of the arguments in a function object. This lets you use a binary function object where you would normally use a unary object.

- **Function binding.** A clever function object can convert a function pointer to a function object.

- **Composition.** You can build expressions out of multiple function objects. This allows you to compose complex function objects from simpler components.

Have we been introduced?

Function adaptors are simply template functions that allow you to combine existing function objects to create new function objects. Since the function adaptors are used to build new function objects, each function adaptor is a function that returns a new function object. The function objects returned by function adaptors are instances of new template classes. (Whew!)

As you probably realized from the last paragraph, the problem with function adaptors is that there are too many things to keep track of! This is the basic process:

1. A function adaptor takes a function object as its argument, so you need to keep track of the argument and return types of one type of function.

2. Then, the function adaptor creates a new function object, which takes its own types of arguments and returns its own function.

On top of that, you're using a function adaptor as a callback for an STL algorithm, so you have to keep track of what sort of function and arguments *it* expects.

This really exposes the downside of a statically typed language!

Table 12-4 might offer some help. It shows the eight function adaptors defined by the STL, along with their argument types and return types. The table also shows the class of the object returned by the adaptor, but that isn't particularly important. When using a function adaptor, you don't specify the *class* of the adaptor, you simply use the function. The only time the return classes are important is if you attempt to develop some function adaptors of your own.

Table 12-4

Function adaptors

Function adaptor	Argument types	Result object type	Result class
not1	bool fn(arg)	bool fn(arg)	unary_negate<>
not2	bool fn(arg1, arg2)	bool fn(arg1, arg2)	binary_negate<>
bind1st	T fn(arg1, arg2), x x is bound to arg1	T fn(arg)	binder1st<>
bind2nd	T fn(arg1, arg2), x x is bound to arg2	T fn(arg)	binder2nd<>
ptr_fun	T (*fn)(arg)	T fn(arg)	pointer_to_unary_function<>
ptr_fun	T (*fn)(arg1, arg2)	T fn(arg1, arg2)	pointer_to_binary_function<>
compose1	T fn1(arg), T fn2(arg)	T fn(arg)	unary_compose<>
compose2	T fn1(arg1,arg2), T fn2(arg), T fn3(arg)	T fn(arg)	binary_compose<>

The remainder of this chapter gives some examples of how these function adaptors work in STL programs.

not1, not2

These two functions are good starting points, because they are conceptually very simple. not1() takes a unary function argument and logically negates its output. not2() takes a binary function argument and logically negates its output. Accordingly, these functions are particularly useful when used as function predicates. The mechanism by which this takes place is fairly simple. When you call not1() or not2(), you must pass it a function object. Both not1() and not2() create a new function object which has a single data member. That data member, defined as *pred*, is a copy of the function object (or pointer) you passed it.

You use the newly created function object by invoking its operator(), just as for any other function object. The function object created by not1() has the following definition for operator():

```
bool operator()(const argument_type& x) const
{
    return !pred(x);
}
```

Likewise, the function object created by not2() has this operator():

```
bool operator()( const first_argument_type& x,
                 const second_argument_type& y) const
{
    return !pred(x, y);
}
```

In both cases, you can see that this is a pretty simple operation. It calls the predicate function that was passed as an argument previously, then inverts the output.

not1() and not2() were probably designed to work with predicate functions. However, you don't have to limit it to functions that return boolean arguments. Any scalar type that can be inverted is naturally fair game, as long as you can think of a sensible use for it.

Listing 12-11 gives an example of how the two not adaptors might be used. In both cases, you use the function adaptor to invert the sense of a function.

Note: Remember that the function object created by not1() or not2() will have the same number and type of arguments as the function it is modifying. This is important because it's often difficult at first to determine when and where not1() and not2() are to be used. For these two adaptors, the logic is simple. If you already have a function that is the right type to use as a predicate function—or whatever else you might want—then it will still be correct when you wrap it up in not1() or not2(). If it wasn't correct before, neither adaptor will make things right. Beyond that, the only thing you need to remember about these functions is that not1() expects a function with one argument and not2() expects a function with two arguments.

Listing 12-11

not1211.cpp: Exercising the two not adaptors

```
//
// NOT1211.CPP
//
// This program is used in Chapter 12 to demonstrate
// the use of the function adaptors not1 and not2.
// Note that the function object mod3 I use here is
// derived from the unary_function<> template class.
// Remember that this is a necessary prerequisite
// for using an adaptor on a function object.
//
```

```
//
// Borland 4.x workarounds
//
#define __MINMAX_DEFINED
#pragma option -vi-

#include <iostream.h>
#include <function.h>
#include <algo.h>

struct mod3 : public unary_function<int,int> {
    bool operator()( int a ) const
    {
        return ( a % 3 ) == 0;
    }
};

int a[] = { 1, 2, 3, 4, 5, 6, 7, 7, 6, 5, 4, 3, 2, 1 };
int *aend = a + ( sizeof(a) / sizeof( *int ) );

main()
{
    cout << "Input = ";
    copy( a, aend, ostream_iterator<int>(cout, " " ) );
    cout << endl;
    int count = 0;
    count_if( a, aend, mod3(), count );
    cout << "count_if( ... mod3 ... )  returned "
        << count
        << endl;
    count = 0;
    count_if( a, aend, not1( mod3() ), count );
    cout << "count_if( ... not1( mod3 ) ... ) returned "
        << count
        << endl;
    int *i = adjacent_find( a, aend, not2( less<int>() ) );
    cout << "adjacent_find with not2( less<int>() )"
        << " found a match at "
        << ( i - a )
        << endl;
    return 1;
}
```

The output from not1211 shows that both adaptors are working properly:

```
Input=12345677654321
count_if( ... mod3 ... )  returned 4
count_if( ... not1( mod3 ) ... ) returned 10
adjacent_find with not2( less<int>() ) found a match at 6
```

bind1st, bind2nd

These two functions create a function object that takes a single argument and returns a single value. This means they are appropriate for use in functions such as transform(), replace_if(), or any other function that expects a single argument predicate.

bind1st() and bind2nd() combine a single input argument with an argument object, and pass the two objects to a binary function. The binary function and the argument object are the two things passed to bind1st() and bind2nd(). The "1st" and "2nd" in the names bind1st() and bind2nd() refer to whether the argument object is bound to the first or second argument of the binary function.

As an example, you can create a function object with a call like this:

```
f = bind2nd( times<int>, 3 );
```

Later, a call to *f* with an argument of *x* is equivalent to making this call:

```
times<int>( x, 3 )
```

This is a very useful tool, since it lets you build more complicated function objects from simple building blocks. Without this ability, you'd have to write custom function objects for all but the most trivial cases.

Listing 12-12

bind1212.cpp: Demonstrating both bind1st() and bind2nd()

```
//
// BIND1212.CPP
//
// This program is used in Chapter 12 to demonstrate
// the use of bind1st() and bind2nd(). In both cases,
// the function is used to bind an integer to a numeric
```

```
// function object, which in turn modifies data in a
// vector.
//

//
// Borland 4.x workarounds
//
#define __MINMAX_DEFINED
#pragma option -vi-

#include <iostream.h>
#include <vector.h>
#include <function.h>
#include <algo.h>

main()
{
    vector<long> lv;
    for ( int i = 0 ; i < 10 ; i++ )
        lv.push_back( i * i );
    cout << "Before: ";
    copy( lv.begin(),
          lv.end(),
          ostream_iterator<long>( cout, " " ) );
    cout << endl;
    transform( lv.begin(),
               lv.end(),
               lv.begin(),
               bind1st( times<long>(), 100L ) );
    cout << "After multiplying by 100: ";
    copy( lv.begin(),
          lv.end(),
          ostream_iterator<long>( cout, " " ) );
    cout << endl;
    transform( lv.begin(),
               lv.end(),
               lv.begin(),
               bind2nd( minus<long>(), 144L ) );
    cout << "After subtracting 144: ";
    copy( lv.begin(),
          lv.end(),
          ostream_iterator<long>( cout, " " ) );
    cout << endl;
    return 1;
}
```

bind1212.cpp uses the bind1st() and bind2nd() operators to create a pair of new function objects. bind1st() creates a function that multiplies a long by 100 and returns the result using this piece of code:

```
bind1st( times<long>(), 100L )
```

bind2nd() creates a function that subtracts 144 from a long using this fragment:

```
bind2nd( minus<long>(), 144L )
```

Both bind1st() and bind2nd() create function objects that take a single argument, which means they are suitable for functions like transform(), as shown in the example. However, they take a somewhat crooked path to get there.

To create a function object that takes a single argument, bind1st() and bind2nd() require an existing function object that takes two arguments. One of the two arguments to the function is supplied as an argument to bind1st() or bind2nd(), the other argument is passed to the resulting function object. This isn't always easy to keep straight, but it's definitely worth the effort.

ptr_fun

ptr_fun() is a nice, simple function adaptor. All it does is take an existing function pointer and convert it to a first-class function object.

Earlier in this chapter, you saw that function pointers could be used in many of the same contexts as function objects, but not all. For instance, function pointers can't be used as the targets of function adaptors. To get around this shortcoming, simply use ptr_fun() to create a function object with the same calling convention, and return type as your function.

Listing 12-13 shows how to use ptr_fun() in a practical program. In this case, the program uses stricmp() to build a predicate function object used when processing C strings (char pointers). Normal STL predicate functions that test for equality of C strings wouldn't work very well, because they would compare the actual value of the pointers to the strings, not the strings themselves. Using a handy batch of function adaptors lets you create a useful predicate function for comparing strings.

Listing 12-13

ptr1213.cpp: ptr_fun lets you treat function pointers as first-class STL objects

```cpp
//
// PTR1213.CPP
//
// This program is used in Chapter 12 to demonstrate
// the use of the ptr_fun() function adaptor. ptr_fun()
// converts an existing function pointer (not a function
// object) to a function object that can be used with
// any of the classes in the STL. In this case, we use
// stricmp() to compare for equality of character strings.
// The first time find_if() is called, you get a demo of
// how *not* to do it. Comparing two pointers for equality
// just isn't going to work. Instead, you have to compare
// the actual strings, which is what happens
// the second time. Note also that stricmp() returns 0
// on a match, so we have to negate it with a not1() to
// return the boolean expected by the STL. Wow!
//

//
// Borland 4.x workarounds
//

#define __MINMAX_DEFINED
#pragma option -vi-

#include <iostream.h>
#include <string.h>

#include <list.h>
#include <algo.h>

main()
{
    list<char *> vec;
    vec.push_back( "IDG" );
    vec.push_back( "M&T" );
    vec.push_back( "SAMS" );
    vec.push_back( "Microsoft" );
//
// This is the *wrong* way to compare strings.
//
    list<char *>::iterator p =
        find_if( vec.begin(),
                 vec.end(),
```

```
                bind2nd( equal_to<char*>(), "m&t" ) );
    int i = 0;
    distance( vec.begin(), p, i );
    cout << "Offset = "
         << i
         << ".  Matched data = "
         << ( p == vec.end() ? "<end>" : *p )
         << endl;
//
// This is the right way to compare strings.
//
    p = find_if( vec.begin(),
                 vec.end(),
                 not1( bind2nd( ptr_fun( stricmp ), "m&t" ) ) );
    i = 0;
    distance( vec.begin(), p, i );
    cout << "Offset = "
         << i
         << ".  Matched data = "
         << ( p == vec.end() ? "<end>" : *p )
         << endl;

    return 1;
}
```

The predicate function called by find_if() in ptr1213.cpp is called with a single argument, which is a character string pointer. If you want to compare it to the string "m&t" using stricmp(), to find the first appearance of that string, your first inclination may be to use bind2nd() like this:

```
bind2nd( stricmp, "m&t" );
```

However, this construct generates a slew of errors, because stricmp can't be the legitimate target of a function adaptor (bind2nd). To make it work properly, you need to encase stricmp in ptr_fun(), so that you create a legitimate function object.

The only thing left to do to make the function object you need is to wrap the whole thing up with not1(), to invert the return value from stricmp(). stricmp() returns 0 on a match, which you will want to convert to a boolean true. The resulting function object is created with this function call:

```
not1( bind2nd( ptr_fun( stricmp ), "m&t" ) )
```

compose1, compose2

These two function adaptors have similar names, but they operate rather differently. compose1() is called to let you cascade function objects. It's used when a unary function is desired. You pass two function objects to compose1(), creating a function object that executes the two arguments in order.

For example, if you have an increment function object and a "doubling" function object, you could put them together like this:

```
compose1( increment<int>(), x2<int>() )
```

The resulting function object would first double its input number, then increment the result of that operation.

The obvious fact that jumps out at this point is that with compose1(), you can cascade as many instances of the function object as you would like in order to perform a long series of operations on an input value.

compose2() can also create function objects that take a single argument. However, compose2() takes three function objects as arguments. It uses fn1, fn2, and fn3 to evaluate the following expression (where x is the argument being passed to the function object):

```
fn1( fn2( x ), fn3( x ) );
```

You can see that compose1 and compose2 are similar in that they both combine multiple function objects. However, they combine the operations in very different ways. Both functions are used to cascade function calls, but only compose2 can cascade binary functions. Listing 12-14 shows comp1214.cpp, which gives a simple demonstration using the two composition functions.

Listing 12-14

comp1214.cpp: Demonstrating the two composition functions

```
//
// COMP1214.CPP
//
// This program is used in Chapter 12 to demonstrate
// the two composition functions. compose2() combines
// three function objects, and compose1() combines two
// function objects.
//

//
// Borland 4.x workarounds
//
```

```
#define __MINMAX_DEFINED
#pragma option -vi-

#include <iostream.h>
#include <string.h>
#include <projectn.h>

#include <algo.h>

double d[]= { 1.0, 2.0, 3.0, 4.0, 5.0 };
double *dend = d + ( sizeof( d ) / sizeof( double ) );

main()
{
    cout << "d[] = ";
    copy( d, dend, ostream_iterator<double>(cout, " "));
    cout << endl
        << "compose2 will perform x = -x * -x\n";
    transform( d,
              dend,
              d,
              compose2( times<double>(),
                        negate<double>(),
                        negate<double>() ) );
    cout << "After compose2: ";
    copy( d, d + 5, ostream_iterator<double>(cout, " " ) );
    cout << endl;
    cout << "compose1 will perform x = ( x * 100 ) + 100\n";
    transform( d,
              dend,
              d,
              compose1( bind1st( plus<double>(), 100.0 ),
                        bind1st( times<double>(), 100.0 ) ) );
    cout << "After compose1: ";
    copy( d, dend, ostream_iterator<double>(cout, " " ) );
    cout << endl;
    return 1;
}
```

The output from comp1214.cpp indicates that the functions worked as expected:

```
d[] = 1 2 3 4 5
compose2 will perform x = -x * -x
After compose2: 1 4 9 16 25
compose1 will perform x = ( x * 100 ) + 100
After compose1: 200 500 1000 1700 2600
```

A note of caution

It's very nice to be able to create new functions without having to code an entirely new function or function object. However, you need to face reality about functions like compose1() or bind1st(). These functions *do* let you create more complex functions, but they quickly become very difficult to test, modify, or even use.

Listing 12-15 shows a program that implements a simple second-order equation using STL function object components. Even though this isn't a complicated function, you'd probably find it difficult to read. And any programmer who had to follow in your footsteps and maintain this code would probably curse your name many times daily! When faced with a situation like this, the only appropriate reaction is to bite the bullet and write a function object. The next person who works on your code will thank you!

Some people have suggested that automatic translation tools similar to yacc or lex could be used to generate these complex compositions. This is a great idea, and perhaps could eventually become a part of C++. However, for now, you are stuck with doing things the hard way.

Listing 12-15
bad1215.cpp: A bad example

```
//
// BAD1218.CPP
//
// This program is used in Chapter 12 to show how difficult it
// can be to work with function objects after a certain level
// of complexity is reached. The function under test here is
// relatively simple, x**2 + x + 5, but the STL function object
// that implements it is fairly horrendous. It works, but
// the hand-coded function object used for comparison purposes
// is much easier to follow.
//

//
// Borland 4.x workarounds
//
#define __MINMAX_DEFINED
#pragma option -vi-

#include <iostream.h>
#include <function.h>
```

```
#include <algo.h>
#include <projectn.h>

int input[]={ 0, 1, 2, 3, 4, 5 };
int output[ 6 ];

struct custom {
    int operator()( int x ) {
        return x * x + x + 5;
    }
};

main()
{
    cout << "This section of the program implements the function\n"
        << "x**2 + x + 5 using STL function objects"
        << endl;
    transform( input,
               input + 6,
               output,
               compose1( bind1st( plus<int>(), 5 ),
                         compose2( plus<int>(),
                                   compose2( times<int>(),
                                             ident<int,int>(),
                                             ident<int,int>() ),
                                   ident<int,int>() ) ) );
    int *p1 = input;
    int *p2 = output;
    for ( ; p1 < ( input + 6 ) ; p1++, p2++ )
        cout << "f("
             << *p1
             << ") = "
             << *p2
             << endl;

    cout << "This section of the program implements the function\n"
        << "x**2 + x + 5 using a custom function object"
        << endl;
    transform( input,
               input + 6,
               output,
               custom() );
    p1 = input;
    p2 = output;
    for ( ; p1 < ( input + 6 ) ; p1++, p2++ )
        cout << "f("
             << *p1
```

```
            << ") = "
            << *p2
            << endl;

    return 1;
}
```

The output from bad1215.cpp shows that both the composition function object and the hand-coded object yield the same results:

```
This section of the program implements the function
x**2 + x + 5 using STL function objects
f(0) = 5
f(1) = 7
f(2) = 11
f(3) = 17
f(4) = 25
f(5) = 35
This section of the program implements the function
x**2 + x + 5 using a custom function object
f(0) = 5
f(1) = 7
f(2) = 11
f(3) = 17
f(4) = 25
f(5) = 35
```

Decomposing the function adaptors shown in bad1215.cpp isn't trivial. (Just be glad you don't have to write the compiler!) But doing so might be instructive. The definition of the function object as written in the program is:

```
fn(x) = compose1( bind1st( plus<int>(), 5 ),
               compose2( plus<int>(),
                      compose2( times<int>(),
                             ident<int,int>(),
                             ident<int,int>() ),
                      ident<int,int>() ) ) );
```

The compiler will start evaluating the innermost expressions first. In this case, the two calls to ident in compose2() can be evaluated. As you might recall from Table 12-1, applying ident to x simply returns x. Doing that for both copies of ident simplifies the expression somewhat.

```
fn(x) = compose1( bind1st( plus<int>(), 5 ),
                  compose2( plus<int>(),
                            compose2( times<int>(),
                                      x,
                                      x ),
                            ident<int,int>() ) ) );
```

The next step is to perform the work required by the innermost copy of compose2. It has three arguments: times<int>(), and the two copies of *x*. By the definition of the compose2() adaptor, that yields the expression *x* * *x*.

```
fn(x) = compose1( bind1st( plus<int>(), 5 ),
                  compose2( plus<int>(),
                            x * x,
                            ident<int,int>() ) ) );
```

Now the compiler can work through to the next innermost expression. Once again, that is an ident function object which will return a copy of *x*:

```
fn(x) = compose1( bind1st( plus<int>(), 5 ),
                  compose2( plus<int>(),
                            x * x,
                            x ) );
```

Now the compiler will apply the last copy of compose2() to its three arguments, which will produce the expression (*x* * *x*) + *x*:

```
fn(x) = compose1( bind1st( plus<int>(), 5 ),
                  ( x * x ) + x ) );
```

The compiler now moves on to bind1st(). This function has two arguments, plus <int>() and 5. Remember that bind1st() will yield a unary function object, which is really a binary function in disguise. The second argument to bind1st will be the object that is always used as the first argument to the given function. The result looks something like this:

```
fn(x) = compose1( plus<int>(),
                  5,
                  ( x * x ) + x ) );
```

Finally, applying compose1() gives this expression:

```
fn(x) = 5 + ( x * x ) + x;
```

FUNCTION OBJECTS SAVE TIME

Many new STL users will be seeing function objects and adaptors for the first time. These objects can save you a lot of coding time, but only if you learn how to use them. That's going to take some practice and experimentation, but I think you'll find that the time you invest will pay you back handsomely.

Part

III

THE PUBLIC INTERFACE: REFERENCE INFORMATION

435

NON-MUTATING SEQUENCE OPERATIONS

Civilization advances by extending the number of important operations we can perform without thinking about them.

— Alfred North Whitehead,
An Introduction to Mathematics

A non-mutating sequence operation performs an operation over a range defined by a pair of iterators. The algorithm starts its work at the location pointed to by the first iterator, and continues until it reaches either a terminating condition or the terminating iterator. You use these functions when you have an input range or a container that you want to process. The functions in this group do things like comparing two sequences for equality, finding one sequence in another, or counting specific elements in a sequence.

These algorithms are collectively referred to by the awkward name *non-mutating* because they don't modify the container pointed to by the iterators. (As you have seen earlier, it's actually possible to sneak a mutating operation past the compiler, but it's usually not a good idea!)

The rest of this chapter is a reference to the non-mutating sequence operations. For almost all the functions described here, you'll find a complete copy of the code that makes up the function. Some of the functions are too long to reproduce, in which case you can find their source code in either algo.h or algobase.h.

In the STL, much of the complexity of an operation is hidden in the supporting code for the container classes, which makes these algorithms seem deceptively simple. Due to their economy of expression, the entire function often fits comfortably in the space normally reserved for just the prototype.

Table 13-1 lists the non-mutating sequence operations. Note that all but one of the operations have a predicate version. In some cases, the predicate version has the same name as the standard version. In other cases, the function name has "_if" appended to it. The reason some functions have to be renamed is that they are template functions with an identical number of arguments, so the compiler can't distinguish between the predicate and normal version. For an example of this, check the argument lists of find() and find_if().

Table 13-1

The non-mutating sequence operations

Function	Predicate	Description
for_each()	None	Apply a function to each element in a sequence
find()	find_if()	Find the first matching element in a sequence
find_end()	find_end()	Return the last iterator in a matching sequence
find_first_of()	find_first_of()	Return the first iterator in a matching sequence
adjacent_find()	adjacent_find()	Find two adjacent matching elements
count()	count_if()	Count the number of matching elements
mismatch()	mismatch()	Find the first two mismatched elements
equal()	equal()	Test two sequences for equality
search()	search()	Search for a sequence
search()	search()	Search for equal values

FOR_EACH

Function

```
template < class InputIterator, class Function >
Function for_each( InputIterator first,
                   InputIterator last,
                   Function f )
{
    while ( first != last )
        f( *first++ );
    return f;
}
```

Arguments

first: An iterator pointing to the first element in a sequence. The algorithm will start performing its operation on the object pointed to by this iterator.

last: An iterator pointing *one past* the last element in a sequence. The algorithm will continue working through the sequence of objects, beginning with the first iterator, until it reaches last.

f: A function object or pointer, used by for_each() to process each element in the sequence defined by the two iterators. It can either be:

- a pointer to a function that takes an argument of the same type as that pointed to by the iterators; or

- a function object that has the same syntax for operator()().

The function object takes a single argument, which is a value argument of type T, where T is the type of object pointed to by the two input iterators.

Return value

for_each() returns a copy of the function object that was applied to each of the objects in the sequence. This can be useful if you're using the function object to hold some value that is accumulated as the function is applied to each element in turn. If you use a function pointer instead of a function object, for_each() will return a copy of the function pointer. In either case, for most applications of for_each(), you'll ignore the return value.

Description

for_each() applies a function to each object in an input sequence. The input sequence is normally a container or built-in array, but it can be any object with iterator-like syntax and semantics. for_each is intended to be a non-mutating function, which means it shouldn't modify the objects pointed to by the iterator. You can (but probably shouldn't) overcome this restriction by creating a function object that uses reference objects as arguments.

for_each() is a nice, simple function that saves you from writing a few lines of code. By examining the function body shown above, you can see it isn't particularly substantial, but using for_each() might save you a bit of time.

Complexity

Since for_each() will call function object *f* once per object in the input sequence, it has linear time complexity. Regardless of how many times it is called, for_each() only needs to make a single copy of the function object. Therefore, this algorithm has constant space complexity.

Example

Listing 13-1

each1301.cpp: A demonstration of the for_each() algorithm.

```
/*
 * EACH1301.CPP
 *
 * This program is used in Chapter 13 to demonstrate the
 * for_each() algorithm. for_each() is called here using a
 * function object called sum_of_squares. sum_of_squares is
 * set up so that each instance has a reference to an
 * integer used to total the values. This shows off one of
 * the advantages of a function object: encapsulated data.
 *
 */

//
// Borland 4.x workarounds
//
#define __MINMAX_DEFINED
#pragma option -vi-

#include <iostream.h>
#include <algo.h>

struct sum_of_squares {
    int &sum;
    sum_of_squares( sum_of_squares &a ) : sum( a.sum ){;}
    sum_of_squares( int &i ) : sum( i ){;}
```

```
        void operator()( int a )
        {
            sum += a * a;
        }
};

main()
{
    int a[] = { 1, 2, 3, 4 };
    int total = 0;
    sum_of_squares sos( total );

    for_each( a, a + 4, sos );
    cout << "sum of squares = " << total << endl;
/*
 * Since for_each() returns a function object, we
 * can use it to retrieve the results just as easily.
 */
    total = 0;
    cout << "sum of squares = "
         << for_each( a, a + 4, sos ).sum
         << endl;
    return 1;
}
```

Example output

```
sum of squares = 30
sum of squares = 30
```

FIND

Function

find() has two versions, standard and predicate. The standard version is as
follows:

```
template < class InputIterator, class T >
InputIterator find( InputIterator first,
                    InputIterator last,
                    const T& value )
```

```
{
    while ( first != last && *first != value )
        ++first;
    return first;
}
```

The predicate version is as follows:

```
template < class InputIterator, class Predicate >
InputIterator find_if( InputIterator first,
                       InputIterator last,
                       Predicate pred )
{
    while ( first != last && !pred( *first ) )
        ++first;
    return first;
}
```

Arguments

first: An iterator pointing to the first element in a sequence. The algorithm will start its search with the object pointed to by this iterator.

last: An iterator pointing *one past* the last element in a sequence. The algorithm will continue working through the sequence of objects pointed to by the first iterator until it either finds a match or reaches this iterator.

value: In the first version of find(), the search will terminate when it finds an object equal to this argument, as defined by operator==().

pred: In the second version of find(), the search termination is determined by calling this predicate function, not by testing an iterator against a predefined value. This allows you the flexibility to create a more complex set of find criteria than can be done using operator==(). pred() returns true when called with an argument that meets the search criteria.

               The predicate function or function object should take a single argument of type T, where T is the type of object pointed to by the two input iterators. It should return a boolean value.

Return value

The find function may terminate for one of two reasons:

1. If it terminates because of a successful find operation, the return value is an iterator pointing to the object responsible for the termination. This object will either be equal to value—for the first version of find()—or will cause the pred() function to return a true value when it is passed as an argument.

2. If no object was able to pass the termination test, the algorithm returns an iterator identical to last, which is one past the end of the input range.

Description

find() searches through an input range for an object that meets the termination test supplied as an argument to the algorithm. In the first version of the algorithm, it simply tests each object in the input sequence with the value argument. If the two objects are equal (using operator==()), the search terminates. In the second version of the function, termination occurs when the predicate function returns true for a particular argument.

In the event that no match occurs, the function returns an iterator pointing to the end of the input range, which is one past the last object tested.

It's reasonable to ask why find() (and the next couple of functions in this section) is categorized as a non-mutating sequence operation. At first glance, the sorting and searching group seems a much better place for this algorithm.

The reason for this seemingly bad placement is that the sorting and searching algorithms all work with *sorted* ranges. That means searching can operate in better than linear $O(N)$ time. The functions in this section, find() and the like, work on *unsorted* ranges. This means they have to perform brute force linear searches. You could say they just don't quite fit in with the elite crowd in sorting and searching!

Complexity

Since find() will perform its test—either operator==() or a call to pred()—once per object in the input sequence, it has linear time complexity. Regardless of how many times it needs to be called, find() need only make a single copy of the predicate function or value object. Therefore, this algorithm has constant space complexity.

Example

Listing 13-2

find1302.cpp: A demonstration of the find() algorithm.

```
/*
 * FIND1302.CPP
 *
 * This program is used in Chapter 13 to demonstrate the
 * find() algorithm. It works by reading in all the words
 * from a text file (find1302.cpp!), then searching for the
 * appearances of "Woodchuck" and "Womprat".
 *
 */

//
// Borland 4.x workarounds
//
#define __MINMAX_DEFINED
#pragma option -vi-

#include <iostream.h>
#include <fstream.h>
#include <cstring.h>

#include <algo.h>
#include <vector.h>

main()
{
    ifstream f( "find1302.cpp" );
    if ( !f ) {
        cerr << "Couldn't open the input file!\n";
        return 1;
    }
    vector<string> v;

    while ( f ) {
        string word;
        f >> word;
        v.push_back( word );
```

```
        }
        f.close();
//
// Search targets : Woodchuck Womprat
//
        vector<string>::iterator i1, i2;
        i1 = find( v.begin(), v.end(), "Woodchuck" );
        i2 = find( v.begin(), v.end(), "Womprat" );
        int n1 = 0, n2 = 0;
        distance( v.begin(), i1, n1 );
        distance( v.begin(), i2, n2 );
        cout << "Woodchuck found at position "
            << n1
            << endl
            << "Womprat found at position "
            << n2
            << endl;
        return 1;
    }
```

Example output

```
Woodchuck found at position 109
Womprat found at position 110
```

FIND_END

Function

find_end() has two versions, standard and predicate. The standard version is as follows:

```
template< class ForwardIterator1,
          class ForwardIterator2 >
ForwardIterator1 find_end( ForwardIterator1 first1,
                           ForwardIterator1 last1,
                           ForwardIterator2 first2,
                           ForwardIterator2 last2 );
```

The predicate version is:

```
template< class ForwardIterator1,
          class ForwardIterator2,
          class BinaryPredicate >
ForwardIterator1 find_end( ForwardIterator1 first1,
                           ForwardIterator1 last1,
                           ForwardIterator2 first2,
                           ForwardIterator2 last2,
                           BinaryPredicate pred );
```

Arguments

first1, last1:   This iterator pair defines the input range to be searched. The range is defined using forward iterators, which precludes searching for sequences in an input stream. Iterators pointing into any STL container or C/C++ array can be used.

first2, last2:   This iterator pair defines the sequence to be searched for in the first sequence.

pred: The standard version of find_end compares the elements in the two lists using operator==(). In the event that you need a more powerful comparison function, you can supply a binary predicate. The predicate will take two arguments, the first being the type of element in the first range, and the second being the type of element in the second range. The function should return a boolean value indicating whether the values are equal.

Return value

find_end() returns an iterator of type ForwardIterator1. The iterator is either last1, if no match was found, or the iterator points to the end of the matched sequence in the input range.

Description

Both find_first_of() and find_end() search through an input sequence to find a match for a test sequence that is passed in the second input range. There can be multiple appearances of the test sequence in the input sequence, and find_end() looks for the last one. If it finds the last appearance of the input sequence, it returns an iterator pointing to the last element in the match. If no match is found, it returns last1.

   Note: This function was added to the ANSI/ISO specification, but at press time, the HP public distribution of the STL does not include find_end().

Complexity

The ANSI/ISO C++ specification dictates that this algorithm must operate in linear time.

Example

Listing 13-3

find1303.cpp: A demonstration of the find_end() algorithm

```
/*
 * FIND1303.CPP
 *
 * This program is used in Chapter 13 to demonstrate
 * the find_end() algorithm.  It uses a pair of
 * character arrays to perform the test.
 *
 */

//
// Borland 4.x workarounds
//
#define __MINMAX_DEFINED
#pragma option -vi-
```

```
#include <iostream.h>
#include <algo.h>

//
// Note that the array was chosen to *not*
// provide a match.
//

char *input = "ABCDEABCDEABCDE";
char *match = "ABCDEF";
const int input_len = sizeof( input ) / sizeof( char );
const int match_len = sizeof( match ) / sizeof( char );

main()
{
    char *result = find_end( input, input + input_len,
                             match, match + match_len );
    cout << "find_end returned an offset of "
         << (result - input)
         << endl;
    return 1;
}
```

FIND_FIRST_OF

find_first_of() has two versions, standard and predicate. Following is the standard version:

```
template<class ForwardIterator1, class ForwardIterator2>
ForwardIterator1 find_first_of( ForwardIterator1 first1,
                                ForwardIterator1 last1,
                                ForwardIterator2 first2,
                                ForwardIterator2 last2 );
Here is the predicate version:
template<class ForwardIterator1,
         class ForwardIterator2,
         class BinaryPredicate >
ForwardIterator1 find_first_of( ForwardIterator1 first1,
                                ForwardIterator1 last1,
                                ForwardIterator2 first2,
                                ForwardIterator2 last2,
                                BinaryPredicate pred );
```

Arguments

first1, last1:   This iterator pair defines the input range to be searched. The input stream is a forward iterator, so any STL container will work properly.

first2, last2:   This iterator pair defines the sequence to be searched for in the first sequence.

pred: The standard version of find_first_of() compares the elements in the two lists using operator==(). If you need a more powerful comparison function, you can supply a binary predicate. The predicate will take two arguments, the first being the type of element in the first range, and the second being the type of element in the second range. The function should return a boolean value indicating whether the values are equal.

Return value

find_first_of() searches the input range for a sequence of elements equal to the test range defined by first2, last2. Equality is defined using operator==() in the first version of this function, and by the predicate function in the second version.

Description

find_first_of() is used to find the first input sequence that matches the test sequence. It returns the first iterator in the test range where the match starts.

Complexity

This routine has linear complexity, running in $O(N)$ time, proportional to the length of the test sequence.

Example

Listing 13-4
find1304.cpp: A demonstration of the find_first_of() algorithm.

```
/*
 * FIND1304.CPP
 *
 * This program is used in Chapter 13 to demonstrate
 * the find_first_of() algorithm. It uses a pair of
 * character arrays to perform the test.
 *
 */

//
// Borland 4.x workarounds
//
#define __MINMAX_DEFINED
#pragma option -vi-

#include <iostream.h>
#include <algo.h>

char *input = "ABCDEABCDEABCDE";
char *match = "EABCDE";
const int input_len = sizeof( input ) / sizeof( char );
const int match_len = sizeof( match ) / sizeof( char );

main()
{
    char *result = find_first_of( input, input + input_len,
                                  match, match + match_len );
    cout << "find_first_of returned an offset of "
         << (result - input)
         << endl;
    return 1;
}
```

ADJACENT_FIND

Function

adjacent_find has two versions, standard and predicate. The standard version
is as follows:

```
template < class InputIterator >
InputIterator adjacent_find( InputIterator first,
                             InputIterator last )
{
    if ( first == last )
        return last;
    InputIterator next = first;
    while( ++next != last )
    {
        if ( *first == *next )
            return first;
        first = next;
    }
    return last;
}
```

The predicate version is very similar:

```
template < class InputIterator, class BinaryPredicate >
InputIterator adjacent_find( InputIterator first,
                             InputIterator last,
                             BinaryPredicate binary_pred )
{
    if ( first == last )
        return last;
    InputIterator next = first;
    while( ++next != last )
    {
        if ( binary_pred( *first, *next ) )
            return first;
        first = next;
    }
    return last;
}
```

Arguments

first: An iterator pointing to the first element in a sequence. The algorithm will start its search with the object pointed to by this iterator.

last: An iterator pointing *one past* the last element in a sequence. The algorithm will continue working through the sequence of objects pointed to by the first iterator until it either finds a match or reaches this iterator.

pred: In the second version of adjacent_find(), the search termination is determined by calling this predicate function, not by comparing two values using operator==(). This allows you the flexibility to create a more complex set of find criteria than can be done using the normal comparison operator. pred() returns true when called with an argument that meets the search criteria.

The predicate function or function object takes two arguments of type T, where T is the type of object pointed to by the input iterators. It should return a boolean value.

Return value

adjacent_find() returns a single iterator. If an adjacent match is found, the iterator will be the first of the matching pair. If no adjacent match is found, the iterator value returned will be equal to last.

Description

adjacent_find() locates a pair of adjacent objects in a container that are equal to one another. In the first version of adjacent_find(), equality is tested for by comparing the objects using operator==(). In the second version, equality is tested for by using a custom predicate function. Naturally, this means that equality can really be anything you like!

The adjacent_find() function generates fairly simple code. The complete body of the function is shown above. You should be aware that both versions of the function return a copy of the last iterator if no match is found. This means that any time you call adjacent_find() you must test the return against the end of your range, to ensure that a match was found—or not found.

Complexity

Both functions have linear time complexity. The average amount of time they take to find a match is directly proportional to the length of the container. The space complexity is constant, as no additional data storage is required, regardless of the length of the input sequence.

Example

Listing 13-5

find1305.cpp: A demonstration of the adjacent_find() algorithm.

```
/*
 * FIND1305.CPP
 *
 * This program is used in Chapter 13 to demonstrate the
 * adjacent_find() algorithm. It works by reading in all the
 * words from a text file (find1305.cpp!), then searching for
 * all adjacent matches.
 * Here are some matches: match match match
 *                        a a b c c d e e e
 *
 */

//
// Borland 4.x workarounds
//
#define __MINMAX_DEFINED
#pragma option -vi-

#include <iostream.h>
#include <fstream.h>
#include <cstring.h>

#include <algo.h>
#include <list.h>

main()
{
    ifstream f( "find1305.cpp" );
    if (!f) {
        cerr << "Couldn't open input file!\n";
        return 1;
    }
    list<string> l;

    while ( f ) {
        string word;
        f >> word;
        l.push_back( word );
    }
    f.close()
    for ( ; ; ) {
```

```
        list<string>::iterator i;
        i = adjacent_find( l.begin(), l.end() );
        if ( i == l.end() )
            break;
        cout << "Adjacent match: "
            << *i
            << endl;
        l.erase( i );
    }
    return 1;
}
```

Example output

```
Adjacent match: *
Adjacent match: match
Adjacent match: match
Adjacent match: a
Adjacent match: c
Adjacent match: e
Adjacent match: e
Adjacent match: ;
```

COUNT

Function

count() has two versions, standard and predicate. The standard version is as follows:

```
template < class InputIterator, class T, class Size >
void count( InputIterator first,
            InputIterator last,
            const T& value,
            Size& n )
{
    while ( first != last )
        if ( *first++ == value )
            ++n;
}
```

The predicate version is as follows:

```
template < class InputIterator, class Predicate, class Size >
void count_if( InputIterator first,
               InputIterator last,
               Predicate pred,
               Size& n )
{
    while ( first != last )
        if ( pred( *first++ ) )
            ++n;
}
```

Arguments

first: An iterator pointing to the first element in a sequence. The algorithm will start counting at the object pointed to by this iterator.

last: An iterator pointing *one past* the last element in a sequence. The algorithm will continue working through the sequence of objects pointed to by the first iterator until it reaches this iterator.

value: In the first version of count(), the algorithm increments counter *n* each time it finds an object in the input sequence equal to this value. Equality is determined by applying operator==() to the sequential object and the value argument.

pred: In the count_if() version of this algorithm, the counter is incremented when the predicate function returns true, instead of testing against a value. This allows you the flexibility to create a more complex set of count criteria than can be done using operator==().

The predicate function or function object should take a single argument of type T, where T is the type of object pointed to by the two input iterators. It should return a boolean value.

n: This is the value that gets incremented for each object in the input sequence that either matches the value argument, or causes the predicate function to return true. *n* is a reference argument, which means it can function as a return value from the function.

Normally, *n* would be returned from the function, but it's not possible to parameterize the return type of a template function. If a template function needs to return a parameterized value to the calling routine, it usually does so using a reference argument, which can be parameterized. That's the case for the count() and count_if() functions.

Return value

count() and count_if() are void functions, so they don't return anything. What you would normally think of as a return value from these functions is *n*, which is a reference argument.

Description

The count() algorithm iterates through a sequence of objects and increments a count for each value that meets certain criteria. In count(), the criteria is equality to a value argument based on operator==(). In count_if(), the count is incremented whenever an object in the input sequence causes the predicate function object to return true.

Note: Neither of these functions initializes *n*, the counter value. They might better have been named increment() or update() in the interests of accuracy. Be sure you initialize the counter value before calling the function.

Complexity

The time complexity of these two functions is linear. The algorithm has to perform either a comparison or a call to the predicate function object exactly once per object in the input sequence.

The space complexity of these two functions is constant. The amount of storage used by the algorithm is determined by the value argument or the predicate function, and is therefore independent of the length of the input sequence.

Example

Listing 13-6

coun1306.cpp: A demonstration of the count_if() algorithm.

```
/*
 * COUN1306.CPP
 *
 * This program is used in Chapter 13 to demonstrate
 * the count_if() algorithm. It works by reading in all
 * the words from a text file (coun1306.cpp), then
 * counting all the words that contain only letters.
 *
 */


//
// Borland 4.x workarounds
//
#define __MINMAX_DEFINED
#pragma option -vi-

#include <iostream.h>
#include <fstream.h>
#include <cstring.h>
#include <ctype.h>

#include <algo.h>
#include <deque.h>

bool my_count( string &a )
{
    for ( int i = 0 ; i < a.length() ; i++ )
        if ( !isalpha( a[ i ] ) )
            return 0;
    return 1;
}

main()
{
    ifstream f( "coun1306.cpp" );
    if ( !f ) {
        cerr << "Error opening input file!\n";
        return 1;
    }
    deque<string> dq;
```

```
while ( f ) {
    string word;
    f >> word;
    dq.push_back( word );
}
f.close();
int n = 0;
count_if( dq.begin(), dq.end(), my_count, n );
cout << "Total words: "
    << dq.size()
    << endl;
cout << "All alpha count: "
    << n
    << endl;
return 1;
}
```

Example output

```
Total words: 169
All alpha count: 62
```

MISMATCH

Function

mismatch() has two versions, standard and predicate. The standard version
is as follows:

```
template < class InputIterator1, class InputIterator2 >
pair< InputIterator1, InputIterator2 >
mismatch( InputIterator1 first1,
          InputIterator1 last1,
          InputIterator2 first2)
{
  while ( first1 != last1 && *first1 == *first2 )
  {
    ++first1;
    ++first2;
  }
  return pair< InputIterator1, InputIterator2 >( first1, first2 );
}
```

The predicate version is as follows:

```
template < class InputIterator1,
           class InputIterator2,
           class BinaryPredicate >
pair< InputIterator1, InputIterator2 >
mismatch( InputIterator1 first1,
          InputIterator1 last1,
          InputIterator2 first2,
          BinaryPredicate binary_pred )
{
  while ( first1 != last1 && binary_pred( *first1, *first2 ) )
  {
    ++first1;
    ++first2;
  }
  return pair< InputIterator1, InputIterator2 >( first1, first2 );
}
```

Arguments

first1:   An iterator pointing to the start of the first input sequence. This algorithm compares two input sequences, with this iterator showing where the first one begins.

last1:   An iterator pointing *one past* the end of the first input sequence. You should note that the two input sequences are assumed to have the same length, so the distance from first1 to last1 also defines the length of the second sequence. Because of this, the algorithm needs to define first2, but not last2.

first2:   The start of the second sequence. As mentioned above, the length of the second sequence is assumed to be the same as that of this sequence.

             Note that the type of the object pointed to by first2 does not necessarily have to be the same type as that pointed to by first1. The two objects will be compared with either operator==() or a binary predicate function. Both are perfectly capable of comparing objects of disparate types.

binary_pred: The first version of mismatch() compares the two
                sequences using operator==(), which is more than ade-
                quate for many comparisons. However, you may want to
                customize your comparison function by using a predicate
                function object.

                The predicate function object takes two arguments, one
                of type T1, and one of type T2. T1 and T2 are the types
                pointed to by the iterators for the two input sequences.
                The binary predicate function performs some sort of
                comparison of the two objects, and returns a boolean
                indicating whether the two match or not.

Return value

mismatch() is one of the functions that returns a pair<> object. pair<> is
that unique STL construct which combines two unconnected objects
together into a single construct, so that it can easily be used to return
multiple objects from a function call.

The pair returned from mismatch() consists of two iterators, one from
each of the two input sequences. If a mismatch is found before the end of
the sequence, the two iterators point to the first two objects that didn't
match. If no mismatch is found, the two iterators point to the last values of
the sequences, which point one past the last value in the sequence.

Remember when using the return value from mismatch() that pair<>
objects don't have a default constructor. This means that the easiest way to
get a return value is usually via the copy constructor, something like this:

```
pair<int *, int *> p = mismatch( a.begin(), a.end(), b.begin() );
```

If you were to try to declare a pair variable by itself for later use, you
would get an error message from the compiler, indicating that no constructor could be found for the pair. The sample code shown below would provoke the error message, with the compiler complaining about the first line.

```
pair<int *, int *> p;
p = mismatch( a.begin(), a.end(), b.begin() );
```

Description

mismatch() iterates through a pair of input sequences, checking each pair of resulting objects for equality. The first version of the function compares the two objects using operator==(), while the second uses a binary predicate function.

If a mismatch is found using either of these two methods, the two iterators that yielded the mismatched objects are returned as a pair. If mismatch() makes it all the way to the end of the sequence with no mismatches, the two last iterators are returned. Remember that the last values actually point one past the last value in the sequence, so they can be easily distinguished from a pair of legitimate iterators.

Complexity

mismatch() has linear time complexity. It has to perform a single operation for each object in the first input sequence. Space complexity is constant.

Example

Listing 13-7

misml1307.cpp: A demonstration of the mismatch() algorithm.

```
/*
 * MISM1307.CPP
 *
 * This program is used in Chapter 13 to demonstrate
 * the mismatch algorithm. The program creates a big
 * vector of doubles, copies them into a set of integers,
 * then runs mismatch to see if there is one. There should
 * be a forced error at the very end of the vector, because
 * a value that won't convert to an integer is used.
 *
 * Note also that this program demonstrates the fact that
 * mismatch() can work with different container types, as
 * well as use iterators that point to different types.
 *
 */
```

```
//
// Borland 4.x workaround
//
#define __MINMAX_DEFINED
#pragma option -vi-

#include <iostream.h>
#include <cstring.h>
#include <ctype.h>

#include <set.h>
#include <vector.h>
#include <algo.h>

main()
{
//
// Fill up the vector with a bunch of doubles
//
    vector<double> a;
    for ( double d = 0.0 ; d < 3000.0 ; d += 100.0 )
        a.push_back( d );
    a.push_back( 3000 + 0.5 );
//
// Insert all the doubles into a set using an
// insertion iterator.
//
    set< int, less<int> > b;
    insert_iterator< set<int, less<int> > > sii( b, b.begin() );
    copy( a.begin(), a.end(), sii );
//
// Now check for a mismatch.
//
    double *mm = mismatch( a.begin(), a.end(), b.begin() ).first;
    if ( mm == a.end() )
        cout << "No mismatch detected!\n";
    else
        cout << "Mismatch at: "
                << *mm
                << endl;
    return 1;
}
```

Example output

```
Mismatch at: 3000.5
```

EQUAL

Function

equal() has two versions, standard and predicate. The standard version is as follows:

```
template < class InputIterator1, class InputIterator2 >
inline bool equal( InputIterator1 first1,
                   InputIterator1 last1,
                   InputIterator2 first2 )
{
    return mismatch( first1, last1, first2 ).first == last1;
}
```

The predicate version is as follows:

```
template < class InputIterator1,
           class InputIterator2,
           class BinaryPredicate >
inline bool equal( InputIterator1 first1,
                   InputIterator1 last1,
                   InputIterator2 first2,
                   BinaryPredicate binary_pred )
{
  return
    mismatch( first1, last1, first2, binary_pred ).first == last1;
}
```

Arguments

first1:   An iterator pointing to the start of the first input sequence. This algorithm compares two input sequences, and this determines where the first one begins.

last1:   An iterator pointing *one past* the end of the first input sequence. You should note that the two input sequences are assumed to have the same length, so the distance from first1 to last1 also defines the length of the second sequence. Because of this, the algorithm needs to define first2, but not last2.

first2:   The start of the second sequence. As mentioned above, the length of the second sequence is assumed to be the same as that of this sequence.

Note: The type of the object pointed to by first2 does not necessarily have to be the same type as that pointed to by first1. The two objects will be compared with either operator==() or a binary predicate function. Both are perfectly capable of comparing objects of disparate types.

binary_pred: The first version of equal() compares the two sequences using operator==(), which is more than adequate for many comparisons. However, you may want to customize your comparison function by using a predicate function object.

The predicate function object takes two arguments, one of type T1, and one of type T2. T1 and T2 are the types pointed to by the iterators for the two input sequences. The binary predicate function performs some sort of comparison of the two objects, and returns a boolean indicating whether or not the two match.

Return value

This algorithm returns a simple boolean value indicating whether every object in the first sequence is equal to the corresponding object in the second sequence. Equality is determined by using either operator==(), or the predicate function.

Description

This algorithm compares two input sequences for equality. "Equality" means that each object in the first sequence is equal to the corresponding object in the second sequence, using either operator==() or the binary predicate function.

equal() is essentially just a wrapper around a call to mismatch(). If mismatch() makes it all the way to the end of the input sequence without finding a mismatch, it means the two input sequences are identical.

Complexity

equal() has linear time complexity. It has to perform a single operation for each object in the first input sequence. Space complexity is constant.

Example

Listing 13-8

eq1308.cpp: A demonstration of the equal() algorithm.

```
/*
 * EQ1308.CPP
 *
 * This program is used in Chapter 13 to demonstrate
 * the equal algorithm. The flexibility of STL
 * algorithms is demonstrated by using equal() to
 * compare a sequence in a vector with a sequence
 * in a set.
 */

#define __MINMAX_DEFINED
#pragma option -vi-

#include <iostream.h>
#include <cstring.h>
#include <ctype.h>

#include <set.h>
#include <vector.h>
#include <algo.h>

main()
{
//
// Fill up the vector with a bunch of doubles
//
    vector<double> a;
    for ( double d = 0.0 ; d < 3000.0 ; d += 100.0 )
        a.push_back( d );
//
// Insert all the doubles into a set using an
// insertion iterator.
//
```

```
        set< int, less<int> > b;
        insert_iterator< set<int, less<int> > > sii( b, b.begin() );
        copy( a.begin(), a.end(), sii );

        bool match = equal( a.begin(), a.end(), b.begin() );
        cout << "Before modification a and b are "
             << ( match ? "" : "not " )
             << "equal\n";

        a[ 1 ] += .5;
        match = equal( a.begin(), a.end(), b.begin() );
        cout << "After modification a and b are "
             << ( match ? "still " : "not " )
             << "equal\n";
        return 1;
    }
```

Example output

```
Before modification a and b are equal
After modification a and b are not equal
```

SEARCH

Function

search() has two versions, standard and predicate. The standard version is as follows:

```
template < class ForwardIterator1, class ForwardIterator2 >
ForwardIterator1 search( ForwardIterator1 first1,
                         ForwardIterator1 last1,
                         ForwardIterator2 first2,
                         ForwardIterator2 last2 );
```

The predicate version is as follows:

```
template < class ForwardIterator1,
           class ForwardIterator2,
           class BinaryPredicate >
```

```
ForwardIterator1 search( ForwardIterator1 first1,
                         ForwardIterator1 last1,
                         ForwardIterator2 first2,
                         ForwardIterator2 last2,
                         BinaryPredicate binary_pred );
```

Arguments

first1:   An iterator pointing to the start of the input sequence. This algorithm searches for the appearance of the second sequence in the sequence starting with this iterator.

last1:   An iterator pointing *one past* the last element in the input sequence. The range defined by first1, last1, defines the input sequence that will be searched for the appearance of the second sequence.

first2:   An iterator pointing to the first element in a sequence. search() attempts to find an appearance of this sequence in the first sequence. You should note that this doesn't necessarily have to be a sequence of a type identical to that pointed to by first1, last1. The two types merely have to either work with operator==() or the binary predicate function object, depending on which version of search() is employed.

last2:   An iterator pointing *one past* the last element in the second sequence. This defines the end of the sequence.

binary_pred: The first version of search() compares the elements in the two input sequences using operator==(). If you don't want to use the default comparison operator, you can define a binary predicate function or function object that will perform a comparison object for you.

The binary predicate function should take an argument of type T1, and a second argument of type T2. T1 and T2 are the types pointed to by the two types of input iterators. The predicate function returns a boolean value, indicating whether or not the two objects passed to it are identical.

Return value

search() returns an iterator pointing to the position in the input sequence where a copy of sequence two was located. If the second sequence wasn't found, the iterator returned is last1, which points one element past the last element in the input sequence.

Description

search() locates the first appearance of the second sequence in the first sequence. The iterator returned by the function points to the location in the first sequence where the second sequence makes its appearance. search() returns last1 if no match is found.

Complexity

Unfortunately, search() has worst-case quadratic behavior. The search algorithm consists of what amounts to a nested loop, resulting in time complexity that goes up in proportion to the product of the lengths of the two sequences. Space complexity is constant.

Example

Listing 13-9

srch1309.cpp: A demonstration of the search() algorithm.

```
/*
 * SRCH1309.CPP
 *
 * This program is used in Chapter 13 to demonstrate
 * the search() algorithm. It simply searches for the
 * appearance of the key in the text, then prints out
 * information on what was found.
 *
 */

//
// Borland 4.x workarounds
//
```

```
#define __MINMAX_DEFINED
#pragma option -vi-

#include <iostream.h>
#include <string.h>

#include <vector.h>
#include <algo.h>

char text[] = "It was the best of times, it "
              "was the worst of times.";
char key[] = "it was";

main()
{
    vector<char> t( text, text + strlen( text ) );
    vector<char> k( key, key + strlen( key ) );
    t.push_back( 0 );

    char *p = search( t.begin(), t.end(), k.begin(), k.end() );
    cout << "Match was found at offset "
        << ( p - t.begin() )
        << endl;
    cout << "Match: "
        << p
        << endl;
    return 1;
}
```

Example output

```
Match was found at offset 26
Match: it was the worst of times.
```

MUTATING SEQUENCE OPERATIONS

Let the great world spin forever down the ringing grooves of change.
— Alfred Lord Tennyson, *Locksley Hall*

Mutating sequence operations share their fundamental mode of operations with their non-mutating siblings. (See Chapter 13.) They all perform an operation over a range defined by a pair of iterators. Each algorithm starts its work at the location pointed to by the first iterator, and continues until it reaches either a terminating condition or the terminating iterator.

The algorithms in this chapter are collectively referred to as *mutating*, because they either can or will modify the objects pointed to by the iterators. In many cases, the copy versions of the algorithms in this chapter don't modify their inputs. Nonetheless, they are classified as mutating, since they still modify the ranges pointed to by their output iterators.

Most of the function descriptions in this chapter include a complete copy of the code that makes up the function. In the STL, much of the complexity of an operation is hidden in the supporting code for the container and iterator classes, which makes these algorithms seem deceptively simple. Due to their economy of expression, the entire function often fits comfortably in the same space normally reserved for the prototype.

One typical case where the code implementing the function isn't shown is when the function uses specializations for several different categories of iterators. For example, the body for one version of reverse() is shown here:

```
template < class BidirectionalIterator >
inline void reverse( BidirectionalIterator first,
                     BidirectionalIterator last)
{
    __reverse( first, last, iterator_category( first ) );
}
```

This version of reverse() doesn't do anything except call a specialized version of reverse() that is parameterized on the iterator category. This technique is used frequently in the STL to provide the optimal version of a function for each iterator type. It makes for a more efficient library, but since this frequently leads to an additional three or four functions per algorithm, it isn't practical to provide full listings.

Table 14-1 gives a brief summary of the mutating sequence operations. Both this set of functions and the ones in Chapter 13 frequently have separate copy and predicate versions, which are noted in the table.

Table 14-1

The mutating sequence operations

Function	Predicate	Description
copy() copy_backward()		Copies a range of elements to a second range
swap()		Swaps two elements
iter_swap()		Swaps two elements pointed to by iterators
swap_ranges()		Swaps two ranges
transform()		Performs an operation on one or two sequences, storing the new result
replace() replace_copy()	replace_copy_if() replace_if()	Replaces selected elements in a range
fill() fill_n()		Fills a range with a specific value
generate() generate_n()		Fills a range with a generated value
remove() remove_copy()	remove_copy_if() remove_if()	Removes specific values from a range
unique() unique_copy()	unique() unique_copy_if()	Eliminates runs of equal values from a range

Function	Predicate	Description
reverse() reverse_copy()		Reverses a sequence
rotate() rotate_copy()		Rotates the elements in a sequence
random_shuffle()		Shuffles a sequence
partition() stable_partition()		Divides a range into two partitions

COPY

Function

```
template < class InputIterator, class OutputIterator >
OutputIterator copy( InputIterator first,
                     InputIterator last,
                     OutputIterator result )
{
    while ( first != last )
        *result++ = *first++;
    return result;
}


template < class BidirectionalIterator1,
           class BidirectionalIterator2 >
BidirectionalIterator2 copy_backward( BidirectionalIterator1 first,
                                      BidirectionalIterator1 last,
                                      BidirectionalIterator2 result) {
    while ( first != last )
        *--result = *--last;
    return result;
}
```

Arguments

first: An iterator pointing to the first element in a sequence. This iterator points to the first object in the input sequence to be copied.

last: An iterator pointing *one past* the final element in the sequence. As always in the STL, the last iterator doesn't point to the last object in a sequence, it points one past it.

result: This iterator points to the destination of the copy algorithm. Since the copy algorithm is going to copy last-first elements, you need to be certain that you have enough room in the destination to accommodate that many values. One way to be sure is to use an insertion iterator as your destination.

When performing copy_backward(), result needs to point one past the end of the output range, not to the start of the output range. A quick look at the source to copy_backward() will show why this is necessary.

Return value

The copy() algorithm returns a copy of the output iterator after the input range has been copied to it. The returned iterator will be positioned one entry past the point where the last copy operation took place. copy_backward() returns an iterator that points to the position of the final element that was copied.

When performing a copy, you need to be careful to avoid overlapping ranges between the source and destination. A quick examination of the source to copy() shows you that problems will occur if the result iterator points to an element in the range first, last. When this is the case, copy() will overwrite portions of the input data before it has been copied.

copy_backward() has a similar problem with overlapping ranges. If the input and output ranges overlap, and result is less than last, the copy operation won't be performed properly.

Note that in both cases you can perform copies of overlapping ranges. You just have to be sure that the result iterator doesn't lie in the input range.

Description

copy() puts a copy of an input range in the destination that is pointed to with an object that obeys iterator syntax. If the iterator points into an STL container, you need to be sure there is enough room allocated in the container to accommodate last-first objects.

The objects are copied to the output container using the assignment operator. The actual behavior of the assignment operator depends on the type of object being copied, of course.

The copy_backward() variant changes the operation slightly. Instead of starting the copy operation at first and working forward to last, copy_backward() starts copying with the element immediately preceding last, and works down to first. result points to the last element in the output sequence.

Complexity

Time complexity for both copy() and copy_backward() is linear with respect to the size of the input range. Space complexity is constant.

Example

Listing 14-1

copy1401.cpp: A demonstration of the copy() algorithm

```
/*
 * COPY1401.CPP
 *
 * This program is used in Chapter 14 to demonstrate the copy
 * algorithm. It does so using the extremely simple example of
 * copying an array to an ostream iterator. Note that this
 * copy operation is a handy way to print the contents of a
 * container.
 *
 */

//
// Borland 4.x workarounds
//
#define __MINMAX_DEFINED
#pragma option -vi-

#include <iostream.h>
#include <algo.h>

main()
{
    char *names[] = { "Abel", "Baker", "Charlie", "Delta" };

    copy( names,
          names + 5,
          ostream_iterator<char*>( cout, " " ) );
    return 1;
}
```

Example output:

```
Abel Baker Charlie Delta
```

SWAP

Function

```
template < class T >
inline void swap( T& a, T& b )
{
    T tmp = a;
    a = b;
    b = tmp;
}


template < class ForwardIterator1, class ForwardIterator2 >
void iter_swap( ForwardIterator1 a, ForwardIterator2 b )
{
__iter_swap( a, b, value_type(a) );
}
```

Arguments

a: swap() and iter_swap() use the same name for their two arguments. In swap(), *a* is the object to be exchanged with *b*. In iter_swap(), *a* is an iterator pointing to the object to be exchanged.

b: In swap(), *b* is the object to be exchanged with *a*. In iter_swap(), *b* is an iterator pointing to the object to be exchanged.

Return value

swap() and iter_swap() are void functions, so they have no return value.

Description

swap() and iter_swap() are basically two versions of the same function. swap() operates directly on the objects specified as parameters, whereas iter_swap() operates on the objects pointed to by the two iterator parameters. Both functions operate by creating a temporary object of type T, then using it to hold one object during the swap.

The implementation of swap() is straightforward, but iter_swap() requires a little more work. iter_swap() gets a pair of iterators as parameters, but doesn't have a template parameter to indicate what type of object the iterators point to. To remedy this problem, iter_swap() calls a helper template function, __iter_swap(). iter_swap() passes value_type(a) as the argument to __iter_swap. value_type(a) returns the type of object pointed to by the iterator, which then allows __iter_swap() to determine the type of object to be swapped.

__iter_swap() is defined as follows in algobase.h:

```
template < class ForwardIterator1,
           class ForwardIterator2,
           class T >
void __iter_swap( ForwardIterator1 a, ForwardIterator2 b, T* )
{
    T tmp = *a;
    *a = *b;
    *b = tmp;
}
```

Complexity

Both functions have constant time and space complexity.

Example

Listing 14-2

swap1402.cpp: A demonstration of the iter_swap() algorithm

```
/*
 * SWAP1402.CPP
 *
 * This program is used in Chapter 14 to demonstrate the
 * iter_swap algorithm. It swaps two elements from a pair
 * of arrays of character strings.
 */

//
// Borland 4.x workarounds
//
#define __MINMAX_DEFINED
#pragma option -vi-
```

```
#include <iostream.h>
#include <algo.h>

main()
{
    char *boys[] = { "Fred", "Ricky", "Pat", "George" };
    char *girls[] = { "Ethel", "Lucy", "Barbara", "Chris" };

    iter_swap( boys + 2, girls + 3 );
    cout << "Boys: ";
    copy( boys,
          boys + 4,
          ostream_iterator<char*>( cout, " " ) );
    cout << "\nGirls: ";
    copy( girls,
          girls + 4,
          ostream_iterator<char*>( cout, " " ) );
    return 1;
}
```

Example output:

```
Boys: Fred Ricky Chris George
Girls: Ethel Lucy Barbara Pat
```

SWAP_RANGES

Function

```
template < class ForwardIterator1, class ForwardIterator2 >
ForwardIterator2 swap_ranges( ForwardIterator1 first1,
                              ForwardIterator1 last1,
                              ForwardIterator2 first2 )
{
    while ( first1 != last1 )
        iter_swap( first1++, first2++ );
    return first2;
}
```

Arguments

first1:   An iterator pointing to the first element in a sequence. swap_ranges() has two sequences of objects to swap, and this iterator defines the start of the first sequence.

last1:   An iterator pointing *one past* the last element in the first sequence. All of the objects starting at first1 and ending just before last1 will be swapped.

first2:   An iterator pointing to the start of the second sequence. Note that swap_ranges() doesn't have a parameter to define the end of the second sequence. This is because the first and second sequences *must* be the same length, so there's no need for an additional parameter.

Return value

swap_ranges() continually increments first2, so a copy of this iterator will always be returned pointing *one past* the last element of the second list that has been swapped. It returns the updated value of first2 after the algorithm completes. first2 will then point *one past* the last element swapped in the second sequence.

Description

swap_ranges() swaps all objects in two sequences. This is done by iterating through the two sequences defined in the arguments to swap_ranges(), and performing an iter_swap() operation at each position.

swap_ranges() is a useful function when you need to exchange a subset of items in a container, or when swapping items between disparate container types. If you're going to swap the entire contents of two containers of the same type, you should first see if the swap() member function of the container is a better choice. The member function swap() of most containers implements a swap by exchanging a few key member variables, resulting in a much faster exchange.

Complexity

The time complexity of swap_ranges() is linear with respect to the length of the sequence to be exchanged. The number of operations it needs to perform, such as dereferences, iterator increments, and so on, are directly proportional to the length of the sequence. The space complexity is constant.

Example

Listing 14-3

swap1403.cpp: A demonstration of the swap_ranges() algorithm

```
/*
 * SWAP1403.CPP
 *
 * This program is used in Chapter 14 to demonstrate the
 * swap_ranges() algorithm. It does so by swapping two
 * randomly selected ranges of iterators.
 */

//
// Borland 4.x workarounds
//
#define __MINMAX_DEFINED
#pragma option -vi-

#include <iostream.h>
#include <algo.h>

main()
{
    char *boys[] = { "Fred", "Ricky", "Pat", "George" };
    char *girls[] = { "Ethel", "Lucy", "Barbara", "Chris" };

    cout << "Boys before: ";
    copy( boys,
          boys + 4,
          ostream_iterator<char*>( cout, " " ) );
    swap_ranges( boys + 1, boys + 4, girls );
    cout << "\nBoys after: ";
    copy( boys,
          boys + 4,
          ostream_iterator<char*>( cout, " " ) );
    return 1;
}
```

Example output:

```
Boys before: Fred Ricky Pat George
Boys after: Fred Ethel Lucy Barbara
```

TRANSFORM

Function

```
template < class InputIterator,
           class OutputIterator,
           class UnaryOperation >
OutputIterator transform( InputIterator first,
                          InputIterator last,
                          OutputIterator result,
                          UnaryOperation op )
{
    while ( first != last )
        *result++ = op( *first++ );
    return result;
}

template < class InputIterator1,
           class InputIterator2,
           class OutputIterator,
           class BinaryOperation >
OutputIterator transform( InputIterator1 first1,
                          InputIterator1 last1,
                          InputIterator2 first2,
                          OutputIterator result,
                          BinaryOperation binary_op )
{
    while ( first1 != last1 )
        *result++ = binary_op( *first1++, *first2++ );
    return result;
}
```

Arguments

first, first1:   An iterator pointing to the first element in the input sequence. The unary version of transform operates on one input sequence, which is started by the first iterator. The binary version of transform operates on two input sequences, and first1 is the starting iterator for the first sequence.

last, last1:	An iterator pointing *one past* the last element in the input sequence. For the unary version of transform, last marks the end of the only input sequence. For the binary version of transform, last1 marks the end of the first input sequence.
first2:	The binary version of transform operates on two input sequences. first2 marks the start of the second input sequence. Note that there is no last2 parameters, since the lengths of the two sequences must be the same.
result:	An iterator pointing to the output iterator. transform() applies a function to the input sequence(s) and places the result in the output sequence. Take care that the output sequence already has space allocated for last-first elements, or be prepared to create the space using an insertion iterator.
op, binary_op:	A function object or function pointer applied to the input sequence(s). The function object is called with either one or two objects as arguments. transform() is capable of handling two different types of input sequences, so there's no requirement that the iterators point to identical object types (in the case of the binary version of transform). The function object returns yet another type of object, which is assigned to the output sequence by way of the assignment operator.

Return value

Both versions of transform() return a copy of the output iterator after the last assignment has been performed. As a result, the output iterator should point to the next element in the output sequence.

Description

The transform algorithm applies a function to one or two input sequences and stores the results in another sequence. In this sense it is similar to the for_each() algorithm. The key difference is that transform() is called with an output iterator that points to an output sequence destined to receive the results of the transform operation.

There are two overloaded versions of transform. The unary version operates on a single input sequence and, accordingly, expects a function object argument that only takes a single argument. The binary version operates on a pair of input sequences, and thus expects a function object argument that takes a pair of objects. Both function objects should return an object value compatible with the output container type.

Complexity

transform has linear time complexity. All of its operations are performed a fixed number of times per input object. It has constant space complexity.

Example

Listing 14-4

trans1404.cpp: A demonstration of the transform() algorithm

```
/*
 * TRANS1404.CPP
 *
 * This program is used in Chapter 14 to demonstrate the
 * transform algorithm. It applies an area function to a queue
 * full of circles, and routes the output to cout via an
 * iostream iterator object.
 *
 */

//
// Borland 4.x workarounds
//
#define __MINMAX_DEFINED
#pragma option -vi-

#include <iostream.h>
#include <deque.h>
#include <algo.h>

struct circle {
    int x_origin;
    int y_origin;
```

```
    int radius;
    circle( int x = 0, int y = 0, int r = 1 ) :
        x_origin(x), y_origin(y), radius( r ){}
};

double area( const circle &c )
{
    return 3.1459 * c.radius * c.radius;
}

main()
{
    deque<circle> a;

    a.push_back( circle( 1, 1, 5 ) );
    a.push_back( circle( 2, 2, 2 ) );
    a.push_back( circle( 0, -100, 15 ) );

    cout << "circle areas: ";
    transform( a.begin(),
               a.end(),
               ostream iterator<double>( cout, " " ),
               area );
    return 1;
}
```

Example output:

```
circle areas: 78.6475 12.5836 707.827
```

REPLACE

The replace() algorithm has four different implementations, which can lead to a bit of confusion. All the replace() functions have one thing in common: they move through a sequence of elements, replacing some with a new value, and leaving other elements alone.

There are two factors that can be varied, leading to the four different functions. The first is how replace() decides which elements to replace, and which to leave unchanged. replace() and replace_copy() both test each element against the value parameter using operator==(). If operator==() returns true, the value is replaced. replace_if() and replace_copy_if() use a different method: they pass each element to a predicate function. If the function returns true, the values are replaced.

The second factor leading to the need for four separate functions is whether the input range is modified in place. Both replace() and replace_if() modify elements directly in the input range. replace_copy() and replace_copy_if() make the modifications as the input sequence is copied to the output range.

Function

```
template < class ForwardIterator, class T >
void replace( ForwardIterator first,
              ForwardIterator last,
              const T& old_value,
              const T& new_value )
{
    while ( first != last ) {
        if ( *first == old_value )
            *first = new_value;
        ++first;
    }
}

template < class ForwardIterator, class Predicate, class T >
void replace_if( ForwardIterator first,
                 ForwardIterator last,
                 Predicate pred,
                 const T& new_value )
{
    while ( first != last ) {
        if ( pred( *first ) )
            *first = new_value;
        ++first;
    }
}

template < class InputIterator, class OutputIterator, class T >
OutputIterator replace_copy( InputIterator first,
                             InputIterator last,
                             OutputIterator result,
                             const T& old_value,
                             const T& new_value )
{
```

```
        while ( first != last ) {
            *result++ = *first == old_value ? new_value : *first;
            ++first;
        }
        return result;
    }


    template < class Iterator,
               class OutputIterator,
               class Predicate,
               class T >
    OutputIterator replace_copy_if( Iterator first,
                                    Iterator last,
                                    OutputIterator result,
                                    Predicate pred,
                                    const T& new_value )
    {
        while ( first != last ) {
            *result++ = pred( *first ) ? new_value : *first;
            ++first;
        }
        return result;
    }
```

Arguments

first: An iterator pointing to the first element in a sequence. All four versions of the replace algorithm operate over an input sequence whose first element is pointed to by this iterator.

last: An iterator pointing *one past* the last element in the input sequence. The replace algorithm operates on every object in the input sequence starting at first and continuing to last-1.

old_value: replace() and replace_copy() look for this value in the input sequence and perform a replacement when they find it. The comparison is done using operator==(), with suitable type conversions applied as needed.

new_value: All four comparison routines use this argument as the new value that is substituted when a replace operation is called for. The new value is inserted into either the original sequence or the output sequence by using the assignment operator.

pred: The standard version of replace() does a comparison of objects in the input sequence against old_value, to decide if a replacement needs to be done. The two if variants of replace, replace_if() and replace_copy_if(), don't use old_value to see if a replacement needs to be performed. Instead, they apply this predicate function object to the input object and check the boolean return value. If the predicate function returns true, a replacement is done.

result: The first two versions of replace, replace() and replace_if(), perform a replacement function in place of the input vector. The two copy variants, replace_copy() and replace_copy_if() don't modify the input sequence. Instead, they perform a copy operation while simultaneously doing the replacement. The contents of the input vector, after appropriate replacements are made, are copied to the output sequence pointed to by this iterator.

Note: This iterator needs to have enough space allocated to hold last-first objects. If it doesn't, it needs to be an insertion iterator, or an object with similar semantics.

Return value

Both replace() and replace_if() are void functions, and return nothing. Both copy versions of the replace algorithm, replace_copy() and replace_copy_if() return a copy of the output iterator that was their copy destination. Since the return value is the output iterator after its final increment, it points *one past* the final insertion point.

Description

The replace() algorithm performs a simple operation; it works its way through an input sequence, replacing any given value with a new value. This seems easy enough, but the STL designers complicated things a bit by providing two optional features: predicate functions and a copy option.

Normally, replacement is done when an element in the input sequence is equal to old_value, an argument to the replace function. However, there are times when this capability is somewhat limiting.

For example, you may want to replace an entire range of objects, instead of just one particular value. When this is the case, you can create a predicate function that returns a true value for any of the objects you want to replace. You can then call replace_if() or replace_copy_if() with this predicate function, and perform your tailored replacement.

The two standard replace functions, replace() and replace_if(), have two variants that perform a copy during the replacement. replace_copy() and replace_copy_if() let you leave the original input sequence intact while storing the new objects—with replacements where called for—in the location of your choice.

Complexity

All four of these functions have linear time complexity. The operations in the main loop of these algorithms are performed once per element in the input range. Space complexity is constant, as it's independent of the input sequence length.

Example

Listing 14-5

repl1405.cpp: A demonstration of the replace() algorithm

```
/*
 * REPL1405.CPP
 *
 * This program demonstrates the replace() algorithm
 * as described in Chapter 14. I perform a simple
 * replace_copy() with the results printed before
 * and after the replacement.
 */

//
// Borland 4.x workarounds
//
#define __MINMAX_DEFINED
#pragma option -vi-
```

```
#include <iostream.h>
#include <cstring.h>

#include <algo.h>
#include <vector.h>

main()
{
    vector<string> leaders;
    vector<string> revised( 3 );

    leaders.push_back( string( "Lenin" ) );
    leaders.push_back( string( "Molotov" ) );
    leaders.push_back( string( "Trotsky" ) );

    cout << "Original leaders of the 1917 revolution: ";
    copy( leaders.begin(),
          leaders.end(),
          ostream_iterator<string>( cout, " " ) );
    cout << endl;

    replace_copy( leaders.begin(),
                  leaders.end(),
                  revised.begin(),
                  string( "Trotsky" ),
                  string( "Stalin" ) );

    cout << "Revised leaders of the revolution: ";
    copy( revised.begin(),
          revised.end(),
          ostream_iterator<string>( cout, " " ) );
    cout << endl;
    return 1;
}
```

Example output:

```
Original leaders of the 1917 revolution: Lenin Molotov Trotsky
Revised leaders of the revolution:  Lenin Molotov Stalin
```

FILL

Function

```
template < class ForwardIterator, class T >
void fill( ForwardIterator first,
           ForwardIterator last,
           const T& value )
{
    while ( first != last )
        *first++ = value;
}

template < class OutputIterator, class Size, class T >
void fill_n( OutputIterator first,
             Size n,
             const T& value)
{
    while ( n-- > 0 )
        *first++ = value;
}
```

Arguments

first: An iterator pointing to the first element in a sequence. The fill procedure will start assigning the value argument to the position in the sequence pointed to by this iterator.

last: The first version of the fill() algorithm uses two iterators to define the range of elements to be initialized to the fill value. last is the second iterator in the pair, and it points *one past* the last element to be affected by the fill operation.

n: The second version of fill doesn't use a last iterator to define the end of its fill range. Instead, it fills the number of elements specified by the scalar value *n*.

value: This is the value that will be stuffed into each object in the sequence.

Return value

Both versions of the fill algorithm are void functions, and return nothing.

Description

The fill algorithm is used to set an entire range of elements to a predefined value. The only difference between the two versions of the algorithm is in how they specify the range to be filled. fill() defines the range using the conventional STL iterator pair; first and last. fill_n() uses a start iterator and a count.

Both versions of the algorithm simply step through the sequence, setting each object pointed to by the iterator as equal to value.

Complexity

The fill algorithm has linear time complexity. It has to execute each of the operations in its inner loop once per iterator in the range. Its space complexity is constant.

Example

Listing 14-6

fill1406.cpp: A demonstration of the fill algorithm

```
/*
 * FILL1406.CPP
 *
 * This program is used in Chapter 14 to demonstrate
 * the fill algorithm. It fills the first 50 elements of
 * a 100 element list with a copy of a string. Note that
 * the value passed to the fill algorithm is not a string
 * object, just a character pointer. This is okay, because
 * there is a string assignment operator that can convert
 * from character pointers without complaint. This is
 * another flexibility win for templates and the STL.
 */
```

```
//
// Borland 4.x workarounds
//
#define __MINMAX_DEFINED
#pragma option -vi-

#include <iostream.h>
#include <cstring.h>
#include <list.h>
#include <algo.h>

main()
{
    list<string> a( 100 );
    fill_n( a.begin(), 50, "<null>" );
    for ( list<string>::iterator i = a.begin();
          i != a.end();
          i++ )
        cout << "\""
             << *i
             << "\" ";
    return 1;
}
```

Example output:

```
"<null>" "<null>" "<null>" "<null>" "<null>" "<null>" "<null>" "<null>" "<null>"
"<null>" "<null>" "<null>" "<null>" "<null>" "<null>" "<null>" "<null>" "<null>"
"<null>" "<null>" "<null>" "<null>" "<null>" "<null>" "<null>" "<null>" "<null>"
"<null>" "<null>" "<null>" "<null>" "<null>" "<null>" "<null>" "<null>" "<null>"
"<null>" "<null>" "<null>" "<null>" "<null>" "<null>" "<null>" "<null>" "<null>"
"<null>" "<null>" "<null>" "<null>" "<null>" "" "" "" "" "" "" "" "" "" "" ""
"" "" "" "" "" "" "" "" "" "" "" "" "" "" "" "" "" "" "" "" "" "" "" "" "" "" ""
"" "" "" "" "" "" "" "" "" "" ""
```

GENERATE

Function

```
template < class ForwardIterator, class Generator >
void generate( ForwardIterator first,
               ForwardIterator last,
               Generator gen )
    {
```

```
    while ( first != last )
        *first++ = gen();
}

template < class OutputIterator,
           class Size,
           class Generator >
void generate_n( OutputIterator first,
                 Size n,
                 Generator gen )
{
    while ( n-- > 0 )
        *first++ = gen();
}
```

Arguments

first: An iterator pointing to the first element in a sequence. The
          generation function object will start assigning the output of the
          generator function to the position in the sequence pointed to
          by this iterator.

last: The first version of the generate() algorithm uses two itera-
          tors to define the range of elements to be initialized by the
          generation function object. last is the second iterator in the
          pair, and it points *one past* the last element to be affected by
          the operation.

n: The second version of generate doesn't use a last iterator to
          define the end of its range. Instead, it generates values for the
          number of elements specified by the scalar value *n*.

gen: This is the generation function object used to create new
          objects to be inserted into the sequence. The generator func-
          tion object can be anything that obeys function object syntax.
          The compiler expects the function object to have no argu-
          ments, and to return some sort of object that can be assigned
          to the object pointed to by the iterator.

Return value

Both versions of the generate algorithm are void functions, and return nothing.

Description

The generate algorithm is very similar to fill. It works its way through a sequence of objects pointed to by an iterator, assigning a new value to each object. Just like the fill algorithm, it has two versions:

- one that uses a pair of iterators to define the range
- one that uses a single iterator to point to the start of a sequence, along with a scalar to define the sequence's length.

Unlike the fill algorithm, however, generate doesn't have to blindly assign a single constant value to the objects it's modifying. Instead, it uses a generator function object to create new values. This provides a handy way to create more complex initialization sequences than can be done by using just a fixed value.

Complexity

The generate algorithm has linear time complexity. It has to execute each of the operations in its inner loop once per iterator in the range. Its space complexity is constant.

Example

Listing 14-7

gen1407.cpp: A demonstration of the generate() algorithm

```
/*
 * GEN1407.CPP
 *
 * This program is used in Chapter 14 to demonstrate
 * the generate algorithm. It fills the first 20 elements of
 * an integer array with the first 20 fibonacci numbers.
 * Remember that f(1) = 1, f(2) = 1, and
```

```
 * f(n) = f(n-1) + f(n-2).
 */

//
// Borland 4.x workarounds
//
#define __MINMAX_DEFINED
#pragma option -vi-

#include <iostream.h>
#include <cstring.h>
#include <algo.h>

struct fibber {
    int n_minus_1;
    int n_minus_2;
    fibber() {
        n_minus_1 = 0;
        n_minus_2 = 1;
    }
    int operator()() {
        int ret_val = n_minus_1 + n_minus_2;
        n_minus_2 = n_minus_1;
        n_minus_1 = ret_val;
        return ret_val;
    }
};

main()
{
    int fibs[ 20 ];
    generate_n( fibs, 20, fibber() );
    copy( fibs, fibs + 20 , ostream_iterator<int>( cout, " " ) );
    return 1;
}
```

Example output:

```
1 1 2 3 5 8 13 21 34 55 89 144 233 377 610 987 1597 2584 4181 6765
```

REMOVE

The remove() algorithm has four different implementations. They all perform the same function, which is to remove certain values from a sequence. The word "remove" can be deceptive in the description of this algorithm, because elements aren't actually removed from the container. Instead, elements are overwritten by having their contents copied over by elements from later in the sequence.

After remove() has done its work, the range will have a new sequence that might have fewer elements than it did before, with unused elements filling in the remainder of its range. For example, this sequence of characters

```
"ABCDEFGABCDEFGABCDEFG"
```

could have every appearance of letter "A" removed. The resulting sequence would then look like this:

```
"BCDEFGBCDEFGBCDEFGEFG"
```

You can see that the range has been compacted down by copying elements, but the length of the range hasn't changed. This concept is explained in detail in the "Description" section for these functions.

The four variations of remove() correspond exactly to the four variations of replace() discussed earlier in this chapter. remove() and remove_copy() both remove elements that are identical to a value passed as a parameter. remove_if() and remove_copy_if() remove elements that cause the predicate function to return true. remove() and remove_if() modify a sequence in place. remove_copy() and remove_copy_if() modify a sequence while copying it to a new location.

Function

```
template < class ForwardIterator, class T >
ForwardIterator remove( ForwardIterator first,
                        ForwardIterator last,
                        const T& value)
{
    first = find( first, last, value );
    ForwardIterator next = first;
    return first == last ?
            first :
            remove_copy( ++next, last, first, value );
}
```

```
template < class ForwardIterator, class Predicate >
ForwardIterator remove_if( ForwardIterator first,
                           ForwardIterator last,
                           Predicate pred )
{
    first = find_if( first, last, pred );
    ForwardIterator next = first;
    rèturn first == last ?
            first :
            remove_copy_if( ++next, last, first, pred );
}


template < class InputIterator,
           class OutputIterator,
           class T >
OutputIterator remove_copy( InputIterator first,
                            InputIterator last,
                            OutputIterator result,
                            const T& value )
{
    while ( first != last )
    {
        if ( *first != value )
            *result++ = *first;
        ++first;
    }
    return result;
}


template < class InputIterator,
           class OutputIterator,
           class Predicate >
OutputIterator remove_copy_if( InputIterator first,
                               InputIterator last,
                               OutputIterator result,
                               Predicate pred )
{
    while ( first != last )
    {
        if ( !pred(*first) )
            *result++ = *first;
        ++first;
    }
    return result;
}
```

Arguments

first: An iterator pointing to the first element in a sequence. The remove algorithm will start performing its operation on the object pointed to by this iterator.

last: An iterator pointing to the last element in the sequence.

value: Two versions of the remove algorithm remove an object from a sequence if it matches this value. Both remove() and remove_copy() test each element in the sequence against this value, removing those that compare equal. The code shown above demonstrates that equality is defined using operator==() for the type of object pointed to by the input iterator.

pred: The remaining two versions of the remove algorithm don't test the input object stream against a specific value. Instead, they check the return value generated by a predicate function that's called with the object's value as a parameter. If the predicate function returns true, the object is removed.

result: The first two versions of the remove algorithm, remove() and remove_if(), do their work in place. That means they will remove objects from the input sequence. The copy variants of the remove() algorithm, remove_copy() and remove_copy_if(), don't modify the input sequence. Instead, they create an output sequence that contains the input stream, less the objects that have been removed.

Accordingly, these two versions of remove need an iterator pointing into the output sequence. The output iterator needs to have at least last-first objects already allocated, so there's room for a complete copy of the input sequence.

Return value

All four versions of this algorithm return an iterator pointing into the next position to be used in the output sequence. For remove() and remove_if(), this iterator is a pointer into the input sequence. For remove_copy() and remove_copy_if(), this iterator is a pointer into the output sequence—which started with iterator result.

Description

The four remove functions are used to selectively delete objects from a container. Each uses one of two different sets of criteria:

- remove() and remove_copy() remove objects that match a value passed to the functions
- remove_if() and remove_copy_if() remove objects that cause the predicate function to return a true value

In addition, the functions use two different methods to store the resulting sequence of objects:

- remove() and remove_if() both modify the input iterator in place
- remove_copy() and remove_copy_if() both make a new copy of the input sequence to an output sequence; all elements that satisfy the remove criteria will have been removed from the output sequence, but not from the input

It's very important when using the remove algorithm to understand that it won't actually *remove* the matched objects from the input sequence. When the algorithm runs, it leaves some unused objects at the end of the sequence, where they can be easily deleted, using member functions of the container they're in.

So, how do you determine how many objects were removed? (Or more correctly, written over.) Easy. The function returns an iterator that points to the current output iterator, which is pointing *one past* the last element to be copied or tested. You can then use the output iterator as the start of a sequence to be deleted.

Complexity

All four versions of the remove algorithm have linear time complexity. The function has to execute each of the operations in its inner loop once per iterator in the range. Its space complexity is constant.

Example

Listing 14-8

rem1408.cpp: A demonstration of the remove() algorithm

```
/*
 * REM1408.CPP
 *
 * This program is used in Chapter 14 to demonstrate the
 * remove algorithm. The program creates a simple list of
 * names, then calls remove() to remove every name that
 * contains the word "Bill". Note that remove() compacts
 * the data in the vector, but leaves some unused
 * objects at the end of the container. It takes a call
 * to erase() to actually free up the extra objects.
 */

//
// Borland 4.x workarounds
//
#define __MINMAX_DEFINED
#pragma option -vi-

#include <iostream.h>
#include <string.h>
#include <vector.h>
#include <algo.h>

bool no_bill( char *s )
{
    if ( strstr( s, "Bill" ) )
        return 1;
    else
        return 0;
}

template<class Stream, class OutputIterator>
void output( Stream &s,
             OutputIterator begin,
             OutputIterator end )
{
    while ( begin != end ) {
        s << *begin++;
        if ( begin != end )
            cout << ", ";
    }
```

```
        cout << endl;
    }

main()
{
    vector<char *> a;
    a.push_back( "Bill Gates" );
    a.push_back( "Bill Clinton" );
    a.push_back( "George Bush" );
    a.push_back( "Abe Lincoln" );
    a.push_back( "Michael Spindler" );

    cout << "Initial vector:\n";
    output( cout, a.begin(), a.end() );
    char **last = remove_if( a.begin(), a.end(), no_bill );
    cout << "\nVector after remove():\n";
    output( cout, a.begin(), a.end() );
    a.erase( last, a.end() );
    cout << "\nVector after erase:\n";
    output( cout, a.begin(), a.end() );
    return 1;
}
```

Example output:

```
Initial vector:
Bill Gates, Bill Clinton, George Bush, Abe Lincoln, Michael Spindler

Vector after remove():
George Bush, Abe Lincoln, Michael Spindler, Abe Lincoln, Michael Spindler

Vector after erase:
George Bush, Abe Lincoln, Michael Spindler
```

UNIQUE

unique() is another algorithm with four distinct implementations. unique()
removes elements using the same system as the remove() algorithm, meaning
that the range gets compacted. Once the algorithm has finished, there will
be unused elements left at the end of the range. It's up to the caller of
unique() to remove those elements from a container or array.

There are two overloaded functions named unique(). The standard version removes one of any pair of adjacent elements that are identical when compared using operator==(). The predicate version removes one of any pair of adjacent elements that return a true value when passed to the binary predicate function.

There are also two overloaded functions named unique_copy(). They have the same characteristics as the functions named unique(), with one exception. Instead of modifying elements in place, they copy the input range to an output range, and perform removal on the fly.

Note: This function should be used on a sorted sequence.

Function

```
template < class ForwardIterator >
ForwardIterator unique( ForwardIterator first,
                        ForwardIterator last )
{
    first = adjacent_find( first, last );
    return unique_copy( first, last, first );
}

template < class ForwardIterator, class BinaryPredicate >
ForwardIterator unique( ForwardIterator first,
                        ForwardIterator last,
                        BinaryPredicate binary_pred )
{
    first = adjacent_find( first, last, binary_pred );
    return unique_copy( first, last, first, binary_pred );
}

template < class InputIterator, class OutputIterator >
OutputIterator unique_copy( InputIterator first,
                            InputIterator last,
                            OutputIterator result );

template < class InputIterator,
           class OutputIterator,
           class BinaryPredicate >
OutputIterator unique_copy( InputIterator first,
                            InputIterator last,
                            OutputIterator result,
                            BinaryPredicate binary_pred );
```

Arguments

first:
: An iterator pointing to the first element in a sequence. The unique algorithm will start looking for unique elements at the location pointed to by first.

last:
: An iterator pointing to the last element in the input sequence. All versions of the unique algorithm assume that the last element to be processed is the element one before the last pointer.

result:
: There are two versions of the unique algorithm that write their results out to a different location from their input. These two functions, both called unique_copy(), copy all unique elements to the sequence pointed to by result. You should be aware that you need to have at least last-first elements in the result sequence to accommodate the maximum number of objects that might be copied into it. An insertion iterator is often a good choice here.

binary_pred:
: Two versions of the unique algorithm use the logical equality operator to determine whether or not two elements are unique. At times--for example, when storing character pointers--this may not be an adequate method of comparison. For cases when you need a different test, you can call a version of unique that uses a function object to test for equality.

: binary_pred can be any sort of object that obeys function pointer syntax. You can expect the function to be called with two arguments of type T, where T is the type of object pointed to by the iterator.

Return value

All four of the unique algorithms return an iterator that points to the next insertion point for the function output. For the two in-place versions of unique(), this is a pointer into the input sequence. For the others, it's a pointer to the output sequence.

Description

The unique algorithm is applied to sorted sequences of objects. It simply steps through an input sequence, and only copies those elements in the list that are unique. After each item is copied to the output sequence, the algorithm skips over any duplicates of that value in the input sequence. Thus, the resulting output sequence is a sorted sequence, with no duplicates.

Note: This function is very similar to the remove algorithm. Just like remove, when it sorts in-place, it doesn't delete the tail-end of the sequence, which means you must do it yourself. This is a necessary outgrowth of the convention that algorithms only know about iterators, not containers.

Also, just like remove, the unique algorithm supports four different variations. The two overloaded versions of function unique() both modify a sequence in place. They also *perform* the same way remove() does; they leave some unused space at the end of the sequence. These two functions are complemented by the two unique_copy() functions. These write their output to a new sequence, creating a new copy of the unique sorted sequence. As always, it's important to be sure the output sequence has enough room to accommodate last-first objects.

Both unique() and unique_copy() support overloaded versions that use a binary predicate function object to test for equality of objects. This function object is simply an object that uses function syntax to take two objects as arguments and returns a boolean value.

Complexity

All four versions of the unique algorithm have linear time complexity. Unique has to execute each of the operations in its inner loop once per iterator in the range, including the binary predicate function. Its space complexity is constant.

Example

Listing 14-9

uniq1409.cpp: A demonstration of the unique() algorithm

```
/*
 * UNIQ1409.CPP
 *
 * This program is used in Chapter 14 to demonstrate the
 * unique algorithm. The container used to supply an input
 * sequence to the unique() algorithm is a multiset.
```

```
 * unique() works with any sort of container, but it
 * can only guarantee removal of all duplicates when its
 * input is already sorted. Given this criteria, input
 * data stored in a multiset is a good choice. The unique
 * algorithm creates an output sequence that is inserted
 * into a list using an insertion iterator.
 */

//
// Borland 4.x workarounds
//
#define __MINMAX_DEFINED
#pragma option -vi-

#include <iostream.h>
#include <cstring.h>
#include <multiset.h>
#include <list.h>
#include <algo.h>

main()
{
    multiset< string, less<string> > a;

    a.insert( "Bill" );
    a.insert( "Mike" );
    a.insert( "Bill" );
    a.insert( "Fred" );
    a.insert( "Andy" );
    a.insert( "Mike" );
    a.insert( "Mike" );

    cout << "Initial multiset :\n";
    copy( a.begin(),
          a.end(),
          ostream_iterator<string>( cout, " " ) );
    cout << endl;

    list<string> b;
    back_insert_iterator< list<string> > i( b );
    unique_copy( a.begin(), a.end(), i );

    cout << "\nList after unique():\n";
    copy( b.begin(),
          b.end(),
          ostream_iterator<string>( cout, " " ) );
    cout << endl;
    return 1;
}
```

Example output:

```
Initial multiset:
Andy Bill Bill Fred Mike Mike Mike

List after unique():
Andy Bill Fred Mike
```

REVERSE

Function

```
template < class BidirectionalIterator >
inline void reverse( BidirectionalIterator first,
                     BidirectionalIterator last );

template < class BidirectionalIterator, class OutputIterator >
OutputIterator reverse_copy( BidirectionalIterator first,
                             BidirectionalIterator last,
                             OutputIterator result)
{
    while ( first != last )
        *result++ = *--last;
    return result;
}
```

Arguments

first: An iterator pointing to the first element in a sequence. This is
            where the reverse algorithm starts its operations.

last: An iterator pointing *one past* the last element in the sequence
            to be reversed.

result: An iterator pointing to the destination of the reverse operation.
            The reverse_copy() function implements a copy version of the
            algorithm. This leaves the input sequence intact while creating
            a reversed copy in the sequence pointed to by this iterator.

Return value

The two versions of the reverse algorithm have different return values. reverse() is a void function that returns nothing. reverse_copy() returns an output iterator pointing *one past* the last element stored into the output sequence.

Description

The reverse algorithm simply reverses the order of the elements in a sequence. Note that, in order to reverse the elements, the input iterators passed to the algorithm must be either bidirectional or random access iterators. This requirement arises for two reasons. First, the last iterator has to be decremented during the reversing process. And second, the algorithm needs to test the last iterator after it's decremented, to see if it has passed the midpoint of the sequence.

The reverse() function is slightly more complicated than reverse_copy() because it has two versions, one for bidirectional iterators, the other for random access iterators. The random access iterator version of reverse() can perform the reversal operation with fewer comparisons, by virtue of the fact that it supports operator<(). The two customized versions of reverse are shown below:

```
template < class BidirectionalIterator >
void __reverse( BidirectionalIterator first,
                BidirectionalIterator last,
                bidirectional_iterator_tag)
{
    while ( true )
        if ( first == last || first == --last )
            return;
        else
            iter_swap( first++, last );
}

template < class RandomAccessIterator >
void __reverse( RandomAccessIterator first,
                RandomAccessIterator last,
                random_access_iterator_tag)
{
    while ( first < last )
        iter_swap( first++, --last );
}
```

Complexity

All the versions of the reverse algorithm have linear time complexity, with
the cost of the function increasing in direct proportion to the size of the
input sequence. Space complexity is constant, since it is unaffected by the
size of the input sequence.

Example

Listing 14-10

rev1410.cpp: A demonstration of the reverse() algorithm

```
/*
 * REV1410.CPP
 *
 * This program is used in Chapter 14 to demonstrate the
 * reverse algorithm. An integer array is initialized with the
 * first 15 squared integers. The array is reversed, with the
 * result being copied into a second array. The two arrays are
 * then added together using the transform function, and the
 * results are plotted.
 *
 */

//
// Borland 4.x workarounds
//
#define __MINMAX_DEFINED
#pragma option -vi-

#include <iostream.h>
#include <iomanip.h>
#include <algo.h>

main()
{
    int a[ 15 ];
    int b[ 15 ];

    for ( int i = 0 ; i < 15 ; i++ )
        a[ i ] = i * i;
    reverse_copy( a, a + 15, b );
    transform( a, a + 15, b, a, plus<int>() );
```

```
//
// Plot the results
//
    for ( i = 0 ; i < 15 ; i++ ) {
        cout << setw( 3 ) << a[ i ] << " ";
        for ( int j = 0 ; j < a[ i ] ; j += 10 )
            cout << '*';
        cout << endl;
    }
    return 1;
}
```

Example output:

```
196 ********************
170 *****************
148 ***************
130 *************
116 ************
106 ***********
100 **********
 98 **********
100 **********
106 ***********
116 ************
130 *************
148 ***************
170 *****************
196 ********************
```

ROTATE

Function

```
template < class ForwardIterator >
inline void rotate( ForwardIterator first,
                    ForwardIterator middle,
                    ForwardIterator last );

template < class ForwardIterator, class OutputIterator >
OutputIterator rotate_copy( ForwardIterator first,
```

```
                              ForwardIterator middle,
                              ForwardIterator last,
                              OutputIterator result )
         {
            return copy( first, middle, copy( middle, last, result) );
         }
```

Arguments

first: An iterator pointing to the first element in a sequence. This iterator points to the start of the sequence where the rotate algorithm can start working.

middle: The middle iterator marks the position in the input sequence that will be moved to the start of the result sequence.

last: An iterator that marks the end of the input sequence.

result: There are two versions of rotate. The first, rotate(), is an in-place version that performs a rotate directly on a sequence. The second version, rotate_copy(), creates a copy of the rotated input sequence in an output sequence, while leaving the input unchanged. rotate_copy() uses the result parameter to locate the start of the output sequence.

As is usually the case with STL algorithms, you will need to be certain that the output sequence has room to contain all of the input objects.

Return value

The in-place function, rotate(), is a void function which returns nothing. The copy version of the rotate algorithm, rotate_copy(), returns an output iterator pointing to the position in the output sequence immediately following the rotated image of the input.

Description

The rotate algorithm performs a circular rotation of the elements in a sequence. The object pointed to by middle is rotated to the first position in the result array. middle+1 is rotated to first+1, and so on. The rotate operation wraps around the end of the sequence when it reaches last, and continues copying the elements from first to middle-1. Eventually, middle-1 is copied to last-1 in the output sequence; this terminates the operation. Figure 14-1 gives a graphical description of which elements are being copied where.

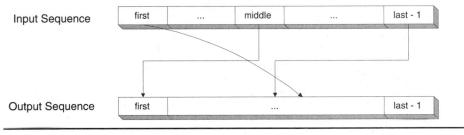

| Input Sequence | first | ... | middle | ... | last - 1 |

| Output Sequence | first | ... | last - 1 |

Figure 14-1
The operation of the rotate algorithm

The rotate algorithm is implemented in two versions. rotate() performs an in-place rotation; rotate_copy() leaves the input sequence alone while rotating into an output sequence. rotate() has unique specializations for forward, bidirectional, and random access iterators.

Complexity

Both implementations of rotate have linear time complexity, with the cost of the function increasing in direct proportion to the size of the input sequence. Space complexity is constant, as it is unaffected by the size of the input sequence.

Example

Listing 14-11

rot1411.cpp: A demonstration of the rotate() algorithm

```
/*
 * ROT1411.CPP
 *
 * This program is used in Chapter 14 to demonstrate the
 * rotate algorithm. The program makes two calls to the
 * rotate algorithm. The first uses rotate_copy()to produce
```

```
 * an output sequence in a new array. The second performs an
 * in-place rotation of the input sequence. They are both
 * printed out, and they had better be identical!
 */

//
// Borland 4.x workarounds
//
#define __MINMAX_DEFINED
#pragma option -vi-

#include <iostream.h>
#include <algo.h>

main()
{
    char *a[] = { "0th", "1st", "2nd", "3rd", "4th",
                  "middle", "6th", "last" };
    char *b[ 8 ];

    cout << "Input: " << endl;
    copy( a, a + 8, ostream_iterator<char*>(cout, " " ) );
    cout << endl << endl;

    rotate_copy( a, a + 5, a + 8, b );
    cout << "Copy output: " << endl;
    copy( b, b + 8, ostream_iterator<char*>(cout, " " ) );
    cout << endl << endl;

    rotate( a, a + 5, a + 8 );
    cout << "In-place output: " << endl;
    copy( a, a + 8, ostream_iterator<char*>(cout, " " ) );
    cout << endl << endl;

    return 1;
}
```

Example output:

```
Input:
0th 1st 2nd 3rd 4th middle 6th last

Copy output:
middle 6th last 0th 1st 2nd 3rd 4th

In-place output:
middle 6th last 0th 1st 2nd 3rd 4th
```

RANDOM_SHUFFLE

Function

```
template < class RandomAccessIterator >
inline void random_shuffle( RandomAccessIterator first,
                            RandomAccessIterator last );

template < class RandomAccessIterator,
           class RandomNumberGenerator >
void random_shuffle( RandomAccessIterator first,
                     RandomAccessIterator last,
                     RandomNumberGenerator& rand )
{
    if ( first == last )
        return;
    for ( RandomAccessIterator i = first + 1;
          i != last;
          ++i )
        iter_swap( i, first + rand( ( i - first ) + 1 ) );
}
```

Arguments

first: An iterator pointing to the first element in a sequence. The shuffle algorithm will start performing swaps on the object pointed to by this iterator.

last: An iterator pointing *one past* the last element in the input sequence. The shuffle algorithm will operate on all the elements in the range: first to last-1.

rand: The second version of random_shuffle employs a user-supplied random number generating function object to decide which elements to swap. The user-supplied function object should be a function that takes a single integer parameter *n*, and returns a random integer between 0 and *n-1*.

Return value

Both versions of random_shuffle are void functions.

Description

random_shuffle() randomly rearranges the elements in a sequence. It does this by iterating through the entire range of elements between first and last-1, performing a single random swap at each location.

Complexity

The time complexity of random_shuffle() is linear, in direct proportion to the number of elements in the input sequence. The space complexity is constant.

Example

Listing 14-12

shuf1412.cpp. A demonstration of the random_shuffle() algorithm

```
/*
 * SHUF1412.CPP
 *
 * This program is used in Chapter 14 to demonstrate
 * the random_shuffle algorithm. It does so by
 * creating a deck of cards, then performing a single
 * shuffle.
 *
 * Note that this program uses the __long_random()
 * function, which is defined in random.cpp. To
 * keep things simple, this program actually includes
 * random.cpp as an include file. You probably won't
 * want to do this in a real programming project.
 */

//
// Borland 4.x workarounds
//
#define __MINMAX_DEFINED
#pragma option -vi-

#include <iostream.h>
#include <vector.h>
#include <algo.h>
#include <random.cpp>
```

```
struct card {
    int value;
    card( int v = 0 ) : value( v ){;}
};

ostream & operator<<( ostream &s, card c )
{
    static count = 0;
    s << "A23456789TJQK"[ c.value % 13 ];
    s << "DCHS"[ c.value / 13 ];
    if ( ( ++count % 13 ) == 0 )
        s << endl;
    else
        s << " ";
    return s;
}

main()
{
    vector<card> a;
    for ( int i = 0 ; i < 52 ; i++ )
        a.push_back( card( i )  );
    cout << "Before shuffling: " << endl;;
    copy( a.begin(), a.end(), ostream_iterator<card>( cout ) );
    cout << endl;

    random_shuffle( a.begin(), a.end() );
    cout << "After shuffling: " << endl;;
    copy( a.begin(), a.end(), ostream_iterator<card>( cout ) );
    cout << endl;

    return 1;
}
```

Example output:

```
Before shuffling:
AD 2D 3D 4D 5D 6D 7D 8D 9D TD JD QD KD
AC 2C 3C 4C 5C 6C 7C 8C 9C TC JC QC KC
AH 2H 3H 4H 5H 6H 7H 8H 9H TH JH QH KH
AS 2S 3S 4S 5S 6S 7S 8S 9S TS JS QS KS

After shuffling:
QH QD 4H JC 6C 2H 3S JS 8C 3C 5D 7H 9S
6D 8S AS 8H KH 2C 9H TS 9D 9C KS 8D 7C
2S KD 5S TD AC 4C TC 5H 6H QS AD 6S TH
KC AH 5C 7S 3D 4S 7D 2D JD JH QC 4D 3H
```

PARTITION

Function

```
template < class BidirectionalIterator, class Predicate >
BidirectionalIterator partition( BidirectionalIterator first,
                                 BidirectionalIterator last,
                                 Predicate pred );

template < class ForwardIterator, class Predicate >
ForwardIterator stable_partition( ForwardIterator first,
                                  ForwardIterator last,
                                  Predicate pred );
```

Arguments

first: An iterator pointing to the first element in a sequence. The partition algorithm will start performing its operation on the object pointed to by this iterator.

last: The iterator pointing one past the end of the sequence.

pred: The predicate function the STL uses to partition the sequence. This should be an object with function object syntax that takes an argument of type T, where T is the type pointed to by the iterators, and returns a bool.

Return value

Both partition functions return an iterator pointing to the first element in the sequence that doesn't satisfy the predicate function. If every element in the sequence satisfies the predicate function, the partition functions return the last iterator.

Description

The partition functions take an input sequence and rearrange it into two groups. The first group consists of all the elements in the sequence that satisfy the predicate function the objects that cause the predicate function to return true when they are passed as inputs). The second group consists of all the objects that don't satisfy the predicate function.

After the algorithm has finished rearranging the objects in the sequence, it returns a pointer to the first object in the second group. This is the dividing point between the two groups. If the return value is equal to last or first, it means every object returned the same value from the predicate function, so the partition didn't succeed in creating two groups.

When partition() completes its rearrangement, the elements in the two groups are not in any defined order. stable_partition() guarantees that the elements in the two partitions have the same relative order as they did before the partition took place.

Complexity

partition() has linear time complexity, proportional to the number of elements in the sequence. stable_partition() has worst case time complexity of $N\log N$. However, if ample memory is available for buffering, stable_partition() is able to perform its work in linear time.

stable_partition() attempts to allocate a buffer large enough to hold a complete copy of the input sequence. The buffer is allocated via a call to get_temporary_buffer(), a template function defined in tempbuf.h. This function uses the set_new_handler() standard library call to prevent an exception from occurring if not enough memory is available.

If get_temporary_buffer() succeeds in allocating the requested amount of data, a worker function called __stable_partition_adaptive() does the partitioning. If the memory allocation failed, a function called __inplace_stable_partition() is called.

partition() has constant space complexity. The space complexity of stable_partition() varies from constant to linear, depending on whether or not it is successful in allocating an internal buffer during its operations.

Example

Listing 14-13

part1413.cpp: A demonstration of the partition() algorithm

```
/*
 * PART1413.CPP
 *
 * This program is used in Chapter 14 to demonstrate the
 * use of the partition algorithm. I implement a
 * divide-and-conquer sorting algorithm that works by
 * simply recursively breaking a sequence down into pieces,
 * then sorting the pieces. This is a very elegant
 * algorithm, except for when the partition fails
 * because the first element is already the least. In that
 * case I make the first element be a partition of 1.
 */

//
// Borland 4.x workarounds
//
#define __MINMAX_DEFINED
#pragma option -vi-

#include <iostream.h>
#include <time.h>
#include <function.h>
#include <algo.h>
#include <conio.h>

const int size = 10;

int a[ size ];

//
// This sorting algorithm is essentially
// identical to a quicksort.
//
void my_sort( int *first, int *last )
{
    cout << "Sorting ("
        << (int)( first - a )
        << ", "
        << (int)( last - a )
        << ") : ";
    copy( first, last, ostream_iterator<int>( cout, " " ) );
    cout << endl;
```

```
    //
    // I try to create two partitions, using the first element in
    // the range as a pivot.
    //
        int *p = partition( first, last, bind2nd( less<int>(), *first ) );
        cout << "Partition at "
            << (int)( p - a )
            << endl;
    //
    // If the subdivide operation failed, it means the first element
    // is already the least, so I make it a partition. Note that
    // partition() can return last if the predicate function always
    // returns true, but that can't happen when comparing integers.
    // If it did, it would mean every integer was less than every other
    // integer!
    //
        if ( p == first )
            p++;
    //
    // Now sort the two pieces. This is a recursive call.
    // Note that I don't sort the pieces if the piece is
    // only one element long! Also note that the pivot
    // element isn't included in either piece. It doesn't
    // need to be, since it is already at its proper place
    // in the sequence.
    //
        if ( ( p - first ) > 1 )
            my_sort( first, p );
        if ( ( last - p ) > 1 )
            my_sort( p, last );
    }

main()
{
    srand( time( 0 ) );
    for ( int i = 0 ; i < size ; i++ )
        a[ i ] = rand();

    cout << "Input: ";
    copy( a, a + size, ostream_iterator<int>( cout, " " ) );
    cout << endl;
    my_sort( a, a + size );
    cout << "After: ";
    copy( a, a + size, ostream_iterator<int>( cout, " " ) );
    cout << endl;
        return 1;
}
```

Example output:

```
Input: 22956 21229 27751 5013 29890 28425 13967 11284 11775 12381
Sorting (0, 10) : 22956 21229 27751 5013 29890 28425 13967 11284 11775 12381
Partition at 6
Sorting (0, 6) : 12381 21229 11775 5013 11284 13967
Partition at 3
Sorting (0, 3) : 11284 5013 11775
Partition at 1
Sorting (1, 3) : 11284 11775
Partition at 1
Sorting (3, 6) : 21229 12381 13967
Partition at 5
Sorting (3, 5) : 13967 12381
Partition at 4
Sorting (6, 10) : 28425 29890 27751 22956
Partition at 8
Sorting (6, 8) : 22956 27751
Partition at 6
Sorting (8, 10) : 29890 28425
Partition at 9
After: 5013 11284 11775 12381 13967 21229 22956 27751 28425 29890
```

SORTING AND SEARCHING

Seek, and ye shall find...

— Matthew Chapter 7, Verse 7

Sorting and searching are almost synonymous with computer programming. In college courses on algorithms, several weeks are typically devoted to the study of these two closely related topics. Donald Knuth's influential series of books, *The Art of Computer Programming*, devotes an entire volume just to sorting and searching.

The STL isn't meant to be an all-inclusive library, so it doesn't attempt to provide sorting and searching algorithms for every possible application. Instead, the functions in this chapter provide a good, general-purpose foundation that can be used where standard algorithms are appropriate. In cases where the utmost efficiency is required, you'll probably want to develop your own customized solutions. For example, if you wanted to write an application that could do a keyword search on the contents of the Library of Congress, you might find the STL lacking! In fact, the STL doesn't offer built-in support for disk-based databases, external sorting and merging, or similar data processing tasks.

On the other hand, if you simply want to alphabetize the symbol table for the C++ compiler you're developing, the STL might be just the ticket. Its predefined algorithms will save you from having to write and debug your own code. Not only are you reasonably assured that the STL algorithms work, you also know they are fairly efficient. To take advantage of the STL's capabilities, your data just has to be stored in an STL container or C/C++ array, so that it can be accessed with STL-compatible iterators.

The algorithms in this chapter perform three basic functions: sorting, searching, and merging. The algorithms in the previous two chapters are usually fairly short, so that an entire function is often only a few lines of code. That isn't the case here; most of these routines are either somewhat longer, or call helper routines that are relatively long themselves. Because of this, you'll see that, in most cases, the reference only gives the function prototype, not the entire body of the function itself. You'll need to refer to the source code in algo.h for those details.

Every one of the functions described in this chapter has two implementations. The first implementation uses operator<() to order the elements in the range. The second version takes a comparison object as an argument, allowing you to customize the ordering of the elements.

Table 15-1 gives a capsule description of the functions documented in this chapter.

Table 15-1

The sorting and searching algorithms

Function	Description
sort()	Sorts a range using roughly $N\log N$ comparisons
stable_sort()	Sorts while preserving relative order of elements
partial_sort()	Puts the first N elements in their proper places
partial_sort_copy()	Copies the first N elements into an output range
nth_element()	Puts element N in its proper place in the range
lower_bound()	Finds the first position where an element can be inserted
upper_bound()	Finds the last position where an element can be inserted
equal_range()	Returns lower_bound() and upper_bound()
binary_search()	Finds an element in the range
merge()	Merges two sorted ranges
inplace_merge()	Merges two consecutive ranges

SORT

Function

```
template < class RandomAccessIterator >
void sort( RandomAccessIterator first,
           RandomAccessIterator last );

template < class RandomAccessIterator, class Compare >
void sort( RandomAccessIterator first,
           RandomAccessIterator last,
           Compare comp );
```

Arguments

first: An iterator pointing to the first object in the input sequence. Note that both iterators in the input sequence need to be random access iterators, the most powerful type of STL iterator.

last: An iterator marking the end of the input sequence. As always in the STL, the last iterator doesn't point to the last object in a sequence, it points one past it.

comp: The first version of the sort algorithm uses operator<() to order the elements in the input sequence. The second version takes a user-supplied comparison function object. This object needs to compare two objects of type T, where T is the type of object pointed to by the iterator. The comparison object should return a boolean value, with the same semantics as operator<()

Return value

Both functions implementing the sort algorithm are void functions, and accordingly have no return values.

Description

The sort algorithm sorts an input sequence using a combination of two sorting techniques. The primary sort on the input sequence is done using a conventional Quicksort, which recursively divides the input range into successively smaller partitions. When the partitions are smaller than a predefined size—16 elements in the HP version of the STL—they are sorted using a conventional insertion sort.

   This sorting algorithm is fairly fast on average, with a time complexity of $N*\log(N)$. However, Quicksort demonstrates pathologically bad performance on input data that has already been sorted, which can increase its time complexity to N^2. If this worst-case performance must be avoided at all costs, you can employ the next algorithm in this chapter, stable_sort.

Complexity

The average time complexity of the sort algorithm is $N*\log(N)$. However, this complexity cannot be guaranteed, and may degrade to N^2 in some cases.

   While it may seem at first glance that these algorithms have constant (and negligible) space complexity, it should be remembered that they're implemented using recursive functions. Since each of these functions need a stack frame, arguments, and local variables, the space complexity of the sort algorithms is actually $\log(N)$. Nonetheless, the amount of automatic storage required should be negligible. $\log(N)$ increases so slowly in comparison to N that even exceptionally large sorts aren't going to generate very deep stack frames.

Example

Listing 15-1

sort1501.cpp: A demonstration of the sort algorithm

```
/*
 * SORT1501.CPP
 *
 * This program is used in Chapter 15 to demonstrate
 * the sort algorithm. It creates an array with
 * 10,000 random elements, then sorts them.  The
 * first and last five elements of the array are
 * printed before and after the sort operation.
 */
```

```
//
// Borland 4.x workarounds.
//
#define __MINMAX_DEFINED
#pragma option -vi-

#include <iostream.h>
#include <stdlib.h>
#include <algo.h>

const int n = 10000;

int data[ n ];

main()
{
    for ( int i = 0 ; i < n ; i++ )
        data[ i ] = rand();

    cout << "Before sorting:\n\n";
    cout << "First 5 elements: ";
    copy( data,
          data+ 5,
          ostream_iterator<int>( cout, " " ) );
    cout << "\n\nLast 5 elements: ";
    copy( data + n - 5,
          data + n,
          ostream_iterator<int>( cout, " " ) );
    cout << endl;

    sort( data, data + n );

    cout << "\n\nAfter sorting:\n\n";
    cout << "First 5 elements: ";
    copy( data,
          data+ 5,
          ostream_iterator<int>( cout, " " ) );
    cout << "\n\nLast 5 elements: ";
    copy( data + n - 5,
          data + n,
          ostream_iterator<int>( cout, " " ) );
    cout << endl;

    return 1;
}
```

Example output:

```
Before sorting:

First 5 elements: 346 130 10982 1090 11656

Last 5 elements:  6209 14530 1616 20563 13125


After sorting:

First 5 elements: 4 6 11 12 12

Last 5 elements:  32754 32757 32761 32765 32767
```

STABLE_SORT

Function

```
template < class RandomAccessIterator >
void stable_sort( RandomAccessIterator first,
                  RandomAccessIterator last );

template < class RandomAccessIterator, class Compare >
void stable_sort( RandomAccessIterator first,
                  RandomAccessIterator last,
                  Compare comp );
```

Arguments

first: An iterator marking the start of the input sequence. This iterator points to the first object in the input sequence. Note that both iterators in the input sequence must be random access iterators.

last: An iterator marking the end of the input sequence.

comp: The first version of the stable_sort algorithm uses operator<() to order the elements in the input sequence. The second version of stable_sort takes a user-supplied comparison function object. This object needs to compare two objects of type T, where T is the type of object pointed to by an iterator. The comparison object should return a boolean value, with the same semantics as operator<().

Return value

Both of the functions implementing the sort algorithm are void functions, and accordingly have no return values.

Description

stable_sort() is defined in the STL specification as an algorithm that on average performs worse than sort(), but has a better worst-case complexity. Tests on the HP release of the STL show that stable_sort() actually performs nearly as well as sort() for average input. stable_sort() usually performs fewer comparisons than sort(), but has to perform more assignments.

Complexity

The time complexity for stable_sort() is guaranteed to be no worse than $N*\log(N)*\log(N)$. If a suitably large buffer is available, the worst-case complexity should drop to $N*\log(N)$. If the buffer is available, space complexity rises to N, as the buffer size is directly proportional to the size of the buffer to be sorted.

Example

Listing 15-2

sort1502.cpp: A demonstration of the stable_sort algorithm

```
/*
 * SORT1502.CPP
 *
 * This program is used in Chapter 15 to demonstrate
 * the stable_sort algorithm. It creates an array with
 * 1024 random elements, then sorts them. To make it
 * interesting, this program compares sort() with
 * stable_sort() by counting comparisons and assignments.
 *
 * Note that this program needs to include an STL C++
 * source file, tempbuf.cpp. The normal way to do this
 * would be to add it to your project, and compile it
 * separately. To simplify building these example programs,
 * it is included here using the preprocessor.
 */
```

```
//
// Borland 4.x workarounds
//
#define __MINMAX_DEFINED
#pragma option -vi-

#include <iostream.h>
#include <stdlib.h>
#include <algo.h>
#include <vector.h>

long foo_count;

struct foo {
    int i;
    foo( int a = 0 ) : i( a ){ foo_count++; }
    foo( const foo &a ){ i = a.i ; foo_count++; }
    void operator=( const foo &a )
    {
        i = a.i;
        foo_count++;
    }
};

long comp_count;

bool int_comp( const foo &a, const foo &b )
{
    comp_count++;
    return a.i < b.i;
}

vector<foo> data( 1024 );

//
// By changing the "#if 0" to "#if 1", you can
// force stable_sort() to run without any temporary
// buffer space, which increases both the number of
// comparisons and assignments it has to make.
//

#include <tempbuf.cpp>
#if 0
pair<foo*, int> get_temporary_buffer(int, foo*) {
    return pair<foo*, int>( 0, 0 );
}
#endif
```

```
main()
{
    long seed = time( 0 );

    srand( seed );
    generate( data.begin(), data.end(), rand );
    comp_count = 0;
    foo_count = 0;
    sort( data.begin(), data.end(), int_comp );
    cout << "Sort performed "
        << comp_count
        << " comparisons, "
        << foo_count
        << " assignments\n";

    srand( seed );
    generate( data.begin(), data.end(), rand );
    comp_count = 0;
    foo_count = 0;
    stable_sort( data.begin(), data.end(), int_comp );
    cout << "Stable sort performed "
        << comp_count
        << " comparisons, "
        << foo_count
        << " assignments\n";

    return 1;
}
```

Example output:

```
Sort performed 12314 comparisons, 9961 assignments
Stable sort performed 9984 comparisons, 13681 assignments
```

Example output when no buffer space available:

```
Sort performed 12220 comparisons, 10067 assignments
Stable sort performed 12427 comparisons, 33490 assignments
```

PARTIAL_SORT

Function

```
template < class RandomAccessIterator >
void partial_sort( RandomAccessIterator first,
                   RandomAccessIterator middle,
                   RandomAccessIterator last);

template < class RandomAccessIterator, class Compare >
void partial_sort( RandomAccessIterator first,
                   RandomAccessIterator middle,
                   RandomAccessIterator last,
                   Compare comp);

template < class InputIterator, class RandomAccessIterator >
RandomAccessIterator
partial_sort_copy( InputIterator first,
                   InputIterator last,
                   RandomAccessIterator result_first,
                   RandomAccessIterator result_last );

template < class InputIterator,
           class RandomAccessIterator,
           class Compare >
RandomAccessIterator
partial_sort_copy( InputIterator first,
                   InputIterator last,
                   RandomAccessIterator result_first,
                   RandomAccessIterator result_last,
                   Compare comp );
```

Arguments

first: An iterator marking the start of the input sequence. The partial sort algorithm will sort elements starting at this location. Note that for the two versions of partial_sort that sort in-place, first and last have to be random access iterators. For the copy versions of the algorithm, first and last can be input iterators.

last: An iterator marking the end of the input sequence. The partial_sort algorithm performs its sort over the range of items defined by the first and last iterators.

middle: All four versions of partial_sort described here locate and sort the first N items in the input range. The partial_sort() functions define N as the number of elements between first and middle. After the sort operation has taken place, the range defined by first through middle will contain the lowest N elements in the input sequence, in sorted order.

result_first: The copy versions of the algorithm also sort the first N elements of the input sequence, but they place their output in the sequence pointed to by this iterator, result_first. This iterator must be a random access iterator pointing to a sequence with enough room for the partial sort result.

result_last: This iterator defines the end of the destination range for the partial sort operation. Normally, the number of elements sorted is defined as N = result_last - result_first. The only time this isn't true is when last - first is less than result_last - result_first. In those cases, N = last - first.

comp: Two of the versions of partial_sort perform their comparisons using operator<(). The other two allow for more flexible comparisons by using a comparison object. The comparison object should use function syntax, taking two arguments of type T, and returning a boolean result.

Return value

The two in-place functions, both overloaded versions of partial_sort(), are void functions and therefore have no return values. The copy functions return an iterator pointing *one past* the end of the sorted range, which will be result_first + N, where N is the smaller of result_last - result_first and last - first.

Description

This algorithm performs a partial sort of the input sequence. It locates the elements which will make up the first N elements in the sorted sequence, and places them in their proper locations. The remaining items in the sequence are left in an indeterminate order. The algorithm supports versions that perform in place sorting as well as versions that copy their result to an output range.

Note that in order to determine which elements belong in the first N places, the algorithm must examine all the elements in the input sequence. This makes this routine only slightly more efficient than a complete sort of the entire sequence.

Complexity

The time complexity for these algorithms is $N*\log(N)$, where N is the length of the input sequence. Space complexity is constant.

Example

Listing 15-3

sort1503.cpp: A demonstration of the partial_sort algorithm

```
/*
 * SORT1503.CPP
 *
 * This program is used in Chapter 15 to demonstrate the
 * partial_sort algorithm. A random deque of integers is
 * partially sorted. The input and output results are
 * displayed using the standard STL copy() algorithm.
 */

//
// Borland 4.x workarounds
//
#define __MINMAX_DEFINED
#pragma option -vi-

#include <iostream.h>
#include <stdlib.h>
#include <algo.h>
#include <deque.h>

main()
{
    deque<int> data( 10 );
    deque<int> result( 5 );

    srand( time( 0 ) );
    for ( int i = 0 ; i < 10 ; i++ )
        data[ i ] = rand();
```

```
cout << "Before sorting:\n";
    copy( data.begin(),
          data.end(),
          ostream_iterator<int>( cout, " " ) );

    partial_sort_copy( data.begin(),
                       data.end(),
                       result.begin(),
                       result.end() );

    cout << "\n\nPartial sort result:\n";
    copy( result.begin(),
          result.end(),
          ostream_iterator<int>( cout, " " ) );
    cout << endl;
    return 1;
}
```

Example output:

```
Before sorting:
2610 14628 31813 14398 14994 2140 6179 1124 12185 21461

Partial sort result:
1124 2140 2610 6179 12185
```

NTH_ELEMENT()

Function

```
template < class RandomAccessIterator >
void nth_element( RandomAccessIterator first,
                  RandomAccessIterator nth,
                  RandomAccessIterator last );

template < class RandomAccessIterator, class Compare >
void nth_element( RandomAccessIterator first,
                  RandomAccessIterator nth,
                  RandomAccessIterator last,
                  Compare comp );
```

Arguments

first: An iterator defining the start of the input sequence.

last: An iterator defining the end of the input sequence.

nth: This iterator points to the position in the input sequence where the partitioning is going to take effect.

comp: The first version of the nth_element algorithm uses operator<() to partition the elements in the input set. When more flexibility is needed than operator<() offers, you can use the second version of the algorithm, which takes a comparison object as an argument. The comparison object should use function syntax, take two arguments of type T, and return a boolean value.

Return value

Both versions of nth_element are void functions, so they have no return value.

Description

nth_element partitions the input sequence around the *n*th element. This means the *n*th element, as indicated by the parameter, will be placed in the exact position in the input sequence where it would go when the sequence was completely sorted. The remaining elements in the input set aren't sorted, but are partitioned into two groups. All elements that appear before the *n*th element in the sequence will be less than it, according to the ordering function. All elements that follow the *n*th element in the input sequence will be greater than it, according to the input function.

nth_element is the type of function that could be used as a building block for more complex sorting routines. It would be relatively simple to sort an input sequence by recursively partitioning input ranges into smaller and smaller partitions, as an implementation of traditional divide and conquer techniques.

Complexity

Time complexity for nth_element is linear, in proportion to the length of the input range. Space complexity is constant.

Example

Listing 15-4
nth1504.cpp: A demonstration of the nth_element algorithm

```
/*
 * NTH1504.CPP
 *
 * This program is used in Chapter 15 to demonstrate
 * the nth_element algorithm. A data array of chars
 * is shuffled into a random sequence, then
 * partitioned around the 13th element.  The 13th element
 * should always be letter 'N'.  After the partitioning,
 * everything before 13 should be less than 'N', and
 * everything after should be greater.
 */

//
// Borland 4.x workarounds
//
#define __MINMAX_DEFINED
#pragma option -vi-

#include <iostream.h>
#include <stdlib.h>
#include <algo.h>

//
// This example program uses the code found in
// random.cpp. In a normal project, you would
// compile this module separately and combine at
// link time. In this example, the source is
// included directly, to simplify building.
//
#include <random.cpp>

char data[] = "ABCDEFGHIJKLMNOPQRSTUVWXYZ";

main()
{
    random_shuffle( data, data + 26 );
    cout << "Shuffled data: "
        << data
        << endl;

    nth_element( data, data + 13, data + 26 );
```

```
cout << "Lower partition: ";
for ( int i = 0 ; i < 13 ; i++ )
    cout << data[ i ];
cout << endl;

cout << "Pivot: "
     << data[ 13 ]
     << endl;

cout << "Upper partition: ";
for ( i = 14 ; i < 26 ; i++ )
    cout << data[ i ];
cout << endl;

return 1;
}
```

Example output:

```
Shuffled data: GLJXSMRYUPEWKFBZNDOQAIVCHT
Lower partition: CADBFEHGIJKLM
Pivot: N
Upper partition: OPQZXSWUVYRT
```

LOWER_BOUND

Function

```
template < class ForwardIterator, class T >
ForwardIterator lower_bound( ForwardIterator first,
                             ForwardIterator last,
                             const T& value );

template < class ForwardIterator, class T, class Compare >
ForwardIterator lower_bound( ForwardIterator first,
                             ForwardIterator last,
                             const T& value,
                             Compare comp );
```

Arguments

first: An iterator defining the start of the input sequence. lower_bound is one of those STL algorithms that is implemented differently, depending on the iterator type. While first and last must be at least forward iterators, the algorithm will perform much more efficiently if first and last are random access iterators.

last: An iterator pointing one past the final element in the sequence.

value: lower_bound seeks to find the first location in the sorted input sequence where this value can be inserted without violating the sequence's order.

comp: lower_bound has two different methods for determining the correct location for the new value object. The first method uses operator<() to determine the correct order for the object. The second method uses this comparison object for ordering. The comparison object needs to have function syntax, taking two objects of type T as arguments and returning a boolean value.

Return value

lower_bound returns an iterator that indicates the first position in the input sequence where the value object can be inserted without violating the ordering relation. If the value is greater than all of the objects currently in the sequence, last is returned, indicating that the object would have to be added to the end of the sequence to maintain its order.

Description

lower_bound is an algorithm that locates the first available position for an object in a sorted sequence. It uses either operator<() or the comparison function object to test for the validity of each position. The value returned gives the first position in the sequence where the new value could be inserted, while still maintaining the ordering relation.

Note: Be sure to remember that this algorithm expects the input data to already be sorted according to the ordering relation! If the data is not sorted, the return value is not very meaningful.

Complexity

If the iterators being used are random access iterators, lower_bound can perform a binary search for the appropriate insertion position, which gives time complexity of log(N). If the iterators are bidirectional iterators or less, a linear search has to be performed, which means the time complexity is N, or is linear with respect to the length of the input sequence. In both cases the space complexity is constant.

Example

Listing 15-5

low1505.cpp: A demonstration of the lower_bound algorithm

```
/*
 * LOW1505.CPP
 *
 * This program is used in Chapter 15 to demonstrate the
 * lower_bound algorithm. A vector of strings is created
 * and then sorted. Once that valid input sequence has
 * been determined, lower_bound() is used to find the
 * correct insertion point for three new strings.
 */

//
// Borland 4.x workarounds
//
#define __MINMAX_DEFINED
#pragma option -vi-

#include <iostream.h>
#include <cstring.h>
#include <algo.h>
#include <vector.h>

main()
{
    vector<string> a;
    a.push_back( "Microsoft" );
    a.push_back( "Apple" );
    a.push_back( "IBM" );
    a.push_back( "Next" );
```

```
a.push_back( "Sun" );
a.push_back( "Symantec" );
a.push_back( "HP" );
a.push_back( "Watcom" );

sort( a.begin(), a.end() );
cout << "Input sequence : "
     << "\n";
copy( a.begin(),
      a.end(),
      ostream_iterator<string>( cout, " " ) );
cout << endl;

string *p = lower_bound( a.begin(),
                         a.end(),
                         "Oracle" );
cout << "lower_bound( \"Oracle\" ) returned "
     << ( p - a.begin() )
     << endl;
a.insert( p, "Oracle" );

p = lower_bound( a.begin(),
                 a.end(),
                 "Novell" );
cout << "lower_bound( \"Novell\" ) returned "
     << ( p - a.begin() )
     << endl;
a.insert( p, "Novell" );

p = lower_bound( a.begin(),
                 a.end(),
                 "Lotus" );
cout << "lower_bound( \"Lotus\" ) returned "
     << ( p - a.begin() )
     << endl;
a.insert( p, "Lotus" );

cout << "Final sequence : "
     << "\n";
copy( a.begin(),
      a.end(),
      ostream_iterator<string>( cout, " " ) );
cout << endl;

return 1;
}
```

Example output:

```
Input sequence :
Apple HP IBM Microsoft Next Sun Symantec Watcom
lower_bound( "Oracle" ) returned 5
lower_bound( "Novell" ) returned 5
lower_bound( "Lotus" ) returned 3
Final sequence :
Apple HP IBM Lotus Microsoft Next Novell Oracle Sun Symantec Watcom
```

UPPER_BOUND

Function

```
template < class ForwardIterator, class T >
ForwardIterator upper_bound( ForwardIterator first,
                             ForwardIterator last,
                             const T& value );

template < class ForwardIterator, class T, class Compare >
ForwardIterator upper_bound( ForwardIterator first,
                             ForwardIterator last,
                             const T& value,
                             Compare comp );
```

Arguments

first: An iterator defining the start of the input sequence. first and last must be at least forward iterators, but upper_bound will perform much more efficiently if first and last are random access iterators.

last: An iterator marking the end of the input sequence.

value: upper_bound looks for the last location in the sorted input sequence where this value can be inserted without violating the sequence's order.

comp: upper_bound has two different methods for determining the correct location for the new value object. The first method uses operator<() to determine the correct order for the object. The second method uses this comparison object for ordering. The comparison object needs to have function syntax, taking two objects of type T as arguments and returning a boolean value.

Return value

upper_bound returns an iterator that indicates the last position in the input sequence where the value object can be placed without violating the ordering relation. If the value is greater than all of the objects currently in the sequence, last is returned, indicating that the object would have to be added to the end of the sequence to maintain its order.

Description

upper_bound is an algorithm that locates the last available position for an object in a sorted sequence. It uses either operator<() or the comparison function object to test for the validity of each position. The value returned gives the last position in the sequence where the new value could be inserted, while still maintaining the ordering relation.

lower_bound() and upper_bound() both determine the correct insertion point for a new object. The only time there will be any difference between the two is if the input sequence has a run of duplicate values. Note also that if you need to have the lower and upper bounds for inserting an object, you can get them both simultaneously with equal_range().

Complexity

If the iterators being used are random access iterators, upper_bound can perform a binary search for the appropriate insertion position, which gives time complexity of $\log(N)$. If the iterators are bidirectional iterators or less, a linear search has to be performed, which means the time complexity is linear with respect to the length of the input sequence. In both cases the space complexity is constant.

Note: Be sure to remember that this algorithm expects the input data to already be sorted according to the ordering relation! If the data isn't properly sorted, any results returned by upper_bound will be meaningless.

Example

Listing 15-6

up1506.cpp: A demonstration of the upper_bound algorithm

```
/*
 * UP1506.CPP
 *
 * This program is used in Chapter 15 to demonstrate
 * the upper_bound algorithm. The lower and upper bounds
 * of some integers are computed and displayed. The
 * only time the lower and upper bounds are going to
 * be different is when there are runs of duplicate
 * values, so the input data is set up to have a few.
 */

//
// Borland 4.x workarounds
//
#define __MINMAX_DEFINED
#pragma option -vi-

#include <iostream.h>
#include <cstring.h>
#include <algo.h>

int a[] = { 0, 0, 0, 2, 2, 2, 4, 4, 4, 4 };
const int nelems = sizeof( a ) / sizeof( int );

main()
{
    cout << "Input sequence : "
         << "\n";
    copy( a, a + nelems, ostream_iterator<int>( cout, " " ) );
    cout << endl;

    int *p1 = lower_bound( a, a + nelems, 0 );
    int *p2 = upper_bound( a, a + nelems , 0 );
    cout << "lower, upper of 0: "
         << ( p1 - a )
```

```
                        << ", "
                        << ( p2 - a )
                        << endl;

            p1 = lower_bound( a, a + 10, 1 );
            p2 = upper_bound( a, a + 10 , 1 );
            cout << "lower, upper of 1: "
                        << ( p1 - a )
                        << ", "
                        << ( p2 - a )
                        << endl;

            p1 = lower_bound( a, a + 10, 4 );
            p2 = upper_bound( a, a + 10 , 4 );
            cout << "lower, upper of 4: "
                        << ( p1 - a )
                        << ", "
                        << ( p2 - a )
                        << endl;

            return 1;
        }
```

Example output:

```
Input sequence :
0 0 0 2 2 2 4 4 4 4
lower, upper of 0: 0, 3
lower, upper of 1: 3, 3
lower, upper of 4: 6, 10
```

EQUAL_RANGE

Function

```
template < class ForwardIterator, class T >
pair< ForwardIterator, ForwardIterator >
equal_range( ForwardIterator first,
            ForwardIterator last,
            const T& value );
```

```
template < class ForwardIterator, class T, class Compare >
pair< ForwardIterator, ForwardIterator >
equal_range( ForwardIterator first,
             ForwardIterator last,
             const T& value,
             Compare comp);
```

Arguments

first: An iterator marking the start of the input sequence. first and last must be at least forward iterators, but equal_range will perform much more efficiently if first and last are random access iterators.

last: An iterator marking the end of the input sequence.

value: equal_range searches for the first and last locations in the sorted input sequence where this value can be inserted without violating the sequence's order.

comp: equal_range has two different methods for determining the correct location for the new value object. The first method uses operator<() to determine the correct order for the object. The second method uses this comparison object for ordering. The comparison object needs to have function syntax, taking two objects of type T as arguments and returning a boolean value.

Return value

equal_range returns two iterators in a pair<> object. The first member of the pair points to the first location in the input sequence where the value could be legally inserted. The second member of the pair points to the last location in the input sequence where the value could be legally inserted. The two iterators can be have the same value, and may both be equal to last.

Remember that the pair object doesn't have a default constructor, so you need to initialize it using an assignment of the return value from this function. This type of code will cause the compiler to generate an error:

```
pair< int *, int * > p;
p = equal_range( a, a + 100, 45 );
```

Instead, you need to write your code like this:

```
pair< int *, int *> p = equal_range( a, a + 100, 45 );
```

Description

equal_range provides a simple way to get the return values from lower_bound and upper_bound simultaneously. It determines those values by using a binary search technique to first find the lower insertion point, then the upper insertion point. Both values are then packed into a pair and returned to the caller.

   equal_range uses advance() to increment the iterator during the search process. If the sequence is defined using random access iterators, advance()—and the entire process—will be considerably more efficient, since the iterator can be incremented by an arbitrary amount simply by adding a scalar to a pointer.

Complexity

The time complexity of equal_range depends on the type of iterator used to define the input sequence. If the iterator is a random access iterator, the complexity is $\log(N)$, where N is the length of the input sequence. For all other iterator types, the complexity is linear in direct proportion to N. The space complexity is constant.

Example

Listing 15-7

eq1507.cpp: A demonstration of the equal_range algorithm

```
/*
 * EQ1507.CPP
 *
 * This program is used in Chapter 15 to demonstrate
 * the equal_range algorithm. The lower and upper bounds
 * of some integers are computed and displayed. Note
 * that this program is almost identical to up1506.cpp,
```

```
 * which does the same thing using dual calls to
 * lower_bound and upper_bound.
 */

//
// Borland 4.x workarounds
//
#define __MINMAX_DEFINED
#pragma option -vi-

#include <iostream.h>
#include <cstring.h>
#include <algo.h>

int a[] = { 0, 0, 0, 2, 2, 2, 4, 4, 4, 4 };
const int nelems = sizeof( a ) / sizeof( int );

main()
{
    cout << "Input sequence : "
         << "\n";
    copy( a, a + nelems, ostream_iterator<int>( cout, " " ) );
    cout << endl;

    pair< int *, int * > p = equal_range( a, a + nelems, 0 );
    cout << "lower, upper of 0: "
         << ( p.first - a )
         << ", "
         << ( p.second - a )
         << endl;

    p = equal_range( a, a + nelems, 1 );
    cout << "lower, upper of 1: "
         << ( p.first - a )
         << ", "
         << ( p.second - a )
         << endl;

    p = equal_range( a, a + nelems, 5 );
    cout << "lower, upper of 5: "
         << ( p.first - a )
         << ", "
         << ( p.second - a )
         << endl;

    return 1;
}
```

Example output:

```
Input sequence :
0 0 0 2 2 2 4 4 4 4
lower, upper of 0: 0, 3
lower, upper of 1: 3, 3
lower, upper of 5: 10, 10
```

BINARY_SEARCH

Function

```cpp
template < class ForwardIterator, class T >
bool binary_search( ForwardIterator first,
                    ForwardIterator last,
                    const T& value )
{
    ForwardIterator i = lower_bound( first, last, value );
    return i != last && !( value < *i );
}

template < class ForwardIterator, class T, class Compare >
bool binary_search( ForwardIterator first,
                    ForwardIterator last,
                    const T& value
                    Compare comp )
{
    ForwardIterator i = lower_bound( first, last, value, comp );
    return i != last && !comp( value, *i );
}
```

Arguments

first: An iterator defining the first element in a sequence. first and
            last must be at least forward iterators, but binary_search will
            perform much more efficiently if first and last are random
            access iterators.

last: An iterator defining the end of the input sequence.

value: binary_search looks for the first location in the sorted input sequence where this value is found.

comp: binary_search needs to use the correct ordering function when searching through the input sequence for a match. If the input sequence was ordered using a comparison object instead of operator<(), the same comparison object needs to be passed to binary_search via this parameter. The comparison object needs to have function syntax, taking two objects of type T as arguments and returning a boolean value.

Return value

binary_search returns a boolean value indicating whether or not the indicated value was found in the input sequence. A value of true indicates that it was found; false indicates that it isn't present.

Description

The two versions of binary_search are called to return a boolean value indicating whether or not a given value is present in the input sequence. Both of these functions are short and simple, because they rely on lower_bound to do all the hard work. All binary_search has to do to locate a value is call lower_bound. If the return from lower_bound is equal to last, a value of false can be returned immediately. Otherwise, the object pointed to by the return from lower_bound is compared to value. If they are the same, value has been located, and a value of true is returned. If not, value was not found in the input range, and the function returns false.

Note: This function expects the input sequence to be sorted, using either operator<() or the specified comparison object. If the sequence is not sorted according to the same algorithm used for the search, the result cannot be trusted.

Complexity

If the iterators being used are random access iterators, lower_bound can perform a binary search for the appropriate insertion position, which gives this algorithm time complexity of $\log(N)$. If the iterators are bidirectional iterators or less, a linear search has to be performed, which means the time complexity is linear with respect to the length of the input sequence. In both cases the space complexity is constant.

Example

Listing 15-8

A demonstration of the binary_search algorithm

```
/*
 * SRCH1508.CPP
 *
 * This program is used in Chapter 15 to demonstrate
 * the binary_search algorithm. It reads in all of
 * the strings from this source file, then attempts
 * to locate a few of them. Remember that the strings
 * will be read in according to the rules the string
 * insertion operator uses for parsing.
 */

//
// Borland 4.x workarounds
//
#define __MINMAX_DEFINED
#pragma option -vi-

#include <iostream.h>
#include <fstream.h>
#include <cstring.h>

#include <algo.h>
#include <vector.h>

void test( vector<string> &v, string s )
{
    bool result;
    result = binary_search( v.begin(), v.end(), s );
    cout << "\"" << s << "\""
        << " was "
        << ( result ? "" : "not " )
        << "found"
        << endl;
}
```

```
main()
{
    ifstream f( "srch1508.cpp" );
    if ( !f ) {
        cerr << "Couldn't open input file!\n";
        return 1;
    }

    vector<string> v;

    while ( f ) {
        string word;
        f >> word;
        v.push_back( word );
    }
    f.close();
    sort( v.begin(), v.end() );
    test( v, "ifstream" );
    test( v, "Woodchuck" );
    test( v, "Barsoom" );
    test( v, v[ 20 ] );

    return 1;
}
```

Example output:

```
"ifstream" was found
"Woodchuck" was not found
"Barsoom" was not found
"#include" was found
```

MERGE

Function

```
template < class InputIterator1,
           class InputIterator2,
           class OutputIterator >
```

```
OutputIterator merge( InputIterator1 first1,
                      InputIterator1 last1,
                      InputIterator2 first2,
                      InputIterator2 last2,
                      OutputIterator result )
{
    while ( first1 != last1 && first2 != last2 )
        if ( *first2 < *first1 )
            *result++ = *first2++;
        else
            *result++ = *first1++;
    return copy( first2, last2, copy( first1, last1, result ) );
}

template < class InputIterator1,
           class InputIterator2,
           class OutputIterator,
           class Compare >
OutputIterator merge( InputIterator1 first1,
                      InputIterator1 last1,
                      InputIterator2 first2,
                      InputIterator2 last2,
                      OutputIterator result,
                      Compare comp )
{
    while ( first1 != last1 && first2 != last2 )
        if ( comp( *first2, *first1 ) )
            *result++ = *first2++;
        else
            *result++ = *first1++;
    return copy( first2, last2, copy( first1, last1, result ) );
}
```

Arguments

first1, first2:　These two iterators point to the start of the two input ranges that are going to be merged. As you can see from examining the source code shown above, these two iterators don't have to be the same type, but the two types of objects they point to need to be tested by a comparison function, as well as assigned to the output object. So, for example, with an appropriate comparison object, you might be able to merge a list of strings with a list of char * objects.

last1, last2:   These two iterators define the end of the two input sequences. The two sequences don't have to be the same length, so last1 and last2 both have to be specified.

result: This is an iterator pointing to the sequence where the merged result is going to be stored. These two versions of the merge algorithm don't attempt to do any sort of in-place merge; instead, they both send their output to a new destination. Accordingly, result needs to be able to accommodate all the items output by the merge algorithm. This number will be the sum of the lengths of the two input ranges:
(last1 - first1) + (last2 - first2).

This is a good place to use an insert iterator. That way the insertion iterator can ensure that the correct amount of space will be available for the use of the merge algorithm.

comp: Like most of the algorithms in this section, merging can be done using the default comparison delivered by operator<(), or by a comparison object of your own creation. The comparison object needs to be an object that obeys function syntax, and takes two objects of type T as argument. The object should return a boolean value, indicating the result of the comparison.

Return value

Both versions of the merge function return an output iterator pointing to the first location after the resulting merged sequence.

Description

The two merge functions combine a pair of sorted sequences into one new sequence. The merging is performed by reading the two input sequences and writing the merged output into a result sequence.

For this function to work properly, the two input sequences need to already be sorted according to the comparison function being used. The output will be the properly merged combination of the two sequences.

Complexity

Time complexity for versions of merge is linear, with respect to the combined length of the two input sequences. Space complexity is constant.

Example

Listing 15-9

merg1509.cpp: A demonstration of the merge algorithm

```
/*
 * MERG1509.CPP
 *
 * This program is used in Chapter 15 to demonstrate
 * the merge algorithm. It creates two sorted arrays
 * of char pointers, then merges them and print the
 * results. As always when sorting pointers, you
 * usually need to define a comparison object to
 * compare the elements found by dereferencing the
 * pointers. In this case, the comparison object is
 * actually a function pointer.
 */

//
// Borland 4.x workarounds
//
#define __MINMAX_DEFINED
#pragma option -vi-

#include <iostream.h>
#include <string.h>
#include <algo.h>
#include <vector.h>

char *dem[] = { "Al", "Bill", "Hillary", "Tipper" };
const int dem_len = sizeof( dem ) / sizeof( char * );

char *rep[] = { "Barbara", "Dan", "George", "Marilyn" };
const int rep_len = sizeof( rep ) / sizeof( char * );

bool comp( const char *a, const char *b )
{
    return strcmp( a, b ) < 0;
}
```

```
main()
{
    vector<char *> result;

    back_insert_iterator< vector< char * > > i( result );
    merge( dem, dem + dem_len, rep, rep + rep_len, i, comp );
    copy( result.begin(),
          result.end(),
          ostream_iterator< char * >( cout, " " ) );
    cout << endl;
    return 1;
}
```

Example output:

```
Al Barbara Bill Dan George Hillary Marilyn Tipper
```

INPLACE_MERGE

Function

```
template < class BidirectionalIterator >
void inplace_merge( BidirectionalIterator first,
                    BidirectionalIterator middle,
                    BidirectionalIterator last );

template < class BidirectionalIterator, class Compare >
void inplace_merge( BidirectionalIterator first,
                    BidirectionalIterator middle,
                    BidirectionalIterator last,
                    Compare comp );
```

Arguments

first: An iterator marking the first element in the first sequence. This
             version of the merge assumes that the two sequences to be
             merged are arranged consecutively as part of a larger sequence.

middle: An iterator marking the end of the first sequence and the start of the second sequence. Since this algorithm assumes the two sequences are arranged back-to-back as part of a larger sequence, one iterator can mark the border between the two sequences. As you can expect from the STL conventions, middle points directly to the start of the second sequence, and one item past the end of the first sequence.

last: An iterator marking the end of the second sequence.

comp: Like most of the other sorting algorithms in the STL, inplace_merge has two different versions. The first version assumes that the two input sequences are sorted using operator<(). The second version assumes the two input sequences are sorted using a user-defined comparison object, which is passed here.

The user-defined comparison object obeys function syntax, and expects two arguments of type T, where T is the type pointed to by the iterators. The function should return a boolean value indicating whether the comparison passed or failed.

Return value

Both versions of inplace_merge are void functions, and consequently don't have a return value.

Description

inplace_merge performs the same function as merge, but it assumes a certain layout of the two input sequences. Instead of working with two sequences that can reside anywhere, and be independent of one another, inplace_merge insists that the two sequences have to be arranged sequentially in memory. This means that, when you increment an iterator *one past* the last element in the first sequence, you'll reach the first element in the second sequence.

Given this order, the two sequences can be defined using just three iterators. first points to the start of the first sequence, middle points to the start of the second sequence, and last points to the end of the second sequence.

Since these two sequences form one contiguous sequence, it's possible to perform an in-place merge, where the resulting merged sequence is copied on top of the two input sequences. Since the resulting sequence can't be longer than the two input sequences, you can be sure there'll always be room for the merge to take place.

Complexity

inplace_merge tries to allocate some buffer space to hold a temporary copy of the merge while working on the two input sequences. If it is successful in allocating this space, both the time and space complexity will be linear, in proportion to the combined length of the two input sequences. If the additional space can't be allocated, the time complexity moves up to $N*\log(N)$, and the space complexity becomes constant.

Example

Listing 15-10

merg1510.cpp: A demonstration of the inplace_merge algorithm

```
/*
 * MERG1510.CPP
 *
 * This program is used in Chapter 15 to demonstrate
 * the inplace_merge algorithm. It is fundamentally
 * the same program as that shown in MERG1509.CPP, with
 * the only difference being that the two input arrays
 * are stored in a single location before merging.
 */

//
// Borland 4.x workarounds
//
#define __MINMAX_DEFINED
#pragma option -vi-

#include <iostream.h>
#include <cstring.h>
#include <algo.h>
#include <vector.h>
```

```
//
// Normally you would not include a source module
// using the preprocessor. This program includes
// tempbuf.cpp to make it easier to build the demos.
//
#include <tempbuf.cpp>

string white_house[] =
    { "Al", "Bill", "Hilary", "Tipper",
      "Barbara", "Dan", "George", "Marilyn" };

main()
{
    inplace_merge( white_house,
                   white_house + 4,
                   white_house + 8 );
    copy( white_house,
          white_house + 8,
          ostream_iterator< string >( cout, " " ) );
    return 1;
}
```

Example output:

```
Al Barbara Bill Dan George Hilary Marilyn Tipper
```

SET

OPERATIONS

16

The algorithms collectively know as set operations perform functions similar to set operations used in logic and mathematics. Set operations are performed on ranges of elements defined by iterators, just like the other STL algorithms. All the set operations have the additional requirement that elements in the input ranges be sorted. And naturally, each algorithm is implemented using a pair of overloaded functions: one uses operator<() to order its elements, the other uses a comparison object.

Table 16-1 lists the functions defined in this group.

Table 16-1

The set operations

Function	Description
includes()	Determines if one range is included in another
set_union()	Generates the union of two ranges
set_intersection()	Generates the intersection of two ranges
set_difference()	Generates the difference of two ranges
set_symmetric_difference()	Generates the symmetric difference of two ranges.

INCLUDES

Function

```
template < class InputIterator1, class InputIterator2 >
bool includes( InputIterator1 first1,
               InputIterator1 last1,
               InputIterator2 first2,
               InputIterator2 last2 );

template < class InputIterator1,
           class InputIterator2,
           class Compare >
bool includes( InputIterator1 first1,
               InputIterator1 last1,
               InputIterator2 first2,
               InputIterator2 last2,
               Compare comp );
```

Arguments

first1, last1: This pair of iterators defines the first ordered sequence. This set can be any arbitrary length, including 0. The includes algorithm tests to see if the second ordered sequence is present in this set.

first2, last2: This pair of iterators defines the second ordered sequence. The algorithm performs a test to see if every element in this set is present in the first set. If every element is, the algorithm will return true.

comp: If the first and second set are ordered using some other comparison than operator<(), it needs to be passed as a function object to the includes function. The comparison object should obey function syntax, meaning it should take arguments of type T1 and T2—where T1 is pointed to by the first pair of iterators, and T2 is pointed to by the second pair of iterators—and return a boolean.

Return value

Both versions of includes() return true if every element in the second ordered set is present in the first ordered set. Otherwise, they both return false.

Description

This algorithm tests one set for inclusion in another set. To make the algorithm relatively efficient, both sets have to be ordered by a comparison function which, by default, is operator<().

Note: This algorithm (like the rest of the algorithms in this chapter) doesn't use operator==() to test for the equality of the members of the two sets. Instead, it's assumed that $a == b$, if it's not the case that $a < b$ or that $b < a$.

When testing the two sequences, the includes algorithm requires that multiple appearances of an element in the second set have corresponding multiple appearances in the first set. So, for example, the sequence { 1, 1, 1, } would return false if tested for inclusion in { 1, 2, 3 }. It would return true if tested for inclusion in { 1, 1, 1, 2, 3 }.

Figure 16-1 shows an example of what inclusion means. If you consider the abstract circles to be STL ranges (or maybe containers), the figure shows two examples of how two ranges can intersect. In the first example, A and B contain some common elements, but others that are unique to each set. In this case, a call to:

```
includes( A.begin(), A.end(),
          B.begin(), B.end() )
```

would return the boolean value false. In the second example, range D is completely included in range C. This means that every element that appears in D also appears in C. Because of this, the corresponding call to includes() would return a boolean true.

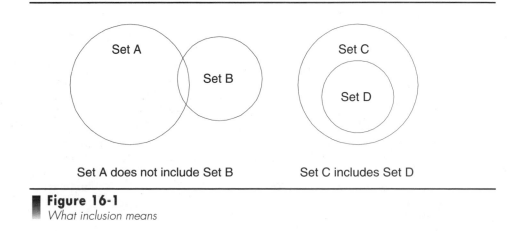

Set A does not include Set B   Set C includes Set D

Figure 16-1
What inclusion means

Complexity

includes has linear complexity in proportion to the sum of the lengths of the two sequences. The space complexity of includes is constant.

Example

Listing 16-1

incl1601.cpp: A demonstration of the includes algorithm

```
/*
 * INCL1601.CPP
 *
 * This program is used in Chapter 16 to demonstrate the
 * includes algorithm. It creates a set that is ordered
 * using a case-insensitive comparison. The program then
 * tests various strings for membership in the set.
 */

//
// Borland 4.x workarounds
//
#define __MINMAX_DEFINED
#pragma option -vi-

#include <iostream.h>
#include <string.h>
#include <ctype.h>
#include <algo.h>
#include <set.h>

//
// The set is missing letter 'm', and is only
// ordered if the comparison object does a
// case-insensitive comparison.
//
char *set_data = "abcdefghijklnopqrstuvwXYZ";

struct upper_comp {
    bool operator()( const char &a, const char &b ) const
    {
        return toupper( a ) < toupper( b );
    }
};
```

```
void test( set< char, upper_comp> & a, char *b )
{
    bool c;
    c = includes( a.begin(),
                  a.end(),
                  b,
                  b + strlen( b ),
                  upper_comp() );
    cout << b
         << " is "
         << ( c ? "" : "not " )
         << "included in the set"
         << endl;
}

main()
{
    set< char, upper_comp > a;

    while ( *set_data )
        a.insert( *set_data++ );
    cout << "Set: ";
    copy( a.begin(),
          a.end(),
          ostream_iterator<char>( cout ) );
    cout << endl;
    test( a, "ABC" ); //Should pass
    test( a, "ZZZ" ); //Should fail
    test( a, "lmn" ); //Should fail
    test( a, "NML" ); //Bad order, should fail
    test( a, "anz" ); //Should pass
    return 1;
}
```

Example output:

```
Set: abcdefghijklnopqrstuvwXYZ
ABC is included in the set
ZZZ is not included in the set
lmn is not included in the set
NML is not included in the set
anz is included in the set
```

SET_UNION

Function

```
template < class InputIterator1,
           class InputIterator2,
           class OutputIterator >
OutputIterator set_union( InputIterator1 first1,
                          InputIterator1 last1,
                          InputIterator2 first2,
                          InputIterator2 last2,
                          OutputIterator result );

template < class InputIterator1,
           class InputIterator2,
           class OutputIterator,
           class Compare >
OutputIterator set_union( InputIterator1 first1,
                          InputIterator1 last1,
                          InputIterator2 first2,
                          InputIterator2 last2,
                          OutputIterator result,
                          Compare comp );
```

Arguments

first1, last1:   The set_union algorithm combines the contents of two ordered sequences and places the result into a new sequence. first1 and last1 define the first sequence in normal STL fashion, where first1 points to the first element and last1 points *one element past* the last element in the sequence.

first2, last2:   These two iterators define the second sequence. Like the first sequence, these elements need to be sorted with either a specific comparison object or the default, operator<(). Note that the two input sequences can be lowly input iterators, since the algorithm operates in a linear fashion from start to finish.

result: As the algorithm proceeds, it places the sorted union of the two input sequences into an output sequence. The result iterator defines the start of that output sequence. Since you won't know in advance how large the sorted union will be, your output iterator should be capable of handling as many as $N1 + N2$ objects, where $N1$ is the length of sequence 1, and $N2$ is the length of sequence 2.

comp: Like most STL algorithms that use sorted sequences, set_union can assume that sets are sorted using the default comparison object, operator<(). If the input was sorted using some other criteria, set_union needs to be informed of this. The correct way to do so is by passing set_union a comparison object which defines the ordering function. The comparison object should use function syntax, and take two objects of type T as input arguments. It returns a boolean result that defines the ordering of the two elements. If the boolean result is true, T1 and T2 should be ordered as T1, T2. A false result means they should be ordered T2, T1.

Return value

As set_union does its work, it continually stores new objects in the location pointed to by result. After each assignment operation, set_union increments result, so that it always points to the next free location in the output sequence. When the two sequences have been completely processed, the algorithm returns a copy of the output iterator, which should now be pointing *one past* the end of the output sequence.

Description

This algorithm combines two sorted sequences into the union of the two sequences. The resulting union is stored in the location pointed to by the result argument. The algorithm lets you know how long the output sequence is by returning the iterator that marks the new end of the output sequence.

Note: The input sequences can look like multisets, with more than one copy of identical elements. If the first sequence has $N1$ copies of an element, and the second sequence has $N2$ copies of an element, the resulting output union will have the greater of $N1$ and $N2$ copies of the specific element. So if each set has just one copy of an element, the union will have one copy as well.

Figure 16-2 gives a graphical depiction of what a union looks like. When you look at two input ranges, the union is the group of elements that are found in both input ranges. In the second case shown in Figure 16-2, the union contains every element from C and D, since there is no overlap.

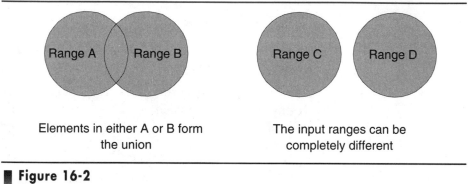

Elements in either A or B form
the union

The input ranges can be
completely different

Figure 16-2
A union of ranges

Complexity

set_union has linear complexity proportional to the sum of the lengths of the two sequences. The space complexity of set_union is constant.

Example

Listing 16-2

un1602.cpp: A demonstration of the set_union algorithm

```
/*
 * UN1602.CPP
 *
 * This program is used in Chapter 16 to demonstrate
 * the set_union algorithm. It executes the set_union
 * algorithm on several pairs of input sets. Note that
 * in one case, the input set is not properly sorted,
 * which will result in a bad output set. The input data
 * to the set_union() function should be sorted, so this
 * program has a short function that checks for that.
 */
```

```
//
// Borland 4.x workarounds
//

#define __MINMAX_DEFINED
#pragma option -vi-

#include <iostream.h>
#include <string.h>
#include <ctype.h>
#include <algo.h>
#include <set.h>

template<class ForwardIterator>
bool sorted( ForwardIterator begin, ForwardIterator end )
{
    ForwardIterator old = begin;
    if ( begin == end )
        return true;
    begin++;
    while ( begin != end )
        if ( *begin++ < *old++ )
            return false;
    return true;
}

void u( char *a, char *b )
{
    cout << a
         << " union "
         << b
         << " = ";
    if ( !sorted( a, a + strlen( a ) ) ) {
        cout << "First range not sorted!\n";
        return;
    } else if ( !sorted( b, b + strlen( b ) ) ) {
        cout << "Second range not sorted!\n";
        return;
    }
    set_union( a,
               a + strlen( a ),
               b,
               b + strlen( b ),
               ostream_iterator<char>( cout, " " ) );
    cout << endl;
}
```

```
main()
{
    u( "abc", "cde" );
    u( "abc", "abc" );
    u( "abc", "cba" ); //Error, not sorted!
    u( "xxxxxxx", "xxx" );
    return 1;
}
```

Example output:

```
abc union cde = a b c d e
abc union abc = a b c
abc union cba = Second range not sorted!
xxxxxxx union xxx = x x x x x x x
```

SET_INTERSECTION

Function

```
template < class InputIterator1,
           class InputIterator2,
           class OutputIterator >
OutputIterator set_intersection( InputIterator1 first1,
                                 InputIterator1 last1,
                                 InputIterator2 first2,
                                 InputIterator2 last2,
                                 OutputIterator result);


template < class InputIterator1,
           class InputIterator2,
           class OutputIterator,
           class Compare >
OutputIterator set_intersection( InputIterator1 first1,
                                 InputIterator1 last1,
                                 InputIterator2 first2,
                                 InputIterator2 last2,
                                 OutputIterator result,
                                 Compare comp);
```

Arguments

first1, last1:   The set_intersection algorithm calculates the intersection of two ordered sequences and places the result into a new sequence. first1 and last1 are iterators that define the start and end of the first sequence.

first2, last2:   These two iterators define the second sequence. These elements need to be sorted with either a specific comparison object, or the default, operator<().

result: As the algorithm proceeds, it places the sorted intersection of the two input sequences into an output sequence. This iterator defines the start of that output sequence. Remember that the size of the result can be as large as the sum of the two input sequences, so plan the space needed by result accordingly.

comp: set_intersection can assume that sets are sorted using the default comparison object, which is operator<(). If the input was sorted using some other function, set_intersection needs to be informed of this. The correct way to do so is by passing set_intersection a comparison object which defines the ordering function.

The comparison object should have function syntax, and take two objects of type T as input arguments. It returns a boolean result that defines the ordering of the two elements. If the boolean result is true, T1 and T2 should be ordered as T1, T2. A false result means they should be ordered T2, T1.

Return value

As set_intersection does its work, it continually stores new objects in the location pointed to by result. After each assignment operation, set_intersection increments the output iterator, so that it always points to the next free location in the output sequence. When the two sequences have been completely processed, the algorithm returns a copy of the output iterator, which now should be pointing *one past* the end of the output sequence.

Description

This algorithm combines two sorted sequences into the intersection of the two sequences as shown in Figure 16-3. The resulting intersection is stored in a location pointed to by the result argument. The algorithm lets you know how long the output sequence is by returning the iterator that marks the new end of the output sequence.

Note: The input sequences can look like multisets, with more than one copy of identical elements. If the first sequence has $N1$ copies of an element, and the second sequence has $N2$ copies of an element, the resulting output union will have the lesser of $N1$ and $N2$ copies of the specific element.

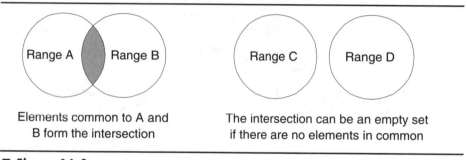

Elements common to A and
B form the intersection

The intersection can be an empty set
if there are no elements in common

Figure 16-3
An intersection of ranges

Why does set_intersection behave this way? It makes sense if you treat each instance of an element as a separate entity. For example, suppose range A has three copies of String1 and range B has two copies. You can match up the first copy of String1 from A and B, and then match up the second copy from A and B. This gives you two elements to add to the intersection. But the third copy of String1 in Range A doesn't have a match, so it isn't added to the intersection.

Range A		*Range B*
String1	Match	String1
String1	Match	String1
String1	No match!	

Complexity

set_intersection has linear complexity proportional to the sum of the lengths of the two sequences. The space complexity of set_intersection is constant.

Example

Listing 16-3

int1603.cpp: A demonstration of the set_intersection algorithm

```
/*
 * INT1603.CPP
 *
 * This program is used in Chapter 16 to demonstrate
 * the set_intersection algorithm. It executes the
 * algorithm on one particular set of data, storing the
 * result in some reserved space in a deque<double>
 * object. There are a couple of interesting points
 * to note here. First, the output sequence is of a
 * different type than the two input sequences, which
 * works fine, since operator=() is able to convert
 * from one type to the other. Second, to see where
 * the end of the output data is, I have to look at the
 * iterator returned from the set_intersection algorithm.
 */

//
// Borland 4.x workarounds
//
#define __MINMAX_DEFINED
#pragma option -vi-

#include <iostream.h>
#include <iomanip.h>
#include <algo.h>
#include <deque.h>

main()
{
    int a[] = { 1, 1, 1, 5, 10 };
    int b[] = { 1, 1, 4, 5 };
    deque<double> c( 10 );
    deque<double>::iterator j;

    j = set_intersection( a, a + 5,
                          b, b + 4,
                          c.begin() );
    cout << "Intersection: ";
    cout.setf( ios::showpoint );
    for ( deque<double>::iterator i = c.begin() ;
          i != j;
          i++ )
      cout << *i << " ";
    cout << endl;
    return 1;
}
```

Example output:

```
Intersection: 1.00000 1.00000 5.00000
```

SET_DIFFERENCE

Function

```
template < class InputIterator1,
          class InputIterator2,
          class OutputIterator >
OutputIterator set_difference( InputIterator1 first1,
                               InputIterator1 last1,
                               InputIterator2 first2,
                               InputIterator2 last2,
                               OutputIterator result );

template < class InputIterator1,
          class InputIterator2,
          class OutputIterator,
          class Compare >
OutputIterator set_difference( InputIterator1 first1,
                               InputIterator1 last1,
                               InputIterator2 first2,
                               InputIterator2 last2,
                               OutputIterator result,
                               Compare comp );
```

Arguments

first1, last1:   The set_difference algorithm takes as input two ordered
                 sequences that it uses to create a difference set. first1 and
                 last1 are iterators that define the start and end of the first
                 sequence. Note that only an input iterator is required here.
                 The algorithm steps through the sequences one step at a
                 time, so more powerful iterators aren't necessary.

first2, last2:   These two iterators define the second sequence. These ele-
                 ments need to be sorted with either a specific comparison
                 object, or the default, operator<().

result:	As the set_difference algorithm proceeds, it places the sorted difference of the two input sequences into an output sequence. This iterator defines the start of that output sequence. Remember that the size of the result can be as large as the length of the first sequence. This is often a good place to use an insertion iterator.
comp:	set_difference can assume that sets are sorted using the default comparison object, operator<(). If the input was sorted using some other function, set_difference needs to be informed of this. The correct way to do so is by passing set_difference a comparison object which defines the ordering function.
	The comparison object should have function syntax, and take two objects of type T as input arguments. It returns a boolean result that defines the ordering of the two elements. If the boolean result is true, T1 and T2 should be ordered as T1, T2. A false result means they should be ordered T2, T1.

Return value

As set_difference does its work, it continually stores new objects in the location pointed to by result. After each assignment operation, set_difference increments the output iterator, so that it always points to the next free location in the output sequence. When the two sequences have been completely processed, the algorithm returns a copy of the output iterator, which now should be pointing *one past* the end of the output sequence.

Description

set_difference looks for all the elements in the first sequence that don't appear in the second sequence. These elements are then placed in sorted order in the result iterator that is passed to the function.

If you need a function that returns both the unique elements of sequence 1 *and* sequence 2, you should call set_symmetric_difference.

The set_difference algorithm lets you know how long the output sequence is by returning the iterator that marks the new end of the output sequence.

Note also that the input sequences can look like multisets, with more than one copy of identical elements. If the first sequence has $N1$ copies of an element, and the second sequence has $N2$ copies of an element, and $N1$ is greater than $N2$, the resulting output union will have the $N1 - N2$ copies of the specific element. If $N2$ is greater then $N1$, the resulting union won't have any copies of the element.

The reason set_difference() works this way corresponds to the logic behind the way set_intersection() handles multiple appearances of an element. Once again, suppose there are two ranges, A and B. Range A has three copies of String1 and B has two copies.

Range A		Range B
String1	Match	String1
String1	Match	String1
String1	No match!	

When calculating the difference of the two ranges, we throw out any elements that appear in Range A and B. So the first and second appearances of String1 in A and B are both discarded. This leaves only the third appearance in Range A, which is now unique. Thus, one copy of String1 is added to the output range. (Note that any extra instances in Range B won't get included, since we are only looking at elements in A not found in B.)

Complexity

set_difference has linear complexity proportional to the sum of the lengths of the two sequences. The space complexity of set_difference is constant.

Example

Listing 16-4

diff1604.cpp: A demonstration of the set_difference algorithm

```
/*
 * DIFF1604.CPP
 *
 * This program is used in Chapter 16 to demonstrate
 * the set_difference algorithm. It simply performs
 * a batch of set_difference algorithms on sorted
```

```
 * strings. Note that one of the test inputs is
 * not sorted, resulting in erroneous output.
 */

//
// Borland 4.x workarounds
//
#define __MINMAX_DEFINED
#pragma option -vi-

#include <iostream.h>
#include <string.h>
#include <algo.h>
#include <set.h>

void diff( char *a, char *b )
{
    cout << a
         << " diff "
         << b
         << " = ";
    set_difference( a, a + strlen( a ),
                    b, b + strlen( b ),
                    ostream_iterator<char>( cout, "" ) );
    cout << endl;
}

main()
{
    diff( "abc", "cde" );
    diff( "abc", "abc" );
    diff( "xxxxxxx", "xxx" );
    diff( "abcdefg", "" );
    diff( "abcdefg", "gfedbca" ); //Error! Not sorted!
    return 1;
}
```

Example output:

```
abc diff cde = ab
abc diff abc =
xxxxxxx diff xxx = xxxx
abcdefg diff  = abcdefg
abcdefg diff gfedbca = abcdef
```

SET_SYMMETRIC_DIFFERENCE

Function

```
template < class InputIterator1,
           class InputIterator2,
           class OutputIterator >
OutputIterator set_symmetric_difference( InputIterator1 first1,
                                         InputIterator1 last1,
                                         InputIterator2 first2,
                                         InputIterator2 last2,
                                         OutputIterator result );


template < class InputIterator1,
           class InputIterator2,
           class OutputIterator,
           class Compare >
OutputIterator set_symmetric_difference( InputIterator1 first1,
                                         InputIterator1 last1,
                                         InputIterator2 first2,
                                         InputIterator2 last2,
                                         OutputIterator result,
                                         Compare comp );
```

Arguments

first1, last1:   The set_symmetric_difference algorithm processes two
                 ordered sequences and places the difference result into a
                 new sequence. first1 and last1 are iterators that define the
                 start and end of the first sequence.

first2, last2:   These two iterators define the second sorted sequence. The
                 algorithm looks for elements that are only present in the
                 first sequence, or only present in this sequence.

result: As the algorithm proceeds, it places the sorted difference of
                 the two input sequences into an output sequence. This itera-
                 tor defines the start of that output sequence. Remember that
                 the size of the result can be as large as the sum of the
                 lengths of the two sequences.

comp: set_symmetric_difference can assume that sets are sorted using the default comparison object, which is operator<(). If the input was sorted using some other function, set_symmetric_difference needs to be informed of this. The correct way to do so is by passing the function a comparison object which defines the ordering function. The comparison object should have function syntax, and take two objects of type T as input arguments. It returns a boolean result that defines the ordering of the two elements. If the boolean result is true, T1 and T2 should be ordered as T1, T2. A false result means they should be ordered T2, T1.

Return value

As set_symmetric_difference does its work, it continually stores new objects in the location pointed to by result. After each assignment operation, set_symmetric_difference increments the output iterator, so that it always points to the next free location in the output sequence. When the two sequences have been completely processed, the algorithm returns a copy of the output iterator, which now should be pointing *one past* the end of the output sequence.

Description

set_symmetric_difference, as shown in Figure 16-4, looks for all the elements in the first sequence that don't appear in the second sequence, and all the elements from the second sequence that aren't found in the first. These elements are then placed, in sorted order, into the result iterator that is passed to the function.

If you need a function that just returns the unique elements of sequence 1, you can call set_difference.

Note also that the input sequences can look like multisets, with more than one copy of identical elements. If the first sequence has $N1$ copies of an element, and the second sequence has $N2$ copies of an element, the resulting output union will be either $N1 - N2$, or $N2 - N1$ copies of the specific element. The logic behind this is nearly identical to that behind set_difference(). The only change is that set_difference() only looks for elements in A not found in B. set_symmetric_difference() also looks for elements in B not found in A.

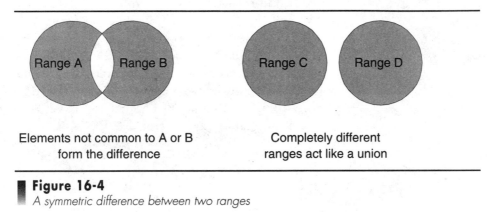

Elements not common to A or B
form the difference

Completely different
ranges act like a union

Figure 16-4
A symmetric difference between two ranges

Complexity

set_symmetric_difference has linear complexity proportional to the sum of the lengths of the two sequences. The space complexity of set_difference is constant.

Example

Listing 16-5

diff1605.cpp: A demonstration of the set_symmetric_difference algorithm

```
/*
 * DIFF1605.CPP
 *
 * This program is used in Chapter 16 to demonstrate
 * the set_symmetric_difference algorithm. It performs
 * the same batch of operations as DIFF1604.CPP, but
 * uses set_symmetric_difference instead of
 * set_difference, so you can compare the output
 * from the two programs.  Note that one of the
 * input sets is invalid in this program as well.
 */
```

```
//
// Borland 4.x workarounds
//
#define __MINMAX_DEFINED
#pragma option -vi-

#include <iostream.h>
#include <string.h>
#include <algo.h>
#include <set.h>

void sdiff( char *a, char *b )
{
    cout << a
         << " sdiff "
         << b
         << " = ";
    set_symmetric_difference( a, a + strlen( a ),
                              b, b + strlen( b ),
                              ostream_iterator<char>( cout, "" ) );
    cout << endl;
}

main()
{
    sdiff( "abc", "cde" );
    sdiff( "abc", "abc" );
    sdiff( "xxxxxxx", "xxx" );
    sdiff( "abcdefg", "" );
    sdiff( "abcdefg", "gfedbca" ); //Error! Not sorted!
    return 1;
}
```

Example output:

```
abc sdiff cde = abde
abc sdiff abc =
xxxxxxx sdiff xxx = xxxx
abcdefg sdiff  = abcdefg
abcdefg sdiff gfedbca = abcdeffedbca
```

HEAP OPERATIONS

17

It takes a heap o' livin' in a house t' make it home,
A heap o' sun an' shadder, an' ye sometimes have t' roam
Afore ye really 'preciate the things ye lef' behind,
An' hunger fer 'em somehow, with 'em allus on yer mind.

— Edgar A. Guest, *Home*

WHAT IS A HEAP?

The heap is a very useful data structure. It provides an easy way to implement a priority queue, which is a data structure used to retrieve data elements in a sorted order (without the expense of completely sorting the elements). Heaps are also used in sorting algorithms like Heapsort.

The internal structure of a heap is modeled on the binary tree, but in practice, heaps are normally stored in arrays. A complete binary tree can be represented simply as an array, by defining the left and right child nodes of element m as elements $2m+1$ and $2m+2$ (when using a zero-based indexing system). Knuth defines a complete binary tree as a tree with nodes 1 through n, where node $k/2$ is always the parent of node k.

The STL uses this array-storage system for heaps, which means heaps can only be stored in containers which support random access iterators. In the initial definition of the STL by the ANSI/ISO committee, this limits heaps to C/C++ arrays, or containers of type vector<T> or deque<T>. vector<T> is probably the best general-purpose container for heaps, as it has fast random access iterators but can grow as necessary.

Figure 17-1 shows the layout of a binary tree made up of an array of 6 members. Every node except the root has a parent node at $(i-1)/2$, and child nodes are found at $2i+1$ and $2i+2$. Navigating the tree is easy, and can be done using simple index math, as opposed to following pointers.

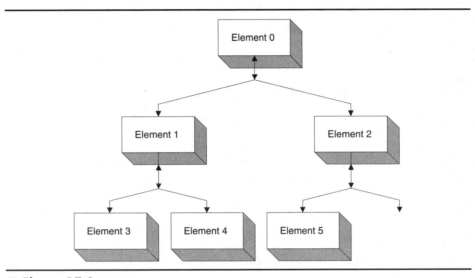

Figure 17-1
The heap structure

A binary tree like this is considered to be a *heap* when the value of each parent node is greater than or equal to its two children. While this might seem like a sorted tree, a valid heap may not look much like a sorted tree at all. This is the key to the strengths of the heap: not having to keep the data structure completely sorted cuts down on the time needed to maintain it.

As Figure 17-2 shows, the elements in a heap aren't exactly sorted. The numbers always get bigger as you move up the tree, and they always get smaller as you move down it, but there is no apparent relationship between siblings on the same level.

While not completely sorted, there is one very useful attribute of this heap structure: you can always count on the largest value in the heap being at the top. In an STL container, this means the largest value in a heap will be at the first location, or container.first(). When used in this fashion, a heap can be termed a *priority queue*.

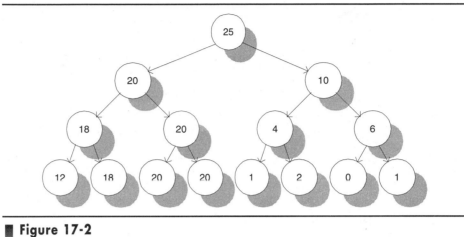

Figure 17-2
A sample heap

Two operations are needed to make a priority queue really handy: you need to be able to remove the highest value from the queue, and to add new values. Both of these operations are defined as STL algorithms: push_heap() and pop_heap().

The final two pieces that round out the heap algorithms are make_heap() and sort_heap(). make_heap() is crucial, as it takes an ordinary unsorted sequence (that supports random access iterators) and converts it to a valid heap. The second function is sort_heap(), which takes a heap and turns it into a fully sorted sequence. All four of these algorithms will be discussed in detail in this chapter. Table 17-1 lists heap operations.

Table 17-1

The heap operations

Function	Description
push_heap()	Adds a new element to an existing heap
pop_heap()	Removes an element from a heap
make_heap()	Makes a range into a heap
sort_heap()	Sorts the elements in a heap

PUSH_HEAP

Function

```
template < class RandomAccessIterator >
void push_heap( RandomAccessIterator first,
                RandomAccessIterator last );

template < class RandomAccessIterator, class Compare >
void push_heap( RandomAccessIterator first,
                RandomAccessIterator last,
                Compare comp );
```

Arguments

first: This iterator points to the first element in a sequence. The iterator needs to be random access, since heap operations rely on indexing for moving through the tree.

last: last defines the end of the input sequence. The input sequence is composed of two parts. The first part, defined by first through last-1, is assumed to be a sequence already ordered as a heap. The second part of the input sequence is the value at last-1, which is the new value to be inserted into the heap.

comp: Like most STL algorithms that assume a sorted sequence, push_heap assumes by default that the items in the heap are ordered using operator<(). For sequences that are ordered using a different algorithm, this argument needs to be passed to push_heap() to provide an alternative ordering function. The comp object must obey function syntax, and should accept two arguments of type T, where T is the type pointed to by first and last. The function object returns true if the correct order of the two objects is T1, T2, and false if the inverse is true.

Return value

Both versions of push_heap are void functions that don't return anything.

Description

push_heap takes an existing heap and adds a new element to it. Adding a new element to a fully sorted sequence, such as a set, can be a costly operation. But adding a new object to a heap is considerably simpler, involving a guaranteed maximum number of exchanges and comparisons.

This algorithm operates somewhat differently from what you might expect. If you were designing a push_heap function from scratch, you might think push_heap would take a new value of type T as an argument. The function would then insert the new value into the heap, expanding the container by one element. The function prototype could look something like this:

```
template < class RandomAccessIterator, class T >
void push_heap( RandomAccessIterator first,
                RandomAccessIterator last,
                T new_value );
```

The problem with this mode of operation is that it requires the algorithm to know something about the container. Adding a new element simply can't be done without either calling container member functions, or updating container data structures.

But STL algorithms operate on containers without knowing how to modify their size. Instead, they view their input data as simply part of a string of objects connected by iterator operators. So the STL has to use a slightly off-beat method for inserting an object into a heap.

The push_heap algorithm operates on a sequence that is defined by the iterators first and last, with length = last-first elements. But only the first len-1 elements in the sequence constitute a valid heap. The last element in the sequence is the new element to be added. This means that adding a new element to a heap will usually take two steps, looking something like this:

```
container.push_back( new_value );
push_heap( container.first(), container.last() );
```

The STL specification describes what push_heap() is supposed to do, but it doesn't impose requirements on how it should accomplish its work. The public release of the STL from Hewlett Packard gives a complete implementation that you can examine to see one approach, which is what is discussed in this chapter. Remember, however, that other compiler vendors are free to implement the heap functions however they care to, as long as the constraints defined in the specification are adhered to. The next section of this chapter will discuss the HP implementation.

HP Details

Adding a new node to a heap isn't too complicated. In HP's implementation, the actual insertion doesn't take place in the code for push_heap, which is simply a one-line function that calls a different helper function:

```
template < class RandomAccessIterator >
inline void push_heap( RandomAccessIterator first,
                       RandomAccessIterator last )
{
    __push_heap_aux( first, last, value_type( first ) );
}
```

The new node still hasn't been added by __push_heap_aux, which does the same thing push_heap() did: it calls another helper function:

```
template < class RandomAccessIterator, class T >
inline void __push_heap_aux( RandomAccessIterator first,
                             RandomAccessIterator last,
                             T* )
{
    __push_heap( first, (last - first) - 1, 0, T( *(last - 1) ) );
}
```

Finally, some real code shows up at the end of the chase. The excerpt below shows all the code from the __push_heap() worker function.

```
_ template < class RandomAccessIterator, class Distance, class T >
void __push_heap( RandomAccessIterator first,
                  Distance holeIndex,
                  Distance topIndex,
                  T value )
{
    Distance parent = ( holeIndex - 1 ) / 2;
    while ( holeIndex > topIndex && *( first + parent ) < value )
    {
        *( first + holeIndex ) = *( first + parent );
        holeIndex = parent;
        parent = ( holeIndex - 1 ) / 2;
    }
    *( first + holeIndex ) = value;
}
```

__push_heap() is a specialized routine that adds a new value to the heap, using the following parameters:

first: An iterator pointing to the start of an existing heap.

holeIndex: The index of an unused object in the heap. When this routine is called from push_heap(), the holeIndex is the index of the last object in the heap. When this routine is first called, the heap actually is only valid from first to last-1. The object pointed to by last is the new object being added to the heap. So why does __push_heap() get to consider that last position in the sequence to be vacant? Because the value of the object being inserted was also passed to __push_heap() as a parameter.

topIndex: The index of the first object in the heap. In this case, the index is 0.

value: The value of the new object to be inserted into the heap.

The code in __push_heap() executes in a loop that starts at the initial holeIndex, and works its way up the heap. At each position, it tests to see if the parent of the holeIndex is greater than or equal to the value being inserted in the heap. If it is, it has found a place where the value can safely be inserted. The loop exits, value is assigned to the position indicated by the holeIndex, and the routine exits.

If the parent of the node indicated by the holeIndex is less than the value being inserted, the routine has to iterate through the loop at least once more. It moves the value of the parent node down into the holeIndex node, then makes the parent node the new holeIndex. This process continues until the holeIndex reaches the appropriate position for the new value, at which point the new value must be assigned to the holeIndex.

Figure 17-3 shows a sample heap that is about to have a new value inserted. Before push_heap() was called, the valid heap ended at the node just before the node labeled "hole." The hole node contained the element to be inserted, with a value of 21. After the program makes its way down to __push_heap(), the new value found is the function's value parameter, and the last index in the heap is considered to be the holeIndex.

In the first pass through the loop, the parent of the holeIndex node is tested, and found to be less than the new value (the parent value was 18, the new value 21). So the parent node and hole node are swapped, yielding the position shown in Figure 17-4. The next test has the same result, since the parent node now has a value of 20, which is still less than the new value of 21. So the holeIndex node and the parent node are swapped again.

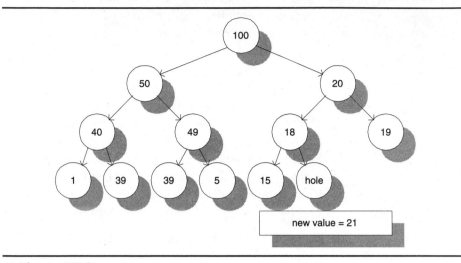

Figure 17-3
A heap about to receive a new value

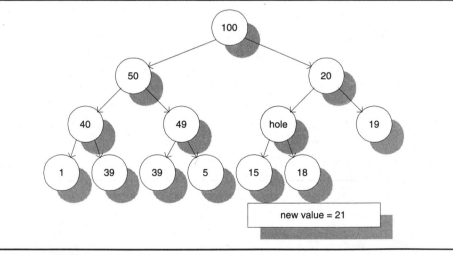

Figure 17-4
After one pass through the loop in __push_heap()

After the second swap, the holeIndex is the child of the heap's top node, which has a value of 100. Since 100 is greater than the new value, the loop exits, and the new value is stored in the holeIndex node. The resulting heap is shown in Figure 17-5.

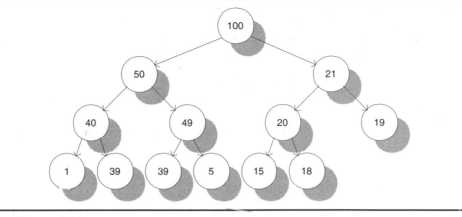

Figure 17-5
The heap when __push_heap() is finished

Note that there are corresponding versions of push_heap_aux() and __push_heap() that use a comparison object instead of operator<(). These routines are essentially identical to the ones shown here.

Why the hole?

If you look up heap operations in a standard reference on algorithms, you will probably find that the routine to insert a new node doesn't look exactly like this. More often than not, the insertion routine adds the new element to the end of the heap. A balancing routine then walks up the heap, swapping the new node with its parent until it floats up to its final destination.

The STL algorithm deviates from this in one small way. Instead of adding the new value to the heap, the STL adds a vacant slot, referred to as the *hole*. There's a big advantage here when the algorithm works its way up the heap. Instead of having to perform a swap of two fully constructed members, the algorithm simply performs an assignment of the parent node into the hole. The parent node then becomes the new hole, at no cost.

Once the hole has percolated up into its final destination, a single assignment of the new value fills the hole. This strategy avoids costly swaps, which require execution of two assignment operators, as well as a copy constructor. This same strategy shows up in the remaining heap adjustment routines, as you will see later in this chapter.

Complexity

If you follow the logic of the __push_heap() function discussed above, you can see that in the worst case, an insertion will have to travel from the bottom of the heap up to the root node. Since this is a complete binary tree, the time complexity of the routine is going to be log(N), where N is the total number of nodes in the heap.

The space complexity of push_heap() is constant.

Example

Listing 17-1

push1701.cpp: A demonstration of the push_heap algorithm

```
/*
 * PUSH1701.CPP
 *
 * This program is used in Chapter 17 to demonstrate the push_heap
 * algorithm. It simply creates a heap in the data[] array,
 * using the first 10 elements. It prints the initial heap, then
 * prints the heap after each of two new elements is added.
 */

//
// Borland 4.x workarounds
//
#define __MINMAX_DEFINED
#pragma option -vi-

#include <iostream.h>
#include <iomanip.h>
#include <algo.h>
#include <heap.h>

int data[] = { 10, 11, 12, 13, 14, 15, 16, 17, 18, 19, -1, -1 };

void print_heap( int *first, int *last );

int main()
{
    make_heap( data, data + 10 );
    cout << "Before:\n";
    print_heap( data, data + 10 );
```

```
        data[ 10 ] = 99;
        push_heap( data, data + 11 );
        cout << "After push_heap( 99 ):\n";
        print_heap( data, data + 11 );

        data[ 11 ] = 10;
        push_heap( data, data + 12 );
        cout << "After push_heap( 10 ):\n";
        print_heap( data, data + 12 );

        return 1;
}


/*
 * This slightly complicated routine is used to print a heap,
 * one row at a time. The calculations needed to make it look
 * tree-like are what take up all the space here.
 */

int print_row( int n, const int *p, int last )
{
        int low = ( 1 << n ) - 1;
        int high = 2 * low;

        int max_row = 0;
        int temp = last;
        for ( ; ; ) {
            temp /= 2;
            if ( temp == 0 )
                break;
            max_row++;
        }
        if ( n > max_row )
            return 0;
        int spaces = ( 2 << ( max_row - n ) ) - 1 ;
        for ( int i = low ; i <= high && i < last ; i++ ) {
            for ( int j = 0 ; j < spaces ; j++ )
                cout << " ";
            cout << setw( 2 ) << p[ i ];
            for ( j = 0 ; j < spaces ; j++ )
                cout << " ";
        }
        cout << endl;
        return 1;
}


/*
```

```
 * This is the print_heap() routine. It prints out the
 * heap, one row at a time.
 */

void print_heap( int *first, int *last )
{
    for ( int i = 0 ; ; i++ )
        if ( !print_row( i, first, last - first ) )
            break;
    cout << "\n";
}
```

Example output:

```
Before:
                19
        18              16
    17      14      15      12
  10  13  11

After push_heap( 99 ):
                99
        19              16
    17      18      15      12
  10  13  11  14

After push_heap( 10 ):
                99
        19              16
    17      18      15      12
  10  13  11  14  10
```

POP_HEAP

Function

```
template < class RandomAccessIterator >
void pop_heap( RandomAccessIterator first,
               RandomAccessIterator last );

template < class RandomAccessIterator, class Compare >
void pop_heap( RandomAccessIterator first,
               RandomAccessIterator last,
               Compare comp );
```

Arguments

first: first is a random access iterator that points to the first element of a heap. This algorithm assumes that the sequence defined by first, last is a valid heap. If it isn't, the results of the algorithm are meaningless.

last: This iterator points one past the last element in the heap. This is the conventional way of defining a sequence in the STL, and it means that the last valid element in the sequence is pointed to by last-1. last-1 is also the pointer to the location where the algorithm returns the highest element from the heap after removing it.

comp: This algorithm works under the assumption that the heap is ordered using operator<(). If the heap is ordered using some other method, the algorithm needs to be informed by the passing of a comparison object as an argument. The comparison object obeys function syntax, taking two arguments of type T, where T is the type pointed to by first and last. The comparison object should return a boolean value indicating whether the two arguments are in the correct order, or need to be reversed.

Return value

Both versions of the pop_heap() algorithm are void functions that have no return value. However, both functions are expected to return the highest value from the heap. Instead of having this be a function return, they place the object in the position pointed to by last-1 and return it that way.

Description

pop_heap is the mirror twin of push_heap(). Where push_heap() added a new value to an existing heap, pop_heap() removes the highest value from the existing heap. And just like push_heap(), it doesn't modify the size of the container, even though the heap is actually shrinking. Instead, it shrinks the heap itself, and moves the highest value in the heap to the last position in the old heap.

This mode of operation might seem kind of odd. If you were to write this function from scratch, it would be a lot more convenient to have the function automatically return the top value from the heap, then resize the container. You might expect the function to have a prototype something like this:

```
template < class Container, class T >
T pop_heap( Container &c );
```

The problem with writing the function this way is that it requires the algorithm to have knowledge of container operations. The function must know how to find the first element of the container, the last element, and how to resize the container. Since STL algorithms traditionally only deal with sequences of objects bound by iterator operations, this is a problem. Even worse, a solution that relied on container member functions would be likely to exclude the use of built-in C++ data types, such as arrays. So this slightly awkward compromise will have to do. If you are going to be using specific containers for heaps, you can easily create a simple wrapper function to provide one-stop convenience for popping the highest value from the heap.

HP Details

Once again, remember that the implementation details being discussed here are specific to HP's release of the STL. Other vendors are free to use whatever methods they desire to create the heap functions, as long as they adhere to the ANSI/ISO specification.

The hierarchy of functions that get called in response to pop_heap() are very much like what you saw in push_heap. When pop_heap is initially called by your program, it simply passes control along to a helper function, __pop_heap_aux().

```
template < class RandomAccessIterator >
inline void pop_heap( RandomAccessIterator first,
                      RandomAccessIterator last)
{
    __pop_heap_aux( first, last, value_type( first ) );
}
```

As you can see here, __pop_heap_aux() does virtually nothing on its own, simply passing control to a helper function, __pop_heap_aux(). __pop_heap_aux() is a little more interesting. It passes control to another worker function called __pop_heap(). The interesting thing about this function call is the minor modification of a couple of parameters:

```
template < class RandomAccessIterator, class T >
inline void __pop_heap_aux( RandomAccessIterator first,
                            RandomAccessIterator last,
                            T* )
{
    __pop_heap( first,
                last - 1,
                last - 1,
                T( *( last - 1 ) ),
                distance_type( first ) );
}
```

The first two parameters passed to __pop_heap() are first and last, which define the first and last elements of the heap. Instead of just passing through the input parameters first and last to __pop_heap(), __pop_heap_aux() takes it upon itself to pass last-1 to mark the end of the heap. This means __pop_heap() will treat the heap as if it had one fewer element than it does right now.

The third parameter to __pop_heap() is called result. This is an iterator pointing to a memory location where the result of __pop_heap() can be stored. In this case, __pop_heap_aux() passes last-1 as the result iterator. This means the value popped off the top of the heap will be stored in last-1.

This set of three parameters tells you what the sequence first, last is going to look like when the __pop_heap() operation is complete. When __pop_heap() starts, a properly ordered heap is contained in the sequence defined by first, last. When __pop_heap() returns, the highest element from that heap will have been removed and stored in location last-1. A new, smaller (by 1 element) heap is now stored in the sequence defined by first, last-1.

The final argument passed to __pop_heap() is the value of the element currently in the location pointed to by last-1. Since the result of the __pop_heap() operation will be written into last-1, __pop_heap() needs the value that is presently stored in that location so it can be added back into the new heap.

```
template < class RandomAccessIterator, class T, class Distance >
inline void __pop_heap( RandomAccessIterator first,
                        RandomAccessIterator last,
                        RandomAccessIterator result,
                        T value,
                        Distance* )
{
    *result = *first;
    __adjust_heap( first,
                   Distance( 0 ),
                   Distance( last - first ),
                   value );
}
```

The source code for __pop_heap() is still frustratingly brief! But you can see that it does one important thing: it writes the top value of the heap out to the location pointed to by result, which is the last element of the original heap. After doing that, it calls the worker routine, __adjust_heap(), which is going to perform all the work necessary to adjust the new, smaller heap.

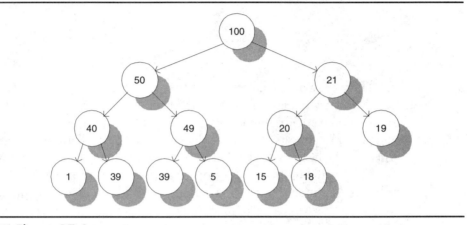

Figure 17-6
A sample heap before the pop operation begins

Figure 17-6 shows a representative heap that will have its top value popped. Once this heap is passed to __pop_heap(), the top value, 100, is stored in the last position, which is currently occupied by a value of 18. The value of 18 is passed to __adjust_heap() as a value parameter. This means the heap looks something like Figure 17-7 when adjust_heap() is called. (Remember that the value of 18 is in a sort of limbo, since it isn't in the heap at this time. It is a value parameter that will get added to the heap when the adjustment is finished.)

__adjust_heap has four parameters, with the following definitions:

first: The start of the heap. This argument is passed in unchanged by __pop_heap(), so it still points to the first element of the original heap.

holeIndex: The index of a location in the heap that can be considered unused. When this routine is called by __pop_heap(), the holeIndex is set to 0. This is because the first location in the heap is the value that was just written out to the result location. Since it has already been stored elsewhere, __adjust_heap() doesn't have to worry about preserving its value, so it can be treated as a vacant spot in the heap.

len: The size of the heap. When called by __pop_heap(), this parameter is set to the length of the new heap, which is the length of the original heap-1.

value: A new value to be inserted into the heap. Since the heap has a hole, __adjust_heap() knows it can insert the new value. It just needs to figure out where to put it. When called by __pop_heap(), value is set to what used to be the least element in the heap. The least element has been destroyed since the highest value was stored there by __pop_heap(). So the argument passed to this function is the only good copy of that value available now.

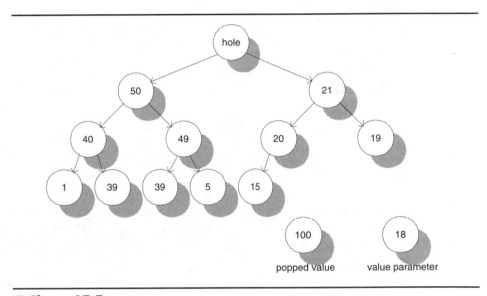

Figure 17-7
The same heap as passed to __adjust_heap()

```
template < class RandomAccessIterator, class Distance, class T >
void __adjust_heap( RandomAccessIterator first,
                    Distance holeIndex,
                    Distance len,
                    T value )
{
    Distance topIndex = holeIndex;
    Distance secondChild = 2 * holeIndex + 2;
    while ( secondChild < len )
    {
```

```
                if (*(first + secondChild) < *(first + (secondChild - 1)) )
                    secondChild--;
                *( first + holeIndex ) = *( first + secondChild );
                holeIndex = secondChild;
                secondChild = 2 * ( secondChild + 1 );
            }
            if ( secondChild == len ) {
                *( first + holeIndex ) = *( first + ( secondChild -1 ) );
                holeIndex = secondChild - 1;
            }
            __push_heap( first, holeIndex, topIndex, value );
        }
```

__adjust_heap() is really a two-part process:

- It has to adjust the heap to deal with a hole that has been inserted into its tree structure.

- Then, it has to call __push_heap() to properly insert a new value into that hole.

The first part of __adjust_heap() is simply a matter of taking the hole and moving it to the bottom of the heap. This is done by selecting the largest of the hole's two children at each level, then exchanging the hole with that child.

Figure 17-8 shows the structure of the sample heap after __adjust_heap() has moved the hole to the bottom of the tree. You can see that the heap now has mostly compensated for the loss of its largest member. The vacancy left at the top has been properly filled in, and what remains looks like a valid heap.

The only thing remaining at this point is the call to __push_heap(). As you saw in the last function definition, __push_heap() inserts a value into the hole after adjusting the heap to be sure it will be properly ordered. The value inserted into the hole is the value parameter that was passed to __pop_heap() by __pop_heap_aux() — originally the last member of the heap.

Pushing this last member back into the heap should be a fairly easy job. Since it was originally the last member, it isn't likely to require too many comparisons and swaps to adjust after it is inserted at the bottom of the heap. Figure 17-9 shows what the sample heap looks like after the value parameter is once again put back into the heap.

At this point, the heap has been reordered, it is now completely valid, and the original top value, 100, is now stored in location last-1. The new heap goes from first to last-1, instead of from first to last.

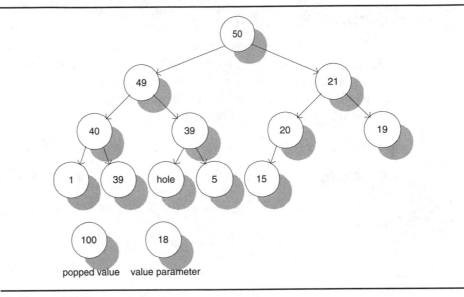

Figure 17-8
The same heap after __adjust_heap() has moved the hole to the bottom of the tree

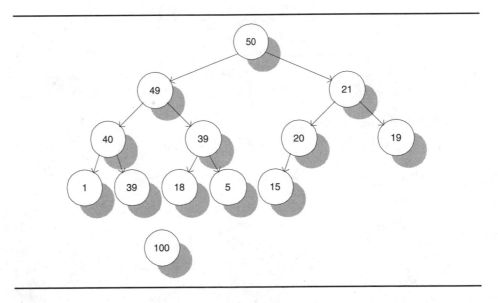

Figure 17-9
The heap after all work is complete

Complexity

The code for __adjust_heap() shows that in the worst case, a pop operation will have to travel from the root of the heap down to a leaf node. Since this is a complete binary tree, the time complexity of the routine is log(N), where N is the total number of nodes in the heap.

The space complexity of push_heap() is constant.

Example

Listing 17-2

pop1702.cpp: A demonstration of the pop_heap algorithm

```
/*
 * POP1702.CPP
 *
 * This program is used in Chapter 17 to demonstrate the pop_heap
 * algorithm. It simply creates a vector with 10 random elements.
 * The vector is then sorted by first making it into a heap,
 * then popping the top element, one by one, until the whole vector
 * has been processed.
 */

//
// Borland 4.x workarounds
//
#define __MINMAX_DEFINED
#pragma option -vi-

#include <iostream.h>
#include <stdlib.h>

#include <algo.h>
#include <heap.h>
#include <vector.h>

int main()
{
    vector< int > a;
    srand( time( 0 ) );

    cout << "Unsorted vector:\n";
    for ( int i = 0 ; i < 10 ; i++ )
```

```
                a.push_back( rand() );
        copy( a.begin(),
              a.end(),
              ostream_iterator<int>( cout, " " ) );
        cout << endl;
        make_heap( a.begin(), a.end() );
        cout << "Sorted vector   :\n";
        while ( a.begin() != a.end() ) {
            pop_heap( a.begin(), a.end() );
            cout << *( a.end() - 1 )
                 << " ";
            a.pop_back();
        }
        return 1;
    }
```

Example output:

```
Unsorted vector:
1688 11981 17696 25360 20555 19946 28631 7361 30974 15930
Sorted vector   :
30974 28631 25360 20555 19946 17696 15930 11981 7361 1688
```

MAKE_HEAP

Function

```
template < class RandomAccessIterator >
void make_heap( RandomAccessIterator first,
                RandomAccessIterator last );

template < class RandomAccessIterator, class Compare >
void make_heap( RandomAccessIterator first,
                RandomAccessIterator last,
                Compare comp );
```

Arguments

first: This is a random access iterator pointing to the start of an input sequence. The current ordering of the input sequence is irrelevant; unsorted input is appropriate at this point.

last: The last iterator defines the end of the input sequence using the normal STL conventions. If last == first, the input sequence is empty.

comp: The default method used to order the elements in the heap is by using operator<(). However, there may be times when you need a more sophisticated comparison. Or, operator<() may not be defined for the particular object. A good example would be when comparing standard C strings, which are represented as character pointers.

              When comp is passed to the make_heap() function, it is expected to follow the syntax of operator<(). This means the function accepts two arguments of type T, where T is the type of object pointed to by the iterator passed to make_heap(). In addition, comp should return a boolean value, indicating whether the correct ordering of the two arguments is arg1, arg2 (true), or arg2, arg1 (false).

Return value

This is a void function; it has no return value.

Description

The make_heap algorithm takes an unordered input sequence and converts it to a heap. To build the heap, make_heap() calls a helper function, __make_heap(), which does the actual work:

```
template < class RandomAccessIterator, class T, class Distance >
void __make_heap( RandomAccessIterator first,
                  RandomAccessIterator last,
                  T*,
                  Distance* )
```

```
    {
        if ( last - first < 2 )
            return;
        Distance len = last - first;
        Distance parent = ( len - 2 ) / 2;

        while ( true ) {
            __adjust_heap( first,
                           parent,
                           len,
                           T( *( first + parent ) ) );
            if ( parent == 0 )
                return;
            parent--;
        }
    }
```

__make_heap() adopts a bottom-up strategy for building the heap. It starts at the bottom of the heap, adjusting the smallest possible sub-heap. It starts making adjustments on the first node that has any children.

Figure 17-10 illustrates how this process would work in a typical heap. The code in __make_heap() selects the first parent to be (len-2)/2, which in this case would be node 4. After calling __adjust_heap(), the sub-heap rooted at node 4 would be ordered properly. Although this doesn't have much effect on the overall heap, it also doesn't take much work.

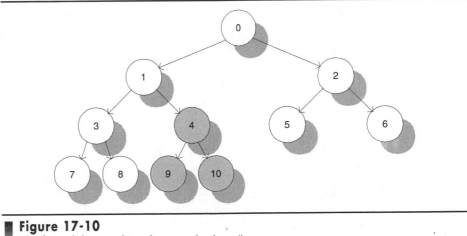

Figure 17-10
The first sub-heap adjusted in __make_heap()

After adjusting the heap rooted at node 4, __make_heap() starts working its way up the heap by backing up to the previous node. It adjusts the sub-heap at 3, then at 2, and continues moving back until it has adjusted node 0. At that point, the heap is completely ordered.

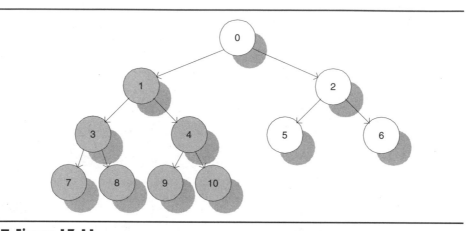

Figure 17-11
Adjusting the sub-heap starting at parent node 1

Complexity

While it may not be immediately obvious, the STL manages to construct a heap from an unsorted array in linear time. Even though it has to do a tree traversal for half the nodes in the heap, most of the sub-heaps aren't very deep. Half of the heaps that are ordered in this process will only have a single pair of children. The STL guarantees that this algorithm makes no more than $3N$ comparisons.

Space complexity for make_heap is constant.

Example

Listing 17-3

make1703.cpp: A demonstration of the make_heap algorithm

```
/*
 * MAKE1703.CPP
 *
 * This program is used in Chapter 17 to demonstrate
 * the make_heap algorithm. It keeps track of the
 * number of operations performed while making the
 * heap, to help demonstrate that the complexity of
 * make_heap() is linear.
 */
```

```
//
// Borland 4.x workarounds
//
#define __MINMAX_DEFINED
#pragma option -vi-

#include <iostream.h>
#include <stdlib.h>

#include <algo.h>
#include <heap.h>
#include <vector.h>


struct bob {
    int x;
    static int comp_count;
    static int ctor_count;
    static int copy_count;
    static int assign_count;

    bob() : x( 0 ){ ctor_count++; }
    bob( int i ) : x( i ){ ctor_count++; }
    bob( const bob &a ) : x( a.x ){ copy_count++; }
    void operator=( const bob& a ){ assign_count++; x = a.x; }
    bool operator<( const bob& a ) {
        comp_count++;
        return x < a.x;
    }
};

int bob::comp_count = 0;
int bob::ctor_count = 0;
int bob::copy_count = 0;
int bob::assign_count = 0;

int main()
{
    srand( time( 0 ) );
    vector< bob > a;
    const int k = 1000;

    for ( int i = 0 ; i < k; i++ )
        a.push_back( bob( rand() ) );
    make_heap( a.begin(), a.end() );
    cout << "Nodes      : " << k              << endl;
    cout << "Comparisons: " << bob::comp_count   << endl;
    cout << "Ctors      : " << bob::ctor_count   << endl;
    cout << "Copies     : " << bob::copy_count   << endl;
    cout << "Assigns    : " << bob::assign_count << endl;
    return 1;
}
```

Example output:

```
Nodes      : 1000
Comparisons: 1642
Ctors      : 1000
Copies     : 2000
Assigns    : 1752
```

SORT_HEAP

Function

```
template < class RandomAccessIterator >
void sort_heap( RandomAccessIterator first,
                RandomAccessIterator last )
{
    while ( last - first > 1 )
        pop_heap( first, last-- );
}

template < class RandomAccessIterator, class Compare >
void sort_heap( RandomAccessIterator first,
                RandomAccessIterator last,
                Compare comp )
{
    while ( last - first > 1 )
        pop_heap( first, last--, comp );
}
```

Arguments

first: This iterator points to the first element in a sequence. The iterator needs to be random access, since heap operations rely on indexing for moving through the tree.

last: last defines the end of the input sequence. The input sequence defined by *first, last* is assumed to already be a heap. If not, the results of sort_heap() are undefined.

comp: Like most STL algorithms that assume a sorted sequence, sort_heap assumes by default that the items in the heap are ordered using operator<(). For sequences ordered using a different algorithm, this argument needs to be passed to sort_heap()

to provide an alternative ordering function. The comp object must obey function syntax, and should accept two arguments of type T, where T is the type pointed to by first and last. The function object returns true if the correct order of the two objects is T1, T2, and false if the inverse is true.

Return value

Both versions of sort_heap() are void functions with no return values.

Description

sort_heap is an algorithm that takes an existing heap and turns it into a sorted sequence. This algorithm takes advantage of the fact that removing the highest value from a heap is a relatively efficient operation. It sorts the heap by iterating through a loop, removing the highest value from the heap, and placing it in the sorted sequence immediately after the newly shortened heap.

You can see from the source code that the algorithm's implementation is fairly simple, since the pop_heap() algorithm places the highest value from the heap at the end. Because the length of the heap decrements by one with each pop_heap() call, the output elements collect in reverse order from the end of the sequence.

Complexity

This algorithm features $N*\log(N)$ time complexity, and constant space complexity.

Example
Listing 17-4

sort1704.cpp: A demonstration of the sort_heap algorithm

```
/*
 * SORT1704.CPP
 *
 * This program is used in Chapter 17 to demonstrate
 * the sort_heap algorithm. It simply creates a character
 * array with 40 random elements, then makes the array
```

```
* into a heap, then sorts it. The array is printed
* out at each step along the way.
*/

//
// Borland 4.x workarounds
//
#define __MINMAX_DEFINED
#pragma option -vi-

#include <iostream.h>
#include <stdlib.h>

#include <algo.h>
#include <heap.h>

int main()
{
    char data[ 41 ];
    srand( time( 0 ) );
    char input_set[] = "ABCDEFGHIJKLMNOPQRSTUVWXYZ"
                       "abcdefghijklmnopqrstuvwxzy";

    for ( int i = 0 ; i < 40 ; i++ )
        data[ i ] = input_set[ rand() % 52 ];
    data[ 40 ] ='\0';
    cout << "Data   = " << data << endl;
    make_heap( data, data + 40 );
    cout << "Heap   = " << data << endl;
    sort_heap( data, data + 40 );
    cout << "Sorted = " << data << endl;
    return 1;
}
```

Example output:

```
Data   = OAodRdpSIEhySooFtuNqcLcPDaHIQYirGpzJhshJ
Heap   = zuytqoprschdaooOphhJRLcPDSHIQYiFGdSJINAE
Sorted = ADEFGHIIJJLNOPQRSSYaccddhhhioooppqrstuyz
```

NUMERIC

OPERATIONS

The concept of number is the obvious distinction between the beast and man. Thanks to number, the cry becomes song, noise acquires rhythm, the spring is transformed into a dance, force becomes dynamic, and outlines figures.

— Joseph Marie de Maistre (1753-1821)

These four functions are part of the original STL release by HP. During the standardization process, the ANSI/ISO committee moved the functions to the numerics section of the C++ standard library, a much more appropriate home for them. They'll probably be a lot less lonely among functions of their own kind.

In the interests of completeness, this chapter will go ahead and document these functions. The STL wasn't trying to be an all-inclusive library for every numeric operation. But the STL numeric functions *do* give you a glimpse of the kind of interface you might design for a template-based numeric library.

ACCUMULATE

Function

```
template < class InputIterator, class T >
T accumulate( InputIterator first,
              InputIterator last,
```

```
                    T init )
{
    while ( first != last )
        init = init + *first++;
    return init;
}

template < class InputIterator, class T, class BinaryOperation >
T accumulate( InputIterator first,
              InputIterator last,
              T init,
              BinaryOperation binary_op )
{
    while ( first != last )
        init = binary_op( init, *first++ );
    return init;
}
```

Arguments

first: This iterator points to the first element in a sequence. It
                 needn't be more powerful than an input iterator, since the only
                 operations performed on it are the dereference, increment, and
                 comparison operations.

last: last points to an element one past the last element to be used in
                 the input sequence.

init: The initial value required by the accumulate algorithm. For
                 example, if you are using accumulate to add up a vector of
                 integers, you would need to provide an init value of 0.

binary_op: There are two different implementations of the accumulate
                 algorithm. The first version repeatedly adds each input element
                 to the initial value, eventually yielding the final results. The
                 second version instead uses a function object to perform some
                 other operation on the input value.

                 binary_op must be an object that obeys function semantics. It
                 should take two arguments, one of type T, and one of the type
                 pointed to by the input iterators. It should return an object of
                 type T, which is updated to supply the new cumulative value. See
                 the source code above for a view of how this function is used.

Return value

Both versions of accumulate return a result that is of the same type as the init parameter, The result will be a copy of init, after either operator+() or the binary_op argument is applied for each value in the input sequence.

Description

accumulate repeatedly applies a function to each member of the input sequence, storing the result in temporary storage. The initial value of the result is determined by an input parameter to the function. The function applied to the input sequence is either operator+(), or a binary function object specified by the caller.

When operator+() or the binary function object is called, the first parameter is a copy of the current intermediate value of the result. The second argument is the next value from the input sequence. The two are processed by the function, and the result is stored in the intermediate result.

Complexity

The time complexity of accumulate is linear, in proportion to the length of the input sequence. Its space complexity is constant.

Example

Listing 18-1

acc1801.cpp: A demonstration of the accumulate algorithm

```
/*
 * ACC1801.CPP
 *
 * This program is used in Chapter 18 to demonstrate
 * the accumulate algorithm. The algorithm in this
 * case repeatedly adds a character from an array
 * to a string, which has the effect of appending the
 * entire character array to the string.
 *
```

```
 * Note that the use of templates allows this program
 * to use the addition operator inside the accumulate
 * algorithm in a different way than you might normally
 * expect. It is definitely not being used in a
 * numeric fashion! Instead, we are using accumulate
 * to add a single character to a C++ string object.
 * This has the effect of appending the character to
 * the string.
 */

//
// Borland 4.x workarounds
//
#define __MINMAX_DEFINED
#pragma option -vi-

#include <iostream.h>
#include <cstring.h>
#include <algo.h>

int main()
{
    char data[]= { 'A', 'B', 'C', 'D', 'E' };

    string x = accumulate( data, data + 5, string( "" ) );
    cout << "Accumulated string = "
        << x
        << endl;
    return 0;
}
```

Example output:

```
Accumulated string = ABCDE
```

INNER_PRODUCT

Function

```
template < class InputIterator1, class InputIterator2, class T >
T inner_product( InputIterator1 first1,
                 InputIterator1 last1,
                 InputIterator2 first2,
                 T init)
{
    while ( first1 != last1 )
        init = init + ( *first1++ * *first2++ );
```

```
          return init;
    }

    template < class InputIterator1,
               class InputIterator2,
               class T,
               class BinaryOperation1,
               class BinaryOperation2 >
    T inner_product( InputIterator1 first1,
               InputIterator2 last1,
               InputIterator2 first2,
               T init,
               BinaryOperation1 binary_op1,
               BinaryOperation2 binary_op2 )
    {
        while ( first1 != last1 )
            init = binary_op1( init,
                        binary_op2( *first1++, *first2++ ) );
        return init;
    }
```

Arguments

first1:   This iterator points to the first element in a sequence. It need only be an input iterator, since the only operations performed on it are the dereference, increment, and comparison operations.

last1:   last points to an element one past the last element to be used in the input sequence.

first2:   The inner_product algorithm accumulates the result of an operation on two input sequences. The second input sequence starts at the location pointed to by this iterator. Note that the algorithm doesn't need the value of last2, since both input sequences must be the same length.

init: The inner_product algorithm requires an initial value, since it is going to accumulate the results of an operation on the two input sequences.

binary_op1, There are two different implementations of the inner_product
binary_op2: algorithm. The first version takes the product of two input elements, then adds it to the accumulated value. This version doesn't require either of the binary_op arguments, since it uses the default values of operator+() and operator*().

The second version of inner_product gives you the opportunity to override these defaults. It applies binary_op2() to the two elements from the input sequences. It then uses binary_op1() with the result to update the accumulated value. The code shown above should make this clear.

Return value

inner_product returns the accumulated value of the two operations as applied to the two input sequences.

Description

inner_product is very similar to the accumulate algorithm. While accumulate adds each element of an input sequence to a total, inner_product adds the product of two input sequences to a total. In the event that the addition and multiplication operations don't do exactly what you want, you can override them with other binary function objects.

Complexity

The time complexity of inner_product is linear, in proportion to the length of the input sequence. Its space complexity is constant.

Example

Listing 18-2

in1802.cpp: A demonstration of the inner_product algorithm

```
/*
 * IN1802.CPP
 *
 * This program is used in Chapter 18 to demonstrate
 * the inner_product algorithm. It uses function
 * objects to perform an operation that is somewhat
 * different from the default version of inner_product.
```

```
 * The default inner product function will sum the
 * products of the two ranges, something like this:
 *
 *   while ( first1 != last1 )
 *       sum = sum + *first1++ * *first2++;
 *
 * This program uses function objects to turn that on
 * its head. It instead implements:
 *
 *   while ( first1 != last1 )
 *       sum = sum = *first1++ / *first2++;
 */


//
// Borland 4.x workarounds
//
#define __MINMAX_DEFINED
#pragma option -vi-

#include <iostream.h>
#include <cstring.h>
#include <algo.h>

double s1[] = { 1, 2, 3, 4, 5 };
double s2[] = { 5, 4, 3, 2, 1 };

int main()
{
    double d = inner_product( s1,
                              s1 + 5,
                              s2,
                              0.0,
                              minus<double>(),
                              divides<double>() );
    cout << "inner_product = "
         << d
         << endl;
    return 0;
}
```

Example output:

```
inner_product = -8.7
```

The calculation of the inner product leads directly to this result:

```
-(1/5) -(2/4) -(3/3) -(4/2) -(5/1) = -.2 -.5 -1 -2 -5 = -8.7
```

PARTIAL_SUM

Function

```
template < class InputIterator, class OutputIterator >
OutputIterator partial_sum( InputIterator first,
                            InputIterator last,
                            OutputIterator result );

template < class InputIterator,
           class OutputIterator,
           class BinaryOperation >
OutputIterator partial_sum( InputIterator first,
                            InputIterator last,
                            OutputIterator result,
                            BinaryOperation binary_op );
```

Arguments

first: This iterator, which only needs to be an input iterator, points to the first element in a sequence.

last: The last iterator points to an element one past the end of the input sequence. If first == last, the input sequence is empty.

result: The partial_sum algorithm generates a sequence of last-first result values. Those values are stored starting at the location pointed to by the result iterator. Since the algorithm only writes to and increments the value of result, this can be a simple output iterator. Note that result must have space allocated to hold last-first values.

binary_op: Normally, partial_sum creates a sum of the values in the input sequence. If some other function needs to be applied to the input sequence, it can be defined with this parameter.

binary_op should obey function syntax. It accepts two arguments, one of the type pointed to by the output iterator, and one of the type pointed to by the input iterator. It returns a value of the type pointed to by the output iterator.

Return value

partial_sum returns a copy of the result iterator. The iterator will have had last-first objects written to it, and should be pointing to the next output element.

Description

The partial_sum algorithm creates a sequence of elements that represent a running total of the elements in the input sequence. This means:

- the first element in the output sequence will be a copy of the first element in the input sequence
- the second output element will be the sum of the first two input elements
- the third output element will be the sum of the first three input elements, and so on
- the last output element will be the sum of the entire input sequence.

If you call the second version of the algorithm, you can substitute a different function for the addition operation, which gives you intermediate results of some other kind. For example, you could use the times<> function object to get a running product instead of a running total.

When the algorithm completes, it returns an iterator pointing to the next item in the output sequence. This will be the first item after the last running total.

Complexity

partial_sum has linear time complexity, in proportion to the length of the input sequence. The space complexity of partial_sum() is constant.

Example

Listing 18-3

part1803.cpp: A demonstration of the partial_sum algorithm

```
/*
 * PART1803.CPP
 *
 * This program is used in Chapter 18 to demonstrate the partial_sum
 * algorithm. The program uses partial_sum() to create a running
 * total of the elements in an array of integers. The output of
 * the algorithm is sent directly to an ostream iterator, so it is
 * displayed on cout.
 */

//
// Borland 4.x workarounds
//
#define __MINMAX_DEFINED
#pragma option -vi-

#include <iostream.h>
#include <algo.h>

int main()
{
    int data[] = { 6, 5, 4, 3, 2, 1 };
    partial_sum( data,
                 data + 6,
                 ostream_iterator<int>( cout, " " ) );
    return 0;
}
```

Example output:

```
6 11 15 18 20 21
```

ADJACENT_DIFFERENCE

Function

```
template < class InputIterator, class OutputIterator >
OutputIterator adjacent_difference( InputIterator first,
                                    InputIterator last,
                                    OutputIterator result );
```

```
template < class InputIterator,
          class OutputIterator,
          class BinaryOperation >
OutputIterator adjacent_difference( InputIterator first,
                                    InputIterator last,
                                    OutputIterator result,
                                    BinaryOperation binary_op );
```

Arguments

first: This iterator that points to the first element in a sequence. The iterator only needs to be an input iterator, since the algorithm steps through the input one element at a time.

last: The last iterator points to an element one past the end of the input sequence.

result: Like partial_sum, adjacent_difference writes a series of values using the result iterator. This iterator should therefore point to an available storage area that can hold last-first objects.

binary_op: Normally, adjacent_difference calculates the difference between adjacent elements in the input sequence. If some other function needs to be applied to the input, it can be defined with this parameter.

                    binary_op should obey function syntax. It accepts two arguments, one of the type pointed to by the output iterator, and one of the type pointed to by the input iterator. It returns a value of the type pointed to by the output iterator.

Return value

adjacent_difference returns a copy of the result iterator. The iterator will have had last-first objects written to it, and should be pointing to the next output element.

Description

The adjacent_difference algorithm creates an output sequence that consists of the differences between adjacent elements in the input sequence. The first element in the output sequence is simply a copy of the first element in the input sequence. The second output element is the difference between the first two input elements. In general:

```
output element n = input element n-1 - input element n
```

The only exception to this rule is for output element 0, which is a copy of input element 0.

If a binary operation is supplied as an argument to adjacent_difference, operator() in the above equation is replaced with the result of the binary operation.

Complexity

adjacent_difference has linear time complexity, in proportion to the length of the input sequence. The space complexity of adjacent_difference is constant.

Example

Listing 18-4

diff1804.cpp: A demonstration of the adjacent_difference algorithm

```
/*
 * DIFF1804.CPP
 *
 * This program is used in Chapter 18 to demonstrate the
 * adjacent_difference algorithm. It simply outputs the
 * adjacent differences between a vector of input data.
 */

//
// Borland 4.x workarounds
//
#define __MINMAX_DEFINED
#pragma option -vi-

#include <iostream.h>
#include <algo.h>
```

```
int main()
{
    int data[] = { 0, 1, 3, 6, 10, 6, 3, 1, 0, 0 };
    cout << "Input data: ";
    copy( data,
          data + 10,
          ostream_iterator<int>( cout, " " ) );
    cout << endl;
    cout << "Adjacent difference: ";
    adjacent_difference( data,
                data + 10,
                ostream_iterator<int>( cout, " " ) );
    cout << endl;
    return 0;
}
```

Example output:

```
Input data: 0 1 3 6 10 6 3 1 0 0
Adjacent difference: 0 1 2 3 4 -4 -3 -2 -1 0
```

MISCELLANEOUS OPERATIONS

What is the use of a book, thought Alice, without pictures or conversations?

— Lewis Carroll, Alice's Adventures in Wonderland

Most STL algorithms fit nicely into one of a few different categories. However—as often happens when you embark on a categorization project—there are a few oddities that don't quite fit anywhere. This chapter consists of the leftovers from the STL algorithm family. But just because these algorithms landed in the miscellaneous chapter, don't think they aren't useful! And don't be surprised if some of the functions described here end up at the top of your list.

MIN AND MAX

Function

```
template <class T>
inline const T& min(const T& a, const T& b)
{
    return b < a ? b : a;
}
```

```
template <class T, class Compare>
inline const T& min(const T& a, const T& b, Compare comp)
{
    return comp( b, a ) ? b : a;

}


template <class T>
inline const T& max(const T& a, const T& b) {
    return  a < b ? b : a;
}


template <class T, class Compare>
inline const T& max(const T& a, const T& b, Compare comp) {
    return comp(a, b) ? b : a;
}
```

Arguments

a, b: The min and max algorithms expect two arguments of type T. The arguments are passed to the function by reference, so you avoid the expense of performing copy operations on the two inputs. Note that if the first version of min or max is used, there should be an operator<() defined for the argument type.

comp: The first version of min or max compares the two arguments using operator<(), and returns the lesser of the two. If you want to make some other comparison, you can supply the function with a comparison object. If you do this, the comparison object is called using function syntax, with b as the first argument and a as the second under min(), and a as the first argument and b as the second under max().

Return value

Both versions of min and max return a reference to one of the two input arguments. The first version returns a reference to the least of the two arguments. The second version returns a reference to b if comp(b,a) returns true, for min, or a if comp(a,b) returns true, for max.

Description

The min() and max() functions were part of the official release of the C standard library blessed by the ANSI committee. But there are shortcomings in C that prevent min() and max() from being implemented in an optimal fashion. In fact, since min() and max() are so short and simple, they are frequently used as demonstration routines to show the superiority of template-based library functions when compared to standard C.

Since there wasn't a standardized C++ library when the STL was first created, the designers thought min and max would be good additions. Both are template functions that return const objects. Since they are implemented inline, they give us the best of C and C++: the most efficient code combined with the safety benefits of function calls.

min() normally returns the lesser of two objects, but the STL adds a twist in the form of a separate function that takes a comparison object. Thus, min() can actually be coerced into defining any sort of binary relationship between two objects. It's probably not a good idea to stray too far from the numeric origins of min(), however. A reliance on an idiosyncratic comparison function could leave you with efficient but indecipherable code.

The same holds true for max(), with the sense of the comparisons reversed.

Complexity

min and max have constant complexity in both time and space.

Example

Listing 19-1

min1901.cpp: A demonstration of the min algorithm

```
/*
 * MIN1901.CPP
 *
 * This program is used in Chapter 19 to demonstrate the min
 * algorithm. It simply works its way through a list of strings,
 * applying min() to adjacent pairs and printing the result.
 */
```

```
//
// Borland 4.x workarounds
//
#define __MINMAX_DEFINED
#pragma option -vi-

#include <iostream.h>
#include <cstring.h>
#include <algo.h>

string data[] = { "Ford",
                  "Chevrolet",
                  "Chrysler",
                  "Toyota",
                  "Honda",
                  "Subaru" };

int main()
{
    for ( int i = 1 ; i <= 5 ; i++ )
        cout << "min( "
             << data[ i - 1 ]
             << ", "
             << data[ i ]
             << " ) = "
             << min( data[ i - 1 ], data[ i ] )
             << endl;
    return 0;
}
```

Example output:

```
min( Ford, Chevrolet ) = Chevrolet
min( Chevrolet, Chrysler ) = Chevrolet
min( Chrysler, Toyota ) = Chrysler
min( Toyota, Honda ) = Honda
min( Honda, Subaru ) = Honda
```

MIN_ELEMENT AND MAX_ELEMENT

Function

```
template <class InputIterator>
InputIterator min_element( InputIterator first,
                           InputIterator last );
```

```
template <class InputIterator, class Compare>
InputIterator min_element( InputIterator first,
                           InputIterator last,
                           Compare comp );

template < class InputIterator >
InputIterator max_element( InputIterator first,
                           InputIterator last );

template < class InputIterator, class Compare >
InputIterator max_element( InputIterator first,
                           InputIterator last,
                           Compare comp );
```

Arguments

first: This iterator points to the first element in the input sequence. first can be a simple input iterator, since the algorithm just walks through the input sequence one element at a time.

last: The last iterator points one past the last element in the input sequence. If first == last, the input sequence is empty.

comp: To determine the least or greatest element in an input sequence, these two functions normally use operator<(). However, there will be times when you want to use something other than this operator to compare two elements. In that case, you can supply a comparison object, which can be a function object, or something as simple as a function pointer. It just needs to obey function syntax, and be able to return a boolean value given two input values of type T. The rules regarding its operation are the same as the rules for min() and max().

Return value

The first two algorithms in this chapter, min and max, return a reference to the minimum or maximum of two values. min_element and max_element assume that you not only want to know the value of an element in a sequence, but the object's position as well. To accomplish this, the function returns an iterator pointing to the minimum or maximum element, instead of returning the element itself.

Returning an iterator also has a nice side-effect; it gives you a feasible way to handle an empty input sequence. When this is the case, the iterator returned will be equal to last, which is clearly an out-of-range value.

Description

min_element finds the minimum element in a sequence, max_element the greatest. The code that does the job is found in algo.h, and is a straight-forward and easy-to-follow implementation. Note that the code doesn't actually keep track of the minimum or maximum element. Instead, it keeps track of the input iterator that points to the minimum element. The core code for min_element is shown here:

```
if ( first == last )
    return first;
InputIterator result = first;
while ( ++first != last )
    if ( *first < *result )
        result = first;
return result;
```

If you use the version of min_element that takes a comparison object, the code looks slightly different:

```
while (++first != last)
    if ( comp( *first, *result ) )
        result = first
```

Complexity

The time complexity of min_element and max_element is linear, in proportion to the length of the input sequence. Its space complexity is constant.

Example

Listing 19-2

min1902.cpp: A demonstration of the min_element algorithm

```
/*
 * MIN1902.CPP
 *
 * This program is used in Chapter 19 to demonstrate the min_element
 * algorithm. This program selects the minimum integer from a
 * selection read from cin.
 *
 * One interesting thing to note is that the istream_iterator
 * can be used in this algorithm. The iterator returned from
 * min_element() points to a valid copy of the minimum value,
 * even though the input stream has presumably all been read in.
 */


//
// Borland 4.x workarounds
//
#define __MINMAX_DEFINED
#pragma option -vi-

#include <iostream.h>
#include <algo.h>


int main()
{
    cout << "Enter a sequence of integers,\n"
         << "terminated by an EOF: ";
    cout << flush;

    istream_iterator<int,ptrdiff_t> ii( cin );
    istream_iterator<int,ptrdiff_t> ieof;
    istream_iterator<int,ptrdiff_t> result;

    result = min_element( ii, ieof );
    if ( result == ieof )
        cout << "Empty input sequence!\n";
    else
        cout << "Minimum value = "
             << *result
             << endl;
    return 0;
}
```

Example output:

```
Enter a sequence of integers,
terminated by an EOF:
1 2 3 4 -4 -3 -2 -1 ^D
Minimum value = -4
```

LEXICOGRAPHICAL_COMPARE

Function

```
template < class InputIterator1, class InputIterator2 >
bool lexicographical_compare( InputIterator1 first1,
                              InputIterator1 last1,
                              InputIterator2 first2,
                              InputIterator2 last2);

template < class InputIterator1,
           class InputIterator2,
           class Compare >
bool lexicographical_compare( InputIterator1 first1,
                              InputIterator1 last1,
                              InputIterator2 first2,
                              InputIterator2 last2,
                              Compare comp );
```

Arguments

first1, last1:   This function compares two sequences. first1 and last1 define the starting and ending points of the first input sequence.

first2, last2:   The starting and ending points of the second input sequence. Note that since this algorithm simply steps through the input sequences, one element at a time, both first2 and last2 can be input iterators.

comp: When comparing elements in the input sequence, this function normally uses operator<(). However, there will be times when you want to use something other than this operator to compare two elements. When this is the case, you can supply a comparison object.

The comparison object can be a function object, or something as simple as a function pointer. It just needs to obey function syntax, and be able to return a boolean value given two input values of type T.

Return value

The function returns true if the first sequence is less than the second sequence. If the first sequence is greater than or equal to the second sequence, the function returns false.

Description

Although this function has been blessed with a forbidding name, it performs a relatively simple task. It compares two sequences of elements in the same way that strcmp() compares two arrays of characters. The actual code used in the function is shown below:

```
while ( first1 != last1 && first2 != last2 )
{
    if ( *first1 < *first2 )
        return true;
    if ( *first2++ < *first1++ )
        return false;
}
return first1 == last1 && first2 != last2;
```

Starting at the first element in each sequence, the function performs a comparison of the two elements. If the element in the first sequence is smaller, it immediately returns true. If the second element is smaller, it immediately returns false. If neither comparison causes a return, the comparison moves on to the next object.

If the comparison continues until the end of one of the sequences is reached, it then returns true if the first sequence is shorter than the second; otherwise it returns false. And looking at the last line of the function above tells you what happens if the two sequences are identical: the function returns false. It only returns true when the first sequence is less than the second, not when the two are equal.

In the code above, you might note that the objects being compared only need to have operator<() defined for this function to work properly. And, like most of the other comparison functions in the STL, you can supply a comparison object which provides a customized comparison of your two objects.

Complexity

The time complexity of lexicographical_compare is linear, in proportion to the length of the input sequence. Its space complexity is constant.

Example

Listing 19-3

lex1903.cpp: A demonstration of the lexicographical_compare algorithm

```
/*
 * LEX1903.CPP
 *
 * This program is used in Chapter 19 to demonstrate the
 * lexicographical_compare function. I do this by creating
 * a functional equivalent of the stricmp() function, which
 * compares two input strings in a case-insensitive manner.
 */

//
// Borland 4.x workarounds.
//
#define __MINMAX_DEFINED
#pragma option -vi-

#include <iostream.h>
#include <string.h>
#include <ctype.h>
#include <algo.h>

bool comp( char a, char b )
{
    return toupper( a ) < toupper( b );
}

void my_stricmp( char *a, char *b )
```

```
    {
        bool result;
        result = lexicographical_compare( a, a + strlen( a ),
                                          b, b + strlen( b ),
                                          comp );
        cout << a
             << " is "
             << (result ? "less than " : "greater or equal to ")
             << b
             << endl;
    }

    int main()
    {
        my_stricmp( "Mark", "mark" );
        my_stricmp( "TEST", "test1" );
        my_stricmp( "test1", "test" );
        my_stricmp( "A", "Z" );
        return 0;
    }
```

Example output:

```
Mark is greater or equal to mark
TEST is less than test1
test1 is greater or equal to test
A is less than Z
```

NEXT_PERMUTATION

Function

```
template < class BidirectionalIterator >
bool next_permutation( BidirectionalIterator first,
                       BidirectionalIterator last);

template < class BidirectionalIterator, class Compare >
bool next_permutation( BidirectionalIterator first,
                       BidirectionalIterator last,
                       Compare comp );
```

Arguments

first: An iterator pointing to the start of a sequence. Note that both permutation functions require bidirectional iterators, since they have to traverse both directions through the input sequence.

last: An iterator that points one past the last member of the input sequence.

comp: The default version of next_permutation uses operator<() to order the elements in the sequence. If you need a different comparison function to order the elements, you can supply it using this parameter. comp should obey function syntax, and should return a boolean value when passed two objects of type T, where T is the type pointed to by the first and last iterators.

Return value

Both versions of next_permutation return true when they can generate a new permutation. The functions return false when all permutations have been generated, and the sequence is returned to its original ordered state.

Description

This algorithm is used to generate permutations. Given an ordered sequence, repeated calls to next_permutation will rearrange all the elements in the set in every possible way. For example, if a sequence originally was at { 0, 1, 2 }, repeated calls to next_permutation would generate the following sequence:

```
0, 2, 1
1, 0, 2
1, 2, 0
2, 0, 1
2, 1, 0
0, 1, 2
```

Notice that the last permutation generated returns the sequence to its original ordering. When next_permutation generates the last permutation, it returns a value of false to indicate that it has completed the job.

Since next_permutation doesn't get to retain any information between calls, it must be able to calculate the next permutation exclusively from the current ordering of the elements. Generating the next permutation requires one swap of a pair of elements, and a reversal of a sequence of elements that terminates at last. Calculating which iterators to swap and where the reversal sequence starts is what most of next_permutation is concerned with.

Complexity

The time complexity of next_permutation is linear, in proportion to the length of the input sequence. Its space complexity is constant.

Example

Listing 19-4

next1904.cpp: A demonstration of the next_permutation algorithm

```
/*
 * NEXT1904.CPP
 *
 * This program is used in Chapter 19 to demonstrate the
 * next_permutation algorithm. It generates all the
 * permutations of the first five letters of the alphabet.
 */

//
// Borland 4.x workarounds
//
#define __MINMAX_DEFINED
#pragma option -vi-

#include <iostream.h>
#include <algo.h>

int main()
{
    char data[] = "ABCDE";
        cout << data << " ";
        while ( next_permutation( data, data + 5 ) )
            cout << data << " ";
        return 0;
}
```

Example output:

```
ABCDE ABCED ABDCE ABDEC ABECD ABEDC ACBDE ACBED ACDBE
ACDEB ACEBD ACEDB ADBCE ADBEC ADCBE ADCEB ADEBC ADECB
AEBCD AEBDC AECBD AECDB AEDBC AEDCB BACDE BACED BADCE
BADEC BAECD BAEDC BCADE BCAED BCDAE BCDEA BCEAD BCEDA
BDACE BDAEC BDCAE BDCEA BDEAC BDECA BEACD BEADC BECAD
BECDA BEDAC BEDCA CABDE CABED CADBE CADEB CAEBD CAEDB
CBADE CBAED CBDAE CBDEA CBEAD CBEDA CDABE CDAEB CDBAE
CDBEA CDEAB CDEBA CEABD CEADB CEBAD CEBDA CEDAB CEDBA
DABCE DABEC DACBE DACEB DAEBC DAECB DBACE DBAEC DBCAE
DBCEA DBEAC DBECA DCABE DCAEB DCBAE DCBEA DCEAB DCEBA
DEABC DEACB DEBAC DEBCA DECAB DECBA EABCD EABDC EACBD
EACDB EADBC EADCB EBACD EBADC EBCAD EBCDA EBDAC EBDCA
ECABD ECADB ECBAD ECBDA ECDAB ECDBA EDABC EDACB EDBAC
EDBCA EDCAB EDCBA
```

Permuting five different letters generates 5! possible results, or 5*4*3*2*1, which is 120.

PREV_PERMUTATION

Function

```
template < class BidirectionalIterator >
bool prev_permutation( BidirectionalIterator first,
                       BidirectionalIterator last );

template < class BidirectionalIterator, class Compare >
bool prev_permutation( BidirectionalIterator first,
                       BidirectionalIterator last,
                       Compare comp );
```

Arguments

first: An iterator pointing to the start of a sequence. Note that both permutation functions require bidirectional iterators, as they have to traverse both directions through the input sequence.

last: An iterator that points one past the last member of the input sequence.

comp: The default version of prev_permutation uses operator<() to order the elements in the sequence. If you need a different comparison function to order the elements, you can supply it using this parameter. comp should obey function syntax, and should return a boolean value when passed two objects of type T, where T is the type pointed to by the first and last iterators.

Return value

Both versions of prev_permutation return true when they can generate a new permutation. The functions return false when all permutations have been generated, and the sequence is returned to its original ordered state.

Description

prev_permutation is the mirror twin of next_permutation. Instead of generating the next permutation in a sequence, it generates the previous permutation. Like next_permutation, it manages to do this without retaining any information about the state of the permutation between successive calls.

Note also that, like next_permutation, this function normally uses operator<() to order the elements in the sequence. You can override this by providing a comparison object as the third argument to prev_permutation.

Complexity

The time complexity of prev_permutation is linear, in proportion to the length of the input sequence. Its space complexity is constant.

Example

Listing 19-5

prev1905.cpp: A demonstration of the prev_permutation algorithm

```
/*
 * PREV1905.CPP
 *
 * This program is used in Chapter 19 to demonstrate the
 * prev_permutation algorithm. It generates all the
 * different permutations of three ones and two zeroes.
 */
```

```
//
// Borland 4.x workarounds
//
#define __MINMAX_DEFINED
#pragma option -vi-

#include <iostream.h>
#include <algo.h>

bool comp( char a, char b )
{
    return a <= b;
}

int main()
{
    char data[] = "11100";
    cout << data << endl;
    while ( prev_permutation( data, data + 5, comp ) )
        cout << data << endl;
    return 0;
}
```

Example output:

```
11100
11010
11001
10110
10101
10011
01110
01101
01011
00111
```

The number of permutations of three objects and two objects is 5! / (3! * 2!), or 120/12. The above list shows that the correct number of permutations has been generated.

CLASS REFERENCE

20

Knowledge is of two kinds. We know a subject ourselves, or we know where we can find information upon it.

— Samuel Johnson

In this first chapter, you'll find straightforward reference information about the public interface to the STL classes and containers. For detailed examples and explanations of how to use the containers, see Chapters 4 through 8.

We'll begin with a quick look at how the current STL distribution differs from the ANSI/ISO specification. After that, this rather lengthy chapter gives reference information for each STL container, beginning with vector<T>; public data and function members of the class are described, and there are notes about some of the more important private members. (Note that these private members are the ones found in the public HP implementation. Different implementations may or may not use the same members.)

WORKAROUNDS: DEVIATIONS FROM THE SPEC

The current distribution of the STL has to deviate from the specification in a few areas. This is due to the fact that most of today's C++ compilers don't support all the features the ANSI/ISO committee has defined for the language.

Default template arguments

All STL containers have a class definition that starts like this:

```
template <class T, template <class U> class Allocator = allocator>
class vector {
```

This means vector<T> should have two template arguments and could, perhaps, be called vector<T,U>. The second argument is the type of the memory allocator used by the class, with a default of class Allocator.

Although this is legal ANSI C++ (as defined today), it is not supported by most compilers. While we wait for templates to have default arguments, existing implementations of the STL must use the C++ preprocessor to select an allocator.

The way to select an allocator in HP's public implementation of the STL is to define the macro *Allocator* to the appropriate class name, before including the header files that define the container. If the macro Allocator is not defined, the header file will use the default allocator. Otherwise, it will use the one defined by the user.

Example file all2001.cpp uses this technique to select the far memory allocator in a small model program. The program first includes the header file faralloc.h, which defines class far_allocator. This class definition isn't enough, though. Before including vector.h, you must define macro Allocator to be a far_allocator.

Note that this workaround is a temporary matter. As C++ compilers come into compliance with the ANSI/ISO specification, this kind of tinkering won't be necessary. Also, your vendor's implementation of the STL may have other solutions to this problem that differ from the one I've described here.

Listing 20-1

all2001.cpp: Demonstrating the way to select a different allocator

```
//
// ALL2001.CPP
//
// This example program is used in Chapter 20 to
// show how allocators are defined in the STL. At some
// point in the future, allocators will be defined
// for objects by way of a second argument to the
```

```
// constructor. The default allocator will be
// defined as the default type used by the class.
// However, default types for templates are not available
// for most compilers at this time, so you have to
// select the allocator using a macro.

//
// Borland 4.x workarounds
//
#define __MINMAX_DEFINED
#pragma option -vi-

//
// Allocator selection is done here.
//
#include <faralloc.h>
//
// The following line must be present *before* you
// include vector.h.!
//
#define Allocator far_allocator

#include <vector.h>
#include <iostream.h>
#include <iomanip.h>

main()
{
    vector<double> a( 8000 );
    vector<double> *b[ 20 ];

    for ( int i = 0; i < 20 ; i++ ) {
        cout << "Allocating number " << i << "\n";
        b[ i ] = new vector<double>( a );
    }
    return 1;
}
```

Normally, a small model program using the default versions of new and delete under MS-DOS can't allocate more than 65K of data memory. This poses an immediate problem for all2001.cpp, since a vector of doubles 8000 entries long is already 64000 bytes in length. Even worse, this program tries to make 20 copies of that 64000-byte vector! In fact, if you try to run all2001.cpp compiled for the small model, without selecting the far allocator, it fails to even allocate vector *a*.

But when compiled as shown above, even the small model code is able to keep seven of these big vectors on hand, as its output shows:

```
Allocating number 0
Allocating number 1
Allocating number 2
Allocating number 3
Allocating number 4
Allocating number 5
Allocating number 6
out of memory
```

The ease with which different memory models can be used is one of the most powerful features designed into the STL. The fact that it is so easy to do, even with this slightly clumsy workaround, is a testament to good design.

Until C++ compilers are updated to work around this problem, you will have to take these somewhat awkward measures to use the far allocator in a small model program. What's worse, once you do this, *every* container you select in this module will use the far memory model. Nonetheless, these inconveniences should be short-lived, since there is a strong incentive for compiler makers to update their products.

Template member functions

Several of the member functions in the container classes are actually template functions themselves. For example, vector <T> parameterized has a constructor that takes two iterator arguments to define an initialization range:

```
template<class InputIterator>
vector(InputIterator first,
       InputIterator last,
       Allocator&=Allocator());
```

Most C++ compilers don't support template member functions yet. (Remember that the constructor is a member function too! Until they do, your implementation of this function will probably look something like this instead:

```
vector(const_iterator first,
       const_iterator last,
       Allocator&=Allocator());
```

This stripped-down version of the constructor lets you construct a new vector from a range of elements in an existing vector, but not from a different container type. This limitation will be lifted as compilers bring themselves into compliance with the C++ specification.

The remainder of this chapter gives a container-by-container reference to the public interface of the STL.

VECTOR<T>

Typedefs

The STL uses a number of standard type definitions that it shares across various containers and functions. The typedefs provide a uniform interface for algorithms to access the containers. For example, we know we can always iterate through a container by writing a *for* loop that looks like this:

```
for ( container<T>::iterator i = x.begin();
      i != x.end();
      i++ )
   ...
```

This works because all the container classes have a typedef statement declaring the type iterator. Imagine how counter-productive it would be for each class to have its own names for various standardized types!

The following type definitions are found in the standard STL header file vector.h.

```
typedef T value_type;
typedef vector_allocator::pointer iterator;
typedef vector_allocator::const_pointer const_iterator;
typedef vector_allocator::reference reference;
typedef vector_allocator::const_reference const_reference;
typedef vector_allocator::size_type size_type;
typedef vector_allocator::difference_type difference_type;
typedef reverse_iterator<const_iterator,
                 value_type,
                 const_reference,
                 difference_type>  const_reverse_iterator;
typedef reverse_iterator<iterator,
                 value_type,
                 reference,
                 difference_type> reverse_iterator;
```

Quite a few of these type definitions won't be used much in day-to-day programming. You'll get the most mileage out of the four iterator definitions.

value_type

```
typedef T value_type;
```

value_type is a synonym for type T, the template parameter for vector<T>. value_type is frequently used in template functions to pass the *type* of a parameter, rather than its *value*.

iterator

```
typedef vector_allocator::pointer iterator;
```

This is one of the more important types defined for vector<T>. Iterators are the primary means we have to access objects in the STL, with vector<T> being no exception to the rule.

This type definition defines an iterator for vector<T> as a pointer in the Allocator class. It is possible to do pointer-like things with it, such as using operator[], without paying a heavy price. And, by this definition, it fills all the requirements of a random access iterator, the most powerful class of iterator.

Note that for a vector, pointers and iterators have the same type definition. This is a consequence of the design of a vector. Since the vector storage is laid out in a contiguous block of memory, normal pointer operations will all work properly.

const_iterator

```
typedef vector_allocator::const_pointer const_iterator;
```

A const_iterator is simply an iterator that refers to a const object. Other than that, its behavior is identical to a standard iterator.

reference

```
typedef vector_allocator::reference reference;
```

A reference is defined in vector.h as identical to a reference for vector_allocator. Normally, the allocator class will define a reference as T&. A reference is returned when you dereference an iterator.

const_reference

```
typedef vector_allocator::const_reference const_reference;
```

A const_reference is the same as a reference, except it returns a reference to a const object.

size_type

```
typedef vector_allocator::size_type size_type;
```

This type defines the size of the largest object that can be created by vector_allocator. For example, if vector<T> is defined using a standard memory model under MS-DOS, size_type is a synonym for the ANSI C type size_t. This will usually be an unsigned int. An unsigned int can hold the largest value passed as the size parameter to malloc().

difference_type

```
typedef vector_allocator::difference_type difference_type;
```

This is another type defined by the allocator. difference_type is used to hold the difference between two pointers in the current allocator. Under MS-DOS standard memory models, this is defined as ptrdiff_t.

reverse_iterator

```
typedef reverse_iterator<iterator,
                         value_type,
                         reference,
                         difference_type> reverse_iterator;
```

The template class *reverse_iterator* creates a new iterator type. In the STL class, reverse_iterator is known as an iterator adaptor. By providing the correct template arguments, this definition creates a new iterator type, which is used to traverse containers in the reverse direction. The definition of the reverse iterator class is found in iterator.h, and is discussed in detail in Chapter 9, "Allocators."

A quick example of iterating in the reverse direction through a container illustrates how typedef reverse_iterator can be used:

```
for (vector<char>::reverse_iterator ri = a.rbegin();
     ri != r.rend();
     ri++ )
    cout << *ri;
```

This code might take some getting used to. Just remember that reverse iterators act like normal iterators in your program. Iteration starts at rbegin() and ends at rend(). You move through the container using operator++(), and you dereference the iterators as usual. The only difference is that all of this takes place in reverse.

const_reverse_iterator

```
typedef reverse_iterator<const_iterator,
                         value_type,
                         const_reference,
                         difference_type>  const_reverse_iterator;
```

This type definition is identical to reverse_iterator, except it creates a reverse_iterator that returns a reference to a constant object.

Important data members

```
Allocator<T> allocator;
iterator start;
iterator finish;
iterator end_of_storage;
```

Remember that these data members are implementation-specific, and are not mentioned in the ANSI/ISO specification.

Allocator<T> allocator

The Allocator class for this template provides a complete interface for memory management, including allocation and freeing of memory, and the use of pointers. Each instance of vector<T> has an allocator object, used to encapsulate memory operations.

As this is a private data member, it won't be used in your programs. However, it is very important to understand the role the allocator plays in the operation of container classes.

iterator start

This private data member points to the start of the raw storage area allocated for objects in the vector<T> object. If no storage has been allocated, the iterator is assigned the singular value 0.

This iterator is not accessible outside the class, but its value can be returned by calling vector<T>::begin().

iterator finish

This private data member points one element past the last element in use in the raw storage area. For example, if vector<char> a has been initialized with three elements, using the push_back() function, finish will point to *a*+4. If no storage has been allocated, finish will have the singular value 0. If storage has been allocated, but no elements have been stored in the container, finish will equal start, and both will point to the start of the array.

This iterator is not accessible outside the class, but its value can be returned by calling vector<T>::end().

iterator end_of_storage

This private data member points one element past the end of the raw storage allocated for the vector. Its value is initialized in the constructors of vector<T>, and in any operation—such as insert()—that causes new storage to be allocated or freed. If no storage has been allocated, end_of_storage is set to the singular value 0.

This iterator is not accessible outside the class. Its value can be inferred by calling member function capacity(), using code similar to this:

```
vector<int>::iterator get_end_ptr( vector<int> &a )
{
  vector<int>::iterator eos;
  eos = a.begin() + a.capacity();
  return eos;
}
```

Copy, construct, destroy

```
vector(Allocator&=Allocator());
vector(size_type n, const T& value = T(),Allocator&=Allocator());
vector(const vector<T>& x,Allocator&=Allocator());
vector(InputIterator first,
       InputIterator last,
       Allocator&=Allocator());
~vector();
vector<T>& operator=(const vector<T>& x);
assign(InputIterator first,InputIterator last);
assign(Size n, const T& t=T());
```

vector<T> has four different constructors, the required destructor, and an assignment operator. These are all public functions and are intended for use as appropriate. In addition, it has a pair of assign() functions that perform the equivalent of operator=() for different data types.

The ANSI/ISO committee made one last-minute change to the constructors for all containers defined in the STL. Each of these constructs had a single parameter added to their argument list, which allows you to pass a specific allocator for use by that object. If you don't specify an allocator (and under normal circumstances, you won't), one is constructed for you using the default allocator constructor.

vector(Allocator&=Allocator())

The default constructor creates a new empty vector<T> object. It either constructs an anonymous allocator, or uses one that you specify as the constructor's sole argument.

This is the default constructor for objects of type vector<T>. It doesn't allocate any memory, so the initial values of start, finish, and end_of_storage are set to 0. The first time a call to push_back() or insert() is made, memory will be allocated to store elements of type T in the vector.

```
int main()
{
    vector<char *> a;
    a.push_back( "Testing" );
...
```

vector(size_type n, const T& value = T(),
Allocator&=Allocator())

This constructor creates a vector<T> with *n* initial elements. The constructor first allocates storage for exactly *n* elements of type T. It allocates the raw storage, then initializes each of the storage areas with the same element. Initialization is done by using the copy constructor to type T, via a call to uninitialized_copy().

Say there is a newly created vector<T>. When can the initial value copied into each element be defined? Only when a second argument to this constructor is specified. If no argument is specified, the default constructor is called to provide a seed value for all the newly created elements.

```
int foo()
{
    vector<String> *sv;
    sv = new vector<String>( 25 );
...
```

vector(const vector<T>& x, Allocator&=Allocator())

The copy constructor creates a new vector that is a copy of the vector<T> parameter, whose elements are identical to those in the source vector *x*.

First, enough raw memory is allocated to store exactly the required number of elements in the new vector. Then each object in the new raw storage is created by using the copy constructor for type T. This is done with the template function uninitialized_copy().

```
vector<foo> *clone( const vector<foo>& x )
{
    vector<foo> *new_vec;
    new_vec = new vector<foo>( x );
    return new_vec;
}
```

template<class InputIterator>
vector(InputIterator first, InputIterator last,
Allocator&=Allocator())

This final constructor for vector<T> copies a range of items from an existing container of any type. It accepts two iterators of type T as its only arguments. They define a range of elements by using the canonical form for the STL. This means the *first* should reference the *first* element in the range, and *last* should point *one past* the last element.

The constructor allocates enough raw storage to hold all elements specified by the range from *first* to *last*. It then calls the copy constructor for each of the elements, using uninitialized_copy().

This template function calls the constructor for the objects by using the placement syntax, which allows the constructor to operate on uninitialized memory.

```
char *p = "Initial data";

int foo()
{
    vector<char> a( p, p + strlen( p ) );
...
```

Note: This is a template member function. Your implementation of the STL may substitute the following function:

```
vector( const_iterator first,
        const_iterator last,
        Allocator&=Allocator()  )
```

~vector()

The destructor for vector<T> frees storage and destroys objects. It has two jobs to do. First, it goes through all the memory currently allocated for the vector (the range between start and finish) and calls the destructor for each element in that range. This is done with the destroy() function, defined as part of the allocator.

Second, once all elements in the vector have been destroyed, the destructor has to free the memory. This is achieved by a call to the deallocate() member function of the allocator. When that is taken care of, the destructor's job is finished.

```
void draw()
{
    vector<shape> shape_v;
    shape_v.push_back( circle() );
    shape_v.push_back( ellipse() );
    ...
    delete shape_v;
}
```

vector<T>& operator=(const vector<T>& x)

The assignment operator copies one vector into another. Its job appears to be identical to the copy constructor. But this function is made more complicated because the existing object may already have storage allocated that contains existing objects. If this is the case, that storage may have to be deleted, and those objects may have to be destroyed.

The assignment operator directs its work into one of three possible directions:

- If the existing vector (*this* in C++ lingo) doesn't have enough storage space allocated to hold a copy of *x*, the operator destroys any existing objects in *this*, deletes their storage, allocates exactly enough new storage to hold a copy of *x*, then performs an uninitialized_copy() function call. That function call will execute the copy constructor for each copy to be made.

- If the existing vector already holds the same or more objects than *x*, all the objects of *x* are copied into the current storage of *this*, and any remaining objects past the length of *x* in *this* are destroyed. The objects that were overwritten aren't destroyed, because they will have had any cleanup performed in the assignment operation.

- Finally, if the existing vector has space, but holds fewer objects than *x*, a slightly different approach is taken: all existing objects have their new values copied from *x*. Then, all remaining raw memory objects are created from *x* using uninitialized_copy().

Regardless of the approach, when it's all over, the start and finish members are updated to reflect the new length.

Finally, the function returns a reference to the resulting vector.

```
vector<employee> staff;
staff = *old_staff;
delete old_staff;
...
```

template<class InputIterator>
void assign(InputIterator first, InputIterator last)

This template member function is nearly identical to the assignment operator: it erases any existing elements in the container, then copies an input range into the now-empty container.

```
deque<int> a;
vector<int> b;
     .
     .
     .
b.assign( a + 2, a + 5 );
```

Note: This is a template member function. Your compiler may have to substitute the following function:

```
void assign(const_iterator first, const_iterator last)
```

template<class Size, class T>
void assign(Size n, const T& t = T())

This assign command initializes the vector with a set of *n* copies of object *t*. If you don't specify an object of type T, a default constructor makes one for you to copy. This function will erase all elements in the vector before inserting the *n* copies of *t*.

```
names.assign( 100, string( "" ) );
```

Note: This is a template member function. Your compiler may have to substitute the following function:

```
void assign(size_type n, value_type& t = value_type() )
```

Iterators

```
iterator begin();
const_iterator begin() const;
iterator end();
const_iterator end() const;
reverse_iterator rbegin();
const_reverse_iterator rbegin() const;
reverse_iterator rend();
const_reverse_iterator rend() const;
```

The member functions listed here all return iterator types. They are used to provide the functions needed to iterate through the container.

Note: Most of these functions come in pairs: a const and non-const version. The const version is used to access elements in an object that has been declared to be const.

```
int sum_odd( const vector<int> &x )
{
    int sum = 0;
    for ( vector<int>::const_iterator i = x.begin();
          i != x.end();
          i++ )
        if ( *i & 1 )
            sum += *i;
    return sum;
}
```

An example of where the const version vector<T>::begin() might be called is shown above. Since the vector argument to function sum_odd() is declared to be const, the compiler selects the const version of begin(). The code fragment shown here is aware of that fact, since it is using a const_iterator type to hold the iterator. If you attempt to use a vector<int>::iterator instead, the compiler generates a warning message.

iterator begin()
const_iterator begin() const

begin() is one of the most commonly used functions in the container classes. It returns an iterator that points to the location of the first element in the vector. The iterator can be dereferenced using either the dereferencing operator, or operator[].

Note: If begin() returns the singular value 0, it indicates that no storage space has been allocated for the vector. If the value of begin() is equal to the value returned by end(), the vector has allocated storage, but has not created any objects. In either case, the iterator returned by begin() should not be dereferenced.

```
void dump( vector<int> &a )
{
    vector<int>::iterator i;
    for ( i = 0 ; i != a.end() ; i++ )
        printf( "%d ", *i );
    printf( "\n" );
}
```

iterator end()
const_iterator end() const

vector<T>::end() provides the counterpoint to the begin() function. Any time you want to iterate through a container, start with the iterator returned by begin(), and terminate when that iterator has been incremented to the point where it equals end().

Note: The const version of end() is used whenever you call end() for a const version of vector<T>.

When testing for the end of a vector, you must test for equality with end(), not for less than end(). The less-than operator for iterators may be undefined, or it may be meaningless. In either case, when the iterator is equal to end(), as defined by operator==(), you have gone past the end of the vector, and it's time to terminate.

Testing for equality versus vector<T>::end() has one good side-effect: in the event that a vector<T> doesn't have any storage allocated yet, end() will return the singular value 0. Fortunately, in this situation, begin() will return 0 as well, so the standard iteration loop will still work properly. It isn't necessary to create a special test case for empty vectors.

```
void print( char *start, char *end )
{
    while ( start != end )
        cout << *start++;
}

void foo( vector<char> & a )
{
    print( a.begin(), a.end() );
}
```

reverse_iterator rbegin()
const_reverse_iterator rbegin() const

Reverse iterators are created by using the reverse_iterator<> iterator adaptor. A reverse iterator looks and acts exactly like a forward iterator, but works its way through the container from finish to start, instead of in the normal start-to-finish order.

Reverse iterators need to be initialized with reverse iterator values, so you shouldn't try to use vector<T>::begin() to start an iterative loop. Use this function instead, which returns a reverse iterator.

```
typedef vector<char> Rstring;

ostream &operator << ( ostream&s, Rstring &x )
{
    Rstring::reverse_iterator ri = x.rbegin();
    while ( ri != x.rend() )
        cout << *ri++;
    return s;
}
```

```
main()
{
    char *s = "Testing";
    Rstring r( s, s + strlen( s ) );

    cout << r << endl;
    return 0;
}
```

Normally, the iterator returned by this function will refer to the last element stored in the vector. In the event that no storage space has been allocated, rbegin() will be equal to the singular value 0. If the vector has storage space allocated, but has no elements initialized at this time, rbegin() will be equal to rend().

reverse_iterator rend()

const_reverse_iterator rend() const

vector<T>::rend() corresponds to the rbegin() function in the same manner that vector<T>::end() corresponds to begin(). If the vector has no storage allocated, rend() will be equal to the singular value 0 when tested with operator==(). In the event that storage has been allocated, but no elements exist, rend() will be equal to rbegin().

```
void psize( vector<double> & x )
{
    cout << "x contains "
        << x.rend() - x.rbegin()
        << " elements";
}
```

Capacity

```
size_type size() const;
size_type max_size() const;
size_type capacity() const;
bool empty() const;
void resize(size_type sz, T c = T() );
void reserve(size_type n );
```

These functions don't affect the contents of the vectors, with the possible exception of resize. Instead, they deal with the storage management features of the vector. For example, they can return information about the amount of data, either present in the vector, or that can be placed into the vector.

size_type size() const

size() returns the current count of elements present in the vector. This is the same number you would get if you calculated the value of end() - begin().

```
for ( i = 0 ; i < a.size() ; i++ )
    cout << a[ i ];
```

size_type max_size() const

Although max_size() is a member of vector<T>, it is a function defined by the allocator currently used by vector<T>. max_size() calculates how many elements of type T could fit into the largest vector possible, using the appropriate allocator, and returns that number.

If you are building a vector<double> object under any MS-DOS implementation that limits objects to 64K, vector<double>::max_size() should return 8192.

```
void zero( vector<int> &a, int n )
{
    if ( n > a.max_size() ) {
        cerr << "Sorry, can't do it!\n";
        return;
    }
    ....
```

It's important to remember that this function doesn't say anything about how reasonable your allocation is. For example, max_size() might indicate that you could create a 1G-byte character vector on a 32-bit computer, but this doesn't mean there is enough memory available to fulfill the request. Even worse, a machine with virtual memory might fill the request, but slow to a crawl due to incessant disk swapping. max_size() is simply a measure of the theoretical capacity of a particular container/allocator combination.

size_type capacity() const

This function determines the current capacity of the vector, given the size of the raw storage area presently allocated. This can be calculated by end_of_storage - start. Since end_of_storage is a private member, you must use this function to calculate how many objects can be inserted into the vector.

```
vector<foo> a( 100 );
assert( a.capacity() == 100 );
```

bool empty() const

vector<T>::empty() tests if the vector contains any constructed elements. If it does, this function returns a false value; otherwise it returns true.

```
cout << "vector a is "
     << ( a.empty() ? "" : "not ";
     << "empty\n";
```

void reserve(size_type n)

vector<T>::reserve() doesn't modify any of the elements in an existing vector. It is called to ensure the reserved raw storage has enough room to hold at least *n* elements. If the vector doesn't have that room available (as measured by the capacity() function), more space will be allocated. The allocation will cause a round of allocation activity. If you know in advance how much space has to be allocated, you're better off performing the allocation and copying when the vector has few or no elements stored in it.

```
main( int argc, char *argv[] )
{
    vector<string> a;
    if ( strcmp( argv[ 1 ], "Employees" ) == 0 )
        a.reserve( 1000 );
    else if ( strcmp( argv[ 1 ], "Management" ) == 0 )
        a.reserve( 100 );
    else if ( strcmp( argv[ 1 ], "President" ) == 0 )
        a.reserve( 1 );
    ...
```

void resize(size_type sz, T c = T())

vector<T>::resize is similar to, but not identical, to reserve(). The ANSI/ISO
specification gives a short piece of code to describe the effects of this function:

```
if ( sz > size() )
    s.insert( s.end(), s.size() - sz, c );
else if ( sz < size() )
    s.erase( a.begin() + sz, s.end() );
```

This code shows us that resize() has three courses of action. The first
parameter indicates the desired size of the element after the function completes.
So if the resize() function is asking for an increase in the number of
elements in the vector, the function adds enough copies of c to change the
vector's size to sz. On the other hand, if resize() is asking for a decrease in
the size of the vector, the appropriate number of elements is removed from
the end of the vector.

If the desired size is the same as the present size of the vector, no action
is taken.

```
inline void make_string_fit( vector<char>& s, int n )
{
    s.resize( n, ' ' );
}
```

Element access

```
reference operator[](size_type n);
const_reference operator[](size_type n) const;
const_reference at(size_type n) const;
reference at( size_type n);
reference front();
const_reference front() const;
reference back();
const_reference back() const;
```

Element access functions are used to access individual elements in the
container. Although these functions can modify the contents of a particular
element, they don't ever cause any resizing or new allocations of memory.
Because of this, you will never invalidate an iterator pointing into your container
by simply using one of these functions.

reference operator[](size_type n)

const_reference operator[](size_type n) const

const_reference at(size_type n) const

reference at(size_type n)

One of the advantages of working with vector<T> is that it has the random-access property; that is, any element of the vector can be accessed by using operator[]. This isn't the case with other containers, where you can only reach a particular element through a process of iteration.

operator[] gives objects of vector<T> the syntax and semantics of ordinary C arrays, except for one slight difference. Ordinarily, a C array can accept an index that is an unsigned integer, or size_t. This is not the case for STL containers. The index passed as an argument to operator[] is defined by the memory allocator in use for that object.

The type of the index operator is thus defined as being a size_type object. size_type is a typedef defined according to the size_type definition from the allocator.

```
vector<foo> a;
...
for ( int i = 0;
      i < a.size( );
      i++ )
   cout << "tag = " << a[ i ];
```

The two at() functions shown here do the same thing as operator[](), but with one important added feature: both functions throw an exception if the size argument is greater than the size of the container.

reference front()

const_reference front() const

The vector<T> member functions front() and back() correspond to the begin() and end() functions. But instead of returning an iterator that references the first and last members of a vector, front() and back() return an actual reference to those values. This provides a quick way to get at the first and last members of a vector.

Unless you have a version of the STL with added bounds checking, you have to ensure front() is only called when the first element of the array actually exists. If you call it for a vector that hasn't allocated any storage space, front() will probably attempt to dereference a null pointer, with results that will vary from system to system. (The results may vary, but you can count on them being unpleasant!)

```
cout << "First value = "
     << a.front()
     << endl;
```

reference back()

const_reference back() const

vector<T>::back() returns a reference to the last element in a vector. If the vector has no elements allocated, the results of back() will be undetermined.

Note: This function provides a capability that either doesn't exist with standard C arrays, or has to be implemented by hand. This is particularly useful in string-like classes made from vector<char>.

```
template<class T>
void reverse_purge( vector<T> &a )
{
    while ( a.size() > 0 ) {
        cout << a.back();
        a.pop_back();
    }
}
```

Modifiers

The functions in this section not only modify individual elements of the vector, they may also modify internal data members such as first or last. This means that when you invoke most of these functions, any outstanding iterators into the container should be considered invalid.

```
void push_back(const T& x);
void pop_back();
void swap(vector<T>& x);
iterator insert(iterator position, const T& x);
void insert( iterator position,
             const_iterator first,
             const_iterator last);
```

```
void insert (iterator position, size_type n, const T& x);
void insert(iterator position,
            InputIterator first,
            InputIterator last );
void erase(iterator position);
void erase(iterator first, iterator last);
```

If the complex access functions cause a memory allocation to occur, they can also cause the raw storage holding the vector to be reallocated, resulting in a bulk copy operation. With these functions, you need to be particularly careful about dangling iterators that can result when a memory allocation takes place.

Any iterators that point into a vector will be invalid after an allocation takes place. If you are writing code that needs to work properly through allocations, you might need to use operator[] with an index instead. As long as new objects are added *after* the index, this method will be safe.

void push_back(const T& x)

vector<T>::push_back() provides one of the specialized functions that the vector container is good at: adding an element to the end of the list. vector<T> can add elements to the end of the list in constant amortized time. Just divide the total time required by the number of elements added. This will average the work needed to add an object to the end of the vector to a constant value.

Whenever the vector runs out of memory, there is a single insertion that takes O(N) time, due to memory resizing (where N is the current number of elements). The next N insertions will each take a fixed amount of time. When the total effort is averaged (amortized) over the number of insertions, the average time is constant. Thus, the STL specification refers to functions like these as having a *constant amortized time complexity*.

push_back() uses the allocator template function construct() to create a new object in the empty raw storage space at the end of the vector. If finish is equal to end_of_storage at the time of the request, a memory allocation operation has to take place. In either case, the copy constructor performs the eventual initialization of the raw memory.

```
void fill_fib( int n, vector<int> &a )
{
    a.push_back( 1 );
    a.push_back( 1 );
    for ( int i = 0 ; i < ( n - 2 ) ; i++ )
        a.push_back( a.back() + a[ a.size() - 2 ] );
}
```

void pop_back()

pop_back() destroys the last element of the vector. Be aware that it makes
no attempt to verify that the vector contains at least one element. If you
call pop_back() on an empty vector, you will be left with an object in an
invalid state. After pop_back() has been called, both size() and end() will
be decremented.

pop_back() decrements the finish member of the vector, and calls allocator function destroy() to execute the destructor for the object. It doesn't try
to free any storage, regardless of how much is being wasted.

If you want to recover wasted space from a vector that is mostly empty,
the best way is to copy it into a new vector. The copy operation will only
allocate as much space as is needed. You can then delete the old vector and
free the resources it is using.

```
while ( a.size() > 0 )
    a.pop_back();
```

void swap(vector<T>& x)

swap() performs a complete swap between two vectors. Because of the internal
structure of vector<T>, this is a very easy operation. You only have to swap the
three private data members of the two vectors: start, finish, and end_of_storage.

Keep in mind that, after the two vectors have been swapped, any dangling iterators pointing into either vector will be invalid, or at a minimum,
slightly confused. An iterator that pointed to element 1 of vector *a* will still
point to the same element after the swap. The problem is, that element will
now be in vector *b*!

```
struct invoices {
    vector<entries> records;
    currency total;
};
...
void sort_receivables( invoices inv[], int n )
{
...
    if ( inv[ i ].total < inv[ j ].total ) {
        inv[ i ].records.swap( inv[ j ].records );
        swap( inv[ i ].total, inv[ j ].total );
    }
...
}
```

iterator insert(iterator position, const T& x)

template<InputIterator>
void insert(iterator position, InputIterator first, InputIterator last)

void insert (iterator position, size_type n, const T& x)

The three different insert functions correspond to the three different vector<T> constructor operations (ignoring the default constructor). Each version of insert() uses its first argument to indicate where the insertion will take place. To insert a new object at the very start of a vector, use the begin() function to provide the insertion point iterator. To add data to the end of a vector, use the end() iterator.

The three functions differ in the type of argument(s) used to specify exactly what is to be inserted:

- const T& x indicates that a single element is to be inserted.

- InputIterator first, InputIterator last indicates a range of elements to be inserted. As always, first will point to the first element to be inserted, and last will point one past the last element.

- size_type n, const T& x indicates that multiple copies of a single object are to be inserted.

Each function has to open up additional storage space to handle new entries. A new memory allocation may be needed, invalidating any dangling iterators. The new elements will be filled in, either by the assignment operator or by the copy constructor, depending on their location in the destination vector.

One of these insert operations returns an iterator, while the others have a void return type. vector<T>::insert(const T& x) returns an iterator that points to the position where the new element was inserted into the vector.

Any insertion operation can exact a high cost. If you insert into a vector that doesn't have any storage space, you'll have to perform a reallocation. Not only must a new block of memory be allocated, but N copy constructors and N destructors must be executed, followed by a memory deallocation.

The cost of this series of events will vary tremendously. It depends on the specifics of the class of object being inserted. Whenever you work with vector<T>, you should be acutely aware of the cost of executing your constructors, assignment operators, and destructors; they will have a great bearing on your performance.

```
char *p = "Insert this at the front";
vector<char> s;
s.insert( s.begin(), 'A' );
s.insert( s.begin(), p, p + strlen( p ) );
s.insert( s.end(), 100, ' ' );
```

Note: The template version of insert may not be supported by your compiler. If this is the case, you will probably have a replacement non-template function that looks like this:

```
void insert( iterator position,
             const_iterator first,
             const_iterator last );
```

The replacement function restricts you to inserting elements from other vectors, instead of elements from any container.

void erase(iterator position)
void erase(iterator first, iterator last)

Like pop_back(), the two erase() functions remove one or more elements from the vector. But unlike pop_back(), they can remove elements from *any* position in the array. This requires considerably more internal work than just deleting the last element of the vector.

These functions do their work in two steps:

- copy the remaining elements after the erasure sequence, to fill the gap created by removing one or more elements
- call the destructor for all slack elements left behind at the end of the vector

The first version of erase() shown here removes a single element from the vector. Note that no range checking is done on the iterator passed in. If the iterator is equal to or greater than end(), the resulting vector will be in an invalid state.

The second version of erase() erases a range of elements from a vector. As usual, the range is defined with first pointing to the first element in the range, and last pointing *one past* the last element to be erased. No range checking will be done on either of these iterators, so it's up to you to ensure they are valid.

```
vector<int> a;
for ( i = 0 ; i < 100 ; i++ )
    a.push_back( i );
a.erase( a.begin() );
a.erase( a.begin() + 10, a.end() );
```

Relational/equality operators

```
template <class T>
bool operator==(const vector<T>& x, const vector<T>& y);

template <class T>
bool operator<(const vector<T>& x, const vector<T>& y);
```

These two functions compare two vectors. The equality operator only returns true if the two vectors have the same number of elements, and all elements are equal. The second function performs a lexicographical (string) comparison of the two vectors, and returns the result.

Note: For a definition of a lexicographical comparison, see two sections below.

template <class T>
bool operator==(const vector<T>& x, const vector<T>& y)

This operator provides an easy way to test whether or not two vectors are equal. First, it compares the size() for both vectors. If they are unequal, false is returned immediately. If the sizes are the same, the two vectors are compared element by element, using the template function equal().

This function uses operator==() for function T to compare elements one at a time. If all elements compare as equal, a true value is returned; otherwise false is returned.

```
void duplicate( vector<foo*> &fp )
{
    vector<foo*> nfp;
    nfp = fp;
    if ( nfp == fp )
        cout << "Assignment operator worked!\n";
}
```

template <class T>
bool operator<(const vector<T>& x, const vector<T>& y)

The previous function had a fairly easy job deciding if two vectors are equal. This function has a harder time of it. To see if one vector is considered to be less than another, we have to perform a lexicographical comparison. This is an element-by-element comparison similar to a string comparison in the standard C library using strcmp().

operator<() doesn't do any work itself; it passes iterators into both vectors to one of the STL standard algorithms, lexicographical_compare(). This function steps through the two vectors one element at a time, and returns a value based on the following code:

```
template <class InputIterator1, class InputIterator2>
bool lexicographical_compare(InputIterator1 first1,
                             InputIterator1 last1,
                             InputIterator2 first2,
                             InputIterator2 last2) {
    while (first1 != last1 && first2 != last2) {
        if (*first1 < *first2) return true;
        if (*first2++ < *first1++) return false;
    }
    return first1 == last1 && first2 != last2;
}
```

The function looks forbidding but, stepping through it, it acts more or less as expected. If an element in the first string is less than the second, true is returned immediately. If the element in the second string is greater, false is returned. Otherwise, move on to the next element.

If you ever fall out of the loop, you've reached the end of one of the vectors. If you've reached the end of vector 1, but not vector 2, you can return true. Otherwise, vector 1 is equal to vector 2, and you must return false.

```
int check_order( vector<char> a[], int n )
{
    for ( i = 1 ; i < n ; i++ )
        if ( a[ i ] < a[ i -1 ] {
            cout << "Vectors out of order!\n";
            return 0;
        }
    return 1;
}
```

DEQUE<T>

classes

The deque<T> container has two nested classes that perform the iterator functions for the container.

class iterator

The iterator class is a public nested class of deque<T>. It is the key to the container as a whole, since it knows how to navigate the map and block architecture of deque<T>.

Iterator classes have to obey pointer syntax. So, in addition to constructors and destructors, deque<T>::iterator must support the following additional functions:

```
reference operator*();
difference_type operator-(const iterator& x) const;
iterator& operator++();
iterator operator++(int);
iterator& operator--();
iterator operator--(int);
iterator& operator+=(difference_type n);
iterator operator+(difference_type n) const;
iterator operator-(difference_type n) const;
reference operator[](difference_type n);
bool operator==(const iterator& x) const;
bool operator<(const iterator& x) const;
```

Unlike classes that use pointers as iterators, each of these operators generates at least a few lines of code. This means deque<T> won't be as efficient as vectors or standard arrays.

class const_iterator

To support C++ const functions, the iterator class needs a near twin defined: class const_iterator. This class is exactly the same as class iterator, except for a couple of minor points:

- class const_iterator has an additional constructor that allows you to create a const_iterator from an iterator

- operator*() returns a reference in the first class, and a const_reference in the other

- operator[]() returns a reference in one class, and a const_reference in the other

Other than that, the two classes are identical.

Typedefs

The STL uses a set of standard type definitions to support uniform access to container classes. When designing a container for the STL, some of these type definitions have to be built from scratch. For example, deque<T> had to define iterator and const_iterator as completely new classes. The rest of the types needed by this class are defined as typedefs, so deque<T> can recycle those already defined elsewhere.

```
typedef T value_type;
typedef Allocator<T>::reference reference;
typedef Allocator<T>::const_reference const_reference;
typedef Allocator<T>::size_type size_type;
typedef Allocator<T>::difference_type difference_type;
typedef reverse_iterator< const_iterator,
                          value_type,
                          const_reference,
                          difference_type> const_reverse_iterator;
typedef reverse_iterator< iterator,
                          value_type,
                          reference,
                          difference_type> reverse_iterator;
```

value_type

```
typedef T value_type;
```

value_type is a synonym for type T, the template parameter for deque<T>. It is frequently used when calling template functions to pass the *type* of a parameter, as opposed to the *value* of a parameter.

reference

```
typedef Allocator<T>::reference reference;
```

A reference is defined in deque.h as identical to a reference for Allocator<T> (data_allocator_type). Normally, the allocator class will define a reference to be T&. A reference is returned when you dereference an iterator.

const_reference

```
typedef Allocator<T>::const_reference const_reference;
```

A const_reference is the same as a reference, except it returns a reference to a const object.

size_type

```
typedef Allocator<T>::size_type size_type;
```

This type defines the size of the largest object created by Allocator<T> (data_allocator_type). For example, if deque<T> is defined using a standard memory model under MS-DOS, size_type is a synonym for the ANSI C type size_t, which will usually be an unsigned int. An unsigned int can hold the largest value passed as an argument to malloc().

difference_type

```
typedef Allocator<T>::difference_type difference_type;
```

This is another type defined by the allocator. difference_type is used to hold the difference between two pointers in the current allocator. Under MS-DOS standard memory models, it is defined as ptrdiff_t.

const_reverse_iterator

```
typedef reverse_iterator< const_iterator,
                          value_type,
                          const_reference,
                          difference_type> const_reverse_iterator;
```

The template class reverse_iterator creates a new iterator type. In the STL class, reverse_iterator is known as an *iterator adaptor*. By providing the correct template arguments, this definition creates a new iterator type that traverses containers in the reverse direction. The definition of the reverse iterator class is found in iterator.h, and is discussed in detail in Chapter 9.

Here's a quick example showing how to iterate in the reverse direction through a container:

```
for (deque<char>::const_reverse_iterator ri = a.rbegin();
     ri != r.rend();
     ri++ )
    cout << *ri;
```

reverse_iterator

```
typedef reverse_iterator< iterator,
                          value_type,
                          reference,
                          difference_type> reverse_iterator;
```

This type definition is identical to that for const_reverse_iterator, except it creates a reverse_iterator that returns a reference to a mutable object.

Important data members

```
iterator start;
iterator finish;
size_type length;
map_pointer map;
size_type map_size;
```

iterator start

deque<T>::start is an iterator that points to the first object stored in the container. If the container is empty, start will be set to the singular value 0.

start performs a second useful function. Iterator objects in deque<T> point to a location in the map object. Thus, start can be used internally to find the location of the first pointer in use in the map table. All pointer locations in map before that pointed to by start have random, invalid data.

start is a protected data member, so you can't access it directly. The begin() function will return a copy of it, however. Anytime you want to iterate through an STL container, your first iterator can be found by calling begin().

iterator finish

finish is a pointer to the last location in use in the container. As is always the case in the STL, finish points to the next location *after* the last location in the container as shown in Figure 20-1. Like start, finish is useful because it contains a pointer back to the last valid location in the map. (Remember, the iterators used in deque<T> keep four internal pointers. Only one actually points to the data element referenced by the iterator.) And in a break with STL convention, the pointer into the map truly points to the last map pointer, not one past!

finish is a protected data member, so you can't access it directly. The end() function will return a copy of it, however. Anytime you want to iterate through an STL container, your termination point can be found by calling end().

Note: If the last object in use is in the last available slot in a data block, finish will still point to that data block (one past the last position), not to the next block (which hasn't been allocated yet).

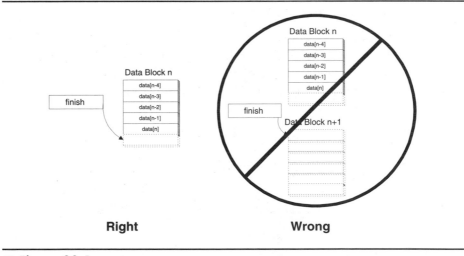

Right   **Wrong**

Figure 20-1
The finish iterator points into the current block, not the next (phantom) block

size_type length

Classes like vector<T> can figure out how many objects they contain using simple pointer math: finish - start + 1. deque<T> could do this too, but the result wouldn't be simple pointer math, it would be fairly complicated iterator math. So deque<T> keeps track at all times of the number of constructed objects it contains, using this data member.

Note: This is a protected data member, but it can be read at any time by calling the size() function.

map_pointer map

The map is a block of pointers to individual data blocks. To determine which map locations hold valid data, you need to look at the node members of the start and finish iterators. All locations outside the range defined by those two iterators are invalid.

The iterators in deque<T> always check their node values against this pointer when it's time to create a new data block at the start of the deque object. If their node member is equal to map, there is no room at the front of the map, and a map reallocation needs to be done.

size_type map_size

This is the current size of the map, the value used to determine whether an iterator is going to go past the end of the map when a new data block is added. If the new value of node would equal map + map_size, there is no room at the end of the map, and a reallocation needs to be performed.

Copy, construct, destroy

```
deque(Allocator&=Allocator());
deque(size_type n,
      const T& value = T(),
      Allocator&=Allocator());
deque( InputIterator first,
       InputIterator last,
       Allocator&=Allocator());
deque(const deque<T>& x, Allocator&=Allocator())
deque<T>& operator=(const deque<T>& x)
~deque()
```

The deque container class has four different constructors, the required destructor and an assignment operator. They are all public functions.

Each of the constructors has as its final argument a reference to an allocator object. This argument always has a default value, which is just an allocator constructed using the default constructor. This allocator argument is not present in HP's release of the STL as this book is being published.

deque(Allocator&=Allocator())

The default constructor creates an empty container. It has no map allocated, so all its iterators and pointers are set to 0. length is also set to 0. The first call to push_front() or push_back() will cause a map reallocation.

```
main()
{
    deque<int *> a;
...
```

deque(size_type n, const T& value=T(), Allocator&=Allocator())

This constructor creates a new deque container that is initialized with *n* copies of value.

Note: If value is not present, the default constructor for type T will be used to supply the initial value.

```
void foo()
{
    deque<string> labels( 100 );
....
```

template <class InputIterator> deque(InputIterator first, InputIterator last, Allocator&=Allocator())

This constructor can be used to copy a range from any container into the newly created iterator. The function is implemented differently in HP's public version of the STL, due to compiler incompatibilities with the C++ standard. Because of these incompatibilities, the two arguments to this version of the constructor have to be simple pointers to objects of type T.

```
char title[]="The Standard Template Library";
deque<char> dq_title( title, title + strlen( title ) );
```

Note: This is a template member function. Your implementation of the STL may substitute the following function:

```
deque( const_iterator first,
       const_iterator last,
       Allocator&=Allocator() );
```

The substitute function will only allow you to construct a deque container using a range from another deque container. If your compiler supports template member functions (as it must to comply with the ANSI/ISO specification), it will support the template version of this function.

deque(const deque<T>& x, Allocator&=Allocator())

This is the copy constructor for the deque container. It creates a new empty deque object, then calls the STL insert() function to copy all elements of *x* into the new deque.

```
int massage( deque<dataset>& a )
{
    deque<dataset> mycopy( a );

    for ( deque<dataset>::iterator i = mycopy.begin();
          i != mycopy.end();
          i++ ) {
    ...
```

deque<T>& operator=(const deque<T>& x)

The assignment operator is similar to the copy constructor, since it has to copy the contents of *x* into itself. However, it can be more efficient than the copy constructor by using all the existing storage it can to hold the new values copied from *x*.

If *x* is shorter than the current length of the deque<T> object, the extra values at the end of the deque will be erased, returning storage for their data blocks back to the system by way of the allocator.

```
static deque<records> my_copy;

int update( deque<records>& a )
{
    my_copy = a;
....
```

~deque()

The destructor of deque<> has to not only free all the storage in the deque(), but also call the destructor for each object stored in the container. It accomplishes this by repeatedly calling pop_back() until the container is empty.

This strategy won't work for vector<T>, because vector objects don't return storage as they free it. However, deque containers free each data block once it is empty, and free the map once it is no longer needed. So, all memory will be freed automatically as long as all objects are removed.

```
int finish( deque<employee> *a ) {
    if ( write_to_disk( a ) != SUCCESS )
        throw( "Failed to write data" );
    else
        delete a;
```

template<class InputIterator>
void assign(InputIterator first, InputIterator last)

This template member function performs a function nearly identical to that of the assignment operator. It erases any existing elements in the container, then copies an input range into the now-empty container.

```
void take end( char *s ) {
    deque<char> a;
    s = s + strlen( s );
    a.assign( s - 10, s );
```

Note: This is a template member function. Your compiler may have to substitute the following function:

```
void assign(const_iterator first, const_iterator last)
```

template<class Size, class T>
void assign(Size n, const T& t = T())

This assign command is used to initialize the deque with a set of *n* copies of object *t*. If you don't specify an object of type T, a default constructor is used to make one for you to copy. This function will erase all of the elements in the vector before inserting the *n* copies of *t*.

```
void erase( deque<string>& ds )
{
    ds.assign( 1, "<empty>" );
    ...
```

Note: This is a template member function. Your compiler may have to substitute the following function:

```
void assign(size_type n, value_type& t = value_type() )
```

Iterators

The member functions listed here all return iterator types. They are used to provide the functions needed to iterate through the container. For example, if you want to step through the entire container using a deque<T> iterator, you use begin() and end() to calculate your start and stop points.

The functions in this section provide you with the ability to modify individual elements in the deque, but don't change the size or arrangement of the deque itself. The functions in the Modifiers group can modify individual elements, but may also modify the vector's private start, finish, and map members. This means that using an Modifiers function may invalidate an iterator you have been using to point into the container. The functions in the Iterator group won't do that.

```
iterator begin();
const_iterator begin() const;
iterator end();
const_iterator end() const;
reverse_iterator rbegin();
const_reverse_iterator rbegin() const;
reverse_iterator rend();
const_reverse_iterator rend() const;
```

Note: Most of the functions described here come in pairs: a const and non-const version. The const versions of the functions have to be used when manipulating a deque<T> item declared as const.

iterator begin()
const_iterator begin() const

begin() is one of the functions supported across all STL containers. It is called to get an iterator that points to the first object in the container. If the container is empty, the iterator returned by begin() will equal the iterator returned by end().

Note: It is conventional in C/C++ programming to assign the singular value 0 to a pointer to indicate that it is invalid. In the STL, an iterator's singular value (meaning the end of a container has been reached) is supplied by the end() member function. This is one place where iterators don't completely obey pointer semantics: they can't be freely compared to the integer value 0.

```
template<class T>
void display_container( const T& a )
{
    for ( T::iterator i = a.begin();
          i != a.end();
          i++ )
        cout << *i << endl;
}
```

iterator end()

const_iterator end() const

deque<T>::end() is complementary to the begin() function. Anytime you want to iterate through a container, you must start with the iterator returned by begin(). You must terminate when that iterator has been incremented to the point where it equals end().

Note: The const version of end() will be used whenever you call end() for a const version of vector<T>.

The code for this function in deque.h is simple; all it does is return a copy of the finish iterator. Any operations on the container that change the number of elements being stored will update the finish iterator, so it is always a good reference value for end().

```
cout << "Number of objects in the container = ";
if ( a.begin() == a.end() )
    cout << 0;
else
    cout << (a.end() - a.begin());
```

reverse_iterator rbegin()

const_reverse_iterator rbegin() const

rbegin() returns a reverse iterator value, which points to the last used location in the container. You need to store the value returned by rbegin() in a deque<T>::reverse_iterator, not a standard iterator.

It isn't possible to test iterators in deque<T> against the scalar value 0. To see if the reverse iterator returned is valid, you have to check whether it is equal to the value returned by rend(). If it is equal, it no longer points to a valid object.

```
template<class T>
void reverse_container( T& a )
{
    T::reverse_iterator ri = a.rbegin();
    T::iterator i = a.begin();
    for ( int i = 0 ; i < a.size() / 2 ; i++ )
        *i++ = *ri++;
}
```

reverse_iterator rend()

const_reverse_iterator rend() const

deque<T>::rend() returns a reverse_iterator that denotes the end of a reverse iteration sequence. The value returned by rend() should not be dereferenced, since it will attempt to access a location in memory not owned by the current container. rend() is used primarily to return a value that can be tested to see if a reverse iterator has reached the end of its container.

```
deque<char>::reverse_iterator ri = a.rbegin();
while ( ri != a.rend() )
    cout << *ri++;
```

Capacity

```
bool empty() const;
size_type size() const;
size_type max_size() const;
void resize( size_type sz, T c = T() );
```

Capacity functions don't affect the contents of deque containers, with the exception of resize(). Instead, they return information on the amount of data either present in the deque, or that can be placed in the deque. The first three are const functions, which don't modify the container in any way during their operation.

bool empty() const

empty() is a simple boolean function that checks to see if the container is empty. There are many different ways to figure this out, but deque<T>::empty() takes a direct approach: it tests the length member to see if it is 0. If it is, the container is empty, and true is returned. Otherwise, false is returned.

```
cout << "First name in list: "
     << ( names.empty() ? "N/A", names.front() )
     << "\n";
```

size_type size() const

size() is called to discover how many objects are stored in the container at a given time. Like empty(), this is done using a direct approach. size() returns the current value in the length() member.

```
for ( i = 0 ; i < a.size() ; i++ )
    cout << a[ i ];
```

size_type max_size() const

max_size() is an allocator function. Its job is to report the maximum number of objects of type T that can fit into a single piece of raw memory, using the current allocator.

```
cout << "max_size = " << a.max_size() << endl;
```

void resize(size_type sz, T c = T())

deque<T>::resize forces the container to be a specific size. If the container's size is less than the requested size, new copies of argument *c* are added to the container until it reaches the size specified by *sz*. If *sz* is less than the desired size, the elements closest to the end of the container are deleted until the container is the correct size.

If the desired size is the same as the present size of the vector, no action is taken.

```
if ( name.size() > 100 )
    name.resize( 100, ' ' );
```

Element access

```
reference operator[](size_type n);
const_reference operator[](size_type n) constn);
reference at( size_type n) const;
reference at( size_type n );
reference front();
const_reference front() const;
reference back();
const_reference back() const;
```

reference operator[](size_type n)

const_reference operator[](size_type n) const

const_reference at(size_type n) const

reference at(size_type n)

operator[] lets you treat a deque<T> object as if it were a standard C array type. This is a great convenience when you are trying to access individual elements. However, deque containers don't have iterators that are as efficient as those for vector<T>. Every operation performed with this operator has to execute many lines of C++ code, so the cost is high in comparison to the same operation on a native pointer.

deque<T>::operator[] returns a reference to an object of type T. The const version will be applied if you are performing the operation on a const deque<T> object.

```
void print_info( deque<pet>& a, size t index )
{
    cout << a[ index ].name << endl;
    cout << a[ index ].species << endl;
    cout << a[ index ].breed << end;
...
```

The two at() functions shown here do the same thing as operator[](), but add one important capability: both functions throw an exception if the size argument is greater than the size of the container.

reference front()
const_reference front() const

This member function returns a reference to the first element. It is simply a convenience, because it is identical to *begin(). You do need to be careful with this function, because it doesn't attempt to verify that the container actually has data. If the container is empty, this function will probably try to dereference a null pointer. This will usually produce an undesired result.

```
cout << "The first student is "
     << students.front()
     << endl;
```

reference back()
const_reference back() const

back() is complementary to front(). Instead of returning a reference to the first element in the container, it returns a reference to the last. Like first(), this function exists solely as a notational convenience, because it is identical to the expression *(end() - 1).

Also like first(), it doesn't attempt to verify whether the container has objects in it. Attempting to access the last element of an empty container will usually have bad consequences.

Modifiers

The functions in this section bear some resemblance to those of previous sections, insofar as they access and modify individual elements of the container. However, since these functions can both add and remove elements from the container, they have the potential to cause map reallocations. This can render existing iterators useless.

```
void push_front(const T& x);
void push_back(const T& x);
void pop_front();
```

```
void pop_back();
void swap(deque<T>& x);
iterator insert(iterator position, const T& x);
void insert(iterator position, size_type n, const T& x);
void insert(iterator position,
            InputIterator first,
            InputIterator last);
void erase(iterator position);
void erase(iterator first, iterator last);
```

Be careful with iterators when using functions from this group. For example, code like this might cause major problems:

```
for ( deque<foo>::iterator i = a.begin();
      i != a.end();
      i++ )
    if ( *i == test_case )
        a.push_back( foo( 16 ) );
```

As you work through this loop, from time to time you can add a new object to the container. If you inadvertently force a map reallocation, you will find *i* is no longer a valid iterator. It's likely that your loop will never exit properly, since *i* will never be equal to a.end().

If you have to write a loop that performs this function, a better solution would be something like this:

```
for ( int i = 0 ; i < a.size() ; i++ )
    if ( a[ i ] == test_case )
        a.push_back( foo( 16 ) );
```

void push_front(const T& x)

push_front() is not a universal STL function. For example, it is not supported in vector<T>. This is because of the difficulty of adding an element to the start of the vector. However, adding elements to the start of a deque container is a low-cost operation, so it is supported by a dedicated function.

The push operation first checks to see if additional memory space is available at the front of the deque. If not, a new block of memory is allocated and added to the map. This operation may require reallocation of the map.

Once the memory is available, the start iterator is decremented, and the copy constructor is invoked with the placement syntax. This forces the new object of type T to be stored at *start. The function increments the length member, which keeps track of the number of objects in the container.

```
template<class T>
void reverse_insert( deque<T> &a,
                         T::iterator start,
                         T::iterator end )
{
    while ( start != end )
        a.push_front( *start++ );
}
```

void push_back(const T& x)

deque<T>::push_back() is the complementary function to push_front(). deque<T> is designed to be symmetrical, not favoring insertions from the front or back. Because of this, the two functions operate in a nearly identical fashion.

First, push_back() has to check if there is an open spot in the last data block. If there isn't, a new data block must be added, and its pointer added to the map. This can cause a map reallocation.

Once the new storage is positively available, the copy constructor is called, using the placement syntax. This creates a new copy of *x* at the end of the container. finish is then incremented, the length member is incremented, and the operation is complete.

```
template<class T>
void append( deque<T>& a, T *data, size_t n )
{
    while ( n-- )
        a.push_back( *data++ );
}
```

void pop_front()

pop_front() is another function available in deque<T>, but not in vector<T>. Removing an object from the front of a deque is relatively easy, but the equivalent operation on a vector<T> is costly.

pop_front() assumes the container has data. If you call this member function for an empty container, bad things will happen. The function calls the allocator function destroy(), which calls the explicit destructor for the address of the object. This destroys the object without freeing the memory.

The start pointer is then incremented, and length is decremented. The function has to check if the first data block is now empty. If it is, the allocator frees it. If the container is now empty, the map is freed as well.

```
int trim_leading_space( deque<char>& a )
{
    int count = 0;
    while ( !a.empty() && a.front() == ' ' ) {
        count++;
        a.pop_front();
    }
    return count;
}
```

void pop_back()

pop_back() is the twin of pop_front(). It has to perform the same operations in a complementary manner. It first calls destroy()—defined along with the allocator class—to delete the object at the end of the container. It then goes through the same memory management process as pop_front(). When it's all over, one data block may have been freed. If the container is empty, the map will also have been freed.

Calling pop_back() on an empty container is a bad idea. In the standard release of the STL, there is no checking to verify if there are objects in the deque<T>. If you call pop_back() in this empty state, the container's allocator could cause errors as it attempts to destroy a non-existent object.

```
template<T>
void nuke( T& a ) //works on vector, deque, and list
{
    while ( !a.empty() )
        a.pop_back();
}
```

void swap(deque<T>& x)

This function is called to exchange one entire deque container with another. It sounds like a big operation, but it's very simple. The source code from deque.h shows that a complete exchange of the two containers can be accomplished by swapping just five members:

```
void swap(deque<T>& x) {
    ::swap(start, x.start);
    ::swap(finish, x.finish);
```

```
    ::swap(length, x.length);
    ::swap(map, x.map);
    ::swap(map_size, x.map_size);
}
```

Since all these members are either scalars or pointer-like objects, this is a quick and easy operation.

```
void shift_change( deque<staff>& on, deque<staff>& off )
{
    cout << "changing crew\n";
    on.swap( off );
}
```

template <class InputIterator>
void insert(iterator position,InputIterator first,
InputIterator last)

iterator insert(iterator position, const T& x)

void insert(iterator position, size_type n, const T& x)

deque<T> supports three different insertion functions. As with vector<T>, these operations are potentially expensive.

To perform an insertion in the middle of a container, memory must be allocated at the start or end of the container. Then, a bulk copy is performed to open space in the middle, at the location pointed to by the position argument to insert(). Finally, the data is copied into the new location.

The big expense in this operation occurs during the bulk copy. Since it is necessary to copy as many as size()/2 objects, this is now an O(N) function. The function will become more and more costly as the size of the container increases. As a result, the function won't scale up well.

If you have an algorithm that requires frequent insertions, and you think the deque<T> object may grow to a large size, consider using list<T> as your container. list<T> performs insertions in constant time, so performance is not affected by the number of objects in the container.

```
void student_deque::add_student( string & name )
{
    deque<string>::iterator i;
    while ( i != end() && name > *i )
        i++;
    insert( i, name );
}
```

Note: The template version of insert may not be supported by your compiler. If this is the case, you will probably have a replacement non-template function that looks like this:

```
void insert( iterator position,
             const_iterator first,
             const_iterator last );
```

The replacement function restricts you to inserting elements from other vectors, instead of elements from any container.

void erase(iterator position)
void erase(iterator first, iterator last)

Like insert(), erase is a second-class citizen in the deque<T> order of things. erasure operations have to bulk copy objects from one end of the container, up to the erasure point. This can require as many as size()/2 copy operations, followed by a batch of destructor calls. As a result, the function will run in O(*N*) time, making it an unattractive operation.

If you have an application that needs to perform many erase() function calls, and you find your deque containers are getting large, try evaluating the list<T> container. It may prove more suitable for your application.

```
a.erase( a.begin(), a.end() - 5 );
```

Relational/equality operators

```
template <class T>
bool operator<(const deque<T>& x, const deque<T>& y);
template <class T>
bool operator==(const deque<T>& x, const deque<T>& y);
```

These two functions enable two containers to be compared. The equality operator will only return true if the two containers have the same number of elements, and all elements are equal. The second function performs a lexicographical (string) comparison of the two deques, and returns the result.

template <class T>
bool operator<(const deque<T>& x, const deque<T>& y)

This function is needed to compare two containers, component by component. It performs a lexicographical comparison. C programmers normally think of this as a *C comparison*. It tests the first objects in the deques, the second objects, and so on, until it either finds two that aren't equal, or runs out of objects in one or both containers.

```
if ( deque_a < deque_b )
    cout << "a is less\n";
```

template <class T>
bool operator==(const deque<T>& x, const deque<T>& y)

This function tests two containers to see if they are equal. Equality, in this case, means they are the same size and all elements compare equal.

```
int write_with_verify( deque<foo> &a )
{
    deque<foo> b;

    data_file << a;
    data_file >> b;
    if ( a == b )
        return 1;
    else
        return 0;
}
```

LIST<T>

classes

There are four new types defined as nested types in class list<T>. The two iterator classes are public definitions that you should expect to use regularly when utilizing lists. The other two types are protected structures, so you probably won't use them.

```
class iterator;
class const_iterator;
struct list_node;
struct list_node_buffer;
```

class iterator

The iterator class is a public nested class of list<T>. It provides two important functions for users of list<T>. First, it shields you from having to handle pointer navigation when moving from link to link. More importantly, it gives list<T> an interface compatible with other STL containers. This means you can easily implement algorithms that work with all sequential classes, despite their inherent differences.

Iterator classes have to obey pointer syntax. So, in addition to constructors and destructors, deque<T>::iterator has to support the following additional functions:

```
reference operator*();
iterator& operator++();
iterator operator++(int);
iterator& operator--();
iterator operator--(int);
bool operator==(const iterator& x) const;
bool operator<(const iterator& x) const;
```

You might notice that it's missing quite a few functions available for normal pointers, or for iterators in vector<T> and deque<T>:

```
difference_type operator-(const iterator& x) const;
iterator& operator+=(difference_type n);
iterator operator+(difference_type n) const;
iterator operator-(difference_type n) const;
reference operator[](difference_type n);
```

These are the functions in random access iterators, but not in bidirectional iterators. list<T> is a container class that doesn't have full-featured random access iterators. Instead, it gets by with the second-class citizenship of bidirectional iterators.

Unlike classes that use pointers as iterators, each of these operators generates at least a few lines of code. Accordingly, list<T> iterator use won't be as efficient as vectors or standard arrays.

class const_iterator

To support C++ const functions, the iterator class must have a near twin defined: class const_iterator. This class is exactly the same as class iterator, except for a couple of minor points:

- class const_iterator has an additional constructor which allows you to create a const_iterator from an iterator
- operator*() returns a reference in one class, and a const_reference in the other

Other than that, the two classes are identical.

struct list_node

```
struct list_node {
    void_pointer next;
    void_pointer prev;
    T data;
};
```

list_node is a protected type defined in class list<T>. The list_node is the storage object which holds the data belonging to the container.

Each data object stored in the list needs a pointer to the nodes before and after it in the list. These pointers are defined as next and prev in this structure.

Since this is a protected structure, you won't normally have access to it when using list<T>. If you need to look at the individual list_node elements of the list, you can see the example programs earlier in this chapter for help on deriving classes from list<T>. Since this structure definition is protected, you will have full access to it in a class derived from list<T>.

struct list_node_buffer

```
struct list_node_buffer {
    void_pointer next_buffer;
    link_type buffer;
};
```

This is another protected structure found inside class list<T>. It creates a list of the buffers added to the buffer pool. The only reason to keep this list on hand is so that, when the time arrives, the code in list<T> can go back and delete all the buffers in the pool.

This process is described more fully in the section of this chapter on allocation.

Typedefs

The STL employs a set of standard type definitions to support uniform access to container classes. When designing a container for the STL, some of these type definitions have to be built up from scratch.

For example, list<T> has to define iterator and const_iterator as completely new classes. The rest of the types needed by this class are defined as typedefs, so list<T> can recycle types that are already defined elsewhere.

```
typedef T value_type;
typedef Allocator<T>::reference reference;
typedef Allocator<T>::const_reference const_reference;
typedef Allocator<list_node>::size_type size_type;
typedef Allocator<list_node>::difference_type difference_type;
typedef reverse_bidirectional_iterator<const_iterator,
                                       value_type,
                                       const_reference,
                                       difference_type>
             const_reverse_iterator;
typedef reverse_bidirectional_iterator<iterator,
                                       value_type,
                                       reference,
                                       difference_type>
             reverse_iterator;
```

value_type

```
typedef T value_type;
```

value_type is a synonym for type T, the template parameter for list<T>. It's frequently used when calling template functions to pass the type of a parameter, as opposed to the value of a parameter.

reference

```
typedef Allocator<T>::reference reference;
```

A reference is defined in list.h as identical to a reference for Allocator<T>. Normally, the allocator class defines a reference as T&. A reference is returned when you dereference an iterator or a pointer.

const_reference

```
typedef Allocator<T>::const_reference const_reference;
```

A const_reference is the same as a reference, except it returns a reference to a const object.

size_type

```
typedef Allocator<list_node>::size_type size_type;
```

This type defines the size of the largest object that can be created by Allocator<list_node>. For example, if list<T> is defined by a standard memory model under MS-DOS, size_type is a synonym for the ANSI C type size_t—usually an unsigned int. An unsigned int can hold the largest value requested from malloc().

difference_type

```
typedef Allocator<list_node>::difference_type difference_type;
```

difference_type is another type defined by the allocator. It can hold the difference between two pointers under the current allocator. Under MS-DOS standard memory models, this is defined as ptrdiff_t.

reverse_iterator

```
typedef reverse_bidirectional_iterator<iterator,
                                       value_type,
                                       reference,
                                       difference_type>
          reverse_iterator;
```

The template class reverse_iterator creates a new iterator type. In the STL, reverse_iterator is known as an iterator adaptor.

By providing the correct template arguments, this definition creates a new iterator type that traverses containers in the reverse direction. The definition of the reverse iterator class is found in iterator.h, and is discussed in detail in Chapter 9, "Allocators."

const_reverse_iterator

```
typedef reverse_bidirectional_iterator<const_iterator,
                                       value_type,
                                       const_reference,
                                       difference_type>
            const_reverse_iterator;
```

This type definition is identical to reverse_iterator, except it creates a reverse_iterator that returns a reference to a constant object.

For example, you must use this type of iterator to write an algorithm that iterates through a const list<T>.

Static data members

All containers in the STL use static instances of their allocator to perform memory allocation and removal. In most cases, the allocator object doesn't take up any space; it simply provides a definition of the member functions used to manage memory.

list<T> has three different static data members to handle allocation and memory model issues. In addition, it has a small collection of members to manage the buffer pool and free list. Note that these are list<T> internals in the HP STL distribution. Your vendor's implementation may differ.

```
static Allocator<list_node> list_node_allocator;
static Allocator<T> value_allocator;
static Allocator<list_node_buffer> buffer_allocator;
static buffer_pointer buffer_list;
static link_type free_list;
static link_type next_avail;
static link_type last;
static size_type number_of_lists;
```

static Allocator<list_node> list_node_allocator

list_node_allocator is a static data member with one important function in list<T>. Whenever a call to get_node() is made, list<T> checks if there are any list_node objects in the free list. If there aren't, it checks the buffer pool. If the buffer pool is empty as well, list_node_allocator. allocate() is called to create a new buffer. This buffer is added to the buffer pool, next_avail and last are updated, and get_node() returns the first list_node in the newly created buffer.

list_node_allocator also calculates the buffer size of list<T>, that is, how many objects of type T can be stored in one buffer in the buffer pool.

static Allocator<T> value_allocator

value_allocator is another instance of an Allocator<> object. It characterizes the Allocator for type <T>. value_allocator is only used in the construct() and destroy() functions. In these functions, value_allocator returns the address of an object of type T in the current memory model. For example, the call to construct() looks like this:

```
construct(value_allocator.address((*tmp).data), x);
```

static Allocator<list_node_buffer> buffer_allocator

buffer_allocator is the final static allocator object defined for list<T>. It's employed in member function add_new_buffer() to allocate a new block of list_node objects that use the appropriate memory model. The complete source of list<T>::add_new_buffer() shows how this allocator object is used, as well as list_node_allocator:

```
void add_new_buffer() {
    buffer_pointer tmp = buffer_allocator.allocate((size_type)1);
    tmp->buffer = list_node_allocator.allocate(buffer_size());
    tmp->next_buffer = buffer_list;
    buffer_list = tmp;
    next_avail = buffer_list->buffer;
    last = next_avail + buffer_size();
}
```

static buffer_pointer buffer_list

list<T> maintains a pool of buffers that supply it with raw memory for the creation of list_node objects. (For more information, see Chapter 5.)

When these buffers are allocated, list<T> must keep track of them so they can be properly deleted when all objects in a given class of list<T> have been destroyed. buffer_list is the root pointer to the list of buffers.

Figure 20-2 shows an overview of the structure of the buffer pool.

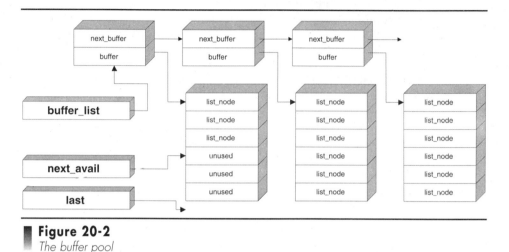

Figure 20-2
The buffer pool

static link_type free_list

Initially, list_node objects are allocated for a container from the buffer pool. When those objects are removed from their list containers and destroyed, the list_node storage block is not returned to the buffer pool. Instead, the objects are added to the free list.

The free list is a list of pointers freed from list<T> containers. Figure 20-3 shows how the free list interacts with the buffer pool.

Like all elements of the buffer pool, the free list is made up of static data members. So, all lists for a given type T share a common storage pool. A given list_node might be added to and deleted from many different lists over its lifetime, but they will all have the same type.

free_list is the root pointer of the free list; it points to the first element in the free list. This will be the first element used the next time a call is made to get_node() to get a new list_node().

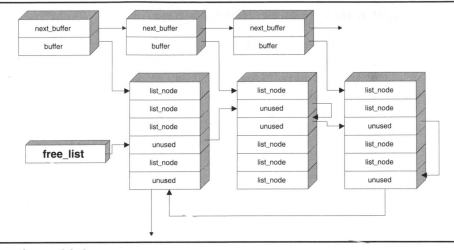

Figure 20-3
The free list

static link_type next_avail
static link_type last

When a new buffer is allocated and added to the buffer pool, it has a certain number of unused list_node-sized memory blocks that can be used to create new list_node objects for a list. At the time the buffer is allocated, two pointers are created that will assist in its management.

The first pointer is next_avail, which points to the next list_node object available to create a list_node. Initially, it points to the start of the memory block allocated for the pool. Each time a list_node object is allocated from the buffer pool, next_avail is incremented. It will now point to the next free node in the block.

There is also a second pointer, *last*. Sooner or later, next_avail will go past the end of the block allocated for the pool, and the last pointer tells you when that point has been reached. In canonical STL fashion, last is initialized to point just past the end of the buffer when it is allocated. You can see this in Figure 20-2.

When the list is created, there are no entries in the buffer pool, so next_avail and last are both initialized to 0. The code doesn't have any problem with this, since the test for being out of memory is to see if next_avail == last. Even when the buffer pool is empty, this condition will be true.

static size_type number_of_lists

This static data member keeps track of the number of lists of type T that have been created. This number is important for deciding when to delete all the memory in the buffer pool. list<T> hangs on to all that memory until there are no more lists in use, at which point all buffers are deleted.

The constructor for an individual list increments this static member as soon as the list is created:

```
list() : length(0) {
    ++number_of_lists;
    node = get_node();
    (*node).next = node;
    (*node).prev = node;
}
```

The destructor for list<T> has to check to see if all the lists have been destroyed. If they have, the buffer pools should be empty, and be safe to destroy as well. The next code excerpt shows the code from the destructor, as defined in list.h.

Note: After all nodes have been destroyed, the destructor checks whether this was the last list of its type to be destroyed. If it was, deallocate_buffers() is called to erase all buffers in the pool. It also erases the buffer pool list.

```
~list() {
    erase(begin(), end());
    put_node(node);
    if (--number_of_lists == 0) deallocate_buffers();
}
```

Data members

The list class has quite a few static data members to provide support for all members of the class. In contrast, it only takes two protected data members to support an individual list. Remember that these members are part of HP's public implementation of the STL. Your vendor may choose to implement list<T> differently, since the data members are not part of the ANSI/ISO implementation.

```
link_type node;
size_type length;
```

link_type node

A linked list needs to have starting and ending points. In the case of list<T>, the starting and ending points of the entire list are stored in a root node, simply named *node*. This root node has storage for an object of type T, but this storage is wasted, as it is never used.

When a list<T> object is first initialized, the prev and next pointers in node are initialized to point to node. node will always be the value used for the end() iterator for a given list. So, in an empty list, the next pointer points to end(). This means the list is empty by default.

node has to be allocated in the constructor, just like any other node. This means the buffer pool is usually initialized during construction of the list<T> container, not when the first node is allocated.

size_type length

Each time a new node is added to the list, length is incremented. When a node is removed from the list, length is decremented. Thus, length will always contain the count of nodes in the list.

Other containers don't need a data member to keep track of the container size, but this isn't practical in list<T>. It's too much work—and O(N) work at that—to calculate the size on the fly. So, the minor expense of maintaining the length member is the price you have to pay.

Copy, construct, destroy

list<T> comes with the typical STL complement of constructors. There is a default constructor that creates an empty list; a copy constructor; and two constructors that initialize the list with either a single value, or a copy of a range of values.

The ANSI/ISO committee made one last-minute change to the constructors for all the containers defined in the STL. Each of these constructors had a single parameter added to their argument list, which allows you to pass a specific allocator for use by that object. If you don't specify an allocator (and under normal circumstances, you won't), one is constructed for you using the default allocator constructor.

```
list(Allocator& = Allocator());
list(size_type n,
     const T& value = T(),
     Allocator& = Allocator());
```

```
list(InputIterator* first,
    InputIterator last,
    Allocator& = Allocator());
list(const list<T>& x, Allocator& = Allocator());
~list();
list<T>& operator=(const list<T>& x);
void assign(InputIterator first, InputIterator last);
void assign(Size n, const T& t =T() );
```

list(Allocator& = Allocator())

The default constructor creates an empty list<T> object. Although the list is empty, it allocates the root node, so the buffer pool should allocate some space. As the empty list has a length of 0, a call to list<T>::size() returns a value 0.

```
int main()
{
    list<foo> a;
...
```

This constructor, along with all the other constructors in this group, increments the static variable list<T>::number_of_lists.

list(size_type n, const T& value = T(), Allocator& = Allocator())

This constructor not only creates a list, it stores *n* copies of the second parameter in the list. The second parameter has a default value created by the default constructor, so you don't have to supply a default parameter.

```
int main()
{
    list<int> a( 50 );
    list<double> b( 100, 1.0 )
...
```

template<class InputIterator>
list(InputIterator first, InputIterator last,
Allocator& = Allocator())

This constructor creates a list, and initializes it with copies of a range of objects of type T. It copies a range of objects from an existing array or vector<T>.

```
void make_list( char *name )
{
    list<char> *a = new list<char>( name, name + strlen( name ) );
...
```

The code in the constructor is simple: the constructor has to initialize the root of the list, member *node*, then call the insert() member function to add all the elements to the list:

```
list(const T* first, const T* last) : length(0) {
    ++number_of_lists;
    node = get_node();
    (*node).next = node;
    (*node).prev = node;
    insert(begin(), first, last);
}
```

Note: This is a template member function. Your implementation of the STL may substitute the following function:

```
list( const_iterator first,
      const_iterator last,
      Allocator&=Allocator()  )
```

list(const list<T>& x, Allocator& = Allocator())

The copy constructor code is nearly identical to the previous constructor. The only difference is, the copy constructor doesn't need the first and last iterators passed as arguments. It can access the start and finish of the argument list<T> using the two member functions begin() and end():

```
list(const list<T>& x) : length(0) {
    ++number_of_lists;
    node = get_node();
    (*node).next = node;
    (*node).prev = node;
    insert(begin(), x.begin(), x.end());
}
```

After the constructor is complete, the two list containers will be defined as identical according to operator==().

```
template<class T>
void print_sorted_copy( list<T> &a )
{
    list<T> b( a );
    b.sort();
    for ( list<T>::iterator i = b.begin();
          i != b.end();
          i++ )
        cout << *i;
}
```

~list()

The destructor removes all existing storage in the list by using member function erase() over the entire range of nodes. It then disposes of the root node and decrements the static member number_of_lists.

If this was the last list of type list<T>, the member function deallocate_buffers() is called to free all buffers added to the pool.

```
void flush( list<foo> *a )
{
    for ( list<foo>::iterator j = a.begin();
          j != a.end();
          j ++ )
        if ( j->value > 0 )
            output << *j;
    delete a;
}
```

list<T>& operator=(const list<T>& x)

The easiest way to write an assignment operator for list<T> would be to delete all existing nodes in the list, then make copies of the argument list nodes. However, while this is easy, it is decidedly less efficient. You would free memory from the original list, only to turn around and reallocate the same memory to hold new nodes.

The code shown here is from list.h, and shows that the STL approach to implementation of the assignment operator takes a more sophisticated approach to this problem.

```
template <class T>
list<T>& list<T>::operator=(const list<T>& x) {
    if (this != &x) {
```

```
            iterator first1 = begin();
            iterator last1 = end();
            const_iterator first2 = x.begin();
            const_iterator last2 = x.end();
            while ( first1 != last1 &&
                    first2 != last2)
                *first1++ = *first2++;
            if (first2 == last2)
                erase(first1, last1);
            else
                insert(last1, first2, last2);
        }
    return *this;
}
```

In the STL, implementation of the assignment operator for list<T> is a little more efficient about storage management. It copies as many entries as it can directly on top of the existing nodes of the array. The copy loop terminates when one of two conditions has occurred. Either when:

- there is no more room in the target array to copy any more nodes; or
- all source nodes have been copied to the destination.

If the first possibility occurs, the remaining nodes are added to the target list, using the member function insert(). If the loop terminates because of the second possibility, the extra nodes in the target list are deleted via erase(). Either way, you've copied the source into the target, and evened up the number of nodes.

Here is an example of how you might use the assignment operator:

```
if ( *(a.begin() ) > *(b.begin() )
    c = a;
else
    c = b;
```

template<class InputIterator>
void assign(InputIterator first, InputIterator last)

This template member function performs a function nearly identical to that of the assignment operator. It erases any existing elements in the list, then copies an input range into the now-empty container. This is a new function specified by the ANSI/ISO committee, so it won't be found in HP's public STL implementation.

```
deque<int> a;
list<int> b;
   .
   .
   .
b.assign( a + 2, a + 5 );
```

Note: This is a template member function. Your compiler may have to substitute the following function:

```
void assign(const_iterator first, const_iterator last)
```

or even:

```
void assign(const T *first, const T* last)
```

template<class Size, class T>
void assign(Size n, const T& t = T())

This assign command is used to initialize a list container with a set of *n* copies of object *t*. If you don't specify an object of type T, a default constructor is used to make one for you to copy. This function will erase all of the elements in the vector before inserting the *n* copies of *t*.

```
names.assign( 100, string( "" ) );
```

Note: This is a template member function. Your compiler may have to substitute the following function:

```
void assign(size_type n, value_type& t = value_type() )
```

Iterators

The member functions listed here all return iterator types. They are used to provide the functions needed to iterate through the container.

```
iterator begin();
const_iterator begin() const;
iterator end();
const_iterator end() const;
```

```
reverse_iterator rbegin();
const_reverse_iterator rbegin();
reverse_iterator rend();
const_reverse_iterator rend() const;
```

Note: All these functions come in pairs: a const and non-const version. The const version is used to access elements in an object declared to be const. An example of where the const version list<T>::begin() might be called is shown here:

```
int sum_odd( const list<int> &x )
{
    int sum = 0;
    for ( list<int>::const_iterator i = x.begin();
          i != x.end();
          i++ )
        if ( *i & 1 )
            sum += *i;
    return sum;
}
```

Since the list argument to function sum_odd() is declared to be const, the compiler selects the const version of begin(). The code fragment shown here is aware of that fact, since it is using a const_iterator type to hold the iterator. If the programmer attempts to use a list<int>::iterator instead, the compiler generates a warning message.

iterator begin()

const_iterator begin() const

begin() is one of the most commonly used functions in the container classes. begin() returns an iterator that points to the location of the first element in the list. The iterator returned by begin() can be dereferenced using the dereferencing operator*().

Note: If begin() == end(), no nodes have been allocated by the list<T> container. When this is the case, the iterator returned by begin() should not be dereferenced.

```
void dump( list<int> &a )
{
    list<int>::iterator i;
    for ( i = a.begin() ; i != a.end() ; i++ )
        printf( "%d ", *i );
    printf( "\n" );
}
```

iterator end()

const_iterator end() const

list<T>::end() is the companion function to list<T>::begin(). Typically, these two functions are used to iterate through a list of nodes. begin() provides the initial iterator for the loop, and end() provides the value used to test for the end of the loop.

There is one important thing to remember about the iterator returned by end(). When testing for the end of a vector, you must test for equality with end(), not for less than the value returned by end(). The less-than operator for iterators might be undefined, or meaningless. In any case, you can continue working with your iterator as long as it doesn't equal end().

```
void print( list<char>::const_iterator start,
            list<char>::const_iterator end )
{
    while ( start != end )
        cout << *start++;
}

void foo( list<char> & a )
{
    print( a.begin(), a.end() );
}
```

reverse_iterator rbegin()

const_reverse_iterator rbegin()

Reverse iterators are created using an iterator adaptor. A reverse iterator is a handy construct that lets you iterate through a loop in reverse order. While this might not sound like a particularly memorable feat, algorithms that accept an iterator as input also accept a reverse iterator. This means you can cause STL algorithms to run backwards through containers just by changing the type of iterator you pass to them!

```
void vectorize( list<foo> &a )
{
    vector<foo> b( a.rbegin(), a.rend() );
    ...
```

reverse_iterator rend()

const_reverse_iterator rend() const

list<T>::rend() corresponds to the rbegin() function, in the same manner that list<T>::end() corresponds to begin(). rend() returns a reference to just before the first element in the list.

Note: You shouldn't attempt to dereference the iterator returned by rend().

```
template<class T>
print_tail( list<T>& a, list<T>::reverse_iterator ri )
{
    while ( ri != a.rend() )
        cout << *ri++ << endl;
}
```

Capacity

```
bool empty() const;
size_type size() const;
size_type max_size() const;
void resize(size_type sz, T c = T() );
```

Capacity functions don't affect the contents of lists; they simply return information regarding the amount of data either present in the list, or that can be placed into the list. All three functions are const functions; they don't modify the list during their operation.

bool empty() const

list<T>::empty() tests to see whether the list contains any constructed elements. If it does, this function returns a false value; otherwise it returns true. The determination is made by simply testing to see if length is 0. If it is, the list is empty.

```
cout << "list a is "
    << ( a.empty() ? "" : "not ";
    << "empty\n";
```

size_type size() const

size() returns the current count of elements present in the list. Because of the way list<T> keeps track of its own element count, this function just returns the length member.

```
list<string>::iterator p = a.begin();
for ( i = 0 ; i < a.size() ; i++ )
    cout << *p++;
```

size_type max_size() const

Although max_size() is a member of list<T>, it is a function defined by the allocator being used by list<T>. max_size() calculates how many elements of type T the container can hold, and returns that number.

Note that a list (and a deque) can hold more than max_size() items but, in general, this is not a good thing to do. For example, a list<double> object under 16-bit MS-DOS implementations might have a max_size() value of 8192. Despite this, you may succeed in inserting 50,000 doubles into the list. However, at this point, you are not guaranteed that your list object will work properly with all STL algorithms. You may also not be able to copy your list to other container types, such as vector<T>.

```
void zero( list<int> &a, int n )
{
    if ( n > a.max_size() ) {
        cerr << "Sorry, can't do it!\n";
        return;
    }
    ....
```

void resize(size_type sz, T c = T())

list<T>::resize sets the size of a container to a specific size. The ANSI/ISO specification gives a short piece of code to describe the effects of this function:

```
if ( sz > size() )
    s.insert( s.end(), s.size() - sz, c );
else if ( sz < size() )
    s.erase( a.begin() + sz, s.end() );
```

This code shows us that resize() has three courses of action. The resize() function's first parameter indicates the desired size of the element after the function completes. This means that if the resize() function is asking for an increase in the number of elements in the container, resize() adds enough copies of *c* to change the vector's size to *sz*.

If resize() is asking for a *decrease* in the size of the container, the appropriate number of elements is removed from the end of the list. If the desired size is the same as the present size of the list, no action is taken.

```
void trim_list( list<string>& l, int n )
{
    if ( l.size() > 100 )
        l.resize( n, string( "" ) );
}
```

Element access

```
reference front();
const_reference front() const;
reference back();
const_reference back() const;
```

These functions are used to access individual elements in the container. Although these functions can modify the contents of a particular element, they don't ever cause any resizing or new allocations of memory. Because of this, you will never invalidate an iterator pointing into your container by simply using one of these functions.

Note: The pair of operator[] functions are missing from this section. If implemented in a list container, operator[] would be an $O(N)$ time function, so it isn't found for this container type.

reference front()

const_reference front() const

The list<T> member functions front() and back() correspond to the begin() and end() functions. However, they don't return an iterator that references the first and last members of a list. front() and back() return an actual reference to those values—a quick way to get at the first and last members of a list.

Unless you have a version of the STL with added bounds checking, you will be responsible for making sure front() is called when the first element of the array exists.

If you call this function for a list that hasn't allocated any nodes, front() will return a reference to the data member of the root node, which will be an uninitialized block of memory. This is probably not a good thing to do.

```
cout << "First value = "
     << a.front()
     << endl;
```

reference back()
const_reference back() const

list<T>::back() is the partner to front(), discussed in the previous definition. back() is used to return a reference to the last object in the list container, which is easily accessible using the prev pointer of the root node.

Unless you have a version of the STL with added bounds checking, you will be responsible for making sure back() is called when the last element of the array exists. If you call this function for a list that hasn't allocated any nodes, back() will return a reference to the data member of the root node. It will actually be an uninitialized block of raw memory. This is not a good thing to do.

```
cout << "last value = "
     << a.back()
     << endl;
```

Modifiers

The functions in this section not only modify individual elements of the vector, but may modify internal data members, such as first or last.

```
void push_front(const T& x);
void push_back(const T& x);
void pop_front();
void pop_back();
iterator insert(iterator position, const T& x);
void insert(iterator position, const T* first, const T* last);
void insert(iterator position,
            const_iterator first,
            const_iterator last);
```

```
void insert(iterator position, size_type n, const T& x);
void erase(iterator position);
void erase(iterator first, iterator last);
void swap(list<T>& x);
```

void push_front(const T& x)

push_front() is supported in deque<T> and list<T>, but not in vector<T>. This is a particularly easy operation to implement in list<T>, because it doesn't have to worry about shuffling maps or pointers, as required in deque<T>. In list<T>, push_front() is implemented with a call to insert(begin(), x).

The insert() function itself is simple:

```
iterator insert(iterator position, const T& x) {
    link_type tmp = get_node();
    construct(value_allocator.address((*tmp).data), x);
    (*tmp).next = position.node;
    (*tmp).prev = (*position.node).prev;
    (*(link_type((*position.node).prev))).next = tmp;
    (*position.node).prev = tmp;
    ++length;
    return tmp;
}
```

The insert() routine isn't trivially short, but its operation is simple to follow. It allocates space with a call to get_node(), makes a copy of the x parameter into the new space, then links it in with the existing data.

An example of how to use push_front() is shown here.

```
template<class T>
void reverse_insert( list<T> &a,
                     T::iterator start,
                     T::iterator end )
{
    while ( start != end )
        a.push_front( *start++ );
}
```

void push_back(const T& x)

list<T>::push_back() is nearly identical to push_front() when implemented for list<T>. push_front() is implemented by calling insert(begin(), x), and push_back() is implemented with a similar function:

```
void push_back( const T& x ){ insert( end(), x ); }
```

push_back() is therefore a nice, low-cost operation in list<T>, just like its sibling. An example is shown here.

```
void pad( list<string>& a, int i )
{
    while ( i-- )
        a.push_back( "~" );
    a.push_back( "<EOF>" );
}
```

void pop_front()

pop_front() is available in list<T> and deque<T>, but not in vector<T>. Removing an object from the front of a vector is costly. From the front of a list, it is trivial.

pop_front() assumes the container has at least one data element. If you call this member on an empty container, bad things will happen. The function calls the allocator function destroy(), which calls the explicit destructor for the address of the object. This destroys the object without freeing the memory. The memory is then returned to the free list by a call to put_node().

The implementation of pop_front() is done by calling erase() with a pointer to begin().

```
int trim_slackers( list<workers>& a )
{
    while ( !a.empty() && a.front().work_ethic == 0 )
        a.pop_front();
return count;
}
```

void pop_back()

pop_back() destroys the last element of the list. Be sure to note that pop_back() makes no attempt to verify that the list contains at least one element. If you call pop_back() on an empty list, you are left with an object in an invalid state. After pop_back() is called, length decrements, and end() returns a reference to a new element of the list.

pop_back() does its work with a simple call to erase(end()). The amount of work needed to accomplish this is constant, regardless of the number of elements in the list.

```
while ( a.size() > 0 )
    a.pop_back();
```

iterator insert(iterator position, const T& x = T())

template<class InputIterator>
void insert(iterator position, InputIterator first,
InputIterator last)

void insert(iterator position, size_type n, const T& x)

In comparison to other containers, list<T> does very well at insertions, so it makes sense that it has a wide variety of insertion member functions. These three functions allow you to insert the following into a random position in the list:

- a single T object
- a range of T objects, based on either pointers or iterators defining a range
- a sequence of *n* identical copies

Regardless of which function you choose, inserting a single object of type T takes place in $O(k)$ time. So, the expense of inserting an object or sequence of objects doesn't change as the length of the list goes up. Of course, this is one of the appealing characteristics of list<T>.

Note that one of the three insert() functions returns an iterator instead of a void. When inserting a single object into the container, this version of insert returns an iterator pointing to the position of the newly created object in the container.

```
list<string>::iterator j;
j = a.find( "Mark Nelson" );
insert( j, string( "Mike Nelson" ) );
```

void erase(iterator position)

void erase(iterator first, iterator last)

Erasing a single element in a list is an $O(k)$ operation. Regardless of the size of the list container, a single erasure has a predetermined amount of work to perform. It has to change the links in the previous and next nodes, call the destructor for the object via destroy(), and dispose of the memory using put_node().

Likewise, erasing a sequence of objects in a list takes $O(N)$ time, where N reflects the size of the range to be erased, not the size of the list. The code to implement this version of erase() makes that obvious—at least, if you believe a single erasure is O(*k*):

```
template <class T>
void list<T>::erase(iterator first, iterator last) {
    while (first != last) erase(first++);
}
```

Note: An iterator pointing into a range that has been erased will no longer be valid. This may not be the case with a vector<T> or deque<T>, but it will definitely be true here.

```
void clear( list<double>& assets )
{
    list<double>::iterator i;
    for( ; ; ) {
        i = find( assets, 0 );
        if ( !i )
            return;
        assets.erase( i );
    }
}
```

void swap(list<T>& x)

list<T>::swap() is easy to implement under the STL. Like the swap() functions implemented for the other containers in the STL, this is actually a very simple function that only appears to be doing a lot of work. All the list<T> member function needs to do in order to swap two entire lists is to swap the root nodes. Since the root nodes are the only link to the rest of the list, exchanging this small amount of data has the effect of swapping the entire list.

```
void swap(list<T>& x) {
    ::swap(node, x.node);
    ::swap(length, x.length);
}
```

list<T> has scads of other data members. As they are all static members, they are shared among every instance of a particular list<T>, and don't need to be swapped.

Note: If you have an iterator pointing into list *a*, and you swap it with list *b*, your iterator will end up pointing into *b*, not *a*.

```
template<class T>
void rotate( list<T>& a )
{
    tape << a;
    a.swap( backup );
}
```

List Operations

```
void splice(iterator position, list<T>& x);
void splice(iterator position, list<T>& x, iterator i);
void splice(iterator position,
            list<T>& x,
            iterator first,
            iterator last);
void remove(const T& value);
void unique();
void merge(list<T>& x);
void reverse();
void sort();
```

void splice(iterator position, list<T>& x)

void splice(iterator position, list<T>& x, iterator i)

void splice(iterator position, list<T>& x, iterator first, iterator last)

All three versions of this function splice elements of the argument list into the list<T>container. The affected elements are removed from list *x*.

The first version of splice() moves the entire contents of *x* into the list<T> container at the iterator position, leaving *x* empty. The second splice() moves a single element, decreasing the length of *x* by 1 and increasing the length of the target list by 1.

The third version removes a range of elements from *x* and moves them into the target list. The length of the target is increased by the appropriate amount, and the length of *x* is decremented by the same amount. All serious work here is done by the private member function transfer().

Like all standard versions of the STL, these functions do no range checking on *x*. You need to ensure in advance you can splice the range you want to.

```
void graduate( list<employee> &new_hires )
{
    staff.splice( new_hires );
    ...
```

void remove(const T& value)

remove() iterates through the entire list, erasing any occurrence of a node equal to *value*. This simple function performs its work in $O(N)$ time, where N is the number of elements in the list:

```
template <class T>
void list<T>::remove(const T& value) {
    iterator first = begin();
    iterator last = end();
    while (first != last) {
        iterator next = first;
        ++next;
        if (*first == value) erase(first);
        first = next;
    }
}
```

The function has to be coded carefully to avoid leaving a pointer dangling after an erase, but it is still relatively simple.

```
main()
{
    list<double> income;
    read_data( income );
    income.remove( 0.0 );
...
```

void unique()

unique is the first of two functions that make an assumption about list<T>. unique() is designed to go through the entire list and remove any duplicate values. This sounds like a difficult job and, ordinarily, it is. However, unique() makes the assumption that the list is already sorted! (Since list<T> has a member function that sorts the list, this isn't as harsh a requirement as it might first sound.) That changes things quite a bit, as the code from list.h shows:

```
template <class T>
void list<T>::unique() {
    iterator first = begin();
    iterator last = end();
    if (first == last) return;
    iterator next = first;
    while (++next != last) {
```

```
                        if (*first == *next)
                            erase(next);
    •              else
                            first = next;
                   next = first;
               }
       }
```

The presence of unique() in the header file as well is why type T needs an operator==() defined. Even if you aren't using unique(), some compilers, such as Borland's, insist on instantiating list<T>::unique(). If operator==() isn't defined, there will be an error.

```
void spell_check( char *file )
    list<string> vocabulary;
    read( file, vocabulary );
    vocabulary.sort();
    vocabulary.unique();
```

void merge(list<T>& x)

Like unique(), list<T>::merge() assumes both *this* and *x* are lists in sorted order. The merge() function takes the contents of *x* and transfers them to *this*, while keeping the resulting list sorted. When the merge operation is complete, *x* will have a length 0. The length of the target list will have increased by the original size of *x*.

```
list<string> stock;

void add_to_stock( list<string>& shipment )
{
    shipment.sort();
    stock.merge( shipment );
}
```

void reverse()

The STL has a built-in reverse() algorithm that can be used effectively with vector<T> or deque<T>. The same algorithm can be applied to list<T> as well, but member function reverse provides a more efficient alternative.

This version of reverse() takes advantage of that fact that it is often easier to break links and move a node than to swap the contents of two nodes. In particular, this is the case when type T is relatively large, especially in comparison to the pointers used as links in list<T>.

The source code for list<T>::reverse() is shown next. The code may appear slightly convoluted, but it's working its way through the list, transferring elements 1 through *N*-1 to the front of the list.

```
template <class T>
void list<T>::reverse() {
    if (size() < 2) return;
    for (iterator first = ++begin(); first != end();) {
        iterator old = first++;
        transfer(begin(), old, first);
    }
}
```

Let's look at Figure 20-4 as an example. If there's a list<int> with five elements, originally filled with integers 0 through 4, the first pass through the loop sets up old to point to element 1, and first to element 2. The function call to transfer() then moves element 1 only to the start of the list.

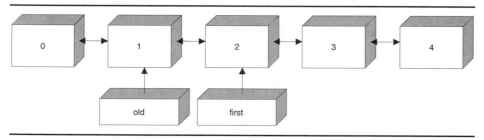

Figure 20-4
A sample list<int> before the first call to transfer()

The second pass through the loop calls transfer() with an iterator pointing to element 2. As a result, it is shifted to the front of the list. See Figure 20-5.

After *N*-1 iterations of the loop, the list<T> is completely reversed. The cost for this operation is measured in terms of O(*N*) manipulations of link pointers.

The standard reverse() algorithm swaps the actual contents of the container. It has to perform *N*/2 of these swaps to reverse a container. Clearly, if the objects stored in the container are large, reversing via the list<T> member function is vastly more efficient, since it only has to manipulate link pointers. However, you might want to test performance for list containers holding smaller objects.

```
list<employee> a;
input >> a;
a.reverse();
output << a;
```

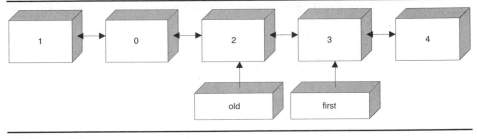

Figure 20-5
Before the second call to transfer()

void sort()

The standard package of algorithms that comes with the STL includes a couple of sort variations, so you might not expect to have a sort() member function as part of a container class. However, the sort code found in algo.h presents a problem. The standard sort algorithms expect random access iterators,
and list<T> can only supply a bidirectional iterator.

Fortunately, there are sort algorithms that don't require random access
iterators, so a specialized sort is provided as a member function of list<T>.
This sort() has $O(N\log N)$ performance, where N is the size of the linked list
to be sorted.

```
main()
{
    list<employees> staff;
    read_in( staff );
    staff.sort();
    promote( staff,.10 );
    return SUCCESS;
}
```

Relational/equality operators

```
bool operator==(const list<T>& x, const list<T>& y);
bool operator<(const list<T>& x, const list<T>& y);
```

These two functions compare two lists. The equality operator only
returns true if the two vectors have the same number of elements, and if all
elements are equal. The second function performs a lexicographical (string)
comparison of the two vectors, and returns the result.

bool operator==(const list<T>& x, const list<T>& y)

This operator provides an easy way to test whether or not two lists are equal. First, it compares the size() for both vectors. If they are unequal, a result of false is returned immediately.

If the sizes are the same, it compares the two vectors element by element, using the template function equal(). This function uses operator==() for function T to compare elements one at a time. If all elements compare as equal, a true value is returned; otherwise false is returned.

```
template<class T>
void process( list<T>& a )
{
    list<T> b( a );
    assert( a == b );
```

bool operator<(const list<T>& x, const list<T>& y)

The previous function has an easy job, trying to decide if two lists are equal. This function has a harder time of it.

To see if one vector is considered to be less than another, you must perform a lexicographical comparison. This is an element-by-element comparison, done in much the same way as a string comparison in the standard C library using strcmp().

operator<() doesn't do any work itself. It passes iterators pointing into both vectors to one of the STL standard algorithms, lexicographical_compare(). This function steps through the vectors, one element at a time, and returns a value based on the following code:

```
template <class InputIterator1, class InputIterator2>
bool lexicographical_compare(InputIterator1 first1,
                             InputIterator1 last1,
                             InputIterator2 first2,
                             InputIterator2 last2) {
    while (first1 != last1 && first2 != last2) {
        if (*first1 < *first2) return true;
        if (*first2++ < *first1++) return false;
    }
    return first1 == last1 && first2 != last2;
}
```

lexicographical_compare() looks forbidding, but it does more or less what you expect. If an element in the first container is less than the second, you can immediately return true. If the element in the second container is greater, you can immediately return false. Otherwise, you must move on to the next element. If you ever exit the loop, you have reached the end of one of the containers. If you reach the end of container 1, but not container 2, you can return true. Otherwise, container 1 is equal to container 2, and you must return false.

An example of how operator<() can be used on list<T> containers is shown here:

```
int check_order( list<char> a[], int n )
{
    for ( i = 1 ; i < n ; i++ )
        if ( a[ i ] < a[ i -1 ] {
            cout << "Lists out of order!\n";
            return 0;
        }
    return 1;
}
```

ASSOCIATIVE CONTAINERS

This section provides reference information on all four associative containers. It describes types, all public members, and some of the more important private members.

To avoid duplication, functions and members that are identical for all four classes have been grouped together whenever possible. Functions or members not found in all four classes are labeled for clarity.

classes

The four associative container classes have only one nested class definition, and it only appears in the two map-based classes.

	Set	Multi-Set	Map	Multi-Map
class value_compare;			√	√

class value_compare

class value_compare is a nested class that compares the key values of objects stored in a map or multimap. It creates a comparison object that can be used much like the comparison object that compares key values for all four classes.

When the associative class is declared, a comparison class is passed as a type parameter. For example, in the declaration

```
set<int,less<int> > a;
```

the type parameter less<int> is the type of a comparison class. An object created from this class is used to compare key values when navigating the red-black tree during insertions or searches.

Note: A map stores objects of type pair<const Key, T>, so you can't compare them directly with a comparison function such as less<int>.

To perform comparisons on objects of value_type, this class uses the original comparison class on the key portions of the pair<> object stored in the container. The definition of the comparison function inside this class shows how this is accomplished:

```
bool operator()(const value_type& x, const value_type& y) const {
    return comp(x.first, y.first);
}
```

In this case, the first member of each of the two objects is the first part of the pair object, or simply the key value.

Typedefs

The STL uses a set of standard type definitions to support uniform access to container classes. When designing a container for the STL, some of these type definitions have to be built up from scratch.

For example, deque<T> has to define iterator and const_iterator as completely new classes. The rest of the types needed by this class are defined as typedefs. Thus, deque<T> can recycle types that are already defined elsewhere.

When you look through this list of typedefs, it may appear that there is a huge difference between the two map containers and the two set containers. In fact, the differences are minimal.

	Set	Multi-Set	Map	Multi-Map
typedef Key key_type;	√	√	√	√
typedef Key value_type;	√	√		
typedef pair<const Key, T> value_type;			√	√
typedef Compare key_compare;	√	√	√	√
typedef Compare value_compare;	√	√		
typedef value_type::reference reference;	√	√	√	√
typedef value_type::const_reference const_reference;	√	√	√	√
typedef value_type::iterator iterator;	√	√	√	√
typedef value_type::const_iterator const_iterator;	√	√	√	√
typedef value_type::reverse_iterator reverse_iterator;			√	√
typedef value_type::const_reverse_iterator const_reverse_iterator;	√	√	√	√
typedef value_type::size_type size_type;	√	√	√	√
typedef value_type::difference_type difference_type;	√	√	√	√

The reason for the variation between the two sets of typedefs is a minor difference in the way the const-ness of the key object is handled in the two families. In neither case can you use an iterator to modify a key already present in the container. This would destroy the ordered nature of the tree, making it unusable.

set<> and multiset<> ensure you won't do this. They always return a const_iterator, regardless of whether you declare your iterator to be of type iterator or const_iterator. Because of this, set<> and multiset<> don't have a definition for const_iterator; they don't need it.

map<> and multimap<> handle things somewhat differently. Their iterators point to a pair<const Key,T> object. The standard iterator shouldn't be a const_iterator, because you can use it to modify the T object. For this reason, these containers have both an iterator and const_iterator definition.

key_type

```
typedef Key key_type;  //All containers
```

This type definition refers to the type of the key used to order the elements in the container. The key value is established by the key type passed in the type definition of the associative container. For example, a multimap<> declaration might look like this:

```
multimap< long, string, less<long> > employees;
```

In this class definition, the typedef for key_type makes it a synonym for the built-in type long.

value_type

```
typedef Key value_type;             //set, multiset
typedef pair<const Key, T> value_type;  //map, multimap
```

The two families of associative containers have two completely different definitions for value_type. This type definition defines what is stored in the container. It also determines what sort of value is returned by dereferencing an iterator.

set<> and multiset<> containers only contain key values. Therefore, their definition for value_type is a synonym for the Key type declared in the type definition. map<> and multimap<> store a pair<> instead of just the key, so they have a different type declaration.

key_compare

```
typedef Compare key_compare;  //All containers
```

This type declaration duplicates the Compare class definition in key_compare. The Compare type is defined in the type declaration for the associative container. A typical value for Compare is less<Key>.

value_compare

```
typedef Compare value_compare;  //set,multiset
```

All associative containers contain a comparison object that can compare two key values. It's used when objects are inserted into the container, or a search operation is taking place.

In addition to the standard comparison objects, associative classes define a value_compare class. This class can test two value_objects for inequality.

Note: This class doesn't test to see if the objects themselves are unequal; it just compares their keys.

The map<> and multimap<> classes have to work to compare two keys in a pair of value_object objects. There isn't this problem with multiset<> and set<>, because their value_object is the same as Key. You can use the compare class employed in the type declaration to compare value_object objects, just as easily as you can for Key objects; after all, they're the same thing!

reference

const_reference

```
typedef value_type::reference reference;             //All
typedef value_type::const_reference const_reference; //All
```

This type definition defines a reference to a value_object. This is a reference to the type of data being stored in the container.

There is a difference in the way references are defined for the set<> family and the map<> family. The value_object in a set<> is the key, and cannot be modified. Because of this, both reference and const_reference for the set<> family are the same const type.

The map<> family is different, because half of the pair<const Key,T> objects it returns as value_type can be modified. The Key member is const, but the T member can be freely modified. Because of this, map<> and multimap<> have both a reference and a const_reference.

iterator

const_iterator

```
typedef rep_type::iterator iterator;             //All
typedef rep_type::const_iterator const_iterator; //All
```

There is an exact parallel here between iterators and references. set<> and multiset<> iterators refer to key objects which are const. Because of this, iterator and const_iterator are equivalent for set<> and multiset<>. The map<> family has a standard iterator that can be dereferenced to point to a value_object, which can then be modified.

reverse_iterator

const_reverse_iterator

```
typedef
rep_type::reverse_iterator reverse_iterator; //All

typedef
rep_type::const_reverse_iterator const_reverse_iterator; //All
```

Once again, there is the same parallel here with the iterator and reference classes. The reverse iterator for set<> and multiset<> is a const iterator, whereas the map<> family of containers has both types of iterators.

All iterators created for use with the four associative containers are rb_tree iterators. They are bidirectional; both forward and reverse iterators are easily supported.

size_type

```
typedef rep_type::size_type size_type;  //All containers
```

size_type is a typedef that gets copied directly from the size_type in class rb_tree. The typedef for rb_tree is, in turn, a copy of the size_type defined in the allocator for this class. size_type is an integer type big enough to hold the size of the largest object that can be created using the memory allocator.

Using the default allocator, size_type is usually a synonym for size_t. Other memory allocators use different types. For example, the 16-bit Borland C++ compiler has a huge memory pointer type, which would define size_type to be synonymous with long.

difference_type

```
typedef rep_type::difference_type difference_type; //All containers
```

This is another type defined by the allocator. difference_type can be used to hold the difference between two pointers under the current allocator. Under MS-DOS standard memory models, this is defined as ptrdiff_t.

Copy, construct, destroy

The four associative classes have three different constructors, plus an assignment operator. In a departure from the rest of the STL, these containers don't have destructors. The cleanup done in the rb_tree destructor handles all the necessary work.

While each class has a unique version of the three constructors and the assignment operator, you can see they are essentially identical. Only the names have been changed:

```
set(const Compare& comp = Compare(), Allocator& = Allocator() );
multiset(const Compare& comp = Compare(),Allocator& = Allocator() );
map(const Compare& comp = Compare(),Allocator& = Allocator() );
multimap(const Compare& comp = Compare(),Allocator& = Allocator());

set(InputIterator first,
    InputIterator last,
    const Compare& comp = Compare(),
    Allocator& = Allocator() );
multiset(InputIterator first,
        InputIterator last,
        const Compare& comp = Compare(),
        Allocator& = Allocator() );
map(InputIterator first,
    InputIterator last,
    const Compare& comp = Compare(),
    Allocator& = Allocator() );
multimap(InputIterator first,
        InputIterator last,
        const Compare& comp = Compare(),
        Allocator& = Allocator() );

set(const set<Key, Compare>& x,
    Allocator& = Allocator() );
multiset(const multiset<Key, Compare>& x,
        Allocator& = Allocator() );
map(const map<Key, T, Compare>& x,
    Allocator& = Allocator() );
multimap(const multimap<Key, T, Compare>& x,
        Allocator& = Allocator() );

set<Key, Compare>& operator=(const set<Key, Compare>& x);
multiset<Key, Compare>& operator=(const multiset<Key, Compare>& x);
map<Key, T, Compare>& operator=(const map<Key, T, Compare>& x);
multimap<Key, T, Compare>&
operator=(const multimap<Key, T, Compare>& x);
```

container(const Compare& comp = Compare(), Allocator& = Allocator())

```
set(const Compare& comp = Compare(),
    Allocator& = Allocator() );
multiset(const Compare& comp = Compare(),
        Allocator& = Allocator());
map(const Compare& comp = Compare(),
    Allocator& = Allocator());
multimap(const Compare& comp = Compare(),
        Allocator& = Allocator());
```

This is the default constructor for the four associative containers. If you don't specify a comparison object (and it isn't likely you'll need to) the compiler constructs a default object using the comparison class you specified in the type declaration.

After the constructor runs, the rb_tree member of the class will have been initialized, and should contain no objects.

```
void sort_lines( ifstream &input )
{
    set< int, string, less< string > > lines;
    .
    .
    .
```

template<class InputIterator>
container(InputIterator first,
InputIterator last,
const Compare& comp = Compare(),
Allocator& = Allocator())

```
template<class InputIterator>
set( InputIterator first,
     InputIterator last,
     const Compare& comp = Compare(),
     Allocator& = Allocator());

template<class InputIterator>
multiset( InputIterator first,
          InputIterator last,
          const Compare& comp = Compare(),
          Allocator& = Allocator());
```

```
template<class InputIterator>
map(InputIterator first,
    InputIterator last,
    const Compare& comp = Compare(),
    Allocator& = Allocator());


template<class InputIterator>
multimap( InputIterator first,
          InputIterator last,
          const Compare& comp = Compare(),
          Allocator& = Allocator());
```

How does this constructor perform the comparisons when navigating the tree? The same way as the default constructor: it takes a function object as an optional argument. If you don't specify the comparison object, the compiler creates one by using the default constructor for the comparison object class. In all likelihood, you can let the default case apply.

The first and second arguments to this constructor consist of pointers to a range of value_type objects. As the object is constructed, these objects are added, one at a time, to the newly created container.

```
void foo( string *first, string *last ) {
{
    multiset< string, string, less<string> > input( first, last );
    .
    .
    .
```

Note: This is a template member function. Your implementation of the STL may substitute a function that looks something like this:

```
container( const T* first,
           const T* last,
           const Compare& comp = Compare(),
           Allocator& = Allocator());
```

container(const container& , Allocator& = Allocator())

```
set( const set<Key,Compare>& x,
     Allocator& = Allocator());
multiset(const multiset<Key,Compare>& x,
         Allocator& = Allocator());
map( const map<Key, T, Compare>& x,
     Allocator& = Allocator());
multimap( const multimap<Key, T, Compare>& x,
          Allocator& = Allocator());
```

The copy constructor for each of the four container types is implemented using the copy constructor of rb_tree. The copy constructor for the red-black tree is able to improve on the brute force copy done in the previous constructor. The reason is that the container knows the tree it is copying from is already ordered properly. This means no tree navigation is necessary as new items are added to the tree.

The net result is that one container can be copied to another at a lower cost than a sequence of insertions. The constructor still has to perform the memory allocations for all the objects being inserted, but the comparison operations are skipped. The savings vary, depending on the relative cost of the two operations.

```
void process( const my_map& employees )
{
    my_map transfers( employees );
    my_map::iterator transfers.find( "Mark Nelson" );
        .
        .
        .
```

container& operator=(const container&)

```
set<Key, Compare>& operator=(const set<Key, Compare>& x);
multiset<Key, Compare>& operator=(const multiset<Key, Compare>& x);
map<Key, T, Compare>& operator=(const map<Key, T, Compare>& x);
multimap<Key, T, Compare>&
operator=(const multimap<Key, T, Compare>& x);
```

Just like the copy constructor, the assignment operator works by calling the assignment operator for the red-black tree class. An example is this code for the assignment operator for map<>:

```
map<Key, T, Compare>& operator=(const map<Key, T, Compare>& x) {
    t = x.t;
    return *this;
}
```

As is the case with the copy constructor, the assignment operator can do the copy more efficiently than with just a straight sequence of insertions. Since the data being copied is already in order, the comparison function never needs to be called, as the tree is copied in order.

This function costs more in execution time than the copy constructor. The existing container has to be erased before the new elements can be copied into it.

```
my_map bonus_payments;

void reward( const my_map& employees )
{
    my_map::iterator employees.find( "Mark Nelson" );
    .
    .
    .
    bonus_payments = employees;
}
```

Iterators

	Set	Multi-Set	Map	Multi-Map
iterator begin();	√	√	√	√
const_iterator begin() const;	√	√	√	√
iterator end();	√	√	√	√
const_iterator end() const;	√	√	√	√
reverse_iterator rbegin();	√	√	√	√
const_reverse_iterator rbegin() const;	√	√	√	√
reverse_iterator rend();	√	√	√	√
const_reverse_iterator rend() const;	√	√	√	√

The functions that return iterators have the same names and semantics as their namesakes in the sequential containers. This uniformity is one of the strengths of the STL. Once you learn how to use iterators, and how to get them, you know how to work with all types of containers.

begin()

```
iterator begin();              //All
const_iterator begin() const;  //All
```

begin() is one of the functions supported across all STL containers. It's called to get an iterator that points to the first object in the container. If the container is empty, the iterator returned by begin() is equal to the iterator returned by end().

```
typedef map< long, double, less<long> > salaries;

double payroll( const salaries& s )
{
    double total = 0;
    salaries::iterator i;
    for ( i = s.begin() ; i != s.end() ; i++ )
        total += (*i).second;
    return total;
}
```

end()

```
iterator end();              //All
const_iterator end() const; //All
```

end() is complementary to the begin() function. Anytime you want to iterate through a container, start with the iterator returned by begin(). Terminate when the iterator has been incremented to the point where it equals end().

```
multiset<foo, my_compare_class>::iterator i;
i = models.lower_bound( test_case );
if ( i == models.end() )
    return;
```

rbegin()

```
reverse_iterator rbegin();              //All
const_reverse_iterator rbegin() const;  //All
```

All associative containers can support reverse iterators without any extra effort, since the underlying object, rb_tree, has bidirectional iterators. Since they *are* bidirectional, creating a reverse iterator is a simple job.

```
print_employees( const staff &employees )
{
    cout << "Employees ranked in order of importance\n";
        << "Highest pay comes first\n";
    for ( staff::reverse_iterator ri = employees.rbegin();
        ri != employees.end();
        ri++ )
        print_employee( ri );
}
```

rend()

```
reverse_iterator rend();                 //All
const_reverse_iterator rend() const;   //All
```

rend() returns a reverse_iterator that denotes the end of a reverse iteration sequence. The value returned by rend() should not be dereferenced, as
it will attempt to access a nonexistent location in the red-black tree.
Primarily, rend() is used to return a value that can be tested to see if a
reverse iterator has reached the end of its container.

```
for ( set<string,less<string> >::reverse_iterator ri = a.rebegin();
    ri != a.rend();
    ri++ )
    cout << (*ri) << endl;
```

Capacity

	Set	Multi-Set	Map	Multi-Map
bool empty() const;	√	√	√	√
size_type size() const;	√	√	√	√
size_type max_size() const;	√	√	√	√

These three functions are standard across the entire line of STL containers,
so you shouldn't encounter any surprises from them.

bool empty() const

empty() is a simple boolean function that checks whether the container is empty. There are many different ways you can determine if a container is empty, but empty() is a nice, straightforward function.

empty() is implemented in all four associative containers by simply calling rb_tree::empty(). The red-black tree class checks its node_count to see if there are 0 nodes in the tree, in which case it returns true. Otherwise, it returns false.

```
cout << "Stocks on hand: ";
if ( Investments.empty() )
    return;
```

size_type size() const

size() is called to find how many objects are stored in the container at a given time. Like empty(), the actual work is done by the red-black tree class, which returns its node count.

```
cout << "Palette entries:"
    << colors.size()
    << endl;
```

size_type max_size() const

max_size() returns the count of the largest possible container. This value is determined by the memory model presently in use, set by the Allocator object.

```
cout << "Container can only hold "
    << container.max_size()
    << " items"
    << endl;
```

Element access

	Set	Multi-Set	Map	Multi-Map
T& operator[](const key_type& k);		√		
const T& operator[] (const key_type& k) const;	√			

This operator is used to make map<> work as an associative array. If an object corresponding to the key value *k* is found in the container, this function returns a reference to it. If no object is found corresponding to the key, a new entry is created using the default constructor of the value object.

This is one of the only functions in the family of associative containers that isn't universally supported in one form or another. It simply doesn't make sense in the other containers, but it is was too good to pass up for the one container it does support.

```
a[ "Bill Gates" ] = 1;
a[ "Steve Jobs" ] = 2;
a[ "Bob Frankenberg" ] = 3;
a[ "Charles Wang" ] = 4;
```

Modifiers

	Set	Multi-Set	Map	Multi-Map
pair<iterator,bool> insert(const value_type& x);	√		√	
iterator insert(const value_type& x);		√		√
iterator insert(iterator position, const value_type& x);	√	√	√	√
void insert(InputIterator first, InputIterator last);	√	√	√	√
void erase(iterator position);	√	√	√	√
size_type erase(const key_type& x);	√	√	√	√
void erase(iterator first, iterator last);	√	√	√	√
void swap(Container& x);	√	√	√	√

These functions modify the structure of the tree. They insert and delete items, which will cause reshaping of the tree, and may invalidate existing iterators.

insert(const value_type& x)
iterator insert(iterator position, const value_type& x)
void insert(InputIterator first, InputIterator last)

```
pair<iterator,bool> insert(const value_type& x); //Set,Map
iterator insert(const value_type& x); //Multiset, Multimap
iterator insert(iterator position, const value_type& x); //All
template<InputIterator>
void insert(InputIterator first, InputIterator last);  //All
```

Although there are four different insert functions defined here, they represent just three different types of insertions.

The first two functions are called to insert a new object into a container. They differ in return type because of the differences between the set<> and map<> containers and their two siblings.

Since set<> and map<> don't allow multiple keys, you have to deal with the possibility that their insertions may fail. This isn't going to happen with multiset<> and multimap<>.

To deal with the possibility of failure, the first form of insert() returns a pair<> instead of just a simple iterator. The second element of the pair is a boolean flag, indicating whether the insertion operation worked.

If the insertion was successful, the returned iterator points to the newly inserted object (as it always will in the second type of insert). If the insertion fails, the returned iterator points to the duplicate key that caused the insertion to fail.

The final two insertion operations are universal across all four container types. insert(iterator, const value_type&) is similar to the first function. The key difference is that it includes a *hint iterator*. This iterator tells the insertion function where to begin searching for an appropriate insertion point.

The nice thing about supplying a hint iterator is that it can significantly cut down your insertion time. Usually, an insertion takes O(logN) time, where N is the number of items in the container. If you supply a hint that points directly to the position where the object should be inserted, it's reduced to constant time, or O(k).

Normally, you could take advantage of this whenever you insert a list of objects that are already sorted. For example, if you iterate through a sorted vector, inserting the objects into a container, you might write code like this:

```
i = a.begin();
for ( j = v.begin(); j != v.end(); j++ )
    i = a.insert( i, *j );
```

The final insert() function inserts a range of objects into the container. It's strictly a convenience, as the code in tree.h performs the insertion into the red-black tree precisely as you would do it yourself:

```
template <class Key, class Value, class KeyOfValue, class Compare>
void rb_tree<Key, Value, KeyOfValue, Compare>::
insert(const Value* first, const Value* last) {
    while (first != last) insert(*first++);
}
```

Note: This final version of insert() is a template member function. Your compiler may have to substitute the following function:

```
void insert(const value_type *first, const value_type *last);
```

void erase(iterator position)

size_type erase(const key_type& x)

void erase(iterator first, iterator last)

These three functions provide the ability to remove elements from the container. The three functions differ in the elements they erase.

erase(iterator) is the simplest of the three; it removes the element in the container pointed to by the single iterator argument. Navigating the tree and adjusting it after the removal is an O(logN) operation.

Note: There is no error checking on this operation, so you have to be sure your iterator points to a valid element in the container.

erase(const key_type&) is called to erase all elements that match the key argument. The actual number found and destroyed is returned as an integer count.

Finally, erase(iterator, iterator) accepts a range of iterators pointing into the tree, and destroys the entire range.

```
pair< my_map::iterator, my_map::iterator> ip =
        a.equal_range( "Bill Gates" );
a.erase( ip.first, ip.second );
```

void swap(Container& x)

```
void swap(set<Key, Compare>& x);
void swap(multiset<Key, Compare>& x);
void swap(map<Key, T, Compare>& x);
void swap(multimap<Key, T, Compare>& x);
```

All four of these functions call the equivalent function in the underlying class of rb_tree. rb_tree<>::swap() is a nice, low-cost operation. It merely has to swap the root of the tree, the comparison object, the duplicate flag, and the count. Relative to the potential size of the tree itself, that makes this function a computational bargain.

```
check( my_map & a, my_map & b )
{
    if ( a.size() > b.size() )
        a.swap( b );
}
```

Observers

	Set	Multi-Set	Map	Multi-Map
key_compare key_comp() const;	√	√	√	√
value_compare value_comp() const;	√	√	√	√

You can use these functions to get copies of the comparison objects in use for the given container.

key_compare key_comp() const

This function returns a copy of the comparison object used to compare keys. If you need to compare keys, and want to be sure you're using the same comparison function as the tree in question, you can access it this way.

The function object returned from this call can be treated in your program as if it were an actual function:

```
my_set::key_compare comp = a.key_comp();
cout << "comp( Mark, Bill ) = "
     << comp( "Mark", "Bill" )
     << endl;
```

value_compare value_comp() const

This function returns a function object as well. Unlike key_comp(), it isn't a user-defined function object. Instead, it's created inside the container class that can compare the key values of two objects. This requires the function object to extract key values from the pair<const Key&, T> stored in the container.

```
main()
{
    typedef map< string, int, less<string> > my_set;
    my_set a;

    cout << "The key value is the string, not the number!"
        << endl;
    a[ "Mark" ] = 100;
    a[ "Bill" ] = 200;
    a[ "John" ] = 300;
    my_set::iterator m = a.find( "Mark" );
    my_set::iterator b = a.find( "Bill" );
    my_set::iterator j = a.find( "John" );
    cout << "Mark = " << (*m).second << endl;
    cout << "Bill = " << (*b).second << endl;
    cout << "John = " << (*j).second << endl;
    my_set::value_compare comp = a.value_comp();
    cout << "John is "
        << ( comp( *j, *b ) ? "" : "not " )
        << "greater than Bill"
        << endl;
    cout << "John is "
        << ( comp( *j, *m ) ? "" : "not " )
        << "greater than Mark"
        << endl;
    return 1;
}
```

Map/set operations

	Set	Multi-Set	Map	Multi-Map
iterator find(const key_type& x) const;	√	√	√	√
const_iterator find (const key_type& x) const;			√	√
size_type count (const key_type& x) const;	√	√	√	√
iterator lower_bound (const key_type& x) const;	√	√	√	√
const_iterator lower_bound (const key_type& x) const;			√	√
iterator upper_bound (const key_type& x) const;	√	√	√	√
const_iterator upper_bound (const key_type& x) const;			√	√
pair<iterator,iterator> equal_range(const key_type& x) const;	√	√	√	√
pair<const_iterator,const_iterator> equal_range(const key_type& x) const;			√	√

The most important feature of associative containers is their ability to store data in a manner conducive to quick and efficient searches. The functions in this section are all dedicated to searching the map or set containers.

find(const key_type& x) const

```
iterator find(const key_type& x) const;
const_iterator find(const key_type& x) const; //map,multimap
```

The find() function is defined for all four associative containers. find() returns an iterator pointing to a record that matches the key passed as the single parameter. If no key is found, the iterator equals end().

For the multiset<> and multimap<> containers, the key may appear more than once in the container. If this is the case, you have no guarantee about *which* appearance of the key is pointed to by the iterator. If you need to know which key value is returned, you are better off using lower_bound(), upper_bound(), or equal_range() to search for your key.

```
bool exists( string &s )
{
    set< string, less<string> >::iterator i;
    i = symbols.find( s );
    if ( i == symbols.end() )
        return false;
    else
        return true;
}
```

size_type count(const key_type& x) const

count() returns a count of the number of elements in the container equal to the parameter *x*. For map<> and set<> this can only be 0 or 1, since these containers insist on unique keys. For multimap<> and multiset<>, the return value from this function can be anything from 0 to size().

Internally, this function is implemented in the rb_tree class by calling equal_range(), then calculating the distance between the two iterators returned by that function.

Note: If no occurrence of the key is found in the tree, equal_range() returns two iterators, both equal to end(), which should yield a distance of 0.

```
cout << "Outstanding traffic ticket count = "
     << tickets.count( "Letterman" )
     << endl;
```

lower_bound(const key_type& x) const

```
iterator lower_bound(const key_type& x) const;
const_iterator lower_bound(const key_type& x) const; //map,multimap
```

This function is defined for all four associative containers, but isn't particularly useful for map<> and set<>. It's used to locate the first occurrence, in iterator order, of key parameter *x* in the container.

Since map<> and set<> don't allow duplicate keys, find() takes care of this function unambiguously. However, when multiset<> or multimap<> are being used, you need to identify the entire range of objects that contain key. find() doesn't work in those cases, since it returns an iterator that could belong to *any* of the appearances.

When you need to identify the entire range of a key's presence in the container, there are two ways to do it. The first is to use the value returned by this function, along with either upper_bound() or count(). In either case, you can use the iterator returned here as a starting point. You can also use the return value from upper_bound() or count() to determine when to stop incrementing.

The second way to define the range a key occupies is to call equal_range(). This returns a pair of iterators, and is equivalent to making a call to lower_bound(), followed by a call to upper_bound().

```
multiset<foo,fooless>::iterator i;
i = fooset.lower_bound( 50 );
cout << "Lowest match of 50 is "
     << (*i)
     << end;
```

upper_bound(const key_type& x) const

```
iterator upper_bound(const key_type& x) const;
const_iterator upper_bound(const key_type& x) const; //map,multimap
```

upper_bound() is the companion function to lower_bound(). In the canonical STL fashion, it points *one past* the last appearance of the key parameter. If there is no appearance of key parameter *x*, it returns an iterator equal to end().

Note: This function is only useful in conjunction with lower_bound(). When called by itself, you can't be sure if there are any appearances of the key. So, the usual place to see upper_bound() called is as the terminating condition of an iteration loop:

```
multimap<grade,string,less<grade> >::iterator j;
for ( j = employees.lower_bound( SALARIED );
      j != employees.upper_bound( SALARIED );
      j++ )
    cout << (*j).second << " ";
```

equal_range(const key_type& x) const

```
pair<iterator,iterator> equal_range(const key_type& x) const;
pair<const_iterator,const_iterator>
equal_range(const key_type& x) const; //map,multimap
```

Like the previous two functions, this isn't a particularly useful function when dealing with a map<> or set<>. It is defined for these classes as well as multiset<> and multimap<>, which means you can write generic code to handle all four types of containers. However, it's only useful when used with the two container types that handle duplicate keys.

This is another function that returns a pair of values using the pair<> template class. It's important to remember that pair<T1,T2> doesn't have a default constructor. You must initialize it using the copy constructor. This means you can't write code like this:

```
pair<set<int>::iterator,set<int>::iterator> pi;
pi = a.equal_range( 22 );
```

This will generate compiler errors warning you that there isn't a valid constructor that can be used in the declaration of pi.

The sample code shown below calls equal_range() at the declaration of the iterator. This allows it to use the copy constructor to initialize the pair<> object.

```
main()
{
    typedef map< string, int, less<string> > my_map;
    my_map a;

    a[ "Bill Gates" ] = 1;
    a[ "Steve Jobs" ] = 2;
    a[ "Bob Frankenberg" ] = 3;
    a[ "Charles Wang" ] = 4;
    pair< my_map::iterator, my_map::iterator> ip =
        a.equal_range( "Bill Gates" );
    cout << (*(ip.first)).first
        << " = "
        << (*(ip.first)).second
        << endl;
    return 1;
}
```

Note: Accessing the elements in the container is also somewhat convoluted. This is an unfortunate side-effect of having to work through *two* pair<> objects to get to the data.

Relational/equality operators

	Set	Multi-Set	Map	Multi-Map
bool operator==(const Container& x, const Container& y);	√	√	√	√
bool operator==(const Container& x, const Container& y);	√		√	√

All four classes implement identical versions of the logical operators. They can be used to compare two containers of exactly the same type.

bool operator==(const Container& x, const Container& y)

```
bool operator==( const set<Key, Compare>& x,
                 const set<Key, Compare>& y);
bool operator==( const multiset<Key, Compare>& x,
                 const multiset<Key, Compare>& y);
bool operator==( const map<Key, T, Compare>& x,
                 const map<Key, T, Compare>& y);
bool operator==( const multimap<Key, T, Compare>& x,
                 const multimap<Key, T, Compare>& y);
```

This function tests whether two containers are equal. Equality in this case means they are the same size, and all elements compare equal.

```
int write_with_verify( multiset<foo,foo_test> &a )
{
    multiset<foo,foo_test> b;

    data_file << a;
    data_file >> b;
    if ( a == b )
        return 1;
    else
        return 0;
}
```

bool operator<(const Container& x, const Container& y)

```
bool operator<( const set<Key, Compare>& x,
                const set<Key, Compare>& y);
bool operator<( const multiset<Key, Compare>& x,
                const multiset<Key, Compare>& y);
bool operator<( const map<Key, T, Compare>& x,
                const map<Key, T, Compare>& y);
bool operator<( const multimap<Key, T, Compare>& x,
                const multimap<Key, T, Compare>& y);
```

This function is called to compare two containers, component by component. It performs a lexicographical comparison—what C programmers normally think of as a string comparison. This means it tests the first objects in the trees, the second objects, and so on, until it either finds two that aren't equal, or runs out of objects in one or both containers.

```
if ( magnitude_in > magnitude_out )
    cerr << "Losses seen\n"
```

STACK<T>

One of the nice features of container adapters is their simple interface. The reference sections for the three STL sequential containers (vector<T>, deque<T>, and list<T>) describe dozens of type definitions, constructors, and member functions. In comparison, the reference section for the stack container adaptor has less than a dozen entries. If you're a little fatigued after reading about the sequential containers, this ought to be a nice change of pace!

Typedefs

value_type

```
typedef Container::value_type value_type
```

This is one of two typedefs defined for stack<T>. It defines value_type as identical to the value_type definition for the underlying container type. Thus, value_type for stack<deque<string> > will be string.

size_type

```
typedef Container::size_type size_type
```

size_type is another type definition lifted directly from the definition of the container. The type of size_type is defined in the container by the Allocator class. Under most standard memory models, size_type will be size_t, the ANSI C type definition.

Important data members

Container c

The stack container adaptor has just a single data member, Container c. This is a protected data member that defines the container that holds the stack. It is of the type specified in the class definition, and is normally a vector<T> or deque<T>. The class of the container must meet the type requirements defined in Chapter 7.

Member and friend functions

bool empty() const

empty() is a boolean public member function. It returns the value given from evaluating c.empty(). Under the definitions for the three sequential STL classes, empty() will be true when the container doesn't contain any objects. Of course, a user-defined class is free to define empty() to mean something completely different, but any such attempt would be unwise.

size_type size() const

This function simply returns the value of c.size(). All of the STL container classes define this member function to return the number of objects held in the container. Note that the value returned by this function isn't used internally by the stack adaptor, but it should be useful to end users of stack<T>.

value_type& top()
const value_type& top() const

The two variations of top() return references to the top item on the stack, which means you can use top() on the left side of an assignment:

```
a.top() = "New value";
```

Note: These two functions do no testing to see if there is a valid item on the stack, so the user should be careful to only call this function when empty() is false.

void push(const value_type& x)

This function pushes a new item onto the stack. A copy of object x is made, which gets inserted into the container using Container::push_back(). It is assumed that the push_back() function will put the value at the end of the container, where it can be removed using pop_back().

void pop()

You might expect a function such as pop() to return the value popped from the stack, but the STL doesn't work this way. Instead, pop() destroys the last item in the container by calling the pop_back() function. If you want to use it at any time, you either have to make a copy of it, or keep a reference to it on hand.

Since pop() is a void function, your code that uses pop() might end up looking something like this:

```
stack< vector<string> > a;
    .
    .
    .
if ( !a.empty() ) {
    string x = a.top();
    a.pop();
    foo( x );
    ...
```

template <class Container>
bool operator==(const stack<Container>& x, const stack<Container>& y)

template <class Container>
bool operator<(const stack<Container>& x, const stack<Container>& y)

These two friend functions perform lexicographical comparisons of two stack<T> objects. They rely on the member operator functions of Container to do the work needed.

QUEUE<T>

queue<T> has the simple interface typical of container adaptors.

Typedefs

value_type

```
typedef Container::value_type value_type
```

This is one of two typedefs defined for queue<T>. It defines value_type as identical to the value_type definition for Container. So if you declare your queue<T> as queue< list<foo> >, value_type should be foo.

size_type

```
typedef Container::size_type size_type
```

size_type is another type definition lifted directly from the definition of the container. The type of size_type is defined in the container by the Allocator class. Under most standard memory models, size_type equals size_t, the ANSI C type definition.

Important data members

Container c

This data member defines the container that holds the queue. It is of the type specified in the class definition, and will usually be a deque<T> or list<T>. This is a protected data member of queue<T>, which encapsulates the container. This means your interface to this container will be restricted to the member functions of queue<T>.

The class of the container must meet the type requirements defined in Chapter 7. deque<T> and list<T> both meet the requirements, as should classes derived from them. You have to ensure that any custom containers you develop have all the required member functions and operators.

Member and friend functions

bool empty() const

empty() is a boolean public member function. It returns the value given from evaluating c.empty(). Under the definitions for the two sequential STL classes that can be used here, empty() will be true when the container holds 0 objects.

size_type size() const

This function returns the value of c.size(). The STL container classes define this member function to return the number of objects held in the container. The queue<T> code doesn't use the size() function; it is there strictly for you as a user of the queue container.

value_type& front()
const value_type& front() const

These two functions return a reference to the oldest item in the queue<T>. The next call to pop() removes this item from the queue. This function returns a reference to the item in the queue, which means you can also use it on the left side of an assignment operator:

```
q.front() = -1;
```

   Note: These two functions do no testing to see if there is a valid item on the stack, so the user should be careful to call this function when empty() is true.

value_type& back()
const value_type& back() const

The two variations of back() return references to the last item of type T inserted into the queue. Like front(), since this function returns a reference, it can be used as the left side of an assignment operator.
   Note: These two functions do no testing to see if there is a valid item on the stack, so the user should be careful to call this function when empty() is true.

void push(const value_type& x)

This function pushes a new item into the FIFO. A copy of object x is made, which gets inserted into the container using Container::push_back(). queue<T> expects push_back() to put the value at the end of the container, which is the behavior defined for STL containers.

Objects that get removed from the container will be removed from the front. Anything inserted using push() will now be the last object removed before the container is emptied.

void pop()

pop() deletes just the first item in the container by calling the container's pop_front() function. If you want to utilize this object before destroying it, you need to make a copy of it using the front() reference function.

template <class Container>
bool operator==(const queue<Container>& x, const queue<Container>& y)

template <class Container>
bool operator<(const queue<Container>& x, const queue<Container>& y)

These two friend functions each perform lexicographical comparisons of two queue<T> objects. They rely on the member operator functions of Container to do the work needed.

PRIORITY_QUEUE<T>

priority_queue<T> has the same type definitions used by the other two container adaptors.

Typedefs

value_type

```
typedef Container::value_type value_type
```

This is one of two typedefs defined for priority_queue<T>. It defines value_type as identical to the value_type definition for Container. For the standard STL sequential classes, this is normally type T.

size_type

```
typedef Container::size_type size_type
```

size_type is another type definition lifted directly from the definition of the container. The type of size_type is defined in the container by the Allocator class. Under most standard memory models, size_type is equal to size_t, the ANSI C type definition.

Important data members

Container c

This data member defines the container that holds the priority_queue. It is of the type specified in the class definition, and is normally a vector<T> or deque<T>.

The class of the container must meet the type requirements defined in the previous section. vector<T> and deque<T> both meet the requirements, as should classes derived from them. It's important to ensure that any custom containers you develop have all the required member functions and operators.

Container c is coerced into being a heap at the time it is first constructed. From that point on, it remains a heap. The only time this has to be dealt with is when an object is either added to or removed from the container. The adaptor manages this transparently, as you can see in the source code found in stack.h.

Member and friend functions

Compare comp

comp is the comparison object discussed in the previous sections. Its only purpose is to provide a comparison operator for heap functions. Normally, the comparison operator is used to test whether one element of type T is less than another.

By reversing the sense of the comparison function object, you can reverse the order in which items come out of the priority queue.

For built-in types, using a comparison object of less<T> results in a priority queue that returns the largest objects first. If you supply class greater<T> instead, the priority queue returns the smallest objects first.

priority_queue(const Compare& x = Compare())

This constructor creates an empty priority_queue. Note that you have the option to provide a constructed comparison object for the class to use.

Normally, there's no reason to use anything other than the default comparison object, particularly if you're using the function objects provided with the STL. In the case of STL function objects, one instance is identical to any other, so there's no reason to construct a unique object.

template<class InputIterator>
priority_queue(InputIterator first,
InputIterator last,
const Compare& x = Compare())

This constructor initializes the priority_queue with an existing list of objects. All objects in the range of first to last—actually just *before* last—are copied into container c.

This presents a small problem because, after the objects have been copied, the container won't necessarily be a valid heap. The source code for the class definition shows how the constructor deals with this problem:

```
priority_queue(InputIterator first,
               InputIterator last,
               const Compare& x = Compare()) : c(first, last),
                                               comp(x) {
    make_heap(c.begin(), c.end(), comp);
}
```

Immediately after constructing *c*, the constructor calls make_heap(), an STL function that sorts the elements of the container into heap order. Once that is done, the first element of the heap is the greatest element, at least by the standards of the comparison object, and future additions and subtractions can be handled properly.

Note: This is a template member function, and may not be supported by your C++ compiler. If your compiler isn't in complete compliance with the ANSI/ISO specification, it may be replaced with a function whose prototype looks like this:

```
priority_queue(const T *first,
               const T *last,
               const Compare& x = Compare());
```

(where T is the type of object stored in the container used to support the priority queue.)

bool empty() const

empty() is a boolean public member function that returns the value given from evaluating c.empty(). Under the definitions for the two sequential STL classes that can be used here, empty() is true when the container holds 0 objects.

size_type size() const

This function returns the value of c.size(). The container classes normally define this member function to return the number of objects held in the container.

value_type& top()
const value_type& top() const

top() returns a reference to top element in the container. The top element is the next element to come off the heap when a call to pop() is made.

Note: This class doesn't ensure there is, in fact, a top element in the container. So, it's up to you not to call top() when the container is empty.

void push(const value_type& x)

This function inserts a copy of the argument x into the container. Since the container is being maintained as a heap, the insertion is a two-step procedure:

- First, the object is added to the end of the heap by a call to push_back(). This adds the object to the end of the container, but doesn't adjust the heap. You now have a container with a heap of size() - 1 objects, and one additional object tagged on the end.

- Next, a call is made to push_heap(). push_heap() takes the last element in the container and properly incorporates it into the heap. As soon as this function completes, the entire container is, once again, a valid heap.

void pop()

pop() is called to remove the highest priority element from the top of the heap. Since the container is a valid heap, the first element is always the largest.

All other containers and adaptors looked at here implement pop_front() by a simple process. They destroy the first element in the container, then adjust internal pointers or data members to free up the memory that was occupied by the first element. After the adjustment, element 1 is now element 0, element 2 is now element 1, and so on.

priority_queue<T> takes a different approach to this. First, it calls an STL function named pop_heap(). This function is the converse of push_heap(). It takes element 0 and moves it to the end of the container. The remaining size() - 1 elements are shuffled until what remains is a valid heap starting at location 0, and spanning size() - 1 elements.

Once pop_heap() has completed its work, the last element in the container is destroyed by a call to pop_back(). The container then has a new value to be found in top(), and is 1 element smaller.

ALLOCATOR REFERENCE

Chapter

The Buddha—the Godhead—resides quite as comfortably in the circuits of a digital computer or the gears of a cycle transmission as he does at the top of a mountain or in the petals of a flower.
— Robert M. Pirsig, *Zen and the Art of Motorcycle Maintenance*

This chapter describes the components required of any allocator: type definitions, class member functions, and template functions. In addition, this section discusses a required specialization of the allocator for void pointers.

Typedefs

```
typedef T value_type;
typedef T* pointer;
typedef const T* const_pointer;
typedef T& reference;
typedef const T& const_reference;
typedef size_t size_type;
typedef ptrdiff_t difference_type;
```

The type definitions specified here are not normally used by the end user of a Container class. However, they form the basis for many type definitions created within the Container class. These you will use frequently.

value_type

value_type should always be defined to be type T in the allocator. This is one type definition that isn't normally employed by Container classes using the allocator. There's no need to utilize value_type to define container<T>::value_type, since the type of object held in the container doesn't change with different memory models.

The definition of value_type in the allocators used in the public release of the STL is the same:

```
typedef T value_type;
```

pointer

const_pointer

This is a critical type definition for the Allocator class. As objects are created and placed in containers, you need to be able to access them. One way is to use pointers. This type definition tells the container what type can be used to return something that *looks* like a pointer. You probably won't care whether it truly *is* a pointer or not, but you'll need to dereference it to get at an object. Accordingly, it has to be a type that returns a reference to an object of type T when dereferenced.

Normally, the Container class picks up the pointer definition from the allocator and uses it unmodified, with a typedef inside the class definition:

```
typedef Allocator<T>::pointer pointer;
```

A good example of how a pointer might be used is found in the list class definition. As Chapter 5, "The list<T> Container," explains, list<T> keeps a linked list of buffer objects. These objects are created using the Allocator parameterized by list_node_buffer. This means the Allocator is doing double duty, since it also creates objects of type T.

list.h defines a typedef for that type of pointer as buffer_pointer:

```
typedef Allocator<list_node_buffer>::pointer buffer_pointer;
```

Subsequent code in the program relies on being able to treat buffer_pointer objects like valid pointers. For example, when cleaning up after a list, all buffer objects have to be deleted. This requires navigating a linked list that is maintained using pointers. The deallocate_buffers() function provides a good example of how this is done:

```
template <class T>
void list<T>::deallocate_buffers() {
    while (buffer_list) {
        buffer_pointer tmp = buffer_list;
        buffer_list = (buffer_pointer)(buffer_list->next_buffer);
        list_node_allocator.deallocate(tmp->buffer);
        buffer_allocator.deallocate(tmp);
    }
    free_list = 0;
    next_avail = 0;
    last = 0;
}
```

The default allocator defines its pointer type to be a simple pointer:

```
typedef T * pointer;
typedef const T * const_pointer;
```

As you would expect, the far and huge allocators have to change this definition to one that selects their specific memory model:

```
typedef T __far * pointer;
typedef T __huge * pointer;
```

reference
const_reference

The two reference types provide a service nearly identical to pointer type. The only difference is, instead of providing a pointer to an object of type T, they return a *reference* to the object.

This type is usually copied directly from the Allocator class to the Container class using a statement in the Container class declaration like this:

```
typedef Allocator<T>::reference reference;
```

Objects like deque<T> that define their own iterators can use reference types as the return value for a dereference operation. For example, deque<T> defines its own iterator class, and uses the following code to implement a dereference operation:

```
reference operator*() const { return *current; }
```

The definitions of reference and const_reference for the default, far, and huge allocators are shown in these next pieces of code:

```
typedef T& reference;
typedef const T& const_reference;

typedef T __far & reference;
typedef const T __far & const_reference;

typedef T __huge & reference;
typedef const T __huge & const_reference;
```

size_type

size_type is another type definition generally copied verbatim into the Container class from the allocator. You will always find a line like this in the Container class definition:

```
typedef Allocator<T>::size_type size_type;
```

size_type defines the type that can hold the size of the largest object in the memory model. For example, under any conventional model of standard 16-bit DOS, including both small and large, size_type is defined as size_t. This, in turn, is defined in several header files as an unsigned int.

size_type is used in the Container classes as the return type from any functions that return an object *count* of some sort. These include public functions such as container<T>::size(). size_type is also used as an argument type for container member functions that accept a count of objects as an argument:

```
template<class T>
reference vector<T>::operator[](size_type n)
{
    return *(begin() + n);
}
```

The three allocators define size_type to the appropriate value for the memory model they support:

```
typedef size_t size_type;        //Default and far allocator
typedef unsigned long size_type; //Huge allocator
```

difference_type

difference_type is defined as the signed integer type capable of representing the difference between any two pointers in the supported memory model.

This is normally an int, although Borland's huge model does require a long integer. All Container classes copy this type directly from the allocator, with a line in the class definition like this:

```
typedef Allocator<list_node>::difference_type difference_type;
```

One place difference_type is used frequently is in iterator operations. Some of these operations are internal to the Container class, and therefore not visible to users of the container. However, it does show up as a return type from an iterator operation.

Classes that define their own iterators and support operator-() or operator+() use difference_type as either an argument type or a return type. These two function prototypes from list.h illustrate this:

```
difference_type operator-(const iterator& x) const;
iterator& operator+=(difference_type n);
```

Member functions

```
pointer allocate(size_type n)
void deallocate(pointer p);
pointer address(reference x);
const_pointer const_address(const_reference x);
size_type init_page_size();
size_type max_size() const;
```

The member functions of Allocator classes are used whenever a Container class wants to manipulate memory. This completely encapsulates memory management. And it's this which gives you the ability to use different memory models simply by changing a type parameter in a template class declaration.

It's also important to remember that you usually won't pay a performance penalty at runtime for using these functions. Most of these template functions are treated as inline functions, and generate the same code as when not using this memory modeling technique.

pointer allocate(size_type n)

This function is used to allocate a raw block of memory big enough to hold *n* objects. It doesn't try to construct objects of type T in the allocated memory; that can be done later. In fact, much of the memory allocation done by STL containers relies on the ability to allocate big blocks of memory, and parcel them out to new objects one at a time, as needed.

Since this is a member function of the Allocator class, it needs to be called using an allocator object. Each container has its own reference to an allocator, which it uses for all memory allocation.

For example, the following constructor from vector<T> allocates a block of memory using the member named allocator:

```
vector(size_type n, const T& value = T()) {
    start = allocator.allocate(n);
    uninitialized_fill_n(start, n, value);
    finish = start + n;
    end_of_storage = finish;
}
```

The public STL implementation carries out this function as a simple one-liner that calls a global template function to actually do the work:

```
pointer allocate(size_type n) {
    return ::allocate((difference_type)n, (pointer)0);
}
```

The global template version of allocate() is defined in the same header file. Its purpose is to provide blocks of memory using the specific pointer family. The code shown below performs this operation for the far memory allocator:

```
template <class T>
inline T __far * allocate(long size, T __far * p) {
    set_new_handler(0);
    T __far * tmp = (T __far *)
        (::operator new((unsigned long)(size * sizeof(T))));
    if (tmp == 0) {
        cerr << "out of memory" << endl;
        exit(1);
    }
    return tmp;
}
```

Note: One very important thing to note here is the crude error handling in the public release of the STL. Enhanced versions from compiler vendors or third-party sources will probably use the C++ exception mechanism to provide better error handling in this function.

void deallocate(pointer p)

Just like Allocator<T>::allocate(), the deallocate() function is a simple one-liner:

```
template <class T>
inline void deallocate(T *buffer) {
    ::operator delete(buffer);
}
```

The function shown above is the version of deallocate() defined for the default allocator. In this case, however, it doesn't rely on a template function to delete the memory. Instead, it calls the global version of operator delete, which takes care of restoring the memory to the heap.

The important thing to note here is the global version of delete is called to restore the memory, but *not* to destroy the objects. It's the responsibility of the Container class to call deallocate() only after all objects in the memory have been destroyed. The destructor from vector.h shown below illustrates this point:

```
~vector() {
    destroy(start, finish);
    allocator.deallocate(start);
}
```

Note that the destroy() function is called first. It goes through all the constructed parts of vector.h, calling the explicit version of the destructor for each object of type T. Once this is complete, it can use the static allocator member of vector<>T to call the deallocate() function to return all memory to the heap.

pointer address(reference x)
const_pointer const_address(const_reference x)

These two closely related functions are used to convert a reference to a pointer. The semantics of the address() function are defined in the STL specification as:

```
*(a.address(r)) == r
```

Because of this, the object returned by the address() function can be dereferenced as if it were an actual pointer.

The definition of this function in all supported allocators of the public release is short and sweet:

```
pointer address(reference x)
{
    return (pointer)&x;
}
```

The function employs the address-of operator to convert a reference to an address. It's used internally by some Container classes to properly coerce arguments to construct() and destroy(). For example, the insert() function of list<> starts like this:

```
iterator insert(iterator position, const T& x) {
    link_type tmp = get_node();
    construct(value_allocator.address((*tmp).data), x);
```

size_type init_page_size()

Many Container classes perform some low-level memory management of their own. For instance, deque<T> allocates big blocks of memory that it fills with constructed objects one by one. Rather than let these classes decide on their own how big a "block" should be, the Allocator class is allowed to make the decision. The result of that decision is returned to the container through this function call.

This function is called by list<T>, deque<T>, and all the associative containers when allocating memory. At the time of this writing, the public release of the STL returns a hard-coded value of 4096 from this function. The best fit for a particular implementation is bound to have system-specific dependencies, such as virtual memory page size, and this function provides a way to encapsulate the information.

As commercial implementations of the STL become available, you can expect to see different values of default page sizes as vendors tune their allocators for specific environments.

size_type max_size() const

max_size() returns a value from Allocator<T> which indicates the maximum number of objects that can be stored in an object using the current memory model. To calculate this, the allocator has to know the size of the objects of type T to be stored, as well as the maximum size of an object in the current memory model.

As an example, a small model program using the default allocator calculates max_size() like this:

```
size_type max_size() const {
    return max(size_type(1), size_type(UINT_MAX/sizeof(T)));
}
```

The equivalent function for the far and huge allocators substitutes ULONG_MAX for UINT_MAX when making this calculation.

In general, max_size() is called by the Container classes to implement their versions of max_size(), a required function for a container. For instance, deque<> defines its version of max_size this way:

```
size_type max_size() const
{
    return data_allocator.max_size();
}
```

Template functions

```
template <class T1,class T2>
void construct(T1* p, const T2& value);

template <class T>
void destroy(T* pointer);
```

These two global functions are used by Allocator classes to construct and destroy objects from predefined memory locations. They detach the twin processes of memory allocation and object construction.

C++ programmers frequently think of these two operations as a unit, linking them together via the new and delete operators. The STL does away with this linkage, preferring to handle the two processes completely independently.

template <class T1,class T2>
void construct(T1* p, const T2& value)

This function is called by the allocator to create a new object in the memory location pointed to by pointer *p*. To do this, it invokes the constructor using the new placement syntax. This offbeat way of constructing an object is discussed in some detail in Chapters 4 and 9.

The next code excerpt shows the definition of the default constructor construct(). The only difference in the definition for the __far and __huge allocators is that function parameter T1* p changes to T1 __far *p or T1 __huge *p.

```
template <class T1, class T2>
inline void construct(T1* p, const T2& value) {
    new (p) T1(value);
}
```

This function is called by the Container classes whenever they need to insert a new object into the container. For example, vector.h has the following definition for the push_back() function, which adds an object to the end of the vector:

```
void push_back(const T& x) {
    if (finish != end_of_storage)
        construct(finish++, x);
    else
        insert_aux(end(), x);
}
```

The only other way to construct an object in a container is by way of the assignment operator, which creates a new object on top of an old one.

template <class T> void destroy(T* pointer)

This function is the mirror opposite of construct(); it destroys an object in an existing memory area. The Container classes use this function whenever an object needs to be destroyed. destroy() uses the somewhat odd call to the explicit destructor, in order to destroy the object. It does this so it can destroy the object without freeing the memory. The destroy() function defined for the far memory allocator is shown here:

```
template <class T>
inline void destroy( T __far * pointer ) {
    pointer->~T();
}
```

The only other method Container classes can employ to delete objects already in memory is to use the assignment operator. The assignment operator destroys an existing object by copying a new one on top of it.

An example of the use of destroy() by deque<T> is shown in the next piece of code. The pop_front() function is called to destroy the first object in the deque<T> container. Unless the pop operation causes an entire buffer to go completely empty, pop_front() leaves the memory that was holding the object in place:

```
void pop_front() {
    destroy(start.current);
    ++start.current;
    --length;
    if (empty() || begin().current == begin().last)
        deallocate_at_begin();
}
```

Specializations

Allocator classes are required to support a single specialized version of the allocator, to support the creation of untyped memory objects. This is simply a block of raw memory that hasn't been initialized at any time, which can be pointed to with a void pointer. This class only has to have a constructor, destructor, and pointer type defined. The Allocator<void>::pointer object has conversions defined so that any pointer type from any Allocator<T> can be converted back and forth from the void type.

The entire class definition for allocator<void> in defalloc.h is shown below:

```
class allocator<void> {
public:
    typedef void* pointer;
};
```

THE STL SPECIFICATION

Note: This specification (July 7, 1995) was written by Alexander Stepanov and Meng Lee, and was provided by Hewlett Packard. It has not been edited or otherwise changed by Mark Nelson or IDG Books.

1 INTRODUCTION

The Standard Template Library provides a set of well structured generic C++ components that work together in a seamless way. Special care has been taken to ensure that all the template algorithms work not only on the data structures in the library, but also on built-in C++ data structures. For example, all the algorithms work on regular pointers. The orthogonal design of the library allows programmers to use library data structures with their own algorithms, and to use library algorithms with their own data structures. The well specified semantic and complexity requirements guarantee that a user component will work with the library, and that it will work efficiently. This flexibility ensures the widespread utility of the library.

Another important consideration is efficiency. C++ is successful because it combines expressive power with efficiency. Much effort has been spent to verify that every template component in the library has a generic implementation that performs within a few percentage points of the efficiency of the corresponding hand-coded routine.

The third consideration in the design has been to develop a library structure that, while being natural and easy to grasp, is based on a firm theoretical foundation.

2 STRUCTURE OF THE LIBRARY

The library contains five main kinds of component:

- algorithm: defines a computational procedure
- container: manages a set of memory locations
- iterator: provides a means for an algorithm to traverse through a container
- function object: encapsulates a function in an object for use by other components
- adaptor: adapts a component to provide a different interface

Such decomposition allows us to dramatically reduce the component space. For example, instead of providing a search member function for every kind of container, we provide a single version that works with all of them as long as a basic set of requirements is satisfied.

The following description helps clarify the structure of the library.

If software components are tabulated as a three-dimensional array, where one dimension represents different data types, e.g. int, double, the second dimension represents different containers, e.g. vector, linked-list, file, and the third dimension represents different algorithms on the containers, e.g. searching, sorting, rotation, if i, j, and k are the size of the dimensions, then $i*j*k$ different versions of code have to be designed. By using template functions that are parameterized by a data type, we need only $j*k$ versions. Further, by making our algorithms work on different containers, we need merely $j+k$ versions. This significantly simplifies software design work and also makes it possible to use components in the library together with user-defined components in a very flexible way.

A user may easily define a specialized container class and use the library's sort function to sort it. A user may provide a different comparison function for the sort either as a regular pointer to a comparison function, or as a function object — an object with an operator() defined that does the comparisons. If a user needs to iterate through a container in the reverse direction, the reverse_iterator adaptor allows that.

The library extends the basic C++ paradigms in a consistent way, so it is easy for a C/C++ programmer to start using the library. For example, the library contains a merge template function. When a user has two arrays, *a* and *b,* to be merged into *c* it can be done with:

```
int a[1000];
int b[2000];
int c[3000];
...
merge( a, a + 1000, b, b + 2000, c );
```

When a user wants to merge a vector and a list, both of which are template classes in the library, and put the result into a freshly allocated uninitialized storage it can be done with:

```
vector<Employee> a;
list<Employee> b;
...
Employee* c = allocate(a.size + b.size, (Employee*)0);
merge(a.begin(), a.end(), b.begin(), b.end(),
      raw_storage_iterator<Employee*, Employee>(c);
```

where begin() and end() are member functions of containers that return the right types of iterators or pointer-like objects that allow the merge to do the job, and raw_storage_iterator is an adapter that allows algorithms to put results directly into uninitialized memory by calling the appropriate copy constructor.

In many cases it is useful to iterate through input/output streams in the same way as through regular data structures. For example, if we want to merge two data structures and then store them in a file, it would be nice to avoid creation of an auxiliary data structure for the result, instead storing the result directly into the corresponding file. The library provides both istream_iterator and ostream_iterator template classes to make many of the library algorithms work with I/O streams that represent homogenous aggregates of data. Here is a program that reads a file of integers from the standard input, removes all those that are divisible by its command argument, and writes the result to the standard output:

```
main( int argc, char** argv) {
    if (argc != 2) throw("usage: remove_if_divides integer\n");
    remove_copy_if(istream_iterator<int>(cin), istream_iterator<int>(),
        ostream_iterator<int>(cout, "\n"),
        not1(bind2nd(modulus<int>(), atoi(argv[1])))));
}
```

All the work is done by remove_copy_if which reads integers one by one until the input iterator becomes equal to the *end-of-stream* iterator that is constructed by the constructor with no arguments. In general, all the algorithms work in a 'from here to there' fashion, taking two iterators that signify the beginning and the end of the input. Then remove_copy_if writes the integers that pass the test onto the output stream through the output iterator that is bound to cout. As a predicate, remove_copy_if uses a function object constructed from a function object, modulus<int>, which takes *i* and *j* and returns *i%j*, as a binary predicate and makes it into a unary predicate by using bind2nd to bind the second argument to the command line argument, atoi(argv[1]). Then the negation of this unary predicate is obtained using function adaptor not1.

A somewhat more realistic example is a filter program that takes a file and randomly shuffles its lines:

```
main(int argc, char**) {
    if (argc != 1) throw("usage: shuffle\n");
    vector<string> v;
    copy(istream_iterator<string>(cin), istream_iterator<string>(),
        inserter(v, v.end()));
    random_shuffle(v.begin(), v.end());
    copy(v.begin(), v.end(), ostream_iterator<string>(cout));
}
```

In this example, copy moves lines from the standard input into a vector, but since the vector is not pre-allocated it uses an insert iterator to insert the lines one-by-one into the vector. (This technique allows all of the copying functions to work in the usual overwrite mode as well as in the insert mode.) Then random_shuffle shuffles the vector and another call to copy copies it onto the cout stream.

3 REQUIREMENTS

To ensure that the different components in a library work together, they must satisfy some basic requirements.

Requirements should be as general as possible, so instead of saying "class X has to define a member function operator++()," we say "for any object *x* of class X, ++*x* is defined. (It is unspecified whether the operator is a member or a global function.) Requirements are stated in terms of well-defined expressions, which define valid terms of the types that satisfy the requirements. For every set of requirements there is a table that specifies an initial set of the valid expressions and their semantics. Any generic algorithm that uses the requirements has to be written in terms of the valid expressions for its formal type parameters.

If an operation is required to be linear time, it means no worse than linear time, and a constant time operation satisfies the requirement.

In some cases we present the semantic requirements using C++ code. Such code is intended as a specification of equivalence of a construct to another construct, not necessarily as the way the construct must be implemented — although in some cases the code given is unambiguously the optimum implementation.

4 CORE COMPONENTS

This section contains some basic template functions and classes that are used throughout the rest of the library.

4.1 Operators

To avoid redundant definitions of operator!= out of operator== and operators>, <=, and >= out of operator< the library provides the following:

```
template <class T>
inline bool operator!=(const T& x, const T& y) {
      return !x == y;
}

template <class T>
inline bool operator>(const T& x, const T& y) {
      return y < x;
}

template <class T>
inline bool operator<=(const T& x, const T& y) {
      return !y < x;
}

template <class T>
inline bool operator>=(const T& x, const T& y) {
    return !x < y;
}
```

4.2 Pair

The library includes templates for heterogeneous pairs of values.

```
template <class T1, class T2>
struct pair {
      T1 first;
      T2 second;
      pair(const T1& x, const T2& y) : first(x), second(y) {}
};

template <class T1, class T2>
inline bool
  operator==(const pair<T1, T2>& x, const pair<T1, T2>& y) {
    return x.first == y.first && x.second == y.second;
}

template <class T1, class T2>
inline bool
  operator<(const pair<T1, T2>& x, const pair<T1, T2>& y){
    return x.first < y.first ||
           !y.first < x.first &&
            x.second < y.second;
}
```

The library provides a matching template function make_pair to simplify their construction. Instead of saying, for example,

```
return pair<int, double>(5, 3.1415926); // explicit types
```

one may say,

```
return make_pair(5, 3.1415926); // types are deduced

template <class T1, class T2>
inline pair<T1, T2> make_pair(const T1& x, const T2& y) {
      return pair<T1, T2>(x, y);
```

5 ITERATORS

Iterators are a generalization of pointers that allow a programmer to work with different data structures (containers) in a uniform manner. To be able to construct template algorithms that work correctly and efficiently on different types of data structures, we need to formalize, not just the interfaces, but also the semantics and complexity assumptions of iterators. Iterators are objects that have operator* returning a value of some class or built-in type T called a *value type* of the iterator. For every iterator type X for which equality is defined, there is a corresponding signed integral type called the *distance type* of the iterator.

Since iterators are a generalization of pointers, their semantics are a generalization of the semantics of pointers in C++. This assures that every template function that takes iterators works with regular pointers. Depending on the operations defined on them, there are five categories of iterators:

1. *input iterators*
2. *output iterators*
3. *forward iterators*
4. *bidirectional iterators and*
5. *random access iterators.*

Forward iterators satisfy all the requirements of the input and output iterators and can be used whenever either kind is specified.

Bidirectional iterators satisfy all the requirements of the forward iterators and can be used whenever a forward iterator is specified.

Random access iterators satisfy all the requirements of bidirectional iterators and can be used whenever a bidirectional iterator is specified.

There is an additional attribute that forward, bidirectional and random access iterators might have, that is, they can be *mutable* or *constant* depending on whether the result of the operator*() behaves as a reference or as a reference to a constant. Constant iterators do not satisfy the requirements for output iterators.

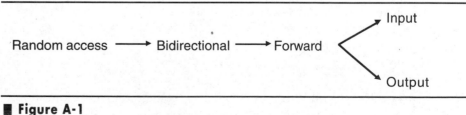

Figure A-1
Relations among iterator categories

Just as a regular pointer to an array guarantees that there is a pointer value pointing past the last element of the array, so for any iterator type there is an iterator value that points past the last element of a corresponding container. These values are called *past-the-end* values. Values of the iterator for which the operator*() is defined are called *dereferenceable*. The library never assumes that past-the-end values are dereferenceable.

Iterators might also have *singular* values that are not associated with any container. For example, after the declaration of an uninitialized pointer *x* (as with int* *x*;), *x* should always be assumed to have a singular value of a pointer. Results of most expressions are undefined for singular values. The only exception is an assignment of a non-singular value to an iterator that holds a singular value. In this case the singular value is overwritten the same way as any other value. Dereferenceable and past-the-end values are always non-singular.

An iterator *j* is called *reachable* from an iterator *i* if and only if there is a finite sequence of applications of operator++ to *i* that makes *i* == *j*. If *i* and *j* refer to the same container, then either *j* is reachable from *i*, or *i* is reachable from *j*, or both (*i* == *j*).

Most of the library's algorithmic templates that operate on data structures have interfaces that use ranges. A range is a pair of iterators that designate the beginning and end of the computation. A range [*i*, *i*] is an empty range; in general, a range [*i*, *j*] refers to the elements in the data structure starting with the one pointed to by *i* and up to but not including the one pointed to by *j*. Range [*i*, *j*] is valid if and only if *j* is reachable from *i*. The result of the application of the algorithms in the library to invalid ranges is undefined.

All the categories of iterators require only those functions that are realizable for a given category in constant time (amortized). Therefore, requirement tables for the iterators do not have a complexity column.

In the following sections, we assume: *a* and *b* are values of X; *n* is a value of the distance type Distance; *u*, *tmp*, and *m* are identifiers; *r* and *s* are lvalues of X; and *t* is a value of value type T.

5.1 Input iterators

A class or a built-in type X satisfies the requirements of an input iterator for the value type T if the following expressions are valid:

Table A-1

Input iterator requirements

expression	return type	operational semantics	assertion/note pre/post-condition
X(a)			a == X(a) Note: a destructor is assumed
X u(a); X u = a;			post: u == a
a == b	convertible to bool		==is an equivalence relation
a != b	convertible to bool	!(a == b)	
*a	convertible to T		pre: a is dereferenceable a == b implies *a == *b
++r	X&		pre: r is dereferencable post: r is dereferenceable or r is past-the-end &r == &++r
r++	X	{ X tmp = r; ++r; return tmp; }	

Note: For input iterators, *r* == *s* does not imply ++*r* == ++*s*. Equality does not guarantee the substitution property or referential transparency.

Algorithms on input iterators should never attempt to pass through the same iterator twice. They should be *single pass* algorithms. *Value type T is not required to be an lvalue type.* These algorithms can be used with istreams as the source of the input data through the istream_iterator class.

5.2 Output iterators

A class or a built-in type X satisfies the requirements of an output iterator if the following expressions are valid:

Note: The only valid use of an operator* is on the left side of the assignment statement. *Assignment through the same value of the iterator happens only once.* Algorithms on output iterators should never attempt to pass through the same iterator twice. They should be *single pass* algorithms. Equality and inequality are not necessarily defined.

Table A-2

Output iterator requirements

expression	return type	operational semantics	assertion/note pre/post-condition
X(a)			*a = t is equivalent to *X(a)=t
			Note: a destructor is assumed
X u(a);			
X u = a;			
*a = t	result is not used		
++r	X&		
r++	X or X&		

Algorithms that take output iterators can be used with ostreams as the destination for placing data through the *ostream_iterator* class, as well as with insert iterators and insert pointers. In particular, the following two conditions should hold:

- first, any iterator value should be assigned through before it is incremented (this is, for an output iterator *i*, *i++*; *i++*; is not a valid code sequence);

- second, any value of an output iterator may have at most one active copy at any given time (for example, *i = j*; *++i = a*; *j = b*; is not a valid code sequence).

5.3 Forward iterators

A class or a built-in type X satisfies the requirements of a forward iterator if the following expressions are valid:

Note: The fact that $r == s$ implies $++r == ++s$ (which is not true for input and output iterators) and the removal of the restrictions on the number of the assignments through the iterator (which applies to output iterators) allows the use of multi-pass one-directional algorithms with forward iterators.

Table A-3

Forward iterator requirements

expression	return type	operational semantics	assertion/note pre/post-condition
X u;			Note: u might have a singular value Note: a destructor is assumed
X();			Note: X() might be singular
X(a)			a == X(a)
X u(a) X u = a		X u; u = a;	post: u == a
a == b	convertible to bool		== is an equivalence relation
a != b	convertible to bool	!(a == b)	
r = a	X&		post: r == a
*a	convertible to T		pre: a is dereferencable a == b implies *a == *b If X is mutable, *a = t is valid
++r	X&		pre: r is dereferencable post: r is dereferencable or r is past-the-end r == s and r is dereferencable implies ++r == ++s &r == &++Rr
r++	X	{ X tmp = r; ++r; return tmp; }	

5.4 Bidirectional iterators

A class or a built-in type X satisfies the requirements of a bidirectional iterator if, to the table that specifies forward iterators, we add the following lines:

Note: Bidirectional iterators allow algorithms to move iterators backward as well as forward.

Table A-4

Bidirectional iterator requirements (in addition to forward iterator)

expression	return type	operational semantics	assertion/note pre/post-condition
$--r$	X&		pre: there exists s such that $r = ++s$ post: s is dereferencable $--(++r) == r$ $--r == --s$ implies $r == s$ $\&r == \&--r$
$r--$	X	{ X *tmp* = r; $--r$; return tmp; }	

5.5 Random access iterators

A class or a built-in type X satisfies the requirements of a random access iterator if, to the table that specifies bidirectional iterators, we add the following lines:

Table A-5

Random access iterator requirements (in addition to bidirectional iterator)

expression	return type	operational semantics	assertion/note pre/post-condition

$r += n$	X&	{ Distance $m = n$;
		if $(m >= 0)$
		  while $(m--)$ $++r$;
		else
		  while $(m++)$ $--r$;
		return r; }	

$a + n$ $n + a$	X	{ X *tmp* = a; return *tmp* += n; }	$a + n == n + a$
$r -= n$	X&	return $r += -n$;	
$a - n$	X	{ X *tmp* = a; return *tmp* -= n; }	
$b - a$	Distance		pre: there exists a value n of Distance such that $a + n = b$ $b == a + (b - a)$
$a[n]$	convertible to T	$*(a + n)$	
$a < b$	convertible to bool	$b - a > 0$	< is a total ordering relation
$a > b$	convertible to bool	$b < a$	> is a total ordering relation opposite to <
$a >= b$	convertible to bool	$!(a < b)$	
$a <= b$	convertible to bool	$!(a > b)$	

5.6 Iterator tags

To implement algorithms only in terms of iterators, it is often necessary to infer both the value type and the distance type from the iterator. To enable this, it is required that for an iterator *i* of any category other than output iterator, the expression value_type(*i*) returns (T*)(0) and the expression distance_type(*i*) returns (Distance*)(0). For output iterators, these expressions are not required.

5.6.1 Examples of using iterator tags

For all the regular pointer types we can define value_type and distance_type with the help of:

```
template <class T>
inline T* value_type(const T*) { return (T*)(0); }

template <class T>
inline ptrdiff_t* distance_type(const T*) {
    return (ptrdiff_t*)(0);
}
```

Then, if we want to implement a generic reverse function, we do the following:

```
template <class BidirectionalIterator>
inline void reverse(BidirectionalIterator first,
                 BidirectionalIterator last {
    __reverse(first, last,
            value_type(first), distance_type(first));
}
```

where __reverse is defined as:

```
template <class BidirectionalIterator, class T, class Distance>
void __reverse(BidirectionalIterator first,
            BidirectionalIterator last,
            T*,
            Distance*) {
    Distance n;
    distance(first, last, n); // see Iterator operations  section
    --n;
    while( n > 0 ) {
        T tmp = *first;
        *first++ = *--last;
        *last = tmp;
        n -= 2;
    }
}
```

If there is an additional pointer type __huge such that the difference of two __huge pointers is of the type long long, we define:

```
template <class T>
inline T* value_type(const T __huge *) { return (T*)(0); }

template <class T>
inline long long* distance_type(const T __huge *) {
    return (long long*)(0);
}
```

It is often desirable for a template function to find out what is the most specific category of its iterator argument, so that the function can select the most efficient algorithm at compile time. To facilitate this, the library introduces *category tag* classes, which are used as compile time tags for algorithm selection. They are:

1. *input_iterator_tag*
2. *output_iterator_tag*
3. *forward_iterator_tag*
4. *bidirectional_iterator_tag and*
5. *random_access_iterator_tag.*

Every iterator *i* must have an expression iterator_category(*i*) defined on it that returns the most specific category tag that describes its behavior. For example, we define that all the pointer types are in the random access iterator category by:

```
template <class T>
inline random_access_iterator_tag iterator_category(const T*) {
    return random_access_iterator_tag();
}
```

For a user-defined iterator BinaryTreeIterator, it can be included into the bidirectional iterator category by saying:

```
template <class T>
inline bidirectional_iterator_tag iterator_category(
                    const BinaryTreeIterator<T>&) {
    return bidirectional_iterator_tag();
}
```

If a template function evolve is well defined for bidirectional iterators, but can be implemented more efficiently for random access iterators, then the implementation is like:

```
template <class BidirectionalIterator>
inline void evolve(BidirectionalIterator first,
                   BidirectionalIterator last)
    evolve(first, last, iterator_category(first));
}

template <class BidirectionalIterator>
void evolve(BidirectionalIterator first,
            BidirectionalIterator last,
            bidirectional_iterator_tag ) {
// ... more generic, but less efficient algorithm
}

template <class RandomAccessIterator>
void evolve(RandomAccessIterator first,
            RandomAccessIterator last,
            random_access_iterator_tag ){
// ... more efficient, but less generic algorithm
}
```

5.6.2 Library defined primitives

To simplify the task of defining the iterator_category, value_type and distance_type for user-definable iterators, the library provides the following predefined classes and functions:

```
// iterator tags

struct input_iterator_tag {};
struct output_iterator_tag {};
struct forward_iterator_tag {};
struct bidirectional_iterator_tag {};
struct random_access_iterator_tag {};

// iterator bases

template <class T, class Distance = ptrdiff_t>
struct input_iterator {};
struct output_iterator {};
// output_iterator is not a template because output iterators
```

```
// do not have either value type or distance type defined.
template <class T, class Distance = ptrdiff_t>
struct forward_iterator {};
template <class T, class Distance = ptrdiff_t>
struct bidirectional_iterator {};
template <class T, class Distance = ptrdiff_t>
struct random_access_iterator {};

// iterator_category

template <class T, class Distance>
inline input_iterator_tag
iterator_category(const input_iterator<T, Distance>&) {
return input_iterator_tag();
}
inline output_iterator_tag
  iterator_category(const output_iterator&) {
    return output_iterator_tag();
}
template <class T, class Distance>
inline forward_iterator_tag
iterator_category(const forward_iterator<T, Distance>&) {
        return forward_iterator_tag();
}
template <class T, class Distance>
inline bidirectional_iterator_tag
iterator_category(const bidirectional_iterator<T, Distance>&) {
        return bidirectional_iterator_tag();
}
template <class T, class Distance>
inline random_access_iterator_tag
iterator_category(const random_access_iterator<T, Distance>&) {
return random_access_iterator_tag();
}
template <class T>
inline random_access_iterator_tag
iterator_category(const T*) {
        return random_access_iterator_tag();
}

// value_type of iterator

template <class T, class Distance>
inline T* value_type(const input_iterator<T, Distance>&) {
return (T*)(0);
}
```

```
template <class T, class Distance>
inline T* value_type(const forward_iterator<T, Distance>&) {
        return (T*)(0);
}
template <class T, class Distance>
inline T* value_type(const bidirectional_iterator<T, Distance>&) {
        return (T*)(0);
}
template <class T, class Distance>
inline T* value_type(const random_access_iterator<T, Distance>&) {
        return (T*)(0);
}
template <class T>
inline T* value_type(const T*) { return (T*)(0); }

// distance_type of iterator

template <class T, class Distance>
inline Distance* distance_type(const input_iterator<T, Distance>&) {
        return (Distance*)(0);
}
template <class T, class Distance>
inline Distance*
  distance_type(const forward_iterator<T, Distance>&) {
    return (Distance*)(0);
}
template <class T, class Distance>
inline Distance* distance_type(const bidirectional_iterator<T, Distance>&) {
        return (Distance*)(0);
}
template <class T, class Distance>
inline Distance* distance_type(const random_access_iterator<T, Distance>&) {
        return (Distance*)(0);
}
template <class T>
inline ptrdiff_t* distance_type(const T*) { return (ptrdiff_t*)(0); }
```

If a user wants to define a bidirectional iterator for some data structure containing double, such that it works on a large memory model of a computer, it can be done by defining:

```
class MyIterator : public bidirectional_iterator<double, long> {
        // code implementing ++, etc.
};
```

Then there is no need to define iterator_category, value_type, and distance_type on MyIterator.

5.7 Iterator operations

Since only random access iterators provide + and - operators, the library provides two template functions, advance and distance. These functions use + and - for random access iterators (and are, therefore, constant time for them); for input, forward, and bidirectional iterators they use ++ to provide linear time implementations. advance takes a negative argument n for random access and bidirectional iterators only. advance increments (or decrements for negative n) iterator reference i by n. distance increments n by the number of times it takes to get from first to last.

```
template <class InputIterator, class Distance>
inline void advance(InputIterator& i, Distance n);

template <class InputIterator, class Distance>
inline void distance(InputIterator first,
                     InputIterator last,
                     Distance& n);
```

distance must be a three argument function storing the result into a reference instead of returning the result, because the distance type cannot be deduced from built-in iterator types such as int*.

6 FUNCTION OBJECTS

Function objects are objects with an operator() defined. They are important for the effective use of the library.

In the places where one would expect to pass a pointer to a function to an algorithmic template, the interface is specified to accept an object with an operator() defined. This not only makes algorithmic templates work with pointers to functions, but also enables them to work with arbitrary function objects. Using function objects together with function templates increases the expressive power of the library as well as making the resulting code much more efficient. For example, if we want to have a by-element addition of two vectors a and b containing double and put the result into a we can do:

```
transform(a.begin(), a.end(), b.begin(), a.begin(), plus<double>());
```

If we want to negate every element of a we can do:

```
transform(a.begin(), a.end(), a.begin(), negate<double>());
```

The corresponding functions will inline the addition and the negation.

To enable adaptors and other components to manipulate function objects that take one or two arguments, it is required that they correspondingly provide typedefs argument_type and result_type for function objects that take one argument, and first_argument_type, second_argument_type, and result_type for function objects that take two arguments.

6.1 Base

The following classes are provided to simplify the typedefs of the argument and result types:

```
template <class Arg, class Result>
struct unary_function {
        typedef Arg argument_type;
        typedef Result result_type;
};

template <class Arg1, class Arg2, class Result>
struct binary_function {
        typedef Arg1 first_argument_type;
        typedef Arg2 second_argument_type;
        typedef Result result_type;
};
```

6.2 Arithmetic operations

The library provides basic function object classes for all of the arithmetic operators in the language.

```
template <class T>
struct plus : binary_function<T, T, T> {
    T operator()(const T& x, const T& y) const {
        return x + y;
    }
};

template <class T>
struct minus : binary_function<T, T, T> {
    T operator()(const T& x, const T& y) const {
        return x - y;
    }
};
```

```
template <class T>
struct times : binary_function<T, T, T> {
    T operator()(const T& x, const T& y) const {
        return x * y;
    }
};

template <class T>
struct divides : binary_function<T, T, T> {
    T operator()(const T& x, const T& y) const {
        return x / y;
    }
};

template <class T>
struct modulus : binary_function<T, T, T> {
    T operator()(const T& x, const T& y) const {
        return x % y;
    }
};

template <class T>
struct negate : unary_function<T, T> {
    T operator()(const T& x) const {
        return -x;
    }
};
```

6.3 Comparisons

The library provides basic function object classes for all of the comparison operators in the language.

```
template <class T>
struct equal_to : binary_function<T, T, bool> {
    bool operator()(const T& x, const T& y) const {
        return x == y;
    }
};

template <class T>
struct not_equal_to : binary_function<T, T, bool> {
    bool operator()(const T& x, const T& y) const {
        return x != y;
    }
};
```

```cpp
template <class T>
struct greater : binary_function<T, T, bool> {
    bool operator()(const T& x, const T& y) const {
        return x > y;
    }
};

template <class T>
struct less : binary_function<T, T, bool> {
    bool operator()(const T& x, const T& y) const {
        return x < y;
    }
};

template <class T>
struct greater_equal : binary_function<T, T, bool> {
    bool operator()(const T& x, const T& y) const {
        return x >= y;
    }
};

template <class T>
struct less_equal : binary_function<T, T, bool> {
    bool operator()(const T& x, const T& y) const {
        return x <= y;
    }
};
```

6.4 Logical operations

```cpp
template <class T>
struct logical_and : binary_function<T, T, bool> {
    bool operator()(const T& x, const T& y) const {
        return x && y;
    }
};

template <class T>
struct logical_or : binary_function<T, T, bool> {
    bool operator()(const T& x, const T& y) const {
        return x || y;
    }
};

template <class T>
struct logical_not : unary_function<T, bool> {
    bool operator()(const T& x const) {
        return !x;
    }
};
```

7 ALLOCATORS

One of the common problems in portability is to be able to encapsulate the information about the memory model. This information includes the knowledge of pointer types, the type of their difference, the type of the size of objects in this memory model, as well as the memory allocation and deallocation primitives for it.

The STL addresses this problem by providing a standard set of requirements for *allocators*, which are objects that encapsulate this information. All of the containers in the STL are parameterized in terms of allocators. That dramatically simplifies the task of dealing with multiple memory models.

7.1 Allocator requirements

In the following table, we assume: X is an allocator class for objects of type T; *a* is a value of X; *n* is of type X::size_type; *p* is of type X::pointer; *r* is of type X::reference; and *s* is of type X::const_reference.

All the operations on the allocators are expected to be amortized constant time.

pointer belongs to the category of mutable random access iterators referring to T. const_pointer belongs to the category of constant random access iterators referring to T. There is a conversion defined from pointer to const_pointer.

For any allocator template Alloc there is a specialization for type void. Alloc<void> has only constructor, destructor, and Alloc<void>::pointer defined. Conversions are defined from any instance of Alloc<T>::pointer into Alloc<void>::pointer and back, so that for any *p*, *p* == Alloc<T>::pointer(Alloc<void>::pointer(*p*)).

Table A-6

Allocator requirements

expression	return type	assertion/note pre/post-condition
X::value_type	T	
X::reference	lvalue of T	
X::const_reference	const lvalue of T	
X::pointer	pointer to T type	the result of operator* of values of X::pointer is of reference
X::const_pointer	pointer to const T type	the result of operator* of values of X::const_pointer is of const_reference; it is the same type of pointer as X::pointer, in particular, sizeof(X::const_pointer) == sizeof(X::pointer)
X::size_type	unsigned integral type	the type that can represent the size of the largest object in the memory model
X::difference_type	signed integral type	the type that can represent the difference between any two pointers in the memory model
X a;		Note: a destructor is assumed
a.address(r)	pointer	*(a.address(r)) == r
a.const_address(s)	const_pointer	*(a.address(s)) == s
a.allocate(n)	X::pointer	memory is allocated for n objects of type T but objects are not constructed. allocate may raise an appropriate exception
a.deallocate(p)	result is not used	all the objects in the area pointed by p should be destroyed prior to the call of the deallocate
construct(p,a)	void	post: *p == a
destroy(p)	void	the value pointed by p is destroyed
a.init_page_size()	X::size_type	the returned value is the optimal value for an initial buffer size of the given type. It is assumed that, if k is returned by init_page_size, t is the construction timer for T, and u is the time that it takes to do allocate(k), then k * t is much greater than u
a.max_size()	X::size_type	the largest positive value of X::difference_type

7.2 The default allocator

```
template <class T>
class allocator {
public:
    typedef T* pointer;
    typedef const T* const_pointer;
    typedef T& reference;
    typedef const T& const_reference;
    typedef T value_type;
    typedef size_t size_type;
    typedef ptrdiff_t difference_type;
    allocator();
    ~allocator();
    pointer address(reference x);
    const_pointer const_address(const_reference x);
    pointer allocate(size_type n);
    void deallocate(pointer p);
    size_type init_page_size();
    size_type max_size();
};

class allocator<void> {
public:
    typedef void* pointer;
    allocator();
    ~allocator();
};
```

In addition to allocator, the library vendors are expected to provide allocators for all supported memory models.

8 CONTAINERS

Containers are objects that store other objects. They control allocation and deallocation of these objects through constructors, destructors, insert and erase operations. In the following table, we assume: X is a container class containing objects of type T; *a* and *b* are values of X; *u* is an identifier; and *r* is a value of X&.

The member function size() returns the number of elements in the container. Its semantics are defined by the rules of constructors, inserts, and erases.

Table A-7

Container requirements

expression	return type	operational semantics	assertion/note pre/post condition	complexity
X::value_type	T			compile time
X::reference				compile time
X::const_reference				compile time
X::pointer	a pointer type pointing to X::reference		pointer to T in the memory model used by the container	compile time
X::iterator	iterator type pointing to X::reference		any iterator of any iterator category except output iterator	compile time
X::const_iterator	iterator type pointing to X::const_reference		a constant iterator of any iterator category except output iterator	compile time
X::difference_type	signed integral type		is identical to the distance type of X::iterator and X::const_iterator	compile time
X::size_type	unsigned integral type		size_type can represent any non-negative value of difference_type	compile time
X u;			post: u.size() == 0	constant
X()			X().size() == 0	constant
X(a)			a == X(a)	linear
X u(a); X u = a;		X u; u = a;	post: u == a	linear
(&a)->~X()	result is not used		post: a.size() == 0. Note: type destructor is applied to every element of a and all the memory is returned	linear
a.begin()	iterator; const_iterator for constant a			constant
a.end()	Iterator; const_iterator for constant a			constant
a == b	convertible to bool	a.size() == b.size && equal(a.begin(), a.end(), b.begin())	== is an equivalence relation. Note: equal is defined in the algorithms section	linear
a != b	convertible to bool	!(a == b)		linear
r = a	X&	if (&r != &a) { (&r) ->X::~X(); new (&r) X(a); return r; }	post: r == a	linear
a.size()	size_type	size_type n=0 distance (a.begin(), a.end(), n); return n;		constant
a.max_size()	size_type		size() of the largest possible container	constant
a.empty()	convertible to bool	a.size() == 0		constant
a < b	convertible to bool	lexicographical_compare(a.begin(), a.end(), b.begin(), b.end())	pre: < is defined for values of T. < is a total ordering relation. lexicographical_compare is defined in the algorithms section	linear
a > b	convertible to bool	b < a		linear
a <= b	convertible to bool	!(a > b)		linear
a >= b	convertible to bool	!(a < b)		linear
a.swap(b)	void	swap(a,b)		constant

begin() returns an iterator referring to the first element in the container. end() returns an iterator which is the past-the-end value.

If the iterator type of a container belongs to the bidirectional or random access iterator categories, the container is called reversible and satisfies the following additional requirements:

Table A-8

Reversible container requirements (in addition to container)

expression	return type	operational semantics	complexity
X::reverse_iterator		reverse_iterator<iterator, value_type, reference, difference_type> for random access iterator reverse_ bidirectional_iterator< iterator, value_type, reference, difference_type> for bidirectional iterator	compile time
X::const_reverse_ iterator		reverse_iterator<const_iterator, value_type, const_reference, difference_type> for random access iterator reverse_ bidirectional_iterator< const_iterator, value_type, const_reference, difference_ type> for bidirectional iterator	compile time
a.rbegin()	reverse_iterator; const_reverse_ iterator for constant a	reverse_iterator(end())	constant
a.rend()	reverse_iterator; const_reverse_ iterator for constant a	reverse_iterator(begin())	constant

8.1 Sequences

A sequence is a kind of container that organizes a finite set of objects, all of the same type, into a strictly linear arrangement. The library provides three basic kinds of sequence containers: vector, list, and deque. It also provides container adaptors that make it easy to construct abstract data types, such as stacks or queues, out of the basic sequence kinds — or out of other kinds of sequences the user might define.

In the following two tables: X is a sequence class; a is a value of X; i and j satisfy input iterator requirements; $[i, j)$ is a valid range; n is a value of X::size_type; p is a valid iterator to a; $q, q1$ and $q2$ are valid dereferenceable iterators to a; $[q1, q2)$ is a valid range; and t is a value of X::value_type.

The complexities of the expressions are sequence dependent.

Table A-9

Sequence requirements (in addition to container)

expression	return type	operational semantics
X(n, t)		post: size() ==n
X a(n, t);		constructs a sequence with n copies of t
X(i, j)		post: size() == distance between i and j
X a(i, j)		constructs a sequence equal to the range [i, j)
a.insert(p, t)	iterator	inserts a copy of t before p. the return value points to the inserted copy
a.insert(p, n, t)	result is not used	inserts n copies of t before p
a.insert(p, i, j)	result is not used	inserts copies of elements in [i, j) before p
a.erase(q)	result is not used	erases the element pointed to by q
a.erase(q1,q2)	result is not used	erases the elements in the range [q1,q2)

vector, list, and deque offer the programmer different complexity trade-offs and should be used accordingly. vector is the type of sequence that should be used by default. list should be used when there are frequent insertions and deletions from the middle of the sequence. deque is the data structure of choice when most insertions and deletions take place at the beginning or at the end of the sequence.

iterator and const_iterator types for sequences have to be at least of the forward iterator category.

All the operations in the above table are provided only for the containers for which they take constant time.

Table A-10

Optional sequence operations

expression	return type	operational semantics	container
a.front()	reference; const_ reference for constant a	*a.begin()	vector, list, deque
a.back()	reference; const _reference for constant a	*a.(--end())	vector, list, deque
a.push_front(x)	void	a.insert(a.begin(), x)	list, deque
a.push_back(x)	void	a.insert(a.end(), x)	vector, list, deque
a.pop_front()	void	a.erase(a.begin())	list, deque
a.pop_back()	void	a.erase(--a.end())	vector, list, deque
a[n]	reference; const_ reference for constant a	*(a.begin() + n)	vector, deque

8.1.1 Vector

vector is a kind of sequence that supports random access iterators. In addition, it supports (amortized) constant time insert and erase operations at the end; insert and erase in the middle take linear time. Storage management is handled automatically, though hints can be given to improve efficiency.

```
template <class T, template <class U> class Allocator = allocator>
class vector {
public:

// typedefs:

    typedef iterator;
    typedef const_iterator;
    typedef Allocator<T>::pointer pointer;
    typedef Allocator<T>::reference reference;
    typedef Allocator<T>::const_reference const_reference;
    typedef size_type;
    typedef difference_type;
    typedef T value_type;
    typedef reverse_iterator;
    typedef const_reverse_iterator;

// allocation/deallocation:
```

```
    vector();
    vector(size_type n, const T& value = T());
    vector(const vector<T, Allocator>& x);
    template <class InputIterator>
    vector(InputIterator first, InputIterator last);
    ~vector();
    vector<T, Allocator>& operator=(const vector<T, Allocator>& x);
    void reserve(size_type n);
    void swap(vector<T, Allocator>& x);

// accessors:

    iterator begin();
    const_iterator begin() const;
    iterator end();
    const_iterator end() const;
    reverse_iterator rbegin();
    const_reverse_iterator rbegin();
    reverse_iterator rend();
    const_reverse_iterator rend();
    size_type size() const;
    size_type max_size() const;
    size_type capacity() const;
    bool empty() const;
    reference operator[](size_type n);
    const_reference operator[](size_type n) const;
    reference front();
    const_reference front() const;
    reference back();
    const_reference back() const;

// insert/erase:

    void push_back(const T& x);
    iterator insert(iterator position, const T& x = T());
    void insert(iterator position, size_type n, const T& x);
    template <class InputIterator>
    void insert(iterator position,
                InputIterator first,
                InputIterator last);
    void pop_back();
    void erase(iterator position);
    void erase(iterator first, iterator last);
};

template <class T, class Allocator>
bool operator==(const vector<T, Allocator>& x,
                const vector<T, Allocator>& y);
template <class T, class Allocator>
bool operator< const vector<T, Allocator>& x,
                const vector<T, Allocator>& y;
```

iterator is a random access iterator referring to T. The exact type is implementation-dependent and determined by Allocator.

const_iterator is a constant random access iterator referring to const T. The exact type is implementation-dependent and determined by Allocator. It is guaranteed that there is a constructor for const_iterator out of iterator.

size_type is an unsigned integral type. The exact type is implementation-dependent and determined by Allocator.

difference_type is a signed integral type. The exact type is implementation-dependent and determined by Allocator.

The constructor template <class InputIterator> vector(InputIterator first, InputIterator last) makes only N calls to the copy constructor of T (where N is the distance between first and last and no reallocations if iterators first and last are of forward, bidirectional, or random access categories. It does at most $2N$ calls to the copy constructor of T and $\log N$ reallocations if they are just input iterators, since it is impossible to determine the distance between first and last and then do copying.

The member function capacity returns the size of the allocated storage in the vector. The member function reserve is a directive that informs vector of a planned change in size, so that it can manage the storage allocation accordingly. It does not change the size of the sequence and takes at most linear time in the size of the sequence. Reallocation happens at this point if, and only if, the current capacity is less than the argument of reserve. After reserve, capacity is greater or equal to the argument of reserve if reallocation happens, and equal to the previous value of capacity otherwise. Reallocation invalidates all the references, pointers, and iterators referring to the elements in the sequence. It is guaranteed that no reallocation takes place during the insertions that happen after reserve takes place till the time when the size of the vector reaches the size specified by reserve.

insert causes reallocation if the new size is greater than the old capacity. If no reallocation happens, all the iterators and references before the insertion point remain valid. Inserting a single element into a vector is linear in the distance from the insertion point to the end of the vector. The amortized complexity over the lifetime of a vector of inserting a single element at its end is constant. Insertion of multiple elements into a vector with a single call of the insert member function is linear in the sum of the number of elements plus the distance to the end of the vector.

In other words, it is much faster to insert many elements into the middle of a vector at once than to do the insertion one at a time. The insert template member function preallocates enough storage for the insertion if the iterators first and last are of forward, bidirectional or random access category. Otherwise, it does insert elements one by one and should not be used for inserting into the middle of vectors.

erase invalidates all the iterators and references after the point of the erase. The destructor of T is called the number of times equal to the number of the elements erased, but the assignment operator of T is called the number of times equal to the number of elements in the vector after the erased elements.

To optimize space allocation, a specialization for bool is provided:

```
class vector<bool, allocator> {
public:

// bit reference:

    class reference {
    public:
        ~reference();
        operator bool() const;
        reference& operator=(const bool x);
        void flip(); // flips the bit
    };

// typedefs:

    typedef bool const_reference;
    typedef iterator;
    typedef const_iterator;
    typedef size_t size_type;
    typedef ptrdiff_t difference_type;
    typedef bool value_type;
    typedef reverse_iterator;
    typedef const_reverse_iterator;

// allocation/deallocation:

    vector();
    vector(size_type n, const bool& value = bool());
    vector(const vector<bool, allocator>& x);
    template <class InputIterator>
    vector(InputIterator first, InputIterator last);
    ~vector();
    vector<bool, allocator>&
        operator=(const vector<bool, allocator>& x);
    void reserve(size_type n);
    void swap(vector<bool, allocator>& x);

// accessors:
```

```
    iterator begin();
    const_iterator begin() const;
    iterator end();
    const_iterator end() const;
    reverse_iterator rbegin();
    const_reverse_iterator rbegin();
    reverse_iterator rend();
    const_reverse_iterator rend();
    size_type size() const;
    size_type max_size() const;
    size_type capacity() const;
    bool empty() const;
    reference operator[](size_type n);
    const_reference operator[](size_type n) const;
    reference front();
    const_reference front() const;
    reference back();
    const_reference back() const;

// insert/erase:

    void push_back(const bool& x);
    iterator insert(iterator position, const bool& x = bool());
    void insert(iterator position, size_type n, const bool& x);
    template <class InputIterator>
    void insert(iterator position,
                InputIterator first,
                InputIterator last);
    void pop_back();
    void erase(iterator position);
    void erase(iterator first, iterator last);
};

void swap(vector<bool, allocator>::reference x,
          vector<bool, allocator>::reference y);

bool operator==(const vector<bool, allocator>& x,
                const vector<bool, allocator>& y);

bool operator<(const vector<bool, allocator>& x,
               const vector<bool, allocator>& y);
```

reference is a class that simulates the behavior of references of a single bit in vector<bool>. Every implementation is expected to provide specializations of vector<bool> for all supported memory models.

At present, it is not possible to templatize a specialization. That is, we cannot write:

```
template <template <class U> class Allocator = allocator>
class vector<bool, Allocator> { /* ... */ };
```

Therefore, only vector<bool, allocator> is provided.

8.1.2 List

list is a kind of sequence that supports bidirectional iterators and allows constant time insert and erase operations anywhere within the sequence, with storage management handled automatically. Unlike vectors and deques, fast random access to list elements is not supported, but many algorithms only need sequential access anyway.

```
template <class T,
          template <class U> class Allocator = allocator>
class list {
public:

// typedefs:

    typedef iterator;
    typedef const_iterator;
    typedef Allocator<T>::pointer pointer;
    typedef Allocator<T>::reference reference;
    typedef Allocator<T>::const_reference const_reference;
    typedef size_type;
    typedef difference_type;
    typedef T value_type;
    typedef reverse_iterator;
    typedef const_reverse_iterator;

// allocation/deallocation:

    list();
    list(size_type n, const T& value = T());
    template <class InputIterator>
    list(InputIterator first, InputIterator last);
    list(const list<T, Allocator>& x);
    ~list();
    list<T, Allocator>& operator=(const list<T, Allocator>& x);
    void swap(list<T, Allocator>& x);
```

```
// accessors:

    iterator begin();
    const_iterator begin() const;
    iterator end();
    const_iterator end() const;
    reverse_iterator rbegin();
    const_reverse_iterator rbegin();
    reverse_iterator rend();
    const_reverse_iterator rend();
    bool empty() const;
    size_type size() const;
    size_type max_size() const;
    reference front();
    const_reference front() const;
    reference back();
    const_reference back() const;

// insert/erase:

    void push_front(const T& x);
    void push_back(const T& x);
    iterator insert(iterator position, const T& x = T());
    void insert(iterator position, size_type n, const T& x);
    template <class InputIterator>
    void insert(iterator position,
                InputIterator first,
                InputIterator last);
    void pop_front();
    void pop_back();
    void erase(iterator position);
    void erase(iterator first, iterator last);

// special mutative operations on list:

    void splice(iterator position, list<T, Allocator>& x);
    void splice(iterator position,
                list<T, Allocator>& x,
                iterator i);
    void splice(iterator position,
                list<T, Allocator>& x,
                iterator first,
                iterator last);
    void remove(const T& value);
    template <class Predicate> void remove_if(Predicate pred);
    void unique();
    template <class BinaryPredicate>
```

```
        void unique(BinaryPredicate binary_pred);
        void merge(list<T, Allocator>& x);
        template <class Compare>
        void merge(list<T, Allocator>& x, Compare comp);
        void reverse();
        void sort();
        template <class Compare> void sort(Compare comp);
};


template <class T, class Allocator>
bool operator==(const list<T, Allocator>& x,
                const list<T, Allocator>& y);


template <class T, class Allocator>
bool operator<(const list<T, Allocator>& x,
               const list<T, Allocator>& y);
```

iterator is a bidirectional iterator referring to T. The exact type is implementation-dependent and determined by Allocator.

const_iterator is a constant bidirectional iterator referring to const T. The exact type is implementation-dependent and determined by Allocator. It is guaranteed that there is a constructor for const_iterator out of iterator.

size_type is an unsigned integral type. The exact type is implementation-dependent and determined by Allocator.

difference_type is a signed integral type. The exact type is implementation-dependent and determined by Allocator.

insert does not affect the validity of iterators and references. Insertion of a single element into a list takes constant time and exactly one call to the copy constructor of T. Insertion of multiple elements into a list is linear in the number of elements inserted, and the number of calls to the copy constructor of T is exactly equal to the number of elements inserted.

erase invalidates only the iterators and references to the erased elements. Erasing a single element is a constant time operation with a single call to the destructor of T. Erasing a range in a list is linear time in the size of the range, and the number of calls to the destructor of type T is exactly equal to the size of the range.

Since lists allow fast insertion and erasing from the middle of a list, certain operations are provided specifically for them:

- list provides three splice operations that destructively move elements from one list to another:

1. void splice(iterator position, list<T, Allocator>& *x*) inserts the contents of *x* before position and *x* becomes empty. It takes constant time. The result is undefined if &x == this.

2. void splice(iterator position, list<T, Allocator>& x, iterator i) inserts an element pointed to by *i* from list *x* before position and removes the element from *x*. It takes constant time. *i* is a valid dereferenceable iterator of *x*. The result is unchanged if position == *i* or position == ++*i*.

3. void splice(iterator position, list<T, Allocator>& *x*, iterator first, iterator last) inserts elements in the range [first, last) before position and removes the elements from *x*. It takes constant time if &*x* == this; otherwise, it takes linear time. [first, last) is a valid range in x. The result is undefined if position is an iterator in the range [first, last).

- remove erases all the elements in the list referred by the list iterator i for which the following conditions hold: *i == value, pred(*i)== true. remove is stable, that is, the relative order of the elements that are not removed is the same as their relative order in the original list. Exactly size() applications of the corresponding predicate are done.

- unique erases all but the first element from every consecutive group of equal elements in the list. Exactly size()-1 applications of the corresponding binary predicate are done.

- merge merges the argument list into the list (both are assumed to be sorted). The merge is stable, that is, for equal elements in the two lists, the elements from the list always precede the elements from the argument list. *x* is empty after the merge. At most size() + *x*.size() - 1 comparisons are done.

- reverse reverses the order of the elements in the list. It is linear time.

- sort sorts the list according to the operator< or a compare function object. It is stable, that is, the relative order of the equal elements is preserved. Approximately $N \log N$ comparisons are done where N is equal to size().

8.1.3 Deque

deque is a kind of sequence that, like a vector, supports random access iterators. In addition, it supports constant time insert and erase operations at the beginning or the end; insert and erase in the middle take linear time. As with vectors, storage management is handled automatically.

```
template <class T,
          template <class U> class Allocator = allocator>
class deque {
public:

// typedefs:

    typedef iterator;
    typedef const_iterator;
    typedef Allocator<T>::pointer pointer;
    typedef Allocator<T>::reference reference;
    typedef Allocator<T>::const_reference const_reference;
    typedef size_type;
    typedef difference_type;
    typedef T value_type;
    typedef reverse iterator;
    typedef const_reverse_iterator;

// allocation/deallocation:

    deque();
    deque(size_type n, const T& value = T());
    deque(const deque<T, Allocator>& x);
    template <class InputIterator>
    deque(InputIterator first, InputIterator last);
    ~deque();
    deque<T, Allocator>& operator=(const deque<T, Allocator>& x);
    void swap(deque<T, Allocator>& x);

// accessors:

    iterator begin();
    const_iterator begin() const;
    iterator end();
    const_iterator end() const;
    reverse_iterator rbegin();
    const_reverse_iterator rbegin();
    reverse_iterator rend();
    const_reverse_iterator rend();
    size_type size() const;
    size_type max_size() const;
    bool empty() const;
    reference operator[](size_type n);
    const_reference operator[](size_type n) const;
    reference front();
    const_reference front() const;
    reference back();
    const_reference back() const;
```

```
// insert/erase:

    void push_front(const T& x);
    void push_back(const T& x);
    iterator insert(iterator position, const T& x = T());
    void insert(iterator position, size_type n, const T& x);
    template <class InputIterator>
    void insert(iterator position,
                InputIterator first,
                InputIterator last);
    void pop_front();
    void pop_back();
    void erase(iterator position);
    void erase(iterator first, iterator last);
};

template <class T, class Allocator>
bool operator==(const deque<T, Allocator>& x,
                const deque<T, Allocator>& y);

template <class T, class Allocator>
bool operator<(const deque<T, Allocator>& x,
               const deque<T, Allocator>& y);
```

iterator is a random access iterator referring to T. The exact type is implementation-dependent and is determined by Allocator.

const_iterator is a constant random access iterator referring to const T. The exact type is implementation-dependent and determined by Allocator. It is guaranteed that there is a constructor for const_iterator out of iterator.

size_type is an unsigned integral type. The exact type is implementation-dependent and determined by Allocator.

difference_type is a signed integral type. The exact type is implementation-dependent and determined by Allocator.

insert and push invalidate all the iterators and references to the deque. In the worst case, inserting a single element into a deque takes time linear in the minimum of the distance from the insertion point to the beginning of the deque and the distance from the insertion point to the end of the deque. Inserting a single element either at the beginning or end of a deque always takes constant time and causes a single call to the copy constructor of T. That is, a deque is especially optimized for pushing and popping elements at the beginning and end.

erase and pop invalidate all the iterators and references to the deque. The number of calls to the destructor is the same as the number of elements erased, but the number of the calls to the assignment operator is equal to the minimum of the number of elements before the erased elements and the number of elements after the erased elements.

8.2 Associative containers

Associative containers provide an ability for fast retrieval of data based on keys. The library provides four basic kinds of associative containers: set, multiset, map and multimap.

All of them are parameterized on Key and an ordering relation Compare that induces a total ordering on elements of Key. In addition, map and multimap associate an arbitrary type T with the Key. The object of type Compare is called the comparison object of a container.

In this section, when we talk about equality of keys we mean the equivalence relation imposed by the comparison and *not* the operator== on keys. That is, two keys $k1$ and $k2$ are considered to be equal if, for the comparison object comp(), comp($k1$, $k2$) == false && comp($k2$, $k1$) == false.

An associative container supports *unique keys* if it may contain at most one element for each key. Otherwise, it supports *equal keys*. set and map support unique keys; multiset and multimap support equal keys.

For set and multiset the value type is the same as the key type. For map and multimap, it is equal to pair<const Key, T>.

iterator of an associative container is of the bidirectional iterator category. insert does not affect the validity of iterators and references to the container, and erase invalidates only the iterators and references to the erased elements.

In the following table: X is an associative container class; a is a value of X; a_uniq is a value of X when X supports unique keys; a_eq is a value of X when X supports multiple keys; i and j satisfy input iterator requirements and refer to elements of value_type; [i, j) is a valid range; p is a valid iterator to a; q, $q1$ and $q2$ are valid dereferenceable iterators to a; [$q1$, $q2$) is a valid range; t is a value of X::value_type; and k is a value of X::key_type.

Table A-11

Reversible container requirements (in addition to container)

expression	return type	assertion/note pre/post-condition	complexity
X::key_type	Key		compile time
X::key_compare	Compare	defaults to less<key_type>	compile time
X::value_compare	a binary predicate type	is the same as key_compare for set and multiset; is an ordering relation on pairs induced by the first component (i.e. Key) for map and multimap	compile time
X(c) X a(c)		constructs an empty container; uses c as a comparison object	constant
X() X a;		constructs an empty container; uses Compare() as a comparison object	constant
X(i, j, c) X a(i, j, c);		constructs an empty container and inserts elements from the range [i, j) into it; uses c as a comparison object	NlogN in general (N is the distance from i to j); linear if [i, j) is sorted with value_comp()
X(i, j) X a(i,j)		same as above, but uses Compare() as a comparison object	same as above
a.key_comp()	X::key_compare	returns the comparison object out of which a was constructed	constant
a.value_comp()	X::value_compare	returns an object of value_compare constructed out of the comparison object	constant
a_uniq.insert(t)	pair<iterator,bool>	inserts t if and only if there is no element in the container with key equal to the key of t; the bool component of the returned pair indicates whether the insertion takes place and the iterator component of the pair points to the element with key equal to the key of t	logarithmic

expression	return type	assertion/note pre/post-condition	complexity
a_eq.insert(t)	iterator	inserts t and returns the iterator pointing to the newly inserted element	logarithmic
a.insert(p,t)	iterator	inserts t if and only if there is no element with key equal to the key of t in containers with unique keys; always inserts t in containers with equal keys; always returns the iterator pointing to the element with key equal to the key of t; iterator p is a hint pointing to where the insert should start to search	logarithmic in general, but amortized constant if t is inserted right after p.
a.insert(i,j)	result is not used	inserts the elements from the range [i,j) into the container	Nlog(size()+N)(N is the distance from i to j) is sorted according to value_comp()
a.erase(k)	size_type	erases all the elements in the container with key equal to k; returns the number of erased elements	log(size())+count(k)
a.erase(q)	result is not used	erases the element pointed to by q	amortized constant.
a.erase(q1,q2)	result is not used	erases all the elements in the range [q1,q2)	log(size())+N where N is the distance from q1 to q2.
a.find(k)	iterator; const_iterator for constant a	returns an iterator pointing to an element with the key equal to k, or a.end() if such an element is not found	logarithmic
a.count(k)	size_type	returns the number of elements with key equal to k	log(size())+count(k)
a.lower_bound(k)	iterator; const_iterator for constant a	returns an iterator pointing to the first element with key not less than k	logarithmic
a.upper_bound(k)	iterator; const_iterator for constant a	returns an iterator pointing to the first element with key greater than k	logarithmic
a.equal_range(k)	pair<iterator, iterator>; pair< const_iterator, const_iterator> for constant a	equivalent to make_pair(a.lower_bound (k),a.upper_bound(k))	logarithmic

The fundamental property of iterators of associative containers is that they iterate through the containers in the non-descending order of keys, where non-descending is defined by the comparison that was used to construct them. For any two dereferenceable iterators *i* and *j* such that distance from *i* to *j* is positive,

```
value_comp(*j, *i) == false
```

For associative containers with unique keys the stronger condition holds,

```
value_comp(*i, *j) == true.
```

8.2.1 Set

set is a kind of associative container that supports unique keys (i.e. it contains at most one of each key value) and provides for fast retrieval of the keys themselves.

```
template <class Key,
          class Compare = less<Key>,
          template <class U> class Allocator = allocator>
class set {
public:

// typedefs:

    typedef Key key_type;
    typedef Key value_type;
    typedef Allocator<Key>::pointer pointer;
    typedef Allocator<Key>::reference reference;
    typedef Allocator<Key>::const_reference const_reference;
    typedef Compare key_compare;
    typedef Compare value_compare;
    typedef iterator;
    typedef iterator const_iterator;
    typedef size_type;
    typedef difference_type;
    typedef reverse_iterator;
    typedef const_reverse_iterator;

// allocation/deallocation:

    set(const Compare& comp = Compare());
    template <class InputIterator>
    set(InputIterator first,
```

```
            InputIterator last,
            const Compare& comp = Compare());
      set(const set<Key, Compare, Allocator>& x);
      ~set();
      set<Key, Compare, Allocator>&
            operator=(const set<Key, Compare, Allocator>& x);
      void swap(set<Key, Compare, Allocator>& x);

// accessors:

      key_compare key_comp() const;
      value_compare value_comp() const;
      iterator begin() const;
      iterator end() const;
      reverse_iterator() rbegin const;
      reverse_iterator rend() const;
      bool empty() const;
      size_type size() const;
      size_type max_size() const;

// insert/erase:

      pair<iterator, bool> insert(const value_type& x);
      iterator insert(iterator position, const value_type& x);
      template <class InputIterator>
      void insert(InputIterator first, InputIterator last);
      void erase(iterator position);
      size_type erase(const key_type& x);
      void erase(iterator first, iterator last);

// set operations:

      iterator find(const key_type& x) const;
      size_type count(const key_type& x) const;
      iterator lower_bound(const key_type& x) const;
      iterator upper_bound(const key_type& x const);
      pair<iterator, iterator> equal_range(const key_type& x) const;
};

template <class Key, class Compare, class Allocator>
bool operator==(const set<Key, Compare, Allocator>& x,
                const set<Key, Compare, Allocator>& y;

template <class Key, class Compare, class Allocator>
bool operator<(const set<Key, Compare, Allocator>& x,
               const set<Key, Compare, Allocator>& y);
```

iterator is a constant bidirectional iterator referring to const value_type. The exact type is implementation-dependent and determined by Allocator.

const_iterator is the same type as iterator.

size_type is an unsigned integral type. The exact type is implementation-dependent and determined by Allocator.

difference_type is a signed integral type. The exact type is implementation-dependent and determined by Allocator.

8.2.2 Multiset

multiset is a kind of associative container that supports equal keys (i.e. it possibly contains multiple copies of the same key value) and provides for fast retrieval of the keys themselves.

```
template <class Key,
         class Compare = less<Key>,
         template <class U> class Allocator = allocator>
class multiset {
public:

// typedefs:

    typedef Key key_type;
    typedef Key value_type;
    typedef Allocator<Key>::pointer pointer;
    typedef Allocator<Key>::reference reference;
    typedef Allocator<Key>::const_reference const_reference;
    typedef Compare key_compare;
    typedef Compare value_compare;
    typedef iterator;
    typedef iterator const_iterator;
    typedef size_type;
    typedef difference_type;
    typedef reverse_iterator;
    typedef const_reverse_iterator;

// allocation/deallocation:

    multiset(const Compare& comp = Compare());
    template <class InputIterator>
    multiset(InputIterator first,
             InputIterator last,
             const Compare& comp = Compare());
    multiset(const multiset<Key, Compare, Allocator>& x);
    ~multiset();
```

```
          multiset<Key, Compare, Allocator>&
              operator=(const multiset<Key, Compare, Allocator>& x);
          void swap(multiset<Key, Compare, Allocator>& x);

    // accessors:

          key_compare key_comp() const;
          value_compare value_comp() const;
          iterator begin() const;
          iterator end() const;
          reverse_iterator rbegin();
          reverse_iterator rend();
          bool empty() const;
          size_type size() const;
          size_type max_size() const;

    // insert/erase:

          iterator insert(const value_type& x);
          iterator insert(iterator position, const value_type& x);
          template <class InputIterator>
          void insert(InputIterator first, InputIterator last);
          void erase(iterator position);
          size_type erase(const key_type& x);
          void erase(iterator first, iterator last);

    // multiset operations:

          iterator find(const key_type& x) const;
          size_type count(const key_type& x const);
          iterator lower_bound(const key_type& x const);
          iterator upper_bound(const key_type& x const);
          pair<iterator, iterator> equal_range(const key_type& x const);
    };

    template <class Key, class Compare, class Allocator>
    bool operator==(const multiset<Key, Compare, Allocator>& x,
                    const multiset<Key, Compare, Allocator>& y);

    template <class Key, class Compare, class Allocator>
    bool operator<(const multiset<Key, Compare, Allocator>& x,
    const multiset<Key, Compare, Allocator>& y);
```

iterator is a constant bidirectional iterator referring to const value_type.
The exact type is implementation-dependent and determined by Allocator.
const_iterator is the same type as iterator.

size_type is an unsigned integral type. The exact type is implementation-dependent and determined by Allocator.

difference_type is a signed integral type. The exact type is implementation-dependent and determined by Allocator.

8.2.3 Map

map is a kind of associative container that supports unique keys (i.e. it contains at most one of each key value) and provides for fast retrieval of values of another type T based on the keys.

```
template <class Key, class T, class Compare = less<Key>,
          template <class U> class Allocator = allocator>
class map {
public:

// typedefs:

    typedef Key key_type;
    typedef pair<const Key, T> value_type;
    typedef Compare key_compare;
    class value_compare
      : public binary_function<value_type,
                               value_type,
                               bool> {
    friend class map;
    protected:
        Compare comp;
        value_compare(Compare c) : comp(c) {}
    public:
        bool operator()(const value_type& x,
                        const value_type& y ){
          return comp(x.first, y.first);
        }
    };
    typedef iterator;
    typedef const_iterator;
    typedef Allocator<value_type>::pointer pointer;
    typedef Allocator<value_type>::reference reference;
    typedef Allocator<value_type>::const_reference const_reference;
    typedef size_type;
    typedef difference_type;
    typedef reverse_iterator;
    typedef const_reverse_iterator;
```

```
// allocation/deallocation:

    map(const Compare& comp = Compare());
    template <class InputIterator>
    map(InputIterator first,
        InputIterator last,
        const Compare& comp = Compare());
    map(const map<Key, T, Compare, Allocator>& x);
    ~map();
    map<Key, T, Compare, Allocator>&
        operator=(const map<Key, T, Compare, Allocator>& x);
    void swap(map<Key, T, Compare, Allocator>& x);

// accessors:

    key_compare key_comp() const;
    value_compare value_comp() const;
    iterator begin();
    const_iterator begin() const;
    iterator end();
    const_iterator end() const;
    reverse_iterator rbegin();
    const_reverse_iterator rbegin();
    reverse_iterator rend();
    const_reverse_iterator rend();
    bool empty() const;
    size_type size() const;
    size_type max_size() const;
    Allocator<T>::reference operator[](const key_type& x);

// insert/erase:

    pair<iterator, bool> insert(const value_type& x);
    iterator insert(iterator position, const value_type& x);
    template <class InputIterator>
    void insert(InputIterator first, InputIterator last);
    void erase(iterator position);
    size_type erase(const key_type& x);
    void erase(iterator first, iterator last);

// map operations:

    iterator find(const key_type& x);
    const_iterator find(const key_type& x) const;
    size_type count(const key_type& x) const;
    iterator lower_bound(const key_type& x);
    const_iterator lower_bound(const key_type& x const);
```

```
        iterator upper_bound(const key_type& x);
        const_iterator upper_bound(const key_type& x) const;
        pair<iterator, iterator> equal_range(const key_type& x);
        pair<const_iterator, const_iterator>
            equal_range(const key_type& x const);
    };

    template <class Key, class T, class Compare, class Allocator>
    bool operator==(const map<Key, T, Compare, Allocator>& x,
                const map<Key, T, Compare, Allocator>& y;

    template <class Key, class T, class Compare, class Allocator>
    bool operator<(const map<Key, T, Compare, Allocator>& x,
                const map<Key, T, Compare, Allocator>& y);
```

iterator is a bidirectional iterator referring to value_type. The exact type is implementation-dependent and determined by Allocator.

const_iterator is a constant bidirectional iterator referring to const value_type. The exact type is implementation-dependent and determined by Allocator. It is guaranteed that there is a constructor for const_iterator out of iterator.

size_type is an unsigned integral type. The exact type is implementation-dependent and determined by Allocator.

difference_type is a signed integral type. The exact type is implementation-dependent and determined by Allocator.

In addition to the standard set of member functions of associative containers, map provides Allocator<T>::reference operator[](const key_type&). For a map *m* and key *k*, *m*[*k*] is semantically equivalent to (*((*m*.insert(make_pair(*k*, T())))).first)).second.

8.2.4 Multimap

multimap is a kind of associative container that supports equal keys (i.e. it possibly contains multiple copies of the same key value) and provides for fast retrieval of values of another type T based on the keys.

```
    template <class Key, class T, class Compare = less<Key>,
            template <class U> class Allocator = allocator>
    class multimap {
    public:

    // typedefs:
```

```
            typedef Key key_type;
            typedef pair<const Key, T> value_type;
            typedef Compare key_compare;
            class value_compare
              : public binary_function<value_type,
                                       value_type,
                                       bool> {
            friend class multimap;
            protected:
                Compare comp();
                value_compare(Compare c) : comp(c) {}
            public:
                bool operator()(const value_type& x,
                                const value_type& y) {
                    return comp(x.first, y.first);
                }
            };
            typedef iterator;
            typedef const_iterator;
            typedef Allocator<value_type>::pointer pointer;
            typedef Allocator<value_type>::reference reference;
            typedef Allocator<value_type>::const_reference const_reference;
            typedef size_type;
            typedef difference_type;
            typedef reverse_iterator;
            typedef const_reverse_iterator;

// allocation/deallocation:

            multimap(const Compare& comp = Compare());
            template <class InputIterator>
            multimap( InputIterator first,
                      InputIterator last,
                      const Compare& comp = Compare());
            multimap(const multimap<Key, T, Compare, Allocator>& x);
            ~multimap();
            multimap<Key, T, Compare, Allocator>&
                operator=( const multimap<Key, T, Compare, Allocator>& x);
            void swap(multimap<Key, T, Compare, Allocator>& x);

// accessors:

            key_compare key_comp() const;
            value_compare value_comp() const;
            iterator begin();
            const_iterator begin() const;
            iterator end();
```

```
        const_iterator end() const;
        reverse_iterator rbegin();
        const_reverse_iterator rbegin();
        reverse_iterator rend();
        const_reverse_iterator rend();
        bool empty() const;
        size_type size() const;
        size_type max_size() const;

    // insert/erase:

        iterator insert(const value_type& x);
        iterator insert(iterator position, const value_type& x);
        template <class InputIterator>
        void insert(InputIterator first, InputIterator last);
        void erase(iterator position);
        size_type erase(const key_type& x);
        void erase(iterator first, iterator last);

    // multimap operations:

        iterator find(const key_type& x);
        const_iterator find(const key_type& x const);
        size_type count(const key_type& x const);
        iterator lower_bound(const key_type& x);
        const_iterator lower_bound(const key_type& x const);
        iterator upper_bound(const key_type& x);
        const_iterator upper_bound(const key_type& x const;
        pair<iterator, iterator> equal_range(const key_type& x);
        pair<const_iterator, const_iterator>
            equal_range(const key_type& x const);
    };

    template <class Key, class T, class Compare, class Allocator>
    bool operator==(const multimap<Key, T, Compare,
                    Allocator>& x,
                    const multimap<Key, T, Compare, Allocator>& y);
    template <class Key, class T, class Compare, class Allocator>
    bool operator<(const multimap<Key, T, Compare, Allocator>& x,
                   const multimap<Key, T, Compare, Allocator>& y);
```

iterator is a bidirectional iterator referring to value_type. The exact type is implementation-dependent and determined by Allocator.

const_iterator is a constant bidirectional iterator referring to const value_type. The exact type is implementation-dependent and determined by Allocator. It is guaranteed that there is a constructor for const_iterator out of iterator.

size_type is an unsigned integral type. The exact type is implementation-dependent and determined by Allocator.

difference_type is a signed integral type. The exact type is implementation-dependent and determined by Allocator.

9 STREAM ITERATORS

To make it possible for algorithmic templates to work directly with input/output streams, appropriate iterator-like template classes are provided. For example,

```
partial_sum_copy(istream_iterator<double>(cin),
                 istream_iterator<double>(),
                 ostream_iterator<double>(cout,"\n");
```

reads a file containing floating point numbers from cin, and prints the partial sums onto cout.

9.1 Istream Iterator

istream_iterator<T> reads (using operator>>) successive elements from the input stream for which it was constructed. After it is constructed, and every time ++ is used, the iterator reads and stores a value of T. If the end of stream is reached (operator void* on the stream returns false), the iterator becomes equal to the *end-of-stream* iterator value. The constructor with no arguments istream_iterator() always constructs an end of stream input iterator object, which is the only legitimate iterator to be used for the end condition. The result of operator* on an end of stream is not defined. For any other iterator value a const T& is returned. It is impossible to store things into istream iterators. The main peculiarity of the istream iterators is the fact that ++ operators are not equality preserving; that is, $i == j$ does not guarantee at all that $++i == ++j$. Every time ++ is used, a new value is read.

The practical consequence of this fact is that istream iterators can be used only for one-pass algorithms, which actually makes perfect sense, since for multi-pass algorithms it is always more appropriate to use in-memory data structures. Two end-of-stream iterators are always equal. An end-of-stream iterator is not equal to a non-end-of-stream iterator. Two non-end-of-stream iterators are equal when they are constructed from the same stream.

```
template <class T, class Distance = ptrdiff_t>
class istream_iterator : public input_iterator<T, Distance> {
friend bool operator==(const istream_iterator<T, Distance>& x,
                       const istream_iterator<T, Distance>& y);
public:
    istream_iterator();
    istream_iterator(istream& s);
    istream_iterator(const istream_iterator<T, Distance>& x);
    ~istream_iterator();
    const T& operator*() const;
    istream_iterator<T, Distance>& operator++();
    istream_iterator<T, Distance> operator++(int);
};

template <class T, class Distance>
bool operator==(const istream_iterator<T, Distance>& x,
                const istream_iterator<T, Distance>& y);
```

9.2 Ostream iterator

ostream_iterator<T> writes (using operator<<) successive elements onto
the output stream from which it was constructed. If it was constructed
with char* as a constructor argument, this string, called a *delimiter string*,
is written to the stream after every T is written. It is not possible to get
a value out of the output iterator. Its only use is as an output iterator in
situations like

```
while (first != last) *result++ = *first++;
```

ostream_iterator is defined as:

```
template <class T>
class ostream_iterator : public output_iterator {
public:
    ostream_iterator(ostream& s);
    ostream_iterator(ostream& s, const char* delimiter);
    ostream_iterator(const ostream_iterator<T>& x);
    ~ostream_iterator();
    ostream_iterator<T>& operator=(const T& value);
    ostream_iterator<T>& operator*();
    ostream_iterator<T>& operator++();
    ostream_iterator<T>& operator++(int);
};
```

10 ALGORITHMS

All of the algorithms are separated from the particular implementations of data structures and are parameterized by iterator types. Because of this, they can work with user-defined data structures, as long as these data structures have iterator types satisfying the assumptions on the algorithms.

Both in-place and copying versions are provided for certain algorithms. The decision whether to include a copying version was usually based on complexity considerations. When the cost of doing the operation dominates the cost of copy, the copying version is not included. For example, sort_copy is not included since the cost of sorting is much more significant, and users might as well do copy followed by sort. When such a version is provided for *algorithm* it is called *algorithm copy*. Algorithms that take predicates end with the suffix _if (which follows the suffix _copy).

The Predicate class is used whenever an algorithm expects a function object that, when applied to the result of dereferencing the corresponding iterator, returns a value testable as true. In other words, if an algorithm takes Predicate pred as its argument and first as its iterator argument, it should work correctly in the construct if (pred(*first)){...}. The function object pred is assumed not to apply any non-constant function through the dereferenced iterator.

The BinaryPredicate class is used whenever an algorithm expects a function object that, when applied to the result of dereferencing two corresponding iterators, or to dereferencing an iterator and type T — when T is part of the signature — returns a value testable as true. In other words, if an algorithm takes BinaryPredicate binary_pred as its argument and first1 and first2 as its iterator arguments, it should work correctly in the construct if (binary_pred(*first, *first2){...}. BinaryPredicate always takes the first iterator type as its first argument, that is, in those cases when T value is part of the signature, it should work correctly in the context of if (binary_pred(*first, value){...}. It is expected that binary_pred will not apply any non-constant function through the dereferenced iterators.

In the description of the algorithms operators, + and - are used for some of the iterator categories for which they do not have to be defined. In these cases the semantics of $a+n$ is the same as that of { X tmp = a; advance(tmp, n); return tmp; } and that of $a-b$ is the same as that of { Distance n; distance(a, b, n); return n; }.

10.1 Non-mutating sequence operations

10.1.1 For each

```
template <class InputIterator, class Function>
Function for_each(InputIterator first,
                  InputIterator last,
                  Function f);
```

for_each applies *f* to the result of dereferencing every iterator in the range [first, last) and returns *f*. *f* is assumed not to apply any non-constant function through the dereferenced iterator. *f* is applied exactly last - first times. If *f* returns a result, the result is ignored.

10.1.2 Find

```
template <class InputIterator, class T>
InputIterator find(InputIterator first,
                   InputIterator last,
                   const T& value);

template <class InputIterator, class Predicate>
InputIterator find_if(InputIterator first,
                      InputIterator last,
                      Predicate pred);
```

find returns the first iterator *i* in the range [first, last) for which the following corresponding conditions hold: $*i$ == value, pred($*i$) == true. If no such iterator is found, last is returned. Exactly find(first, last, value) - first applications of the corresponding predicate are done.

10.1.3 Adjacent find

```
template <class InputIterator>
InputIterator adjacent_find(InputIterator first,
                            InputIterator last);

template <class InputIterator, class BinaryPredicate>
InputIterator adjacent_find(InputIterator first,
                            InputIterator last,
                            BinaryPredicate binary_pred);
```

adjacent_find returns the first iterator *i* such that both *i* and *i* + 1 are in the range [first, last) for which the following corresponding conditions hold: **i* == **i* + 1, binary_pred(**i*, **i* + 1) == true. If no such iterator *i* is found, last is returned. At most, max((last - first) - 1, 0) applications of the corresponding predicate are done.

10.1.4 Count

```
template <class InputIterator, class T, class Size>
void count(InputIterator first,
           InputIterator last,
           const T& value,
           Size& n);

template <class InputIterator, class Predicate, class Size>
void count_if(InputIterator first,
              InputIterator last,
              Predicate pred,
              Size& n);
```

count adds to *n* the number of iterators *i* in the range [first, last) for which the following corresponding conditions hold: **i* == value, pred(**i*) == true. Exactly last - first applications of the corresponding predicate are done.

count must store the result into a reference argument instead of returning the result, because the size type cannot be deduced from built-in iterator types such as int*.

10.1.5 Mismatch

```
template <class InputIterator1, class InputIterator2>
       pair<InputIterator1, InputIterator2>
   mismatch(InputIterator1 first1,
            InputIterator1 last1,
            InputIterator2 first2);

template <class InputIterator1,
          class InputIterator2,
          class BinaryPredicate>
pair<InputIterator1, InputIterator2>
   mismatch(InputIterator1 first1,
            InputIterator1 last1,
            InputIterator2 first2,
            BinaryPredicate binary_pred);
```

mismatch returns a pair of iterators i and j such that j == first2 + i - first1, and i is the first iterator in the range [first1, last1) for which the following corresponding conditions hold: !(*i == *(first2 + (i - first1))), binary_pred(*i, *(first2 + (i - first1))) == false. If such an iterator i is not found, a pair of last1 and first2 + (last1 - first1) is returned. At most, last1 - first1 applications of the corresponding predicate are done.

10.1.6 Equal

```
template <class InputIterator1, class InputIterator2>
bool equal(InputIterator1 first1,
           InputIterator1 last1,
           InputIterator2 first2;

template <class InputIterator1,
          class InputIterator2,
          class BinaryPredicate>
bool equal(InputIterator1 first1,
           InputIterator1 last1,
           InputIterator2 first2,
           BinaryPredicate binary_pred);
```

equal returns true if, for every iterator i in the range [first1, last1), the following corresponding conditions hold: *i == *(first2 + (i - first1)), binary_pred(*i, *(first2 + (i - first1))) == true. Otherwise, it returns false. At most, last1 - first1 applications of the corresponding predicate are done.

10.1.7 Search

```
template <class ForwardIterator1, class ForwardIterator2>
ForwardIterator1 search(ForwardIterator1 first1,
                        ForwardIterator1 last1,
                        ForwardIterator2 first2,
                        ForwardIterator2 last2);

template <class ForwardIterator1,
          class ForwardIterator2,
          class BinaryPredicate>
ForwardIterator1 search(ForwardIterator1 first1,
                        ForwardIterator1 last1,
                        ForwardIterator2 first2,
                        ForwardIterator2 last2,
                        BinaryPredicate binary_pred);
```

search finds a subsequence of equal values in a sequence. search returns the first iterator i in the range [first1, last1 - (last2 - first2)) such that, for any non-negative integer n less than last2 - first2, the following corresponding conditions hold: $*(i + n)$ == $*(first2 + n)$, binary_pred($*(i + n)$, $*(first2 + n)$) == true. If no such iterator is found, last1 is returned. At most, (last1 - first1) * (last2 - first2) applications of the corresponding predicate are done. The quadratic behavior, however, is highly unlikely.

10.2 Mutating sequence operations

10.2.1 Copy

```
template <class InputIterator, class OutputIterator>
OutputIterator copy(InputIterator first,
                    InputIterator last,
                    OutputIterator result);
```

copy copies elements. For each non-negative integer n < last - first, $*(rcsult + n)$ = $*(first + n)$ is performed. copy returns result + (last - first). Exactly last - first assignments are done. The result of copy is undefined if result is in the range [first, last).

```
template <class BidirectionalIterator1,
          class BidirectionalIterator2>
BidirectionalIterator2
    copy_backward(BidirectionalIterator1 first,
                  BidirectionalIterator1 last,
                  BidirectionalIterator2 result);
```

copy_backward copies elements in the range [first, last) into the range [result - (last - first), result) starting from last - 1 and proceeding to first. It should be used instead of copy when last is in the range [result - (last - first), result). For each positive integer n <= (last - first), $*(result - n)$ = $*(last - n)$ is performed. copy_backward returns result - (last - first). Exactly last - first assignments are done. The result of copy_backward is undefined if result is in the range [first, last).

10.2.2 Swap

```
template <class T>
void swap(T& a, T& b);
```

swap exchanges values stored in two locations.

```
template <class ForwardIterator1, class ForwardIterator2>
void iter_swap(ForwardIterator1 a, ForwardIterator2 b);
```

iter_swap exchanges values pointed by the two iterators *a* and *b*.

```
template <class ForwardIterator1, class ForwardIterator2>
ForwardIterator2 swap_ranges(ForwardIterator1 first1,
                             ForwardIterator1 last1,
                             ForwardIterator2 first2);
```

For each non-negative integer n < (last1 - first1) the swap is performed: swap(*(first1 + n), *(first2 + n)). swap_ranges returns first2 + (last1 - first1). Exactly last1 - first1 swaps are done. The result of swap_ranges is undefined if the two ranges [first1, last1) and [first2, first2 + (last1 - first1)) overlap.

10.2.3 Transform

```
template <class InputIterator,
          class OutputIterator,
          class UnaryOperation>
OutputIterator transform(InputIterator first,
                         InputIterator last,
                         OutputIterator result,
                         UnaryOperation op );
```

```
template <class InputIterator1,
          class InputIterator2,
          class OutputIterator,
          class BinaryOperation>
OutputIterator transform(InputIterator1 first1,
                         InputIterator1 last1,
                         InputIterator2 first2,
                         OutputIterator result,
                         BinaryOperation binary_op);
```

transform assigns through every iterator *i* in the range [result, result + (last1 - first1)) a new corresponding value equal to op(*(first1 + (*i* - result))) or binary_op(*(first1 + (*i* - result)), *(first2 + (*i* - result))). transform returns result + (last1 - first1). Exactly last1 - first1 applications of op or binary_op are performed. op and binary_op are expected not to have any side effects. result may be equal to first in case of unary transform, or to first1 or first2
    in case of binary transform.

10.2.4 Replace

```
template <class ForwardIterator, class T>
void replace(ForwardIterator first,
          ForwardIterator last,
          const T& old_value,
          const T& new_value);

template <class ForwardIterator, class Predicate, class T>
void replace_if(ForwardIterator first,
          ForwardIterator last,
          Predicate pred,
          const T& new_value);
```

replace substitutes elements referred by the iterator *i* in the range [first, last) with new_value, when the following corresponding conditions hold: **i* == old_value, pred(*i) == true. Exactly last - first applications of the corresponding predicate are done.

```
template <class InputIterator, class OutputIterator, class T>
OutputIterator replace_copy(InputIterator first,
                    InputIterator last,
                    OutputIterator result,
                    const T& old_value,
                    const T& new_value );

template <class Iterator,
       class OutputIterator,
       class Predicate,
       class T>
OutputIterator replace_copy_if(Iterator first,
                    Iterator last,
                    OutputIterator result,
                    Predicate pred,
                    const T& new_value );
```

replace_copy assigns to every iterator *i* in the range [result, result + (last - first)) either new_value or *(first + (*i* - result)) depending on whether the following corresponding conditions hold: *(first + (*i* - result)) == old_value, pred*(first + (*i* - result)) == true. replace_copy returns result + (last - first). Exactly last - first applications of the corresponding predicate are done.

10.2.5 Fill

```
template <class ForwardIterator, class T>
void fill(ForwardIterator first, ForwardIterator last,
        const T& value);

template <class OutputIterator, class Size, class T>
void fill_n(OutputIterator first, Size n, const T& value);
```

fill assigns value through all the iterators in the range [first, last) or [first, first + *n*). Exactly last - first or *n* assignments are done.

10.2.6 Generate

```
template <class ForwardIterator, class Generator>
void generate(ForwardIterator first,
            ForwardIterator last,
            Generator gen);

template <class OutputIterator, class Size, class Generator>
void generate_n(OutputIterator first, Size n, Generator gen);
```

generate invokes the function object gen and assigns the return value of gen through all the iterators in the range [first, last) or [first, first + *n*). gen takes no arguments. Exactly last - first or *n* invocations of gen and assignments are done.

10.2.7 Remove

```
template <class ForwardIterator, class T>
ForwardIterator remove(ForwardIterator first,
                    ForwardIterator last,
                    const T& value);
```

```
template <class ForwardIterator, class Predicate>
ForwardIterator remove_if(ForwardIterator first,
                          ForwardIterator last,
                          Predicate pred);
```

remove eliminates all the elements referred to by iterator i in the range [first, last) for which the following corresponding conditions hold: $*i$ == value, pred($*i$) == true. remove returns the end of the resulting range. remove is stable, that is, the relative order of the elements that are not removed is the same as their relative order in the original range. Exactly last - first applications of the corresponding predicate are done.

```
template <class InputIterator, class OutputIterator, class T>
OutputIterator remove_copy(InputIterator first,
                           InputIterator last,
                           OutputIterator result,
                           const T& value);
```

```
template <class InputIterator,
          class OutputIterator,
          class Predicate>
OutputIterator remove_copy_if(InputIterator first,
                              InputIterator last,
                              OutputIterator result,
                              Predicate pred);
```

remove_copy copies all the elements referred to by the iterator i in the range [first, last) for which the following corresponding conditions do not hold: $*i$ == value, pred($*i$) == true. remove_copy returns the end of the resulting range. remove_copy is stable, that is, the relative order of the elements in the resulting range is the same as their relative order in the original range. Exactly last - first applications of the corresponding predicate are done.

10.2.8 Unique

```
template <class ForwardIterator>
ForwardIterator unique(ForwardIterator first,
                       ForwardIterator last);
```

```
template <class ForwardIterator, class BinaryPredicate>
Forward-Iterator unique(ForwardIterator first,
                        ForwardIterator last,
                        BinaryPredicate binary_pred);
```

unique eliminates all but the first element from every consecutive group of equal elements referred to by the iterator i in the range [first, last) for which the following corresponding conditions hold: $*i == *i - 1$ or binary_pred($*i$, $*i - 1$) == true. unique returns the end of the resulting range. Exactly (last - first) - 1 applications of the corresponding predicate are done.

```
template <class InputIterator, class OutputIterator>
OutputIterator unique_copy(InputIterator first,
                           InputIterator last,
                           OutputIterator result);


template <class InputIterator,
          class OutputIterator,
          class BinaryPredicate>
OutputIterator unique_copy(InputIterator first,
                           InputIterator last,
                           OutputIterator result,
                           BinaryPredicate binary_pred);
```

unique_copy copies only the first element from every consecutive group of equal elements referred to by the iterator i in the range [first, last) for which the following corresponding conditions hold: $*i == *i - 1$ or binary_pred($*i$, $*i - 1$) == true. unique_copy returns the end of the resulting range. Exactly last - first applications of the corresponding predicate are done.

10.2.9 Reverse

```
template <class BidirectionalIterator> void
reverse(BidirectionalIterator first, BidirectionalIterator last);
```

For each non-negative integer $i <=$ last - first/2, reverse applies swap to all pairs of iterators first + i, (last - i) - 1. Exactly (last - first)/2 swaps are performed.

```
template <class BidirectionalIterator, class OutputIterator>
OutputIterator
    reverse_copy(BidirectionalIterator first,
                 BidirectionalIterator last,
                 OutputIterator result );
```

reverse_copy copies the range [first, last) to the range [result, result + (last - first)) such that for any non-negative integer $i <$ (last - first) the following assignment takes place: *(result + (last - first) - *i*) = *(first + *i*). reverse_copy returns result + (last - first). Exactly last - first assignments are done. The result of reverse_copy is undefined if [first, last) and [result, result + (last - first)) overlap.

10.2.10 Rotate

```
template <class ForwardIterator>
void rotate(ForwardIterator first,
            ForwardIterator middle,
            ForwardIterator last);
```

For each non-negative integer *i* < (last - first), rotate places the element from the position first + *i* into position first + (*i* + (last - middle)) % (last - first). [first, middle) and [middle, last) are valid ranges. At most last - first swaps are done.

```
template <class ForwardIterator, class OutputIterator>
OutputIterator rotate_copy(ForwardIterator first,
                           ForwardIterator middle,
                           ForwardIterator last,
                           OutputIterator result);
```

rotate_copy copies the range [first, last) to the range [result, result + (last - first)) such that for each non-negative integer *i* < (last - first) the following assignment takes place: *(result + *i* + (last - middle)) % (last - first)) = *(first + *i*). rotate_copy returns result + (last - first). Exactly last - first assignments are done. The result of rotate_copy is undefined if [first, last) and [result, result + (last - first)) overlap.

10.2.11 Random shuffle

```
template <class RandomAccessIterator>
void random_shuffle(RandomAccessIterator first,
                    RandomAccessIterator last);

template <class RandomAccessIterator, class RandomNumberGenerator>
void random_shuffle(RandomAccessIterator first,
                    RandomAccessIterator last,
                    RandomNumberGenerator& rand);
```

random_shuffle shuffles the elements in the range [first, last) with uniform distribution. Exactly (last - first) - 1 swaps are done. random_shuffle can take a particular random number generating function object rand such that rand takes a positive argument n of distance type of the RandomAccessIterator and returns a randomly chosen value between 0 and n-1.

10.2.12 Partitions

```
template <class BidirectionalIterator, class Predicate>
BidirectionalIterator
    partition(BidirectionalIterator first,
              BidirectionalIterator last,
              Predicate pred);
```

partition places all the elements in the range [first, last) that satisfy pred before all the elements that do not satisfy it. It returns an iterator i such that for any iterator j in the range [first, i), pred(*j) == true, and for any iterator k in the range [i, last), pred(*j) == false. It does at most (last - first)/2 swaps. Exactly last - first applications of the predicate is done.

```
template <class BidirectionalIterator, class Predicate>
BidirectionalIterator
    stable_partition(BidirectionalIterator first,
                     Bidirectional Iterator last,
                     Predicate pred);
```

stable_partition places all the elements in the range [first, last) that satisfy pred before all the elements that do not satisfy it. It returns an iterator i such that, for any iterator j in the range [first, i), pred(*j) == true, and for any iterator k in the range [i, last), pred(*j) == false. The relative order of the elements in both groups is preserved. It does at most last - first * log(last - first) swaps, but only linear number of swaps if there is enough extra memory. Exactly last - first applications of the predicate are done.

10.3 Sorting and related operations

All the operations in this section have two versions: one that takes a function object of type Compare and one that uses an operator<.

Compare is used as a function object which returns true if the first argument is less than the second, and false otherwise. Compare comp is used throughout for algorithms assuming an ordering relation. It is assumed that comp will not apply any non-constant function through the dereferenced iterator. For all algorithms that take Compare, there is a version that uses operator< instead. That is, comp(*i, *j) == true defaults to *i < *j == true. For the algorithms to work correctly, comp has to induce a total ordering on the values.

A sequence is sorted with respect to a comparator comp if for any iterator i pointing to the sequence and any non-negative integer n such that $i + n$ is a valid iterator pointing to an element of the sequence, comp(*$i + n$, *i) == false.

In the descriptions of the functions that deal with ordering relationships, we frequently use a notion of equality to describe concepts such as stability. The equality to which we refer is not necessarily an operator==, but an equality relation induced by the total ordering. That is, two elements, a and b, are considered equal if and only if !($a < b$) && !($b < a$).

10.3.1 Sort

```
template <class RandomAccessIterator>
void sort(RandomAccessIterator first,
        RandomAccessIterator last);

template <class RandomAccessIterator, class Compare>
void sort(RandomAccessIterator first,
        RandomAccessIterator last,
        Compare comp);
```

sort sorts the elements in the range [first, last). It does approximately $N\log N$ (where N equals to last - first) comparisons on the average. If the worst case behavior is important stable_sort or partial_sort should be used.

```
template <class RandomAccessIterator>
void stable_sort(RandomAccessIterator first,
                RandomAccessIterator last);

template <class RandomAccessIterator, class Compare>
void stable_sort(RandomAccessIterator first,
                RandomAccessIterator last,
                Compare comp);
```

stable_sort sorts the elements in the range [first, last). It is stable, that is, the relative order of the equal elements is preserved. It does at most $N(logN)^2$ (where N equals to last - first) comparisons; if enough extra memory is available, it is NlogN.

```
template <class RandomAccessIterator>
void partial_sort(RandomAccessIterator first,
                  RandomAccessIterator middle,
                  RandomAccessIterator last);

template <class RandomAccessIterator, class Compare>
void partial_sort(RandomAccessIterator first,
                  RandomAccessIterator middle,
                  RandomAccessIterator last,
                  Compare comp);
```

partial_sort places the first middle - first sorted elements from the range [first, last) into the range [first, middle). The rest of the elements in the range [middle, last) are placed in an undefined order. It takes approximately (last - first) * log(middle - first) comparisons.

```
template <class InputIterator, class RandomAccessIterator>
RandomAccessIterator
    partial_sort_copy(InputIterator first,
                      InputIterator last,
                      RandomAccessIterator result_first,
                      RandomAccessIterator result_last);

template <class InputIterator,
          class RandomAccessIterator,
          class Compare >
RandomAccessIterator
    partial_sort_copy(InputIterator first,
                      InputIterator last,
                      RandomAccessIterator result_first,
                      RandomAccessIterator result_last,
                      Compare comp);
```

partial_sort_copy places the first min(last - first, result_last - result_first) sorted elements into the range [result_first, result_first + min(last - first, result_last - result_first)). It returns either result_last or result_first + (last - first) whichever is smaller. It takes approximately (last - first) * log(min(last - first, result_last - result_first)) comparisons.

10.3.2 Nth element

```
template <class RandomAccessIterator>
void nth_element(RandomAccessIterator first,
                RandomAccessIterator nth,
                RandomAccessIterator last);

template <class RandomAccessIterator, class Compare>
void nth_element(RandomAccessIterator first,
                RandomAccessIterator nth,
                RandomAccessIterator last,
                Compare comp);
```

After *n*th_element, the element in the position pointed to by *n*th is the element that would be in that position if the whole range were sorted. Also for any iterator *i* in the range [first, *n*th) and any iterator *j* in the range [*n*th, last) it holds that !(*$*i > *j$*) or comp(*$*i, *j$*) == false. It is linear on the average.

10.3.3 Binary search

All of the algorithms in this section are versions of binary search. They work on non-random access iterators minimizing the number of comparisons, which will be logarithmic for all types of iterators. They are especially appropriate for random access iterators, since these algorithms do a logarithmic number of steps through the data structure. For non-random access iterators they execute a linear number of steps.

```
template <class ForwardIterator, class T>
ForwardIterator lower_bound(ForwardIterator first,
                           ForwardIterator last,
                           const T& value);

template <class ForwardIterator, class T, class Compare>
ForwardIterator lower_bound(ForwardIterator first,
                           ForwardIterator last,
                           const T& value,
                           Compare comp);
```

lower_bound finds the first position into which value can be inserted without violating the ordering. lower_bound returns the furthermost iterator *i* in the range [first, last) such that, for any iterator *j* in the range [first, *i*), the following corresponding conditions hold: *$*j$* < value or comp(*$*j$*, value) == true. At most, log(last - first) + 1 comparisons are done.

```
template <class ForwardIterator, class T>
ForwardIterator upper_bound(ForwardIterator first,
                            ForwardIterator last,
                            const T& value);

template <class ForwardIterator, class T, class Compare>
ForwardIterator upper_bound(ForwardIterator first,
                            ForwardIterator last,
                            const T& value,
                            Compare comp);
```

upper_bound finds the furthermost position into which value can be inserted without violating the ordering. upper_bound returns the furthermost iterator *i* in the range [first, last) such that, for any iterator *j* in the range [first, *i*), the following corresponding conditions hold: !(value < **j*) or comp(value, **j*) == false. At most, log(last - first) + 1 comparisons are done.

```
template <class ForwardIterator, class T>
pair<ForwardIterator, ForwardIterator>
    equal_range(ForwardIterator first,
                ForwardIterator last,
                const T& value);

template <class ForwardIterator, class T, class Compare>
pair<ForwardIterator, ForwardIterator>
    equal_range(ForwardIterator first,
                ForwardIterator last,
                const T& value,
                Compare comp);
```

equal_range finds the largest subrange [*i*, *j*) such that the value can be inserted at any iterator *k* in it. *k* satisfies the corresponding conditions: !(**k* < value) && !(value < **k*) or comp(**k*, value) == false && comp(value, **k*) == false. At most, 2 * log(last - first) + 1 comparisons are done.

```
template <class ForwardIterator, class T>
bool binary_search(ForwardIterator first,
                   ForwardIterator last,
                   const T& value);

template <class ForwardIterator, class T, class Compare>
bool binary_search(ForwardIterator first,
                   ForwardIterator last,
                   const T& value,
                   Compare comp);
```

binary_search returns true if there is an iterator i in the range [first last) that satisfies the corresponding conditions: !($*i$ < value) && !(value < $*i$) or comp($*i$, value) == false && comp(value, $*i$) == false. At most, log(last - first) + 2 comparisons are done.

10.3.4 Merge template

```
template <class InputIterator1,
 class InputIterator2,
 class OutputIterator>
OutputIterator merge(InputIterator1 first1,
                     InputIterator1 last1,
                     InputIterator2 first2,
                     InputIterator2 last2,
                     OutputIterator result);

template <class InputIterator1,
          class InputIterator2,
          class OutputIterator,
          class Compare>
OutputIterator merge(InputIterator1 first1,
                     InputIterator1 last1,
                     InputIterator2 first2,
                     InputIterator2 last2,
                     OutputIterator result,
                     Compare comp);
```

merge merges two sorted ranges [first1, last1) and [first2, last2) into the range [result, result + (last1 - first1) + (last2 - first2)). The merge is *stable*, that is, for equal elements in the two ranges, the elements from the first range always precede the elements from the second. merge returns result + (last1 - first1) + (last2 - first2). At most, (last1 - first1) + (last2 - first2) - 1 comparisons are performed. The result of merge is undefined if the resulting range overlaps with either of the original ranges.

```
template <class BidirectionalIterator>
void inplace_merge(BidirectionalIterator first,
                   BidirectionalIterator middle,
                   BidirectionalIterator last);

template <class BidirectionalIterator,class Compare>
void inplace_merge(BidirectionalIterator first,
                   BidirectionalIterator middle,
                   BidirectionalIterator last,
                   Compare comp);
```

inplace_merge merges two sorted consecutive ranges [first, middle) and [middle, last) putting the result of the merge into the range [first, last). The merge is stable, that is, for equal elements in the two ranges, the elements from the first range always precede the elements from the second. When enough additional memory is available, at most (last - first) - 1 comparisons are performed. If no additional memory is available, an algorithm with $O(N \log N)$ complexity may be used.

10.3.5 Set operations on sorted structures

This section defines all the basic set operations on sorted structures. They even work with multisets containing multiple copies of equal elements. The semantics of the set operations is generalized to multisets in a standard way by defining union to contain the maximum number of occurrences of every element, intersection to contain the minimum, and so on.

```
template <class InputIterator1, class InputIterator2>
bool includes(InputIterator1 first1,
              InputIterator1 last1,
              InputIterator2 first2,
              InputIterator2 last2);

template <class InputIterator1,
          class InputIterator2,
          class Compare>
bool includes(InputIterator1 first1,
              InputIterator1 last1,
              InputIterator2 first2,
              InputIterator2 last2,
              Compare comp);
```

includes returns true if every element in the range [first2, last2) is contained in the range [first1, last1). It returns false otherwise. At most (last1 - first1) + (last2 - first2) * 2 - 1 comparisons are performed.

```
template <class InputIterator1,
          class InputIterator2,
          class OutputIterator>
OutputIterator set_union(InputIterator1 first1,
                         InputIterator1 last1,
                         InputIterator2 first2,
                         InputIterator2 last2,
                         OutputIterator result);
```

```
template <class InputIterator1,
          class InputIterator2,
          class OutputIterator,
          class Compare>
OutputIterator set_union(InputIterator1 first1,
                         InputIterator1 last1,
                         InputIterator2 first2,
                         InputIterator2 last2,
                         OutputIterator result,
                         Compare comp);
```

set_union constructs a sorted union of the elements from the two ranges. It returns the end of the constructed range. set_union is stable, that is, if an element is present in both ranges, the one from the first range is copied. At most ((last1 - first1) + (last2 - first2)) * 2 - 1 comparisons are performed. The result of set_union is undefined if the resulting range overlaps with either of the original ranges.

```
template <class InputIterator1,
          class InputIterator2,
          class OutputIterator>
OutputIterator set_intersection(InputIterator1 first1,
                                InputIterator1 last1,
                                InputIterator2 first2,
                                InputIterator2 last2,
                                OutputIterator result);

template <class InputIterator1,
          class InputIterator2,
          class OutputIterator,
          class Compare>
OutputIterator set_intersection(InputIterator1 first1,
                                InputIterator1 last1,
                                InputIterator2 first2,
                                InputIterator2 last2,
                                OutputIterator result,
                                Compare comp);
```

set_intersection constructs a sorted intersection of the elements from the two ranges. It returns the end of the constructed range. set_intersection is guaranteed to be stable, that is, if an element is present in both ranges, the one from the first range is copied. At most ((last1 - first1) + (last2 - first2)) * 2 - 1 comparisons are performed. The result of set_intersection is undefined if the resulting range overlaps with either of the original ranges.

```
template <class InputIterator1,
          class InputIterator2,
          class OutputIterator>
OutputIterator set_difference(InputIterator1 first1,
                              InputIterator1 last1,
                              InputIterator2 first2,
                              InputIterator2 last2,
                              OutputIterator result);


template <class InputIterator1,
          class InputIterator2,
          class OutputIterator,
          class Compare>
OutputIterator set_difference(InputIterator1 first1,
                              InputIterator1 last1,
                              InputIterator2 first2,
                              InputIterator2 last2,
                              OutputIterator result,
                              Compare comp);
```

set_difference constructs a sorted difference of the elements from the
two ranges. It returns the end of the constructed range. At most, ((last1 -
first1) + (last2 - first2)) * 2 - 1 comparisons are performed. The result of
set_difference is undefined if the resulting range overlaps with either of the
original ranges.

```
template <class InputIterator1,
          class InputIterator2,
          class OutputIterator>
OutputIterator
    set_symmetric_difference(InputIterator1 first1,
                             InputIterator1 last1,
                             InputIterator2 first2,
                             InputIterator2 last2,
                             OutputIterator result);


template <class InputIterator1,
          class InputIterator2,
          class OutputIterator,
          class Compare>
OutputIterator
    set_symmetric_difference(InputIterator1 first1,
                             InputIterator1 last1,
                             InputIterator2 first2,
                             InputIterator2 last2,
                             OutputIterator result,
                             Compare comp);
```

set_symmetric_difference constructs a sorted symmetric difference of the elements from the two ranges. It returns the end of the constructed range. At most, ((last1 - first1) + (last2 - first2)) * 2 - 1 comparisons are performed. The result of set_symmetric_difference is undefined if the resulting range overlaps with either of the original ranges.

10.3.6 Heap operations

A heap is a particular organization of elements in a range between two random access iterators [*a*, *b*). Its two key properties are:

1. *a* is the largest element in the range
2. *a* may be removed by pop_heap, or a new element added by push_heap, in O(logN) time.

These properties make heaps useful as priority queues. make_heap converts a range into a heap and sort_heap turns a heap into a sorted sequence.

```
template <class RandomAccessIterator>
void push_heap(RandomAccessIterator first,
               RandomAccessIterator last);

template <class RandomAccessIterator,
          class Compare>
void push_heap(RandomAccessIterator first,
               RandomAccessIterator last,
               Compare comp);
```

push_heap assumes the range [first, last - 1) is a valid heap and properly places the value in the location last - 1 into the resulting heap [first, last). At most, log(last - first) comparisons are performed.

```
template <class RandomAccessIterator>
void pop_heap(RandomAccessIterator first,
              RandomAccessIterator last);

template <class RandomAccessIterator, class Compare>
void pop_heap(RandomAccessIterator first,
              RandomAccessIterator last,
              Compare comp);
```

pop_heap assumes the range [first, last) is a valid heap, then swaps the value in the location first with the value in the location last - 1 and makes [first, last - 1) into a heap. At most, 2 * log(last - first) comparisons are performed.

```
template <class RandomAccessIterator>
void make_heap(RandomAccessIterator first,
               RandomAccessIterator last);

template <class RandomAccessIterator, class Compare>
void make_heap(RandomAccessIterator first,
               RandomAccessIterator last,
               Compare comp);
```

make_heap constructs a heap out of the range [first, last). At most, 3*(last - first) comparisons are performed.

```
template <class RandomAccessIterator>
void sort_heap(RandomAccessIterator first,
               RandomAccessIterator last);

template <class RandomAccessIterator, class Compare>
void sort_heap(RandomAccessIterator first,
               RandomAccessIterator last,
               Compare comp);
```

sort_heap sorts elements in the heap [first, last). At most, $N\log N$ comparisons are performed, where N is equal to last - first. sort_heap is not stable.

10.3.7 Minimum and maximum

```
template <class T>
const T& min(const T& a, const T& b);

template <class T, class Compare>
const T& min(const T& a, const T& b, Compare comp);

template <class T>
const T& max(const T& a, const T& b);

template <class T, class Compare>
const T& max(const T& a, const T& b, Compare comp);
```

min returns the smaller and max the larger. min and max return the first argument when their arguments are equal.

```
template <class InputIterator>
InputIterator max_element(InputIterator first,
                          InputIterator last);

template <class InputIterator, class Compare>
InputIterator max_element(InputIterator first,
                          InputIterator last,
                          Compare comp);
```

max_element returns the first iterator i in the range [first, last) such that, for any iterator j in the range [first, last), the following corresponding conditions hold: $!(*i < *j)$ or $comp(*i, *j) ==$ false. Exactly max(last - first - 1, 0) applications of the corresponding comparisons are done.

```
template <class InputIterator>
InputIterator min_element(InputIterator first,
                          InputIterator last);

template <class InputIterator, class Compare>
InputIterator min_element(InputIterator first,
                          InputIterator last,
                          Compare comp);
```

min_element returns the first iterator i in the range [first, last) such that, for any iterator j in the range [first, last), the following corresponding conditions hold: $!(*j < *i)$ or $comp(*j, *i) ==$ false. Exactly max(last - first - 1, 0) applications of the corresponding comparisons are done.

10.3.8 Lexicographical comparison

```
template <class InputIterator1, class InputIterator2>
bool lexicographical_compare(InputIterator1 first1,
                             InputIterator1 last1,
                             InputIterator2 first2,
                             InputIterator2 last2);

template <class InputIterator1, class InputIterator2, class Compare>
bool lexicographical_compare(InputIterator1 first1,
                             InputIterator1 last1,
                             InputIterator2 first2,
                             InputIterator2 last2,
                             Compare comp);
```

lexicographical_compare returns true if the sequence of elements defined by the range [first1, last1) is lexicographically less than the sequence of elements defined by the range [first2, last2). It returns false otherwise. At most, min((last1 - first1), (last2 - first2)) applications of the corresponding comparison are done.

10.3.9 Permutation generators

```
template <class BidirectionalIterator>
bool next_permutation(BidirectionalIterator first,
                      BidirectionalIterator last);

template <class BidirectionalIterator, class Compare>
bool next_permutation(BidirectionalIterator first,
                      BidirectionalIterator last,
                      Compare comp);
```

next_permutation takes a sequence defined by the range [first, last) and transforms it into the *next* permutation. The next permutation is found by assuming that the set of all permutations is lexicographically sorted, with respect to operator< or comp. If such a permutation exists, it returns true. Otherwise, it transforms the sequence into the smallest permutation, that is, the ascendingly sorted one, and returns false. At most, (last - first)/ 2 swaps are performed.

```
template <class BidirectionalIterator>
bool prev_permutation(BidirectionalIterator first,
                      BidirectionalIterator last);

template <class BidirectionalIterator, class Compare>
bool prev_permutation(BidirectionalIterator first,
                      BidirectionalIterator last,
                      Compare comp);
```

prev_permutation takes a sequence defined by the range [first, last) and transforms it into the *previous* permutation. The previous permutation is found by assuming that the set of all permutations is lexicographically sorted, with respect to operator< or comp. If such a permutation exists, it returns true. Otherwise, it transforms the sequence into the largest permutation, that is, the descendingly sorted one, and returns false. At most, (last - first)/ 2 swaps are performed.

10.4 Generalized numeric operations

10.4.1 Accumulate

```
template <class InputIterator, class T>
T accumulate(InputIterator first, InputIterator last, T init);

template <class InputIterator, class T, class BinaryOperation>
T accumulateInput(Iterator first,
                  InputIterator last,
                  T init,
                  BinaryOperation binary_op);
```

accumulate is similar to the APL *reduction* operator and Common Lisp *reduce* function, but it avoids the difficulty of defining the result of reduction on an empty sequence by always requiring an initial value. Accumulation is done by initializing the accumulator acc with the initial value init, and then modifying it with acc = acc + *i or acc = binary_op(acc, *i) for every iterator i in the range [first, last) in order. binary_op is assumed not to cause side effects.

10.4.2 Inner product

```
template <class InputIterator1, class InputIterator2, class T>
T inner_product(InputIterator1 first1,
                InputIterator1 last1,
                InputIterator2 first2,
                T init);

template <class InputIterator1,
          class InputIterator2,
          class T,
          class BinaryOperation1,
          class BinaryOperation2>
T inner_product(InputIterator1 first1,
                InputIterator1 last1,
                InputIterator2 first2,
                T init,
                BinaryOperation1 binary_op1,
                BinaryOperation2 binary_op2);
```

inner_product computes its result by initializing the accumulator acc with the initial value init and then modifying it with acc = acc + (*$i1$) * (*$i2$) or acc = binary_op1(acc, binary_op2(*$i1$, *$i2$)) for every iterator $i1$ in the range [first, last) and iterator $i2$ in the range [first2, first2 + (last - first)) in order. binary_op1 and binary_op2 are assumed not to cause side effects.

10.4.3 Partial sum

```
template <class InputIterator, class OutputIterator>
OutputIterator partial_sum(InputIterator first,
                           InputIterator last,
                           OutputIterator result);

template <class InputIterator,
          class OutputIterator,
          class BinaryOperation>
OutputIterator partial_sum(InputIterator first,
                           InputIterator last,
                           OutputIterator result,
                           BinaryOperation binary_op);
```

partial_sum assigns to every iterator i in the range [result, result + (last - first)) a value correspondingly equal to ((...(*first + *(first + 1)) + ...)+ *(first + (i - result))) or binary_op(binary_op(..., binary_op(*first, *(first + 1),..., *(first + (i - result))). partial_sum returns result + (last - first). Exactly (last - first) - 1 applications of binary_op are performed. binary_op is expected not to have any side effects. result may be equal to first.

10.4.4 Adjacent difference

```
template <class InputIterator, class OutputIterator>
OutputIterator
    adjacent_difference(InputIterator first,
                        InputIterator last,
                        OutputIterator result);

template <class InputIterator,
          class OutputIterator,
          class BinaryOperation>
OutputIterator
    adjacent_difference(InputIterator first,
                        InputIterator last,
                        OutputIterator result,
                        BinaryOperation binary_op);
```

adjacent_difference assigns to every element referred to by iterator *i* in the range [result + 1, result + (last - first)) a value correspondingly equal to *(first + (*i* - result)) - *(first + (*i* - result) - 1) or binary_op(*(first + (*i* - result)), *(first + (*i* - result) - 1)). result gets the value of *first. adjacent_ difference returns result + (last - first). Exactly (last - first) - 1 applications of binary_op are performed. binary_op is expected not to have any side effects. result may be equal to first.

11 ADAPTORS

Adaptors are template classes that provide interface mappings. For example, insert_iterator provides a container with an output iterator interface.

11.1 Container adaptors

It is often useful to provide restricted interfaces to containers. The library provides stack, queue and priority_queue through the adaptors that can work with different sequence types.

11.1.1 Stack

Any sequence supporting operations back, push_back and pop_back can be used to instantiate stack. In particular, vector, list and deque can be used.

```
template <class Container>
class stack {
friend bool operator==(const stack<Container>& x,
                       const stack<Container>& y);
friend bool operator<(const stack<Container>& x,
                      const stack<Container>& y);
public:
    typedef Container::value_type value_type;
    typedef Container::size_type size_type;
protected:
    Container c;
public:
    bool empty() const { return c.empty(); }
    size_type size() const { return c.size(); }
    value_type& top() { return c.back(); }
    const value_type& top() const { return c.back(); }
    void push(const value_type& x) { c.push_back(x); }
    void pop() { c.pop_back(); }
};
```

```
template <class Container>
bool operator==(const stack<Container>& x,
                const stack<Container>& y) {
    return x.c == y.c;
}

template <class Container>
bool operator<(const stack<Container>& x,
               const stack<Container>& y) {
    return x.c < y.c;
}
```

For example, stack<vector<int> > is an integer stack made out of vector, and stack<deque<char> > is a character stack made out of deque.

11.1.2 Queue

Any sequence supporting operations front, back, push_back and pop_front can be used to instantiate queue. In particular, list and deque can be used.

```
template <class Container>
class queue {
friend bool operator==(const queue<Container>& x,
                       const queue<Container>& y);
friend bool operator<(const queue<Container>& x,
                      const queue<Container>& y);
public:
    typedef Container::value_type value_type;
    typedef Container::size_type size_type;
protected:
    Container c;
public:
    bool empty() const { return c.empty(); }
    size_type size() const { return c.size(); }
    value_type& front() { return c.front(); }
    const value_type& front() const { return c.front(); }
    value_type& back() { return c.back(); }
    const value_type& back() const { return c.back(); }
    void push(const value_type& x) { c.push_back(x); }
    void pop() { c.pop_front(); }
};

template <class Container>
bool operator==(const queue<Container>& x,
                const queue<Container>& y) {
    return x.c == y.c;
}
```

```
template <class Container>
bool operator<(const queue<Container>& x,
               const queue<Container>& y) {
    return x.c < y.c;
}
```

11.1.3 Priority queue

Any sequence with random access iterator and supporting operations front, push_back and pop_back can be used to instantiate priority_queue. In particular, vector and deque can be used.

```
template <class Container,
          class Compare = less<Container::value_type> >
class priority_queue {
public:
    typedef Container::value_type value_type;
    typedef Container::size_type size_type;
protected:
    Container c;
    Compare comp;
public:
    priority_queue(const Compare& x = Compare()) : c(), comp(x) {}
    template <class InputIterator>
    priority_queue(InputIterator first,
                   InputIterator last,
                   const Compare& x = Compare()) : c(first, last),
                                                   comp(x) {
        make_heap(c.begin(), c.end(), comp;
    }
    bool empty() const { return c.empty(); }
    size_type size() const { return c.size(); }
    const value_type& top() const { return c.front(); }
    void push(const value_type& x) {
        c.push_back(x);
        push_heap(c.begin(), c.end(), comp);
    }
    void pop() {
        pop_heap(c.begin(), c.end(), comp);
        c.pop_back();
    }
};

// no equality is provided
```

11.2 Iterator adaptors

11.2.1 Reverse iterators

Bidirectional and random access iterators have corresponding reverse iterator adaptors that iterate through the data structure in the opposite direction. They have the same signatures as the corresponding iterators. The fundamental relation between a reverse iterator and its corresponding iterator i is established by the identity

```
&*(reverse_iterator(i)) == &*(i - 1).
```

This mapping is dictated by the fact that, while there is always a pointer past the end of an array, there might not be a valid pointer before the beginning of an array.

```
template <class BidirectionalIterator,
          class T,
          class Reference = T&,
          class Distance = ptrdiff_t>
class reverse_bidirectional_iterator :
    public bidirectional_iterator<T, Distance> {
    typedef reverse_bidirectional_iterator<BidirectionalIterator,
                                           T,
                                           Reference,
                                           Distance> self;
    friend bool operator==(const self& x, const self& y);
protected:
    BidirectionalIterator current;
public:
    reverse_bidirectional_iterator() {}
    reverse_bidirectional_iterator(BidirectionalIterator x) :
        current(x) {}
    BidirectionalIterator base() { return current; }
    Reference operator*() const {
        BidirectionalIterator tmp = current;
        return *--tmp;
    }
    self& operator++() {
        --current;
        return *this;
    }
    self operator++(int) {
        self tmp = *this;
        --current;
        return tmp;
```

```
        }
    self& operator--() {
        ++current;
        return *this;
    }
    self operator--(int) {
        self tmp = *this;
        ++current;
        return tmp;
    }
};


template <class BidirectionalIterator,
          class T,
          class Reference,
          class Distance>
inline bool operator==(
    const reverse_bidirectional_iterator<BidirectionalIterator,
                                         T,
                                         Reference,
                                         Distance>& x,
    const reverse_bidirectional_iterator<BidirectionalIterator,
                                         T,
                                         Reference,
                                         Distance>& y ) {
    return x.current == y.current;
}


template <class RandomAccessIterator,
          class T,
          class Reference = T&,
          class Distance = ptrdiff_t>
class reverse_iterator :
    public random_access_iterator<T, Distance> {
    typedef reverse_iterator<RandomAccessIterator,
                             T,
                             Reference,
                             Distance> self;
    friend bool operator==(const self& x, const self& y);
    friend bool operator<(const self& x, const self& y);
    friend Distance operator-(const self& x, const self& y);
    friend self operator+(Distance n, const self& x);
protected:
    RandomAccessIterator current;
public:
    reverse_iterator() {}
    reverse_iterator(RandomAccessIterator x ): current(x) {}
```

```
        RandomAccessIterator base() { return current; }
        Reference operator*() const {
            RandomAccessIterator tmp = current;
            return *--tmp;
        }
    self& operator++() {
        --current;
        return *this;
    }
    self operator++(int) {
        self tmp = *this;
        --current;
        return tmp;
    }
    self& operator--() {
        ++current;
        return *this;
    }
    self operator--(int) {
        self tmp = *this;
        ++current;
        return tmp;
    }
    self operator+(Distance n) const {
        return self(current - n);
    }
    self& operator+=(Distance n) {
        current -= n;
        return *this;
    }
    self operator-(Distance n) const {
        return self(current + n);
    }
    self& operator-=(Distance n) {
        current += n;
        return *this;
    }
    Reference operator[](Distance n) {
        return *(*this + n);
    }
};

template <class RandomAccessIterator,
          class T,
          class Reference,
          class Distance>
inline bool operator==(
```

```
            const reverse_iterator<RandomAccessIterator,
                                   T,
                                   Reference,
                                   Distance>& x,
            const reverse_iterator<RandomAccessIterator,
                                   T,
                                   Reference,
                                   Distance>& y ) {
    return x.current == y.current;
}

template <class RandomAccessIterator,
          class T,
          class Reference,
          class Distance>
inline bool operator<(
    const reverse_iterator<RandomAccessIterator,
                                   T,
                                   Reference,
                                   Distance>& x,
    const reverse_iterator<RandomAccessIterator,
                                   T,
                                   Reference,
                                   Distance>& y) {
    return y.current < x.current;
}

template <class RandomAccessIterator,
          class T,
          class Reference,
          class Distance>
inline Distance operator-(
    const reverse_iterator<RandomAccessIterator,
                                   T,
                                   Reference,
                                   Distance>& x,
    const reverse_iterator<RandomAccessIterator,
                                   T,
                                   Reference,
                                   Distance>& y {
    return y.current - x.current;
}

template <class RandomAccessIterator,
          class T,
          class Reference,
          class Distance>
```

```
inline reverse_iterator<RandomAccessIterator,
                        T,
                        Reference,
                        Distance>
    operator+( Distance n,
            const reverse_iterator<RandomAccessIterator,
                                   T,
                                   Reference,
                                   Distance>& x) {
    return reverse_iterator<RandomAccessIterator,
                            T,
                            Reference,
                            Distance>(x.current - n);
}
```

11.2.2 Insert iterators

To make it possible to deal with insertion in the same way as writing into an array, a special group of iterator adaptors, called insert iterators, is provided in the library. With regular iterator classes,

```
while (first != last) *result++ = *first++;
```

causes a range [first, last) to be copied into a range starting with result. The same code with result being an insert iterator will insert corresponding elements into the container. This device allows all of the copying algorithms in the library to work in the *insert mode* instead of the regular overwrite mode.

An insert iterator is constructed from a container and, possibly, one of its iterators pointing to where insertion takes place if it is neither at the beginning nor at the end of the container. Insert iterators satisfy the requirements of output iterators. operator* returns the insert iterator itself. The assignment operator=(const T& x) is defined on insert iterators to allow writing into them; it inserts x right before where the insert iterator is pointing. In other words, an insert iterator is like a cursor pointing into the container where the insertion takes place.

back_insert_iterator inserts elements at the end of a container, front_insert_iterator inserts elements at the beginning of a container, and insert_iterator inserts elements where the iterator points to in a container. back_inserter, front_inserter, and inserter are three functions making the insert iterators out of a container.

```
template <class Container>
class back_insert_iterator : public output_iterator {
protected:
    Container& container;
public:
    back_insert_iterator(Container& x) : container(x) {}
    back_insert_iterator<Container>&
    operator=(const Container::value_type& value){
        container.push_back(value);
        return *this;
    }
    back_insert_iterator<Container>& operator*() { return *this; }
    back_insert_iterator<Container>& operator++() { return *this; }
    back_insert_iterator<Container>& operator++(int) {
        return *this;
    }
};

template <class Container>
back_insert_iterator<Container> back_inserter(Container& x) {
    return back_insert_iterator<Container>(x);
}

template <class Container>
class front_insert_iterator : public output_iterator {
protected:
    Container& container;
public:
    front_insert_iterator(Container& x) : containerx {}
    front_insert_iterator<Container>&
    operator=(const Container::value_type& value) {
        container.push_front(value);
        return *this;
    }
    front_insert_iterator<Container>& operator*() { return *this; }
    front_insert_iterator<Container>& operator++() {
        return *this;
    }
    front_insert_iterator<Container>& operator++(int) {
        return *this;
    }
};

template <class Container>
front_insert_iterator<Container> front_inserter(Container& x) {
    return front_insert_iterator<Container>(x);
}
```

```
template <class Container>
class insert_iterator : public output_iterator {
protected:
    Container& container;
    Container::iterator iter;
public:
    insert_iterator(Container& x,
                    Container::iterator i)
                        : container(x), iter(i) {}
    insert_iterator<Container>&
      operator=(const Container::value_type& value ){
        iter = container.insert(iter, value);
        ++iter;
        return *this;
    }
    insert_iterator<Container>& operator*() { return *this; }
    insert_iterator<Container>& operator++() { return *this; }
    insert_iterator<Container>& operator++(int) {
        return *this;
    }
};

template <class Container, class Iterator>
insert_iterator<Container>
inserter(Container& x, Iterator i) {
    return insert_iterator<Container>(x, Container::iterator(i));
}
```

11.2.3 Raw storage iterator

raw_storage_iterator is provided to enable algorithms to store the results
into uninitialized memory. The formal template parameter OutputIterator is
required to have construct(OutputIterator, const T&) defined.

```
template <class OutputIterator, class T>
class raw_storage_iterator : public output_iterator {
protected:
    OutputIterator iter;
public:
    raw_storage_iterator(OutputIterator x) : iter(x) {}
    raw_storage_iterator<OutputIterator, T>& operator*() {
        return *this;
    }
    raw_storage_iterator<OutputIterator, T>&
      operator=(const T& element) {
```

```
            construct(iter, element);
            return *this;
        }
        raw_storage_iterator<OutputIterator, T>& operator++() {
            ++iter;
            return *this;
        }
        raw_storage_iterator<OutputIterator, T> operator++(int) {
            raw_storage_iterator<OutputIterator, T> tmp = *this;
            ++iter;
            return tmp;
        }
    };
```

11.3 Function adaptors

Function adaptors work only with function object classes with argument types and result type defined.

11.3.1 Negators

Negators not1 and not2 take a unary and a binary predicate correspondingly and return their complements.

```
template <class Predicate>
class unary_negate
  : public unary_function<Predicate::argument_type, bool> {
protected:
    Predicate pred;
public:
    unary_negate(const Predicate& x) : pred(x) {}
    bool operator()(const argument_type& x) const {
        return !pred(x);
    }
};

template <class Predicate>
unary_negate<Predicate> not1(const Predicate& pred) {
    return unary_negate<Predicate>(pred);
}
```

```
template <class Predicate>
class binary_negate
  : public binary_function<Predicate::first_argument_type,
                           Predicate::second_argument_type,
                           bool> {
protected:
    Predicate pred;
public:
    binary_negate(const Predicate& x) : predx {}
    bool operator()(const first_argument_type& x,
                    const second_argument_type& y ) const {
        return !pred(x, y);
    }
};


template <class Predicate>
binary_negate<Predicate> not2(const Predicate& pred) {
    return binary_negate<Predicate>(pred);
}
```

11.3.2 Binders

Binders bind1st and bind2nd take a function object *f* of two arguments and a value *x* and return a function object of one argument constructed out of *f* with the first or second argument correspondingly bound to *x*.

```
template <class Operation>
class binder1st :
  public unary_function<Operation::second_argument_type,
                        Operation::result_type> {
protected:
    Operation op;
    Operation::first_argument_type value;
public:
    binder1st(const Operation& x,
              const Operation::first_argument_type& y)
                : op(x), value(y) {}
    result_type operator()(const argument_type& x) const {
        return op(value, x);
    }
};

template <class Operation, class T>
binder1st<Operation> bind1st(const Operation& op,
                             const T& x) {
```

```
        return
            binder1st<Operation>(op,
                            Operation::first_argument_type(x);
    }

    template <class Operation>
    class binder2nd
      : public unary_function<Operation::first_argument_type,
                            Operation::result_type> {
    protected:
        Operation op;
        Operation::second_argument_type value;
    public:
        binder2nd(const Operation& x,
                const Operation::second_argument_type& y)
                  : op(x),value(y) {}
        result_type operator()(const argument_type& x) const {
            return op(x, value);
        }
    };

    template <class Operation, class T>
    binder2nd<Operation> bind2nd(const Operation& op, const T& x) {
        return
            binder2nd<Operation>(op,
                            Operation::second_argument_type(x));
    }
```

For example, find_if(v.begin(), v.end(), bind2nd(greater<int>(), 5)) finds the first integer in vector v greater than 5; find_if(v.begin(), v.end(), bind1st(greater<int>(), 5)) finds the first integer in v less than 5.

11.3.3 Adaptors for pointers to functions

To allow pointers to unary and binary functions to work with function adaptors the library provides:

```
    template <class Arg, class Result>
    class pointer_to_unary_function
      : public unary_function<Arg, Result> {
    protected:
        Result (*ptr)(Arg);
    public:
        pointer_to_unary_function(Result *(x)(Arg)) : ptr(x) {}
        Result operator()(Arg x) const { return ptr(x); }
    };
```

```
template <class Arg, class Result>
pointer_to_unary_function<Arg, Result> ptr_fun(Result *(x)(Arg) {
    return pointer_to_unary_function<Arg, Result>(x);
}

template <class Arg1, class Arg2, class Result>
class pointer_to_binary_function
  : public binary_function<Arg1, Arg2, Result> {
protected:
    Result (*ptr)(Arg1, Arg2);
public:
    pointer_to_binary_function(Result *(x)(Arg1, Arg2)) : ptr(x) {}
    Result operator()(Arg1 x, Arg2 y) const {
        return ptr(x, y);
    }
};

template <class Arg1, class Arg2, class Result>
pointer_to_binary_function<Arg1, Arg2, Result>
ptr_fun(Result (*x)(Arg1, Arg2) {
    return pointer_to_binary_function<Arg1, Arg2, Result>(x);
}
```

For example, replace_if(v.begin(), v.end(), not1(bind2nd(ptr_fun(strcmp), "C")), "C++") replaces all the "C" with "C++" in sequence v.

Compilation systems that have multiple pointer to function types have to provide additional ptr_fun template functions.

12 MEMORY HANDLING

12.1 Primitives

To obtain a typed pointer to an uninitialized memory buffer of a given size the following function is defined:

```
template <class T>
inline T* allocate(ptrdiff_t n, T*); // n >= 0
```

The size in bytes of the allocated buffer is no less than n*sizeof(T).

For every memory model there is a corresponding allocate template function defined with the first argument type being the distance type of the pointers in the memory model.

For example, if a compilation system supports __huge pointers with the distance type being long long, the following template function is provided:

```
template <class T>]
inline T __huge* allocate(long long n, T __huge *);
```

Also, the following functions are provided:

```
template <class T>
inline void deallocate(T* buffer);

template <class T1, class T2>
inline void construct(T1* p, const T2& value) {
    new (p) T1(value);
}

template <class T>
inline void destroy(T* pointer) {
    pointer >~T();
}
```

deallocate frees the buffer allocated by allocate. For every memory model there are corresponding deallocate, construct and destroy template functions defined, with the first argument type being the pointer type of the memory model.

```
template <class T>
pair<T*, ptrdiff_t> get_temporary_buffer(ptrdiff_t n, T*);

template <class T>
void return_temporary_buffer(T* p);
```

get_temporary_buffer finds the largest buffer not greater than $n*$sizeof(T), and returns a pair consisting of the address and the capacity (in the units of sizeof(T)) of the buffer. return_temporary_buffer returns the buffer allocated by get_temporary_buffer.

12.2 Specialized algorithms

All the iterators that are used as formal template parameters in the following algorithms are required to have construct(ForwardIterator, const T&) defined.

```
template <class ForwardIterator>
void destroy(ForwardIterator first, ForwardIterator last) {
    while (first != last)
        destroy(first++);
}

template <class InputIterator, class ForwardIterator>
ForwardIterator
  uninitialized_copy(InputIterator first,
                     InputIterator last,
                     ForwardIterator result) {
    while (first != last)
        construct(result++, *first++);
        return result;
}

template <class ForwardIterator, class T>
void uninitialized_fill(ForwardIterator first,
                        ForwardIterator last,
                        const T& x) {
    while (first != last)
        construct(first++, x);
}

template <class ForwardIterator, class Size, class T>
void uninitialized_fill_n(ForwardIterator first,
                          Size n,
                          const T& x) {
    while (n--)
        construct(first++, x);
}
```

13 ACKNOWLEDGMENTS

The following people contributed to the design of the STL:

Pete Becker
David Jacobson
Mehdi Jazayeri
Tom Keffer
Andy Koenig
Milon Mackey
Doug Morgan

Dave Musser
Nathan Myers
Larry Podmolik
Bob Shaw
Carl Staelin
Bjarne Stroustrup
Mark Terribile Parthasarathy Tirumalai
Mike Vilot
John Wilkes

The present library is a descendant of several earlier libraries (in Scheme, Ada, and C++) which were designed jointly with **Dave Musser**. He contributed to all the aspects of the STL work: design of the overall structure, semantic requirements, algorithm design, complexity analysis and performance measurements.

Andy Koenig was responsible for explaining to us that C++ has an underlying abstract machine and that the generic library should fit this machine. He also convinced us that we should attempt to turn our work into a C++ standard proposal.

During the writing of the proposal, **Bjarne Stroustrup** has been a constant supporter and has given us a lot of technical advice, especially on the language-dependent parts of the library.

Andy and Bjarne have answered hundreds of urgent messages and phone calls of the form: Could we do this?

Dan Fishman and **Mary Loomis** created an environment for us, where we were able to concentrate on the design without any distractions.

Bill Worley was responsible for starting this project and supported it throughout his tenure as our lab director.

Rick Amerson and **Dmitry Lenkov** have given us advice and support.

14 BIBLIOGRAPHY

M. Ellis and B. Stroustrup, *The Annotated C++ Reference Manual*, Addison-Wesley, New York, 1990.

D. Kapur, D. R. Musser, and A. A. Stepanov, "Tecton, A Language for Manipulating Generic Objects," *Proc. of Workshop on Program Specification*, Aarhus, Denmark, August 1981, *Lecture Notes in Computer Science*, Springer-Verlag, vol. 134, 1982.

D. Kapur, D. R. Musser, and A. A. Stepanov, "Operators and Algebraic Structures," *Proc. of the Conference on Functional Programming Languages and Computer Architecture*, Portsmouth, New Hampshire, October 1981.

A. Kershenbaum, D. R. Musser, and A. A. Stepanov, "Higher Order Imperative Programming," *Technical Report 88-10*, Rensselaer Polytechnic Institute, April 1988.

A. Koenig, "Associative Arrays in C++," *Proc. USENIX Conference*, San Francisco, CA, June 1988.

A. Koenig, "Applicators, Manipulators, and Function Objects," *C++ Journal*, vol. 1, #1, Summer 1990.

D. R. Musser and A. A. Stepanov, "A Library of Generic Algorithms in Ada," *Proc. of 1987 ACM SIGAda International Conference*, Boston, December, 1987.

D. R. Musser and A. A. Stepanov, "Generic Programming," invited paper, in P. Gianni, Ed., *ISSAC 88 Symbolic and Algebraic Computation Proceedings, Lecture Notes in Computer Science*, Springer-Verlag, vol. 358, 1989.

D. R. Musser and A. A. Stepanov, *Ada Generic Library*, Springer-Verlag, 1989.

D. R. Musser and A. A. Stepanov, "Algorithm-Oriented Generic Libraries," *Software Practice and Experience*, vol. 247, July 1994.

M. Stahl and U. Steinmller, "Generic Dynamic Arrays," *The C++ Report*, October 1993.

J. E. Shopiro, "Strings and Lists for C++," *AT&T Bell Labs Internal Technical Memorandum*, July 1985.

A. A. Stepanov and M. Lee, "The Standard Template Library," *Technical Report HPL-94-34*, Hewlett-Packard Laboratories, April 1994.

B. Stroustrup, *The Design and Evolution of C++*, Addison-Wesley, New York, 1994.

BIBLIOGRAPHY

Barreirro, Javier, et. al: *Hash Tables for the Standard Template Library*, Internet distribution, January 30, 1995. Published at ftp://butler.hpl.hp.com/stl

Fraley, Bob: *A STL Hash Table Implementation*, Internet distribution, February 16, 1995. Published at ftp://butler.hpl.hp.com/stl

Horstmann, Cay S: *Evaluating Class Libraries*, The C++ Report, Volume 7, Number 4. (May 1995), pp 62-72.

Kernighan, Brian W., and Ritchie, Dennis M: *The C Programming Language*. Prentice-Hall, Englewood Cliffs, N.J. 1978. ISBN 0-13-110163-3.

Knuth, Donald: *The Art of Computer Programming, Volume 3/Sorting and Searching*. Addison-Wesley, Reading, MA. 1973. ISBN 0-201-03803-X

Plauger, P.J.: *The Draft Standard C++ Library*. Prentice Hall, Englewood Cliffs, NJ. 1995. ISBN 0-13-117003-1.

Sedgewick, Robert: *Algorithms in C*. Addison-Wesley, Reading, MA. 1990. ISBN 0-201-51425-7.

Stepanov, Alexander, and Lee, Meng: *The Standard Template Library*. Internet distribution, July 7, 1995. Published at ftp://butler.hpl.hp.com/stl

Stevens, Al: *C Programming*. Dr. Dobb's Journal, Volume 20, Issue 3. (March 1995) pp 115-124.

Stroustrup, Bjarne: *The C++ Programming Language, Second Edition*. Addison Wesley, Reading, MA. 1994. ISBN 0-201-53992-6.

Stroustrup, Bjarne: *The Design and Evolution of C++.* Addison-Wesley, Reading, MA. 1994. ISBN 0-201-54330-3.

Stroustrup, Bjarne: *Making a vector fit for a standard.* The C++ Report, Volume 6 Number 8 (October 1994), pp 30-35.

Vilot, Michael J.: *An introduction to the Standard Template Library.* The C++ Report, Volume 6 Number 8 (October 1994), pp 22-29.

Working Paper for Draft Proposed International Standard for Information Systems - Programming Language C++. Internet distribution, April 26, 1995. Published at ftp://ftp.research.att.com/dist/stdc++/WP.

INDEX

Page entries in **bold** type indicate a reference definition for the topic.

M

ORDER FORM

Order Center: **(800) 762-2974** *(8 a.m.–6 p.m., EST, weekdays)*

5/8/95

Quantity	ISBN	Title	Price	Total

Shipping & Handling Charges

	Description	First book	Each additional book	Total
Domestic	Normal	$4.50	$1.50	$
	Two Day Air	$8.50	$2.50	$
	Overnight	$18.00	$3.00	$
International	Surface	$8.00	$8.00	$
	Airmail	$16.00	$16.00	$
	DHL Air	$17.00	$17.00	$

*For large quantities call for shipping & handling charges.
**Prices are subject to change without notice.

Ship to:

Name _____

Company _____

Address _____

City/State/Zip _____

Daytime Phone _____

Payment: ☐ Check to IDG Books (US Funds Only)

☐ VISA   ☐ MasterCard   ☐ American Express

Card # _____ Expires _____

Signature _____

Subtotal _____

CA residents add
applicable sales tax _____

IN, MA, and MD
residents add
5% sales tax _____

IL residents add
6.25% sales tax _____

RI residents add
7% sales tax _____

TX residents add
8.25% sales tax _____

Shipping _____

Total _____

Please send this order form to:

IDG Books Worldwide
7260 Shadeland Station, Suite 100
Indianapolis, IN 46256

Allow up to 3 weeks for delivery.
Thank you!

IDG Books Worldwide License Agreement

Important -- read carefully before opening the software packet(s). This is a legal agreement between you (either an individual or an entity) and IDG Books Worldwide, Inc. (IDG). By opening the accompanying sealed packet(s) containing the software disk(s), you acknowledge that you have read and accept the following IDG License Agreement. If you do not agree and do not want to be bound by the terms of this Agreement, promptly return the book and the unopened software packet(s) to the place you obtained them for a full refund.

1. License. This License Agreement (Agreement) permits you to use one copy of the enclosed Software program(s) on a single computer. The Software is in "use" on a computer when it is loaded into temporary memory (i.e., RAM) or installed into permanent memory (e.g., hard disk, CD ROM, or other storage device) of that computer.

2. Copyright. The entire contents of this disk(s) and the compilation of the Software are copyrighted and protected by both United States copyright laws and international treaty provisions. The individual programs on the disk(s) are copyrighted by the authors of each program respectively. Each program has its own use permissions and limitations. You may only (a) make one copy of the Software for backup or archival purposes, or (b) transfer the Software to a single hard disk, provided that you keep the original for backup or archival purposes. To use each program, you must follow the individual requirements and restrictions detailed for each in this Book. Do not use a program if you do not want to follow its Licensing Agreement. None of the material on this disk(s) or listed in this Book may ever be distributed, in original or modified form, for commercial purposes.

3. Other Restrictions. You may not rent or lease the Software. You may transfer the Software and user documentation on a permanent basis provided you retain no copies and the recipient agrees to the terms of this Agreement. You may not reverse engineer, decompile, or disassemble the Software except to the extent that the foregoing restriction is expressly prohibited by applicable law. If the Software is an update or

has been updated, any transfer must include the most recent update and all prior versions. Each shareware program has its own use permissions and limitations. These limitations are contained in the individual license agreements that are on the software disks. The restrictions include a requirement that after using the program for a period of time specified in its text, the user must pay a registration fee or discontinue use. By opening the package which contains the software disk, you will be agreeing to abide by the licenses and restrictions for these programs. Do not open the software package unless you agree to be bound by the license agreements.

4. Limited Warranty. IDG Warrants that the Software and disk(s) are free from defects in materials and workmanship for a period of sixty (60) days from the date of purchase of this Book. If IDG receives notification within the warranty period of defects in material or workmanship, IDG will replace the defective disk(s). IDG's entire liability and your exclusive remedy shall be limited to replacement of the Software, which is returned to IDG with a copy of your receipt. This Limited Warranty is void if failure of the Software has resulted from accident, abuse, or misapplication. Any replacement Software will be warranted for the remainder of the original warranty period or thirty (30) days, whichever is longer.

5. No Other Warranties. To the maximum extent permitted by applicable law, IDG and the author disclaim all other warranties, express or implied, including but not limited to implied warranties of merchantability and fitness for a particular purpose, with respect to the Software, the programs, the source code contained therein and/or the techniques described in this Book. This limited warranty gives you specific legal rights. You may have others which vary from state/jurisdiction to state/jurisdiction.

6. No Liability For Consequential Damages. To the extent permitted by applicable law, in no event shall IDG or the author be liable for any damages whatsoever (including without limitation, damages for loss of business profits, business interruption, loss of business information, or any other pecuniary loss) arising out of the use of or inability to use the Book or the Software, even if IDG has been advised of the possibility of such damages. Because some states/jurisdictions do not allow the exclusion or limitation of liability for consequential or incidental damages, the above limitation may not apply to you.

7. U.S.Government Restricted Rights. Use, duplication, or disclosure of the Software by the U.S. Government is subject to restrictions stated in paragraph (c) (1) (ii) of the Rights in Technical Data and Computer Software clause of DFARS 252.227-7013, and in subparagraphs (a) through (d) of the Commercial Computer--Restricted Rights clause at FAR 52.227-19, and in similar clauses in the NASA FAR supplement, when applicable.

Alternate Disk Format Available.

The enclosed disks are in 3 1/2" 1.44MB, high-density format. If you have a different size drive, or a low-density drive, and you cannot arrange to transfer the data to the disk size you need, you can obtain the programs on 5 1/4" 1.2 MB high-density disks or 3 1/2" 720K low-density disks or 800K low-density disks by writing to the following address: IDG Books Disk Fulfillment Department, Attn: Programmer's Guide to the Standard Template Library, IDG Books Worldwide, 7260 Shadeland Station, Indianapolis, IN 46256, or call 800-762-2974. Please specify the size of disk you need, and please allow 3 to 4 weeks for delivery.